EFFECTIVE TEACHING IN HIGHER EDUCATION:
Research and Practice

EFFECTIVE TEACHING IN HIGHER EDUCATION:
Research and Practice

Edited by

Raymond P. Perry
and
John C. Smart

AGATHON PRESS
New York

The following chapters in this book were originally published in the specified volumes of
Higher Education: Handbook of Theory and Research,
and were copyrighted in the year of publication by Agathon Press:
"Perceived Control in College Students: Implications for Instruction in Higher Education," by
R.P. Perry, Vol. VII, 1991; "A Motivational Analysis of Academic Life in College," by M.V. Covington, Vol. IX, 1993; "Matrix Representations: Research, Theory, and Practice," by K.A. Kiewra, Vol. X, 1994; "Effective Teaching Behaviors in the College Classroom," by H. Murray, Vol. VII, 1991; "Instructional Interventions: A Review of the Literature on Efforts to Improve Instruction," by M. Wiemer and L.F. Lenze, Vol. VII, 1991; "Students' Evaluations of University Teaching: A Multidimensional Perspective," by H. Marsh and M. Dunkin, Vol. VIII, 1992; "The Dimensionality of Student Ratings of Instruction: What We Know and What We Do Not," by P.C. Abrami, S. d'Apollonia, and S. Rosenberg, Vol. XI, 1996.

Library of Congress Cataloging in Process Information
Effective teaching in higher education : research and practice /
edited by Raymond P. Perry and John C. Smart.
p. cm.
Includes bibliographical reference and indexes.
ISBN 0-87586-116-4. -- ISBN 0-87586-117-2 (pbk.)
1. College teaching--United States. 2. College teachers--Rating of--
United States. I. Perry, Raymond P. II. Smart, John C.
LB2331.E42 1996
378.1'25--dc20   96-19577
                                                              CIP

To my parents, Bernice and Paul Perry, who got me started, and to my wife Judy, and our son Jason, who kept me going — all great teachers. (R.P.P.)

To my parents, J.C. and Mabel, who taught me right from wrong; to my mentor, Charles F. Elton, who kindled my love of research; and to my wife Bunty and children, Dawn and David, who make it all worthwhile. (J.C.S.)

CONTENTS

The Contributors   *ix*

Introduction
Raymond P. Perry and John C. Smart   *1*

PERSPECTIVES ON STUDENTS

Perceived Control in College Students: Implications for Instruction in Higher Education
Raymond P. Perry   *11*

A Motivational Analysis of Academic Life in College
Martin V. Covington   *61*

Turning Work into Play: The Nature and Nurturing of Intrinsic Task Engagement
Martin V. Covington and Sonja Wiedenhaupt   *101*

The Matrix Representation System: Orientation, Research, Theory, and Application
Kenneth A. Kiewra   *115*

Teaching Effectively: Which Students? What Methods?
Raymond P. Perry   *154*

PERSPECTIVES ON FACULTY

Effective Teaching Behaviors in the College Classroom
Harry G. Murray   *171*

Instructional Interventions: A Review of the Literature on Efforts to Improve Instruction
Maryellen Weimer and Lisa Firing Lenze   *205*

Students' Evaluations of University Teaching: A Multidimensional Perspective
Herbert W. Marsh and Michael J. Dunkin   *241*

The Dimensionality of Student Ratings of Instruction: What We Know and What We Do Not
Philip C. Abrami, Sylvia d'Apollonia, and Steven Rosenfield   *321*

Identifying Exemplary Teachers and Teaching: Evidence from Student Ratings
Kenneth A. Feldman   *368*

Good Teaching Makes a Difference —And We Know What It Is
W. J. McKeachie   *396*

CONCLUSION

Exploring the Implications: From Research to Practice
Maryellen Weimer   *411*

Author Index   *437*

Subject Index   *447*

THE CONTRIBUTORS

PHILIP C. ABRAMI is a professor and the director of the Centre for the Study of Classroom Processes at Concordia University in Montreal, Quebec. His research interests include postsecondary instruction and evaluation, the social psychology of education (especially small group teaching); and meta-analysis.

MARTIN V. COVINGTON is a professor of psychology at the University of California and Research Psychologist, Institute of Personality and Social Research, University of California, Berkeley. His research interests embrace a combination of educational, social, developmental, and cognitive psychology with a special problem focus on (1) the psychology of creativity and the enhancement of achievement motivation and positive self-regard among students; (2) the development of instructional systems to promote prosocial and academic problem-solving skills; and (3) the investigation of fear-of-failure dynamics and text anxiety in schools. Professor Covington is senior author of the *Productive Thinking Program*, a course for elementary school students in learning to think. He has also written several books and numerous research and journal articles. Professor Covington is a recipient of the Berkeley Distinguished Teaching Award and is past president of the International Society for Test Anxiety Research.

MICHAEL J. DUNKIN is founding Professor of Teacher Education at the University of New South Wales—St. George Campus in Sydney, Australia. He was formerly Director of the Centre for Teaching and Learning at the University of Sydney. He is best known for his writings and research on teaching and teacher education and was the author, with Bruce J. Biddle, of *The Study of Teaching*. More recently he wrote the chapter on research on teaching in higher education for the third edition of *The Handbook of Research on Teaching* and edited *The International Encyclopedia of Teaching and Teacher Education*. He currently edits the journal *Teaching and Teacher Education: An International of Research and Studies*. His recent research has focused on orientations to teaching of newly appointed and award-winning university teachers. He has also published research in the area of determinants of academic career advancement of Australian academics.

SYLVIA D'APOLLONIA is an adjunct professor at the Centre for the Study of Classroom Processes and instructor at Dawson College in Montreal, Quebec. Her research interests included postsecondary instruction (especially science education) and meta-analysis.

KENNETH A. FELDMAN is professor of sociology at the State University of New York at Stony Brook. He is a consulting editor for *Research in Higher Education* and has published many articles in that journal; his work has also appeared in a wide array of other professional journals. His book with Theodore M. Newcomb, *The Impact of College on Students,* has been republished as part of a series on the foundations of higher education. With Michael Paulsen, he recently co-edited an ASHE reader entitled *Teaching and Learning in the College Classroom.* A member of the editorial board of the *Journal of Higher Education* since 1994, he is a recipient of the 1994 Wilbert J. McKeachie Career Achievement award of the Special Interest Group in Faculty Evaluation and Development (SIGFED) of the American Educational Research Association, the 1995 American Educational Research Association Distinguished Research Award for the Postsecondary Education Division, and the 1996 Research Achievement Award from the Association for the Study of Higher Education.

KENNETH A. KIEWRA is an Associate Professor of Educational Psychology and Director of the Academic Success Center at the University of Nebraska-Lincoln. He received his Ph.D. in Educational Psychology and Instructional Design from Florida State University in 1982. He served as an Assistant Professor of Educational Psychology from 1982 to 1986 at Kansas State University and as Associate Professor of Psychology from 1986 to 1988 at Utah State University. Kiewra's research investigates note taking and text representations. He is a past president of the Midwestern Educational Research Association, the former Chair of the Special Interest Group on Academic Studying, and a member of four editorial boards.

LISA FIRING LENZE is an adjunct assistant professor in higher education at the University of Rochester and faculty development consultant for the Higher Education Publishing Division of the National Education Association. Formerly she was program assistant for the Instructional Development Program at Penn State University. She is the author or co-author of a number of recently published articles that address discipline-specific knowledge of teaching and instructional interventions to enhance teaching. Her co-authored book on student feedback about teaching is entitled *Learning from Students: Early Term Student Feedback in Higher Education.*

HERBERT W. MARSH is Professor of Education (Research) at the University of Western Sydney (Macarthur) in Australia. His current research interests are students' evaluations of teaching effectiveness, self-concept, school effectiveness, and covariance structural modeling. He has published extensively in these areas in a wide variety of educational and psychological research journals. He is the author of the set of three self-concept instruments, the Self Description Questionnaire (SDQ) I, II, and III, and the student evaluation instrument Students' Evaluations of Educational Quality (SEEQ).

WILBERT J. MCKEACHIE is Professor of Psychology and former Director of the Center for Research on Learning and Teaching at the University of Michigan. His primary activities have been teaching, research on college teaching, and training college teachers. He is past president of the American Psychological Association, the American Association of Higher Education, the American Psychological Foundation, and the Center for Social Gerontology. He is also past chairman of the Committee on Teaching, Research, and Publication of the American Association of University Professors, of the Division of Educational, Instructional, and School Psychology of the International Association of Applied Psychology, and of the Division of Psychology of the American Association for the Advancement of Science. Dr. McKeachie has written a number of books and articles, the best known of which is *Teaching Tips: Strategies, Research, and Theory for College and University Teachers* (D.C. Heath/Houghton Mifflin), now in its ninth edition.

HARRY G. MURRAY is a professor of psychology at the University of Western Ontario, London, Canada. His research over the past 20 years has focused on teacher effectiveness in higher education and evaluation and improvement of university teaching. He has won awards for outstanding teaching from the University of Western Ontario and the Ontario Confederation of University Faculty Associations. He also serves as editor of *Instructional Evaluation,* consulting editor for *Research in Higher Education,* and a member of the editorial board of *The Canadian Journal of Higher Education.*

RAYMOND J. PERRY is a professor of psychology and Director of Research for the Centre for Higher Education Research and Development at the University of Manitoba. His research activities have focused on teaching and learning in higher education, with an emphasis on teaching effectiveness and student motivation and achievement. Dr. Perry's research contributions have won awards from the Max Planck Society and the Alexander Von Humboldt Society in Germany, and the NATO Senior Scientist Committee. He has been a visiting scholar at UCLA, Stanford University, the Max Planck Institute (Munich), and the UNESCO Institute for Education (Hamburg). He serves on the editorial boards of *Research in Higher Education, The Canadian Journal of Higher Education,* and the *Journal of Educational Psychology.* He was the invited editor of a special June 1990 edition of the latter journal entitled "Instruction in Higher Education."

STEVEN ROSENFIELD is an adjunct professor at the Centre for the Study of Classroom Processes and instructor at Vanier College in Montreal, Quebec. His research interests include postsecondary instruction (especially mathematics education).

JOHN C. SMART is professor of higher education at The University of Memphis. He serves as editor of *Research in Higher Education* and *Higher Education: Handbook of Theory of Research.* His research over the past two decades has focused on college effects on students, disciplinary differences among faculty, and the effects of institutional culture and decision-making approaches on the organizational effectiveness of colleges and universities.

MARYELLEN WEIMER returned to the classroom as a full-time faculty member in the fall of 1994. She teaches communication courses at the Berks campus of Penn State, where she is also a facilitator of teaching-learning initiatives. Previously she was the Associate Director of the National Center on Postsecondary Teaching, Learning and Assessment, a five-year, $5.9 million U.S. Department of Education research and development center. For ten years before that she directed Penn State's Instructional Development Program and still holds a faculty appointment in the Higher Education Program.

Dr. Weimer has published in articles in many professional journals, and since 1987 has edited *The Teaching Professor*, a monthly newsletter on college teaching with 20,000 subscribers. Her books include *Improving College Teaching* (Jossey-Bass, 1990), a 1993 Sage book on teaching for new faculty, and, most recently, *Teaching on Solid Ground: Using Scholarship to Improve Practice,* co-edited with Robert Menges and published in 1995 by Jossey-Bass. She is currently working on a book on teaching and learning in large classes.

SONJA WIEDENHAUPT is a Ph.D. candidate in psychology at the University of California. Her areas of research focus on the roles of interest and motivation in learning, the mechanisms for enhancing intrinsic engagement, and the writing process. She is a recipient of the Berkeley Outstanding Graduate Student Instructor Award.

Introduction

Raymond P. Perry and John C. Smart

Institutions of higher learning have come of age during the latter half of the 20th century. In a true sense they have joined McLuhan's (1964) "global village," required to be increasingly accountable for their traditional roles, while simultaneously expected to be responsive to society's changing priorities and pressures. Addressing these issues will require postsecondary institutions to be more proficient at creating new knowledge and at communicating it—their historical research and teaching mandates. And as intellectual capacity, knowledge generation, and technological innovation become more critical to a country's economic vitality, it is the universities and colleges that will assume greater responsibility for the strategic development of these resources.

In the global marketplace, higher education will provide an essential infrastructure with which a country can harness its technological and creative potentials. As part of this expanding "knowledge industry," postsecondary institutions will be expected to place a greater emphasis on teaching, so that new developments can be more quickly communicated to the broader community. Inevitably, for both research universities and postsecondary institutions whose primary role is teaching, this means that increased attention will be directed at how teaching can be done more effectively and more efficiently to ensure the rapid and direct transfer of information. Thus, long-standing commitments to teaching proficiency are likely to intensify as part of society's broader concerns about technology transfer.

Interest in teaching is becoming increasingly evident in postsecondary institutions throughout North America, as policies on tenure, promotion, and merit are revised to give teaching greater emphasis, e.g. Cornell University (*The Chronicle of Higher Education*, Dec.2, 1992). The University of California system, for example, is considering legislation by which faculty could be appointed to the rank of full professor on teaching performance alone (*The Chronicle of Higher Education*, July 29, 1992), and Stanford University has issued a report in which teaching would be given greater emphasis in the hiring and promotion of faculty (*The Chronicle of Higher Education*, Oct. 19, 1994). In Florida, the Miami-Dade community college system has recently funded an endowed chair in teaching to signify the importance it attaches to pedagogy. And along with these administrative changes, entire units are being established expressly for the evaluation and improvement of teaching. In a brief two year period in Canada (1990-1992), the

University of Alberta, Queen's University, Simon Fraser University, and the University of Victoria, to name but a few, have put in place programs or centers for the improvement of teaching.

Teaching Proficiency: The Evidence and Its Accessibility

As a new Ph.D. in 1971, I (R.P.P.) was profoundly struck by the lack of resources available to assist me in my development as a college teacher. There was no office of instruction to provide guidance on teaching strategies or on the latest innovations in the research literature. Assistance from one's peers or more senior colleagues was limited, since they were very busy with their own careers. Added to this was the fact that seeking help implied teaching inadequacies—a significant dilemma since it could undermine one's self-worth and the value of all those years spent in graduate school. More importantly for new faculty, it could potentially risk unfavorable information coming forward in future tenure and promotion decisions. Undoubtedly, these were not unique experiences for a generation of academics beginning their academic careers in the late 1960s and early 1970s.

The research literature on college teaching was extensive, but highly technical and poorly organized. Few systematic reviews of the literature existed in which major issues were highlighted and conclusions drawn. Even less available was literature that translated the research evidence into practical teaching strategies for the typical classroom instructor. Fortunately, my training as a social psychologist helped me with the methodological complexities of the research literature, though it might have been much different, I suspect, had I been in English, History, or Philosophy. As well, there were a few review articles that made the empirical findings more manageable. In particular, McKeachie's (1963) and Costin, Greenough, and Menges' (1971) reviews of the literature on student ratings and McKeachie's *Teaching Tips* (1969) were of great assistance in getting me through those early teaching experiences.

But much has changed in the two decades since I first started teaching. Significant and rapid advances have been made in the research on college teaching, far surpassing the developments of the previous 50 years. Such outlets as the *Annual Review of Psychology, Higher Education: Handbook of Theory and Research, The Journal of Educational Psychology, The Journal of Higher Education*, and *Research in Higher Education*, to name but a few, have been particularly instrumental in making this information available. In the process the research has become more complex and technical, but at the same time, more potentially useful to and of benefit for the academic community. At the institutional level, similar progress has been manifested in the establishment of campuswide standing committees on instruction and centers for improving teaching whose express purpose is to assist faculty in teaching-related issues. And at the organizational level, several new associations and societies have emerged as interest in college teaching grows exponentially. In the 1970s, for example, the Professional and Organizational Development (POD) society became active and two new groups were added to the American Educational Research Association (AERA) devoted to college teaching: the

Special Interest Group on Faculty Evaluation and Development (SIGFED) and Division J on postsecondary education. Division K, Teaching and Teacher Education, was subsequently formed in the 1980s and has college teaching as part of its mission.

And yet, it comes as a great surprise to many faculty and administrators that any research on college teaching exists at all, let alone that it is extensive and of long-standing duration. Some of the earliest studies were done over 70 years ago in the 1920s when Herman Remmers (e.g., Remmers, 1928) and his group at Purdue first started looking at the complexities of college teaching through the use of student ratings (McKeachie, 1990). It is equally surprising to those same academics that the research is of such high quality, adhering to the rigors of sound experimental design and statistical analysis. It seems clear, therefore, that it is not the quantity or the quality of the research *per se* that has slowed the transfer of the empirical evidence, but rather other factors that have limited its application.

In part, the responsibility for ignoring this wealth of scientific knowledge lies with the instructors themselves who feel secure in the knowledge that they know all there is to know about teaching, simply because they are actively engaged in the teaching process. Personal experience and shared myths about teaching are often deemed sufficient to equip oneself to teach effectively. This situation is all the more peculiar given that faculty, unlike school teachers, receive little or no training in pedagogy, yet spend between 30 to 70 percent of their professional careers devoted to teaching, depending on the nature of their institution. In contrast, considerable time and effort is allocated to the development of sophisticated research skills that may only be used a small proportion of the time, or by relatively few faculty. For junior faculty, this problem is particularly exacerbated since they have little personal experience to guide them in their efforts to become proficient teachers.

In part, the responsibility lies with researchers who have devoted little time to translating their findings into practical strategies for assisting the classroom instructor. As a consequence valuable knowledge accumulates in research networks, journals, and libraries, but little of it is synthesized and transformed for potential users. And finally, responsibility lies with the faculty developers who have not made the technical knowledge available to their respective constituents. This requires considerable time and effort to package the information so that research findings can be meaningfully incorporated into routine teaching practices. A good example of bridging this gap between research and classroom practice is *The Teaching Professor*, an international monthly newsletter edited by Maryellen Weimer.

So it is not surprising, then, that many myths about college teaching continue to survive, despite empirical evidence to the contrary. Two of these myths are described here for illustration purposes. For many college professors and administrators, the myth persists that effective teaching borders on the mystical, frequently imbued with the trappings of an art form. As such, it is assumed that the critical qualities guiding superior teaching performance are predetermined; that a select few are blessed with such gifts. From this premise follow several related propositions that are detrimental to improving the quality of instruction on many campuses. For example, little value would be attached to training programs, if performance is assumed to be predetermined by genetic-like qualities. While it seems plausible that a fortunate few may be so blessed, it is equally probable that many others have the capacity to become proficient teachers with proper training. Like the sporting arena, there may be some whose biological gifts allow them to excel with little effort, but there are also many more who become proficient through systematic preparation and training.

But effective teaching can be studied scientifically, its qualities systematically documented, and its "secrets" successfully imparted through proper training programs. The work of leading researchers in the area, such as those whose chapters follow and others (e.g., Boice, 1992; Centra, 1979; Menges, 1990), empirically attests to this position. In response to this myth, for example, Gage (1978) has taken the position that teaching may, in fact, be an art form, but then raises the question as to whether there may be a scientific basis for it. His analyses and conclusions are illuminating, providing further reasons to reject the myth. Nevertheless, the myth persists and undermines faculty development efforts.

Another common myth among faculty and administrators is that those involved with faculty development only presume to have "correct" solutions for improving teaching. There is deep suspicion that these purported knowledge experts have nothing substantive to offer, and perhaps even less than the "experiential" experts, colleagues whose teaching insights are grounded on the fact that they have taught for a number of years. Considerable antipathy arises, particularly in seasoned instructors, to the suggestion that there are right and wrong, good and bad techniques involving teaching proficiency. Those subscribing to this myth act as if "anything goes"; that there is no common consensus about what constitutes effective college teaching.

In fact, there is a voluminous research literature that documents specific relationships between teaching methods and important educational outcomes. It clearly indicates that there are a finite number of teaching skills that contribute to academic objectives such as student motivation or scholastic achievement, as clearly demonstrated in the following chapters. Furthermore, proponents of this "anything goes" myth argue that, since little is known factually, there should be no self-proclaimed knowledge experts advising others on "correct" solutions. A more reasoned approach would be to recognize that there is some consensus about what constitutes important educational outcomes and that there is good empirical evidence about which teaching skills promote these outcomes. Thus, the task for the instructor is to decide which outcomes are relevant to his or her situation and which related skills are appropriate for him or her to master. For the faculty developer, the task remains to facilitate the instructor's mastery, once the instructor has identified pertinent goals and behaviors.

Accordingly, this book is directed at the misinformation and the mythology surrounding teaching proficiency in postsecondary institutions. It is intended to bridge the ever-widening gap between research and practice, bringing critical empirical evidence to bear on matters of practical importance to both classroom instructors and academic administrators. It does so by having recognized scholars, who have achieved outstanding reputations for their research, provide comprehensive syntheses of the rapidly-expanding literature. In so doing, practical applications are described both within each chapter and separately with summary chapters at the end of each section (i.e., Perry & McKeachie) and at the end of the book (Weimer). As such, this book extends previous initiatives to make the research literature more accessible to researchers, classroom instructors, and administrators alike. It is hoped the present project makes the accumulated knowledge more meaningful and the teaching more manageable.

Audience and Focus

One major group for which this book is intended is faculty in all postsecondary institutions who regularly teach as part of their job description. For these professors the material in this book can benefit their daily teaching practices. The consistent empirical finding that the organization and clarity of lectures are directly related to student achievement, for example, provides a clear message on how to plan lectures. Similarly, evidence showing specific linkages between student attributes and performance can assist faculty in using the most appropriate teaching methods with different types of students. In each case the solution is based on sound empirical findings, not anecdotal speculation—an important issue for academics whose professional training has taught them to base their decisions on the weight of the evidence.

Besides professors, this book is intended for faculty developers, academic administrators, and policy-makers who are equally committed to issues involving teaching proficiency. Faculty (instructional) developers are officially charged by the institution with the enhancement of teaching proficiency at the level of the individual faculty member. They are responsible for bringing empirical evidence, conventional wisdom, and practical experience to bear on teaching matters of relevance to the professor. Also important in this respect are members of instruction committees and academic administrators who are primarily responsible for policy issues and personnel decisions related to teaching proficiency. For these administrative groups, the task is not so much to assist individual instructors in their day-to-day teaching activities, as it is to implement accumulated wisdom and empirical findings according to institutional protocols and procedures. Their duties can range from course assignments and program implementation to tenure and promotion decisions, each based on teaching priorities and intended to have educational benefits for students, faculty, and the institution alike. For each of these groups, professors, faculty developers, instruction committees, and administrators, the material presented in this book should be of considerable assistance in achieving their objectives for the advancement of teaching.

In addition to this Introduction and an evaluative concluding chapter, this volume is divided into two sections that consider teaching proficiency from a student and a faculty perspective. The Student Perspective section addresses the issue of student diversity in relation to teaching, a fundamental question raised annually by instructors as they contemplate meeting their classes for the first time. Ensuring that instructional quality is optimal for each student has always been a concern for faculty, but now with access to higher education increasing, it promises to become an even greater challenge. To the usual differences between students involving intelligence, motivation, impulsivity, boredom, etc. are now added others such as race, gender, age, and ethnicity, to name but a few. Being able to find common reference points with such diversity is bound to occupy much of the instructor's planning activities.

In the Student Perspective section, Covington, Covington and Weidenhaupt, and Perry provide two typologies for classifying college students, namely self-worth and perceived control, which can be used to find some commonalty between students. Classifying students into educationally meaningful groups is important to the extent that it enables appropriate teaching methods to be matched to each student. Without identifying such commonalities, teaching could become an unmanageable task because the number of methods required to teach each student individually would be beyond the capacity of a single instructor. Thus, teaching could be enhanced if classroom diversity can be reduced by classifying students into educationally meaningful groups, so that they can be taught in a manner best suited to their unique qualities. From Covington's and Perry's perspectives, then, teaching methods would vary depending on differences between students in their self-worth or perceived control.

With respect to teaching methods, Kiewra believes that instruction is most effective when the course material is made meaningful for students through the use of matrix representations. These structures are intended to organize knowledge so that the facts, as well as the interrelationships between them, are better understood by the students. Kiewra provides a detailed account of how knowledge representations such as lists, outlines, and matrices can be constructed so that course material becomes more organized and meaningful for students. As such, his chapter describes how a professor can become more organized, a teaching behavior shown consistently to be a significant component of effective instruction, as discussed in several chapters in the next section on the faculty perspective (Feldman; Marsh and Dunkin; Murray).

The Faculty Perspective section focuses on specific teaching behaviors that comprise effective instruction. Murray, Marsh and Dunkin, Abrami *et al.*, and Feldman describe a finite set of teaching behaviors that have been empirically related to student achievement. Both correlational and experimental evidence is presented demonstrating that effective teaching is, at least in part, the result of instructors being organized, clear, knowledgeable, expressive, etc. Written by some of the most widely respected experts in the field, these chapters provide comprehensive, state-of-the-art reviews of the burgeoning literature on college teaching that has emerged since the middle half of the 20th century. For instructors, administrators, and faculty developers, rational, empirically based answers are provided to such questions as: How can I be a more effective teacher? Are student ratings valid and reliable? Can their use be defended administratively? Are some faculty better suited for some classes and not others?

Rounding out this section, Weimer and Lenze provide a systematic review of various efforts to improve instruction in postsecondary institutions, including workshops, seminars, programs, consultation, grants for instructional improvement projects, resource materials, and colleagues helping colleagues. This chapter is particularly useful for administrators and faculty developers in providing practical background for the development of instructional interventions on a campus-wide basis. Completing each section are summary chapters for the student (Perry) and the faculty (McKeachie), while the Conclusion is a summarizing chapter for the book as a whole (Weimer).

These three chapters provide several examples of effective teaching from the empirical literature and underscore the necessity for developing research-informed teaching practices. Weimer's chapter in particular provides a kind of detailed summary of each chapter in the entire book, and for that reason some readers may find it useful to read her concluding chapter first.

Acknowledgments

Needless to say, a project of this scope cannot be undertaken without the support of a wide spectrum of individuals, each contributing in their own special way. Most importantly, the authors of the chapters have ensured that the quality and the integrity of the material is of a very high level. In the process, they delivered their chapters in a timely and responsible fashion, making the editors' role in the development of the book exceedingly more manageable. Equally noteworthy were the reviewers whose insightful commentaries and rapid feedback assisted the authors in their task. Institutional support for the project was provided by the University of Manitoba at several levels, notably by the Vice-President Academic, James Gardner, and his predecessor, Fred Stambrook, reflecting the University's broad commitment to the development of faculty as teachers. As well, Sheryl Bond, the past Director of the Centre for Higher Education Research and Development had the foresight to encourage initiatives like this at a time when teaching was not at the forefront of higher education's priorities. In particular, Raymond Currie, Dean of the Faculty of Arts, was instrumental in creating a favorable philosophical and organizational climate in which a book of this nature was feasible. And, finally, Diane Benoit's unstinting secretarial support brought the book to rapid completion.

Many others who have contributed over the years, in their own ways, to the evolution of this book cannot all be listed here, but nevertheless are appreciated for their support. We cannot close without expressing our deep appreciation to our wives, Judy and Bunty, and to our children, Jason and Dawn and David, for giving us balance and perspective throughout this undertaking.

References

Boice, R. (1992). *The New Faculty Member.* San Francisco: Jossey-Bass.

Centra, J. A. (1979). *Determining Faculty Effectiveness.* San Francisco: Jossey-Bass.

The Chronicle of Higher Education, (July 29, 1992). University of California to stress teaching and service. Washington, DC: The Chronicle of Higher Education, Inc.

The Chronicle of Higher Education, (December 2, 1992). Cornell wants vigorous evaluation of teaching in tenure cases. Washington, DC: The Chronicle of Higher Education, Inc.

The Chronicle of Higher Education, (October 19, 1994). Panel of Stanford's Curriculum Committee recommends "moderate" changes. Washington, DC: The Chronicle of Higher Education, Inc.

Costin, F., Greenough, W. T., and Menges, R. J. (1971). Student ratings of college teaching: Reliability, validity, and usefulness. *Review of Educational Research* 41: 511-535.

Gage, N. L. (1978). *The Scientific Basis of the Art of Teaching*. New York: Teachers College Press, Columbia University.

McKeachie, W. J. (1963). Research on teaching at the college and university level. In N. L. Gage (Ed.), *Handbook of Research and Teaching* (pp. 1118-1172). Chicago: Rand McNally.

McKeachie, W. J. (1969). *Teaching Tips: A Guidebook for the Beginning Teacher* (6th edition). Lexington, MA: D. C. Heath.

McKeachie, W. J. (1990). Research on college teaching: The historical background. *Journal of Educational Psychology* 82: 189-200.

McLuhan, M. (1964). *Understanding Media: The Extensions of Man*. New York: McGraw-Hill.

Menges, R. J. (1990). Using evaluative information to improve instruction. In P. Seldin and associates (Eds.), *How Administrators Can Improve Instruction: Moving from Talk to Action in Higher Education*. San Francisco: Jossey-Bass.

Remmers, H. H. (1928). The relationship between students' marks and students' attitudes towards instructors. *School and Society* 28: 759-760.

PERSPECTIVES ON STUDENTS

Perceived Control in College Students: Implications for Instruction in Higher Education

Raymond P. Perry

College students are repeatedly confronted by personal, academic, and societal pressures throughout their educational development. In writing an essay, giving an oral presentation, or forming adult relationships, students are expected to acquire new skills and to apply them effectively to future endeavors. Their success in overcoming these academic challenges is dependent on a variety of factors, two of the most salient being the attributes they bring with them to the classroom and the quality of instruction they receive. Although both factors are critical to achievement in higher education, surprisingly little systematic inquiry has been undertaken to explore their combined effects. For the most part researchers have considered either student attributes or instruction; only infrequently have they been studied jointly.

Several aspects of this issue are of immediate practical concern to the college teacher. Before meeting a class for the first time, a professor often wonders about who the students will be and how to motivate them. In raising these questions, the professor is seeking information to guide decisions about teaching methods, content coverage, textbook selection, and course structure and assignments. The professor frequently relies on previous classroom experiences and on general assumptions arising from the students' appearance, demeanor, and demographic characteristics. Knowing that some students are career-oriented and highly motivated, while others are apathetic and disinterested, can have a strong bearing on the instructional practices adopted. Ultimately, success in organizing the course often rests on how well the professor can adapt methods of instruction to important student attributes.

This chapter was supported by grants from the office of the Vice-President, Academic, University of Manitoba, and from the Max-Planck-Institut, Munich, Germany. Robert C. Calfee, Stanford University, Harry Murray, the University of Western Ontario, and Franz E. Weinert, Max-Planck-Institut, provided critical feedback on the chapter, as did Judy Chipperfield and Jamie-Lynn Magnusson, University of Manitoba. The opinions expressed, however, are solely those of the author. I would also like to thank Dieter Schonwetter and Ward Struthers for their work on the figures and tables. Correspondence concerning this article should be sent to Raymond P. Perry, Centre for Higher Education Research and Development, University of Manitoba, Winnipeg, Manitoba, Canada, R3T 2N2.

The purpose of this chapter is to explore the nature of this relation between student characteristics and college instruction. The relation is predicated on the assumption that there is an optimal match between instructional practices and students' characteristics. Such a match would ensure that an instructional practice produces an acceptable level of performance in students possessing a specified level of some attribute. Thus, for highly motivated students, an instructional method having high information density may provide sufficient challenge to facilitate achievement. For unmotivated or anxious (students, however, this same practice may prove so threatening that it impairs their performance. In one case the match is satisfactory; in the other it is not. The task for educators and researchers alike is to understand these matches so that instruction can be optimized for various subgroups in a college classroom.

This relation between instruction and student characteristics will be examined primarily in terms of lecturing and perceived control. Lecturing is a ubiquitous teaching method in the higher education system, and perceived control is increasingly recognized as an important factor in students' academic achievement. Many pedagogical methods comprising college instruction rely on oral communication despite the growing availability of other alternatives such as computer-assisted learning, intelligent-tutoring systems, and hypermedia. Of the oral methods, lecturing continues to be the most common and will likely remain popular, especially as student enrollments increase and financial support for universities diminishes. A recent review of college teaching (Dunkin and Barnes, 1986) indicated that, although much instructional innovation has occurred in higher education, lecturing continues to predominate. More will be said about the lecture method in Section II.

Perceived personal control has become a predominant concept in psychological theory and research during the last few decades. It has been linked to depression, crowding, marital relations, academic achievement, health, aging, stress, cancer and a variety of other psychological phenomena. It refers to an individual's *perceived* capacity to influence and to predict events in the environment. This emphasis on perceived rather than objective capacity reflects a phenomenological distinction between what the individual believes about his/her capacity in contrast to what actually exists. Some people believe they possess a greater capacity to influence events than they have in reality, while others believe they have less capacity than they actually have. These differences, in turn, determine a variety of cognitive, emotional, and behavioral developments. Thus, someone with a strong sense of personal control will think, feel, and respond differently to challenge than someone with little personal control.

The essential feature of this definition is that personal belief patterns are thought to mediate self-regulatory mechanisms necessary for adaptation to the environment. In a classroom, for example, a student's achievement on a math test would be enhanced by perceptions that focus attention, increase working memory capacity, and reduce emotional interference. In contrast, perceptions that disrupt attention, limit memory, and upset emotional equilibrium, would lead to poor performance. These belief patterns can be either stable and enduring, not unlike personality traits, or temporary and transient, very much the product of environmental circumstance.

Perceptions of personal control play a pivotal role in students' educational attainment, possibly being as important as intelligence, social class, or discipline knowledge. Of course, it is an empirical question as to how these variables are linked together and which may be the most important. One view is that each variable contributes jointly to academic achievement in a relatively equal fashion. Another is that perceived personal control is a superordinate construct, the product of other factors such as intelligence, pre-existing domain expertise, and social class. So, for example, a bright, middle-class student, having considerable background knowledge in mathematics may have greater perceived control in a math course because of these attributes than a student with low intelligence, lacking background information, and belonging to a lower social class.

In the educational domain perceived control would involve beliefs and perceptions about strategies, plans, behaviors, and events contributing specifically to academic achievement. In students, these beliefs are thought to produce major differences in scholastic attainment. For example, Stipiek and Weisz (1981) reviewed research using Crandall, Katkovsky, and Crandall's (1965) Intellectual Achievement Responsibility Scale which measures how much personal responsibility school children take for their intellectual achievement. They showed that those taking greatest responsibility for their achievement, internal-locus children, did consistently better than external-locus children on several academic indicators. These findings are characteristic of a rapidly expanding research literature linking students' perceived control with their achievement motivation and scholastic performance (e.g., Dweck and Reppucci, 1973; Garber and Seligman, 1980; Schunk, 1983).[1]

In relative terms, perceived control is likely to play a *more* important role for academic development at the college level than at the elementary or secondary levels. Almost immediately upon entering college, a student assumes more responsibility for his/her education than previously: in choosing courses, in completing assignments, and in seeking remedial assistance. During class, greater independent effort is expected in note-taking, in comprehending the lecture material, and in mastering the content of the course. Furthermore, an increased emphasis is placed on competition and on success as instrumental factors in career-attainment. Bursaries, awards, and scholarships are dependent on this process, and access to professional schools and career choice are tied to it. Finally, self-concept and academic success become increasingly intertwined so that one's identity is very much linked to one's scholastic record. Feeling good about oneself often hinges precariously on how well one did on the last test!

---

[1]Similar belief patterns in teachers could also affect students' performance, though through a more indirect route involving effective teaching. Teachers' perceived control should improve the quality of their teaching which would then enhance students' performance and, in turn, possibly their perceived control. In fact, increasing students' perceived control could be, itself, argued to be an important goal of effective teaching, in addition to more traditional educational objectives such as achievement. Research on perceived control in teachers is sparse in comparison to students, although some work has been done, i.e., Gibson and Dembo's (1984) self-efficacy scale for teachers.

Virtually omitted from the research, however, has been a consideration of how students' perceived control and instruction are related. It is commonly acknowledged that effective teaching in the college classroom should take into account student differences, but the predominant research emphasis has been on the student *or* on instruction—rarely on how the combination of the two affect student performance. Differences between students in both cognitive and noncognitive domains (e.g., Messick, 1979) are known to determine scholastic achievement and are assumed to influence how students respond to various types of instruction. Yet little has been done in higher education to examine this issue generally, or more specifically in the case of perceived control and instruction. Questions of interest from this interactive perspective would include: Does perceived control in college students influence performance differently depending on the quality of instruction they receive? What teaching methods are likely to increase students' mastery of course content given pre-existing levels of perceived control? This interaction approach enables a far richer conceptual analysis of classroom dynamics than focusing on only one component, namely the student *or* the teacher.

To answer such questions requires the inclusion of both instruction and student variables in the same study. In its simplest form the research design would include an instruction variable having two levels (e.g., effective, ineffective) and a student perceived control variable also having two levels (e.g., internal and external locus of control), along with an achievement measure (see Section I for a detailed description of locus of control). A main effect approach has often been used in which either instruction or perceived control are deemed important, precluding the need to consider the other variable. An instruction main effect indicates that effective teaching produces more achievement in all students, both internals and externals, whereas a perceived control main effect shows that internals perform better than externals in both teaching conditions. In either case one variable is considered sufficiently powerful to explain the performance outcomes without the inclusion of another variable. However, an instruction by perceived control interaction is also possible with this design, having several forms: for internal-locus students, effective teaching could increase achievement more than ineffective teaching, without a similar improvement taking place in external-locus students; or, internals and externals could perform equally well with effective teaching, but internals could do better than externals with ineffective teaching. Several other alternatives are also possible, the important point being that one variable qualifies the other; that the two variables combined are essential to understand the achievement patterns.

A recent study by Perry and Magnusson (1987a) illustrates this interaction approach. Students' perceived control was temporarily altered by subjecting them to one of two feedback conditions designed to induce perceptions of mastery (contingent feedback) or of helplessness (noncontingent feedback). Whereas mastery entails a strong sense of control over one's surroundings, helplessness implies severe loss of control. Following these manipulations, both groups observed a half-hour videotaped lecture presented by either an effective or ineffective instructor, and then wrote a 30-item test on the material. Instructor effectiveness was defined in terms of expressiveness, a teaching behavior considered central to the lecture method and shown to influence student achievement (e.g., Abrami, Leventhal, and Perry, 1982; Marsh and Ware, 1982). For mastery students, performance was better with expressive than unexpressive instruction (see Figure 1). This was not the case for helpless students who failed to improve their performance with expressive instruction. Thus, students experiencing temporary loss of control over their academic performance appear unable to benefit from effective instruction. More about this interaction will be discussed below in Section III.

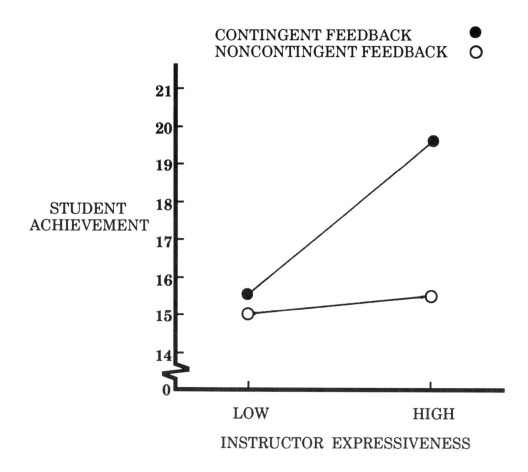

Mastery may result from contingent feedback, internal locus of control, Type A behavior, etc.

Helplessness may result from noncontingent feedback, external locus of control, etc.

FIGURE 1. A perceived control by instruction interaction in which helpless (noncontingent feedback) students are unable to benefit from effective (high expressive) teaching.

If noncontingent feedback reliably inhibits learning during effective instruction, then it raises a number of issues having important research and practical implications. One issue concerns the duration of the effect and whether it is transitory or long-lasting. Since students repeatedly have experiences which can cause loss of control, it would be reassuring to find that the effect is not enduring. A dissipation of the effect in one instance, however, does not mean that it does so in all circumstances; or that certain personal attributes, such as learning disabilities or an external locus of control, do not exacerbate the problem. A second issue concerns whether other teaching behaviors than expressiveness are also ineffective with helpless students. The prognosis for scholastic achievement in helpless students would be exceedingly pessimistic if it were true for most other behaviors as well. An inability to benefit from instruction in general would lower scholastic achievement and, therefore, would threaten access to higher education for some minority groups, such as women, visible minorities, and the physically disabled, who are repeatedly subjected to loss of control. It would also increase the probability that these groups would leave college even after gaining access. A third issue involves assisting students who suffer loss of control. Strategies or techniques such as attributional retraining (Perry and Penner, 1990) may be developed which could help these students derive some benefit from effective instruction.

Almost 20 years ago, McKeachie (1974) drew attention to the relation between student characteristics and instruction in the form of aptitude-treatment interactions (ATIs). According to Cronbach and Snow (1977, p. 6), an aptitude is "any characteristic of a person that forecasts his probability of success under a given treatment." In general, an ATI may occur if variability on some aptitude predisposes subjects to respond differently to one treatment compared to another (e.g., see Figure 1). Within an educational context, ATIs reflect pedagogical reasoning in which individual students are considered to have different capacities, each potentially requiring a different instruction method. Thus, academic attainment is not simply due to student aptitudes or to instruction methods separately; rather, a combination of the two produces optimal learning conditions.[2]

Several weaknesses in the higher education literature revealed by McKeachie's review continue to plague current research endeavors involving student attributes and instruction. First, studies of college classrooms were relatively few in comparison to studies of elementary and secondary classrooms, in part a reflection of U.S. government

---

[2]It is generally acknowledged that studying individual differences in the classroom is both ethically and morally desirable to the extent that it allows the development of instructional practices that optimize academic development for all students. In practice, however, the ATI approach has received mixed support. Several critics (e.g., Bracht, 1970; Goldberg, 1972) have argued that empirical evidence and practicality do not favor an ATI approach. They point to inconsistent research findings (e.g., Tallmadge, Kasten, and Shearer, 1971) and practical problems with trying to institute ATI solutions in the classroom. In contrast, Cronbach and Snow (1977) and others (Salomon, 1972; Tobias, 1976) have presented strong arguments supporting ATIs and have posited improved conceptual frameworks for studying them. Poor experimental methodology and inappropriate theoretical applications have been identified as major reasons for weak results in the past. More recent developments in theory (Snow, 1986) and in methodology (Whitener, 1989) have given further impetus to the ATI approach.

funding priorities of programs such as Head Start and Follow Through (Medley, 1977). Second, the method of instruction was defined in very global terms, often without a sound empirical basis. For example, in Domino's (1971) study of two teaching styles, teacher-centered instruction was defined as homework assignments, class attendance, discipline, and a structured presentation of course content; student-centered instruction de-emphasized these features in favor of student discussion. These early studies (e.g., Koran, Snow, and McDonald, 1971) were not able to take advantage of the extensive empirical evidence currently available for developing a suitable manipulation of instruction (e.g., Travers, 1973; Wittrock, 1986). Unfortunately, more recent studies continue to ignore this literature in specifying operational definitions of instruction. Third, little attention has been given to the critical ATIs in the college classroom. It seems reasonable to assume that some student differences are more important than others and that research efforts should focus on ATIs involving these more fundamental attributes. Although the ATI reported by Domino has been subjected to further scrutiny (e.g., Dowaliby and Schumer, 1973; Peterson, 1979), few other ATIs have been systematically investigated. Finally, even less effort has been devoted to a detailed, fine-grained analysis of ATIs. A micro-analytic ATI approach would enable the cognitive, affective, and motivational processes associated with specific aptitudes and instruction methods to be examined. Thus, in the case of perceived control, the analysis could include a consideration of causal attributions, emotional arousal, or information processing activities. It could also involve an examination of how they are linked to a particular method of instruction. This approach would provide a clearer understanding of the ATI in question and should improve the development of effective instruction methods.

Little has happened in higher education research since 1974 to invalidate McKeachie's claim that there is "a quiescence in the area of research on cognitive variables interacting with treatments" (p. 165). However, the research on perceived control and instruction presented in this chapter features several improvements to the existing literature. To begin with, it is based on the premise that a core of critical aptitude-treatment interactions exist in the college classroom and that they should be a focus of interest. Of course, it is acknowledged that ATIs other than the one between perceived control and instruction are important, but they are not considered in this chapter. In addition, instruction is defined using the extensive research on teaching effectiveness which has emerged in the last 15 years (see Section II below). This evidence identifies specific teaching behaviors as being associated with particular instruction methods which have been directly linked to student achievement and other academic indicators. Finally, a microanalytic approach is used to study the relation between perceived control and instruction. This involves a detailed analysis of students' cognitive, affective, and motivational processes from several theoretical perspectives including information processing, attribution theory, and control theory. These emphases, along with the questions addressed, constitute a significant departure from ATI approaches taken in earlier studies.

The chapter is divided into three major sections. The first and second sections review the theoretical and empirical literature related to perceived control and to effective college teaching. Because each topic has developed historically independently of the other, each is presented here in a separate section. The third section is devoted to the relation between perceived control and instruction, specifically to how the two topics are conceptually linked and what empirical evidence exists for the relation.

I. PERCEIVED CONTROL

The concept of perceived control is grounded in a rapidly expanding literature referred to as social cognition. Within this general body of knowledge, some researchers have focused on people's beliefs about their self-regulatory systems and the relation of these systems to adaptation. Perceived personal control is a key concept in this area of investigation because it deals with people's perceptions of how their personal attributes influence their social world. Its modern development begins with the works of White (1959), Rotter (1966), and De Charms (1968) who posited the terms competence motivation, internal/external locus of control, and personal causation respectively, to describe these belief patterns. More recently, other researchers have delineated the concept with such terms as learned helplessness (Seligman, 1975), mastery (Dweck, 1975), reactance (Wortman and Brehm, 1975), self-efficacy (Bandura, 1977), Type A/B behavior (Glass, 1977), primary/secondary control (Rothbaum, Weisz, and Snyder, 1982), action theory (Kuhl, 1985) and mindfulness (Langer, 1989) to name just a few.

Common to all these constructs is the premise that beliefs about personal causation are related to actual causation. If, for example, an individual believes that he/she has low ability for some task, then the ensuing cognitive, emotional, and motivational deficits could lead to lower performance. Conversely, a belief in high ability could have an opposite effect, namely to increase performance. The purpose of this section is to provide an introduction to these issues so that the perceived control construct can be meaningfully applied to the college classroom (see Section III). It is beyond the scope of this chapter to review all constructs in detail, but some major commonalities will be identified and some examples relevant to the college classroom presented.

A Taxonomy of Perceived Control

Perceived control is directly or indirectly featured in many constructs appearing in the psychological literature. This plethora of alternatives creates confusion for those interested in selecting a suitable construct for research purposes. It can be counterproductive, for example, to choose the Type A/B behavior construct to study perceived control in learning-disabled students who repeatedly experience loss of control and failure in their academic pursuits. The Type A construct would be inappropriate because it describes individuals who are preoccupied with control and who are constantly seeking to influence events, an unlikely profile for learning-disabled students. One resolution to choosing a suitable alternative is to reduce this burgeoning list of constructs to a smaller number of categories. Unfortunately, such a classification system has yet to emerge in the research literature. To this end, a rudimentary taxonomy is proposed here for organizing the growing array of constructs. Only a select sample of constructs is presented to illustrate the taxonomy; other constructs in the research literature can be incorporated as required.

TABLE. 1. A taxonomy for constructs involving perceived personal control

	STABLE	UNSTABLE
CONTROL	Locus of Control (Rotter, 1966) Personal Causation (DeCharms, 1968) *Type A/B Behavior (Matthews, 1982) Health Hardiness (Kolbasa, 1983) Optimism (Scheier & Carver, 1985) **Action Control Theory (Kuhl, 1986) 1	2 Competence Motivation (White, 1959) Reactance (Wortman & Brehm, 1975) Primary/Secondary Control (Rothbaum, Weisz, & Snyder, 1982)
LOSS OF CONTROL	Explanatory Style 3 (Peterson & Seligman, 1984) Helplessness (Dweck, 1975)	4 Helplessness (Seligman, 1975)

*Type A/B behavior can be placed in Cell 1 if the behavior is deemed relatively enduring to the point of reflecting personality traits, or Cell 3 if the emphasis is on negative aspects associated with coronary heart disease.

**Action theory can also be placed in Cell 3 if certain components are of interest and emphasized, i.e., state orientation.

Two dimensions for grouping the various constructs are readily apparent, namely controllability and stability (see Table 1). The controllability dimension describes the degree to which a construct involves perceptions of control versus lack of control over environmental events. At one end of this continuum are constructs emphasizing the acquisition and retention of control, as for example, internal locus of control (Rotter, 1966); at the other end are constructs stressing the loss of control such as learned helplessness (Seligman, 1975). The primary difference between these two extremes is emphasis rather than exclusiveness. That is, some constructs feature control and give little attention to loss of control, whereas others do just the opposite. Thus, each construct may be predicated on the assumption that both control and loss of control are two sides of the same coin, but that one is of greater interest than the other.

The stability dimension describes the degree to which people's perceptions of control are temporary or enduring. Temporary or unstable perceptions of control are considered to be highly susceptible to environmental influence, and therefore quite changeable, whereas stable perceptions are relatively enduring and more impervious to environmental factors. Self-efficacy (Bandura, 1977) and learned helplessness (Seligman, 1975) exemplify constructs concerned with unstable perceptions of control, whereas locus of control (Rotter, 1966) and explanatory style (Peterson and Seligman, 1984) emphasize stability. In this respect the distinction between the two extremes may have a parallel in state versus trait constructs of anxiety in which the former is temporary, usually caused by transient environmental factors, and the latter more enduring, the result of longstanding personality factors. As such, a person's position on the continuum is likely to be relative across settings and time.

Several points are worth noting about this taxonomy. First, each of the two dimensions is a continuum and not the dichotomy implied by the extreme categories in Table 1. Consequently, constructs could occupy intermediate positions between the two extremes on each dimension, as in the case of the locus of control construct having a less extreme position than the Type A/B behavior construct on the controllability dimension. Second, the constructs depicted are not an exhaustive list, but rather a select sample. The constructs chosen are those which highlight perceived control and which are currently topical. Accordingly, new constructs can be added to the taxonomy, as for example, the health hardiness construct (Kobasa, 1983); or others which are only indirectly concerned with perceived control, such as the self-worth construct (Covington, 1984). Third, the placing of the constructs in particular cells is not immutable, partly because of the ambiguities of some constructs (e.g., Type A/B behavior). For our purposes, constructs from two of the cells in the taxonomy will be described in greater detail. These cells were chosen specifically because of their relevance to the research on the college classroom presented in Section III.

Control/Stable (Cell 1).
The constructs in this cell are concerned with people's perceptions of their ability to manipulate environmental events across settings and time. Perceived personal control is represented, implicitly or explicitly, as an enduring set of beliefs and behaviors which can have a direct influence over the surrounding environment. "Being in control" rather than "being out of control" is emphasized as a relatively stable entity somewhat similar to a trait, locus of control being a good example of a construct having these properties. It was first proposed by Rotter (1966) in the context of his social learning theory (Rotter, Chance, and Phares, 1972) and refers to a person's generalized expectancies about the relation between his/her attributes or actions and outcomes in the surrounding environment. Individuals having an *internal* locus of control believe that their efforts typically produce desired results. They perceive a direct connection between their own actions and ensuing consequences, and are therefore likely to strive for valued objectives. Individuals having an *external* locus of control see little connection between their efforts and events taking place around them. Factors outside themselves such as luck, fate, and pow-

erful others are seen as the critical determinants of outcomes. The construct has generated considerable interest in the psychological literature, contributing to over 600 published articles by 1975 (Rotter, 1975), and continues to stimulate lively debate (Lefcourt, 1976; 1984; Phares, 1976; Strickland, 1989).

Loss of Control/Unstable (Cell 4).

The constructs in this category primarily involve perceptions about loss of control. Perceived personal control is represented by a set of beliefs and behaviors reflecting very little influence over environmental outcomes and events. A sense of being "out of control" rather than "in control" is the predominant characteristic of these constructs, most recently epitomized by the learned helplessness construct (Garber and Seligman, 1980; Seligman, 1975). Helplessness, or loss of control, occurs when a person learns that one's actions have little influence over events in the surrounding environment. That is, outcomes are perceived as independent of, or not contingent on, the person's responses. These perceptions of uncontrollability generalize inappropriately to other situations in which the person's behavior can determine events. They cause cognitive, motivational, and emotional deficits which result in withdrawal, passivity, and submissiveness. Consequently, the person makes no attempt to respond in new situations, even though his/her behavior would produce desired outcomes. Similar expectations of uncontrollability can result from failure and aversive stimulation. The helplessness construct created sufficient activity in the 70s that a special edition of the *Journal of Abnormal Psychology* was devoted to it (Huesmann, 1978). Strong interest in the construct has been maintained in the 1980s (e.g., Garber and Seligman, 1980; Peterson and Seligman, 1984) and promises to continue in the 1990s.

Helplessness theory has several advantages for studying perceived control in the college classroom (Perry and Dickens, 1984). First, it has ecological validity because noncontingent feedback occurs frequently in the classroom. The complexities of the classroom ensure that students will experience noncontingent feedback periodically, some students more than others, and some feedback of greater importance. Some instructors, for example, give immediate feedback after an examination, while others allow considerable time to pass before informing students, or give no feedback whatsoever. Lack of feedback and delayed feedback can both create perceptions of noncontingency between response and outcome. Test difficulty can also contribute to noncontingency perceptions when it causes students to perceive little relation between their studying and their performance. Thus, some students may study very hard, expect a good grade, and fail; others may study very little, believe they did poorly, and do very well. In each case noncontingent feedback is generated, making loss of control more probable. Similarly, teacher praise can lead to noncontingency if the praise, a positive outcome, does not follow desirable academic behaviors in students. Brophy's (1981) empirical analysis of elementary classrooms shows that noncontingent praise from the teacher is a common experience for many students. Some teachers rewarded only 11 percent of students' correct responses, while periodically changing the criterion of success; others were unable to learn how to give contingent praise!

Second, helplessness theory provides a reliable and effective method for manipulating students' perceived control in contrast to paper-and-pencil measures. Researchers studying control have often relied on assessing people's perceptions using a variety of paper-and-pencil measures (see Table 1, p. 19) and differentiating levels of control with a median-split procedure. Although it is readily acknowledged by educational researchers that perceived control has both internal and external origins, most attention has been given to internal, stable determinants assessed with paper-and-pencil measures, such as the Intellectual Achievement Responsibility Scale (Crandall, Katkovsky, and Crandall, 1965), the Nowicki-Strickland Children's Locus of Control Scale (Nowicki and Strickland, 1973), the Multidimensional-Multiattributional Causality Scale (Lefcourt, Von Baeyer, Ware and Cox, 1979). For college classroom studies, this approach is particularly weak if it is assumed that the majority of students are relatively internal in their perceived control due to the attrition of less successful external-locus students (Rotter, 1975). By implication, internal differences in perceived control would account for less variability in achievement outcomes than external factors affecting control between students. In contrast, the direct manipulation of control strengthens causal analysis because students can be randomly assigned to control conditions. In addition, manipulating perceived control also places greater emphasis on the environmental origins of uncontrollability.

Finally, helplessness theory has generated considerable research activity which can assist in conceptual development and in the interpretation of empirical results. In particular, the literature offers guidance on the appropriate experimental designs, instrumentation, and statistical analyses necessary to demonstrate loss of control. As such, the model provides a useful template with which to compare results. For example, Perry's procedure for inducing loss of control follows directly from the helplessness model, producing results consistent with the empirical literature and revealing considerable reliability from study to study (e.g., Perry and Dickens, 1984, 1988; Perry and Tunna, 1987).

This is not to suggest that Seligman's helplessness theory is flawless (e.g., Miller and Norman, 1979; Rothbaum et al., 1982), or that other constructs are not suitable for studying the perceived control by instruction interaction. Kuhl (1981; 1985), for example, offers a useful addition to control theory by making a distinction between functional and motivational helplessness. *Functional helplessness* is caused by the development of state-oriented cognitions which can interfere with a variety of information-processing activities such as selective attention, working memory capacity, emotional equilibrium and other self-regulatory mechanisms. *Motivational helplessness* refers to beliefs about uncontrollability in which a person perceives that he/she does not have the capacity to produce a certain outcome, or that he/she has the ability but it will not cause the desired outcome. These beliefs generalize to other settings and reduce motivation to respond. From this brief description, it should be apparent that Kuhl's analysis has obvious implications for the college classroom. His and other control constructs (Table 1) may also be usefully applied to understanding the interaction between perceived control and instruction; however, to date this has not been systematically undertaken.

This brief overview of perceived personal control gives only a superficial introduction to the increasing number of constructs now appearing in the research literature. Table 1 should alert researchers to the large number available and to the importance of selecting the appropriate one for their topic of interest. Their choice should be guided by at least three considerations. First, the emphasis on either being in or out of control should correspond to the phenomenon under investigation. If, for example, the issue concerns perceptions of control and achievement-striving in bright, highly motivated graduate students, then the construct selected should *not* feature loss of control (e.g., learned helplessness) as the central focus, but rather should highlight control (e.g., Type A/B behavior). Similarly, the control perceptions being investigated should reflect the stability of the phenomenon being studied. A construct which is based on transient perceptions of control should not be used to examine enduring (i.e.., stable) control perceptions. Finally, ecological validity should be considered so that the construct is best suited to the context in which it is being applied. For example, the Intellectual Achievement Responsibility Scale (Crandall, et al., 1965) and the Multidimensional-Multiattributional Causality Scale (Lefcourt, et al., 1979) are appropriate for studying academic achievement in school children and college students respectively, whereas the Jenkins Activity Scale is relevant to heart disease patients.

II. DIMENSIONS OF EFFECTIVE TEACHING

The effectiveness of teaching has fueled debate in higher education for centuries, much concern coming from professors who experience the daily pressures of teaching, but who are neither expert in pedagogy, nor skilled in research on instruction (Perry, 1990). As a consequence, solutions to problems involving teaching and learning are more often based on intuition, speculation, and anecdotal evidence than on empirical fact. In contrast, the published research on college teaching is comprehensive and informative, and has a lengthy history, beginning over 65 years ago and spanning most of the 20th century (McKeachie, 1990). Unfortunately, those who teach are frequently unaware of this literature and do not use it; and those who are responsible for assisting teachers in these matters, instructional developers, largely ignore it (Wilson, 1990). Similarly, college administrators routinely fail to consult the empirical evidence when making instruction or personnel decisions about class size, course assignments, grading distributions, or teacher evaluations.

Inattentiveness to this literature is also evident in researchers who are expected to incorporate suitable operational definitions of instruction in their studies. In some cases, the manipulation is so artificial that it bears little resemblance to reality; more frequently, no empirical evidence is provided to verify that the manipulation has legitimate educational consequences. Both problems have plagued the research on college teaching, their resolution being the proper use of the empirical literature to formulate operational definitions. In pursuit of this objective, at least three criteria should be taken into account: contextual constraints; ecological validity, and empirical verification.

Contextual constraints refer to situational determinants found in college classrooms which restrict the potential range of instruction methods available. Dahllof (1971) suggests that within specific educational settings, societal, organizational, structural, personal, and practical factors dictate the teacher's choices of instruction methods. These "frame-factors" quickly reduce an infinite range of instruction options available to a teacher to a relatively small number of alternatives. For example, frame-factors operating in a college classroom of 100 second and third year non-majors are likely to cause the instructor to select the lecture method as the best alternative. Its suitability would be determined by: societal and institutional norms specifying achievement rather than affect as an important educational outcome; economic restrictions making teaching assistants unavailable for small-group seminars; efficiency factors making the lecture particularly powerful for disseminating large amounts of information, and personal attributes equipping some instructors with effective lecturing skills. For obvious reasons, the seminar or discussion method would be much less suitable for teaching the class.

Ecological validity refers to the degree to which various aspects of a study resemble or simulate the phenomenon under investigation, particularly important for the generalizability of the results. When defining a method of instruction, ecological validity requires that the experimental representation reflect the critical elements of the method as it occurs in the educational setting. Frame-factors are important to consider here to the extent that they are salient features in the actual classroom and often dictate the suitability of a particular method. Failure to do so weakens the applicability of the results. Unfortunately, researchers have not given sufficient attention to this issue. In some cases, the manipulation amounts to nothing more than superficial information-induction, i.e., a fictitious teacher is simulated through a written description and is portrayed as competent or incompetent, effective or ineffective, and so on. Subjects are asked to respond to the simulation as if it were an actual teacher. Although this approach may be unavoidable in some instances, researchers should exercise greater care in selecting ecologically valid procedures and should limit their interpretations to the constraints of the manipulation.

Empirical verification requires the provision of research evidence to support the conclusion that a particular instruction method is effective. Such evidence would include a broad range of variables related to students' educational attainment, including cognitive, affective, motivational, and behavioral outcomes. Thus, for example, a method may be deemed effective because it facilitates information processing, improves attitudes towards studying, or increases class attendance. For the most part, the empirical evidence describing effective teaching methods in higher education has been generated using three different approaches: descriptive, correlational, and experimental. The remainder of this section provides a brief outline of these approaches; for a more extensive analysis, see Murray (1991 and this volume).

Descriptive Approach

Some researchers have attempted to describe the components of teaching based on the perceptions of students and faculty. Their approach is guided by the assumption that students and faculty have acquired considerable knowledge and understanding of instructional processes after spending thousands of hours in classrooms observing dozens of teachers. These experiences lead to the development of cognitive schemata in which various teaching practices are linked with specific educational outcomes. These schemata then contribute to teacher-student exchanges in the classroom. Thus, in a lecture method schema, students may associate a well-organized presentation with the promise of better achievement, thereby making the students feel more confident about success and willing to engage in teacher-student interactions. Researchers using this approach believe that accessing information about these schemata provides valuable insight into what constitutes effective teaching. [3]

Procedurally, this approach involves interviews and questionnaires requiring students, alumni, or professors to describe the properties of effective teaching. The researcher uses either structured or nonstructured formats to obtain the attributes of the ideal teacher, the characteristics essential for good teaching, or the qualities of the best teachers (Feldman, 1976). Statistical analyses of these data have enabled several dimensions to be identified. For example, in his comprehensive review of the literature, Feldman (1976) reported the five most highly ranked dimensions found with structured methods to be: knowledge, stimulation of interest, clarity of explanation, enthusiasm, and preparation-organization; and with nonstructured methods to be: concern for students, knowledge, stimulation of interest, availability, and encouragement of questions and discussion. Other dimensions identified by researchers using structured or nonstructured methods include: organization/planning, interaction, clarity, and enthusiasm (Centra, 1990); knowing when students understand, stimulating interest, responding to questions, achieving course objectives, and clarifying complex topics (Pohlmann, 1976); and pedagogical skill and rapport (Frey, 1978).

Table 2 provides a detailed illustration of this descriptive approach based on Marsh's (1984) development of the Students' Evaluations of Educational Quality questionnaire. The right-hand column lists nine factors describing general dimensions of effective teaching. Each factor is defined by specific evaluation items used to rate teaching effectiveness. Factor loadings are given for both student (S) and faculty (F) responses to each evaluation item. Thus, the Enthusiasm dimension consists of five items having factor loadings for both students and faculty: e.g., "enthusiastic about teaching" loaded 55 for students and 42 for faculty. As can be seen from the list, considerable overlap exists between Table 2 and the dimensions reported by other researchers. For example, both enthusism and organization are listed by Feldman and Centra, and rapport by Pohlmann and Frey.

---

[3]Critics of this approach argue that students' knowledge of instructional processes is distorted by insufficient discipline expertise and by unsubstantiated beliefs and attitudes about teaching. These subjective impressions of teaching, known as implicit theories of instruction, have been examined by Whitely and Doyle (1976) and others (Abrami, Dickens, and Leventhal, 1981; Larson, 1979) to determine the extent to which they distort objective evaluations of teaching. Conclusive evidence is lacking as to whether students use their implicit theories in their assessments. Statistical procedures can be used to control some problems; however, it is unclear whether students' implicit theories are, indeed, invalid or whether they correspond reasonably well to more objective representations.

These data are representative of hundreds of factor analyses performed to identify dimensions of effective teaching. [See Centra (1990), Feldman (1976), Kulik and Mc-Keachie (1975), and Marsh (1984) for comprehensive reviews of this literature.] They routinely show that, although some differences exist in the number and type of dimensions found, considerable consistency is evident for certain ones. For the researcher, they offer valuable guidance for constructing experimental manipulations of instruction. However, they offer little insight into whether these perceived dimensions of teaching effectiveness are linked to actual educational outcomes such as student cognition or achievement. This can only be addressed with correlational and experimental studies.

Correlation Approach

Identifying the qualities of effective teaching invariably leads to questions about their relation to students' educational attainment. Researchers have attempted to examine this linkage in correlational studies by comparing instructional practices with academic outcomes such as student satisfaction, motivation, or achievement. This approach usually involves specification of instructional variables based on logic or empirical evidence, perhaps derived from descriptive studies like those discussed above. So, for example, the dimensions in Table 2 can be used to operationally define specific teaching behaviors exhibited by instructors in classrooms which could then be correlated to class attendance, student performance, or achievement. Significant correlations would provide empirical evidence for which dimensions are associated with important educational objectives. However, they would offer little insight into why they are effective.

Table 3 presents several teaching behaviors which have been designated as effective with the correlational approach based on their relation to student achievement. They are derived from Cohen's (1987) and Feldman's (1989; 1990) meta-analyses of field studies examining the linkage between specific behaviors and achievement outcomes in courses. Typically in these studies students' opinions of instruction are obtained with a number of rating items which are transformed into general teaching behaviors using factor analyses. Each dimension is therefore defined in terms of specific, low-inference behavioral rating items and can then be correlated with achievement outcomes at the end of the course. Organization, for example, comprises "presenting and organizing course material" and "planning class activities in detail." As a higher-order construct, it correlates +.55 (+.57) with student achievement. This means that roughly 30 percent of the achievement variance in the course is explained by the organization dimension.

Murray (1991) and his associates (e.g., Erdle and Murray, 1986; Murray and Lawrence, 1980; Murray and Smith, 1989) have conducted some of the best studies of this type. They typically compare low-inference teaching behaviors measured by a specially designed scale, the Teacher Behaviors Inventory, with students' ratings of teaching effectiveness. In one typical study, Murray (1983) had trained observers attend several lectures to assess the frequency of specific teaching behaviors of instructors. He then correlated these frequencies with ratings of instruction made by students in the instructors' courses. Substantial correlations were found between the frequency of teaching behaviors such as clarity and enthusiasm and students' ratings of effectiveness.

TABLE 2. Factor analyses of students' evaluations of teaching effectiveness (S) and the corresponding faculty self-evaluations of their own teaching (F) in 329 courses (*reprinted from Marsh [84] by permission of the American Psychological Association.*)

Evaluation items (paraphrased)	1 S	1 F	2 S	2 F	3 S	3 F	4 S	4 F	5 S	5 F	6 S	6 F	7 S	7 F	8 S	8 F	9 S	9 F
1. Learning/Value																		
Course challenging/stimulating	42	40	23	25	09	-10	04	04	00	-03	15	27	09	05	16	23	29	20
Learned something valuable	53	77	15	02	10	-02	09	04	01	01	10	08	10	04	17	09	16	06
Increased subject interest	57	70	12	05	08	07	08	07	02	-03	18	-01	19	-04	19	05	14	-02
Learned/understood subject matter	55	52	12	12	13	12	05	03	03	11	02	-01	13	07	14	-04	-23	-11
Overall course rating	36	33	25	29	16	09	12	08	09	02	12	16	13	-08	14	27	08	16
2. Enthusiasm																		
Enthusiastic about teaching	15	29	55	42	16	00	07	02	21	15	10	00	05	16	01	09	05	06
Dynamic & energetic	08	03	60	70	15	01	11	06	08	05	06	05	07	16	01	05	05	03
Enhanced presentations with humor	10	04	66	58	-04	06	05	16	13	02	12	02	14	07	02	-18	-07	-10
Teaching style held your interest	09	12	59	64	23	20	16	08	06	00	03	14	10	05	06	03	-02	-03
Overall instructor rating	12	27	40	54	23	09	14	08	23	02	11	16	10	-08	05	27	08	16
3. Organization																		
Instructor explanations clear	12	00	07	24	55	42	20	09	05	04	10	06	13	01	06	23	-08	-03
Course materials prepared & clear	06	06	03	-02	73	69	09	01	10	-02	09	04	06	03	10	03	01	12
Objectives stated & pursued	19	10	-05	-08	49	41	03	05	08	05	14	08	25	27	06	01	06	06
Lectures facilitated note taking	-03	02	20	09	58	53	-17	07	-02	05	11	04	15	06	08	01	-04	-05
4. Group Interaction																		
Encouraged class discussions	04	06	10	02	01	03	84	86	03	00	00	00	06	00	06	-03	00	-03
Students shared ideas/knowledge	02	08	06	-07	-04	-01	85	88	05	13	05	01	03	-02	08	-10	-02	01
Encouraged questions & answers	03	-04	06	09	14	06	62	16	16	-02	15	03	07	11	08	21	00	01
Encouraged expression of ideas	07	01	02	06	01	-11	73	75	20	09	05	07	09	12	05	09	00	-02
5. Individual Rapport																		
Friendly towards students	-04	10	17	06	00	-06	13	12	68	78	-01	-05	13	02	10	-05	-07	01
Welcomed seeking help/advice	04	-10	05	02	02	07	06	00	85	75	-04	04	06	06	05	20	03	-04
Interested in individual students	07	10	11	09	00	07	14	16	69	77	-01	-09	12	03	08	-09	03	09
Accessible to individual students	02	-13	-11	-11	16	09	09	-02	62	43	20	25	08	13	00	14	04	07
6. Breadth of Coverage																		
Contrasted implications	-05	02	12	01	05	03	08	01	-03	01	72	84	08	-03	14	02	08	-06
Gave background of ideas/concepts	08	03	08	10	16	07	-03	-02	02	-02	71	78	01	08	11	-01	03	03
Gave different points of view	04	-06	04	09	11	11	08	16	06	01	72	55	07	17	01	-06	04	08
Discussed current developments	23	29	08	-04	-04	-04	05	12	09	00	50	48	06	05	16	10	-01	-02
7. Examinations/Grading																		
Examination feedback valuable	-03	01	08	09	06	-11	09	05	08	12	-04	03	72	62	05	-03	09	03
Eval. methods fair/appropriate	06	02	00	-03	03	14	07	06	14	00	10	17	69	64	11	11	-08	04
Tested emphasized course content	08	00	-01	04	11	21	01	01	06	00	11	-04	70	58	07	10	-02	-03
8. Assignments																		
Reading/texts valuable	-06	09	-03	-03	03	07	-01	-06	03	01	07	-07	01	11	91	70	02	04
Added to course understanding	12	01	-01	-12	01	04	09	21	01	17	-02	08	07	05	81	56	06	10
9. Workload/Difficulty																		
Course difficulty (Easy-Hard)	-06	00	06	-01	04	-05	-04	02	-01	00	08	00	-04	08	10	04	85	74
Course workload (Light-Heavy)	14	-04	-09	-01	03	02	04	05	00	04	06	01	03	01	00	-04	88	86
Course pace (Too Slow-Too Fast)	-20	07	12	00	04	18	-12	-09	06	02	-03	-07	04	08	05	-04	62	32
Hours/week outside of class	14	00	07	00	-11	00	07	02	00	00	-04	03	04	-08	05	05	73	46

Note. Factor loadings in boxes are the loadings for items designed to measure each factor. All loadings are presented without decimal points. Factor analyses of student ratings and instructor self-ratings consisted of a principal-components analysis, Kaiser normalization, and rotation to a direct oblimin criterion. The analyses were performed with the commercially available Statistical Package for the Social Sciences (SPSS) routine (see Nie, Hull, Jenkins, Steinbrenner, & Bent, 1975).

TABLE 3. The relation between student ratings of a specific teaching behavior and achievement

Effective Teaching Behavior[a]	Relation to Achievement[b]
Organization	
Structure (Cohen, 1987)	.55 (30.3%)
No. 5: Teacher's preparation; organization	
of the course (Feldman, 1989):	.57 (32.5%)
1. The presentation of the material is well organized.	
2. The instructor planned the activities of each class period in detail.	
Clarity	
Skill (Cohen, 1987)	.51 (26.0%)
No. 6: Clarity and understandableness (Feldman, 1989)	.56 (31.4%)
1. The instructor makes good use of examples and illustrations to get across difficult points.	
2. The teacher effectively synthesizes and summarizes the material.	
Interaction	
Interaction (Cohen, 1987)	.45 (20.3%)
No. 16: Teacher's encouragement of questions discussion, and openness to the opinions of others (Feldman, 1989):	36 (13.0%)
1. Students felt free to ask questions or express opinions.	
2. The instructor stimulated class discussions.	
Feedback	
Feedback (Cohen, 1987)	.29 (8.4%)
No. 15: Nature, quality, and frequency of feedback from the teachers to students (Feldman, 1989):	23 (5.3%)
1. The teacher told students when they had done a good job.	
2. The teacher is prompt in returning tests and assignments.	
Stimulation[c]	
No. 1: Teacher's stimulation of interest in the course and its subject matter (Feldman, 1989):	.38 (14.4%)
1. The instructor gets students interested in the subject.	
2. It was easy to remain attentive.<	
Elocution[c]	
No. 7: Instructor's elocutionary skills (Feldman, 1989):	35 (12.3%)
1. The teacher has the ability to speak distinctly and be clearly heard	
2. The instructor changed pitch, volume, or quality of speech.	

[a]Different terminology has been used in the literature to describe similar dimensions. For each dimension listed here, the term used by Cohen (1987) and Feldman (1989; 1990) in their meta-analysis is given. In addition, two specific examples of low-inference rating items for each dimension are presented from Feldman (1989).

[b]The values in this column are the average correlation coefficients between student ratings of each teaching behavior and student achievement based on Cohen's (1987) and Feldman's (1989) meta-analyses. The numbers in brackets refer to the percent of variance explained by each dimension. \

[c]These dimensions were reported only by Feldman (89).

Several methodological advantages are achieved by the correlational approach in comparison with the descriptive approach. First, both the teaching behaviors and the products of effective instruction can be theoretically or empirically derived by the researcher. This process avoids the selection of idiosyncratic or irrelevant teaching behaviors and ensures the use of legitimate indicators of educational attainment. Second, observational studies reduce problems with the generalizability of results by using actual classrooms. The data are gathered in the setting of interest, not in a laboratory, thereby obviating external validity concerns. Finally, trained observers, particularly in Murray's research, provide an independent assessment of instruction that is not confounded with ratings of the quality of instruction made by students in the course. This procedure ensures that teaching behaviors are determined separately from end-of-course outcomes generated by the students. Nevertheless, this approach has some limitations, the primary one being its inability to demonstrate causality and to explain why the variables are correlated. These weaknesses are addressed more appropriately by the experimental approach.

Experimental Approach

Some researchers are interested in the causal analysis of instruction; others in why these linkages exist. In the experimental approach, instruction is deemed to be an independent variable having direct effects on specific academic outcomes. It can be operationally defined as an independent variable either through classification procedures or through direct manipulation. Thus, levels of instruction can be identified by selecting instructors who represent a given level, or by training instructors to enact that level. This approach has a distinct advantage over the others because it enables cause-and-effect relationships to be determined and because it provides a more fine-grained account of teaching-learning processes. Under proper conditions, for instance, it could show that instructor clarity enhances student achievement because long-term memory is facilitated during a lecture.[4]

The experimental approach adheres to the principles of the scientific method and can be applied to either laboratory or field settings, provided the basic requirements for internal and external validity are met (Cook and Campbell, 1979). Internal validity refers to whether conditions exist which can be used to establish a causal relationship; external validity, to whether the relationship holds across settings of research interest. Laboratory studies can provide strong experimental controls which enhance internal validity, thereby improving the causal analysis of instruction. These strict controls, how-

---

[4]This type of analysis of instruction has been more frequently carried out by researchers studying elementary and secondary classrooms due, in part, to government funding initiatives such as Head Start and Follow Through in the U.S. (cf., and Good, 1986). Much less has been done in higher education, as demonstrated in three different decade reviews of research on teaching (Gage, 1963; Travers, 1973; Wittrock, 1986). Of more than 100 chapters in these volumes, only three dealt with instruction in the college classroom, and only one of the three authors has made any sustained contributions to research on teaching in higher education (McKeachie, 1963).

ever, can impose artificial conditions so that representativeness may be lacking in the experimental manipulations, the subject populations, or the dependent measures, thereby causing external validity to suffer. For example, the superficial manipulation of instruction using written descriptions in some studies bears little resemblance to teaching practices occurring in classrooms. The effects may be very powerful, but the results impractical, because they cannot be applied to teaching methods being used in the actual classroom.

In contrast, field studies have much better external validity because they are usually carried out in the setting of interest. Nevertheless, the interpretation of results from these studies is suspect if internal validity is lacking. The failure to randomly assign subjects to experimental conditions, or to match the groups, and the inability to properly manipulate instruction as the independent variable are two common internal validity threats plaguing field studies. Without internal validity, the identification of causal relationships is prevented, making the question of external validity irrelevant. Ideally, the causal analysis of instruction requires studies to have both internal and external validity. In practice, few laboratory or field studies accomplish both satisfactorily, although attempts to enhance both types should be made to whatever extent is possible.

Laboratory analogs are one compromise solution used by researchers to address both types of validity. As laboratory studies, they emphasize internal validity, but differ significantly from the typical laboratory study in stressing external validity as well. Compared to an analog study, the average laboratory study lacks representativeness, typically because of the selection of insignificant instruction variables; the ineffective manipulation of instruction; the use of irrelevant achievement tasks; the absence of important psychological constructs, and inattention to secondary setting factors such as classroom incentives, opportunities for study and note-taking, the presence of other students, etc. Instruction effects may be demonstrated in studies having these flaws, but at considerable cost to generalizability and practical application. In contrast, external validity is enhanced in laboratory analogs through experimental realism (Aronson and Carlsmith, 1968), thereby achieving closer correspondence to actual classroom conditions. Internal validity is also improved in analog studies through the direct manipulation of instruction as an independent variable, the random assignment of subjects to experimental conditions, the precise measurement of educational outcomes, and so on.

The "Dr. Fox" study (Naftulin, Ware, and Donnelly, 1973) is one example of an experimental analog which allows for a causal analysis of instructional effects (Perry, Abrami, and Leventhal, 1979). The analog is presented here in some detail because it provides the basis for the paradigm used to study the perceived control by instruction interaction in the next section. It tests the widely held assumption that an entertaining, charismatic instructor can receive favorable student ratings in the absence of adequate course content. Critics use this argument to claim that student ratings are invalid because favorable evaluations are incompatible with a lecture devoid of content, even if the instructor is charismatic. The merits of this issue have been debated for several decades, as for example, Guthrie (1954) arguing that the entertainment aspect is unimportant in contrast to Royce (1956) suggesting some significance to "superficial popularity."

The "Dr. Fox" effect, also referred to as Educational Seduction, has been empirically tested only recently in a series of experimental studies which systematically varied two teaching behaviors with specific behavioral criteria (e.g., Perry, Abrami, Leventhal, and Check, 1979; Williams and Ware, 1976). Instructor expressiveness was defined in terms of physical movement, voice inflection, eye contact, and humor; and lecture content was defined by the number of teaching points covered in a specific period of time. The basic experimental design for testing the assumption pairs instructor expressiveness (low, high) with the density of lecture content (low, high) in a 2 x 2 factorial design having two dependent measures, student ratings and achievement. Educational seduction would be represented by the high expressive, low content instructor who produces favorable student ratings in the absence of suitable achievement. Abrami, Leventhal, and Perry's meta-analysis (1982) of this research reveals only weak empirical support for the assumption in contrast to what its adherents claim (e.g., Williams and Ware, 1976). Although it may occur on some occasions, it does not appear to be very robust in the typical college classroom. This research underscores the need for closer empirical scrutiny of other common fallacies about teaching and student evaluation in higher education. More importantly, it identifies some fundamental causal linkages between two teaching behaviors and student achievement.

Perry (1982; 1985) has argued that the Dr. Fox paradigm offers the potential for a systematic, empirical analysis of college instruction in a laboratory setting. In part, this has been accomplished in his research through the direct manipulation of critical teaching behaviors and the random assignment of subjects to classroom conditions. It is also achieved through experimental realism as reflected in the independent and dependent variables. The teaching behaviors are derived from a basic core of teaching dimensions identified during several decades of research. Other independent variables, such as classroom incentive, study opportunity, and instructor reputation, are selected with ecological validity in mind as well. The achievement tests and evaluation questionnaires also correspond to actual classroom measures. The multiple-choice achievement test is based on the lecture content presented and the student ratings questionnaire is similar to measures commonly used throughout North America. Other ecologically relevant factors included in the analog are: the presentation of an actual college professor, in color and life-size, using a seven-foot video screen; the length of the lecture and the choice of topics; the physical features of the laboratory designed to correspond to a college classroom, e.g., room size and seating, presence of a desk, a blackboard, and book-shelving.

Although recent technological advances have greatly aided analog simulations, the causal analysis of college teaching remains very much incomplete. Little attention has been given to cognitive or affective outcomes in students, some of which are considered to be critical objectives for effective instruction. Existing research has been restricted to a relatively small number of instruction outcomes such as student ratings, achievement, study habits, and course selections, without considering more complex processes like students' beliefs, expectations, emotions, motivations, and learning strategies. Furthermore, students' cognitive predispositions, motivation, and other psychological attributes have generally been ignored. More importantly, the analysis to date has lacked an integrated conceptual model which stipulates the critical variables involved in learning and which describes their causal linkages and sequential development. It is insufficient to demonstrate that a teaching behavior affects student achievement without also examining its effect on related cognitive and affective processes, and their relation to subsequent academic performance.

III. PERCEIVED CONTROL AND INSTRUCTION

It has been suggested that the interaction between students' perceived control and classroom instruction represents one of the significant aptitude-treatment interactions (ATIs) affecting scholastic performance in higher education (Perry, 1981; 1985). As with any interaction, it can take many forms, several of which are of research interest here. The remainder of this chapter explores the conceptual issues and empirical evidence primarily related to the interaction depicted in Figure 1 (p. 15).

For this analysis, perceived control is represented as a continuum ranging from helplessness to mastery at the extremes, with an individual occupying some point on it. Persons in the *helpless* category would experience a psychological state of severe uncontrollability, often accompanied by overt manifestations of apathy, passivity, failure, and/or withdrawal. A student in this state would believe that he/she has little influence over his/her academic performance and psychologically would feel "out of control." Overt symptoms may include boredom, apathy, inattentiveness, and failure in one or more courses. A range of constructs could be used to study perceived control within this perspective (see Table 1, p. 19), from the stable, traitlike approach proposed by Dweck (1975), to the environmentally determined, state approach taken by Seligman (1975). Persons in the *mastery* category would exhibit heightened psychological control in conjunction with overt manifestations of assertiveness, striving, and goal-directed behavior. A student in this category would take primary responsibility for his/her academic performance and believe he/she determines subsequent success or failure. The student would feel psychologically "in control" and be highly motivated to succeed academically. Constructs appropriate for studying perceived control in this category could include Type A/B behavior and self-efficacy.

Rotter (1975) speculates that the nature of academic development predisposes students with lower perceived control (e.g., externals) to quit the education system, resulting in a greater proportion of those remaining who have control (e.g., internals). If his analysis is correct, and if perceived control is determined by both stable personality and transient environmental factors, then a greater proportion of variance in scholastic performance would be determined by these transient classroom variables. Thus, fewer students would fall within the helpless category at the higher levels of education, and environmental factors would increasingly determine students' loss of control. Accordingly, perceived control is viewed here as a continuum which can be used to differentiate college students. Most would typically be located between the two extremes, helplessness and mastery, with the distribution skewed towards the mastery end.

Effective instruction will be viewed here as comprising a finite number of teaching behaviors specified by existing frame-factors. As discussed in Section II, the literature reveals several teaching behaviors which have been subjected to empirical verification, through descriptive, correlational, and experimental research, and which appear to have reasonable ecological validity. Educational seduction researchers have focused on two of these behaviors, instructor expressiveness and lecture content, and found them to have significant effects on student ratings of instruction and on student achievement. Both have been used to examine the perceived control by instruction interaction depicted in Figure 1 (p. 15). The remainder of this chapter describes how expressiveness, in particular, interacts with students' perceived control to influence academic achievement. Cognitive and affective outcomes are not presented here due to space limitations, but are discussed at length in the original studies.

A Conceptual Framework

The interaction presented in Figure 1 clearly shows that students who experience loss of control are unable to benefit from effective instruction. Specifically, helpless students performed no better with an expressive than with an unexpressive instructor. Before examining the empirical evidence for this interaction, however, some attention must be given to understanding why this pattern would occur. Perry and his associates (e.g., Perry and Dickens, 1984; Perry and Magnusson, 1987a; Perry and Penner, 1990; Perry and Tunna, 1988) have attempted to account for it by exploring two related issues: What makes some teaching behaviors effective? How does loss of control reduce their effectiveness? The answers to these questions can be found within an information processing framework.

According to Perry and Magnusson (1987a), certain teaching behaviors are thought to be effective because they prime central information processing activities. In turn, these instruction-activated mechanisms determine important educational objectives such as knowledge acquisition, motivation, and achievement. The constituent elements of expressiveness, for example, are believed to activate selective attention in students: physical movement and voice intonation produce stimulus modulation; humor causes periodic bursts of laughter; and eye contact conveys intense interest in and/or challenge of the student. These four constituent elements operationally define expressiveness for research purposes but do not exhaust the entire list of characteristics. Some elements have obvious attention-eliciting properties, while others are more indirect, as in the case of humor and eye contact. They operate at a reasonably simple level by serving to orient the students to the material being presented. Expressiveness is effective, therefore, because it engages selective attention, a key mechanism in the central information processing system and a critical factor in the storage and retrieval of achievement-related material.

Other effective teaching behaviors are assumed to activate different components of the central information-processing system. The challenge for researchers is to determine which components are primed by a specific teaching behavior. Figure 2 presents several teaching behaviors which have been defined as effective in relation to student achievement. The behaviors are taken from Feldman's (1989) meta-analyses, based on field studies in which various teaching behaviors were correlated with achievement outcomes. For each general teaching behavior, specific actions are indicated, based on *low-inference rating items*, and are linked to the corresponding cognitive operations which they engage. Expressiveness is separated from the others because it is one of the few teaching behaviors that have been subjected to systematic experimental analysis (Perry, 1985), thereby having a direct causal effect on student achievement.

As can be seen in Figure 2, several hypothetical linkages are possible between effective teaching behaviors and students' cognitive functioning. Instructor organization, for example, involves teaching activities intended to structure course material into units more readily accessible from students' long-term memory. An outline for the lecture provides encoding schemata and advanced organizers which enable students to incorporate new, incoming material into existing structures. Presenting linkages between content topics serves to increase the cognitive integration of the new material and to make it more meaningful, both of which should facilitate retrieval. Linkages to cognitive operations can also be hypothesized for other teaching behaviors as demonstrated by the clarity and interaction examples. Even teaching behaviors having little direct capacity to activate attention or memory mechanisms could affect storage and retrieval by altering factors indirectly linked to the central information-processing system. So, teacher warmth or rapport may be effective because it creates a nurturant environment that lowers negative emotional arousal (e.g., anxiety, frustration, fear). By eliminating high levels of arousal, which can often impair attention, memory capacity, or retrieval, teacher warmth indirectly influences information-processing activities.

Two considerations guided the instruction-cognition linkages illustrated in Figure 2. First, only teaching behaviors associated with achievement were selected because extensive research has been done on this outcome. Of course, effective instruction produces other desirable educational outcomes than achievement, such as student affect and motivation, but much less is known about these consequences. Second, only those behaviors suited to the videotape format in Perry et al.'s (1986) laboratory analog were selected. Such behaviors constitute a major part of the lecture method and can be readily subjected to experimental analyses. Other behaviors, such as feedback and rapport, do not lend themselves well to this type of simulation, but may be linked to student achievement through information processing activities. Since very little is known regarding the nature of these linkages, it would appear fruitful to begin to study them based on results gained with the expressiveness teaching behavior.

Thus, insight into the first question raised by Figure 1, namely "why are some behaviors effective?," is achieved by linking teaching behaviors with cognitive operations of the information-processing system. Figure 2 presents an example of this analysis in which specific teaching behaviors activate various cognitive elements responsible for students' learning and achievement. The key focus in this analysis is identifying effective teaching behaviors and relating them to specific cognitive processes. The model is strictly hypothetical at this time, since preliminary empirical evidence is only available for the expressiveness variable.

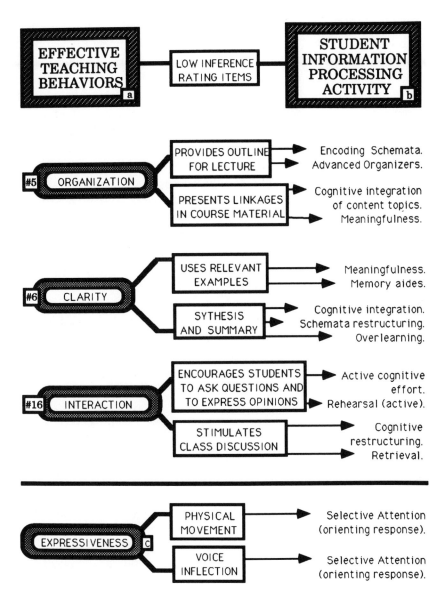

FIGURE 2. Some possible information processing activities initiated by effective teaching behaviors

[a]Each teaching dimension or behavior is taken from Feldman (1989) and is listed here with its respective number (e.g., 5,6, see Appendix A). Specific activities associated with each dimension are defined according to low-inference rating items found on student evaluation questionnaires.

[b]These consequences are a representative sample and are not meant to be exhaustive.

[c]Expressiveness is separated from the other dimensions to denote that its operational definition has been precisely articulated (Perry et al., 1979) and that it has a *causal* effect on achievement.

It is presumed that these instruction effects occur in normally motivated students, but that they may vary if students independently regulate their own cognitive activities. In highly motivated students, information processing is often internally activated regardless of instructional quality. Consequently, Type-A, or mastery-oriented students would automatically engage cognitive operations, such as selective attention, in the absence of effective instruction. In poorly motivated students (e.g., helpless, learning-disabled), self-regulated information processing would be unlikely because of severe cognitive impairment. Thus, both teaching behaviors and students' self-regulation are expected to influence information processing activities. Accordingly, a teaching behavior could be ineffective either because students' regulatory behaviors make it redundant or because cognitive deficits prevent it from initiating information processing.

This model may offer some guidance to practitioners who wish to modify their teaching in response to student characteristics which inhibit scholastic performance. For example, an instructor teaching a required, introductory course may initially view lack of student interest as the major impediment to learning. Thus he/she may decide initially to adopt an expressive teaching style to gain the students' attention. In comparison, organization and skill may be deemed less effective teaching behaviors at this early stage of the course. Once attention to and interest in the material has developed, expressiveness may receive less emphasis in favor of organization and skill. In a small honors course, however, expressiveness would have much less impact because students are already highly motivated and would be actively attending to the material. Instead, rapport may be a more effective behavior because it reduces high levels of achievement anxiety commonly found in such students, thereby reducing the interference of emotional arousal with information processing.

Turning to the second question raised by Figure 1 (p. 15), it becomes apparent why loss of control could interfere with effective instruction. Simply put, it impairs information-processing activities normally primed by effective instruction. This reasoning is compatible with learned helplessness theory (Seligman, 1975; see Table 1, p. 19) in which noncontingent outcomes cause people to believe that their behavior has no effect on goal attainment. These beliefs create severe cognitive, motivational, and affective deficits manifested in withdrawal, apathy, and submissiveness.

Applied to the model of instruction in Figure 2, these deficits provide one plausible explanation for why loss of control impedes effective instruction. Expressive teaching, for example, would have little effect on selective attention if it were diverted to repetitive thinking or rumination. Preoccupation with lack of ability and failure can create *worry cognitions* such as, "I can't," or "I'm a failure," which prevent attention from being directed to the acquisition and storage of information. Also, if the student believed that he/she lacked ability, that it was pointless to try, or that failure was inevitable, then severe motivational deficits may prevent the activation of attention by expressive teaching. Thus, attention would be either consumed with repetitive cognitions, or incapacitated by demotivating cognitions.

Affective deficits could also impair selective attention. Physiological arousal associated with some intense emotional states would focus attention on bodily functioning, thereby redirecting attention. A similar analysis seems feasible for the other effective teaching behaviors presented in Figure 2. The critical issue would be to explain how deficits induced by loss of control impede the information-processing activities activated by specific teaching behaviors.

A Laboratory Analog

The empirical evidence for the perceived control by instruction interaction originated in a series of studies carried out by Perry and his associates at the University of Manitoba. The studies shared a common-core experimental design which was intended to manipulate college students' perceived control before introducing them to classroom instruction variables. The experimental paradigm incorporated a variety of student variables in addition to perceived control, manipulated several teaching behaviors, and assessed students' cognitive, affective, and behavioral reactions. Before reviewing the results of these studies, some consideration will be given to the paradigm and its underlying assumptions.

To begin with, the college classroom, like other social settings, is presumed to operate according to psychological and behavioral dynamics that are reasonably lawful and predictable. As such, the scientific method is well suited to study these dynamics, particularly experimental and quasi-experimental procedures (Shulman, 1986). Even if teaching is considered an "art form," Gage (1978) has argued compellingly that it can still be subject to scientific inquiry. Second, teaching is an important event in the college classroom because it reliably affects a set of desirable academic outcomes. Recent research by Brophy and Good (1986), Doyle (1986), and others, documents teaching's contribution to learning in elementary and secondary classrooms. Although supporting evidence in postsecondary research is sparse by comparison, it seems reasonable to assume that teaching also plays a substantial role.

Third, from a multitude of teaching behaviors that could potentially occur in the college classroom, only a small number are manifest due to societal, institutional, professional and personal values and priorities. An experienced teacher in a suburban school, for example, is faced with a limited number of options if he/she wishes to use recitation for math instruction with a large class of seventh grade students. Thus, these frame-factors (Dahllof, 1971) dictate the most suitable teaching methods as well as the appropriate teaching behaviors. Fourth, lecturing is one of the predominant instructional methods in higher education and comprises specific teaching behaviors. Much of the teaching effectiveness research in higher education has focused on lecturing and provides details about constituent behaviors, such as expressiveness. Finally, the critical dimensions involved in a particular teaching method can be determined from implicit theories of instruction (Gage, 1978), from their common occurrence in the classroom (Murray, 1983), and from their effect on student achievement (Perry, 1981).

These assumptions guided the development of a laboratory paradigm in combination with procedures derived from the Educational Seduction analog. The basic paradigm involves two phases which operationally define the critical variables in the ATI

(Figure 3). During a pretest prior to the first phase, students are introduced to the procedures and given a questionnaire concerning their demographic characteristics and pertinent psychological factors including achievement motivation, locus of control, Type A/B behavior, and so on. The initial step in phase 1 is intended to manipulate students' perceived control temporarily with an aptitude test and a special answer sheet which provides immediate feedback. Perceived control is varied by giving students either contingent or noncontingent feedback on each multiple-choice question (see Perry et al. [1984; 1986] for a complete description). In some studies additional feedback conditions include an aptitude test/no-feedback condition and a no-test/no-feedback condition. Thus, the perceived control manipulation can have up to four feedback conditions: contingent, noncontingent, no-feedback, no-test. A questionnaire follows the aptitude test, completing phase one. The questionnaire includes manipulation checks of the feedback variable, causal attributions for test performance, affective reactions to the performance, and other items of interest (see Perry and Dickens, 1984, for further details).

When the results of the perceived control manipulation are compared across studies, a very clear pattern emerges. Negative noncontingent feedback repeatedly lowers perceived control in comparison with other feedback conditions, namely contingent, noncontingent-positive, and no feedback. For these three feedback conditions, perceived control is relatively comparable. Increasing the amount of negative noncontingent feedback lowers perceived control accordingly. Interestingly, positive noncontingent feedback does not reduce control, in contrast to what Seligman's (1975) theory would predict, but is consistent with other empirical evidence showing only negative noncontingent outcomes lower control (Miller and Norman, 1979; Rothbaum et al., 1982).

A similar pattern emerges for the students' causal attributions for their aptitude test performance. Multivariate analysis of variance and discriminant function analysis reveal that noncontingent feedback produces a causal attribution profile different from those produced by other feedback conditions. Specifically, students who received noncontingent feedback were generally less likely to attribute ability and effort to their performance than those who received contingent or no-feedback. Overall, the aptitude test procedure produced a consistent pattern across these studies. Noncontingent feedback caused students to report less control over their performance and to take less responsibility for it, revealing a helplessness-mastery dichotomy between noncontingent and contingent students. Thus, the procedure ensures empirically reliable results congruent with helplessness theory. It also possesses better ecological validity for college classrooms than other helplessness tasks, which typically use simplistic, low-level intellectual tasks administered to each subject separately. It is evident from these phase 1 results that the aptitude test provides an empirically and ecologically valid manipulation of students' perceived control.

The second phase of the laboratory paradigm (Figure 3) involves manipulating the quality of instruction (A) using videotaped lectures in a simulated college classroom. The students are presented with a half-hour videotaped lecture on a large video-screen, after which they write an achievement test on the material and complete a performance questionnaire related to the postlecture test. In previous studies instruction has been manipulated with two teaching behaviors selected from Educational Seduction studies, namely instructor expressiveness and lecture content, which are defined according to criteria outlined by Perry et al. (1979). High expressiveness and high content both represented effective instruction and low expressiveness and low content, ineffective instruction. The instructor was a professor who had won a teaching award, and the lecture was based on actual material presented in his classes. The achievement test (B) was a 30-item multiple-choice exam, and the performance questionnaire (C) comprised attribution and affect measures related to the achievement test.[5]

Evidence for the Interaction

The laboratory analog described in Figure 3 provided the basis for a common core experimental design (Figure 3, Phase 2) used to test the interaction. Ten studies incorporating this design are described below, each having several independent and dependent variables and each addressing a variety of issues. They are divided into two categories which highlight the environmental and the cognitive origins of perceived control. Environmental determinants are external to the individual, often transient, and can recur in the same situations or in different ones. Cognitive determinants reside within the individual, are relatively more stable, and may be linked to life-span development, not unlike personality traits.

Environmental origins. The first studies incorporating the laboratory analog were intended to empirically demonstrate that an interaction between perceived control and instruction exists (Perry and Dickens, 1984; 1988; Perry and Magnusson, 1987a; Perry, Magnusson, Parsonson and Dickens, 1986). They were based on the premise that students experience periodic shifts in control during their normal academic development. This perspective emphasized external, environmental events as major factors responsible for temporary increases or decreases in students' perceived control. Learned helplessness theory was selected as the appropriate construct for this approach and was incorporated into the first phase of the laboratory paradigm described previously (see Figure 3, phase 1). Perceived control was manipulated using two or more feedback procedures on the aptitude test, one of which was always noncontingent feedback.

---

[5]Four criteria were used to select the two teaching behaviors from empirical research: their common occurrence in the college classroom (e.g., Marsh, 1984); their centrality in students' implicit theories of teaching (e.g., Whitely and Doyle, 1976); their prominence in the lecture method, and their direct effect on student achievement. Both behaviors have been the focus of attention in the Educational Seduction literature which provides consistent empirical evidence for their effects on student achievement. Abrami, Leventhal, and Perry's (1982) meta-analysis of this literature indicated that content and expressiveness accounted for a meaningful amount of the achievement variance: 16 percent and 4.3 percent respectively. Although expressiveness accounted for less variance, it was statistically respectable according to Cohen (1977), particularly in half of the studies in which it explained 8.6 percent of the variance. Even when it didn't account for any variance as a main effect, it did influence achievement as a simple main effect in various experimental conditions (e.g., Perry, Abrami, and Leventhal, 1979, low incentive). Thus, both teaching behaviors appear to be appropriate for studying instruction in the college classroom.

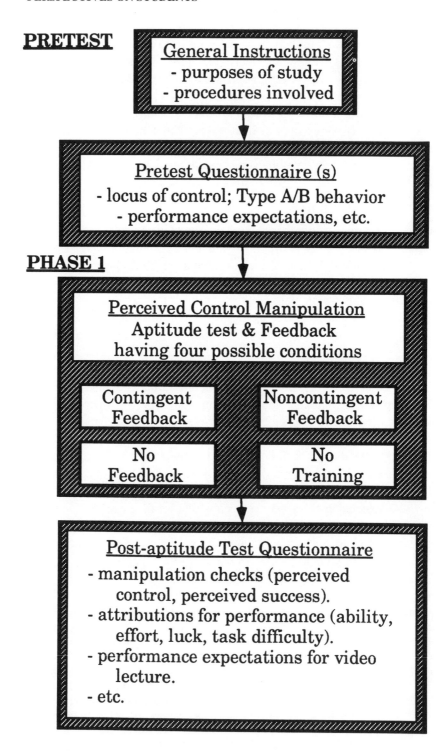

FIGURE 3. Experimental procedures used in the laboratory analog

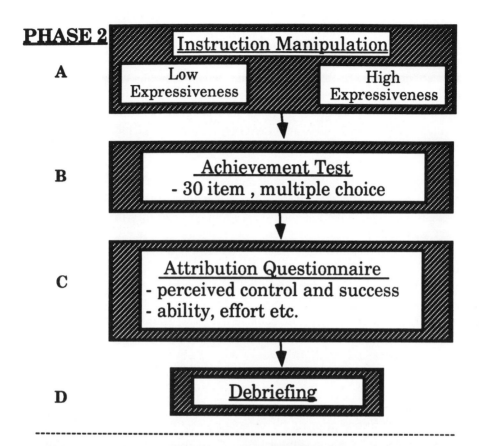

Factorial Design		Lecture Expressiveness	
		Low	High
Aptitude	Contingent	DVs	DVs
Test	Noncontingent	DVs	DVs
Feedback	No Feedback	DVs	DVs
Manipulation	No Training	DVs	DVs

Perry and Dickens (1984) initially demonstrated the interaction between perceived control and instruction using three feedback conditions on the aptitude test: contingent, noncontingent, and no-feedback, in addition to a no-test, lecture-only condition. The first two conditions were intended to create perceptions of mastery and helplessness. The no-feedback condition was included as a critical methodological comparison group with which to contrast the first two. Students were required to answer the aptitude test on a standard IBM sheet which recorded responses without providing feedback. This procedure is representative of testing situations in which students receive feedback belatedly or never, and as such, is ecologically valid. If perceived control differences are found between the contingent and noncontingent groups, then it is important to show also that the contingent group's performance is comparable to, or greater than, the no-feedback group, and that the noncontingent group's is less than the no-feedback group.

Perry and Dickens were also interested in whether the interaction would change in different classroom incentive conditions. They reasoned that motivation to do well may counteract transient loss of control, thereby enabling students to benefit from expressive instruction. Half the students were told before the experiment began, and again during the experiment, that they would receive extra credits for participating if they attained 65 percent or higher on the post-lecture achievement test. The other half received no incentive instructions. All students were subsequently presented with the first and second phases of the laboratory paradigm. That is, they wrote the aptitude test, receiving either contingent, noncontingent, or no feedback, viewed a half-hour lecture by an unexpressive or expressive instructor, then wrote an achievement test on the lecture material (see Figure 3). The perceived control manipulation (Phase 1) produced uniform results in both incentive conditions prior to the videotaped lecture, with contingent and no-feedback students reporting more control over their aptitude test performance and taking more responsibility for it than the noncontingent students.

The postlecture results (Phase 2), however, differed dramatically on the basis of incentive conditions. In the no-incentive conditions, contingent-feedback students performed better with the expressive compared with the unexpressive instructor, whereas performance for noncontingent-feedback students showed no improvement with expressive instruction. These results conform to the interaction described in Figure 1 (p. 15). In contrast, expressive instruction did *not* improve the performance of either contingent or noncontingent students in the incentive conditions! But these results were due to the performance of *all* students being better, including those having unexpressive instruction. In essence, the incentive manipulation appears to have heightened motivation generally, creating a ceiling effect in which performance increased to an optimal level, regardless of the quality of instruction or of the students' level of perceived control. High motivation appears to have primed selective attention, enabling students to compensate for poor quality instruction or loss of control by activating attention on their own initiative. Under such circumstances, expressiveness cannot be regarded as an effective teaching behavior.

Perry and Magnusson (1987a) extended this analysis to determine whether students' loss of control would continue to disrupt effective instruction after a period of time elapsed. A two-lecture sequence was devised in which the first experimental session involved the perceived control and instruction manipulations (phases 1 and 2, Figure 3) followed one week later by an instruction-only manipulation, a repeat of phase 2 procedures with a different lecture topic. After receiving either contingent or noncontingent feedback on the aptitude test, students watched a half-hour lecture on "repression mechanisms" presented by an unexpressive or expressive instructor. One week later they returned to observe a second lecture on "sex roles" presented again by either an unexpressive or expressive instructor. The Lecture 1 results replicated Perry and Dickens' findings in that contingent students performed better with the expressive instructor, whereas no comparable increase occurred for noncontingent students (Figure 1). Lecture 2 results for contingent students revealed a similar pattern as Lecture 1 in which expressive instruction led to better performance than unexpressive instruction. For noncontingent students no differences in performance occurred between expressive and unexpressive instruction; however, the pattern changed from Lecture 1 in that performance for Lecture 2 was elevated in *both* instruction conditions, suggesting that the effects of uncontrollability dissipate with time through the intrusion of other psychological factors.

On the basis of these findings, Perry, Magnusson, Parsonson, and Dickens (1986) examined the type of noncontingent feedback in relation to loss of control. They reasoned that, during their academic development, some students receive primarily negative noncontingent feedback, some negative and positive, and others mostly positive noncontingent feedback. Accordingly, an instructor is likely to have a heterogeneous mix of students with qualitatively different feedback experiences determining their loss of control and response to instruction. Helplessness theory predicts that uncontrollability should occur in each case because noncontingent feedback is involved, but the theory gives little insight into the severity of uncontrollability. Perry et al. (1986) presented students with either positive and negative, or primarily positive, noncontingent feedback on the aptitude test to augment Perry and Dickens's (1984) negative noncontingent feedback conditions. Mixed positive and negative noncontingent feedback reduced students' perceived control and caused them to take less responsibility for their aptitude performance in contrast to students receiving either primarily positive noncontingent feedback or contingent feedback. The mixed feedback students did not perform better with an expressive compared to an unexpressive instructor, whereas the positive noncontingent and contingent feedback students did achieve more.

In a related study, Perry and Dickens (1988) administered four types of aptitude test feedback prior to a lecture: primarily negative noncontingent feedback, positive and negative noncontingent feedback, contingent feedback, and no feedback. They also varied the amount of feedback students received by using a short, medium, and long aptitude test. Negative noncontingent feedback reduced students' control over their aptitude test performance in contrast to the other three feedback conditions, and caused them to take less responsibility for it. Moreover, uncontrollability intensified in direct relation to the amount of noncontingent feedback received. In turn, these differences in uncontrollability determined the students' level of achievement from effective instruction. That is, achievement deteriorated according to the degree of students' uncontrollability: those being most out of control achieved the least. Similar decreases in achievement did not occur in the other feedback conditions receiving expressive instruction.

What these studies show is that good teaching can fail with some students. Specifically, college students who experience temporary loss of control are unable to benefit from effective instruction, performing no better than if they had received ineffective instruction. The results conformed to the analysis in Figure 2 (p. 35) in which cognitive deficits, induced by loss of perceived control, prevent teaching behaviors from engaging information-processing activities. In the studies presented, expressive teaching did not enhance learning and performance in helpless students, suggesting that selective attention may have been impaired. These results, however, do not imply that information processing is activated only by expressive instruction, since other factors can intercede to counteract the deficits caused by loss of control. For example, heightened motivation in Perry and Dickens' study led to better performance in *both* instruction conditions and in helpless students. Thus, students need not be passive participants in the teaching/learning processes described in Figure 2, but can act to compensate for loss of control under some conditions. This issue is dealt with more fully in the next sections which introduce several cognitive factors having the capacity to ameliorate learning deficiencies associated with loss of control.

Cognitive origins. As discussed previously, perceived control has both environmental and personal origins, the latter typified by such constructs as internal and external locus of control and Type A/B behavior (see Table 1, p. 19). A prominent feature of these constructs is their internal and relatively enduring qualities. In college classrooms these qualities are likely to cause differences in perceived control between students in addition to any differences in control produced by environmental factors. If so, these personal determinants may interact with the quality of instruction in a similar way as do environmental determinants. That is, students having more control because of their personality make-up would benefit from effective instruction, whereas those having less control would not. This reasoning suggests a more complex model of the college classroom in which both personal and environmental determinants of perceived control interact with instruction.

Magnusson and Perry (1989) examined the role of cognitive schemata in the perceived control by instruction interaction using a modified version of Crandall et al.'s IAR scale. They reasoned that differences in control associated with internal and external locus would lead to a similar pattern of results as reported by Perry and Dickens (1984) for environmentally determined perceived control. For students who received no prelecture aptitude test (i.e., no test-no feedback condition, Figure 3), an internal locus led to better achievement when instruction was expressive compared with unexpressive, but an external locus prevented a similar improvement in performance. Thus, low perceived control appears to impede the achievement-enhancing effect of expressive instruction whether it is the result of environmental events or enduring, cognitive schemata. When noncontingent feedback was presented prior to the lecture, external-locus students were also unable to benefit from expressive instruction as would be expected. But in contrast, internal-locus students who received the same noncontingent feedback performed better with the expressive than the unexpressive instructor, suggesting that their pre-existing cognitive schemata acted as a buffer against the detrimental effects of noncontingent feedback. Interestingly, external-locus students did better with the expressive instructor when contingent feedback was presented prior to the lecture, suggesting in a remedial sense that contingent feedback can offset the limitations imposed by external-locus cognitive schemata.

A similar pattern emerges for Type A/B behavior, a construct having some affinity to locus of control. Type A individuals are portrayed as aggressive, ambitious, time-urgent, and preoccupied with retaining control in contrast to Type B individuals, who are relatively free of these qualities, and less goal-oriented (Matthews, 1982). Perry and Tunna (1988) argued that, like an internal locus, Type A behavior should buffer students against the detrimental effects of noncontingent feedback. Because Type A students would intensify their efforts to regain control after receiving noncontingent feedback, they would not suffer cognitive impairment and would continue to benefit from expressive instruction. As predicted, following noncontingent feedback, Type A students achieved more with an expressive compared with an unexpressive instructor, whereas Type B students did not do better. Following contingent feedback, however, Type B students' performance improved with the expressive instructor, as did Type A students'. These results parallel those of Magnusson and Perry (1989) in that both internal and Type A students were not hampered by noncontingent feedback and ensuing loss of control, enabling them to perform better with the high expressive instructor; and that both external and Type B students benefited from contingent feedback, resulting in better performance with the high expressive instructor.

Based on these results, Perry and Penner (1990) modified the college classroom analog to study two related issues: the duration of the effects and the responsibility for learning. Previous research into the perceived control by instruction interaction involved administering the achievement test immediately after the lecture. This procedure limits the temporal analysis of the effects which could dissipate shortly after the lecture. The issue is relevant, for example, to the Magnusson and Perry (1989) and Perry and Magnusson (1987a) studies which indicated that external-locus students benefited from contingent feedback initially, but which did not show whether the effect was maintained. The analog in these studies also restricted the responsibility for learning because of its instructor-centered focus. Achievement responsibility during a normal lecture is ideally shared by both the instructor and the student, whereas outside the classroom the onus is on the student. The analog in the earlier studies could assess this shared in-class responsibility, but could not properly consider student-initiated learning outside the classroom.

The duration of the effect and the responsibility for learning issues were addressed by modifying the analog in two ways. First, the postlecture achievement test was given one week later to determine whether the results were stable. Second, the students were assigned homework readings which were also tested one week later, along with the lecture material. The homework assignment placed the responsibility for learning on the students, requiring them to work independently of the instructor. The results showed that external-locus students, who had received contingent feedback, performed much better on the lecture test one week later if they had an expressive rather than an unexpressive instructor. As well, they did better on the homework test at that same time. Interestingly, more students who had initially received expressive instruction returned for the delayed testing session. These results replicate and extend Magnusson and Perry's (1989) and Perry and Tunna's (1988) findings for external-locus and Type B students who also received contingent feedback prior to the lecture. They reveal the same pattern after one week instead of immediately following the lecture, and for both lecture and homework material rather than only lecture material.

A second objective of Perry and Penner's study was to determine whether direct assistance could be provided to students who may suffer from low perceived control. As demonstrated by Magnusson and Perry (1989) and Perry and Tunna (1988), external-locus and Type B students were able to achieve more from expressive than unexpressive instruction if they first received contingent feedback prior to the lecture. These results were consistent with helplessness theory which predicts that contingent feedback increases perceived control, and with Perry and associates' research which shows that students having control benefit from effective instruction. Although contingent feedback appears to have positive benefits, it has not generally been considered to be a remedial intervention.

Attributional retraining, however, has received widespread interest as a treatment for correcting dysfunctional behavior. It is based on the premise that certain attributions are responsible for the behavior and that they can be replaced with more suitable ones. Forsterling's (1985) review of the literature reveals its successful application to students experiencing academic failure. An example would be to change a lack-of-ability attribution for failing a history test to a lack-of-effort attribution. According to attribution theory (Weiner, 1979; 1986), the former would reduce achievement-striving, making failure more likely, whereas the latter would enhance it and subsequent success. Perry and Penner (1990) gave half of the students attributional retraining prior to the videotaped lecture, while the other half received no such training. External-locus students who had attributional retraining performed better on the delayed achievement test than those who had no training. Achievement increased with respect to both the lecture and the homework material. Not surprisingly, internal-locus students did not benefit from attributional retraining presumably because they already had the appropriate cognitive schemata.

These three studies demonstrate that, like transient environmental events, stable cognitive schema involving perceived control influence students' academic achievement depending on the quality of instruction. External locus of control limited the effectiveness of expressive instruction in a manner similar to noncontingent feedback (see Figure 1, p. 15). Thus, whether loss of control is defined as temporary (state) or enduring (traitlike), it appears to interfere with effective instruction. In addition, the studies show that, when factors determining stable and transient perceived control are combined, the pattern of results described in Figure 1 can change. Some students (e.g., internal locus, Type A) seem to be buffered against loss of control because of their psychological make-up. When confronted with loss of control, they intensify their efforts to regain control and consequently continue to benefit from effective instruction.

Other students (e.g., external-locus) who have generally less control can be assisted so that they, likewise, are able to derive the benefits of effective instruction. Attributional retraining appears to offer considerable promise for assisting these students.

Finally, it was shown that the expressive teaching behavior has wide-ranging, relatively enduring effects on student achievement. On a test administered one week after the presentation, the students performed better on lecture-related material and on homework material not covered in the lecture. As well, expressive instruction led to more students attending the delayed testing session one week following the lecture. These results provide strong empirical verification of the significance of expressiveness as a key teaching behavior, affecting two different types of student achievement as well as attendance.

Causal attributions. These studies also highlight the importance of causal attributions, whether they are part of stable cognitive schemata, or are newly created through attributional retraining. A closer analysis of causal attributions in the perceived control by instruction interaction was undertaken by Perry and Magnusson (1987b; 1989a,b). This research departs from the other studies by focusing on specific attributions and on students' evaluations of their aptitude test performance. Both factors are important elements of Weiner's attribution theory (1979; 1986) and critical to achievement-striving. The evaluation of performance is instrumental to causal search, with negative, unexpected, and important outcomes initiating most activity. In the academic achievement domain, failure on an important test is likely to initiate causal search for most students. As well, different attributions have unique effects on the cognitive, affective, and behavioral antecedents of performance. Research consistently shows, for example, that lack of ability and lack of effort attributions for failure can reduce or enhance achievement-striving.

Three causal attributions, ability, effort, and test difficulty, were examined in relation to failure and success, creating six outcome–causal attribution linkages, e.g., failure–lack of ability, failure–lack of effort, etc. Each linkage was induced in the context of the aptitude test prior to the lecture (i.e., phase 1, Figure 3). This procedure enables the effects of these explanatory schemata on achievement to be observed in different instruction conditions. So, for example, the failure–lack of ability and failure–lack of effort schemata could be compared to determine their effects on student performance in conjunction with either expressive or unexpressive instruction. As such, the procedure simulates common student experiences with which an instructor must deal in a normal teaching episode.

Perry and Magnusson (1989a) informed students prior to the aptitude test that their performance would be primarily due to either ability, effort, or test difficulty. Immediate feedback was given to all students using a special answer sheet designed to induce loss of control through noncontingent failure. Students were also asked to evaluate their success on the aptitude test. They then received a videotaped lecture presented by an expressive or unexpressive instructor, after which they wrote an achievement test. These procedures resulted in a causal attribution (ability, effort, test difficulty) by perceived success (failure, success) by instructor expressiveness (low, high) factorial design. The two expressiveness conditions represented ineffective and effective instruction respectively. It should be noted that perceived success was defined by the students' subjective evaluations of their performance which was predetermined for all students as failure (20 correct out of 50). Thus, some students had to resort to distortion in order to report that their poor performance was a success, as might be expected from attribution theory.

The results indicated that the three causal attributions differentially affected postlecture achievement depending on students' subjective evaluations of their performance (distortion, nondistortion) and on the quality of instruction. When instruction was ineffective, students who distorted failure as success performed better using an effort attribution rather than ability or test difficulty attributions. In contrast, the ability attribution led to more achievement in students who accurately judged their performance as failure. These findings show that some attributions are more instrumental to achievement-striving than others, consistent with attribution theory. In addition, they indicate that a student's perceptions of performance (distortion vs. nondistortion) interact with the causal attributions to influence achievement-striving. When instruction was effective, however, no achievement differences emerged between the three attribution groups for either distortion or nondistortion students, although ability leads to marginally better performance. Effective instruction appears to have had a *compensatory* effect in the effort and test difficulty groups by making their achievement comparable to the ability group. It would seem, therefore, that attribution differences in achievement-striving are more pronounced with ineffective instruction and that effective instruction serves to compensate for achievement-striving deficits.

Perry and Magnusson (1987b) repeated this study using similar procedures with the exception that noncontingent failure feedback on the aptitude test was replaced with noncontingent success feedback (38 correct out of 50). They were interested in whether noncontingent success would generate similar patterns of results given that causal search is less likely with positive outcomes in Weiner's theory. Their results replicated the previous study for effective instruction in that the three attributions produced comparable achievement in distortion (success judged to be failure) and in nondistortion (success judged to be success) students. Again, it would appear that effective instruction is having a compensatory effect by elevating performance in all attribution groups to comparable levels. For ineffective instruction, the effort attribution group performed better than the test difficulty group in distortion students. This finding is similar to Perry and Magnusson (1989a); however, unlike that study, no achievement differences occurred between the attribution groups in the nondistortion students. For the most part, therefore, the patterns of results were comparable in the two studies, although they were more pronounced for noncontingent failure than noncontingent success, as might be expected from attribution theory.

In a sequel to these two studies, Perry and Magnusson (1989b) again altered the feedback procedure on the aptitude test by not giving feedback about performance. This modification was achieved simply by having the students respond to the aptitude test on a standard IBM answer sheet which does not provide any feedback. It corresponds to commonly used testing practices in higher education which lead to much delayed, or no feedback at all. All other aspects of their study were similar to the first two, resulting in the same causal attribution (ability, effort, test difficulty) by perceived success (failure, success) by instructor expressiveness (low, high) factorial design. Because feedback was not immediate and known, the distortion-nondistortion distinction was not appropriate, and hence the terms "failure" and "success" were used to describe the students' perceptions of their performance.

The results revealed that with ineffective instruction, the effort and test difficulty attribution groups performed better than the ability group in the high success students. No achievement differences occurred between the attribution groups with the failure students. Thus, it would appear that attributing success to hard work or an easy test enhances achievement-striving and/or that attributing success to high ability actually lowers achievement-striving. The latter analysis is tenable if high ability engenders less effort, a profile not uncommon among underachievers. For effective instruction, the ability group performed better than the test difficulty group with high success students, whereas achievement was comparable in the three attribution groups with low success students. Consequently, depending on the quality of instruction, causal attributions affected performance in high success students but were of little consequence in failure students regardless of instruction. Interestingly, the ability attribution had totally opposite effects in success students, resulting in the worst performance of the three attribution groups with ineffective instruction and the best performance with effective instruction.

These studies begin to provide some clarification of how attributional schemata influence achievement in different instruction conditions. Causal attributions produced greater variability in performance when instruction was poor, failure predominant, and performance was distorted by students. Under these conditions an effort attribution led to the best performance and test difficulty, to the worst. When instruction was good, achievement differences between attribution groups disappeared, suggesting that effective instruction can compensate for attributional schemata, which may have adverse achievement consequences. This compensatory effect of expressive instruction is consistent with the analysis outlined in Figure 3 regarding instruction-activated cognitive processes. That is, selective attention was likely activated by expressive instruction in all groups, leading to comparable achievement gains.

IV. SOME IMPLICATIONS FOR RESEARCH AND PRACTICE

It has been argued that students' academic development in higher education is, in part, a function of critical aptitude-treatment interactions. In contrast to single variable explanations of scholastic performance, variable combinations can provide a more precise and complete analysis of the complexities of the college classroom. The focus of this chapter has been on how one of these determines achievement, namely the relation between perceived control and instruction. The research reported here systematically documents the nature of this interaction and gives some insight into the possible mechanisms accounting for it. A consistent pattern emerges throughout the data that students who suffer loss of control are unable to benefit from effective instruction as defined by instructor expressiveness (Figure 1, p. 15). Of course, this pattern can be modified by other variables, and other patterns may also be of interest.

Before discussing the interaction at length, some consideration should be given to the single variable effects of perceived control and instruction. Persons interested in main effects may want general information about each variable which could be applied broadly across situations, or which could be considered in the absence of the second variable. Instructors, for example, may wish to know whether expressive teaching can be used to achieve certain curriculum objectives. In a history course, having few students who feel threatened about the material, expressive instruction may be effective in activating their flagging attention. In a statistics course which creates severe apprehension in most of the students, it would have relatively little functional value. In contrast, those interested in interaction effects seek information specifically about the relation between the two variables. In either case the laboratory analog potentially offers useful data to the teacher for classroom instruction and to the researcher for empirical analysis.

The contingency feedback manipulation provides reliable information about one cause of loss of control. It is clear from our studies that noncontingent failure feedback on some tests can induce uncontrollability, suggesting that students perceive their performance to be independent of their efforts and abilities. It is not an uncommon experience for a student to do poorly on a test after considerable preparation and effort, but not to know why; or to do well, and be unable to explain the reasons. These perceptions of noncontingent failure can create a predictable pattern of helplessness. Compared with other students, noncontingent-feedback students in our studies differed in how they explained their past performance and in how well they did in subsequent tests. They reported less perceived control, and placed less emphasis on internal factors and more on external factors, in explaining their performance. This external-locus orientation can decrease personal responsibility for academic outcomes, a pattern documented by Dweck (1975) in helpless school children. As a consequence, achievement deteriorates in direct relation to the degree of uncontrollability, particularly when the lecture material is presented by an effective instructor.

The expressiveness main effects provide valuable insights into some aspects of effective college teaching. Initial studies on Educational Seduction revealed that expressive instruction caused students to rate the quality of teaching higher and to learn more from it (Abrami et al., 1982). Our subsequent research gives a clearer picture of its cognitive, motivational and behavioral consequences. First, expressive compared with unexpressive instruction generates a more internal attributional orientation in students toward their achievement. They are more likely to emphasize internal causes (e.g., ability, effort) and to deemphasize external ones (e.g., luck) in explaining their test performance. It also engenders more confidence in students about their achievement and leads them to believe that they tried harder on the test. From an attribution theory perspective, this internal-locus orientation should increase expectations in students about their future success, create positive affect toward their achievement strivings, and cause them to take greater responsibility for their performance.

Lastly, expressive instruction has direct consequences for student achievement, enhancing performance immediately after a lecture and for a period of one week. This effect is not restricted only to instructor-initiated learning in which the teacher is primarily held responsible for presenting the course curriculum. It also includes student-initiated learning which places responsibility on the student to work on material outside the classroom. Motivational effects of expressive instruction are also reflected in student attendance rates which remained stable at a second experimental session. These cognitive, motivational, and behavioral patterns produced by expressive instruction resemble aspects of the mastery orientation described by Dweck (1975). If this profile is verified by field research, then effective instruction in higher education has greater benefits for students than simply conveying the course curriculum.

It should be reiterated that several conceptual and methodological problems have plagued research on college teaching. Those recurring most frequently are: the inadequate definition of instruction and other variables of interest; the failure to validate the constructs with suitable empirical evidence; and the lack of detailed analyses of reported effects. Perry and his associates have tried to avoid these errors by using a laboratory analog which enables instruction to be manipulated directly with videotapes. Ecological validity is also enhanced by designating lecturing as the representative instruction method and by selecting expressiveness as a key component of that method. Descriptive, correlational, and experimental studies provided the empirical verification of expressiveness as an effective teaching behavior. Expressiveness was found to be considered an important component of effective instruction by both students and faculty, to be positively correlated with students' rating of effective instruction, and to directly influence student achievement.

Similar criteria were used to operationally define perceived control. From an extensive analysis of the constructs available (Table 1, p. 19), several were selected as being ecologically valid for the classroom and as having documented empirical support. Conceptualizing perceived control within an environmental perspective was achieved with learned helplessness theory. It allowed students' perceptions to be directly manipulated so that specific conditions could be created. An individual differences perspective was also included in the analog by using standardized questionnaires, particularly the internal and external locus of control construct. Defining perceived control in these two ways enabled both the environmental and the individual origins of the construct to be examined independently and jointly.

Finally, a more precise analysis of the interaction was possible because the laboratory setting afforded the use of powerful experimental procedures. This was accomplished with measures of cognitive, affective, and motivational outcomes, administered at multiple times throughout the teaching sequence, as illustrated in Figure 3 (p. 40). The discussion of these results was restricted primarily to academic achievement due to space limitations, but the data for the other measures are available to the reader in the original sources. It was also achieved by incorporating other independent variables which, in some instances, helped clarify the basic interaction, as with the incentive manipulation (Perry and Dickens, 1984). In others, they revealed new issues for consideration, as exemplified by the explanatory schemata variable (Perry and Magnusson, 1989a,b). These additional measures and manipulations create a greater capacity to understand the basic interaction and more confidence in the effect. Similarly, better procedures for operationally defining the core constructs enable some of the pitfalls of earlier research to be avoided, thereby enhancing both internal and external validity.

Perceived Control and Instruction

The research presented in this chapter documents how loss of control can place college students at risk scholastically by interfering with effective instruction. Common academic experiences such as failing an exam are sufficient to cause uncontrollability, calling attention to a myriad of classroom factors which may threaten similar consequences. Although it is not surprising to find some students unable to benefit from effective teaching, these studies isolate perceived control as a major contributing factor. They suggest, for example, that giving helpless students better instruction to improve their achievement is not likely to be in their best interest. Rather, a more direct, personalized intervention may be required (e.g., Perry and Penner, 1990). A better understanding of this critical interaction should clarify why some students are at risk in higher education.

The empirical data provide reliable information about the specific nature of the interaction and about its implications for related issues. It shows that effective teaching enhances achievement when students perceive having some control over past test performances. Otherwise, lack of control results in poor performance in the presence of effective instruction. This pattern is not restricted simply to academic achievement, but has also been found for causal attributions and affect measures reported elsewhere (see Perry and Dickens, 1984). Significantly, the pattern holds for both transient and stable control constructs, the critical factor being how the student feels about perceived control regardless of its origins. Of course, even though the interaction is similar for these two kinds of control, the ensuing consequences are likely to differ. For example, it appears that the disruption of effective instruction caused by transient loss of control is short-lived, dissipating within a week's time.

From this basic analysis several important issues emerge. First, an interesting development was the discovery of a "buffer effect" in which certain cognitive schemata appear to protect students against the negative consequences of loss of control. Both internal-locus and Type A students performed well with effective instruction even though they suffered loss of control from noncontingent failure feedback. One implication of this finding is that other buffering schemata may exist; another is that a strong preoccupation with having control is likely the common denominator. Several constructs presented in Table 1 (p. 19) are possible candidates. Obviously, this *plasticity*, or ability of the student to recover from transient loss of control, has implications for a student's survival in higher education.

Second, related to the buffer effect is the role of explanatory schemata in teaching and learning. Weiner's theory predicts that the causal attributions used by students to explain their past successes and failures have very different consequences for future performance. Clearly, our research shows that these outcome-attribution linkages, i.e., explanatory schemata, produce variable achievement patterns, depending on the quality of instruction. With ineffective instruction some explanatory schemata appear to compensate for poor quality by increasing achievement to levels similar to that produced by effective instruction. Ineffective instruction makes these schemata more critical for performance than does effective instruction which tends to reduce differences by elevating achievement in all students. More will be said about these compensatory effects below.

Finally, attributional retraining appears to have considerable potential for remediating the deficits associated with stable loss of control. As our results indicate, attributional retraining improved the performance of external students with respect to both instructor- and student- responsible material one week after the lecture and assignment were given. This finding is encouraging because stable loss of control is obviously more difficult to change than transient loss of control and is more likely to affect a broader range of academic situations. It suggests that the limitations in effective instruction depicted in the interaction may be eliminated for both transient and stable loss of control. With transient loss of control, the instructor could simply wait for the deficits to dissipate, and for stable loss of control could intervene more directly with remedial procedures such as attributional retraining.

Instruction and Cognition

The perceived control by instruction interaction rests on the premise that effective teaching behaviors engage components of the information processing system responsible for learning and performance. As Figure 2 (p. 35) illustrated, each behavior is presumed to activate different components of the system. Although some support for such linkages has been found with instructor expressiveness, the model is far from complete. Further research is needed having two objectives: to systematically document these linkages between teaching behaviors and information processing activities, and to examine the extent to which compensatory effects may alleviate instruction and student deficits. The first objective is complicated by the fact that many teaching behaviors may activate the same cognitive component, and that one behavior could engage several mechanisms jointly. Added to these complexities is that actual teaching episodes usually involve several behaviors occurring together.

The second objective can be examined in terms of both student and instruction variables. Compensatory effects refer to the capacity of one variable in the interaction to ameliorate qualities of the other variable which impair student achievement. Weinert and Helmke (1987) use the term *functional compensation* to describe this propensity of one variable to accommodate for the other. A compensation effect due to a student variable can occur if satisfactory performance is attained in spite of poor instruction. Perry and Dickens (1984) demonstrated this in college students using an incentive manipulation in their laboratory analog. They found that high incentive caused all students to perform well so that achievement was comparable in both the expressive and the unexpressive conditions. Apparently, student motivation activated selective attention in both conditions, thereby compensating for unexpressive teaching; but also making expressive teaching redundant.

A compensatory effect due to an instruction variable can occur if suitable performance is achieved despite student learning disabilities. Perry and Magnusson (1987b; 1989a, 1989b) addressed this issue by comparing the effects of students' explanatory schemata in both expressive and unexpressive conditions. When instruction was ineffective, some schemata produced lower achievement than others, but when instruction was effective, these differences disappeared. Performance improved to a comparable level in most schemata groups, suggesting that expressive instruction compensated for some learning deficits associated with certain schemata. A plausible explanation is that expressive instruction activated critical attention processes which are normally impaired by these explanatory schemata.

Thus, cognitive processes should receive a prominent role in pursuing these two research objectives. They offer considerable potential for analyzing both the student- and instruction-determined compensatory effects and the causal linkages between various teaching behaviors and student achievement. Included in this cognitive focus should be the information processing system as well as attribution theory which is discussed more fully in the next section. With this emphasis the model will have much more utility for explaining student achievement in higher education.

A Micro-Analysis of Instruction

It was argued earlier that one problem plaguing research on college teaching was a lack of a systematic analyses of instruction effects. Field experiments and laboratory analogs have identified some causal effects, but have not provided the precise details of these linkages. Attribution theory may offer the conceptual structure to remedy this problem. Attribution theory was first introduced by Heider (1958) in an attempt to account for how people understand and explain their social environment. It is based on the premise that people have a need to make sense of their world and that making sense of it has a functional value: it improves one's chances of survival. Essentially, he proposed that people's explanations for events and outcomes of things around them are part of a rational process which determines how they think and act in the future. Attributing successful test performance to effort could make a student respond differently to subsequent tests than if luck were deemed the reason. These causal attributions serve as both an explanation for an event and as a stimulus for ensuing behavior. Subsequent research by Kelley (1967; 1972), Jones and Davis(1965), Weiner (1972; 1979) and others (see Ross and Fletcher, 1986) has led to further development of Heider's original propositions.

Weiner's attribution theory (1985; 1986) is particularly relevant to the college classroom because of its primary emphasis on achievement motivation. According to Weiner, people routinely seek to explain outcomes in their environment, especially those that are novel, important, or aversive. This causal search process generates explanations or attributions that have a direct influence on cognitive, affective, and behavioral reactions. The attributions can be classified according to three dimensions: locus of causality; stability; controllability. The locus dimension refers to causes within (e.g., ability) or outside (e.g., luck) the person; stability pertains to whether causes are unstable (e.g., effort) or stable (e.g., task difficulty); controllability describes the degree to which a cause can be manipulated or influenced by a person, e.g., effort versus luck. Although other dimensions have been suggested, such as intentionality and globality, locus, stability, and controllability constitute the basic model.

The three dimensions are combined into a locus by stability by controllability taxonomy which can be used to classify any causal attribution. Weiner stresses that this taxonomy is intended for explication purposes only and that the dimensions should not be thought of as dichotomies, but rather as three continua. The location of an attribution in a particular category of the taxonomy determines its capacity to produce subsequent reactions in a person. Once placed in a category, the attribution acquires the dimensional properties associated with that category. Thus, it is the dimensions per se which dictate cognitive, affective, and behavioral reactions. For example, the stability dimension influences expectations because a stable explanation (e.g., ability) of an outcome (e.g., success) implies the likely reoccurrence of that outcome, whereas an unstable explanation (e.g., luck) makes its reoccurrence less probable. Specific emotional reactions are also linked to the three dimensions, as in the case of the locus dimension and pride. An internal attribution (e.g., ability) for success will generate pride because personal qualities were responsible for the performance, whereas an external attribution (e.g., luck) will not engender pride, but possibly gratitude. Together, expectations and emotional arousal determine a person's motivational state which, in turn, serves to influence behavior.

Applied to the college classroom, Weiner's theory identifies critical variables and describes their sequential associations. Attribution, expectation, affect, motivation, and achievement are specified as important elements and their causal linkages outlined in detail. Thus, the theory offers several major advantages for studying the relations between perceived control and instruction: a primary emphasis on achievement; a broad range of cognitive, affective, and motivational outcomes, and a well-developed causal framework which explicitly links the various components. By combining Weiner's theory with recent advances in instructional simulations (e.g., Biddle and Anderson, 1986; Perry and Dickens, 1984), a more precise analysis of instruction effects can be undertaken. These developments provide a suitable basis for a micro-analytic approach to ATI's in the college classroom, long ignored in research on college teaching (McKeachie, 1974).

Some of potential benefits of attribution theory are already evident in data from our own studies. As dependent variables, causal attributions have given us a glimpse of how students think about their academic achievement in the form of internal and external locus profiles (e.g., Perry and Dickens, 1984; 1988). And as independent variables, they reveal how students' explanatory schemata create divergent performance patterns with different types of instruction (Perry and Magnusson, 1987b; 1989a, 1989b). Thus, dependent and independent variables derived from Weiner's theory have begun to give a clearer understanding of the relation between perceived control and instruction in the college classroom. What is now needed is further development of this application.

Finally, attribution theory has considerable heuristic value for integrating the various control constructs described in Table 1 (p. 19) and in the literature more generally. Causal attributions are either implicit or explicit elements in many of these constructs and essentially serve as critical moderating variables which explain the psychological dynamics of being in or out of control. Their prominent role in various theories of achievement motivation and scholastic performance make them particularly important for understanding students' academic achievement.

References

Abrami, P. C., Leventhal, L., and Dickens, W. J. (1981). Multidimensionality of student ratings of *Instructional Evaluation* 6:12–17.

Abrami, P. C., Dickens, W. J., Perry, R. P., and Leventhal, L. (1980). Do teacher standards for assigning grades affect student ratings of instruction? *Journal of Educational Psychology* 72: 107–117.

Abrami, P. C., Leventhal, L., and Perry, R. P. (1982). Educational seduction. *Review of Educational Research* 52: 446–464.

Abramson, L. Y., Garber, J., and Seligman, M. (1980). Learned helplessness in humans: An attributional analysis. In J. Garber and M. Seligman (eds.), *Human Helplessness: Theory and Applications* (pp. 3–34). New York: Academic Press.

Aronson, E., and Carlsmith, J. M. (1968). Experimentation in Social Psychology. In G. Lindzey and E. Aronson (eds.), *Handbook of social psychology* (2nd ed.). Reading, Mass.: Addison-Wesley.

Bandura, A. (1977). Self-efficacy: Toward a unified theory of behavioral change. *Psychological Review* 84: 191–215.

Biddle, B. J., and Anderson, D. S. (1986). Theory, methods, knowledge, and research on teaching. In M. Wittrock (ed.), *Third Handbook of Research on Teaching* (pp. 230–252). New York: Macmillan.

Bracht, G. H. (1970). Experimental factors related to aptitude-treatment interactions. *Review of Educational Research* 40: 627–645.

Brophy, J. E. (1981). Teacher praise: A functional analysis. *Review of Educational Research* 51: 5–32.

Brophy, J. E., and Good, T. L. (1986). Teacher behavior and student achievement. In M. Wittrock (ed.), *Third Handbook of Research on Teaching* (pp. 328–375). New York: Macmillan. \

Centra, J. A. (1990). Faculty evaluation and faculty development. In J. Smart (ed.), *Higher Education: A Handbook of Theory and Research* (Vol. 6). New York: Agathon.

Cohen, J. (1977). *Statistical power analysis for the behavioral sciences*. New York: Academic Press.

Cohen, P. A. (1987). A critical analysis and reanalysis of the multisection validity meta-analysis. Paper presented at the annual meeting of the American Educational Research Association, Boston.

Cook, T. D., and Campbell, D. T. (1979). *Quasi-experimentation: Design and Analysis Issues for Field Settings*. Chicago: Rand McNally.

Costin, F., Greenough, W. T., and Menges, R. J. (1971). Student ratings of college teaching: Reliability, validity, and usefulness. *Review of Educational Research* 41: 511–535.

Covington, M. V. (1984). The motive for self-worth. In R. Ames and C. Ames (eds.), *Research on Motivation in Education: Student Motivation* (Vol. 1) (pp. 77–113). New York: Academic Press.

Crandall, V. C., Katkovsky, W. E., and Crandall, V. J. (1965). Children's beliefs in their control of reinforcements in intellectual achievement behavior. *Child Development* 36: 91–109.

Cronbach, L. J., and Snow, R. E. (1977). *Aptitudes and Instructional Methods: A Handbook for Research on Instructional Methods*. New York: Irvington.

Dahllof, U. (1971). *Ability Grouping, Content Validity, and Curriculum Process Analysis*. New York: Teachers College Press, Columbia University.

de Charms, R. (1968). *Personal Causation*. New York: Academic Press.

Domino, G. (1971). The interactive effects of achievement orientation and teaching style on academic achievement. *Journal of Educational Psychology*, 62: 427–431.

Dowaliby, F. J., and Schumer, H. (1973). Teacher-centered versus student-centered mode of college instruction as related to manifest anxiety. *Journal of Educational Psychology* 64: 125–132.

Doyle, W. (1986). Classroom discourse. In M. Wittrock (ed.), *Third Handbook of Research on Teaching* (pp.

392–431). New York: Macmillan.

Dunkin, M. J., and Barnes, J. (1986). Research on teaching in higher education. In M. Wittrock (ed.), *Third Handbook of Research on Teaching* (pp. 754–777). New York: Macmillan.

Dweck, C. S. (1975). The role of expectations and attributions in the alleviation of learned helplessness. *Journal of Personality and Social Psychology*, 31: 674–685.

Dweck, C. S., and Reppucci, N. D. (1973). Learned helplessness and reinforcement responsibility in children. *Journal of Personality and Social Psychology*, 25: 109–116.

Erdle, S., and Murray, H. G. (1986). Interfaculty differences in classroom teaching behaviors and their relationship to student instructional ratings. *Research in Higher Education* 24: 115–127.

Feldman, K. A. (1976). The superior college teacher from the students' view. *Research in Higher Education* 5: 243–288.

Feldman, K. A. (1989). The association between student ratings of specific instructional dimensions and student achievement: Refining and extending the synthesis of data from multisection validity studies. *Research in Higher Education* 30: 583–645.

Feldman, K. A. (1990). An afterword for \'\'The Association Between Student Ratings of Specific Instructional Dimensions and Student Achievement: Refining and Extending the Synthesis of Data from Multisection Validity Studies." *Research in Higher Education* 31:315–317.

Forsterling, F. (1985). Attributional retraining: A review. *Psychological Bulletin* 98: 495–512.

Frey, P. (1978). A two-dimensional analysis of student ratings of instruction. *Research in Higher Education* 9: 60–91.

Gage, N. L. (ed.). (1963). *First Handbook of Research on Teaching*. Chicago: Rand McNally.

Gage, N. L. (1978). *The Scientific Basis of The Art of Teaching*. New York: Teachers College Press, Columbia University.

Garber, J., and Seligman, M. (eds.). (1980). *Human helplessness: Theory and Applications*. New York: Academic Press.

Gibson, S., and Dembo, M. H. (1984). Teacher efficacy: A construct validation. *Journal of Educational Psychology* 76: 569–582.

Glass, D. C. (1977). *Behavior Patterns, Stress, and Coronary Disease*. Hillsdale, N.J.: Erlbaum.

Goldberg, L. R. (1972). Student personality characteristics and optimal college learning conditions: An extensive search for trait-by-treatment interaction effects. *Instructional Science* 1: 153–210.

Guthrie, E. R. (1954). *The Evaluation of Teaching: A Progress Report*. Seattle: University of Washington.

Heider, F. (1958). *The Psychology of Interpersonal Relations*. New York: Wiley.

Huesmann, L. R. (ed.). (1978). Special Issue: Learned Helplessness as a Model of Depression. *Journal of Abnormal Psychology* 87: 1–198.

Jones, E. E., and Davis, K. E. (1965). From acts to dispositions: The attribution process in person perception. In L. Berkowitz (ed.), *Advances in Experimental Social Psychology* (Vol. 2, pp. 219–266). New York: Academic Press.

Kelley, H. H. (1967). Attribution theory in social psychology. In D. L. Vine (ed.), *Nebraska Symposium on Motivation*. Lincoln, Neb.: University of Nebraska Press.

Kelley, H. H. (1972). *Causal Schemata and The Attribution Process*. Morristown, N.J.: General Learning Press.

Kobasa, S. C. (1983). The hardy personality: Toward a social psychology of stress and health. In G. S. Sanders and J. Suls (eds.), *Social Psychology of Health and Illness* (pp. 3–31). Hillsdale, N.J.: Erlbaum.

Koran, M. L., Snow, R. E., and McDonald, F. J. (1971). Teacher aptitude and observational learning of a teaching skill. *Journal of Educational Psychology* 62: 219–228.

Kuhl, J. (1981). Motivational and functional helplessness: The moderating effect of state versus action orientation. *Journal of Personality and Social Psychology* 40: 155–170.

Kuhl, J. (1985). Volitional mediators of cognition-behavior consistency: Self-regulatory processes and action versus state orientation. In J. Kuhl and J. Bechmann (eds.), *Action Control: From Cognition to Behavior* (pp. 101–128). New York: Springer-Verlag.

Kulik, J. A., and McKeachie, W. J. (1975). The evaluation of teachers in higher education. In F. Kerlinger (ed.), *Review of Research in Education* (vol. 3). Ithasca, IL.: Peacock.

Langer, E. J. (1989). *Mindfulness*. Reading, MA.: Addison-Wesley.

Larson, J. R. (1979). The limited utility of factor analytic techniques for the study of implicit theories in student ratings of teacher behavior. *American Educational Research Journal* 16: 201–211.

Lefcourt, H. M. (1976). *Locus of Control: Current Trends in Theory and Research*. Hillsdale, NJ.: Erlbaum.

Lefcourt, H. M. (1984). *Research With The Locus of Control Construct: Vol. 3: Extensions and limitations*. New York: Academic Press.

Lefcourt, H. M., Von Baeyer, C. L., Ware, E. E. and Cox, D. J. (1979). The Multidimensional-Multiattributional Causality Scale: The development of a goal-specific locus of control scale. *Canadian Journal of Behavioral Science* 11: 286–304. \

Magnusson, J-L., and Perry, R. P. (1989). Stable and transient determinants of perceived control: Implications for instruction in the college classroom. *Journal of Educational Psychology*, 81, 362–370.

Marsh, H. W. (1984). Students' evaluations of university teaching: Dimensionality, reliability, validity, potential biases, and utility. *Journal of Educational Psychology* 76: 707–754.

Marsh, H. W., and Ware, J. E. (1982). Effects of expressiveness, content coverage, and incentive on multidimensional student rating scales: New interpretations of the Dr. Fox Effect. *Journal of Educational Psychology* 74: 126–134.

Matthews, K. A. (1982). Psychological perspectives on the Type A behavior pattern. *Psychological Bulletin* 91: 293–323.

McKeachie, W. J. (1963). Research on teaching at the college and university level. In N. L. Gage, *First Handbook of Research on Teaching* (pp. 1118–1172). Chicago: Rand McNally.

McKeachie, W. J. (1974). Instructional psychology. In M. R. Rosenzweig and L. W. Porter (eds.), *Annual Review of Psychology* (vol. 25). Palo Alto, CA.: Annual Reviews, Inc.

McKeachie, W. J. (1990). Research on college teaching: The historical background. *Journal of Educational Psychology* 82.

McKeachie, W. J., Lin, Y., and Mann, W. (1971). Student ratings of teacher effectiveness: Validity studies. *American Educational Research Journal* 8: 435–445.

Medley, D. M. (1977). *Teacher Competence and Teacher Effectiveness: A Review of Process-Product Research*. Washington, D.C.: American Association of Colleges for Teacher Education.

Messick, S. (1979). Potential uses of noncognitive measurement in education. *Journal of Educational Psychology* 71: 281–292.

Miller, I. W., and Norman, W. H. (1979). Learned helplessness in humans: A review and attribution theory model. *Psychological Bulletin* 86: 93–118.

Murray, H. G. (1983). Low-inference classroom teaching behaviors and student ratings of college teaching effectiveness. *Journal of Educational Psychology* 75: 138–149.

Murray, H. G. (1991). Teaching effectiveness in higher education. In J. Smart (ed.), *Higher Education: A Handbook of Theory and Research* (Vol. 7). New York: Agathon Press. (*Reprinted in this volume.*)

Murray, H. G., and Lawrence, C. (1980). Speech and drama training for lecturers as a means of improving university teaching. *Research in Higher Education* 13: 73–90.

Murray, H. G., and Smith, T. A. (1989). *Effects of midterm behavioral feedback on end-of-term ratings of teaching effectiveness*. Paper presented at the annual meeting of the American Educational Research Association, San Francisco.

Naftulin, D. H., Ware, J. E., and Donnelly, F. A. (1973). The Dr. Fox lecture: A paradigm of educational seduction. Journal of Medical Education 48: 630–635.

Nowicki, S., and Strickland, B. R. (1973). A locus of control scale for children. *Journal of Consulting Psychology* 40: 148–154.

Perry, R. P. (1981). *Educational Seduction: Some Implications for Teaching Evaluation and Improvement*. Vancouver, B.C.: Centre for Improving Teaching and Evaluation Monograph Series (Report #7), University of British Columbia.

Perry, R. P. (1982). The Dr. Fox effect: More than a validity issue. *Instructional Evaluation* 6: 37–41\

Perry, R. P. (1985). Instructor expressiveness: Implications for improving teaching. In J. Donald and A. Sullivan (eds.), *Using Research to Improve Teaching* (pp. 35–49). San Francisco: Jossey-Bass.

Perry, R. P. (1990). Introduction to the special section: Instruction in higher education. *Journal of Educational Psychology* 82: 183–188.

Perry, R. P., Abrami, P. C., and Leventhal, L. (1979). Educational seduction: The effect of instructor expressiveness and lecture content on student ratings and achievement. *Journal of Educational Psychology* 71: 109–116.

Perry, R. P., Abrami, P. C., Leventhal, L., and Check, J. (1979). Instructor reputation: An expectancy relationship involving student ratings and achievement. *Journal of Educational Psychology* 71: 776–787.

Perry, R. P., and Dickens, W. J. (1984). Perceived control in the college classroom: Response-outcome contingency training and instructor expressiveness effects on student achievement and causal attributions. *Journal of Educational Psychology* 76: 966–981.

Perry, R. P., and Dickens, W. J. (1988). Perceived control and instruction in the college classroom: Some implications for student achievement. *Research in Higher Education* 27: 291–310.

Perry, R. P., and Magnusson, J-L. (1987a). Effective instruction and students' perceptions of control in the college classroom: Multiple-lectures effects. *Journal of Educational Psychology* 79: 453–460. \

Perry, R. P., and Magnusson, J-L. (1987b, June). Perceptions of failure and instructional quality: Some conditions determining perceived control and achievement in college classrooms. Paper presented at the Canadian Psychological Association annual meeting, Vancouver.

Perry, R. P., and Magnusson, J-L. (1989a). Causal attributions and perceived performance: Consequences for college students' achievement and perceived control in different instructional conditions. *Journal of Educational Psychology* 81: 164–172.

Perry, R. P., and Magnusson, J-L. (1989b, June). Students' attributional style and effective teaching: Implications for instructional practise. Paper presented at the International Society for the Study of Individual Differences, Heidelberg.

Perry, R. P., Magnusson, J-L., Parsonson, K., and Dickens, W. J. (1986). Perceived control in the college classroom: Limitations in instructor expressiveness due to noncontingent feedback and lecture content. *Journal of Educational Psychology* 78: 98–\ 107.

Perry, R. P., and Leventhal, L. (1980). Learned helplessness in the classroom: Are teacher behaviors involved? *Proceedings, XXII International Congress of Psychology*, Leipzig, GDR.

Perry, R. P., and Penner, K. S. (1990). Enhancing academic achievement in college students through attributional retraining and instruction. *Journal of Educational Psychology* 82:\

Perry, R. P., and Tunna, K. (1988). Perceived control, Type A/B behavior, and quality of instruction. *Journal of Educational Psychology* 80: 102–110.

Peterson, P. L. (1979). Aptitude x treatment interaction effects of teacher structuring and student participation in college instruction. *Journal of Educational Psychology* 71: 521–533.

Peterson, C., and Seligman, M. E. P. (1984). Causal explanations as a risk factor for depression: Theory and evidence. *Psychological Review* 91: 347–374.

Phares, E. J. (1976). *Locus of Control in Personality*. Morristown, NJ.: General Learning Press.

Pohlmann, J. T. (1976). A description of effective college teaching in five disciplines as measured by student ratings. *Research in Higher Education* 4: 335–346.

Ross, M., and Fletcher, G. (1985). Attribution and social perception. In G. Lindzey and E. Aronson (eds.), *Handbook of Social Psychology* (pp. 73–122). New York: Random House.

Rothbaum, F., Weisz, J. R., and Snyder, S. S. (1982). Changing the world and changing the self: A two-process model of perceived control. *Journal of Personality and Social Psychology* 42: 5–37.

Rotter, J. B. (1966). Generalized expectancies for internal versus external control of reinforcement. *Psychological Monographs* 80: 1–28.

Rotter, J. B. (1975). Some problems and misconceptions related to the construct of internal versus external control of reinforcement. *Journal of Consulting and Clinical Psychology* 40: 313–321.

Rotter, J. B., Chance, J. E., and Phares, E. J. (eds.). (1972). *Applications of a Social Learning Theory of Personality*. New York: Holt, Rinehart, and Winston.

Royce, J. D. (1956). Popularity and the teacher. *Education* 77: 233–237.

Salomon, G. (1972). Heuristic models for the generation of aptitude-treatment interaction hypotheses. *Review of Educational Research* 42: 327–343.

Scheier, M. F., and Carver, C. S. (1985). Optimism, coping, and health: Assessment and implications of generalized outcome expectancies. *Health Psychology* 4: 219–247.

Schunk, D. H. (1981). Modeling and attributional effects on children's achievement: A self-efficacy analysis. *Journal of Educational Psychology* 73: 93–105.

Seligman, M. (1975). *Helplessness: On Depression, Development, and Death*. San Francisco: Freeman.

Shulman, L. S. (1986). Paradigms and research programs in the study of teaching: A contemporary perspective. In M. Wittrock (ed.), *Third Handbook of Research on Teaching*. New York: Macmillan.

Snow, R. E. (1986). Individual differences and the design of educational programs. *American Psychologist* 41: 1029–1039.

Stipiek, D. J., and Weisz, J. R. (1981). Perceived control and academic achievement. *Review of Educational Research* 51: 101–138.

Strickland, B. R. (1989). Internal-external control expectancies: From contingency to creativity. *American Psychologist* 44: 1–12.

Tallmadge, G., Kasten, E. A., Shearer, J. W. (1971). Interactive relationships among learner characteristics, types of learning, instructional methods, and subject matter variables. *Journal of Educational Psychology, 62*, 31–38.

Tobias, S. (1976). Achievement treatment interactions. *Review of Educational Research* 48: 61–74. \

Travers, R. M. W. (ed.). (1973). *Second Handbook of Research on Teaching*. Chicago: Rand McNally.

Weiner, B. (1972). *Theories of Motivation*. Chicago: Rand McNally.

Weiner, B. (1979). A theory of motivation for some classroom experiences. *Journal of Educational Psychology* 71: 3–25.

Weiner, B. (1985). An attributional theory of achievement motivation and emotion. *Psychological Review* 92: 548–573.

Weiner, B. (1986). *An Attributional Theory of Motivation and Emotion*. New York: Springer-Verlag.

Weinert, F. E., and Helmke, A. (1987). Compensating effects of student self-concept and instructional quality on academic achievement. In F. Halisch and J. Kuhl (eds.), *Motivation, Intention, and Volition* (pp. 233–247). Berlin: Springer-Verlag.

White, R. (1959). Motivation reconsidered: The concept of competence. *Psychological Review* 66: 297–333.

Whitely, S. E., and Doyle, K. O. (1976). Implicit theories in student ratings. *American Educational Research Journal* 13: 241–253.

Whitener, E. M. (1989). A meta-analytic review of the effect on learning of the interaction between prior achievement and instructional support. *Review of Educational Research* 59: 65–86.

Williams, R. G., and Ware, J. E. (1976). Validity of student ratings of instruction under different incentive conditions: A further study of the Dr. Fox effect. *Journal of Educational Psychology* 68: 48–56.

Wilson, R. C. (1990). Commentary: The education of a faculty developer. *Journal of Educational Psychology* 82: 272–274.

Wittrock, M. (ed.). (1986). *Third Handbook of Research on Teaching*. New York: Macmillan.

Wortman, C. B., and Brehm, J. W. (1975). Responses to uncontrollable outcomes: An integration of reactance theory and the learned helplessness model. In L. Berkowitz (ed.), *Advances in Experimental Social Psychology* (vol. 8) (pp. 277–336). New York: Academic Press.

A Motivational Analysis of Academic Life in College

Martin V. Covington

"The curriculum does not matter. If it did matter, we could not do anything about it.
If we could do something about it, we would not know what to do."
Carnegie Foundation for the Advancement of Teaching, 1977

INTRODUCTION

Of course the curriculum matters; but yes, admittedly, we do not always know what alterations to make if we could. One reason is our imperfect understanding of the very processes of change that we hope to initiate in our students, encouraging changes from novice to expert and shedding an emotional dependency on authority so they may become independent learners. Although recently there has been a dramatic upturn nationwide in the commitment of university faculty to the enhancement of creative and independent thinking at the undergraduate level (Carnegie Foundation for the Advancement of Teaching, 1989), the particular educational policies and practices that best promote these goals are not always clear.

We are at a particular handicap when it comes to understanding the part that *motivation* plays in the process of growing up educated, and how best to respond to those who advocate that the highest goal of university life is to instill a "love of learning" and a willingness to continue learning over a lifetime. Peter Drucker puts it this way: "We know nothing about motivation. All we can do is write books about it." Drucker is correct to the extent that knowing *how* to motivate individuals is not the same as knowing *what* is motivation. As a concept, motivation can be more easily described in terms of its observable effects (e.g., persistence, purposeful action) than it is to define. But leaving aside various definitional issues (see Covington, 1992), and here is where Drucker is misled, we do in fact know at least *something* about how to motivate individuals to higher effort and about those conditions that encourage a love of learning. The essence of our knowledge is that a willingness to continue learning depends heavily on the individual's reasons (motives) for learning in the first instance.

The overall purpose of this chapter is to explore the implications of this proposition for policy and practice at the university and college level. In the first section, we will review what is known about motivation, what factors affect it, and how it in turn enters into and influences the larger achievement process. This considerable body of evidence is organized around the traditional view of *motives-as-drives*, internal needs or states that impel individuals to action. This perspective views motivation as residing largely within the individual, and treats these internal factors as an enabling device—a means to an end, with the end inevitably being improved status, better test performance, or a higher grade point average. This drive perspective dominates popular thinking whenever schools are admonished to motivate (drive) students to do better in response to those highly publicized comparisons of achievement scores, especially in science and mathematics, among students from the leading industrial nations, a contest which puts American students dead last. As one politician confided to Stanford education professor, Michael Kirst (1990), "I just want the little buggers to work harder." Presumably by increasing the rewards for being industrious and threatening sufficient punishments if effort is not forthcoming, schools can arouse otherwise indifferent students to renewed action. This same mentality regarding the motivating properties of rewards and punishments also prevails at the college level albeit in more sophisticated and less crudely expressed forms.

In the second section, we will consider more promising directions for enhancing achievement motivation among undergraduate students, an undertaking that is best conceived of in terms of an alternative metaphor: *motives-as-goals*. Researchers in this tradition assume that all actions are given meaning, direction, and purpose by the goals individuals seek out, and that the quality and intensity of behavior will change as these goals change. Considered from this perspective, motivation is a unique human resource to be encouraged for its own sake, not simply a means to increased school achievement. The topic of motivational change invariably raises the question of the extent to which motives are the property of individuals or of the circumstances in which individuals find themselves, a point to be considered later.

MOTIVES AS DRIVES

Educational decisions depend ultimately on answering three classic questions: *what* is worth knowing (curriculum issues)? *how* do we best impart this preferred knowledge (instructional issues)? and, finally, the question that puts students at the heart of the educational enterprise: *why*, or for what reasons, do students learn? The question of *why* provides us with the necessary motivational dimension. *Why*, for example, does Alice, a sophomore transfer student who must work long hours in the school cafeteria as part of her financial aid package, still find time to organize a Young Socialists Club on campus, compete for the lead in the school play, and have enough energy left over to maintain a 4.0 grade point average? And why does Ted who could do anything well, given his extraordinary intellectual gifts, appear content with choosing only those courses that offer him the most units for the least amount of work. To be sure, Alice's reasons (motives) for her extraordinary accomplishments may be far from positive—perhaps she is attempting to outperform others for fear that she might not prove worthy of perfection. In this case, keeping busy has the virtue of making one feel important and if Alice can't quite manage to do it all, then the implicit assumption is that she must be doing something significant. Similarly, Ted's lack of involvement may not be as aimless as appearances suggest. Rather it may stem from a basically healthy search for alternative, nontraditional means of self-expression. In any event, it is natural to describe these different behaviors as *driven*, with Alice compelled to aggrandize her status even at the risk of exhaustion and Ted seeking to connect with a lifestyle worthy of his talents.

The view of motives-as-drives had its origins beginning in the first decades of the present century (e.g., Woodworth, 1918, for review see also Bolles, 1967; Weiner, 1972, 1990) in laboratory and animal research which stressed physiological needs as the most important instigators of behavior. Simply put, organisms become aroused (motivated), and then goal-directed in an effort to reduce a physiological imbalance, typically represented by states of hunger or thirst, in order to return the body to a state of equilibrium (homeostasis). As valuable as this need-reduction view was for initiating research on motivation, its limitations became increasingly apparent when applied to human beings. The fact is that humans do not act solely to reduce stress, but will on occasion actually seek out stimulation, something any African safari guide or amusement park operator will tell us. More than anything, humans are active explorers and manipulators of their environment. This common sense observation eventually led researchers to postulate the existence of the so-called *stimulus motives* (Harlow, 1953; Hebb, 1961). These motives, like basic tissue needs, are likely unlearned, but their particular expression is conditioned heavily by social rules and conventions. It is easy to imagine that the ultimate expression of the need to control, explore, and manipulate is reflected in those processes required to land a new job, to decipher the meaning of the Dead Sea Scrolls, or to corner silver trading on the Chicago Commodities Exchange. These behaviors are thought to reflect *learned drives* or psychological motives, including a need for power, belongingness, and achievement. The term *drive* is applicable here because individuals often seem driven, even compelled by an internal state or demand for action; and *learned* because the strength and direction of such behavior is controlled to a great extent by custom.

Need Achievement Theory

The most important of the earlier learned-drive approaches to achievement motivation, and still enormously influential today, was developed by John Atkinson (1957, 1964) and his long-time colleague David McClelland (1958, 1961), beginning in the late 1950s. This theory holds that the need for achievement is the consequence of a conflict between two opposing forces: the desire to *approach* success and a fear of failure which results in a disposition (or motive) to *avoid* situations that are likely to devalue the individual. These twin motives were described largely in emotional terms with the anticipation of *pride* characterizing the approach motive and the anticipation of *shame* at failing, characterizing the avoidance motive. In essence, for Atkinson and McClelland the answer to the question of *why* individuals choose certain jobs and not others, or why they pursue tasks with more or less vigor, depended on the quality of the feelings that accompany success and failure.

Atkinson argued that individuals differ markedly in the degree to which they are characterized by these opposing motives. For instance, for those persons whose optimism, or hope for success, outweighs a fear of failure, the conflict is minimal and is typically resolved in a positive direction; by contrast, things are resolved in an opposite fashion for those persons for whom fear overpowers hope. These latter individuals, or *failure acceptors*, as they have recently been described (Covington and Omelich, 1991), are unwilling to volunteer their ideas in class, enter the achievement arena only reluctantly, and prefer either the easy course assignment because the probability of failure is low, or the exceedingly difficult task because they will not feel too badly if they fail at something for which so few others could be expected to succeed (Atkinson and Litwin, 1960; Lewin, Dembo, Festinger, and Sears, 1944; Moulton, 1965). By comparison, success-oriented persons prefer neither the easy nor the difficult assignment, but rather those tasks of intermediate difficulty for which the likelihood of success is exquisitely balanced off against the probability of failure, thus ensuring themselves enough successes to sustain future hope, yet without cheapening the rewards of success by too easy a victory.

Besides focusing on internal states, Atkinson's theory also exemplifies another important feature of the concept of motives-as-drives in that motives are viewed largely as an enabling factor, with the overriding objective being success at the chosen task. Another aspect of the motives-as-drives tradition is reflected in a decidedly entrepreneurial spirit which according to McClelland (1961, 1965) involves competing with standards of excellence, if not directly with other individuals, which amounts to a contest to outdo one's adversaries (Combs, 1957; Greenberg, 1932). This competitive element, not to be confused with striving to overcome one's own limitations or seeking out knowledge for its own sake, reflects what Nicholls (1989) and others (Ames, 1981, 1984; Ames and Ames, 1984; Dweck, 1986) have called an *ego-involved* or *performance* (as opposed to *learning*) mentality. For ego-involved students, noteworthy performance is a way to enhance one's status, commonly one's intellectual or ability standing, and usually at the expense of others. Thus intrinsic reasons for learning are largely missing from the need achievement tradition.

Over the years the need achievement model has evolved in several distinctive ways. First, Atkinson and McClelland have more fully developed their views on how approach and avoidance motives interact with other related motives, including the need for social approval and for power (Veroff and Veroff, 1972; Winter, 1973). The resulting *dynamics of action* model (Atkinson, 1981; McClelland, 1980, 1985) suggests that many motives operate simultaneously and on a moment-to-moment basis within the same individual, a perspective that allows for more dynamic predictions that can be measured in terms of the *percentage* of time that, say, success-oriented individuals spend on various tasks compared with earlier predictions which recognized only all-or-nothing choices among tasks.

Second, Nuttin and Lens (Nuttin, 1984; Nuttin and Lens, 1985) have infused the need achievement model with a decidedly goal-directed orientation in which they argue that the individual's perceptions of the future, especially subjective notions of time, form the fundamental motivational space within which all human beings operate. Success-oriented individuals aspire to more complex, distant goals than do failure-threatened individuals (DeVolder and Lens, 1982) and they are more likely to divide the task of achieving those goals into small steps of intermediate difficulty, like stepping stones, so that the chances of ultimate success are maximized. Raynor (1969, 1970) has characterized these kinds of plans as *partially contingent pathways*, meaning that success at one step creates the opportunity to move to the next, but failure does not necessarily preclude advancement. This is because success-oriented persons create backup plans in case their initial strategies fall short. And they also entertain alternative goals if the original objective becomes impossible such as becoming a paramedic instead of a physician, or working as a paralegal rather than as an attorney.

This research holds important implications for both educational theory and practice. For one thing, it suggests that the ability to plan may be an essential part of what we speak of as motivation; indeed, it may be that *motives* are actually just *plans* but by a different name. For another thing, the research of Nuttin and Lens along with that of others (Findley and Cooper, 1983; Skinner, Wellborn, and Connell, 1990; Stipik and Weiss, 1981) makes the point that believing oneself to be in personal control of events is central to all noteworthy accomplishments. In this connection, Pintrich and his colleagues (Eccles, 1983; Pintrich, 1988, 1989, 1990; Pintrich and DeGroot, 1990) have identified several factors essential to task involvement that are linked to the effective regulation of plans and to realistic goal setting: (1) An expectancy factor that includes beliefs about one's ability to perform well; (2) a value factor that includes the reasons for being involved, what we have called motives; and, (3) an emotional component, "How do I feel about this task?"

The legacy of Atkinson's need achievement model is clearly evident in these most recent developments in motivation theory.

Attribution Theory

Beginning in the early 1970s a significant reinterpretation of Atkinson's model was offered by Bernard Weiner and his colleagues (Weiner et al., 1971; Weiner, 1972, 1974) guided by the principles of attribution theory which are based on the proposition that the way individuals perceive the causes of their successes and failures influences their subsequent achievement. According to Weiner, the important difference between success-oriented and failure-threatened individuals is not so much variations in emotional reaction (pride vs. shame) as the differences in their cognitions. Failure-prone persons tend to attribute their failures to inadequate ability and their successes to external factors such as luck, chance, or mood. By comparison, success-oriented persons typically ascribe their failures to insufficient effort since they believe themselves to be capable enough; and, by extension, they attribute their successes to a combination of skill (ability) and diligence. This latter attributional pattern promotes a highly positive interpretation of achievement outcomes: Success inspires greater confidence in one's ability and promotes a sense of control, whereas failure merely signals the need to try harder (Man and Hrabal, 1988). On the other hand, failure-prone individuals find themselves in a "no-win" situation: Failure implies that success is unlikely, and not worth pursuing; and, on those infrequent occasions when success does occur, it is discounted as the result of forces outside one's ability to control.

The weight of accumulated evidence supports these attributional differences between success-oriented and failure-prone persons (Arkin, Detchon, and Maruyama, 1982; Leppin, Schwarzer, Belz, Jerusalem, and Quast, 1987; Meyer, 1970; Weiner and Kukla, 1970, Experiment 4; Weiner et al., 1971; Weiner, Heckhausen, Meyer, and Cook, 1972). The findings are especially compelling for the predominance of low-ability attributions among failure-prone students (Covington and Omelich, 1979a).

This cognitive reinterpretation of Atkinson's need achievement model prompted a subtle, but important, shift in the focus of motivational research from the question of *why* to one of *how*—that is, *how* individuals interpret events like failure—and also suggests that what is most important to future achievement is the meaning that individuals attribute to their failures (and successes) and not simply the frequency of their occurrence.

These different attributional patterns are thought to enter into the achievement process in the ways portrayed in Figure 1.

First, consider the plight of failure-threatened students (upper portion of Figure 1). Students who interpret failure as caused by insufficient ability are likely to: (1) experience shame (low ability'shame), shame being an ability-linked emotion (Covington and Omelich, 1984a); and, (2) reduce their expectations for future success (low ability'lowered expectation). Lowered expectations occur because among adults, at least, ability is typically perceived to be a fixed, immutable factor, and because ability is also believed to be the preemptive cause of academic success. In short, if someone is not very smart, he or she can only do so well despite having tried hard (Harari and Covington, 1981). The presence of shame eventually inhibits achievement via the expectancy linkage (shame'low expectation'poor performance) because shame triggers renewed self-doubts about one's ability whenever students begin studying again (Covington and Omelich, 1990). According to Figure 1, lower expectations per se also undercut future performance, a lineage that depends largely on the fact that self-doubting students persist less in their work on a problem (Battle, 1965).

Now consider the achievement dynamics of success-oriented persons (lower portion of Figure 1). Individuals who interpret failure as caused primarily by insufficient effort experience feelings of guilt for not having tried hard enough, guilt being an effort-linked emotion (Covington and Omelich, 1984a). In moderation, feelings of guilt mobilize further effort (Hoffman, 1982; Wicker, Payne, and Morgan, 1983), especially among bright individuals who often feel keenly the responsibility associated with brilliance (guilt'increased performance) (Weiner and Kukla, 1970). Also because effort level is perceived of as modifiable, expectations for future success remains high among success-oriented students even in the face of failure because they believe that success is within their grasp if only they try harder. Such optimism (increased expectations) guarantees a measure of persistence which eventually pays off in the form of higher achievement (low effort'higher expectations'improved performance).

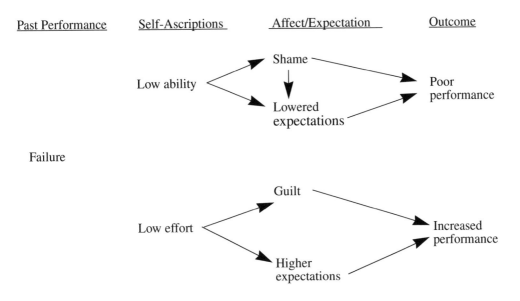

FIGURE 1. Attribution model of achievement motivation. (Source: Adapted from Covington, 1989).

From this overall analysis we now see why failure can drive some individuals to renewed effort and others to despair, depending on the prevailing self-perceived causes of failure. Also it is clear why some individuals reject success despite the fact that it is so sought after. When success is seen as due to external factors beyond one's control—the generosity of an instructor, luck, or the help of others—doing well adds little to one's confidence that success can be repeated.

Cognitive theorists have focused principally on the role of effort in the dynamics portrayed in Figure 1, and as a consequence, several important effort-related linkages have been well established. First, as already noted, if individuals do not exert enough effort in a failing cause, they are more likely to remain optimistic since one can always try harder the next time (Fontaine, 1974; McMahan, 1973; Meyer, 1970; Rosenbaum, 1972; Valle, 1974; Weiner et al., 1972). Second, trying hard mitigates feelings of guilt (for not trying), thereby reinforcing the value of effort (Brown and Weiner, 1984). Third, and perhaps of greatest significance, it is widely accepted that student effort is modifiable through the actions of teachers. For example, many teachers believe that the greater the rewards offered, the harder students will try and that distributing rewards on a competitive basis is the most effective means to drive students to greater effort. Although these particular beliefs are largely misplaced (a point to be discussed later), it is clearly the case that teachers do value effort. They reward least those students who succeed without trying and punish most those who fail for lack of trying (Covington and Omelich, 1979b; Eswara, 1972; Rest, Nierenberg, Weiner, and Heckhausen, 1973; Weiner and Kukla, 1970). For this reason, according to cognitive theorists, students should come to value effort as a major if not the main source of personal worth, and to the extent that students disregard this work ethic, they will experience chagrin and rejection by others.

But it is also clear, abundantly so, that students do not always respond as expected to this dominant work ethic. Many students postpone assignments and generally act in ways contrary to their own best interests insofar as getting high grades are concerned. But why should this be if teachers generously reward trying hard, and are quick to punish inactivity?

There is more afoot here than can be accounted for easily by cognitive reinforcement mechanisms alone. For example, despite the evidence cited above, attributing a prior failure to inadequate effort does not guarantee that a student will remain optimistic about his or her future chances. Such inaction may also reflect the fact that the student has become demoralized and has given up. In effect, the explanations people harbor for their successes and failures are not necessarily synonymous with their reasons for achieving or not achieving. In short, attributions are no simple substitute for the concept of motivation.

Self-Worth Theory

The self-worth theory of achievement motivation (Covington, 1984a, 1984b, 1985b, 1992; Covington and Beery, 1976) attempts to create a theoretical rapport between the cognitive tradition with its emphasis on self-perceptions of causality, especially effort attributions, and the drive theory formulations of Atkinson's earlier need achievement model, along with research on the topics of fear-of-failure and defensive dynamics (e.g., Birney, Burdick, and Teevan, 1969; Snyder, Stephan, and Rosenfeld, 1976). Self-worth theory holds that the search for self-acceptance is the highest priority among humans and that in schools (at least as presently constituted) self-acceptance typically becomes equated with the ability to achieve competitively. In effect, individuals come to believe themselves only as worthy as their accomplishments competitively defined. Thus individuals may approach success (in Atkinson's terms) not only to benefit from the social and personal rewards of high accomplishment, but also to aggrandize their reputations for high ability. And, if success become unlikely, as is typically the case when rewards are distributed on a competitive basis—with the greatest number going to those who perform best—then the first priority is to avoid failure, or at least avoid the implications of failure that one is incompetent.

Self-worth theory stresses those aspects of personal worth that are tied to a sense of competency and those feelings of worthlessness arising out of disclosures of incompetency. A growing body of evidence underscores the importance of ability perceptions among college students as the most salient aspect of their academic self-definition. As only one example, Covington and Omelich (1984a) asked students to analyze retrospectively any one of their courses from a previous semester. Students rated their ability to deal with the subject matter in the course, estimated how hard they had worked, and judged how much positive self-regard they enjoyed as a student. They also reported the course grade they received. By far the most important contributor to feelings of self-regard were self-estimates of ability, a factor which accounted for more than 50\% of the variance. The actual grade received in the course proved to be a distant second as a contributor to feelings of worthiness. And, of lesser importance still was the amount of effort expended. Although those students who worked harder did in fact feel slightly more worthy, hard work was no substitute for a reputation of brilliance when it came to defining academic self-worth. The importance of ability status has also been corroborated in several related studies. For instance, Brown and Weiner (1984) concluded that college students prefer to achieve because of ability rather than effort. Moreover, among those studies that permit estimates of the relative contributions of ability and effort to a sense of worth, ability cognitions accounted for most of the variation in shame (Covington and Omelich, 1984a; Weiner and Kukla, 1970). Finally, analyses of actual college test-taking experiences indicated that ability cognitions were the dominant factor affecting pride and shame reactions as well as actual achievement level (Covington and Omelich, 1979a, 1981, 1982).

The cognitive model stresses those aspects of worthiness associated with hard work, whereas self-worth theory stresses those aspects associated with feelings of competency. But are these two sources of worth necessarily incompatible? Cannot students achieve via hard work and in the process also increase their sense of competency and feelings of control over events? Yes, possibly, but it is unlikely—at least not if the rewards for learning are distributed on a competitive basis where failure is the most frequent outcome. Under competitive conditions learning becomes an ability game: The fewer the rewards available the more they come to depend on ability. And in the circumstance, effort becomes a threat because if one tries hard and fails anyway, then explanations for failure go to low ability. But, try or not, teachers still reward effort and students are expected to comply with this work ethic. Herein lies the dilemma for students: To try hard and fail leads to shame and feelings of worthlessness; but not trying leads to feelings of guilt and teacher punishment.

A number of studies using different methodologies have confirmed this effort dilemma for college students. For example, we collected a number of self-report measures from students over several successive midterm examinations and subjected these data to multivariate path analysis (Covington and Omelich, 1981). For those students who experienced failure (i.e., falling below their competitively derived aspirations), shame not only followed directly from diminutions in self-perceived ability status, but most important from the standpoint of an effort dilemma, the reciprocal linkage between degree of effort expended and feelings of competency (high effort'low ability) increased in saliency as failures accumulated from one midterm to the next. This means that the more individuals study as a response to having failed previously, the more likely it is that any future failures will be interpreted by them and others as a matter of incompetency.

Several companion studies (Covington and Omelich, 1979b; Covington, Spratt, and Omelich, 1980) which employed a role-playing methodology further illustrate this effort dilemma. Students rated the degree of shame they would expect (hypothetically) if they had failed a test under several different circumstances. Those failures that elicited the greatest shame were preceded by high effort (study), whereas those failures that elicited lesser degrees of shame were associated with little or no study preparation. These same students were then asked to assume the role of teachers and punish hypothetical students under each of the same conditions of failure. As "teachers" these subjects now assigned the *greatest* degree of punishment to precisely those failures that previously had offered them (as students) the greatest emotional protection from diminished self-perceptions of ability (i.e., failure without effort); and, conversely, these "teachers" punished far less those failures that triggered the greatest sense of shame among students (i.e., failure after trying hard). Excuses served to moderate this conflict of classroom values. "Teachers" punished least of all those low-effort failures in which lack of study was blamed on illness, exactly the same condition (low-effort/ excuse) that elicited the least shame among students. Also alleged explanations for why studying hard did not paid off—in this case, because the test emphasized material not studied by the student—resulted in substantial reductions in both teacher punishment and student shame. This series of studies not only illuminates the motivational dynamics involved when students face the threat of failure, but also indicates how students can avoid the threat: By not trying or at least trying but with excuses available. As Covington and Beery (1976) have observed:

> Thus there emerges from this complex interplay among students, peers, and teacher a "winning" formula in the anticipation of failure that is designed to avoid personal humiliation and shame on the one hand and to minimize teacher punishment on the other: try, or at least *appear* to try, but not too energetically and with excuses handy. It is difficult to imagine a strategy better calculated to sabotage the pursuit of personal excellence. (p.84)

Failure-avoiding Strategies
Over the last two decades researchers have investigated a number of defensive ploys which college students use in attempts to avoid failure. These self-serving tactics are intended to shift the presumed causes of failure from internal (ability) factors to external causes beyond the individual's control or responsibility; in effect, they work by obscuring the causes of failure which calls to mind Nietzsche's celebrated remark that, "Those who know they are profound strive for clarity. Those who would like to seem profound to the crowd strive for obscurity." These latter tactics can be divided into two groups.

First, consider those ploys described collectively as "self-handicapping" strategies (Berglas and Jones, 1978; Tucker, Vuchinich and Sobell, 1981); self-handicapping because ironically enough they set up the very failures that individuals are attempting to avoid, but at least they are failures "with honor," that is, readily explained, if not always excused. Perhaps the most celebrated and certainly the most frequently employed self-handicapping strategy is procrastination (Silver and Sabini, 1981, 1982). Some observers estimate that a near-majority of college students procrastinate on a regular basis

(Rothblum, Solomon, and Murakami, 1986; Solomon and Rothblum, 1984) while other more pessimistic estimates run as high as 90 percent (Ellis and Kraus, 1977). By postponing study for a test or work on a term paper until the very last minute, students can argue that their performance is not representative of what they could really do, if they had only "not run out of time." An additional benefit of procrastination is that if the student should do well despite having studied only briefly, then a reputation for brilliance will be enhanced. Students have also been known to take on so many tasks that they cannot give sufficient time to any one of them. This variation on the procrastination theme not only allows students to score points for being energetic, but being busy makes one feel important despite the mediocre performances that are likely to result.

Another self-handicapping strategy involves setting one's academic goals so high, say, hoping to maintain a perfect grade point average while carrying a double major, that failure is virtually guaranteed, but a failure that would befall most every other student as well. "If I cannot succeed," the implied argument runs, "then the problem is in the goal, not in me." This reasoning depends on being able to convince oneself that failed tasks are inherently difficult, a mental sleight of hand that appears easily accomplished if we can judge from the research of Bennett and Holmes (as reported in Snyder, 1984). These investigations gave college students a vocabulary test. One-half of the students were told, falsely, that they had failed, while the remaining students were given no feedback at all. A significantly greater percentage of the first group estimated that their friends had also failed the test. From a self-worth perspective these results are to be expected because, indeed, "misery loves company," and the more the better, since the failure of the many obscures the failure of the individual.

Another tactic involves admitting to a minor or nonthreatening handicap such as test-taking anxiety, while avoiding disclosure of a greater real or imagined weakness— in this case, incompetency. The test-anxious student is the perfect blameless victim. Anxiety is real enough and does, in fact, disrupt learning so the affliction is credible; also everyone has experienced anxiety to some degree and as a result the sufferer can convert imagined scorn at being disclosed as stupid into instant sympathy and concern. All in all, the temptation is too great for some students not to use the symptoms of anxiety to personal advantage. For example, when Smith, Snyder, and Handelsman (1982) gave test-anxious subjects legitimate reason to report symptoms of anxiety following a test, they did so more often than another group of equally anxious individuals who were given no permission. By contrast, low test-anxious students reported no more feelings of anxiety whether or not they were given permission to do so. Thus anxiety symptoms among anxious individuals may or may not appear depending upon circumstances and on their potential for self-justification.

Researchers have also documented the use of failure-avoiding strategies in numerous situations outside formal academic settings whenever one's reputation for ability is at stake, whether ability be musical aptitude and the failure to perform well in a public piano recital (Covington, 1982) or physical prowess and the failure to maintain a competitive edge in high school wrestling competition (Burton and Martens, 1986).

A second cluster of failure-avoiding tactics, unlike self-handicapping strategies, seemingly accents the positive by attempting to guarantee success, but success not so much for the sake intrinsic satisfaction as a way to avoid failure. The premier case is that of the *overstriver* (Beery, 1975; Covington and Beery, 1976). We will consider over-strivers in more detail in the next section. Meantime, suffice it to say that in terms of Atkinson's need achievement model overstrivers reflect simultaneously a desire to approach success largely for its high status value and a desire to avoid failure given the implication that one is not worthy of perfection. As we will see, this hybrid quality of hope and fear can drive some individuals to extraordinary accomplishments.

Another technique for ensuring success is to set one's academic aspirations low enough so as to avoid outright failure by means of what Birney, Burdick, and Teevan (1969) refer to as the *confirming interval*. The confirming interval is that range between the highest test score or grade one can reasonably hope to achieve and the lowest accept-able outcome. Students often manipulate the lower bounds of this range, raising it on occasion when they feel confident of outcomes and lowering it in anticipation of a par-ticularly difficult exam. This latter maneuver can protect them from experiencing feel-ings of failure despite the fact that at best their performances may be only mediocre. Indeed, chronic low-goal setting often leads to a prolonged state of mediocrity where success is defined only by not losing.

Covington (1992) has summarized the lessons to be learned from this collection of defensive strategies and the fact of their universality and pervasiveness. "Humans stop at little; lying, cheating, even failing is not too high a price to pay. Yet, in the process failure-threatened students become their own worst enemies. No matter how adroitly they maneuver, they still harbor doubts about their ability because they are unwilling to test the limits by trying their hardest. They fear that they *might* be inadequate, but what they fear most is finding out" (pp. 88\N89).

Individual Student Differences
The self-worth dynamics described so far do not apply equally to all students. Individu-als enter college already disposed to deal with academic stress in various distinctive ways and to protect, or if necessary, to salvage a belief in themselves, especially those individuals who have tied their sense of worth to competitive excellence. This process of coping is not uniform nor are the outcomes identical, but rather it results in an almost endless variety of adaptation and maladaptation. How are we to make sense of such complexity? One response of the social scientist is to identify the fewest, most salient dimensions along which all students can be located and then aggregate them in clusters with each student type reflecting (hopefully) different styles of coping.

The development of student typologies in higher education has become something of a cottage industry with a long and distinguished history. One of the first major typol-ogies was that developed by Clark and Trow (1960, 1966) who differentiated students in terms of their subculture membership—vocational, collegiate, nonconformist, and the like (for a critique, see Ellis, Parelius, and Parelius, 1971; Peterson, 1965; Warren, 1968). Other typologies have followed, most notably the classification schema created by Holland and his colleagues (Holland, 1966, 1973; Osipow, Ashby, and Wall, 1966;

Folsom, 1969) which was intended to reflect broad occupational choices among students, including enterprising, artistic, and intellectual (investigative) types. Yet other approaches have been rooted more firmly in traditional personality research as represented by the Omnibus Personality Inventory which was used by its developers, Heist and Yonge (1968), and others (Elton, 1967; Korn, 1968) to study changes in student coping styles over the course of their college careers. Katchadourian and Boli (1985) have rightly pointed out that most of these typologies are based on a phenomenological approach in which student types are defined either by institutional or group membership, or informally by the students themselves. This means that student types are not always defined in terms of a common set of dimensions so that, for example, nonconformists might describe themselves in terms of the social causes they espouse while intellectually oriented individuals might locate themselves around different philosophical positions.

My approach to typology development, like that of Katchadourian and Boli (1985) who studied careerism and intellectualism among college students, is more analytical. Katchadourian and Boli explicitly classified students on two dimensions, one reflecting a preference/nonpreference for career preparation and the other a preference/nonpreference for an intellectual life of discovery. Thus the four types of students resulting from this 2 \x 2 matrix were based on an interplay of careerism and intellectualism variables and nothing else. I, too, catalogued students on two, independent dimensions, those of *approach* and *avoidance*, dynamic poles which served as the bedrock of Atkinson's need achievement model.

As originally proposed, Atkinson's theory featured a two-dimensional quadripolar model of the kind presented in Figure 2. Individuals could be placed either high or low on either an approach or on a failure-avoiding dimension.

They could also be located high on *both* dimensions. This two-dimensional approach had the advantage of allowing for conflicting motivational tendencies represented by those individuals located high on both dimensions, that is, driven simultaneously by hope and fear (Student A). Also, students could remain seemingly indifferent to achievement events as reflected by the relative absence of *both* hope and fear (Student D).

However, despite the heuristic value of Atkinson's quadripolar model, few researchers have maintained the distinction of two independent dimensions (for exceptions, see Atkinson and Litwin, 1960; Feather, 1965). Instead, most have adopted a unidimensional, bipolar interpretation of achievement motivation in which approach and avoidance tendencies represent extreme polar opposites on only one dimension (e.g., Feather, 1961, 1963; Littig, 1963; Litwin, 1966; Moulton, 1965). By this reckoning approach and avoidance tendencies become blended within the same person so that everyone can be placed somewhere along a single continuum, differing only in relative amounts of hope and fear. Not only does this procedure confound the two approach and avoidance elements of the original model in unknown ways, and disregard the possibility of conflicting tendencies, but it also creates an awkwardness when trying to describe those persons for whom approach and avoidance tendencies balance off equally—the presumed zero point midway between high avoidance and high approach. Is a complete absence of motivation best represented by the resultant canceling of two extreme motives? Probably not. A bipolar model leaves no room for genuine indifference.

In an effort to reestablish Atkinson's original quadripolar model, we analyzed the learning characteristics and achievement styles of some 400 Berkeley undergraduates (Covington and Omelich, 1991) employing a newly developed battery of achievement motive measures which including self-ratings of perceived ability, proneness to anxiety arousal, and the quality of one's study habits and skills. A series of stepwise discriminant analyses confirmed Atkinson's original quadripolar model. Four distinct groups emerged, separated one from the other along two independent axes, one labeled approach and the other, avoidance. First, these data confirmed the classic distinction between success-oriented and failure-avoiding persons as behaviorally distinct (students B and C, respectively: see Figure 2). Success-oriented students rated themselves markedly higher on general ability than did failure avoiders, exhibited far less anxiety about their schoolwork, and harbored few fears of being unmasked as incompetent. Moreover, success-oriented individuals exhibited superior study skills, although they often spent less time preparing for tests than did many failure-avoiding students. Second, two hybrid groups also emerged: students high in both approach and avoidance tendencies (Student A), or *overstrivers*; and students low in both approach and avoidance tendencies (Student D), or *failure-acceptors* as we have called them (Covington and Omelich, 1985).

In self-worth terms, overstrivers attempt to avoid failure by succeeding! Although a seemingly clever response to academic threat, this strategy is basically defensive and eventually can prove self-defeating. Basically, overstrivers are conflicted over the prospects for success. On the one hand, success is sought after because it reassures them, but on the other, it perpetuates fear because overstrivers know they cannot succeed indefinitely, test-after-test, since their goal is not merely excellence, but perfection. Consistent with this self-worth interpretation, overstrivers were found to combine behaviors associated with both pure-approach and pure-avoidance tendencies (see Figure 2). As to the approach dimension, overstrivers possessed superior study strategies, persisted in their work (but to a fault), and gave themselves high marks for ability. As to avoidance tendencies, overstrivers were unsure of their claims on brilliance, and as a result experience considerable anxiety whenever they studied for a test.

From a self-worth perspective, failure-accepting students are those individuals who have given up the struggle to maintain a sense of worth via ability, and because of repeated failures in school, have become convinced to a certainty of their incompetency. We will consider shortly the causal dynamics involved in this progression from defensive failure-avoidance to failure-acceptance. Failure-accepting individuals combine those behaviors and beliefs associated with both low-approach and low-avoidance tendencies. The relative absence of approach tendencies in this group was associated with a life of self-derogation where ability is concerned and with inferior study skills, while the relative absence of avoidance tendencies was associated with a pervasive lack of achievement affect (see also Covington and Omelich, 1985). This group expressed neither much pride in their successes, nor much shame in their failures. It appears that these students have resigned themselves to mediocrity as a way of life. Naturally, other interpretations of inaction are always possible, if only because of the inherent difficulty of explaining a negative event (in this case the relative absence of behavior). It is also possible that these individuals have simply chosen not to participate in what they perceive to be a useless contest, and have sought other alternative sources of personal satisfaction such as self-discovery or the pursuit of socially meaningful achievements (Roberts and Covington, 1991).

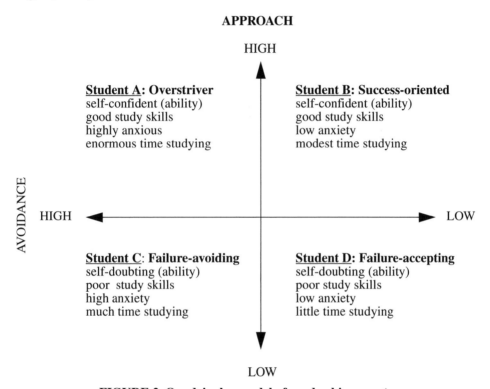

FIGURE 2. Quadripolar model of need achievement

Integration

Recapping so far, we began with a review of research on the concept of achievement motivation organized around the metaphor of motives-as-drives. In the process we considered three successive waves of theory development—the need achievement model, a cognitive reinterpretation of need achievement, and then the marriage of these two approaches according to the tenets of self-worth theory. But how do these many factors—cognitive, motivational, and affective—all interact and play themselves out, causally, in real-life college classrooms? For answers we must look beyond the results of isolated correlational studies that merely establish simple associations between variables taken two at a time. Nor can we rely only on experimental laboratory studies conducted under artificial conditions. In the last analysis, we must investigate multiple variables operating simultaneously as they influence one another and impact jointly on distant achievement outcomes over extended periods of time and for the same persons.

To this end, a series of multivariate achievement studies was conducted at Berkeley in college classrooms. The time frames involved extended over meaningful periods in the academic life of students, ranging from an analysis of a single study/test cycle (Covington and Omelich, 1981) to investigations of several successive midterm examinations in the same course (Covington and Omelich, 1979a, 1984b, 1988; Covington, Omelich, and Schwarzer, 1986). In all cases, we ask several basic questions: Do emotional, cognitive, and motivational factors combine lawfully to influence achievement? And do different types of students respond differently to the challenges and threats inherent in college achievement?

The results of one representative study from our laboratory are reported here in some detail, supplemented by the work of other American as well as European investigators whose findings complement and extend this research. This particular study (Covington and Omelich, 1988) tracked 432 Berkeley undergraduates enrolled in an introductory psychology course over three midterm tests during which time some 200 observations were made per student. Among other things, these students were asked to rate the amount of anxiety they were experiencing at various points in the course, attribute reasons for their successes and failures following each test, indicate how frequently their study was compromised by intrusive worries, describe the sources of this worry, and judge their ability to handle the subject matter following each study session and each test. The general model around which this massive data set was organized is presented in Figure 3.

The horizontal dimension includes a temporal, stagewise sequence through which antecedent factors from each of three different psychological domains play out their respective roles in the achievement process. First, consider the domain of motives. Depending on their dominant motivational orientation (some combination of approach and avoidance tendencies), students will be more or less concerned about their ability status, an issue that becomes especially salient for some students during the first few class meetings when they learn about the course requirements (appraisal stage). Students who believe the course to be within their intellectual capabilities are likely to view it as a challenge, whereas those who doubt their ability to succeed (e.g., failure-avoiders) will likely become threatened. According to theory, for this latter group perceptions of threat in turn trigger varying degrees of defensiveness as students prepare for each successive test (preparation stage). Similarly, those antecedent factors associated with the *cognitive* domain, such as the quality of one's study skills, also contribute to feelings of threat and challenge, with good study habits likely to offset the presence of threat (Tobias, 1985, 1986). Finally, regarding the emotional domain, anxiety aroused during the appraisal stage, will interfere with subsequent study and also eventually disrupt the recall of what was originally learned (anxiety'poor study'poor performance).

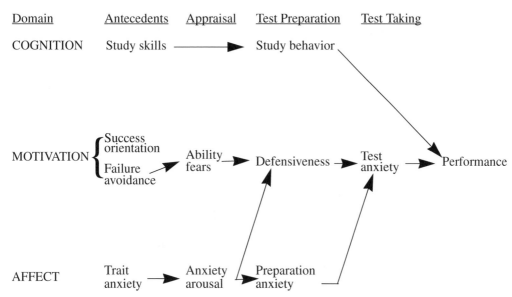

FIGURE 3. Interactive model of achievement dynamics: Motivational, cognitive, and emotional components

Not only do these three time-ordered strands exert a forward-reaching influence individually on a common outcome (in this case, test performance), but they also are likely to interact among themselves as students progress from one stage of the model to the next. These interactions can take many forms. Sometimes the relationship may be *compensatory* as when, for example, good study habits (cognitive strand) offset the negative influence of anxiety (emotional strand) on performance. Other times the relationship among domains may be *additive* or even *multiplicative*. For instance, for some students the presence of anxiety, far from disrupting achievement, may actually mobilize them to study harder than ever.

Having provided the general rationale for the various time-ordered linkages we investigated, it remains only to say that the data were analyzed according to multiple prediction procedures (Anderson and Evans, 1974) in which the numerous (multiple) kinds of information gathered at each stage in the model were used to predict eventual scores on achievement tests. There are several advantages to this approach. First, not only was a longitudinal perspective created, but, second, we were able to investigate the *relative* importance of various factors as predictors of test outcome, say, emotions versus cognitions (worries), at any point in the study/test cycle. Third, because we proposed a testable model in advance of actual data collection, we were justified in interpreting the results of the multiple prediction analysis in causal terms. Thus the arrows in Figure 3 imply cause-and-effect relationships as well as the direction of influence.

Failure-avoiding Students.
Prior research indicated that failure-avoiding students feel inadequately prepared (Covington and Omelich, 1988), harbor considerable doubts about their ability to succeed

(Laux and Glanzmann, 1987; Salamé, 1984; Schmalt, 1982), and experience excessive achievement anxiety (Carver and Scheier, 1988; Hagtvet, 1984). This portrait was confirmed in all aspects by the Berkeley data. But how does this failure-avoiding legacy of fear and doubt enter into the achievement process itself?

During the appraisal stage various apprehensions were magnified out of all proportion for failure-avoiders (compared with the self-reports of success-oriented students), especially those worries associated with being revealed as incompetent and of not doing well enough to stay in school. These ability-linked doubts reverberated in a forward-reaching cascade (from left to right) across the entire model. Worries not only lingered, but intensified during the test preparation stage especially as the first test grew closer, and became manifest as defensively oriented thoughts that diverted the attention of failure-avoiding students from the study task at hand. They hoped, for example, that there would be no test ("I wish the test would somehow go away"), they externalized blame in anticipation of failure ("If I had a better teacher, I might do better"), and they sought relief from anxiety by minimizing the importance of any projected failure ("This course is less important than I originally thought"). Not surprisingly, such thoughts were accompanied by emotional tension and occasionally physiological reactions (upset stomach, dizziness) which in turn added their own unique contribution to the disruption of effective study.

Through this confection of denial, subterfuge and magical thinking we can sense the quiet desperation that serves as a seedbed for the many classic failure-avoiding strategies catalogued earlier, including procrastination and irrationally high goal-setting. As a consequence, failure-avoiding students find themselves largely unprepared even though on average they spent as much or more time studying (or at least going through the motions) as did success-oriented students.

In the final test-taking stage fears of incompetency were triggered anew, sometimes by seeing other students finishing the test early ("I'm so slow, I must really be dumb") or by the obsessive rehearsing of past failures, which recalls to mind a classic definition of anxiety: "The interest paid on trouble before it is due." Unlike mild emotional responses whose arousal depends on cues largely incidental to test-taking such as merely walking into an examination room, the kinds of reactions of which I speak here do not lose their potency once the test begins, but rather continue to preoccupy students even after the test is over in the form of self-criticism and rebuke.

Overall these dynamics place failure-avoiding students in harm's way for two reasons: They learn relatively less to begin with; then, what little they do learn is recalled only imperfectly—they forget the most basic facts and sometimes cannot even remember the questions they are trying to answer. Ironically enough, some failure-avoiding students appear deliberately, and repeatedly, to put themselves in jeopardy. Reagan (1991) studied a select group of community college students who continued to enroll for coursework, semester after semester, despite a record of failing grades. For these students, the majority of whom were identified as failure-avoiding, the noxious gauntlet of repeated failure was more than offset by the sense of self-importance and prestige afforded them by being enrolled in a college level course of study. Needless to say, it was their status as college students, and not their grades, that formed the basis for their projected public image.

Overstriving Students

Although overstrivers share much in common with other failure-prone students that is negative, they do possess certain redeeming qualities; namely, superior study skills and high ability despite their relentless self-doubts. As a result, rather than disrupting their study, anxiety acted to focus their considerable study skills. Overstrivers spent more time studying by far than any other type of student investigated; they were the first to begin studying sometimes weeks before the exam, and the last to stop often just before the instructor threatens to withhold the test unless they put away their notes. Basically this slavish devotion to study, which is more to be pitied than admired, occurs because overstrivers have no choice but to succeed. They dare not procrastinate, nor can they settle for less than perfection because they are betting on success, not on excused failure, as the way to prove their worth.

Eventually, however, the defensively driven character of such meticulous, excessive study catches up with overstrivers. As tension mounts during the test-taking stage, they suffer a massive failure to recall what they had spent so much time overlearning. The student who justifiably laments, "but I knew it cold before the exam," is likely an overstriver. Several hours after the first midterm was administered, all students in the Berkeley sample were invited back to retake parts of the test (Covington and Omelich, 1987a). It was overstrivers (those individuals who combined high anxiety and good study habits) who improved most on retesting, presumably due to the dissipation of a temporary blockage of otherwise superior mental functioning. This "anxiety-blockage" phenomenon is likely heightened by the fact that the presence of anxiety discourages deep-level processing during original learning, and favors instead superficial rote memorization. Information stored in such a mindless fashion is more subject to forgetting later since it was not organized around memorable principles and concepts in the first place (Covington, 1985c).

Failure-accepting Students

I have characterized failure-acceptors as individuals who have given up the struggle to define their worth in terms of competitive achievement via high ability, and as a consequence have become dispirited and apathetic. Although, as mentioned earlier, such indifference is potentially subject to many interpretations, the results of the Berkeley study are consistent with the notion of a general state of resignation. Not only are these undergraduates relatively lacking in the proper study skills, but they also studied far less than did other groups, and reported low levels of anxiety and worry at all stages of the study/test cycle (Covington and Omelich, 1985). This pattern parallels findings from the literature on learned helplessness which has been described as the loss of hope or the will to act that accompanies a belief that no matter how hard one tries, failure is the inevitable outcome (Abramson, Seligman, and Teasdale, 1978; Coyne and Lazarus, 1980; Miller and Norman, 1979; Seligman, 1975). Interestingly, it has been shown that the trigger for such despair is not the fact that trying hard does not work, that is, a non-contingent relationship between effort and outcome, but rather the fact that despair follows from the personal implication that one is incompetent (Covington, 1985a). Thus the phenomenon of learned helplessness becomes yet another instance of the larger self-worth legacy whenever individuals anchor their sense of worth to ability status and to competitive achievement. Feelings of incompetency give rise to task-irrelevant worry about ability which in turn interferes with effective information processing (Carver, 1979; Kuhl, 1981, 1984; Lavelle, Metalsky, and Coyne, 1979).

Success-oriented Students

Success-oriented students are especially intriguing for the fact that the measures included in the Berkeley study did a relatively poor job of predicting the test scores of these students. It appears that the dynamics that uniquely describe success-oriented students were not well represented in the model presented in Figure 3. Even self-estimates of ability, a highly salient factor among all the failure-prone groups, was only marginally related to the achievement of success-oriented individuals. It is likely that in a competitive climate, ability factors become exaggerated for those individuals who are already self-doubting, whereas self-confident individuals continued learning for its own sake, a goal for which variations in perceived ability are less importance to success (Roberts and Covington, 1991). In any event, there is mounting evidence that success-oriented individuals can accommodate to a wide range of achievement conditions, and still do a uniformly superior job. For instance, in an attempt to minimize test-taking anxiety, Covington and Omelich (1987b) arranged a set of test items so that either the easier items were presented first, assuming that students would be encouraged by their initial successes, or hard items presented first on the grounds that failure at a difficult task would hold fewer implications for ability and therefore render the remainder of the test less threatening. Not only did success-oriented students perform equally well under all item orders (including a random order of difficulty), but their performances were invariably superior to those of either failure-avoiders, overstrivers, or failure-acceptors. Also regarding the matter of uniform superiority, we know that the performance of intrinsically motivated students is less influenced by the presence of tangible rewards, because these individuals are already performing at their best, and are less likely to suffer a performance decrement if tangible rewards are withdrawn (Harackiewicz and Manderlink, 1984; Harackiewicz, Abrahams, and Wageman, 1987).

We can draw several broad conclusions from the Berkeley data. First, the achievement process is best viewed as a complex interaction of numerous factors—self-protective cognitions, emotions, and motivational dispositions—\ whose relationships to one another and ultimately to achievement outcomes (test performance) change as individual students move progressively through different stages of the study/test cycle. These relationships also vary lawfully depending on the kinds of students under observation.

Second, this study also clarified the relationship between the so-called *skill-deficit* and *retrieval-deficit* theories of anxiety which provide quite different explanations for the general finding of a negative correlation between measures of test anxiety, on the one hand, and achievement test scores on the other (Schwarzer, Seipp, and Schwarzer, 1989; Seipp, 1991; Seipp and Schwarzer, 1990). The retrieval-deficit position holds that anxiety interferes with the recall of information during test taking when students must remember, or retrieve, what they learned earlier (Deffenbacher, 1977, 1986; Liebert and Morris, 1967; Mandler and Sarason, 1952). By contrast, skill-deficit proponents argue that poor performance is largely the result of inadequate study, and that test-anxious individuals actually have little to retrieve (Culler and Holahan, 1980). By this reckoning, anxious feelings are merely a noncausal by-product of recognizing that one is unprepared and likely to fail. Some researchers have treated the skill-deficit and retrieval-deficit positions as incompatible (e.g., Kirkland and Hollandsworth, 1980). But we now know that both kinds of deficiencies can operate to varying degrees within the same individual depending on the type of students involved. Both deficits are present among failure-avoiding students; overstrivers are relatively more handicapped by the failure to retrieve, while failure-acceptors suffer most heavily during the acquisition phase of the study/test cycle.

These findings hold considerable implications for the treatment of test anxiety. According to this analysis, no single therapeutic intervention will be equally effective for all students. This point has not always been fully appreciated by university-based counseling and guidance centers. Until a closer match is created between the choice of therapy and the particular sources of disruption, the record of therapeutic intervention will remain spotty (Hembree, 1988). Naveh-Benjamin (1985) convincingly demonstrated this point when he deliberately matched and mismatched different kinds of students with different therapeutic interventions. He provided relaxation therapy for anxious students who already possessed good study skills (akin to our overstrivers) and for anxious skill-deficient students he provided study practice. With these proper matches, both groups improved their school work. But not so for two identical comparison groups to whom Naveh-Benjamin gave the same treatments but in the reverse order.

Third, and finally, we can now appreciate why some researchers have found little or no correspondence between academic performance and the possession of good study skills (e.g., Schuman, Walsh, Olson, and Etheridge, 1985). Students do not always prepare adequately, even though they may know how, because effort is potentially threatening to their sense of worth. Clearly, knowing how best to study is a highly important ingredient for success in college, but this knowledge can only benefit students fully if the prevailing achievement context is nonthreatening.

Repeated Failures

The student typology presented in Figure 2 (p. 75) must retain a measure of fluidity. The boundaries between groups are intended to be semipermeable, reflecting the fact that in real life students are often in flux and transition. Sometimes fearful students reverse course and become more success-oriented as the result of counseling, while other students may change precipitously and in a negative direction when a single failure forces an overstriver to give up all pretense of being successful.

Researchers in both the United States and Europe have begun investigating the processes by which otherwise able college students become increasingly discouraged about their ability to succeed, a dynamic that is inevitably triggered by repeated academic failure (for a review, see Stiensmeier-Pelster and Schürmann, 1990). In a second wave of analysis of the Berkeley data base described above, Covington and Omelich (1990) followed the fortunes of those undergraduates who failed (i.e., fell short of their grade goals) on several successive midterms. Following each disappointment, these students were asked to rate their chances for success the next time, to estimate their ability to succeed, and to judge the importance of ability as a factor in doing well. They also rated the degree of shame they felt at having failed and attributed various causes to their failures, including bad luck, insufficient effort, and instructor indifference.

Following the first failure, students typically registered surprise, especially if failure was unexpected, a finding consistent with the work of Schwarzer and his colleagues (Schwarzer, Jerusalem, and Schwarzer, 1983; Schwarzer, Jerusalem, and Stiksrud, 1984) who tracked German high school students over a two-year period. For some of the Berkeley students, typically those who were success-oriented, surprise was mixed with a resolve to do better the next time (which they usually did). But for other students, feelings of shame dominated their reactions to failure, particularly among those who rated themselves low in ability to begin with. A greater tendency to blame others for their failures was also detected among these students as they began preparing for the second examination. As one failure followed another, feelings of shame continued unabated and often intensified, driven by a progressive decrease in the students' self-perceived levels of ability. Most destructive by far was the fact that as self-estimates of ability dwindled, estimates of the importance of ability as a causal factor in attaining success increased. Thus these hapless students believed themselves deficient, increasingly so, in the very factor—ability—that was becoming more and more important in their minds. Again, these dynamics were most obvious among those students who initially held themselves in the lowest self-regard.

The key to resisting this slide into despondency appears to be the extent to which the individuals' suspicions of incompetency crystallize to a certainty. To the degree that students remain uncertain about their ability status, they will continue to strive and in some cases can be driven to extraordinary achievements in an effort to reduce uncertainty in a positive direction (Coopersmith, 1967). Maintaining a state of uncertainty regarding one's ability in the face of repeated failures depends in turn on how credible are the excuses one gives for failure. Insuring that excuses are credible in the eyes of others is an exceedingly complex undertaking which requires that explanations "fit the constraints of reason" (Heider, 1958); that is, they must not only appear logical (free of egotistic reasoning) but excuse-givers must also be convinced themselves that others will agree with these inflated views of their ability, a condition referred to as *egocentrism* (Jones and Nisbett, 1971).

Covington and Omelich (1978) investigated the conditions under which college students are most likely to act in an egotistic fashion. Egotism was defined as rating one's own ability higher than the ability of others under identical circumstances of failure. The results indicated that students overestimate their own ability compared with their estimates of the ability of others whenever logical excuses are available to explain their own poor performance (such as having failed due to illness) even though everyone had exactly the same excuse! Also in these situations students believed outsiders would agree with their overstated self-estimates thus closing the circle of self-deception. It is only when low ability was a compelling explanation for failure (when, for instance, the student tried hard and failed anyway) that these undergraduates moderated their inflated views of self and brought them more in line with those they attributed to others.

This study supports the view that individuals tend to aggrandize their ability status whenever reason permits. It is in this sense (of Self-worth theory) that the need for self-justification can be said to be the primary psychological reality and rational considerations secondary and supportive, or as Reuven Bar-Levav puts it, "In general, people are led by their feelings, and then they unknowingly invent rationalizations to explain their actions or decisions to themselves and to justify them to others."

Another revealing aspect of this experiment concerns the presence of pervasive sex differences. The findings as just described apply to male students both high and low in self-perceptions of ability as well as to high self-confident females. However, compared with these three groups, women with low self-confidence underestimated their ability status in all conditions of failure, whether their estimates were justified or not, and believed that observers would agree with these excessively pessimistic views. Far from aggrandizing ability, then, these women denigrated their talents beyond what was rationally indicated. The defensive tendency reported among males is scarcely surprising given the consistent evidence that males are more likely to tie their sense of worth to ability, especially their ability to compete for and hold jobs (Snyder, Stephan, and Rosenfeld, 1976; Streufert and Streufert, 1969; Wolosin Sherman, and Till, 1973). By contrast there is considerable evidence that many females view the struggle for intellectual status as less role appropriate (Dweck, Davidson, Nelson, and Enna, 1978; Nicholls, 1975; Stephan, Rosenfield and Stephan, 1976). This suggests that women may be more vulnerable to the dynamics of learned helplessness and more quickly give up the struggle to maintain a positive self-image based on ability.

DIRECTIONS FOR CHANGE: MOTIVES AS GOALS

This self-worth perspective on motivation and college academics is troubling. Basically it portrays college classrooms as battlefields where the rules favor sabotage, lackluster effort, and self-deception. Naturally, it can be properly argued that this accounting is far too pessimistic, and that on balance American universities and colleges approximate the more idealized view of schools as places where "teachers gladly teach and students gladly learn." No reasonable person would contend that these disturbing dynamics are solely the product of a system of higher education gone awry. From the larger perspective, these failures are as much or more a consequence of the processes and risks of growing up in an increasingly dangerous and unforgiving world as they are the result of misappropriated educational policy. Still, according to self-worth theory, certain aspects of academic life do represent potential threats to learners and to the development of the talent necessary for America's economic, political, and social survival. What are these sources of peril? And in what directions might we find relief? First, we should note that we are not dealing simply with a matter of inadequate motivation. According to self-worth theory, poor performance is as much the result of being *overmotivated*, but for the wrong reasons, as it is of not being motivated at all. The real threat to learning occurs whenever the individual's sense of worth becomes tied to the ability to achieve competitively. If pride in success and shame in failure depend largely on self-perceptions of ability, then students' involvement in learning will last only for as long as they continue to succeed as a means to aggrandize ability. But once failure threatens a self-image of competency, with its legacy of shame and anger, students will likely withdraw from learning.

By this analysis, the best solutions require changing the reasons for learning, not simply intensifying motivation driven out of a competitive climate. This does not mean that we should stop rewarding noteworthy achievements or no longer withhold rewards when students work beneath their capacity. To argue otherwise would fly in the face of a world dominated by contingent incentives. Boggiano points to the pervasiveness of such contingencies when she observes that "If you sell enough items then you will receive a commission; if you succeed on the GRE then you will be admitted to graduate school; if you publish enough research then you will receive tenure" (Boggiano and Pittman, in press).

What I am arguing for is an alternative basis for rewarding behavior, one that shifts the payoff away from being competitive to becoming competent. Gardner (1961) makes this same point when he proposes that we measure excellence, not as a comparison among individuals, but rather as a comparison between myself at my best and myself at my worst. "It is this latter comparison which enables me to assert that I am being true to the best that is in me—or forces me to confess that I am not" (p. 128).

Another way to envision this transformation is to set aside the dominant metaphor of *motives-as-drives* in favor of *motives-as-goals*—incentives that draw, not drive, individuals toward action (Covington, 1992; Bolles, 1967). Clearly, the distinction between drives and goals is elusive and the concepts somewhat overlapping. For instance, we could just as well describe Alice's compulsive behavior in our earlier example, not as driven, but as goal-oriented—with the dubious goal of aggrandizing her own importance by outdoing others. Yet goals and drives are not the same, and in the difference lie several advantages favoring the concept of goals for educators. First, goals are more malleable than the kinds of deeply rooted inclinations of which drive theory speaks, and by rewarding some goals and not others, instructors can change the reasons students learn, which is to say, change their motives. Second, goal-setting stands as a practical surrogate for motives. We need not await final definitions of the kind Drucker found missing in his appraisal of motivation research before we take steps to solve more immediate problems that are basically motivational in nature. Third, goals (as contrasted to drives) become educational objectives in their own right;

thus, motives are not merely the handmaidens to higher achievement, but also give meaning and purpose to achievement.

What goals are worth encouraging? They are scarcely new; but they are honored more in the breach than in the observance because educators rarely arrange reward contingencies in ways that favor them directly. The first goal is that of self-mastery, becoming the best one can be; the second, defined by Nicholls (1989) as a commitment to solving society's problems, involves helping others. The third goal concerns the expression of creativity and the satisfaction of curiosity. How might we arrange learning so these positive reasons are promoted systematically? Several broad guidelines have emerged from the research literature over the past years. Three are considered here.

Engaging Tasks

College assignments themselves must be worthy of sustained curiosity, and challenge the highest levels of thought and creativity of which students are presently capable. What task characteristics promote these positive ends (Malone, 1981)?

First, tasks are engaging to the degree they feature multiple goals that unfold progressively as work proceeds. Diggory (1966) describes the enormous staying power of such self-initiated complexity:

> If [the individual] chooses an activity he never attempted before, his first attempts will be purely exploratory…[but] once this exploration ends and he begins a more or less systematic attempt to produce something, he very likely will set implicit or explicit aspirations for his successive attempts….Now he tries to produce a result that is as good as the last one, but quicker. Next he may disregard time altogether and try to improve the product. Later he may concentrate on the smoothness of the project and attempt to swing elegantly through a well-ordered and efficient routine. He may discover and invent new processes or adapt new materials or new methods of work. To the casual uninterested observer this may all seem repetitive and dull, but the operator, the worker, may be intensely interested because he never has exactly the same goals on two successive trials….(p.125–126)

This passage also conveys something of the tremendous need for humans to improve themselves, to do things better, or at least differently, a disposition which is taken full advantage of by the college instructor in physics who announces to her students (upon their having developed an efficient solar cell), "Now I want you to make it cheaper," "smaller," and so forth. The civil engineering professor also turns this human potential to advantage when he identifies, one by one, the various negative consequences of his students' decision to dam the upper Nile basin as a way to convert the Egyptian desert to productive farmlands—severe erosion of the Nile delta and rising salt levels in the Mediterranean basin—all unforeseen, but not unpredictable consequences if his students had but paid closer attention to the supplementary readings on oceanographics, biology, and atmospheric physics. The professor's next assignment to his students is to correct the problems that they themselves have created.

Second, tasks are engaging of creativity to the extent they challenge preconceived notions, require students to detect familiar forms in unfamiliar settings, and to be puzzled by the obvious. Science curricula provide especially rich opportunities for identifying and rewarding creative styles of thought, ranging from practicing the art of problem discovery to becoming sensitized to the dynamics of serendipity, the ability to find something of value when you are looking for something else (Shapiro, 1986). Then there are opportunities to practice the skills involved in conceiving of and modifying unlikely, farfetched, but potentially useful ideas (Covington, 1986) such as the unlikely notion of moving ships *over* the water, not through the water (Hovercraft). Introducing controversies and staging debates that require students to take sides or to entertain unpopular or fanciful perspectives are excellent methods to keep students sufficiently challenged to remain open and receptive to further learning.

Third, intrinsic task involvement is enhanced by the social reinforcers that accompany cooperative learning. Not only can all players win when learning becomes a cooperative venture (Ames, 1981; Harris and Covington, 1989; Slavin, 1983, 1984), but learning takes place in a social context where most meaningful adult work occurs anyway, and also becomes part of what Lave (1988) calls *authentic activities* where learners become apprentices who hone the skills of their craft through group collaboration and social interaction. Consider the field of mathematics. Shoenfeld (1989) argues for the teaching of mathematics as basically an empirical, group-defined discipline, one consisting of data and mutual discovery and sharing much like biology and physics. From such a vantage point learning mathematics becomes a group enterprise in which truth becomes "that for which the majority of the community believes it has compelling arguments. In mathematics truth is socially negotiated, as it is in science" (p. 9).

Finally, tasks are inherently self-absorbing to the extent they allow the student to exercise control over the degree of challenge. The quintessential, everyday example is the game of tag (Eifferman, 1974). Here players adjust the risks of being caught as well as the chances of catching others by altering the distance they stay away from whoever is it, in the first instance, and deciding whom to chase, in the second instance. The drama and excitement generated by the manageable challenges of playing tag need not be limited only to young players, nor need they function merely for recreational purposes, but also lie at the heart of what has been called *serious games* (Abt, 1971/1987; Covington, 1992).

Providing Sufficient Reinforcers

Arranging exciting learning opportunities is a necessary first step in shifting the reasons for learning in more positive directions, but more is needed. Students must also be rewarded for their efforts at self-mastery, for preparing to help others, and for problem discovery. The kinds of rewards associated with these intrinsic reasons for learning have a special motivating property: their absolute nature. These rewards do not depend on how many others succeed or fail, but rather on the kinds of tasks chosen—with the greatest number of rewards going to the realistic goal setter—and on whether or not one's performance meets or surpasses the prevailing (or absolute) standards of excellence. In short, these rewards are plentiful and open to all.

A number of grading schema have been developed to accommodate absolute standards (for reviews, see Block, 1977, 1984; Block and Burns, 1976; Kulik, Kulik, and Cohen, 1979; Kulik, Kulik, and Shwalb, 1982), the most sophisticated being a *grade-choice arrangement* (Covington, 1989). Here students work for any grade they wish and stop whenever they have accumulated sufficient credit, so many points needed for an A, so many points for a B, and so forth. Points are awarded depending on how many tasks the individual undertakes, the complexity of these assignments, and the quality of work performed.

Motivationally speaking, a number of benefits derive from the use of absolute grading systems. For one thing, the presence of absolute standards is known to encourage perceptions of fairness in grading (Covington and Omelich, 1984b). For another, they also enhance perceptions of personal control over events because students know what they must do and how well they must perform for a given grade (Ames, Ames, and Felker, 1980; Crockenberg, Bryant, and Wilce, 1976; Williams et al., 1976). It is this positive covariation between the amount of work expended by students and the rewards (grades) attained that forestalls feelings of learned helplessness. In this connection, a sense of personal control and autonomy has been linked to increased task engagement. In a study involving 10 college courses including three English classes, three biology classes, and four social science classes, Garcia and Pintrich (1991) found that those courses rated highest on an autonomy dimension by students (e.g., "Students can negotiate with the instructor over the nature of the course requirements") were also judged highest for eliciting intrinsic task involvement. Moreover, feelings of task engagement increased as the year progressed among those courses rated in the highest quartile for autonomy, while self-perceptions of engagement actually declined in the same period among the lowest quartile classes.

However, for all the potential advantages of absolute grading systems, several issues remain. One concerns the sheer frequency of rewards. There is considerable evidence that the reinforcing value of rewards depends on their scarcity; that is, the fewer the rewards the more sought after they become (for a review, see Covington, 1992). What, then, will happen when rewards are made freely available? Will not their value be cheapened? No, not necessarily. Scarcity becomes valuable largely in those situations where students are playing an ability game. The fewer the rewards, the more ability becomes a factor in attaining them and in turn the more their attainment signals high ability. By contrast, when rewards are distributed on an absolute merit basis, especially for work performed on inherently satisfying tasks, pride in accomplishment comes to depend more on how hard one worked and on whether or not learners believe themselves to have measured up favorably to the instructor's standards. This phenomenon was demonstrated in a study conducted by Covington and Jacoby (1983) in which several hundred introductory psychology students completed various work projects for their grade. These projects required that students create their own solutions to contemporary issues, dilemmas, and puzzles within the field of psychology including devising an explanation for the *moon illusion* (the fact that the moon appears larger on the horizon than at its zenith) and designing toys to help accelerate young children through various intellectual stages of development. All projects were graded in absolute terms, but the level of standards employed varied. One group was always given full credit as long as they met a minimum standard, whereas a second group was required to meet increasingly stringent standards of excellence depending on the grade they sought (i.e., grade-choice arrangement). Those students who received full credit for a minimal effort produced inferior products, were less satisfied with their final course grade, and felt themselves less deserving than those other students who had worked much harder. Moreover, for students in this latter group course satisfaction was undiminished despite the fact that a disproportionate number of their classmates also received the same high grades. In short, when much is demanded of students and much given by them in response, especially in response to meaningful problems, students tend to feel satisfied no matter how many others also achieve at or above the same grade level.

Success-Oriented Assessment

When competitive-based grades are used as motivators to arouse or goad students to greater effort then task engagement, even performance itself, is likely to suffer, especially among failure-prone students (Covington, 1992; Deci, 1975; Deci and Ryan, 1987; Goldberg, 1965). These students tend to give up in the face of poor grades because they interpret failure as the result of inability for which they believe there is no remedy. At the same time, rewarding failure-prone students with higher grades than they expect, as a positive incentive, is likely to be met with disbelief if not suspicion because they do not expect to succeed, and when they do succeed, success is typically attributed to factors beyond their control such as luck.

By contrast, when grades are treated as a source of information or feedback (as in absolute merit systems) they can take on intrinsic properties. Students come to seek out information, and even respond well to negative feedback as long as it provides a constructive basis for self-improvement (Butler and Nisan, 1986). In this connection, one of the most promising forms of assessment involves performance-based appraisals. For the reader unfamiliar with them, performance-based assessments are best explained by example (Frederiksen and Collins, 1989). Consider the concept of *verbal aptitude*, which traditionally is assessed by administering verbal analogies or tests of vocabulary skill. In performance terms, however, verbal aptitude might be defined as the ability to formulate and express arguments in meaningful contexts such as requiring students to develop arguments favoring their side of the law in a small claims court action. Such tasks are reminiscent of those described earlier as *authentic activities* with the addition that, following work on the assignment, students are provided sample answers (feedback) of varying quality, ranging from "exemplary" or "acceptable" to "incomplete" so that it becomes clear to students just how a particular performance is being judged and how they can improve. Hopefully, performance-based testing will encourage students to become their own critics, to notice what is distinctive about their own work, and what is still missing and needs to be accomplished (Levin, 1990). At its most profound, the assessment function becomes an integral part of the instructional process itself (deLange Jzn, 1987).

A DILEMMA RESOLVED

Motivationally speaking, these guidelines for change emphasize a task-focused approach, not an ability-focused approach to learning, with assessment procedures designed to maximize the achievement of *all* students. But this vision of the educational mission and particularly the nontraditional role and function of testing and grades is at fundamental odds with the purpose of schooling as a selection device for identifying those students most capable of further learning. Many educators stress the predictive role of grades as imperfect, yet useful, indices of how efficiently a person will learn similar material on future occasions. They also argue that competitive sorting provides an orderly way to distribute individuals proportionately across the available jobs in our society, some of which are more attractive than others (for a critique, see Deutsch, 1975, 1979). Competitive grading has long been the primary mechanism for assigning talent according to job demands and availability, a reality which has infuriated many educational reformers, among them Campbell (1974) who points out that the whole frantic scramble to win over others is essential for the kinds of institutions that our schools have become, "bargain-basement personnel screening agencies for business and government" (p. 145–146). Campbell's remark perhaps more than any other lays bare the fundamental incompatibility of the mission confronting all of education: Schools—elementary, secondary, and postsecondary alike—are not only places of learning, but also places for sorting out those capable of learning the most. And teachers are caught in the middle. When teachers view their primary job to maximize the academic potential of each student, they recognize hard work and reward persistence on task. But when they are asked to recommend those students who are most suitable for highly prestigious jobs, it is ability not dedication that becomes the dominant criteria (Kaplan and Swant, 1973). Naturally, this selection function is not lost on students. Little wonder that so many of them define their worth in terms of their ability to compete successfully.

The vital question becomes how can institutions of higher learning balance the seemingly incompatible goals of intrinsic task engagement and learning for its own sake against the demands for externally regulated talent selection? I believe the key to resolving this dilemma is the fact that for students at least the paramount issue regarding their own feelings of well being is not so much a matter of the presence of competitive pressure, even severe pressure, as it is a perceived lack of opportunities for intrinsic satisfaction. Meaningful academic work appears to be the critical factor for mitigating the otherwise abrasive gauntlet of competition. Our anecdotal evidence suggests that when students succeed at valued tasks over which they have some choice and control, and can gain the respect of their peers and coworkers, and the admiration of their mentors, then final course grades even those that are computed competitively are far less important in determining the perceived value of a course than for those students who are also judged competitively, but who have little opportunity to satisfy intrinsic interests and curiosities. The experience of Berkeley undergraduates indicates that intrinsic satisfaction comes largely from opportunities to work in field placements, or to volunteer for community service in conjunction with regular course offerings, and the opportunity to produce things of value in classes including creating needed educational material such as new bibliographies or instructional manuals (Promoting Student Success at Berkeley, 1991).

It may seem improbable that individuals can actively pursue intrinsic goals in institutions that also rank order their output publicly and competitively. But we know they can. At present the best evidence on this point comes from research with children. Ames and Archer (1987) observed elementary school youngsters who perceived themselves either to be in a mastery-oriented classroom—striving for the sake of self-improvement through effort—or in classrooms dominated by a performance-orientation—striving to do better than someone else by reason of ability. These researchers also observed classroom combinations of both performance- and mastery-orientations. As long as mastery goals were in evidence, the presence of competition did not diminish intrinsic task engagement. Students still explained their successes and failures in terms of variations in effort expended—a decidedly task-oriented attribute; they also used sophisticated planning strategies in their work, and chose problems where "you can learn a lot of new things but will also have some difficulty and make many mistakes." Also, it appears that the use of competitive or norm-based feedback which establishes one's rank order status in the larger group is at times actually sought out by students and can actually benefit learning especially in the early stages of work on a task as long as other forms of feedback are also available, including samples of work reflecting various absolute levels of quality and information about different styles of thinking or permissible approaches to the problem (Butler, in press).

These findings are central to the process of educational reform at all levels, because if striving for personal excellence requires the virtual absence of competitive comparisons, then change would be impossible. This line of reasoning suggests an important future research agenda: Asking the question of how much or how little an emphasis must be placed on a mastery or merit-based orientation, and for what kinds of students, in order to offset the inevitable press of competition. Perhaps far fewer and less radical changes are needed to tip the classroom balance in favor of spontaneity, involvement, and creativity than was once thought. Yet the answers will likely be complex. For example, will reducing competition actually rob some students of their will to achieve? This query is especially relevant for overstrivers whose reasons for succeeding may actually depend on the presence of a threat to their worth. Although educators are in no position presently to answer these kinds of questions fully, at least they are the proper questions to ask when it comes to reshaping the educational experience of our youth.

CONCLUSIONS

The reader may well ask if there is anything particularly new about the motivational guidelines proposed here since virtually all the examples are standard teaching practice at the postsecondary level. For instance, project-oriented courses (those that feature authentic tasks) are much in evidence on university and college campuses especially in the professional schools and in the applied arts and sciences including architecture and engineering. Similarly, opportunities already abound for students to participate in field-work which allow them to integrate theory and practice as well as to clarify career objectives. Nor is there much that is new about the educational philosophy underlying these recommendations that draw heavily on the notion of *reflective inquiry* first made popular by John Dewey (1916, 1963) in the early part of this century and developed more fully by Hullfish and Smith (1961) and by Pratte (1988).

What *is* new, however, is that these familiar teaching practices that evolved mostly through trial-and-error experimentation are now being legitimized within a network of empirically grounded, conceptually based theories. Theory helps teachers recognize what is profound about the commonplace; it tells them when they are on the right track, when they are not, and what corrections may be needed. Moreover, current motivation theory is quite sophisticated. No longer are investigators content with searching for simple correspondences between variables, say, demonstrating that as anxiety level increases, academic performance tends to decrease. These discoveries were a good start, but now we know that such general relationships are controlled by moderator variables including the reasons for learning and the causal attributions that students make. Until relatively recent times notions of achievement motivation were so poorly defined and their linkage to classroom success and failure so imperfectly delineated as to provide little in the way of guidance to educators who have been vexed by a host of puzzles. But all that has begun to change. For instance, instructors may wonder, if high achievement enhances one's status, then why is there only a mar-ginal relationship between GPA and satisfaction as a student? We now know the answer is that the relationship between self-acceptance and academic performance depends on the reasons students learn, some of which can be self-defeating and dissat-isfying, such as achieving to avoid feelings of inferiority. As a second example, why should otherwise highly successful students be devastated after only *one* failure; should not one's accumulated successes count for more than that? No, not always, especially if one is driven to succeed out of a fear of failing. Here even an isolated failure confirms what overstrivers have feared all along, that they are unworthy of per-fection. And third, why should some failure-threatened students perform best when the odds of failing are greatest? Should not a hopeless cause increase their despair? From a self-worth perspective, there is no puzzle here. Vying against long odds per-mits threatened students to perform at their best because failing at an exceedingly dif-ficult task holds few implications for ability. Similarly, why should students with low self-confidence reject success when it occurs? Because they fear the implied obliga-tion that success must be repeated, and they doubt their ability to do so. Finally, why should failure devastate some individuals and mobilize others to greater action? From an attributional perspective, the answer is clear. Failure affects individuals differently depending on their causal explanations, with success-oriented individuals believing failure to be reversible through renewed effort, while failure-threatened students see increased effort as a waste of time.

As a group, these examples illustrate that the relationship between motives and performance is complex; and at times, the predictions of motivation theory are counterintuitive, but lawful nonetheless. It is this lawfulness that permits educators to begin redressing those conditions described by the Carnegie Foundation for the Advancement of Teaching whose quote opens this chapter. Leaving aside the issue of whether or not we can do anything to improve schooling—resistance to reform being what is—at least we have a surer and growing grasp on what we should do if we could.

References

Abramson, L. Y., Seligman, M. E. P., and Teasdale, J. D. (1978). Learned helplessness in humans: Critique and reformulation. *Journal of Abnormal Psychology* 87: 49–74.

Abt, C. C. (1971/1987). *Serious Games*. New York: Lanham.

Ames, C. (1981). Competitive versus cooperative reward structures: The influence of individual and group performance factors on achievement attributions and affect. *American Educational Research Journal* 18: 273–388.

Ames, C. (1984). Achievement attributions and self-instructions under competitive and individualistic goal structures. *Journal of Educational Psychology* 76: 478–487.

Ames, C., and Ames, R. (1984). Systems of student and teacher motivation: Toward a qualitative definition. *Journal of Educational Psychology* 76: 535–556.

Ames, C., Ames, R., and Felker, D. (1980). Effects of self-concept on children's causal attributions and self-reinforcement. *Journal of Educational Psychology* 71: 613–619.

Ames, C., and Archer, J. (1987). Mothers\' beliefs about the role of ability and effort in school learning. *Journal of Educational Psychology* 79: 409–414.

Anderson, J. G., and Evans, F. B. (1974). Causal models in educational research: Recursive models. *American Education Research Journal* 11: 29–39.

Arkin, R. M., Detchon, C. S., and Maruyama, G. M. (1982). Roles of attribution, affect, and cognitive interference in test anxiety. *Journal of Personality and Social Psychology* 43: 1111–1124.

Atkinson, J. W. (1957). Motivational determinants of risk-taking behavior. *Psychological Review* 64: 359–372.

Atkinson, J. W. (1964). *An Introduction to Motivation*. Princeton, NJ: Van Nostrand.

Atkinson, J. W. (1981). Studying personality in the context of an advanced motivational psychology. *American Psychologist* 36: 117–128.

Atkinson, J. W., and Litwin, G. H. (1960). Achievement motive and test anxiety conceived as motive to approach success and motive to avoid failure. *Journal of Abnormal and Social Psychology* 60: 52–63.

Barnard, J. W., Zimbardo, P. G., and Sarason, S. B. (1968). Teachers\' ratings of student personality traits as they relate to IQ and social desirability. *Journal of Educational Psychology* 59: 128–132.

Battle, E. S (1965). Motivational determinants of academic task persistence. *Journal of Personality and Social Psychology* 2: 209–218.

Beery, R. G. (1975). Fear of failure in the student experience. *Personnel and Guidance Journal* 54: 190–203.

Berglas, S., and Jones, E. (1978). Drug choice as a self-handicapping strategy in response to noncontingent success. *Journal of Personality and Social Psychology* 36: 405–417.

Birney, R. C., Burdick, H., and Teevan, R. C. (1969). *Fear of Failure*. New York: Van Nostrand.

Block, J. H. (1977). Motivation, evaluation, and mastery learning. *UCLA Educator* 12: 31–37.

Block, J. H. (1984). Making school learning activities more playlike: Flow and mastery learning. *The Elementary School Journal* 85: 65–75.

Block, J. H., and Burns, R. B. (1976). Mastery learning. In L. S. Schulman (ed.), *Review of Research in Education*. Itasca, IL: Peacock.

Boggiano, A. K., and Pittman, T. S. (eds.), (in press). *Achievement and Motivation: A Social-Development Perspective*. New York: Cambridge University Press.

Bolles, R. C. (1967). *Theory of Motivation*. New York: Harper and Row.

Brown, J., and Weiner, B. (1984). Affective consequences of ability versus effort ascriptions: Controversies, resolutions, and quandaries. *Journal of Educational Psychology* 76: 146–158.

Burton, D., and Martens, R. (1986). Pinned by their own goals: An exploratory investigation into why kids drop out of wrestling. *Journal of Sport Psychology* 8: 1983– 1997.

Butler, R. (in press). What young people want to know when: Effects of mastery and ability goals on interest in different kinds of social comparisons. *Journal of Personality and Social Psychology*.

Butler, R., and Nisan, M. (1986). Effects of no feedback, task-related comments, and grade on intrinsic instruction and performance. *Journal of Educational Psychology* 78: 210–216.

Campbell, D. N. (1974, October). On being number one: Competition in education. *Phi Delta Kappan* 143–146.

Carnegie Foundation for the Advancement of Teaching (1977). *Missions of the College Curriculum: A Contemporary Review with Suggestions*. San Francisco: Jossey-Bass.

Carnegie Foundation for the Advancement of Teaching (1989). *The Condition of the Professoriate: Attitudes and Trends*. New York: The Carnegie Corporation.

Carse, J. P. (1986). *Finite and Infinite Games*. New York: Ballantine.

Carver, C. S. (1979). A cybernetic model of self-attention processes. *Journal of Personality and Social Psychology* 37: 1251–1281.

Carver, C. S., and Scheier, M. F. (1988). A control-process perspective on anxiety. *Anxiety Research* 1: 17–22.

Clark, B. R., and Trow, M. (1960). Determinants of college student subcultures. Unpublished paper, Center for the Study of Higher Education, Berkeley.

Clark, B. R., and Trow, M. (1966). Determinants of the subcultures of college students—The organizational context. In T. M. Newcomb and E. Wilson (eds.), *College Peer Groups*. Chicago: Adeline.

Combs, A. W. (1957). The myth of competition. *Childhood Education*. Washington, DC: Association for Childhood Education International.

Coopersmith, S. (1967). *The Antecedents of Self-Esteem*. San Francisco: Freeman.

Covington, M. V. (1982, August). Musical chairs: Who drops out of music instruction and why? Proceedings of the National Symposium on the Applications of Psychology to the Teaching and Learning of Music: The Ann Arbor Symposium. Session III: Motivation and Creativity. Ann Arbor: University of Michigan.

Covington, M. V. (1984a). Motivated cognitions. In S. G. Paris, G. M. Olson, and H. W. Stevenson (eds.), *Learning and Motivation in the Classroom*. Hillsdale, NJ: Erlbaum.

Covington, M. V. (1984b). The motive for self-worth. In R. Ames and C. Ames (eds.), *Research on Motivation in Education*, Vol. 1. New York: Academic Press.

Covington, M. V. (1985a). Anatomy of failure-induced anxiety: The role of cognitive mediators. In R. Schwarzer (ed.), *Self-Related Cognitions in Anxiety and Motivation*. Hillsdale, NJ: Erlbaum.

Covington, M. V. (1985b). The role of self-processes in applied social psychology. *Journal of the Theory of Social Behavior* 15: 355–389.

Covington, M. V. (1985c). The effects of multiple-testing opportunities on rote and conceptual learning and retention. *Human learning* 4: 57–72.

Covington, M. V. (1986). Instruction in problem solving and planning. In S. L. Friedman, E. K. Scholnick, and R. R. Cocking (eds.), *Intelligence and Exceptionality*. Norwood, NJ: Ablex.

Covington, M. V. (1989). Self-esteem and failure in school: Analysis and policy implications. In A. M. Mecca, N. J. Smelser, and J. Vasconcellos (eds.), *The Social Importance of Self-Esteem*. Berkeley:

University of California.

Covington, M. V. (1992). *Making the Grade: A Self-Worth Perspective on Motivation and School Reform.* New York: Cambridge.

Covington, M. V., and Beery, R. G. (1976). *Self-Worth and School Learning.* New York: Holt, Rinehart and Winston.

Covington, M. V., and Jacoby, K. E. (1983). Productive thinking and course satisfaction as a function of an independence-conformity dimension. Paper presented at the meeting of the American Psychological Association, Montreal.

Covington, M. V., and Omelich, C. L. (1978). Sex differences in self-aggrandizing tendencies. Unpublished manuscript, Department of Psychology, University of California, Berkeley.

Covington, M. V., and Omelich, C. L. (1979a). Are causal attributions causal? A path analysis of the cognitive model of achievement motivation. *Journal of Personality and Social Psychology,* 37: 1487–1504.

Covington, M. V., and Omelich, C. L. (1979b). Effort: The double-edged sword in school achievement. *Journal of Educational Psychology* 71: 169–182.

Covington, M. V., and Omelich, C. L. (1981). As failures mount: Affective and cognitive consequences of ability demotion in the classroom. *Journal of Educational Psychology* 73: 796–808.

Covington, M. V., and Omelich, C. L. (1982). Achievement anxiety, performance, and behavioral instruction: A cost/benefits analysis. In R. Schwarzer, H. M. van der Ploeg, and C. D. Spielberger (eds.), *Advances in Test Anxiety Research*, Vol. 1. Hillsdale, NJ: Erlbaum.

Covington, M. V., and Omelich, C. L. (1984a). Controversies or consistencies? A reply to Brown and Weiner. *Journal of Educational Psychology* 76: 159–168.

Covington, M. V., and Omelich, C. L. (1984b). Task-oriented versus competitive learning structures: Motivational and performance consequences. *Journal of Educational Psychology* 76: 1038–1050.

Covington, M. V., and Omelich, C. L. (1985). Ability and effort valuation among failure-avoiding and failure-accepting students. *Journal of Educational Psychology* 77: 446–459.

Covington, M. V., and Omelich, C. L. (1987a). "I knew it cold before the exam\'\'": A test of the anxiety-blockage hypothesis. *Journal of Educational Psychology* 79: 393–400.

Covington, M. V., and Omelich, C. L. (1987b). Item difficulty and test performance among high-anxious and low-anxious students. In R. Schwarzer, H. M. van der Ploeg, and C. D. Spielberger (eds.), *Advances in Test Anxiety Research*, Vol. 5. Hillsdale, NJ: Erlbaum.

Covington, M. V., and Omelich, C. L. (1988). Achievement dynamics: The interaction of motives, cognitions and emotions over time. *Anxiety Journal* 1: 165–183.

Covington, M. V., and Omelich, C. L. (1990). The second time around: Coping with repeated failures. Unpublished manuscript, Department of Psychology, University of California, Berkeley.

Covington, M. V., and Omelich, C. L. (1991). Need achievement revisited: Verification of Atkinson's original 2 x 2 model. In C. D. Spielberger, I. G. Sarason, Z. Kulcsár, and G. L. Van Heck (eds.), *Stress and Emotion: Anxiety, Anger, and Curiosity,* Vol. 14. Washington, DC: Hemisphere.

Covington, M. V., Omelich, C. L., and Schwarzer, R. (1986). Anxiety, aspirations, and self-concept in the achievement process: A longitudinal model with latent variables. *Motivation and Emotion* 10: 71–88.

Covington, M. V., Spratt, M. F., and Omelich, C. L. (1980). Is effort enough, or does diligence count too? Student and teacher reactions to effort stability in failure. *Journal of Educational Psychology* 72: 717–729.

Coyne, J. C., and Lazarus, R. S. (1980). Cognitive style, stress perception, and coping. In I. L. Kutash and L. B. Schlesinger (eds.), *Handbook on Stress and Anxiety.* San Francisco: Jossey-Bass.

Crockenberg, S., Bryant, B., and Wilce, L. (1976). The effects of cooperatively and competitively structured learning environments on inter and intrapersonal behavior. *Child Development* 47: 386–396.

Culler, R. E., and Holahan, C. J. (1980). Test anxiety and academic performance: The effects of study-related behaviors. *Journal of Educational Psychology* 72: 16–20.

Csikszentmihalyi, M. (1975). *Beyond Boredom and Anxiety.* San Francisco: Jossey-Bass.

de Lange Jzn, J. (1987). *Mathematics, Insight and Meaning.* Vakgroep Onderzoek Wiskundeonderwijs en

Onderwijscomputercentrum, Rikjsuniversiteit Utrecht.

De Volder, M., and Lens, W. (1982). Academic achievement and future time perspective as a cognitive-motivational concept. *Journal of Personality and Social Psychology* 42: 566–571.

Deci, E. L. (1975). *Intrinsic Motivation.* New York: Plenum.

Deci, E. L., and Ryan, R. M. (1987). The support of autonomy and the control of behavior. *Journal of Personality and Social Psychology* 53: 1024–1037.

Deffenbacher, J. L. (1977). Relationship of worry and emotionality to performance on the Miller Analogies Test. *Journal of Educational Psychology* 69: 191–195.

Deffenbacher, J. L. (1986). Cognitive and physiological components of test anxiety in real-life exams. *Cognitive Therapy and Research* 10: 635–644.

Deutsch, M. (1975). Equity, equality, and need. *Journal of Social Issues* 31: 137–149.

Deutsch, M. (1979). Education and distributive justice. *American Psychologist* 34: 391–\ 401.

Dewey, J. (1916). *Democracy and Education.* New York: Macmillan.

Dewey, J. (1963). *Experience and Education.* New York: Collier. (Original work published 1938)

Diggory, J. C. (1966). *Self-evaluation: Concepts and Studies.* New York: Wiley.

Dweck, C. S. (1986). Motivational processes affecting learning. *American Psychologist* 41: 1040–1048.

Dweck, C. S., Davidson, W., Nelson, S., and Enna, B. (1978). Sex differences in learned helplessness: II. The contingencies of evaluative feedback in the classroom and III. An experimental analysis. *Developmental Psychology* 14: 268–276.

Eccles, J. (1983). Expectancies, values and academic behaviors. In J. T. Spence (ed.), *Achievement and Achievement Motives.* San Francisco: Freeman.

Eifferman, R. R. (1974). It's child's play. In L. M. Shears and E. M. Bower (eds.), *Games in Education and Development.* Springfield, IL: Charles C. Thomas.

Ellis, A., and Kraus, W. J. (1977). *Overcoming Procrastination.* New York: Institute for Rational Living.

Ellis, R. A., Parelius, R. J., and Parelius, A. P. (1971). The collegiate scholar: education for elite status. *Sociology of Education* 44: 27–58.

Elton, C. F. (1967). Male career role and vocational choice: Their prediction with personality and aptitude variables. *Journal of Counseling Psychology* 14(2): 99–105.

Eswara, H. S. (1972). Administration of reward and punishment in relation to ability, effort, and performance. *Journal of Social Psychology* 87: 139–140.

Feather, N. T. (1961). The relationship of persistence at a task to expectation of success and achievement-related motives. *Journal of Abnormal and Social Psychology* 63: 552–561.

Feather, N. T. (1963). Persistence at a difficult task with an alternative task of intermediate difficulty. *Journal of Abnormal and Social Psychology* 66: 604–609.

Feather, N. T. (1965). The relationship of expectation of success to Achievement and test anxiety. *Journal of Personality and Social Psychology* 1: 118–126.

Findley, M. J., and Cooper, H. M. (1983). Locus of control and academic achievement: A literature review. *Journal of Personality and Social Psychology* 44: 419–427.

Folsom, C. H., Jr. (1969). An investigation of Holland's theory of vocational choice. *Journal of Counseling Psychology* 16(3): 260–266.

Fontaine, G. (1974). Social comparison and some determinants of expected personal control and expected performance in a novel task situation. *Journal of Personality and Social Psychology* 29: 487–496.

Frederiksen, N., and Collins, J. R. (1989). A systems approach to educational testing. *Educational Researcher* 18(9): 27–32.

Garcia, T., and Pintrich, P. R. (1991). *The Effects of Autonomy on Motivation, Use of Learning Strategies and Performance in the College Classroom.* Paper presented at the annual meetings of the American Educational Research Association, San Francisco.

Gardner, J. W. (1961). *Excellence: Can We Be Equal and Excellent Too?* New York: Harper and Row.

Goldberg, L. R. (1965). Grades as motivants. *Psychology in the Schools* 2: 17–24.

Greenberg, P. J. (1932). Competition in children: An experimental study. *American Journal of Psychology* 44: 221–250.

Hagtvet, K. A. (1984). Fear of failure, worry and emotionality: Their suggestive causal relationships to mathematical performance and state anxiety. In H. M. van der Ploeg, R. Schwarzer, and C. D. Spielberger (eds.), *Advances in Test Anxiety Research*, Vol. 3. Hillsdale, NJ: Erlbaum.

Harackiewicz, J. M., Abrahams, S., and Wageman, R. (1987). Performance evaluation and intrinsic motivation: The effects of evaluative focus, rewards, and achievement orientation. *Journal of Personality and Social Psychology* 53: 1015–1023.

Harackiewicz, J. M., and Manderlink, G. (1984). A process analysis of the effects of performance-contingent rewards on intrinsic motivation. *Journal of Experimental Social Psychology* 20: 531–551.

Harari, O., and Covington, M. V. (1981). Reactions to achievement behavior from a teacher and student perspective: A developmental analysis. *American Educational Research Journal* 18: 15–28.

Harlow, J. F. (1953). Mice, monkeys, men, and motives. *Psychological Review, 60,* 23– 32.

Harris, A. M., and Covington, M. V. (1989). Cooperative team failure: A double threat for the low performer? Unpublished manuscript, Department of Psychology, University of California at Berkeley.

Hebb, D. O. (1961). Distinctive features of learning in the higher mammal. In J. F. Delafresnaye (ed.), *Brain Mechanisms and Learning*. London: Oxford University Press.

Heider, F. (1958). *The Psychology of Interpersonal Relations*. New York: Wiley.

Hembree, R. (1988). Correlates, causes, effects, and treatment of test anxiety. *Review of Educational Research* 58: 47–77.

Heist, P. A., and Yonge, G. (1968). *Manual for the Omnibus Personality Inventory, Form F*. New York: Psychological Corporation.

Hoffman, M. L. (1982). Development of prosocial motivation: Empathy and guilt. In N. Eisenberg-Borg (ed.), *Development of Prosocial Behavior*. New York: Academic Press.

Holland, J. L. (1966). *Psychology of Vocational Choice*. Waltham, MA: Blaisdell.

Holland, J. L. (1973). *Making Vocational Choices: A Theory of Careers*. Englewood Cliffs, NJ: Prentice-Hall.

Hullfish, G., and Smith, P. (1961). *Reflective Thinking: The Method of Education*. New York: Dodd, Mead.

Jones, E. E., and Nisbett, R. E. (1971). The actor and the observer: Divergent perceptions of the causes of behavior. In E. E. Jones, D. E. Kanouse, H. H. Kelley, R. E. Nisbett, S. Valins, and B. Weiner (eds.), *Attribution: Perceiving the Causes of Behavior*. Morristown, NJ: General Learning Press.

Kaplan, R. M., and Swant, S. G. (1973). Reward characteristics in appraisal of achievement behavior. *Representative Research in Social Psychology* 4: 11–17.

Katchadourian, H. A., and Boli, J. (1985). *Careerism and Intellectualism Among College Students*. San Francisco: Jossey-Bass.

Kirkland, K., and Hollandsworth, J. (1980). Effective test taking: Skills-acquisition versus anxiety-reduction techniques. *Journal of Counseling and Clinical Psychology* 48: 431–439.

Kirst, M. (1990, March). *Stanford Magazine* p. 110.

Korn, H. A. (1968). Differences in student responses to the curriculum. In J. Katz and Associates (eds.), *No time for youth: Growth and Constraint in College Students*. San Francisco: Jossey-Bass.

Kuhl, J. (1981). Motivational and functional helplessness: The moderating effect of action versus state orientation. *Journal of Personality and Social Psychology* 40: 155–170.

Kuhl, J. (1984). Volitional aspects of achievement motivation and learned helplessness: Toward a comprehensive theory of action-control. In B. A. Maher (ed.), *Progress in Experimental Personality Research*, Vol 13. New York: Academic Press.

Kulik, J. A., Kulik, C. C., and Cohen, P. A. (1979). A meta-analysis of outcome studies of Keller's personalized system of instruction. *American Psychologist* 34: 307–318.

Kulik, C. C., Kulik, J. A., and Shwalb, B. J. (1982). Programmed instruction in secondary education: A meta-analysis of evaluation findings. *The Journal of Educational Research* 75: 307–318.

Laux, L., and Glanzmann, P. (1987). A self-presentational view of test anxiety. In R. Schwarzer, H. M. van der Ploeg, and C. D. Spielberger (eds.), *Advances in Test Anxiety Research*, Vol. 5. Hillsdale, NJ: Erlbaum.

Lave, J. (1988). *Cognition in Practice*. Boston: Cambridge.

Lavelle, T. L., Metalsky, G. I., and Coyne, J. C. (1979). Learned helplessness, test anxiety, and acknowledgment of contingencies. *Journal of Abnormal Psychology* 88: 381–387.

Leppin, A., Schwarzer, R., Belz, D., Jerusalem, M., and Quast, H. -H. (1987). Causal attribution patterns of high and low test-anxious students. In R. Schwarzer, H. M. van der Ploeg, and C. D. Spielberger (eds.), *Advances in Test Anxiety Research*, Vol. 5. Hillsdale, NJ: Erlbaum.

Levin, B. B. (1990). Portfolio assessment: Implications for the communication of effort and ability in alternative forms of assessment. Unpublished paper, School of Education, University of California at Berkeley.

Lewin, K., Dembo, T., Festinger, L., and Sears, P. (1944). Level of aspiration. In J. McV. Hunt (ed.), *Personality and the Behavior Disorders*, Vol. 1. New York: Ronald.

Liebert, R. M., and Morris, L. W. (1967). Cognitive and emotional components of test anxiety: A distinction and some initial data. *Psychological Reports* 20: 975–978.

Litwin, L. W. (1963). Effects of motivation on probability preference. *Journal of Personality* 31: 417–427.

Littig, G. H. (1966). Achievement motivation, expectancy of success, and risk-taking behavior. In J. W. Atkinson and N. T. Feather (eds.), *A Theory of Achievement Motivation*. New York: Wiley.

Malone, T. W. (1981). Toward a theory of intrinsically motivating instruction. *Cognitive Science* 4: 333–369.

Man, F., and Hrabal, V. (1988). Self-concept of ability, social consequences anxiety, and attribution as correlates of action control. In F. Halisch and J. H. L. van den Bercken (eds.), *Achievement and Task Motivation*. Lisse, The Netherlands: Swets and Zeitlinger/Erlbaum.

Mandler, G., and Sarason, S. (1952). A study of anxiety and learning. *Journal of Abnormal and Social Psychology* 47: 166–173.

McClelland, D. C. (1958). Methods of measurement human motivation. In J. W. Atkinson (ed.), *Motives in Fantasy, Action, and Society*. Princeton, NJ: Van Nostrand.

McClelland, D. C. (1961). *The Achieving Society*. Princeton, NJ.

McClelland, D. C. (1965). Toward a theory of motive acquisition. *American Psychologist* 20: 321–333.

McClelland, D. C. (1980). Motive dispositions: The merits of operant and respondent measures. In L. Wheeler (ed.), *Review of Personality and Social Psychology*, Vol. 1. Beverly Hills, CA: Sage.

McClelland, D. C. (1985). How motives, skills, and values determine what people do. *American Psychologist* 40: 812–825.

McMahan, I. D. (1973). Relationships between causal attributions and expectancy of success. *Journal of Personality and Social Psychology* 28: 108–114.

Meyer, W. -U. (1970). Selbstverantwortlichkeit und leistungs. Unpublished doctoral dissertation, Ruhr Universität, Bochum, Germany.

Miller, I. W., and Norman, W. H. (1979). Learned helplessness in humans: A review and attribution-theory model. *Psychological Bulletin* 86: 93–118.

Moulton, R. W. (1965). Effects of success and failure on level of aspiration as related to achievement motives. *Journal of Personality and Social Psychology* 1: 399–406.

Naveh-Benjamin, M. (1985). A comparison of training programs intended for different types of test-anxious students. Paper presented at symposium on information processing and motivation, American Psychological Association, Los Angeles.

Nicholls, J. G. (1975). Causal attributions and other achievement-related cognitions: Effects of task outcome, attainment values, and sex. *Journal of Personality and Social Psychology* 31: 379–389.

Nicholls, J. G. (1989). *The Competitive Ethos and Democratic Education*. Cambridge: Harvard University Press.

Nuttin, J. (1984). *Motivation, Planning and Action: A Relational Theory of Behavior Dynamics*. Hillsdale, NJ: Erlbaum.

Nuttin, J., and Lens, W. (1985). *Future Time Perspective and Motivation: Theory and Research Method*. Hillsdale, NJ: Erlbaum.

Osipow, S. H., Ashby, J. D., and Wall, H. W. (1966). Personality types and vocational choice: A test of Holland\'s theory. *Personnel and Guidance Journal* 45: 37–42.

Peterson, R. E. (1965). On a typology of college students. Research Bulletin, RB-65–9. Princeton, NJ: Educational Testing Service.

Pintrich, P. R. (1988). A process-oriented view of student motivation and cognition. In J. S. Stark and L. Mets (eds.), *Improving Teaching and Learning Through Research* New Directions for Institutional Research, 57. San Francisco: Jossey-Bass.

Pintrich, P. R. (1989). The dynamic interplay of student motivation and cognition in the college classroom. In C. Ames and M. Maehr (eds.), *Advances in Motivation and Achievement*, Vol. 6. Greenwich, CT: JAI Press.

Pintrich, P. R., and De Groot, E. V. (1990). Motivational and self-regulated learning components of classroom academic performance. *Journal of Educational Psychology* 82: 33–40.

Pratte, R. (1988). *The Civic Imperative: Examining the Need for Civic Education.* New York: Teachers College *Promoting student success at Berkeley: Guidelines for the future* (1991). (Report of the Commission on Responses to a Changing Student Body). Berkeley: University of California.

Raynor, J. O. (1969). Future orientation and motivation of immediate activity: An elaboration of the theory of achievement motivation. *Psychological Review* 76: 606–610.

Raynor, J. O. (1970). Relationships between achievement-related motives, future orientation, and academic performance. *Journal of Personality and Social Psychology* 15: 28–33.

Reagan, D. (1991). The academic dismissal student and the self-worth theory of achievement motivation. Unpublished doctoral dissertation.

Rest, S., Nierenberg, R., Weiner, B., and Heckhausen, H. (1973). Further evidence concerning the effects of perceptions of effort and ability on achievement evaluation. *Journal of Personality and Social Psychology* 28: 187–191.

Roberts, B., and Covington, M. V. (1991). The myth of Hermes. Unpublished manuscript, Institute of Personality Assessment and Research, University of California, Berkeley.

Rosenbaum, R. M. (1972). A dimensional analysis of the perceived causes of success and failure. Unpublished doctoral dissertation, University of California, Los Angeles.

Rothblum, E. D., Solomon, L. J., and Murakami, J. (1986). Affective, cognitive and behavioral differences between high and low procrastinators. *Journal of Counseling Psychology* 33: 387–394.

Salamé, R. (1984). Test anxiety: Its determinants, manifestations and consequences. In H. M. van der Ploeg, R. Schwarzer, and C. D. Spielberger (eds.), *Advances in Test Anxiety Research*, Vol. 3. Hillsdale, NJ: Erlbaum.

Schmalt, H. D. (1982). Two concepts of fear of failure motivation. In R. Schwarzer, H.M. van der Ploeg, and C. D. Spielberger (eds.), *Advances in Test Anxiety Research*, Vol. 1. Lisse: Swets and Zeitlinger.

Schoenfeld, A. H. (1989). Reflections on doing and teaching mathematics. Paper presented at a conference, Mathematical Thinking and Problem Solving, Berkeley.

Schuman, H., Walsh, E., Olson, C., and Etheridge, B. (1985). Effort and reward: The assumption that college grades are affected by quantity of study. *Social Forces* 63: 945–966.

Schwarzer, R., Jerusalem, M., and Schwarzer, C. (1983). Self-related and situation-\ related cognitions in test anxiety and helplessness: A longitudinal analysis with structural equations. In R. Schwarzer, H. M. van der Ploeg, and C. D. Spielberger (eds.), *Advances in Anxiety Research*, Vol. 2. Hillsdale, NJ: Erlbaum.

Schwarzer, R., Jerusalem, M., and Stiksrud, A. (1984). The developmental relationship between test anxiety and helplessness. In H. M. van der Ploeg, R. Schwarzer, and C D. Spielberger (eds.), *Advances in Test Anxiety Research,* Vol. 3. Hillsdale, NJ: Erlbaum.

Schwarzer, R., Seipp, B., and Schwarzer, C. (1989). Mathematics performance and anxiety: A meta-analysis. In R. Schwarzer, H. M. van der Ploeg, and C. D. Spielberger (eds.), *Advances in Test Anxiety Research*, Vol. 6. Lisse, Netherlands: Swets and Zeitlinger.

Seipp, B. (1991). Anxiety and academic performance: A meta-analysis of findings. *Anxiety Journal* 4: 27–42.

Seipp, B., and Schwarzer, C. (1990, July). Anxiety and academic achievement: A meta-\ analysis of findings. Paper presented at the 11th International Conference of the Society for Test Anxiety Research (STAR), Berlin.

Seligman, M. E. P. (1975). *Helplessness: On Depression, Development, and Death.* San Francisco: Freeman.

Shapiro, G. (1986). *A Skeleton in the Darkroom: Stories of Serendipity in Science.* New York: Harper and Row.

Silver, M., and Sabini, J. (1981). Procrastinating. *Journal for the Theory of Social Behavior* 11: 207–221.

Silver, M., and Sabini, J. (1982, January). When it's not really procrastination. *Psychology Today* 16: 39–42.

Skinner, E. A., Wellborn, J. G., and Connell, J. P. (1990). What it takes to do well in school and whether I've got it: A process model of perceived control and children's engagement and achievement in school. *Journal of Educational Psychology* 82: 22–32.

Slavin, R. E. (1983). When does cooperative learning increase student achievement? *Psychological Bulletin* 94: 429–445.

Slavin, R. E. (1984). Students motivating students to excel: Cooperative incentives, cooperative tasks, and student achievement. *The Elementary School Journal* 85: 53–64.

Smith, T. W., Snyder, C. R., and Handelsman, M. M. (1982). On the self-serving function of an academic wooden leg: Test anxiety as a self-handicapping strategy. *Journal of Personality and Social Psychology* 42: 314–321.

Snyder, C. R. (1984, September). Excuses, excuses: They sometimes actually work—to relieve the burden of blame. *Psychology Today* 18: 50–55.

Snyder, M. L., Stephan, W. G., and Rosenfeld, C. (1976). Egotism and attribution. *Journal of Personality and Social Psychology* 33: 435–441.

Solomon, L. J., and Rothblum, E. D. (1984). Academic procrastination: Frequency and cognitive-behavioral correlates. *Journal of Counseling Psychology* 31: 503–509.

Stiensmeier-Pelster, J., and Schürmann, M. (1990). Performance deficits following failure: Integrating motivational and functional aspect of learned helplessness. *Anxiety Research* 2(3): 211–222.

Stipiek, D. J., and Weisz, J. R. (1981). Perceived personal control and academic achievement. *Review of Educational Research* 51: 101–137.

Streufert, S., and Streufert, S. C. (1969). Effects of conceptual structure, failure, and success on attribution of causality and interpersonal attitudes. *Journal of Personality and Social Psychology* 11: 138–247.

Tobias, S. (1985). Test anxiety: Interference, defective skills, and cognitive capacity. *Educational Psychologist* 20: 135–142.

Tobias, S. (1986). Anxiety and cognitive processing of instruction. In R. Schwarzer (ed.), *Self-Related Cognitions in Anxiety and Motivation.* Hillsdale, NJ: Erlbaum.

Topman, R. M., and Jansen, T. (1984). "I really can't do it, anyway\'\': The treatment of test anxiety. In H. M. van der Ploeg, R. Schwarzer, and C. D. Spielberger (eds.), *Advances in Test Anxiety Research*, Vol. 3. Hillsdale, NJ: Erlbaum.

Tucker, J. A., Vuchinich, R. E., and Sobell, M. B. (1981). Alcohol consumption as a self-handicapping strategy. *Journal of Abnormal Psychology* 90: 220–230.

Valle, V. A. (1974). Attributions of stability as a mediator in the changing of expectations. Unpublished doctoral dissertation, University of Pittsburgh.

Veroff, J., and Veroff, J. B. (1972). Reconsideration of a measure of power motivation. *Psychological Bulletin* 78: 279–291.

Warren, J. R. (1968). Student perceptions of college subcultures. *American Educational Research Journal* 5: 213–232.

Weiner, B. (1972). *Theories of Motivation: From Mechanism to Cognition.* Chicago: Markham.

Weiner, B. (1974). *Achievement Motivation and Attribution Theory.* Morristown, NJ: General Learning Press.

Weiner, B. (1990). History of motivational research in education. *Journal of Educational Psychology* 82: 616–622.

Weiner, B., Frieze, L., Kukla, A., Reed, L., Rest, S., and Rosenbaum, R. (1971). Perceiving the causes of success and failure. In E. E. Jones, D. E. Kanouse, H. H. Kelley, R. E. Nisbett, S. Valins, and B. Weiner (eds.), *Attribution: Perceiving the Causes of Behavior.* Morristown, NJ: General Learning Press.

Weiner, B., Heckhausen, H., Meyer, W., and Cook, R. (1972). Causal ascriptions and achievement behavior: A conceptual analysis of effect and reanalysis of locus of control. *Journal of Personality and Social Psychology* 21: 239–248.

Weiner, B., and Kukla, A. (1970). An attributional analysis of achievement motivation. *Journal of Personality and Social Psychology* 15: 1–20.

Wicker, F. W., Payne, G. C., and Morgan, R. D. (1983). Participant descriptions of guilt and shame. *Motivation and Emotion* 7: 25–39.

Williams, J. P. (1976). Individual differences in achievement test presentation and evaluation anxiety. Unpublished doctoral dissertation, University of Illinois at Urbana-\ Champaign.

Winter, D. G. (1973). *The Power Motive*. New York: The Free Press.

Wolosin, R. J., Sherman, S. J., and Till, A. (1973). Effects of cooperation and competition on responsibility attribution after success and failure. *Journal of Experimental Social Psychology* 15: 1–20.

Woodworth, R. S. (1918). *Dynamic Psychology*. New York: Columbia University Press.

Turning Work into Play: The Nature and Nurturing of Intrinsic Task Engagement

Martin V. Covington and Sonja Wiedenhaupt

"*Work*—whatever a body is obliged to do.
Play—whatever a body is not obliged to do."
Mark Twain.

INTRODUCTION

In the prior chapter of this volume, the first author explored the prospects for transforming the quality of academic life of many colleges and universities in America from being largely an obligatory struggle driven by the pressures of competitive sorting—*work* by Twain's definition, to becoming places devoted to intrinsic involvement, that is, the joyful pursuit of intellectual inquiries which carry no immediate obligation to perform, nor any necessity for tangible payoffs except for the sake of satisfying one's curiosity or for the productive exercise of the mind—*play*, by Twain's definition. By *play* we do not mean a frivolous experience, but rather seeing an activity as sufficiently interesting in its own right, quite apart from grading considerations, to commit all of one's resources, unreservedly, even joyously. The issues of change implied in this vision of college academic life concern the topic of achievement motivation and the time-honored distinction between intrinsic and extrinsic motivation (Deci, 1975; Deci and Ryan, 1985; Maehr, 1989; Maehr and Stallings, 1972). They also raise the question of whether or not such a playful spirit can coexist to any degree, let alone flourish, whenever the highest loyalties are accorded a work ethic based on proving one's competitive superiority.

In this companion chapter, a sequel of sorts, we hope to extend our understanding of how such a transformation might be possible, and explore what new instructional forms might be required. We also ask if the changes we seek in order to tip the balance of schooling in favor of involvement, spontaneity, and creativity are less radical and invasive than has been widely thought. In the process, our goal is not only that of turning work—defined here as the obligatory struggle to achieve competitive superiority—into play, but also to ennoble the prospects for work, that is, to lift work above its more commonly accepted meaning as a chore. Compared to play, work need not be contrastingly bad. Not when we recognize that work involves sustained, meaningful activity as in the phrase "the collective works of Robert Frost," or implies the nobility of "good works," or the quality of "workmanship." Unfortunately, it is these uplifting interpretations of work that all too easily have become the casualties of much of college life as presently structured.

Before we precede, it would be useful to review briefly the basic arguments pursued in the previous chapter that have led us to this point. They can be summarized as follows:

1. Not only do college educators risk discouraging intrinsic impulses by rewarding students with good grades for creative behaviors they might perform anyway (Kohn, 1993), but the typical method for distributing grades across students is also highly abrasive (Covington, 1992). First, as part of a competitive gauntlet, instructors often limit the number of rewards available, with fewer rewards than students; then, second, they reward most those students who perform best. According to self-worth theory (Covington, 1984; Covington and Beery, 1976), this competitive arrangement is a potential threat to the student's sense of worth. In the circumstance, students come to perceive themselves to be only as worthy as their ability to achieve competitively, and since only a few can win at this game, the majority of students must content themselves with the dubious satisfaction of avoiding failure, or in the event of failing, at least avoiding the implication of failure—that they are incompetent. Thus students are placed in a kind of double jeopardy when it comes to the prospects of promoting intrinsic engagement in college; not only are some students punished by rewards when they succeed, but also because of the scarcity of these rewards, many other students must struggle to avoid failure rather than to approach success (Covington and Omelich, 1979). Neither situation bodes well for the promotion of learning for its own sake.

2. We also argued that colleges and universities operate largely as a selection device for identifying those students most capable of further learning. We conceded that this practical reality will not soon be overturned. Competitive grading is here to stay. Indeed, grading students competitively has long been justified as one of the primary mechanisms in our society for assigning talent according to job demands and the availability of jobs, some of which are more attractive than others. (For a critique of this view see Combs, 1957; Covington, 1992; Deutsch, 1979).

Given these realities, we wondered in concluding the previous chapter if it is at all possible for institutions of higher education to encourage the goals of intrinsic task engagement and learning for its own sake both in the face of fear-of-failure dynamics and the demands for externally regulated talent selection.

One of the main obstacles to change implied by this question is the presumed vulnerability of intrinsic motivation to extrinsic rewards. (For reviews, see Kohn, 1993; Olsen, 1991). This presumption depends in part on definitions. Intrinsic motivation has been defined variously as a tendency to engage in activities for their own sake, just for the pleasure derived in performing them, or for the sake of curiosity. The key element linking all such definitions is that the rewards for performance reside in the actions themselves, that is, the act is its own reinforcement. Put differently, the repetition of the action such as satisfying one's curiosity does not depend as much on external inducements as on an internal state or need. The meaning of intrinsic motivation is further delimited by its presumed opposite: extrinsic motivation. Extrinsic motivation is said to involve the performance of an action, not out of any intrinsic satisfaction derived from the action itself, but for the sake of extrinsic payoffs—grades, gold stars, praise, and other kinds of bribes—extrinsic because these rewards are essentially unrelated to the act of learning itself. Here learning becomes the means to an end, not an end in itself.

Whenever intrinsic and extrinsic motivation are contrasted by social science researchers, the former almost invariably becomes defined negatively by the absence of extrinsic forces, not by its own unique presence, that is, an individual is thought to be intrinsically driven whenever she or he does something *without expecting* a payoff. It is this approach to defining intrinsic motivation as actions taken in the absence of extrinsic influences that has contributed heavily to the impression that intrinsic and extrinsic motivation are not just independent processes, but incompatible as well, namely that the presence of extrinsic reasons for achieving necessarily precludes the possibility of learning for its own sake. If this proposition is true and not just the definitional creature of a laboratory research paradigm, then the prospects for arousing intrinsic motivation in college would seem dim indeed, given the unrelenting and largely abrasive presence of competitive sorting and the scramble for extrinsically-conditioned rewards in the form of grades.

This proposition is consistent with what we may call a bipolar or unidimensional model of achievement motivation (Covington, 1992). This model suggests that both intrinsic and extrinsic tendencies blend within the same individual so that everyone can be placed somewhere along a single continuum, ranging from a high intrinsic orientation at one end of the continuum to a high extrinsic orientation at the other end; hence the term bipolar. Thus a state of incompatibility is thought to exist for the fact that to the degree a person is either intrinsically or extrinsically driven, he or she cannot be the other.

By the same token, it can be argued that situations, like people, can also be described in bipolar terms; that is, to the extent that a given situation depends on the presence of extrinsic rewards to sustain involvement, the less likely it is to favor intrinsic reasons for learning. If both individuals and situations reflect such incompatibilities in motivation, then we wonder about the prospects for reform as long as grading pressures prevail, especially those pressures derived from the need to establish competitive superiority. The degree to which our concerns are valid depends in large part on the actual nature of the relationship between intrinsic and extrinsic motivation and on just how incompatible these systems may actually prove to be.

Fortunately, recent findings from our laboratory (Covington and Omelich, 1991) suggest that achievement motivation can be more accurately described in terms of a quadripolar (as opposed to a bipolar) model, an approach which leads to more optimistic conclusions about the possibilities for encouraging intrinsic engagement in the face of competitive sorting. This quadripolar model suggests that intrinsic and extrinsic motivation are two independent dimensions, such that an individual can be placed somewhere along the intrinsic continuum, from high to low, as well as along an extrinsic continuum, from high to low (see Figure 2 in the prior chapter). This arrangement implies that intrinsic and extrinsic tendencies coexist independently within the same individual, so that in theory at least, all persons possess a capacity for intrinsic engagement, to one degree or another, irrespective of the extent to which they may otherwise be driven by the prospects of external reinforcement in the form of praise, recognition, and grades. Likewise, situations may also elicit both intrinsic and extrinsic reasons for achieving, a condition which not only suggests that intrinsic forces can coexist in the presence of extrinsic distractors, but also that intrinsic task engagement can be enhanced directly in its own right, irrespective of the presence of grading pressures.

The specific purpose of this chapter is threefold. First, we will address the question of the nature of the relationship between intrinsic and extrinsic motivation and present evidence favorable to a quadripolar interpretation.

Second, we will address the question of just how malleable is the willingness of individuals to seek out information for its own sake without expecting any reward, or of being open to experience without knowing in advance where these inquiries may lead. This question raises anew the classic issue of whether motivation is best considered to be the trait-like property of individuals—an immutable, internal state or need that impels persons to action, or conversely, the property of specific situations or tasks, not of persons, that beguile individuals into temporary states of involvement for the sake of curiosity and challenge. If individual differences in the capacity for intrinsic engagement are relatively impervious to situational influence, then we should properly be less optimistic about rearranging classroom assignments in ways that promote a renewed emphasis on task engagement. If, on the other hand, the potential for intrinsic arousal resides largely within tasks, then we are on firmer ground in arguing for structural changes in the ways we teach. We will consider two possibilities for the direct encouragement of intrinsic task engagement by altering the nature of tasks themselves. The first strategy involves introducing elements of novelty, intrigue and surprise into classroom assignments. The second strategy involves arranging classroom assignments around students' interests.

Third, and finally, we will conclude the chapter by considering the implications of these various findings for educational policy and reform at the university and college level.

The Berkeley Teaching/Learning Project

The data to be presented were generated from the Berkeley Teaching/Learning Project (Covington, 1992). As part of the ongoing mission of the Project, each year students in a large-enrollment introductory psychology course taught by the first author serve as participants in research designed to explore various questions basic to the academic life of the Berkeley campus and of colleges and universities more generally. Previous research topics have included studies of the dynamics of test-taking anxiety (e.g., Covington, 1985; Covington and Omelich, 1987, 1988) and investigations into the decision-making processes involved in career choice (Roberts and Covington, 1991).

The present data were gathered over two consecutive yearly offerings of the introductory course with enrollments of some 500 freshman each term. As one of the main course requirements students undertook a series of written projects for grade credit designed to promote insights into the subject-matter of contemporary psychology as well as to introduce some of the theoretical issues and problems facing the field. The issues raised were real and representative of the kinds of enduring problems and topics which confront practicing professionals and researchers. For example, students wrote essays describing Jean Piaget's classic theory of human development, and in particular speculated on the kinds of experiences that propel children through Piaget's stages of intellectual growth. Another project required students to write an essay on the use of rewards and punishments to control and shape human behavior.

After being introduced to each project, but before beginning work, students were administered a Likert-type, self-report questionnaire designed to tap their reasons (motives) for undertaking the task. Subsequent factor analyses of these data yielded several distinct item clusters or factors, one of which reflected a purely extrinsic concern for maximizing one's grade, which we dubbed *Grade Focus* (e.g., "I did this project to improve my chances for a good grade"; "It seemed an easy way to gain points"). Three of the remaining factors reflected concepts typically associated with a state of intrinsic task engagement: 1) a commitment to increasing one's knowledge; to improve with practice, and to *master* a subject-matter domain ("I wanted to see how well I was understanding the course material"); 2) the degree to which students expressed personal *interest* in the subject matter topic ("I am interested in children and how they think"); and 3) the degree to which the individual undertook the task for the sake of *fun* and challenge ("I felt challenged").

The Nature of Intrinsic Engagement

An analysis of these four motives across several student projects provided data supportive of the quadripolar model which asserts, as will be recalled, that intrinsic and extrinsic motives operate independently of one another. First, for starters, students consistently reported that all three reasons for intrinsic task engagement figured into their decision to work, despite the fact that extrinsic Grade Focus was given the highest priority by all students.

Second, assuming a state of coexistence, we were curious to know just how the substantial presence of an extrinsic Grade Focus Factor might influence intrinsic reasons for performing. How much, if at all, an extrinsic preoccupation with grades interferes with or overrides such inclinations as self-mastery and the expression of personal interest can be judged indirectly from the magnitude and direction of the correlations between the Grade Focus factor, on the one hand, and the three components of intrinsic task engagement we investigated, on the other.

To begin with, consider the mastery motive. The extent to which self-mastery (e.g., "becoming the best one can be") emerged as a salient work motive was unrelated to the degree of concern over grades. In effect, students could be heavily preoccupied with grades and still harbor mastery motives. This same pattern of neutrality with respect to grades also held in the case of personal interest. Even a substantial preoccupation with grades did not necessarily preclude the emergence of personal interest as a reason for task engagement.

So far these data provide considerable reassurance, given our initial concern that the presence of grades and the threat implied by poor grades would suppress intrinsic motivation. This appears not to be so. And, in the case of personal interest, these findings become especially significant, given the highly positive motivational benefits which derive from being task-engaged by reason of personal interest. But more on this point later.

Finally, consider the more purely affective or emotional component of intrinsic motivation: experiencing joy at overcoming a challenge. Here the relationship between the expression of personal exhilaration and degree of Grade Focus was more complex and depended on the motivational orientation of students. Consider those students whom we described in the prior chapter as Success-oriented; that is, individuals who prefer striving for success in contrast to attempting to avoid failure, and in the bargain valuing intrinsic reasons for learning. The extent to which Success-oriented students engaged in the work assignments for the sake of fun and discovery was unrelated to the degree of grading pressure they felt. Not so, however, for many failure-prone students, especially those we previously described as Overstrivers and Failure-acceptors. For these two groups the degree to which fun was a motivating presence was sharply curtailed as concerns over their grade increased. In short, in these cases grading pressure interfered with intrinsic engagement and probably for different reasons. As will be recalled, Overstrivers are driven to succeed not out of any particular love for learning, but for defensive reasons—in order to avoid failure. But because the risk of failure is ever-present in such a contest, any enjoyment derived from work for Overstrivers is severely curtailed. On the other hand, Failure-accepting students are not particularly attracted to success, but neither are they overly concerned about failure. We believe these students to be essentially disconnected from the cultural and intellectual values associated with college life. Because of such indifference, the presence of grades for these students likely acts as a reason, or even an excuse, not to work, certainly not to work very hard and without much pleasure.

Apart from this qualification regarding limits on the expression of task enjoyment, our overall findings encourage considerable optimism. It appears that intrinsic motives, at least those associated with achieving a sense of mastery and the expression of personal interest, can emerge spontaneously and operate largely unfettered for most students in an achievement arena dominated by extrinsically driven rewards. This is not to suggest that current grading practices in college, which all too often are competitively based, should remain unchallenged on the grounds that they do not necessarily preclude intrinsic task engagement. It is clear that much can be done to alter grading practices in ways that do more than merely maintain a neutral presence, but actually contribute to the goals of intrinsic engagement (Covington and Omelich, 1984). The point is that the mere presence of grades and grading pressure, even severely self-induced pressure, does not necessarily foreclose the spontaneous emergence of intrinsic engagement.

In this connection, the question now arises, "Can we arrange classroom assignments so as to maximize intrinsic engagement, on the one hand, and minimize the threat of failure, on the other?" It is to this inquiry that we now turn. If the potential for intrinsic arousal depends in large part on the characteristics of the task, then we are on firmer ground in arguing for structural changes in the ways we teach.

Nurturing Intrinsic Task Engagement

Novelty vs. Familiarity

Novelty has the power to arrest, beguile, and challenge for the sake of surprise and intrigue alone, and therefore, at an emotional level at least, novelty captures the essence of intrinsic engagement. Yet novelty is not always welcome. In the minds of some students, novelty is also equated with unfamiliarity and lack of structure, and as a consequence, can elicit feelings of being placed at risk. Given this potentially double-headed countenance, we were interested to determine whether or not casting a task in a novel form would, in fact, encourage greater intrinsic task involvement and allay the fear of failure which accompanies course work for many students.

As already mentioned, an important source of grade credit in the introductory psychology course was a series of student projects. Several of these projects were recast in two forms, one version requiring a traditional essay of the kind quite familiar to students, and the other version requiring students to take a novel, intriguing approach which would not necessarily be elicited by the demands of a regular essay. For example, the essay version of the Piaget growth and development task described earlier was altered so that in addition to merely identifying those experiences mentioned in the textbook that might stimulate intellectual growth, students were also challenged to design a toy or game that might actually achieve these ends. Similarly, the essay assignment concerning the use of rewards and punishments to shape human behavior was modified so that the writer became the example by requiring students variously to list the kinds of rewards that make college a positive experience for them (i.e., positive reinforcement), the kinds of punishment they may be attempting to avoid by working hard and doing well (i.e., negative reinforcement), and the kinds of schedules of reinforcement on which they find themselves while studying and keeping up with their classwork.

Initially, all students previewed both forms of a given project prior to knowing which form they would be assigned, and were asked to make a number of comparative rankings, including among them a manipulation check to assure us that the novel version of the task was, indeed, uniformly perceived as more surprising, different, and unusual. This proved to be the case. Students were then assigned randomly to one form of the task or the other, with the assignments counterbalanced so that those students administered the novel version on one occasion, thereafter received the essay version of a new task on a subsequent occasion, and vice versa.

What, then, if any, was the value of perceived novelty for enhancing intrinsic task engagement, and for minimizing divisive reasons for achieving? Not surprisingly, the answer is complex, but on the whole, lawful and quite positive. For all the benefits that novelty conveys, and they are considerable, as we will shortly see, an invitation for problem redefinition offered by the novelty condition nonetheless initially proved to be a potential threat and this was true for all students. For one thing, before beginning work most students rated the novel version of the task as far more difficult, and the sources of difficulty were legion: Students were less clear about where and how to begin working; they anticipated that it would be harder to come up with ideas as well as to express them; and they were concerned that their ideas might be foolish. For another thing, perhaps most ominous of all, students expected that they would get a lower grade for their efforts if assigned the novel version of the task. Yet despite all these misgivings, they preferred to work on the novel version!

By contrast, students tended to judge the essay task to be safer and easier, if not quicker, to accomplish, since they had long ago mastered the mechanics of writing essays based on simply rephrasing information from a textbook, and with a most attractive prospect that they would likely receive a higher grade for their troubles. Yet, as it turned out, the safer bet possessed fewer psychic rewards than those provoked by novelty.

Basically, the presence of novelty as a task attribute transforms an assignment from being seen largely, if not solely, as just another way to improve one's grade, into an opportunity to explore one's own ideas, to think deeply about issues, and in this particular instance, to satisfy one's curiosity both with regard to the broader psychological issues raised, but also for the benefits of learning to think like a psychologist. Overall, the impression one gains is that once the novel task was assigned and work had begun, a grade focus gave way to a sense of pleasure, fun, and the playful use of the mind. The eclipsing of a grade focus under the novelty condition (might we say, in favor of turning work into play) occurred among all students, although the benefits were most pronounced among Success-oriented individuals, who took further advantage of their already substantial readiness to be intrinsically engaged to becoming even more involved. By contrast, Failure-avoiding students (those individuals who tend to blame others as a way to discount their failures) enjoyed different benefits under the novelty condition. This group felt less of a sense of obligation to perform for fear of disappointing others, a sentiment which would have undercut personal satisfaction with their efforts. Also, the novelty condition reduced a preoccupation among Failure-avoiding students to compare their own ideas unfavorably to those of other students. Since Success-oriented students were least likely among all the groups to engage in such comparisons, with or without a novelty manipulation, they showed no particular change on this dimension. Not so, however, for Overstrivers who appeared to seize on novelty as an opportunity to proved themselves "a top student in the class" and to "see how much better they are than others." Clearly the playful elements introduced by novelty offered different psychic invitations for different students, decidedly positive for most, but for a minority, sometimes negative. Yet despite this one negative note, the general consequences of novelty were positive for all groups of students and consistent with all the classic indicators of intrinsic task engagement, including being oblivious to the passage of time.

How, then, are we to understand the attraction of novelty and a decided preference for it—of being drawn to, indeed, beguiled by a situation which, at least initially, also stirs the fear of failure? For us, the answer involves more than the use of novelty as simply a convenient means to induce intrinsic task engagement, and speaks to a further refinement of the basic concept of intrinsic motivation which goes beyond those traditional definitions presented earlier. This additional perspective can be put in a nutshell: As a process, state, or condition, intrinsic task engagement occurs when the prospects for satisfying one's curiosity or for expressing new ideas outweigh the risk of falling short of one's grade goal. The operative term here is "outweighed," and was manifest in the present experiment by the preference of virtually all students for the novel form of the task, despite initial misgivings, especially over grades. But why, under the circumstances, should novelty be judged so favorably by students, especially among failure-prone students? Simply put, because the invitation for intrigue, surprise, and challenge prevailed. And, it is just such a positive intrinsic set which eventually overcame initial doubts and worries about the quality and value of one's work. Perhaps the most dramatic example of this transformation is that despite the fact that the novelty students experienced greater self-doubts of ability as they began work, these sentiments largely failed to elicit negative ability-linked emotions such as shame and anxiety, emotions which were found far more frequently among the essayists, presumably because these latter students did not have the buffer of a manageable challenge and the prospects for fun as they proceeded. In the case of the present research, at least, the novelty manipulation provided an invitation which simply could not be denied; a challenge which eventually was overcome by hard work and resolve. Such hard-won successes at the risk of failure undoubtedly was the reason that novelty students were far more positive in recollecting their affective moods during work, choosing to describe their efforts as "determined," and their demeanor "attentive," "interested," "excited," and even "inspired."

Will such positive outcomes always be true of induced novelty? Obviously not. One can easily imagine tasks that are so removed from the student's own experiences and preparation that any feelings of intrigue and challenge will give way to confusion, self-doubt, and even panic. And sometimes even if an assignment is within the conceptual reach of students, the importance of a grade may loom so large as to override any positive benefits of novelty. From an educational perspective, the induction of novelty is a calculated risk, but one that appears to be worth taking when it comes to the encouragement of intrinsic task engagement.

In order to place novelty as a motivating device in proper perspective, we must also consider its counterpart: the conservative and prudent alternative represented in this research by the simple essay task. Although working on the novel task courted various risks, so, too, did working on the essay task, but for different reasons. Certainly boredom was not one of them, since few students could remain indifferent to the consequences of being graded no matter what version of the task they received. Frustration and defensiveness is the more appropriate description of risk in the case of the essay task. For example, the essayists were more likely to concede that, despite their initial judgment of the relative simplicity of the task, they variously felt that they: ran out of time to do full justice to the project, were in too much of a hurry to finish, and did just enough to receive full credit. Although to some degree these confessions likely reflect the actual, sometimes cruel, realities of time management and mismanagement in college, they also contain considerable maneuvering room for the sake of disassociating oneself from the most threatening interpretation of failure: being intellectually inadequate to the task. How much more comforting is it to blame a poor performance on time pressures or on an insufficient commitment of effort than on personal inadequacies?

Interest-centered Learning

When educators consider how best to arrange the conditions of learning so as to maximize intrinsic engagement, one candidate inevitably leaps to mind: organizing learning around student interests, whether this means teaching fractions to third-graders as the means to calculate the odds in a boxing match, or assigning book reports on the topic of Mars to aspiring young astrophysicists. (For a current treatment of the role of interest in learning, see Renninger, Hidi, and Krapp, 1991). Given the widespread popularity of this motivational strategy at all educational levels and the general dearth of hard evidence as to its actual effectiveness, we decided to explore the dynamics of interest-based learning and especially its potential role in offsetting the negative consequences of grading pressures.

As part of the self-report questionnaire which accompanied all student projects, we established the degree to which students were personally interested in the specific content themes of a given project.

Overall, the results of this inquiry were most gratifying. Degree of subject-matter related interest proved to be a powerful predictor for many of the behaviors associated with intrinsic task engagement. For instance, as personal interest in a project increased so, too, did the frequency of self reports describing students as being caught up in the act of learning, of experiencing feelings of wonder and joy at their discoveries, and of even having a serendipitous experience—that is, discovering unexpectedly something of value in their work beyond what was initially anticipated. Incidently, the perception of time proved to be an intriguing phenomenon in this context. Although high task-interested students judged themselves to be in no hurry to finish, they nonetheless also agreed that time flew as they worked. In effect, what we appeared to have here is an interplay between perceptions of time compression, on the one hand, and time expansion on the other—variously savoring the processes of discovery which expands the sense of time available and reluctant to stop, yet oblivious to the passage of time.

Now, what of the impact of topical interest on the realities of being graded and on the role of grades as a motivational device? The findings can be summarized in two parts, depending on whether interest is high or low.

First, when interest is high, the importance of grades as a goad to perform is substantially diminished since other reasons for learning, largely intrinsic in nature, emerged to sustain student involvement such as feelings of having done well and of achieving mastery. And, even when these same task-interested students acknowledged that they would be graded—nothing obscures this fact of academic life for long—they believed that the presence of grades actually inspired them to do their best. This uplifting sentiment stands in stark contrast to the reactions of those students who showed little task interest. Rather than believing themselves maximally challenged by the presence of grades, this latter group perceived grades as a way only to insure a minimum amount of effort! This reaction illustrates the second part of our findings: When task interest is low, grades become the most prominent justification or imperative for undertaking a task. And, we do not refer here to that largely benign and wholly natural interpretation of the Grade Focus factor as the desire to get good grades, but with grades perceived as an obligatory, competitive means for testing one's sense of worth. It is these latter perceptions that in turn lead low task-interested students to worry about grades as they work, of not feeling smart enough to do well, of perceiving the chances of doing well as remote, and complaining that they did not get enough grade credit given the amount of work required.

There remains one further point with respect to the relationship between task interest and grading which concerns the so-called *overjustification effect* (Lepper and Greene, 1975; Morgan, 1981; Kassin and Lepper, 1984). A great deal of research has shown that rewarding individuals unnecessarily for doing something they already enjoy doing can undermine their intrinsic involvement in the task. This is thought to happen because an already justifiable activity becomes suspect by the promise of additional rewards—hence, the term overjustification—so that the individual reasons, in effect, "if someone has to pay me to do this, then it must not be worth doing for its own sake" (Covington, 1992, pg. 146).

In principle, instructors can avoid discouraging student initiative by simply not rewarding expressions of creativity and ingenuity that arise spontaneously since they need no particular encouragement. But what of the more general case typified by colleges and universities where students are obliged to participate, but are unlikely to do so without the threat of a poor grade? Does the presence of grades in such circumstances automatically degrade further any initial enthusiasm for an assignment? No, not always according to our data. Not as long as initial interest in the task is high. Indeed, the presence of grading under conditions of high interest may even enhance intrinsic engagement—witness our previously reported finding that high task-engaged individuals see grades as a stimulus to do their best. Moreover, it appears that under conditions of high interest, grades become irrelevant as a means to induce student participation in the first place. Specifically, high task-interested students in our study were significantly more likely to express determination to work on a given task whether it was graded or not — a near perfect operational definition of intrinsic engagement!

But these positive reactions to grades and grading pressure were largely absent among students whose task interest was low. In this circumstance grades prove to be a negative presence. For low task-interested students the realization of being graded undercut further what little initial enthusiasm they might have had for a project. Projects remained a chore for this group precisely because, according to their reasoning, it *was* graded. Undercutting enthusiasm for learning is bad enough, but what may be even worse is that rewarding students with the promise of high grades is unlikely to kindle interest in subject-matter topics where none existed before, or as one student put it, "I may get a good grade, but this topic still does not interest me." This is hardly reassuring for those instructors among us who have hoped to encourage student interest in a particular subject-matter area by fostering an increasing sense of competency. Clearly the further development of interests depend on more than simply doing well in the pursuit of those interests (Alexander, Kulikowich, and Schulze, 1994; Sansome, 1986). If grading and extrinsic evaluation are involved in this process then the perceived causes of good grades will heavily influence not only how competent students come to believe themselves to be, but the growth of interest as well.

Conclusions

College instructors often lament that students are largely grade-driven. Yet, the fundamental message of the research presented here is that grades need be only as important as instructors choose them to be. Other markers of excellence besides grades can be encouraged, principally those indicators associated with intrinsic engagement, including feelings of satisfaction and accomplishment for a job well done. Moreover, as we have seen, the emergence of intrinsic task engagement can occur spontaneously even in the presence of competitive grading pressures. Furthermore, not only does intrinsic involvement arise irrespective of competitive pressure but the presence of these intrinsic inducements, once they are in place, can in turn mitigate the otherwise harsh realities of competitive sorting, and even change the meaning of grades for the better. We have seen evidence of this in several different ways. First, in the case of our experiment on the manipulation of novelty, we found students willing to risk the possibility of receiving a poor grade, just for the opportunity to engage in an intriguing, thought provoking and challenging task. Second, organizing assignments around personal interests was also shown to help transform grades from being perceived as a highly controlling presence (designed according to some students to ensure a minimum of effort) when task interest was low, to becoming a stimulant for doing one's best work when personal interest was high. And, not only did perceptions of grades as a motivational device shift in a more positive direction when task interest was high, but the perceived need for grades as a motivator diminished as well.

It is our experience both in the process of conducting this research and from informal observations that students will gladly undertake academic work apart from any grade they might receive so long as it is seen as meaningful and valued. When students succeed at valued tasks over which they have some voice and control, and gain the respect of their peers and coworkers, and the admiration of their mentors, then final course grades, even those that are computed on a competitive basis, are far less important in determining the perceived value of the course and of one's capabilities as a student, than for those individuals who are also judged competitively, but who have little opportunity in their course work to satisfy intrinsic interests and curiosities.

However, if the process of turning student work into play is to succeed, then instructors must work hard, too. A renewed commitment of instructional time, energy and resources is required. As one example, we have already noted that novelty cuts two ways—both enlivening students, thanks to its potential for intrigue; yet also potentially threatening students, due to its unknown character. In order to redress the balance between these two factors in a more positive direction, students not only need be given permission to respond creatively in the face of unfamiliar territory, and be rewarded for doing so, but instructors must also provide sufficient guidance and support so that any initial misgivings about personal inadequacies will give way to a state of task engagement, not ego absorption.

References

Alexander, P. A., Kulikowich, J. M., and Schulze, S. K. (1994). How subject-matter knowledge affects recall and interest. *American Educational Research Journal* 31(2): 313-337.

Combs, A. W. (1957). The myth of competition. *Childhood Education*. Washington, D.C.: Association for Childhood Education International.

Covington, M. V. (1984). The motive for self-worth. In R. Ames and C. Ames (eds.) *Research on Motivation in Education* (Vol. 1). New York: Academic Press.

Covington, M. V. (1985). Test anxiety: Causes and effects over time. In H. M. van der Ploeg, R. Schwarzer and C. D. Spielberger (eds.), *Advances in Test Anxiety Research* (Vol. 4). Hillsdale, NJ: Erlbaum.

Covington, M. V., and Beery, R. G. (1976). *Self-Worth and School Learning*. New York: Holt, Rinehart and Winston.

Covington, M. V., and Omelich, C. L. (1979). Effort: The double-edged sword in school achievement. *Journal of Educational Psychology* 71: 169-182.

Covington, M. V., and Omelich, C. L. (1984). Task-oriented versus competitive learning structures: Motivational and performance consequences. *Journal of Educational Psychology* 76: 1038-1050.

Covington, M. V., and Omelich, C. L. (1987). Item difficulty and test performance among high-anxious and low-anxious students. In R. Schwarzer, H. M. van der Ploeg, and C. D. Spielberger (eds.), *Advances in Test Anxiety Research* (Vol. 5). New Jersey: Erlbaum.

Covington, M. V., and Omelich, C. L. (1988). Achievement dynamics: The interaction of motives, cognitions and emotions over time. *Anxiety Journal* 1: 165-183.

Covington, M. V., and Omelich, C. L. (1991). Need achievement revisited: Verification of Atkinson's original 2 x 2 model. In C. D. Spielberger, I. G. Sarason, Z. Kulcsár, and G. L. Van Heck (eds.), *Stress and Emotion: Anxiety, Anger, and Curiosity* (Vol. 14). Washington, DC: Hemisphere.

Covington, M. V. (1992). *Making the Grade: A Self-Worth Perspective on Motivation and School Reform*. New York: Cambridge University Press.

Deci, E. L. (1975). *Intrinsic Motivation*. New York: Plenum.

Deci, E. L., and Ryan, R. M. (1985). *Intrinsic Motivation and Self-Determination in Human Behavior*. New York: Plenum.

Deutsch, M. (1979). Education and distributive justice. *American Psychologist*, 34: 391-401.

Kassin, S. M., and Lepper, M. R. (1984). Oversufficient and insufficient justification effects: Cognitive and behavioral development. In M. L. Maehr and J. Nicholls (eds.), *Advances in Motivation and Achievement*, Vol. 3. New York: JAI Press, Inc.

Kohn, A. (1993). *Punished by Rewards*. New York: Houghton Mifflin Co.

Lepper, M. R., and Greene, D. (1975). Turning play into work: Effects of adult surveillance and extrinsic rewards on children's intrinsic motivation. *Journal of Personality and Social Psychology* 28: 129-137.

Maehr, M. L. (1989). Thoughts about motivation. In C. Ames and R. Ames (eds.), *Research on Motivation in Education* (Vol. 3). New York: Academic Press.

Maehr, M. L., and Stallings, W. M. (1972). Freedom from external evaluation. *Child Development* 43: 177-185.

Morgan, M. (1981). The overjustification effect: A developmental test of self-perception interpretations. *Journal of Personality and Social Psychology* 40: 809-821.

Olsen, C. (1991). *Achievement Orientation and Context Effects on Intensive Motivation for Learning a Task*. Unpublished doctoral dissertation, University of California at Berkeley.

Renninger, K. A., Hidi, S., and Krapp, A. (1992). *The Role of Interest in Learning and Development*. New Jersey: Lawrence Erlbaum Associates.

Roberts, B., and Covington, M. V. (1991). *The myth of Hermes*. Unpublished manuscript, Institute of Social and Personality Research, University of California, Berkeley.

Sansome, C. (1986). A question of competence: The effects of competence and task feedback on intrinsic interest. *Journal of Personality and Social Psychology* 51(5): 918-931.

The Matrix Representation System: Orientation, Research, Theory, and Application[*]

Kenneth A. Kiewra

Suppose that you are a biology instructor teaching students about human bones. You line several bones across the floor so that students can examine each one carefully. In so doing, students might learn specific information about particular bones (e.g., a rib bone is curved) and general information about all bones (e.g., bones have a white color) but little about the structures that bones form. That bones form the human skeleton in general or that the hands, feet or ribcage in particular is obscured.

Knowing that bones interrelate to form a hand or skeleton is an example of structural knowledge. Structural knowledge is knowledge about the interrelationships among concepts or ideas (Jonassen, Beissner, and Yacci, 1993). Interrelated information is more meaningful than the sum of its parts just as an assembled puzzle is more meaningful than a random collection of its pieces. According to Mandler (1983), "meaning does not exist until some structure or organization is achieved."

This chapter is about representing structural knowledge spatially so that the interrelationships among ideas—the entire skeleton, the assembled puzzle—are apparent. Spatial representations present ideas two dimensionally so that relations within and across topics are easily seen. Text and outline representations, although most common, present information linearly, one idea at a time, like bones lined up across the floor. They often separate or conceal important relationships.

This chapter focuses on a single representation system developed by Du Bois and Kiewra (1989) for displaying structural knowledge. Their system, called the Matrix

[*]I greatly appreciate the helpful comments I received from two anonymous reviewers and the editor, Ray Perry, who read an earlier draft of this chapter. Special thanks are also extended to colleagues Daniel Robinson, Mississippi State University, and Nelson Du Bois, SUNY Oneonta, who helped plan and organize the chapter and critiqued earlier drafts of it. Nelson Du Bois should also be recognized as the chief architect of the Matrix Representation System. Last, I appreciate the work of Ken Jensen, who developed the chapter's graphics.

Representation System, displays structural knowledge spatially using three simple patterns: hierarchy, sequence, and matrix. The matrix is the system's cornerstone because it develops from a hierarchy or sequence representation. Therefore, discussion centers on the matrix representation.

There are other ways to represent structural knowledge. Many of these are detailed by Jonassen et al. (1993). Although this chapter acknowledges and occasionally compares other representation techniques to the Matrix Representation System, its purpose is to orient the reader to this system, and describe its theoretical underpinnings, research evidence, and applications.

ORIENTATION

This section provides an orientation to the Matrix Representation System. First, an example is presented along with a description of general advantages. Second, its structure and construction are discussed. Next, its utility is described. Fourth, its advantages over linear representations are presented. Last, the Matrix Representation System is compared with other spatial representation systems.

Example and General Advantages

Read the following passage about moths and butterflies.

Lepidoptera

    Moths and butterflies are insects belonging to the order Lepidoptera. The moth has two sets of wings that are folded down over its body like a roof when it rests. Moths have feathery antennae and spin a fuzzy cocoon. Moths generally have subdued colors and fly at twilight or night. They go through four stages of development: egg, caterpillar, pupa and adult.

    Butterflies are brightly colored. They fly during the day. They have two sets of wings that remain vertical or outstretched at rest. Their antennae are long and thin with knobs at the end. They proceed through four stages of development: egg, caterpillar, pupa and adult.

This passage has a linear, list-like structure. It presents ideas successively. Consequently, a reader focuses on individual ideas (e.g., a moth's antennae are feathery) rather than the information's overriding structure and interrelationships.

Now examine the representation presented in Figure 1. It was developed using the Matrix Representation System. Its two-dimensional structure has several advantages over the passage. First, it presents the information's overriding structure or framework. Two things are immediately apparent. One, the information is organized hierarchically. Subsumed beneath the superordinate concept Lepidoptera are the subordinate concepts moths and butterflies. Two, moths and butterflies are described along several common categories (e.g., wings and rest).

A second advantage is that within-topic (e.g., moths) relations are easily identifiable. Reading down the moths column, for example, the reader might relate the *feathery* antennae and *fuzzy* cocoon because of their similar texture. Reading down the butterflies

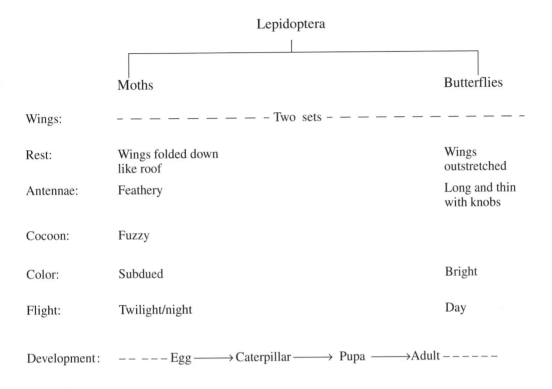

FIGURE 1. Lepidoptera representation based upon the Matrix Representation System.

column, the reader might relate the butterfly's *bright* colors to its *daytime* flight by reasoning that bright colors are only observable at daytime.

A third advantage is that across-topic relations are apparent. The representation encourages readers to compare and contrast the topics (i.e., moths and butterflies) by reading across the representation. Common elements are the two sets of wings and the four stages of development. Differences pertain to rest, antennae, color, and flight. Examining differences, a major pattern emerges: moths have more subtle characteristics than butterflies. Moths have subdued colors; butterflies have bright colors. Moths fly at night while butterflies fly by day. A moth's wings fold down whereas a butterfly's wings extend outward. The moth's antennae are feathery but the butterfly's are long with knobs. Realizing this general pattern should help in understanding and interrelating facts.

The fourth advantage is that relations within the representation's cells are evident. The developmental stages of moths and butterflies are illustrated in a left-to-right sequence with directional arrows joining the stages. Last, missing information is easily spotted. In a glance it is obvious that information about the butterfly's cocoon is missing.

Structure and Construction

As seen in the previous example, the Matrix Representation System depicts four types of structural relations: superordinate-subordinate, temporal, within-topic, and across-topic.

These are represented using three simple patterns: hierarchy, sequence, and matrix.

A hierarchy shows superordinate-subordinate relations in a top-down fashion. Types, parts, or characteristics of something are connected with vertical lines to superordinate ideas above. A sample hierarchy from psychology about operant conditioning is shown in the top three rows in Figure 2. It indicates that there are two types of operant conditioning: reinforcement and punishment, and that each of these has positive and negative subtypes.

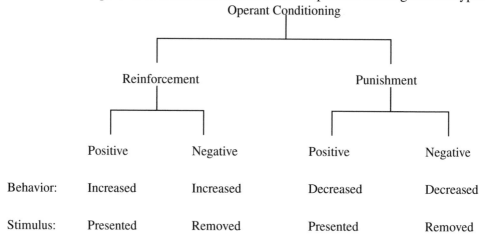

FIGURE 2. Hierarchy extended to form a matrix.

A sequence shows temporal relations. Steps, events, phases, or changes in a process are depicted in a left-to-right sequence with directional arrows between them. A sample sequence pertaining to operant conditioning is shown in the top two rows of Figure 3. This sequence indicates that positive reinforcement occurs when a behavior is followed by a presented stimulus followed by an increased behavior.

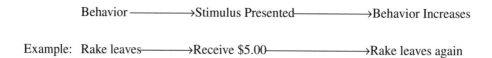

FIGURE 3. Sequence extended to form a matrix.

A matrix is a grid or cross-classification table representing information along two dimensions. Column headings designate *topics*; row headings designate *repeatable categories* (or features) common to the topics. Within the intersecting *cells* (or slots) are *details*. Matrices are developed from a hierarchy or sequence representation that is extended downward by adding repeatable categories and details. Return to Figures 2 and 3 and notice that each was extended downward to form a matrix.

In the Figure 2 matrix, the topics are the four operant concepts: positive and negative reinforcement, and positive and negative punishment. The repeatable categories are behavior and stimulus. The details corresponding to the intersection of topics and repeatable categories appear in the matrix cells. Within-topic relations are observed by reading vertically beneath each topic. For instance, positive reinforcement involves both an increase in behavior and the presentation of a stimulus. Across-topic relations are observed by reading horizontally across the topics. Here, two key patterns emerge: reinforcement involves an increase in behavior whereas punishment involves a decrease in behavior; positive techniques involve a presented stimulus whereas negative techniques involve a removed stimulus.

In the Figure 3 matrix, the topics are the steps in positive reinforcement (i.e., behavior, stimulus presented and behavior increases), the repeatable category is example, and the details are the three example parts. Within-topic relations are formed by matching portions of the definition (the steps) to corresponding portions of the example. For instance, raking leaves is an example of behavior and receiving $5 is an example of a presented stimulus. Across-topic relations are formed when the example parts are learned as a sequence of events and not in isolation.

How can a learner tell which representation is appropriate? Certain alert words in lecture or text specify the appropriate representation. Words such as types, parts, components, characteristics, and kinds signal a hierarchical representation. The phrases "three types of saws," "two characteristics of leaves," and "kinds of cells," for example, all signal a hierarchical structure. Words such as steps, stages, phases, next, before, procedure, and period signal a sequential representation. The phrases "eight phases of the moon," "the next character introduced," and "experimental procedure," for example, all signal a sequential structure. Comparative words such as whereas, however, contrast, and similar signal a matrix representation. The phrase "women on the other hand" signals a matrix structure comparing women with the previous topic—perhaps men. Adjectives like deciduous and liberal also signal a potential comparison with yet unstated topics. If there are deciduous trees, there must be other types (i.e., evergreens); if there are liberal views, there must be conservative and moderate views too.

It is important to remember that even though the initial representation is a hierarchy or sequence, all hierarchy or sequence representations can be extended into a matrix representation. Although it is possible that a text only reports the two types of Lepidoptera or the four stages in the development of butterflies, this information is potentially embellished with the addition of repeatable categories and related details. For instance, the wings, antennae, and color are important repeatable categories for comparing moths and butterflies. Similarly, the appearance, activity and location of the butterfly throughout the stages are germane to its development.

Utility

The Matrix Representation System uses three simple patterns to represent structural knowledge. I contend that these three patterns have widespread utility. As evidence, I briefly introduce the five types of content structures proposed by Meyer (1985) through prose analysis (and illustrated by Jonassen et al., 1993) and show that the Matrix Representation System can represent all of them.

The *descriptive* structure focuses on hierarchical relationships. A descriptive text, for example, might describe the Finger Lakes Wine Region with respect to characteristics such as topography, climate, and wines. A hierarchical representation appears in Figure 4.

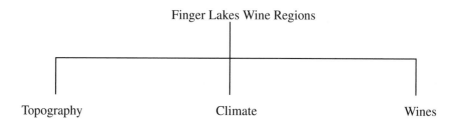

FIGURE 4. Hierarchy representing a descriptive structure.

The *collection plan* structure describes the attributes of a group of topics. The topics might be arranged hierarchically or sequentially. The topics are described along repeatable categories within a matrix framework as shown in Figure 5.

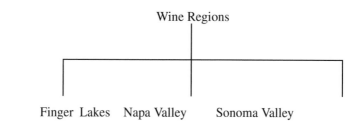

Topography:

Climate:

Wineries:

FIGURE 5. Matrix framework representing a collection plan structure.

Text arranged by *causation* specifies the antecedent conditions that produce consequences. For example, how varying weather conditions affect wine quality. Such relations are captured using a sequence representation as shown in Figure 6.

Weather and Wine Quality

Early freeze————————————→Frozen grapes————————————→ Sour wine

FIGURE 6. Sequence representing a causation structure.

Problem/Solution structures are also sequential. The sequential structure is antecedent event, problem, and solution. A sequence representation depicting a problem/solution structure for photography appears in Figure 7.

Photography Troubleshooting

Insufficient light————————→ Dark print————————————→ Decrease shutter speed

FIGURE 7. Sequence representing a problem/solution structure

The *comparison* structure relates two or more topics across several features. The topics are sequentially related or coordinate topics at the same level in a hierarchy. In either case, their comparative nature is illustrated by developing a matrix representation. A matrix framework for comparing computer models is shown in Figure 8.

Computer Models

Macintosh   IBM

Ease of use:

Software availability:

Cost:

Compatibility:

FIGURE 8. Matrix framework for comparison structure

How useful is the Matrix Representation System? Musgrave and Cohen (1971), for example, believe that all information has an underlying topic-repeatable category structure. Du Bois and Kiewra (1989) believe that most information ultimately has a topic-repeatable category structure and that information's underlying structure is hierarchical or sequential. It is from these structures that a matrix is potentially developed.

Lepidoptera

I. Moths
   A. Wings - Two sets
   B. Rest - Wings folded down like roof
   C. Antennae - Feathery
   D. Cocoon - Fuzzy
   E. Color - Subdued
   F. Flight - Twilight/night
   G. Development
     1. Egg
     2. Caterpillar
     3. Pupa
     4. Adult

II. Butterflies
   A. Color - Bright
   B. Flight - Day
   C. Wings - Two sets
   D. Rest - Wings outstretched
   E. Antennae - Long and thin with knobs
   F. Development
     1. Egg
     2. Caterpillar
     3. Pupa
     4. Adult

Figure 9. Outline representation of Lepidoptera passage.

Advantages Over Linear Representations

Earlier, the advantages of the Matrix Representation System compared with text were illustrated. In this section its advantages compared with linear representations such as lists or outlines are examined.

Figure 9 is an outline representation of the Lepidoptera passage. Compare it with the matrix representation in Figure 1 (p. 117). In terms of content, they are informationally equivalent (Larkin and Simon, 1987) because they include the same ideas. In terms of structure, however, they are computationally different (Larkin and Simon, 1987) because relational information is drawn more easily from the matrix. In particular, the matrix is more computationally efficient because it: a) reduces clutter by minimizing labels and details, b) localizes information, and c) facilitates perceptual enhancement (Larkin and Simon, 1987).

The outline is more cluttered. It presents each label (e.g., wing and rest) twice. The matrix presents a label (repeatable category) one time. The matrix also requires fewer details within its slots than the outline. Common information (e.g., about wings and development) need only appear once in the matrix. The elimination of repetitive labels and details in the matrix reduces clutter and also emphasizes the shared characteristics between topics.

The matrix localizes related information better than the outline. Notice how information about wings, for example, is adjacent in the matrix but separated by several intervening ideas in the outline. Both representations localize information within topics (e.g., moths) but only the matrix localizes information across topics (i.e., moths and butterflies) making coordinate relations more apparent.

Perceptual enhancement occurs when the "big picture" (Winn, 1988) or overriding structure is readily apparent. At a glance, it is evident from the matrix that two types of Lepidoptera are compared along seven dimensions. On two dimensions they are similar, on four dimensions they are different, and on one dimension there is missing information. Upon closer inspection an important pattern emerges from the matrix. It appears that butterflies have more pronounced characteristics than moths. The overriding structure and important pattern develop far more slowly, if at all, from the outline. Its one-dimensional structure obscures these pictures.

Turn now to the next page for another example about fish represented in outline (Figure 10) and matrix (Figure 11) form. Examine those and determine whether the matrix holds an advantage in terms of reducing clutter, localizing information, and facilitating perpetual enhancement.

The labels for social group, color, size and diet appear a total of 24 times in the outline but only four times in the matrix. If more fish are studied, then the number of labels increases for the outline but not for the matrix. Because some information is identical for certain fish (i.e., size and diet), the matrix reports these details one time. Consequently, it contains less information within its cells than the outline. In this case, six repetitive details are eliminated from the matrix. Of course, reducing labels and details not only reduces clutter but emphasizes the shared characteristics among fish.

In terms of localization, the outline separates related information. For example, when examining fish size, there are three intervening facts (pertaining to diet, social group, and color) between each size designation. This is not true with the matrix where all fish sizes appear together in one row. Because there is no intervening information, the matrix reduces the amount of search necessary to locate information.

The fish matrix facilitates perceptual enhancement more than the outline. Only with the matrix representation does the "big picture" or integrative patterns emerge readily. Examining the matrix vertically, it is immediately clear that fish at 200 feet eat algae, are 150 cm in length, and are dark colored. The outline surrenders this information only with greater search and effort. Examining the matrix both vertically and horizontally, the major patterns emerge. As fish swim deeper they consume larger prey, increase in size, become lighter in color, and tend to swim in larger social groups. Extracting this pattern from the outline involves extensive data manipulation. The pieces of the puzzle are there, but lie scattered and unattached—like bones lined up across the floor. A matrix representation comparing the outline and matrix with regard to informational and computational efficiency appears in Figure 12.

Depth of Fish

I. 200 ft
  A. Lup Fish
    1. Social Group - Small
    2. Color - Black
    3. Size - 150 cm
    4. Diet - Algae
  B. Hat Fish
    1. Social Group - Solitary
    2. Color - Brown
    3. Size - 150 cm
    4. Diet - Algae

II. 400 ft
  A. Arch
    1. Social Group - Solitary
    2. Color - Blue
    3. Size - 300 cm
    4. Diet - Minnows
  B. Bone
    1. Social Group - School
    2. Color - Orange
    3. Size - 300 cm
    4. Diet - Minnows

III. 600 ft
  A. Scale
    1. Social Group-School
    2. Color - Yellow
    3. Size - 500 cm
    4. Diet - Flounders
  B. Tin
    1. Social Group - Small
    2. Color - Tan
    3. Size - 500 cm
    4. Diet - Flounders

FIGURE 10. Outline representation for Depth of Fish.

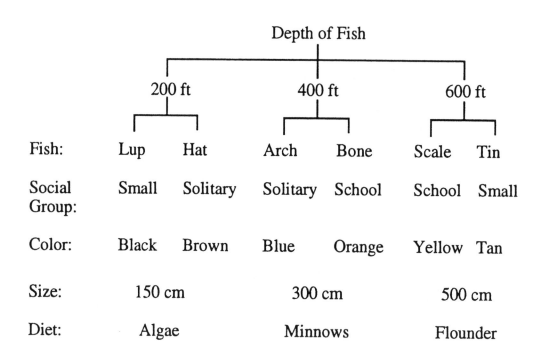

FIGURE 11. Matrix representation for Depth of Fish.

Comparison With Other Spatial Representation Systems

Researchers and practitioners have developed several alternative types of text representations for displaying structural knowledge (see Jonassen et al., 1993). These include, among others, lists, outlines, matrices, tree diagrams, flow charts, concept maps, networks, graphs, numerical tables, topographical maps, pictures and illustrations.

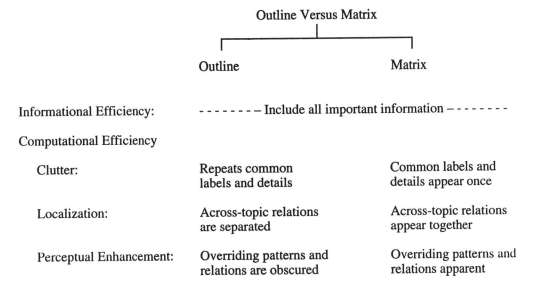

FIGURE 12. Matrix representation comparing outline and matrix.

Some of these are isomorphic; they present a representation nearly identical with its source. Topographical maps, illustrations, and pictures are isomorphic representations. These are powerful representations when a visual depiction is helpful such as showing the parts of a flower (Kiewra, Du Bois, Weiss and Schantz, 1992), or how brakes operate (Mayer and Gallini, 1990). The others are abstract representations in the sense they comprise the essential qualities of a larger thing. Some of these are one dimensional such as lists and outlines and are therefore limited, like text, because they present information sequentially. The others present information in a two-dimensional or spatial form. Some of these have highly specific purposes such as graphs and numerical tables which display numerical data. Others, I believe, have limited utility with respect to reducing clutter, localizing information, and facilitating perceptual enhancement. This is demonstrated by examining the three most popular abstract representation systems: semantic maps, concept maps, and networks (see Jonassen et al., 1993) along these dimensions.

Semantic maps represent concepts hierarchically. They position the primary or superordinate concept in the center and subordinate concepts around the primary concept. Related ideas are listed below the corresponding subordinate concept. An example of a concept map for the fish material introduced previously is shown in Figure 13.

The semantic map is informationally equivalent to the matrix in Figure 11. Computationally, it appears more cluttered, less localized, and less perceptually enhancing. The semantic map contains 30 labels versus four for the matrix. Because common information is listed separately for each fish, the semantic map contains 30 details versus 21 for the matrix. In terms of localization, the semantic map physically separates related information (e.g., about diet) whereas the matrix positions related information along the same row. The overriding pattern and relationships readily apparent in the matrix are obscured in the semantic map which fails to provide perceptual enhancement.

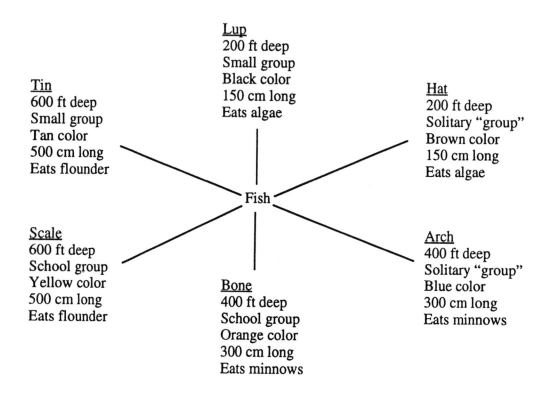

FIGURE 13. Semantic map for Depth of Fish

Concept maps (Novak and Gowin, 1984) and networks (Holley and Dansereau, 1984; Lambiotte, Dansereau, Cross, and Reynolds, 1989) are similar because both represent concepts and specify the links between concepts. Their primary difference is that the link names are invented by the concept map builder but chosen from a menu of six designated links by the network builder. A concept map/network for the fish material is found in Figure 14.

The same problems inherent in the semantic map are found with the concept map/network. First, 30 labels are used and common details are listed separately. The additional labels and details add clutter and shroud common characteristics between fish relative to the matrix. Second, related information is separated physically rather than located adjacently. Last, the concept map/network does not aid perceptual enhancement. The overriding pattern and interrelationships are hidden.

In summary, neither of these representations appear as effective as the matrix for representing information about fish. Of course, research is needed to determine the relative benefits of representation systems for various learning tasks.

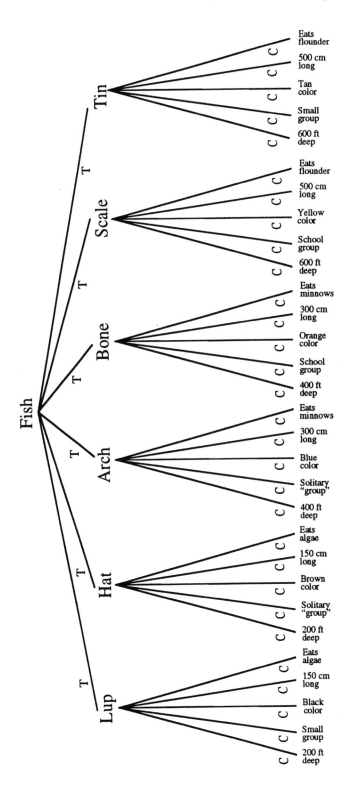

Note:　T = type and C = characteristic

FIGURE 14. Concept map/network for Depth of Fish

THEORY

Why should the matrix representation system facilitate learning? This question is examined in terms of how information is processed in memory. Two sequential memory processes are necessary for learning: attention and encoding. Each of these have two subprocesses. Attention depends on the sequential subprocesses of pattern recognition and selective attention. Encoding has two components: organization and integration. Figure 15 shows the relations among these processes and subprocesses.

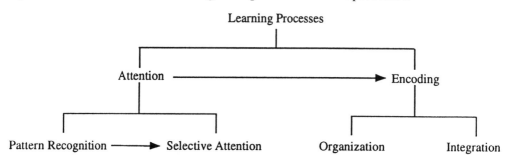

FIGURE 15. Learning processes supporting the Matrix Representation System

Learning begins when information is received through our senses and identified through pattern recognition. Pattern recognition occurs almost instantaneously and without effort. Familiar concepts are recognized by their physical properties. At a carnival, for example, you might recognize at once a giant ferris wheel, a row of game booths, and a concession area housing several merchants.

During selective attention, attention is focused on selected aspects of the environment. At the carnival, for example, you might attend selectively to the concession area focusing on merchant names, the signs displaying prices, and the lengths of service lines.

Organization occurs when selected ideas are restructured in a coherent manner. Organization is also called building internal connections (Mayer, 1984) because the learner makes logical connections among available ideas. At the carnival you might organize selected ideas regarding food as shown in Figure 16. In this case, your organizing framework is the types of food. Subsumed beneath each food type are the representative merchants. The framework's slots house information about the line length and food prices associated with each merchant. Inherent in this organizational structure are several internal connections. You realize, for example, that prices range from $3.00 to $6.00; that lines are either short or long, but most are long; and that low prices are associated with long lines whereas high prices are associated with short lines.

Integration occurs when new knowledge is related with previous knowledge already in memory. This process is also called *building external connections* (Mayer, 1984) because the learner connects new information with previously acquired knowledge outside the current learning context. In considering what to eat at the carnival, for example, you might recall that you dislike tacos, that pizza from the Pizza Parlor gives you heart-

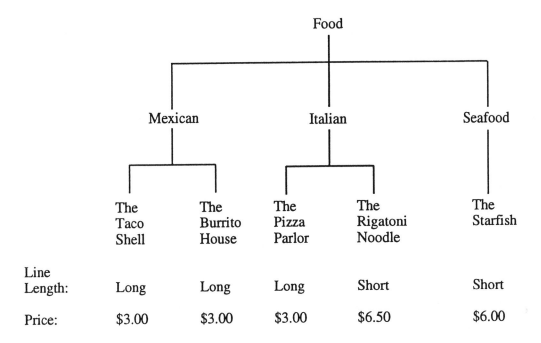

FIGURE 16. Representation showing organized food information

burn, and that you disdain long lines. Integration provides a context for new learning and serves to make new knowledge more meaningful.

I believe that the matrix can facilitate information processing with respect to these four subprocesses. Each subprocess is examined in turn.

Pattern Recognition

One advantage the matrix has over an outline or text is that more structural knowledge is available from the matrix upon immediate viewing. Information's structure is at once apparent. It is quickly apparent, for example, whether information is organized hierarchically or sequentially. If it is hierarchical, the numbers of levels, topics, and subtopics are known at a glance. Furthermore, the number of repeatable categories pertaining to the topics is known instantly. The structure of knowledge must be sewn together from a text and even an outline. Initial processing of a matrix representation is simultaneous; initial processing of an outline or text is successive—one idea at a time.

Few attentional resources are necessary to identify a matrix's informational structure just as few resources are necessary to perceive these three dots (∴) as a triangle. In this sense, the matrix provides valuable information before the learner even sets out to process it. Because minimal mental effort is spent uncovering the information's structure in a matrix or other well designed representation, Waller (1981) contends that such representations present a "visual argument." Through visual argument, ideas are transmitted via a spatial arrangement of words rather than ongoing written language. By "seeing" ideas, readers are relieved of the burden of searching and untangling complex relationships embedded in text.

Glance back at the operant conditioning representation in Figure 2 (p. 118). Immediately, the information's structure is apparent. There is a top-level concept (i.e., operant conditioning) subsuming two concepts (i.e., reinforcement and punishment). Each of these subsume two more concepts. These most subordinate concepts are described along two repeatable categories.

Selective Attention

During selective attention, learners focus attention on a few selected ideas. Because the matrix generally contains a subset of the text's ideas, it directs attention better than the text (Kiewra and Sperling-Dennison, 1992). A matrix might also facilitate selective attention better than an outline even though both representations incorporate identical ideas. Recall that only the matrix's streamlined structure reduces repetitive labels and details (see Figures 10 and 11, p. 124).

Perhaps most importantly, the matrix's structure guides the route of selective attention. Its spatial structure encourages students to search for hierarchical, sequential, and coordinate relations. Returning to Figure 2, a student attends to hierarchical relations (e.g., there are positive and negative types of reinforcement) and coordinate relations (e.g., reinforcement results in an increase in behavior, whereas punishment results in a decrease in behavior).

Organization

To paraphrase Tukey (1990), the purpose of a matrix representation is to organize information, not store facts. A matrix should serve more than an attention function, it should aid the learner in connecting ideas. The hallmark of an effective matrix should be its ability to facilitate relational understanding.

There are a variety of types of connections that a student might learn from studying a matrix. These include sequential, hierarchical, within-topic and across-topic (i.e., coordinate). Based on the algebraic representation in Figure 17, sequential relations exist among a, b, and c. Hierarchical relations exist between b and d, e, and f. Across-topic relations exist among d, e, and f as observed among g, h, and i; and j, k, and l. Within-topic relations exist among d, g, and j; e, h, and k; and f, i, and l.

In some instances, a matrix has facilitated organization (Kiewra and Sperling-Dennison, 1992) and in other instances it has not (Kiewra, Du Bois, Staley, and Robinson, 1992). Contradicting findings may be the result of the learner's activities. No matter how well organized or developed a matrix is, internal connections are formed by the learner who searches the matrix in appropriate ways. A matrix that represents across-topic relations is essentially useless if the learner does not search the rows of the matrix and operate on the information within the rows to form such relations. In other words, the matrix is a tool that facilitates, but does not ensure, internal connections. If the learner, for example, studies the four subordinate concepts in Figure 2 independently by examining

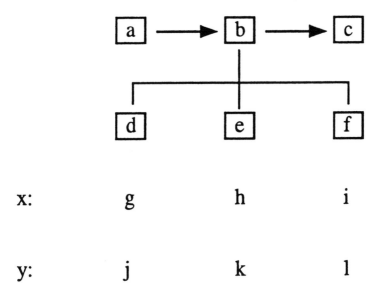

FIGURE 17. Algebraic representation illustrating various relation types.

the matrix in a vertical fashion only, then he/she would not understand the concepts' interrelationships.

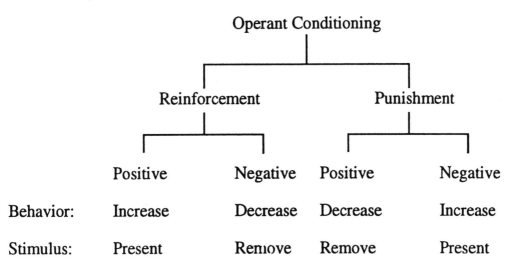

FIGURE 18. Revised operant conditioning representation; information is sorted but generally unrelated.

Contradictory findings can also be attributed to the nature of the learning materials. Matrices that merely sort arbitrary information should not be more effective than lists or outlines in building internal connections. Consider the revised operant conditioning representation in Figure 18. This representation merely sorts information. No relationships or patterns emerge when the information is searched horizontally. In this case, the matrix offers little help in building internal connections.

A third factor possibly producing conflicting results is the type of dependent measure used to assess organization. Matrices should primarily affect the learning of across-topic relations. The matrix's two-dimensional structure accents these relations that are ordinarily obscured in linear representations. Organizational tests that fail to tap across-topic relations are, in part, invalid.

Integration

The matrix can support integration in two ways. First, learners can acquire new information more easily if they have an organized structure in memory for assimilating new knowledge. The notion is consistent with Schema theory (Rumelhart, 1980; Rumelhart and Ortony, 1977) which contends that information in memory is organized categorically along various features (as is a matrix). For example, a building schema might include the categories house, school, and office and the features size and location. The schema's slots or cells store new information intersecting the category members and their features (e.g., most houses are located in the suburbs).

Second, integration can occur when a completed matrix is extended or embellished with previously acquired knowledge. A matrix representation can be modified in three ways: horizontally, vertically, or within its cells. As an example, return to Figure 2 (p. 118). Suppose the learner has past knowledge about another operant technique such as extinction. This concept is added by extending the matrix horizontally. The learner's personal examples of behaviors warranting the various techniques are added by extending the matrix vertically and including the repeatable category "example." Previous knowledge that the stimulus should be presented immediately for positive reinforcement is recorded within the matrix cell intersecting positive reinforcement and stimulus. These integrative adaptations are shown in the boxed portion of Figure 19.

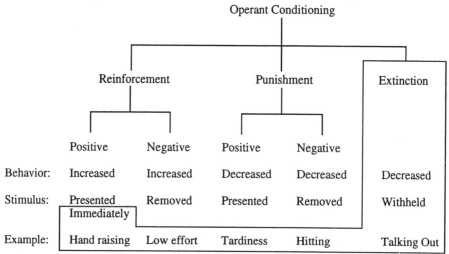

FIGURE 19. Representation including external connections.

REVIEW OF RESEARCH

In this section, research on matrix representations is reviewed versus more linear representations such as text and outlines. The guiding framework is the theoretical ideas presented previously: attention and encoding.

Attention

Attention has two subprocesses: pattern recognition and selective attention. During pattern recognition, the reader rapidly perceives the information's structure. I know of no research investigating pattern recognition for matrix representations. Pattern recognition can be assessed by providing students via computer an outline, text, or matrix representation and inquiring about the information's structure. For example, students might be asked whether the overriding structure is hierarchical or sequential, or about the number of topics, subtopics, features (repeatable categories), and details that appear. Assessing the time needed to respond to such questions can determine if a matrix is previewed more rapidly and accurately than an outline or text.

An experiment, similar in methodology, determined how rapidly different representations are searched during the selective attention phase. Robinson (1994) presented a question to students before they viewed an outline, text, or matrix representation presented by computer. Answering the question depended upon locating two or more details in the representations. For instance, a question might ask which of four snakes is shortest in length. This information was spread over four text paragraphs, four outline sections, or presented within the same matrix row. Students located relevant information and formulated a response more rapidly when viewing the matrix than when viewing the text or outline. This is evidence that selective attention is more rapidly applied to across-topic information in a matrix than a text or outline.

Selective attention was assessed in three experiments conducted by Kiewra and Sperling-Dennison. Their experiments investigated the utility of representations as sup-

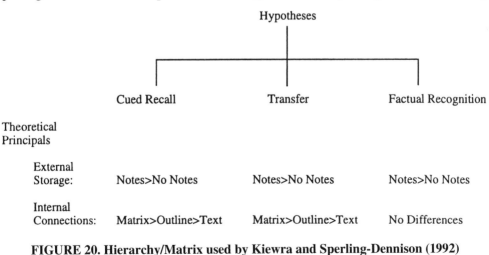

FIGURE 20. Hierarchy/Matrix used by Kiewra and Sperling-Dennison (1992)

plements to a research article. In the first experiment (Kiewra and Sperling-Dennison, 1992), graduate students assigned to one of two groups studied a two-and-a-half page research article for 45 minutes. The article, adapted from the *Journal of Educational Psychology* (1988, *80*: 595–597), pertained to different forms of note taking. One group received only the article; the other group received the article plus four representations. Three of these were hierarchy/matrices; the other was a sequence/hierarchy. One of the representations appears in Figure 20. The others pertained to the experimental method and results described in the research article.

A cued-recall test was administered immediately following the study period. Some items could be answered from the representations (represented items) and some could only be answered from the text (nonrepresented items). Results indicated that students studying the text-plus-representations recalled more represented information. The authors contend that the representations served a selective attention function as evidenced by the superior performance of the representation group on the represented items. Having this information represented outside the text drew students' attention to it.

Experiment 2 (Kiewra and Sperling-Dennison, 1992) was designed to further test representation's selective attention function. A group that received the text with pertinent information underlined (that which appeared in the representations) was added. The research question was whether underlining served as powerful an attention function as representations. A significant group by item type interaction revealed that with respect to represented information the ordering of means was text-plus-representationsΠ underlined text Π text only. With respect to nonrepresented information, the ordering of means was opposite. This interaction indicates that representations served a superior selective attention function, but at same cost. They produced the least recall for nonrepresented information.

A third experiment (Sperling-Dennison and Kiewra, 1993) added yet another group to the previous groups. Participants in this group studied outlines that were informationally equivalent to the spatial representations. This group was added to assess whether it was the structure of the spatial representations that produced consistent selective attention effects over text and underlined text.

Results indicated that both outline and spatial representation groups outperformed the text-only group on represented facts items. For nonrepresented facts items, however, there were no differences among groups. These results indicate that outlines and spatial representations both serve a selective attention function relative to studying the text. However, the outline and matrix proved equal in their ability to aid selective attention.

In summary, spatial representations serve an attention focusing function relative to text or underlined text. They are, however, no more effective than outlines that select and display the same information. In terms of search time, however, a matrix representation is attended to more rapidly than an outline or text.

Encoding

Encoding is the process whereby new information is stored in memory. It is possible to assess whether encoded information is stored as isolated facts, organized structures, or integrated with previous knowledge. Recall tests commonly assess memory for facts. Relational tests or writing tasks assessing coherence measure organization. Problem solving tasks assess integration. Integration produces the meaningful learning necessary to solve new problems (Mayer, 1984). In the following subsections, research is reviewed regarding how matrix representations affect a) memory for factual details, b) relational learning, c) written discourse, and d) problem

Memory for factual details. The fish representations presented as Figures 10 and 11 (see p. 124) were used in a series of experiments by Kiewra and his colleagues assessing memory for factual details.[*] In each experiment, participants read or heard a short passage about six fictitious fish. Five different facts were presented about each fish pertaining to its depth, social group, color, length, and diet. The text presented this information in a linear format and did not reveal how this information interrelated. In fact, the passage obscured the similarities between fish (e.g., both the Hat and the Lup fish are 150 cm long and eat algae) and the overriding patterns among all the fish (e.g., fish swimming at progressively deeper depths are lighter in color, larger in size, and consume larger prey).

In the first experiment (Kiewra, Du Bois, Staley, and Robinson, 1992), the comparison of interest was between those studying a matrix (Figure 11) versus those studying an outline (Figure 10) for 15 minutes. The representations were informationally, but not computationally, equivalent (Larkin and Simon, 1987). The two-dimensional matrix contained fewer labels, placed like information in closer proximity, and provided greater perceptual enhancement than the outline. The interrelationships or patterns among ideas were more apparent in the matrix.

A memory test was administered immediately following the study episode and again two days later. As seen in the graph in Figure 21, the matrix group outperformed the outline group for both immediate and delayed recall. Performance on delayed testing also declined more for the outline group than for the matrix group. These findings indicate that the matrix produced greater immediate and delayed recall than the outline and that learning from the matrix was relatively resistant to memory loss over a moderate two-day delay

In a second experiment (Kiewra, Du Bois, Staley, and Robinson, 1992), the matrix and outline representations were examined in terms of efficiency and long-term retention. To assess efficiency, participants studied representations for 5, 10, or 15 minutes. It was thought that the matrix, given its perceptual advantages, would have its biggest advantage over the outline at 5 minutes. To assess long-term retention, memory tests were administered immediately after study and again five days later. The matrix proved relatively effective for remembering facts. Students studying the matrix statistically outperformed those studying the text, and descriptively outperformed those studying the outline. The matrix's advantage over the outline was most apparent with delayed testing. This observed advantage following a five-day delay supports and extends the findings

---

[*]After the chapter was typeset, Kiewra and his colleagues reclassified their "memory for factual details" test as a "between-concepts relations" test. Their rationale was that the test measures memory for *related* facts more than for *independent* facts. A sample test item is "what two fish eat algae?"

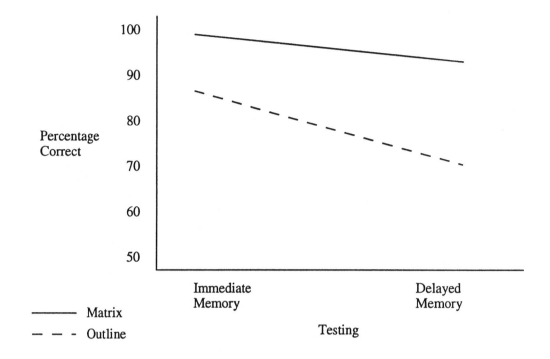

FIGURE 21. Comparison of outline and matrix representations for immediate and delayed memory tests (Kiewra, Du Bois, Staley, and Robinson, 1992).

from the first experiment where the test was delayed two days. In both experiments the matrix facilitated long-term retention.

Finally, with regard to efficiency, there was mild support favoring the matrix over the outline when study time was brief. Although results were not significant, following a five-minute study period the matrix group averaged 94 percent correct versus 83 percent correct for the outline group. After 10 minutes of study, the groups performed virtually the same (94 percent for the matrix group and 92 percent for the outline group).

A third experiment (Kiewra, Levin, Kim, Meyers, Renandya, and Hwang, 1994) investigated whether a matrix for fish could be enhanced by using pictures or mnemonic pictures in place of verbal descriptions. In the picture conditions, the row headings designated social grouping, the column headings designated depth, and along the bottom appeared a series of rulers against which the fish could be measured. Each fish was drawn to its relative size, and in its appropriate color. Solitary fish were pictured alone; those in small groups were pictured in pairs; those in schools were pictured among several fish. The food for each fish was also drawn to resemble the actual food in appearance and relative size. The mnemonic pictures were drawn to help students recall the names of the fish and associate the names with related characteristics. The Hat fish, for example, was drawn to resemble a dark brown hat. The tin fish looked like a tin can and was colored light tan. The "mnematrix" (mnemonic picture matrix) appears in Figure 22.

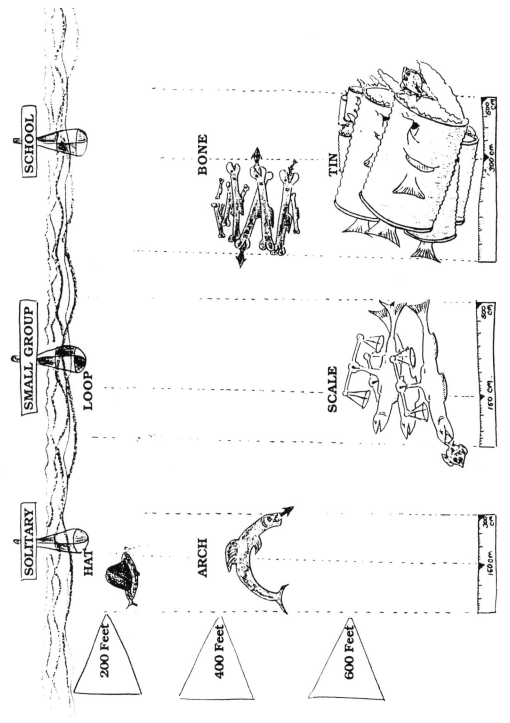

FIGURE 22. "Mnematrix" for Depth of Fish.

The three matrix forms (verbal, picture, and mnematrix) were compared with three corresponding outline forms, and to a read-only control group. Groups studied their instructional materials for 10 minutes before taking several memory tests. Results indicated that the mnematrix group outperformed the text-only control group across memory tests. The conventional matrix group also outperformed the control group on a memory test assessing color. Mnemonic pictures proved generally effective. They boosted memory whether they were presented in matrix or outline form. This study showed first that a matrix can incorporate other instructional aids such as pictures and mnemonics, and that the combination of pictures, mnemonics, and matrix is a powerful one under these conditions.

In summary, the following conclusions can be drawn from the memory studies reported here. First, the matrix was superior to the outline for immediate retention and particularly long-term retention. Second, the matrix was somewhat more efficient than the outline. More information was learned more quickly from the matrix. Third, the matrix can incorporate pictures and mnemonics that bolster memory performance. Studies by Day (1988), Jones, Amiran, and Katims (1985), and Kiewra, Du Bois, Christian, McShane, Meyerhoffer, and Roskelley (1991) also support the memory advantage of matrix representations versus linear representations or *Memory for relationships*. In the experiments reviewed earlier pertaining to learning from a research article (Kiewra and Sperling-Dennison, 1992; Sperling-Dennison and Kiewra, 1993), relational learning was also assessed. Participants were administered tests assessing relationships among ideas. A sample test question was, "what are the internal connection hypotheses for recall, transfer and recognition tests." (See Figure 20.) In general, results indicated that studying the research article plus representations produced higher relational performance than studying the research article only or the research article with important (represented) ideas underlined. However, the outline representations and spatial representations had similar effects on relational learning.

Relational learning was also assessed in experiments involving fish learning (Kiewra, Du Bois, Staley, and Robinson, 1992). Relational items probed the overriding relationships between fish characteristics. One relational question, for example, asked about the relationship between depth and length. In Experiment 1, matrix, outline, and text groups did not differ significantly on relational performance. The practical differences among means, however, was noteworthy. The matrix group averaged 75 percent correct whereas the outline group averaged 65 percent correct, just barely above the text-only control group (62 percent). When study times were varied in Experiment 2, both matrix and outline representations boosted relational performance beyond that of studying the text alone. No relational performance differences were found, however, between outline and matrix studiers.

Two other experiments by Kiewra and colleagues investigated relational learning. In each experiment, participants viewed a 19-minute videotaped lecture about five types of creativity. The lecture contained 1,881 words and 121 idea units, and was delivered at a rate of about 100 wpm. For each type of creativity, nine different features (e.g., definition, motivation, distinguishing characteristics, and myths) were discussed in varying order.

In the first experiment (Kiewra, Du Bois, Christian, and McShane, 1988), college students viewed the lecture and then reviewed either a set of complete notes for 25 minutes or reviewed mentally . Those studying notes either reviewed a verbatim text of the lecture, outline notes, or matrix notes. All materials contained all 121 idea units. The outline contained 758 words; the matrix contained 610 words. The matrix contained 45 cells that were the intersections of the five types of creativity and their nine common features.

Following the review period, students were administered a 30-item transfer test. It comprised 10 relational items (e.g., which two types of creativity take a lifetime to develop?) and 20 conceptual items where novel examples of the types of creativity were presented for classification. On the transfer test, only the matrix group (M=63 percent) significantly outperformed the text group (M=36 percent). The matrix group scored somewhat higher than the outline group (M=56 percent). The authors contended that the matrix's advantage for transfer performance occurred because the matrix best facilitated across-topic relations among the five types of creativity. An increased understanding of similarities and differences among creativity types helped students answer relational items (how are types of creativity similar or different?) and concept items whose solution involved making subtle comparisons among the creativity types.

A second study (Kiewra, Du Bois, Christian, McShane, Meyerhoffer, and Roskelley, 1991) introduced the matrix to lecture note taking. College students viewed the 19-minute creativity lecture while either recording notes in an outline framework, a matrix framework, or on lined paper in a conventional manner. The blank outline and matrix frameworks were identical to those used in the study by Kiewra, Du Bois, Christian, and McShane (1988) but contained no details. Instead, blank spaces were provided for students to record ideas. The matrix framework appears in Figure 23.

Type of Creativity	Expressive	Adaptive	Innovative	Emergentive	School
Definition					
Time Demand to Display Creativity					
Time Demand to Develop Creativity					
Motivation					
Distinguishing Characteristics					
Related Characteristics					
Examples					
Myths					
Myths Expelled					

FIGURE 23. Matrix framework for note taking (Kiewra, Du Bois, Christian, McShane, Meyerhoffer, and Roskelly, 1991).

With respect to relational performance, mean scores did not vary significantly. However, the pattern of scores mirrored those from the earlier study (Kiewra, Du Bois, Christian, and McShane, 1988) and supports the predicted advantage of the matrix for relational performance *M*s=73 percent, 68 percent, and 64 percent for matrix, conventional, and outline notes, respectively).

In summary, the results from these studies indicate that the matrix is superior to text for relational learning. Relative to the outline, however, the matrix shows only a trend toward producing higher relational performance. One problem inherent in these studies, however, is that students were not trained in how to study representations. In fact, students in one study (Kiewra, Du Bois, Christian, and McShane, 1988) were actually observed transforming a provided matrix into an outline. As mentioned previously, the matrix's contribution to relational learning depends on a) students seeking internal connections, b) meaningful relationships being presented within the matrix, and c) dependent measures assessing relationships, particularly across topics. Another means for assessing relational learning is by examining the organization of written.

Written discourse. Four experiments were conducted (Benton, Kiewra, Whitfall, and Dennison, 1993) that examined, in part, whether different note forms affect the organizing processes of writing. In all four experiments, college students viewed the 19-minute videotaped lecture about creativity described earlier. In Experiments 1 and 2, participants recorded notes on matrix or outline frameworks or recorded conventional notes or no notes. Following the lecture, students had 25 minutes to write a compare-and-contrast essay about three types of creativity. One half of the students in each note-taking group wrote essays with their notes available, whereas the other half wrote without notes. In Experiment 1, the writing task was administered immediately after the lecture. In Experiment 2, it was administered following a one-week delay. In Experiments 3 and 4, participants listened to the lecture without recording notes. Afterward they completed the essay assignment with or without notes made available by the experimenters. Those writing with notes were provided with one of three sets of complete notes differing only in form: conventional, outline, or matrix. The writing assignment was immediate in Experiment 3 and delayed one week in Experiment 4.

There were two results of interest. In Experiment 1, students with matrix notes wrote essays containing more cohesive ties than students with outline notes. Cohesive ties are a measure of organization. They are words or phrases that correctly compare or contrast one element of text with another (Halliday and Hasan, 1976). Words and phrases like *similar, however, whereas* and *on the other hand* are examples of cohesive ties. The use of cohesive ties is indicative of a cohesive writing style that interrelates information for the reader. It is contrasted with a linear style where ideas are presented sequentially and independent from potentially related ideas.

In Experiment 4, those writing from matrix notes produced more coherent essays than those writing without notes following a one-week delay. Coherence, like cohesive ties, is an indication of organization. Coherence was measured based upon the Bamberg (1983) coherence scale that globally assesses written discourse along a continuum essentially ranging from incomprehensible to fully coherent where the essay clearly identifies topics, flows smoothly, and provides a clean sense of closure.

Although the matrix did not uniformly produce higher quality writing throughout the four experiments, it was the only form of notes that affected the organization of written discourse. These findings support Langer's (1984) finding that the degree to which topic-related knowledge is organized influences writing quality.

The benefit of matrix notes for increasing organization in written discourse was also seen among college students who read a lengthy text about personality disorders and then reviewed outline, matrix, or text materials. Students reviewing matrix materials wrote responses to compare and contrast essay items that contained more comparisons and more cohesive ties than students reviewing outlines (Robinson, 1993).

In summary, matrices facilitate the organization subprocess of encoding as seen through written discourse. Students who use matrices produce essays that are more coherent, comparative, and cohesive.

Problem solving. Effective problem solving depends on effective problem representation. For example, Bovenmeyer, Lewis, and Mayer (1987) found that students who represent the elements in a word problem generate more correct solutions than those who do not generate a representation. For purposes of this chapter, studies are reviewed where problem solvers use a matrix representation versus another form of representation (e.g., list or hierarchy) in attempts to problem solve. The reported studies show a clear advantage for the matrix across different problem types.

Early investigations of the matrix for problem solving were conducted by Schwartz and his colleagues (Polich and Schwartz, 1974; Schwartz, 1971; Schwartz and Fattaleh, 1972). They presented who-done-it-type deductive reasoning problems for which solvers had to match values along several dimensions by reasoning deductively from sentence clues. In one problem, participants were given a list of statements pertaining to a) the names of men in a hospital, b) their illness, and c) their room numbers. Sentences only presented partial information such as the man in Room 101 has asthma or Mr. Jones has cancer.

The problem entailed determining what disease Mr. Young had. Results showed that when sentence information was represented in a matrix, rather than in a list or hierarchy, problems were solved more accurately. This was particularly true when problem size increased (Polich and Schwartz, 1974) because the matrix permitted the greatest number of relations to be deduced correctly and simultaneously.

A study reported by Day (1988) showed how studying a medication schedule represented in a matrix form (Figure 24) produced more accurate problem solving than studying it in list form (Figure 25). The list contained the names of the six drugs in a column with a dosage alongside each drug (e.g., one tablet four times a day). The matrix also listed the drugs in a column but used time designations (i.e., breakfast, lunch, dinner, and bedtime) as repeatable categories. A check mark in the matrix cells indicated when a drug should be taken (e.g., Lanoxin at breakfast). After studying the list or matrix, students were asked problems (e.g., If you leave home in the afternoon and will not be back until breakfast time the next day, how many Inderal should you take along?). Results showed a superior effect for studying the matrix. The matrix was superior, Day concluded, because, unlike the outline, it presented the union of medication and time information.)

	Breakfast	Lunch	Dinner	Bedtime
Lanoxin	✔			
Inderal	✔	✔		
Quinaglute	✔	✔	✔	✔
Carafate	✔	✔	✔	✔
Zantac	✔			✔
Coumadin				✔

FIGURE 24. Matrix medication schedule (Day, 1988).

Inderal	—	1 tablet 3 times a day
Lanoxin	—	1 tablet every a.m.
Carafate	—	1 tablet before meals and at bedtime
Zantac	—	1 tablet every 12 hours (twice a day)
Qunaglute	—	1 tablet 4 times a day
Coumadin	—	1 tablet a day

FIGURE 25. List medication schedule (Day, 1988).

A matrix representation was compared with a hierarchical representation for problem solving in a study by McGuinness (1986). Participants first memorized a two-level hierarchy or a 4 × 4 matrix showing family relations. The representations contained 16 names of family members. The birth order and nuclear descendants were given for each member.

After memorizing the representations, students were given word problems to solve pertaining to the representations. These had to be solved from memory. Results showed that participants studying the matrix responded to the test items more than twice as fast as those studying the hierarchy. This was true, however, only when problem solution involved searching the matrix in a horizontal manner across topics. In this case the information needed for solution was available in a single package by searching a single matrix row; the same information could be extracted only by searching over many intervening facts throughout the hierarchy. When solution depended on locating information within a single topic, the hierarchy and matrix were equally effective because information was equally accessible within a matrix column or within a single arm of the hierarchy. These results confirm the earlier point that matrix representations particularly facilitate across-topic comparisons.

The matrix has shown transferability across problems (Novick, 1990). Students received a probability problem and a matrix framework (an empty matrix) to aid in problem solution. When they later received a deductive reasoning problem (the patient/room/disease problem described earlier), these students were more likely to generate a matrix to aid solution than were students who had not received the original matrix problem. Although transfer was local (within the same experimental setting), it is encouraging to see that students used the matrix spontaneously and capably without training to solve new problems.

In summary, the matrix proved effective for problem solving. Problem solving is facilitated when meaningful learning—the integration of old and new knowledge—occurs (Mayer, 1984). In each case, the matrix representation allowed learners to see all the data in a meaningful way. John Tukey (1990) said that the greatest possibilities of visual displays lie in their vividness and inescapability of the intended message. A visual display can make you notice what you never intended to see.

MATRIX APPLICATIONS

In this section, how matrices are used to facilitate learning from lecture or text is illustrated. Also demonstrated is how they aid concept and rule learning, and support problem solving, critical thinking, and writing. Last, a method for teaching matrix use and construction is presented.

Learning from Lecture and Text

As a college instructor, I commonly present matrix representations to help students acquire lecture and text information. In lectures about memory, for example, I present a matrix comparing the three memory stores (sensory, short term, and long term) with respect to capacity, forgetting, and storage modality. Another example is a matrix comparing the temporal and capacity limitations of short-term memory in terms of evidence, and strategies for overcoming the limitation.

I also introduce generic matrix frameworks early in the educational psychology course usable throughout the course. Understanding a discipline's structure in advance is instrumental in focusing attention and facilitating encoding. One educational psychology framework organizes research evidence from various studies. All studies have a purpose, method, results, and conclusions. Another framework organizes competing theories. All learning theories have theorists, supporting data, and implications for education.

Generic frameworks exist in all fields. For example, history's structure is always a sequence of events. Cutting across all historical events are the generic repeatable categories: who, what, where, when, why, and so what. In literature, stories are compared along common repeatable categories such as plot, setting, and main characters or the phases of a story: introduction, conflict, climax, and resolution. In physics, all mechanical problems involve a) the external force on the object, b) qualities of the object itself, c) surface features, and d) the resulting movement.

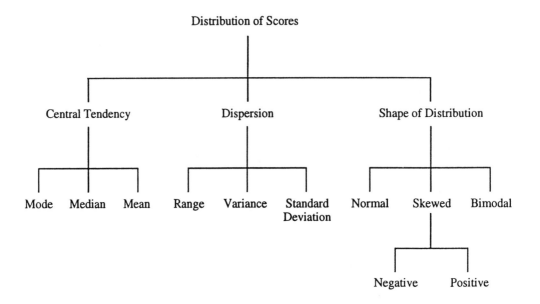

FIGURE 26. Hierarchical representation overviewing a section from a measurement text.

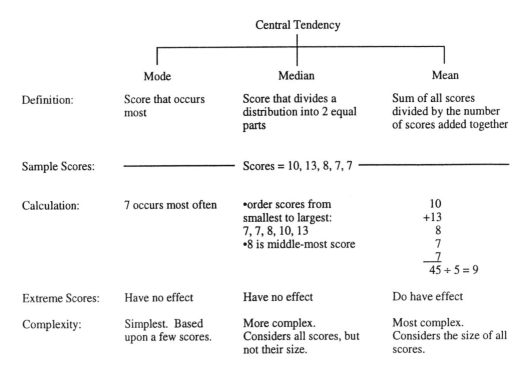

FIGURE 27. Matrix representation focusing on one portion of Distribution of Scores representation.

When my educational psychology students read a measurement chapter about distribution of scores, I supply four representations. Two of these are shown in Figures 26 and 27. Figure 26 is a hierarchy that overviews the structure among concepts. Figure 27 is a matrix that develops one arm of that hierarchy by comparing the three measures of central tendency. As you might suspect, the other representations compare the three dispersion concepts (i.e., range, variance, and standard deviation) and the four distribution shapes (i.e., normal, negatively skewed, positively skewed, and bimodal), respectively.

Concept Learning

Concept learning occurs when novel concept examples are correctly identified from among nonexamples (Gagné, 1985). For instance, the concept of triangle is acquired when triangles are identified from among a host of geometric shapes. A matrix aids concept learning two ways. First, its two-dimensional structure facilitates concept comparison. The geometric shapes matrix in Figure 28, for example, allows easy comparison of characteristics and examples across concepts. Second, a matrix representation can include a diverse range of examples beneath each concept. A range of examples is necessary to promote concept generalization. If a child saw only the single triangle example shown in Figure 28, the child might have difficulty recognizing triangles of different sizes, colors, and shapes (e.g., scalene and right).

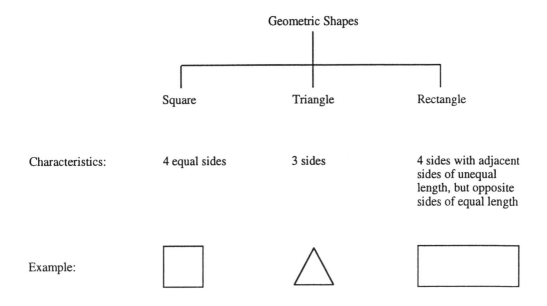

FIGURE 28. Matrix for learning geometric shapes.

The importance of experiencing a range of examples is perhaps best illustrated by a 36-year old doctor friend who had developed a rash he was unable to diagnose. Reluctantly (because he had to pay) he sought the counsel of a dermatologist who made the diagnosis instantaneously: shingles. Throughout medical school and his fledging practice, my friend had seen examples of shingles only in an acute phase among elderly patients (where it most commonly occurs). My friend's diagnostic powers could have been strengthened had a sequence-matrix been used during medical training. The topics are the disease stages from inception to restoration. The repeatable categories are various age levels. Within the matrix cells are pictures (examples) and details describing the disease throughout its progression for varying aged patients.

Rules

Rules are condition-action statements that govern our behavior in a variety of settings (Gagné, 1985). An example is the rule "if the case is objective (condition), then use *whom* (action)." This rule, if properly learned, is generalized to any situation such that a person uses *whom* appropriately in instances where the conditions apply. Another example is the mathematical rule "if there are parentheses, then do the operation in the parentheses first." This rule permits learners to approach correctly all problems like the following by first completing the operation within the parentheses: $6-(7+13)=-14$

In college instruction, many rules are learned such as the statistical rule "if a data set contains ordinal data, then a nonparametric (and not a parametric) test is appropriate." Students in a physical education class learning tennis may acquire the rule "if your opponent is at the baseline and hits a short ball, then progress to the net and volley."

How can the matrix assist in rule learning? Rules, like concepts, are best learned in families. For example, the communitive and associative rules of addition comprise a family of rules. If learned together, students can readily observe and confront similarities and differences between the rules. Because the matrix is effective for displaying coordinate information, it is ideal for presenting rules from within a family. An example follows in Figure 29.

Students often have trouble determining whether to use a comma or a semicolon. The rules for comma and semicolon use are actually better understood when presented together along with examples than if presented separately (as is common in most grammar texts). If these rules were learned separately, the learner might have trouble understanding and applying them. The learner might wonder what is meant by a main clause and coordinating conjunction. Presented as a family, with examples, it is evident that main clauses are parts of a sentence that can stand alone and that coordinating conjunctions such as *but* join main clauses. It is also apparent how the rules are similar (both include main clauses) and how they are different (the comma is used only with the coordinating conjunction).

Problem Solving and Critical Thinking

Problem solving and critical thinking is facilitated by representing the problem spatially (e.g., Day, 1988). In this section, examples of how a representation aids problem solving and critical thinking are presented.

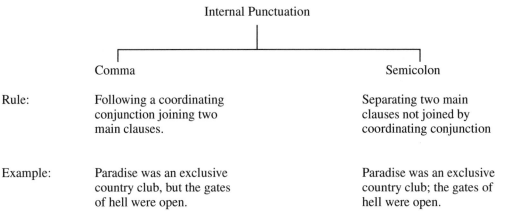

FIGURE 29. Matrix for learning comma and semicolon rules.

Try to solve the following algebra problem:

Two train stations are 50 miles apart. At 1 p.m. on Sunday a train pulls out from each of the stations and the trains start toward one another. Just as the trains pull out from the stations a hawk flies into the air in front of the first train and flies ahead to the front of the second train. When the hawk reaches the second train, it turns around and flies toward the first train. The hawk continues in this way until the trains meet. Assume that both trains travel at the speed of 25 miles per hour and that the hawk flies at a constant speed of 100 miles per hour. How many miles will the hawk have flown when the trains meet?

This is the type of problem that often makes students tremble. In reality it is a rather simple distance/rate/time problem. Once the given information is represented, the problem practically solves itself. The ideal representation for problem solution is a matrix. There are three main topics for comparison: Train A, Train B, and the Hawk. They should be compared with respect to the repeatable categories of distance, rate, and time as shown in Figure 30.

	Train A	Train B	Hawk
Distance:	25 miles	25 miles	?
Rate:	25 mph	25 mph	100 mph
Time:	?	?	?

FIGURE 30. Matrix for solving Trains and Hawk algebra problem.

Having developed this representation it is simple to derive the time that the trains traveled and the hawk flew (i.e., one hour). Knowing that the hawk flew 100 mph for one hour, the total distance for the hawk is computed (i.e., 100 miles) and the problem solved. Earlier, it was shown that the matrix is helpful for solving deductive reasoning problems and problems associated with adhering to a medication schedule.

Critical thinking depends on having a complete and organized body of knowledge from which to reason. That body of knowledge must be well understood in order to reason beyond it. For example, recall the information presented earlier about fish (see Fiure 11, p. 124). If that information were memorized as discrete facts, but its patterns were unnoticed, then it would be impossible for someone to think critically beyond that information. Only when the inherent patterns are understood could one reason beyond the information and speculate as to what fish are like at the unexplored depth of 1,200 feet. Understanding the existing patterns inherent in the matrix one can speculate that fish at that depth are 800–1,000 cm long, in schools, white-colored, and consumers of prey larger than flounders. This sort of extrapolation beyond existing data is possible only when existing data make sense. The matrix then has the potential to aid local understanding and facilitate reasoning beyond the data.

Facial Expressions

	Smile →	Surprise →	Laugh →	Fear →	Shyness →	Anger →	Laugh →	Guilt
Age:	2-3 mo.	4 mo.	4-5 mo.	5-7 mo.	6-8 mo.	8 mo.	1st yr.	2nd yr.
Response Inducement:	adult face	unusual situation	silly adult face	loud noise	new person	take away cookies	at event they cause	bad behavior

FIGURE 31. Matrix representation facilitating critical thinking.

Consider now the material from a college developmental psychology textbook about the development of facial expressions. Figure 31 is a matrix representation of that material. Upon examination of Figure 31, two trends or patterns that were not specified in the text are apparent. Notice that the first three expressions are positive and the next three are negative. Also notice that before age one, expressions are induced by environmental stimuli; after age one, they are induced by the child. These are perhaps important developmental patterns. Learners can now think critically about these data and speculate why such patterns exist. Is this evidence that children are inherently innocent but learn negative emotions? Does the facial musculature of infants constrain them to form positive expressions which in turn are met by social approval and reinforcement? Are facial expressions governed by cognitive or physical development? These critical issues are only explorable once the patterns of existing knowledge are known.

Writing

The planning phase is one of the primary components of the writing process (Flower and Hayes, 1977). However, novice writers often write off the top of their heads. Expert writers, on the other hand, are more planful, often writing from representations they construct. This section includes two examples showing how a matrix facilitates writing.

Suppose students were asked the following essay question on a test in developmental psychology. How could they plan their response?

> Trace the Piagetian stages of development with respect to age of onset, and social and cognitive characteristics.

Many students asked this type of question explode with any or all information available to them about the topic. Again, they are not planful. Developing and completing the matrix framework in Figure 32 can aid the planning and writing processes.

Piagetian Stages

Sensorimotor——→Preoperational———→Concrete———→Formal

Age of Onset:

Social
Characteristics:

Cognitive
Characteristics:

FIGURE 32. Matrix framework for writing Piagetian essay.

Now consider this essay question from history:

> Christopher Columbus's voyages to the new world were more characteristic of French and British exploration than those of the Spanish. Explain how this is so with respect to goals, methods, and relations with Native Americans.

Having the necessary information available in an organized form (as shown in Figure 33) is certainly important, but does not ensure a well structured essay. How the writer traverses the matrix in responding to the question is also important. In this last example, it is inappropriate for the writer to simply report the contents of each matrix cell or to discuss Columbus's, and the French and British explorations independent of one another. The question calls for a comparison of Columbus's voyages with those typical of other countries. To best answer this question, the writer should first discuss Columbus's goals, how they were similar to French and British goals, and then how they differed from the Spanish. Next the writer should discuss methods and relations with Native Americans using the same comparative format. There is evidence that students who use a matrix do produce essays that are more coherent and cohesive (Benton, Kiewra, Whitfall, and Dennison, 1993) and include more and better topic sentences (Jones, Amiran, and Katims, 1985).

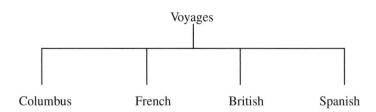

Goals:

Methods:

Relations with
Native Americans:

FIGURE 33. Matrix framework for writing Voyages essay

Teaching Students to Construct Representations

As instructors we can help students learn by providing them with effective learning materials. For example, by providing students with matrix materials about fish (recall Figure 11, p. 124) rather than the passage alone, learning is facilitated. Doing just that, however, is like giving a person a fish to eat for a day instead of teaching him/her how to fish for a lifetime. Certainly instructors should provide the best instructional materials they can, but should also teach students how to learn.

How then are strategies such as the development and application of the matrix taught to college students? One method is through an adjunct course on study skills. An adjunct course, however, separates the strategy from the content areas where it is applicable. The best place for study skills instruction is within content areas. Study skills instruction works best when it makes contact with domain specific knowledge (Perkins and Salomon, 1989). Such training belongs in the math, English, economics, and science curriculums.

Teaching students how to learn, or in this case teaching them to generate and use representations, can and should occur simultaneously with good teaching in the content areas. The process of embedding strategy instruction into content instruction resembles that used by an experienced tradesperson who is training an apprentice. While the tradesperson works, he/she speaks aloud so that personal thoughts and actions become public and explicit for the watchful apprentice.

College instructors can teach students to make and use representations by following a few basic rules that an experienced tradesperson working with an apprentice knows well. First, commonly model the use of representations during instruction. Second, while using representations explain why they are being used (e.g., "to compare several topics or to discern overriding patterns") and how to develop and use them relative to the content being learned (e.g., "because all birds of prey have special weapons for attack, we can make weapons a repeatable category"). This sort of conditional knowledge (Paris, Lipson, and Wixon, 1983) is crucial for strategy instruction. Students must know how and why to use a strategy.

Third, give students opportunities to practice the strategy. This should proceed through successive approximations. After modeling matrix use many times, for example, provide students with a matrix framework prior to a lecture or reading assignment and have them complete it. Later, prompt students to find topics, repeatable categories, and details for a unit of information. Through these types of experiences the skill of generating and using representations is gradually transferred to the students. With practice and feedback they can spontaneously and autonomously generate effective representations.

In summary, an effective instructor teaches the matrix techniques by embedding its use in content instruction. The techniques are modeled, and thoughts and actions are made explicit to students. Multiple opportunities are provided for students to gradually learn and automatize the skills through successive practice and feedback.

References

Bamberg, B. (1983). What makes a text coherent? *College Composition and Communication* 18: 417–429.

Benton, S. L., Kiewra, K. A., Whitfall, J., and Dennison, R. (1993). Encoding and external-storage effects on writing processes. *Journal of Educational Psychology* 85: 267–280.

Bovenmeyer Lewis, A., and Mayer, R. E. (1987). Students\' misconception of relational statements in arithmetic word problems. *Journal of Educational Psychology* 79: 363–371.

Day, R. S. (1988). Alternative representations. In G. Bower (ed.), *The Psychology of Learning and Motivation* 22: 261–303. New York: Academic Press.

Du Bois, N. F., and Kiewra, K. A. (1989). Promoting competent study skills: Some new directions. Paper presented at the National Conference on the Freshman Year Experience, Columbia, SC.

Flower, L. S., and Hayes, J. R. (1977). Problem-solving strategies and the writing processes. *College English* 39: 449–461.

Gagné, R. M. (1985). *The Conditions of Learning*, New York: CBS College Publishing.

Halliday, M. A. K., and Hasan, R. (1976). *Cohesion in English*. London: Longman.

Holley, C. D., and Dansereau, D. F. (1984). Networking: The technique and the empirical evidence. In C. D. Holley and D. F. Dansereau (eds.), *Spatial Learning Strategies: Techniques, Applications and Related Issues*. New York: Academic Press.

Jonassen, D. H., Beissner, K., and Yacci, M. (1993). *Structural Knowledge: Techniques for Representing, Conveying, and Acquiring Structural Knowledge*. Hillside, NJ: Lawrence Erlbaum Associates.

Jones, B. F., Amiran, M. R., and Katims, M. (1985). Teaching cognitive strategies and text structures within language arts programs. In J. Siegel, S. Chipman, and R. Glaser (eds.), *Thinking and Learning Skills: Relation to Basic Research* (Vol. 1). Hillsdale, NJ: Lawrence Erlbaum Associates.

Kiewra, K. A., and Sperling-Dennison, R. A. (1991). How supplemental representations affect learning from a research article. Paper presented at the annual conference of the American Educational Research Association, Chicago, IL.

Kiewra, K. A., Du Bois, N. F., Christian, D., and McShane, A. (1988). Providing study notes: A comparison of three types of notes for review. *Journal of Educational Psychology* 80: 595–597.

Kiewra, K. A., Du Bois, N. F., Christian, D., McShane, A., Meyerhoffer, M., and Roskelley, D. (1991). Notetaking functions and techniques. *Journal of Educational Psychology* 83: 240–245.

Kiewra, K. A., Du Bois, N. F., Staley, R. K., and Robinson, D. H. (1992). Outline versus matrix representations: Memory, integration, and application effects. Paper presented at the annual conference of the American Educational Research Association, San Francisco, CA.

Kiewra, K. A., Du Bois, N. F., Weiss, M. E., and Schantz, S. (1992). Abstract and illustrative text supplements. Paper presented at the annual conference of the American Educational Research Association, San Francisco, CA.

Kiewra, K. A., Levin, J. R., Kim, S., Meyers, T., Renandya, W. A., and Hwang, Y. (1994). Fishing for text facilitators: The lure of the mnematrix. Paper presented at the annual conference of the American Educational Research Association, New Orleans, LA.

Lambiotte, J. G., Dansereau, D. F., Cross, D. R., and Reynolds, S. B. (1989). Multirelational semantic maps. *Educational Psychology Review* 1: 331–365.

Langer, J. A. (1984). The effects of available information on response to school writing tasks. *Research in the Teaching of English* 18: 27–44.

Larkin, J. H., and Simon, H. A. (1987). Why a diagram is (sometimes) worth ten thousand words. *Cognitive Science* 11: 65–99.

Mandler, J. (1983). Stories: The function of structure. Paper presented at the annual convention of the American Psychological Association, Anaheim, CA.

Mayer, R. E. (1984). Aids to text comprehension. *Educational Psychologist* 19: 30–42.

Mayer, R. E., and Gallini, J. K. (1990). When is an illustration worth ten thousand words? *Journal of Educational Psychology* 82: 715–726.

McGuinness, C. (1986). Problem representation: The effects of spatial arrays. *Memory and Cognition* 14: 270–280.

Meyer, B. J. F. (1985). Signaling the structure of text. In D. H. Jonassen (ed.), *Technology of Text* (Vol. 2). Englewood Cliffs, New Jersey: Educational Technology Publications.

Musgrave, B. S., and Cohen, J. (1971). The relationship between prose and list learning. In E. Z. Rothkopf and P. E. Johnson (eds.), *Verbal Learning and the Technology of Written Instruction*. New York: Teacher College Press.

Novak, J. D., and Gowin, D. B. (1984). *Learning How To Learn*. New York: Cambridge University Press.

Novick, L. R. (1990). Representation transfer in problem solving. *Psychological Science* 1: 128–132.

Paris, S. G., Lipson, M. Y., and Wixon, K. K. (1983). Becoming a strategic reader. *Contemporary Educational Psychology* 8: 293–316.

Perkins, D. N., and Salomon, G. (1989). Are cognitive skills context-bound? *Educational Researcher* 18: 16–25.

Polich, J. M., and Schwartz, S. H. (1974). The effect of problem size on representation in deductive problem solving. *Memory and Cognition* 2: 683–686.

Robinson, D. H. (1993). The effects of multiple graphic organizers on students\' comprehension of a chapter-length text. Doctoral dissertation, University of Nebraska–Lincoln, NE.

Robinson, D. H. (1994). Computational efficiency of graphic organizers: Speed of search. Paper presented at the annual conference of the American Educational Research Association, New Orleans, LA.

Rumelhart, D. E. (1980). Schemata: The building blocks of cognition. In R. J. Spiro, B. C. Bruce, and W. F. Brewer (eds.), *Theoretical Issues in Reading Comprehension: Perspectives From Cognitive Psychology, Linguistics, Artificial Intelligence, and Education*. Hillsdale, NJ: Lawrence Erlbaum.

Rumelhart, D. E., and Ortony, A. (1977). The representation of knowledge in memory. In R. C. Anderson, R. J. Spiro, and W. E. Montague (eds.), *Schooling and Acquisition of Knowledge*. Hillsdale, NJ: Lawrence Erlbaum.

Schwartz, S. H. (1971). Modes of representation and problem solving: Well evolved is half solved. *ournal of Experimental Psychology* 91: 347–350.

Schwartz, S. H., and Fattaleh, D. L. (1972). Representation in deductive problem solving: The matrix. *Journal of Experimental Psychology* 95: 343–348.

Sperling-Dennison, R. A., and Kiewra, K. A. (1993). Studying text supplements: Attention focusing and internal connection effects. Paper presented at the annual conference of the American Educational Research Association, Atlanta, GA.

Tukey, J. W. (1990). Data-based graphics: Visual display in the decades to come. *Statistical Science* 5: 327–329.

Waller, R. (1981). Understanding network diagrams. Paper presented at the annual conference of the American Educational Research Association, Los Angeles, CA.

Winn, W. (1988). Recall of the pattern, sequence, and names of concepts presented in instructional diagrams. *Journal of Research in Science Teaching* 25: 375–386.

Teaching Effectively:
Which Students? What Methods?

Raymond P. Perry

Upon meeting a class for the first time, university professors are often struck by the pronounced differences in students seated before them. Race, gender, age, social class, ethnicity, and religion are but a few overt signs of that diversity, augmented by less apparent, but equally important differences in intelligence, motivation, impulsivity, boredom, and so on. Alongside the enthusiastic, determined, and responsible students sit apathetic, bored, and failure-prone students, intermingled with still others possessing various attributes of the first two groups. Not surprisingly, a fundamental challenge facing faculty is how to teach to this complex diversity, so that learning opportunities are optimized for all students.

Addressing this issue usually begins with the instructor asking two basic questions: Who are these students? What are the best methods to help them learn? It is these two questions which, in part, provide the impetus for the three preceding chapters and which are the focus of the present one. One obvious benefit in asking these two questions is that appropriate teaching methods can be matched with those students best suited to prosper from them. Thus, illustrations, demonstrations, and examples may be effective techniques for teaching the concrete learner, and metaphors and paradoxes, the abstract thinker. However, as is readily apparent, answering these questions is not a simple task.

For example, take the first question regarding student diversity. There are dozens of ways in which students likely differ, some of which will never become fully known to the professor. It is almost impossible to take each and every one of these differences into account when planning a lecture. Almost immediately, therefore, the professor is hard pressed to simplify these differences between students, so that only those differences most central to the learning process are attended to. Accordingly, professors resort to devising their own idiosyncratic classification systems for grouping students that are based on personal experience, expectations, collegial exhortations, and speculation. Invariably these classification systems evolve without the benefit of theory and empirical evidence widely available in the literature. While such systems may be of some practical value to the professor, they are likely to have much better utility if properly informed by scientific research.

The preceding chapters by Covington, Covington and Weidenhaupt, Kiewra, and Perry exemplify the kind of research evidence that faculty can use in their teaching efforts. The present chapter examines how this evidence can address the two questions raised earlier about student classification systems and effective teaching methods. In doing so, it is hoped that some useful insights can be gained from applying research findings to the practical issues which arise when professors prepare to teach. In particular, this chapter should interest those in higher education who are directly or indirectly concerned with the academic progress of students, namely classroom instructors, instructional developers, policy planners, and academic administrators. More generally, this chapter underscores the larger perspective that research can make important contributions to college teaching practices and that research *should* inform those practices.

TURNING RESEARCH INTO PRACTICE

The chapters by Covington, Covington and Weidenhaupt, Kiewra, and Perry reflect the broader study of teaching and learning in higher education that has evolved over the past 70 years (cf. McKeachie, 1990). Although that literature is too voluminous to summarize here, it can be found in a variety of scientific sources including *Research in Higher Education, Review of Higher Education, Journal of Educational Psychology,* and so on. For classroom instructors, this literature is potentially of great value because the information it contains can be applied to the problems they face in carrying out their daily teaching responsibilities. For example, Covington's and Perry's chapters describe classification systems which can be used by instructors to understand better the types of students they must teach. As for effective teaching methods, all four chapters provide useful insights into strategies to enhance student motivation and achievement. In turning to these issues specifically, each chapter is summarized and some practical issues highlighted.

Classifying Students: What Students?

It goes without saying that classifying objects into categories is a fundamental preoccupation of humans, ostensibly helping us deal more effectively with our environment. Of course there are potential dangers in this process when the criteria used for classification are inappropriate and when the resulting categories lead to inaccurate generalizations. Obvious examples of the dangers inherent in social discourse include instances of race, gender, and age discrimination. In the college classroom, classifying students into different types helps the instructor answer the question "who are these students?" As such, it has the advantage of potentially simplifying the teaching process and of helping the instructor understand the students better. In this connection, Dahllof (1971), for example, has proposed the existence of a simple classification system in the form of "steering groups" which are used by instructors to gage the impact of their teaching. Instructors are believed to direct their teaching to a specific group of students in the classroom, i.e., a steering group, which, more or less, determines the teaching/learning dynamics of the entire class. Problems can result if the steering group is not representative of the class, receives excessive emphasis, or is too discordant.

Anecdotal evidence suggests that college instructors may use any number of criteria for classifying their students, the most common being ability grouping. Ideally, the criteria should be directly related to the goals of education generally, and to the objectives of the classroom specifically. Both Covington's and Perry's chapters describe student typologies which incorporate educationally relevant criteria involving student motivation, cognition, and affect. Each typology is grounded on established psychological principles and is supported by empirical evidence. As such, they provide a scientifically validated view of student differences in contrast to the informal, unsubstantiated typologies often used by instructors.

Aside from giving instructors greater insights into their students and into classroom dynamics more generally, the two typologies have a second advantage. They enable teaching methods to be better matched to each type of student. Thus, the highly motivated, independent learner may need only minimal instruction from the professor to tackle some assignment, whereas the unmotivated, helpless student may require the professor's direct involvement throughout. In more extreme instances, this may mean special programs for gifted students or remedial interventions for those students academically at risk (Perry, Menec, and Struthers, 1995; Perry and Penner, 1990). Accordingly, Covington's and Perry's typologies enable instructors to answer the question "who are these students?" based on educationally meaningful criteria and on empirically-derived findings. Both are discussed, in turn, as they relate to classroom practice.

Covington's Self-Worth Typology

According to Self-Worth Theory, humans strive, as a fundamental goal, to maintain and to enhance their self-worth. This goal motivates people to act to ensure that their ability or competence is highly valued by themselves and by others as well. Most notable examples of this process involve achievement situations in which success and failure are featured and which are commonly assumed to reflect on a person's abilities. Covington's typology is based on the simple premise that, in classrooms, students are motivated in specific ways to optimize their self-worth. These motivations are the basis for the systematic differences which characterize the four student groups in his typology.

In brief, Covington proposes that students can be divided into four distinct types using a quadripolar model of need achievement (see Figure 1). The four types are defined by two dimensions which describe a success orientation (approach) and a failure-avoiding orientation (avoidance) to achievement situations. The two dimensions range from low to high, thereby allowing each student to be depicted as low-high success oriented and low-high failure avoiding. The resulting quadrants create four prototypical student types referred to by Covington as Overstrivers, Success-Oriented, Failure-Avoiding, and Failure-Accepting.

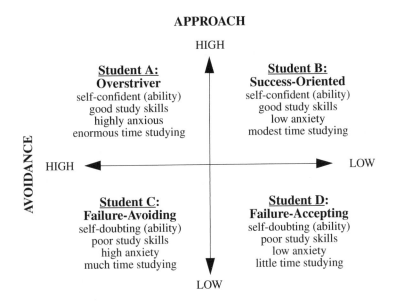

FIGURE 1. Quadripolar model of need achievement

As to be expected, the four types have some qualities in common, but it is their differences that are most notable, as represented by the diagonals in Figure 1. Success-Oriented students and Overstrivers share several similar qualities, but the former are virtual mirror opposites to their Failure-Avoiding counterparts. Possessing many of the qualities of the ideal student, Success-Oriented students have confidence in their academic abilities, exhibit good study skills, experience low anxiety in testing situations, and devote a moderate amount of time to their studies. In contrast, Failure-Avoiding students lack confidence in their abilities, have poor study skills, are highly anxious, and spend excessive amounts of time studying. The Overstriver/Failure-Accepting diagonal also depicts two student types with very different qualities. Overstrivers are self-confident, have good study skills, are highly anxious and spend considerable time in their studies, whereas Failure-Accepting students are not confident, have inadequate study skills, have little anxiety, and devote only minimal time to their studies. Thus, while the four types have a common purpose in mind, to aggrandize their self-worth, they go about it in very different ways.

The merits of Covington's typology rest partly on its validity and practicality. In part, its validity can be assessed from its conceptual underpinnings and, in part, from its empirical verification. The typology's conceptual framework is derived primarily from Self-Worth Theory (Covington, 1984), but also has links to several other prominent psychological theories, notably attribution theory (Weiner, 1974) and learned helplessness theory (Seligman, 1975). Empirical evidence is presented throughout Covington's chapter attesting to Self-Worth Theory itself and to the derived typology, although further empirical verification is needed, as in the case of Success-Oriented students. As for practicality, the typology is of merit in its simplicity and its ecological relevance to college classrooms, both of which make it readily usable for instructors. An accompanying questionnaire further enhances its practicality for those instructors who wish a precise analysis of their students based on quantifiable scores. Using this questionnaire, an instructor can determine whether a particular student is an Overstriver, Success-Oriented, Failure-Avoiding, or Failure-Accepting; whether the majority of the class is one of these types, and so on. Otherwise, a reasonable understanding of Covington's chapter should be of some practical assistance in making more global distinctions.

Of course, assessing the merits of Covington's typology should also involve relative comparisons with classification systems currently being used by instructors. Although research is lacking in this respect, anecdotal evidence would suggest that, for the most part, such naive systems are poorly formulated, highly idiosyncratic, and usually have not been subjected to critical analysis. This means, then, that they are of questionable validity and of limited practical value. At the very least, Covington's typology has something important to offer instructors: an incentive to get them thinking about their own systems. More significantly, however, it has something to contribute as a legitimate typology of college students which should ultimately assist instructors in their teaching practices.

Covington's typology can benefit instructors because it provides a reasonably simple and concise description of student differences, thereby reducing some of the complexities of the classroom. In answer to the question "Who are these students?" the instructor can rest assured that however many differences may exist, the typology describes an important motivational difference and in this connection identifies four specific types of students. As such, it could be used to guide decisions about teaching methods, reading materials, homework assignments, and lesson plans. In a class made up of Overstrivers and Failure-Avoiding students, for example, an instructor may use a textbook of moderate difficulty and allocate considerable class time to discussing it in order to allay these students' typically high levels of anxiety about learning. Or, the instructor may develop test materials designed to minimize anxiety by using study questions, take-home exams, and so on. In reality, however, classrooms will typically consist of all four types, thereby possibly forcing an instructor to target a specific type (cf., steering group), while recognizing that not all the students may benefit from the teaching practice chosen. The typology is also of benefit because it offers a clear explanation for why student differences exist: motivation. In striving to maintain self-worth in achievement settings, students are motivated differently, giving rise to the four distinct student types.

Perry's Perceived Control Typology. Like Covington, Perry offers a typology for classifying college students that is firmly grounded in psychological theory and empirical research. The typology is based on the premise that students differ in their perceived control over their academic performance and that these differences engender divergent thoughts, feelings, and actions. Perceived personal control refers to one's perceived capacity to influence and to predict events in the environment. Essentially, students are differentiated along a continuum of perceived control which varies from "low control" to "high control" at either end (Perry and Dickens, 1984). The "no control" category has similarities to helplessness and related psychological states, suggesting a perceived inability or an unwillingness to influence events, and likewise, "control" is akin to mastery, suggesting a confidence in one's ability to determine outcomes.

Helpless college students believe their ability is responsible for their failures; emphasize grades rather than learning *per se* in their academic tasks; develop negative emotions toward academic tasks; attempt to withdraw from failure situations physically and psychologically; fail to develop effective problem-solving strategies; forget prior success, and lose concentration and focus for learning tasks. In contrast, mastery college students believe lack of effort is responsible for their failures; emphasize competence rather than grades; welcome academic challenges; intensify their efforts when failing; develop effective problem-solving strategies; remember past successes and consider them relevant to future success, and focus attention and concentration on learning tasks (Perry et al., 1995). Essentially, this helpless-mastery continuum depicts students as having gradations of control, with three categories being dominant: low control (helpless), moderate control, and high control (mastery). Obviously, the existence of a control continuum suggests infinite gradations, all of which may not be meaningfully distinguished, and hence unique groupings are assumed, though there may be more than the three described here.

TABLE 1. A taxonomy for constructs involving perceived personal control

	STABLE	UNSTABLE
C O N T R O L	Locus of Control (Rotter, 1966) Personal Causation (DeCharms, 1968) *Type A/B Behavior (Matthews, 1982) Health Hardiness (Kolbasa, 1983) Optimism (Scheier & Carver, 1985) **Action Control Theory (Kuhl, 1985) 〔1〕	Competence Motivation (White, 1959) Reactance (Wortman & Brehm, 1975) Primary/Secondary Control (Rothbaum, Weisz, & Snyder, 1982) Self-efficacy (Bandura, 1977) 〔2〕
LOSS OF CON-TROL	Explanatory Style (Peterson & Seligman, 1984) 〔3〕 Helplessness (Dweck, 1975)	〔4〕 Helplessness (Seligman, 1975)

*Type A/B behavior can be placed in Cell 1 if the behavior is deemed relatively enduring to the point of reflecting personality traits, or Cell 3 if the emphasis is on negative aspects associated with coronary heart disease.

**Action control theory can also be placed in Cell 3 if certain components are of interest and emphasized, i.e., state orientation.

High control students are most likely to believe that they have personal control over their academic performance; that they are largely responsible for their academic successes and failures, with their future resting primarily on their own shoulders. Psychological constructs such as internal locus of control (Rotter, 1966), Type A behavior (Matthews, 1982), Optimism (Scheier and Carver, 1985) and others (see Table 1) reflect this belief in one's ability to master the environment. Conversely, low control students believe that they can do little to influence the course of events around them; that they are helpless and unable to do anything about their circumstances. External locus of control, Type B behavior, and learned helplessness (Seligman, 1975) represent the belief patterns of such students, suggesting an inability to do anything to rectify their situation. And finally, moderate control students seem to combine attributes of both mastery and helpless students, believing that they have control over some aspects of their performance but not others. Of course, tied to these control differences between groups are distinct thoughts, feelings, and actions.

Although Covington's and Perry's typologies highlight different psychological constructs, self-worth versus perceived personal control, they have much in common. Both are rooted in the scientific method and are supported by theory and research. Both also reflect the ecological realities of the college classroom, and consequently, provide a fairly accurate profile of students that instructors can relate to. As with Covington's typology, instructors can readily adapt Perry's to their teaching practices, basing various decisions on their perceptions of perceived control differences between students. Thus, an emphasis on predictability would be important for low control students, in the use of a course outline and behavioral objectives, or in dutifully avoiding the rescheduling of tests, assignments, etc. For high control students, these practices would not be so critical; on the contrary, some element of *un*predictability may be necessary to maintain student interest! Accordingly, both typologies are reasonably valid and practical, particularly in comparison to more common experientially based, idiosyncratic typologies. The challenge, it seems, is for college instructors to make greater use of typologies such as these in making decisions about their teaching practices.

Effective Teaching: What Methods?

As noted earlier, knowing something about one's students helps a professor in planning which teaching practices to use. Matching a particular practice with those students who will benefit most ensures that optimal learning conditions are attained. Thus, students who are bright, independent, autonomous learners may be highly motivated by challenging, Socratic teaching, whereas unmotivated, dependent, and unfocused learners may be threatened by the same instruction, preferring instead a more didactic, low-key approach. The higher education literature is replete with recommendations about effective teaching, much of it based on personal experience, speculation, and anecdotal observation. Less of it, however, is based on the scientific method in which theory and empirical evidence are used to identify effective teaching practices. Less yet is given to whether a practice is effective for all students, or for some but not others: the classic aptitude–treatment interaction issue (see Perry's chapter, p. 11).

What is noteworthy about the chapters by Covington, Covington and Weidenhaupt, Kiewra, and Perry is that the teaching practices they present are, in fact, based on established theory and research. With the exception of Kiewra, they also place emphasis on the aptitude–treatment interaction issue, directly or in directly, as it relates to student differences. Thus, some teaching practices are recommended for all students, whereas other practices are recommended for only some students, as suggested by Covington's and Perry's typologies. Several of these teaching practices may be familiar to readers, others may not; however, common to all is their grounding in logic, theory, and empirical evidence. The remainder of this chapter is devoted to discussing the various practices described by each author.

Foster Self-Worth. According to Covington's Self-Worth Theory, students are committed to maintaining their sense of competence at all costs. This preoccupation can become self-defeating and lead to harmful educational consequences when their self-worth becomes inextricably linked to competing academically with other students. In these instances it is commonly assumed that success implies high ability, and failure, low ability. In reality, however, this perception frequently jeopardizes students' sense of self-worth since few students can be consistently successful and at the top. Covington advises that this potentially damaging psychodynamic must be taken into account when considering appropriate teaching practices. An effective practice would be one that encourages students to compete against themselves rather than against one another for limited rewards (grades). Ultimately, the objective is to have students motivated for the right reasons in which cooperation and *self*-competitiveness are stressed, thereby avoiding between-student rivalries. Motivating students for the wrong reasons is deemed no better than not motivating them at all.

Covington recommends at least three teaching practices that would contribute to overall effective instruction. The first one is the use of engaging and challenging tasks. Typically, such tasks have multiple goals progressively linked to the final objective; they challenge preconceived notions and expectations, and they encourage cooperative learning. A second recommended practice ensures that sufficient reinforcers are available to all students. The use of an absolute grading standard exemplifies this practice in which students work to a recognized level of performance for a specified grade, independent of the grades the other students have received. A third practice entails the use of systematic feedback, given routinely and tied specifically to performance. In this way the feedback serves a constructive function in enhancing self-improvement, even in the case of negative information. In each of these instances the practice is tied to Self-Worth Theory and is supported with relevant empirical findings.

The challenge for university professors is to decide whether Self-Worth Theory offers an appropriate conceptual framework for their own teaching practices. If so, they can then decide whether the three preceding practices are suitable for them and whether Self-Worth principles can be implemented into their other teaching practices. In part, this requires a careful review of each of their current teaching practices to determine the feasibility of implementing Self-Worth principles, much like is demonstrated below with perceived control principles in Perry's section. In each instance, the practice could be adjusted so that it involves a task-focused rather than an ability-focused approach to student learning, the goal being to optimize achievement motivation in every student. For example, the organization of lecture materials is a teaching practice which can create an ability-focused approach to student learning. When organization is poor, only those students having superior talents for organizing lecture material will understand it and benefit academically. However, if the professor organizes the material well, or provides the students with effective techniques for structuring the course content, such as those described by Kiewra in his chapter, then all students have a better opportunity to do well. Thus, an ability-focused approach to learning is reduced, replaced with a more task-focused approach.

Modifying existing teaching practices or developing new ones would be much simpler if one could assume that the benefit to all students is the same. Unfortunately this is not the case because college students differ considerably, giving rise to situations involving aptitude-treatment interactions. Thus, the professor is faced with the task of developing practices that benefit as many students as possible; having many practices, one for each different type of student, may be preferred ideally, but is realistically impractical. Covington's typology makes the problem somewhat more manageable by identifying a key factor underlying student differences and then describing the types of students explicitly. Considerable advantage can be gained, therefore, in developing a teaching practice to match his four types of students and being able to anticipate its eventual impact.

Organizing content. A different approach to effective teaching is offered by Kiewra who focuses on how course material is best represented or communicated to students by the professor. His thesis is that information needs to be organized for optimal learning through the use of a knowledge representation system known as the matrix. Without organization, knowledge lacks meaning much like a puzzle when it is in its separate pieces. According to Kiewra, knowledge is both factual and structural, the former concerned with things, events, ideas; the latter, with the interrelationships between them. Information becomes more meaningful when the interrelationships between the parts, that is the structure, is also understood by students. Representation systems such as lists, outlines, and matrices allow the interrelationships to be concretely displayed with the result that knowledge becomes more meaningful. Because knowledge comprehension requires both facts and structure, professors are responsible for teaching both the specifics as well as their interrelationships.

Some insight into the potential benefits for professors using matrix representations may be gained from the research on effective college teaching. Efforts made by professors to bring order and structure to their course materials, of which matrix representations would be one example, have been referred to as instructor organization in the literature (see chapters in this volume by Feldman, Marsh, and Murray). Professors are deemed to vary in this aspect of teaching, from being highly organized to highly disorganized. Abundant empirical evidence is now available attesting to the significance of instructor organization for student learning. For example, in a comprehensive re-analysis of several meta-analyses involving effective college teaching Feldman (1989) reported a correlation of +.57 between instructor organization and student achievement. This means that professors who are organized also have students who do better than professors who are not organized. While not proving definitively a causal connection, this correlational evidence suggests one possible interpretation in which better organization by the professor enables students to achieve more. Such an interpretation would also suggest that matrix representations, as one aspect of instructor organization, should also contribute to improved academic performance. Accordingly, matrix representations can be placed in the larger context of college instruction as a specific teaching practice.

In a similar vein, Kiewra's matrix representations can also be related to Covington's Self-Worth Theory and Perry's perceived control construct. In Covington's terms, knowledge comprehension can become an ability issue in the classroom if some students are more capable of organizing course materials. Should those students do better academically, then there may be a tendency to interpret learning and performance in terms of pre-existing ability differences between students, thereby making it an ability-focused issue. The professor's use of matrix representations provides all students with the same structures and conceptual frameworks, thereby reducing differences between students in their ability to organize. Moreover, if the professor can actually *teach* matrix representations as an academic skill to students, then the benefits in self-worth terms are further enhanced. Thus, understanding the course content becomes an effort issue in the repeated application of matrix representations to the material, making any pre-existing ability-linked differences between students less important.

In Perry's terms, any teaching practice, such as matrix representations, which makes students' academic tasks more predictable and controllable should benefit their performance. To the extent that matrix representations make the material more understandable, students are better able to predict how well they will do. To the extent that matrix representations can be used by students to understand the material better, they will also enhance students' confidence in their own ability to master the material. Both of these developments are likely to contribute to an increased sense of control. More will be said of this link between teaching practices and perceived control in the following section.

Enhancing perceived control. Differences between college students in their perceived control can have serious consequences for their academic development. Helpless students are more prone to be distracted and bored, to miss assignments and cut classes, and eventually to fail their courses. Mastery students, on the other hand, are more motivated about learning, more willing to complete their assignments, and more likely to excel in their courses. It is not surprising, therefore, that these differences present a serious challenge for professors in their teaching effectiveness. As Figure 2 shows, mastery students perform better with effective than with ineffective instruction, but helpless students show no appreciable improvement in their performance. The paradox in this situation is that those students most in need do not benefit from better quality teaching!

Fortunately, recent empirical evidence suggests that all is not lost for helpless students. Professors have recourse to several alternatives to assist these students, from developing new practices to revising old ones, in each case the objective being to increase perceived

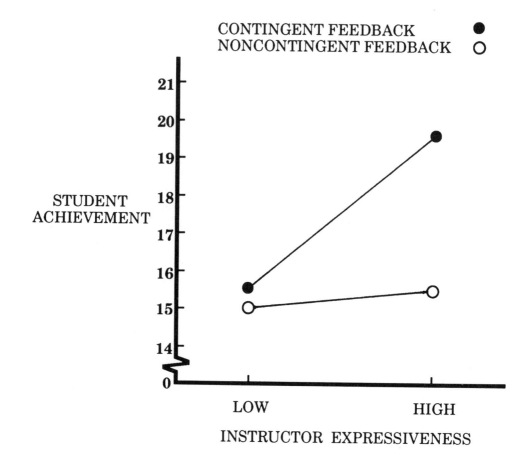

Mastery may result from contingent feedback, internal locus of control, Type A behavior, etc.

Helplessness may result from noncontingent feedback, external locus of control, etc.

FIGURE 2. A perceived control by instruction interaction in which helplessness (noncontingent feedback) students are unable to benefit from effective (high expressive) teaching.

control. Although effective instruction did not increase students' achievement in Figure 2, it has been shown in other studies to produce an internal locus of control under some conditions. Presumably, repeated exposure to this type of teaching could increase helpless students' perceived control to the point at which students become more mastery-oriented and are thereby able to benefit from effective instruction. If so, then teaching behaviors other than instructor expressiveness might also be effective with helpless students such as those described by Feldman, Marsh, and Murray in this volume. Thus, being organized, clear, interactive, expressive, etc., could serve to increase helpless students' internal locus which,

TABLE 2. Teaching Practices Assumed to Enhance Student Development

Teaching Practice	Intended Objective	Perceived Control Consequences	Resolutions
1. Snap Quiz	• to motivate student through anticipation of anxiety • to focus student's attention on course • to emphasize importance of keeping up in course • to accustom student to unexpected academic demands and challenges	positive • anticipation and excitement about meeting challenge • increased commitment to excelling in course negative • uncertainty and loss of control • anxiety, threat, and foreboding directed toward course and professor • problems with assignments and attending classes	• determine degree of positive versus negative developments • if largely positive, then continue • for small minority who have problems—approach directly • if largely negative, then modify by: a) aborting or b) approaching class directly • if b), then discuss intended objectives (column 2) • if b), provide interventions for enhancing perceived control
2. Rescheduling tests and assignments	• to adjust course progress to unexpected developments • to ensure test-related material is recovered	positive • relief, surprise negative • uncertainty, loss of control • disappointment, anger	• avoid rescheduling • negotiate when possible • provide options
3. Restructuring course outline	• to ensure essential material dealt with properly • to emphasize new issues that emerge in course • to be flexible to unique qualities of students • to adust to unexpected events (illness, weather, etc.)	positive • greater sense of determining course development • receptiveness of the instructor negative • uncertaintly and unpredictability • disinterest, apathy, anxiety • confusion regarding assignment, deadlines, etc.	• see 1 (snap quiz) above • negotiate with students regarding restructuring

in turn, may eventually improve their performance.

Instead of adopting new teaching practices, the professor may wish to modify existing ones with the sole purpose of enhancing perceived control in students. In this case the professor would review each existing teaching practice to determine whether it encourages in students a sense of predictability over academic tasks and/or a belief that they have some influence over their successes and failures. Table 2 provides a concrete example of how this might be done. The first column lists specific teaching practices comprising a professor's teaching repertoire followed by their intended objectives in the second column. The third column describes the possible positive and negative consequences of each objective for students' perceived control. Finally, the fourth column provides some possible resolutions to decrease the negative impact of the teaching practice on students' perceived control and/or to increase its positive impact.

The snap quiz in Table 2, for example, is a teaching practice often used by professors to motivate students, to focus their attention on course material, to stress the importance of keeping current, or to accustom the student to unexpected demands. Although all positive, these objectives may not necessarily have the same positive consequences, as depicted in column three. Positive consequences for students' perceived control may occur in the form of heightened anticipation for challenge and increased commitment to the course. Yet, negative consequences are also possible in the form of uncertainty and loss of control, negative emotions, and course withdrawal. A similar analysis can be applied to the rescheduling of tests and assignments which is usually intended to readjust course objectives to unexpected developments and to ensure that test-related material is properly covered prior to the test. Similar to snap quizzes, this practice can also have both positive and negative consequences for a student's perceived control. It may relieve certain time pressures on students, but it can lead to disappointment and anger, and create uncertainty and loss of control as well.

Anticipating these consequences enables a professor to make changes that are intended to maintain a student's perceived control. If the consequences to snap quizzes or rescheduling are largely positive, then the practice can be continued. If, however, they are negative, then certain modifications may be called for. One option is to avoid snap quizzes and rescheduling entirely. This may be particularly appropriate for difficult courses, such as physics or statistics, or for required courses. Another option is to give students some predictability and influence over what takes place in order to increase their perceived control. In the case of snap quizzes, this may involve negotiating a limit on how often they occur, allowing students to drop one or more poor ones, etc. In the case of rescheduling this may require negotiating an alternative date, providing other options, and so on. In each instance the objective to making these changes is to achieve an optimal level of perceived control so that students' performance is enhanced.?

RESEARCH AND PRACTICE

The preceding chapters by Covington, Covington and Weidenhaupt, Kiewra, and Perry provide a rich assortment of information pertaining to teaching and learning in the college classroom. The present chapter has attempted to show how some of this information can be applied to practical issues faced by college instructors in going about their daily teaching routines. Of the many possible issues that could be addressed with the information from these chapters, only two were dealt with in this chapter. Specifically, individual differences between students and effective teaching practices were the topics of concern. Obviously, many other practical issues could have been selected for illustration from the preceding chapters such as dealing with at-risk students or developing active, independent learning styles. However, the objective was to demonstrate that research can, and should, be linked more directly to practice and that practice stands to gain from this initiative. Hopefully, this objective has been attained, and in doing so, demonstrates how research can be linked with other practical issues than the two discussed here.

In raising the aforementioned issues, this chapter has focused primarily on classroom instruction. The exclusion of faculty developers, academic administrators, and policy planners should not imply that the information presented in the preceding chapters is of little relevance for them, but rather that the classroom is where it all begins. Space restrictions prevent attempts to discuss more than the two issues presented, let alone issues related to other interested groups. However, this does not suggest that the information has little value for these groups. On the contrary, the information is of great importance and should be more systematically considered than it has here.

In the case of faculty developers, the information in the preceding chapters is relevant to the extent that their duties are to assist faculty to become more proficient in their teaching. Helping faculty translate information like that presented in the preceding chapters could be of immense value, since faculty are unlikely to have the expertise, or the time, to do it themselves. This chapter represents an example of this type of endeavor, as does Maryellen Weimer's widely circulated newsletter *The Teaching Professor* (e.g., Weimer, 1992). Similarly, academic administrators and policy planners should be conversant with the type of information presented in the preceding chapters so that their policies and procedures can strengthen, not conflict with, good teaching practices. Policies mandating the use of grading curves, for example, must be balanced against the advantages absolute grading practices advocated by Covington. For each group the message is the same: research is important for teaching proficiency. It behooves each party to recognize this message and to be more proactive in supporting the linkage between research and practice.

References

Covington, M.V. (1984). The motive for self-worth. In C. Ames and R. Ames (eds.), *Research on Motivation in Education*, Vol. I. New York: Academic Press.

Covington, M. V. (1993). A motivational analysis of academic life in college. In J. Smart (ed.), *Higher Education: Handbook of Theory and Research*, Vol. IX (pp. 50-93). New York: Agathon Press. (*Reprinted in this volume.*)

Covington, M. V., and Weidenhaupt, S. (1995). Turning work into play: The nature and nurturing of intrinsic task engagement. In R. Perry and J. Smart (eds.), *Effective Teaching in Higher Education: Research and Practice* (p. 101 in this volume). New York: Agathon Press.

Dahllof, U. (1971). *Ability Grouping, Content Validity, and Curriculum Process Analysis*. New York: Teachers' College Press, Columbia University.

de Charms, R. (1968). *Personal Causation*. New York: Academic Press.

Dweck, C. S. (1975). The role of expectations and attributions in the alleviation of learned helplessness. *Journal of Personality and Social Psychology* 31: 674-685.

Feldman, K. (1989). The association between student ratings of specific instructional dimensions and student achievement: Refining and extending the synthesis of data from multisection validity studies. *Research in Higher Education* 30: 583-645.

Kiewra, K. A. (in press). The matrix representation system: Orientation theory, application, and research. In J. Smart (ed.), *Higher Education: Handbook of Theory and Research*, Vol. X. New York: Agathon Press. (*Reprinted in this volume.*)

Kolbasa, S. C. (1983). The hardy personality: Toward a social psychology of stress and health. In G. S. Saunders and J. Suls (Eds.), *Social Psychology of Health and Illness* (pp. 3-31). Hillsdale, N.J.: Erlbaum.

Kuhl, J. (1985). Volitional mediators of cognition-behavior consistency: Self-regulatory processes and action versus state orientation. In J. Kuhl and J. Bechman (Eds.), *Action control: From Cognition to Behavior* (pp. 101-128). New York: Springer-Verlag.

Matthews, K. A. (1982). Psychological perspectives on the Type A behavior pattern. *Psychological Bulletin* 91: 293-323.

McKeachie, W. J. (1990). Research on college teaching: The historical background. *Journal of Educational Psychology* 82: 189-200.

Perry, R. P. (1991). Perceived control in college students: Implications for instruction in higher education. In J. Smart (ed.), *Higher Education: Handbook of Theory and Research*, Vol. VII (pp. 1-56). (*Reprinted in this volume.*)

Perry, R. P., and Dickens, W. J. (1984). Perceived control in the college classroom: Response - outcome contingency training and instructor expressiveness effects on student achievement and causal attributions. *Journal of Educational Psychology* 76: 966-981.

Perry, R. P., Menec, V. H., and Struthers, W. C. (in press). Motivation from a teaching perspective. In R. Menges and M. Weimer (eds.), *What College Teachers Need to Know*. San Francisco: Jossey-Bass.

Perry, R. P., and Penner, K. S. (1990). Enhancing academic achievement in college students through attributional retraining and instruction. *Journal of Educational Psychology* 82: 262-271.

Peterson, P. L., and Seligman, M. E. P. (1984). Causal explanations as a risk factor for depression: Theory and evidence. *Psychological Review* 91: 347-374.

Rothbaum, F., Weisz, J. R., and Snyder, S. S. (1982). Changing the world and changing the self: A two-process model of perceived control. *Journal of Personality and Social Psychology* 42: 5-37.

Rotter, J. B. (1966). Generalized expectancies for internal versus external control of reinforcements. *Psychological Monographs* 80: 1-28.

Scheier, M. F., and Carver, C. S. (1985). Optimism, coping, and health: Assessment and implications of generalized outcome expectancies. *Health Psychology* 4: 219-247.

Seligman, M. E. P. (1975). *Helplessness: On Depression, Development, and Death*. San Francisco: Freeman.

Weimer, M. (1992). *The Teaching Professor*. Madison, WI.: Magna Publications, Inc.

Weiner, B. (Ed.) (1974). *Achievement Motivation and Attribution Theory*. Morristown, NJ: General Learning Press.

White, R. (1959). Motivation reconsidered: The concept of competence. *Psychological Review* 66: 297-333.

Wortman, C. B., and Brehm, J. W. (1975). Responses to uncontrollable outcomes: An integration of reactance theory and the learned helplessness model. In L. Berkowitz (Ed.), *Advances in Experimental Social Psychology* (vol. 8) (pp. 277-336). New York: Academic Press.

PERSPECTIVES ON FACULTY

Effective Teaching Behaviors in the College Classroom[*]

Harry G. Murray

INTRODUCTION

Do teachers differ significantly in their impact on student cognitive and affective development? If so, why do some teachers have more impact on students than others? What are the characteristics that differentiate between more effective and less effective classroom teachers? What is it that successful teachers actually *do* (or less successful teachers fail to do) in the classroom? These are the types of questions addressed in the field of study known as teacher effectiveness research, or process-outcome research. In general, teacher effectiveness research is defined as the study of relationships between instructional activities of teachers (the processes of teaching), and educational changes that occur in students (the outcomes of teaching). The types of outcome measures studied in this area of research include those of a cognitive nature (e.g., gains in knowledge, improvement of problem solving skill), as well as those of an affective or attitudinal nature (e.g., increased motivation to learn, change in self-concept).

Although a huge volume of research exists on characteristics of effective teachers at the elementary and secondary school levels (cf., Dunkin and Biddle, 1974; Brophy and Good, 1986), research on teacher effectiveness in higher education has been more limited and more recent. The purpose of this chapter is to provide a selective but representative review of empirical research on teacher effectiveness at the college and university level. Both observational and experimental studies are included, with special emphasis on research having clear implications for improvement of teaching. Also, an attempt is made to determine the extent to which teacher effectiveness depends on context. For example, are the characteristics that contribute to effective teaching of large lecture classes the same as those that contribute to success in small discussion groups? Similarly, are there differences between academic disciplines in what constitutes effective teaching?

---

[*]Kenneth Feldman, Philip Abrami, and Raymond Perry reviewed an earlier draft of this chapter, and their comments were very helpful. The final version is solely the responsibility of the author.

Classroom Teaching Behaviors

Whereas much of the previous research on college teaching effectiveness has focused on "presage" or preinstructional factors such as teacher knowledge, attitudes, and planning, the present review will deal solely with teaching activities that occur inside the classroom. Moreover, within the classroom domain, preference will be given to studies investigating specific "low-inference" teaching behaviors rather than global, "high-inference" characteristics. Rosenshine and Furst (1971) define a low-inference teaching behavior as a concrete, denotable action of the instructor that can be recorded with little or no inference on the part of an observer. Examples of low-inference classroom teaching behaviors are: "signals the transition from one topic to the next," "addresses individual students by name," and "gestures with arms and hands." In contrast, a high-inference teacher characteristic is one that can be assessed only through observer inference or judgment. Examples of high-inference classroom variables are: "clarity," "student-centeredness," and "task orientation."

Most of the large body of research published on the reliability, validity, and utility of student ratings of university teaching has dealt with high-inference rather than low-inference teacher characteristics, and thus is not discussed at length in the present review. Excellent reviews of the student ratings literature have been provided by Marsh (1984) and McKeachie (1979), among others. The present review includes only those studies involving either systematic observation or experimental manipulation of specific, low-inference classroom teaching behaviors.

There are several advantages in focusing on low-inference instructional behaviors. For one thing, such behaviors are relatively easy to record and operationalize for purposes of observational research, and relatively easy to manipulate for purposes of experimental research. For another, it is easier to give an instructor diagnostic feedback for improvement of teaching if one focuses on specific, concrete behaviors rather than vague generalities. Finally, it can be argued that classroom teaching behaviors represent the "leading edge" of teaching, the point of direct contact between teacher and student, and thus are more likely to have an impact on student development than other types of teacher characteristics. Good planning and good intentions on the part of the teacher will go for nought unless these plans and intentions are translated into effective classroom behaviors. This does not imply, however, that teaching can or should be understood solely in behavioral or "mechanical" terms. In addition to data on classroom teaching behaviors and their effects, we need to understand the "thought" behind teaching, including goals, planning, and decision making, and we need a theory of why it is that certain teaching behaviors affect students in certain ways.

In apparent contradiction to the above rationale for studying low-inference teaching behaviors, Kulik and Kulik (1979) suggest that what a teacher does in the classroom has relatively little influence on the amount learned by students. The main factor determining student learning, according to the Kuliks, is individual studying by students outside the classroom, and the best way to improve student learning is to focus on manipulations such as frequent quizzing and required remediation that affect how and how much students study. In response to this critique, it should first be noted that the impact of teaching behaviors on student learning is, above all, an empirical question, and data relevant to this question are reviewed below. Second, although not explicitly acknowledged by Kulik and Kulik, it seems entirely possible that classroom teaching behaviors might be included among the variables that influence the amount of studying by students outside the classroom. If this were the case, classroom teaching could be assumed to influence student learning in two separate ways—that is, by facilitating information processing in the classroom and by motivating students to study outside the classroom.

It goes without saying that research on teacher characteristics, and particularly that on classroom teaching behaviors, can contribute both theoretically and practically to higher education. This type of research helps us to understand what effective teaching is, why it is effective, and how it impacts on student development. Furthermore, knowledge of factors underlying effective teaching can provide guidelines on how to train or select college teachers, how to evaluate teaching, and how to improve the performance of current teachers. For example, research on low-inference teaching behaviors can be applied to the development of student instructional rating forms that focus on specific, denotable characteristics of instructors, and thus are more useful in providing diagnostic feedback than the typical global rating forms in current use (Murray, 1987). This same type of research can be applied to the design of in-service faculty training programs that focus on a limited set of classroom behaviors known to contribute significantly to overall teaching effectiveness (Murray and Lawrence, 1980).

Do Teachers Make a Difference?

Research on specific classroom behaviors that differentiate between effective and ineffective college teachers presupposes that teachers do in fact differ in effectiveness, or impact on student development. It makes no sense to look for characteristics underlying differential teacher effectiveness if there are no differences in effectiveness to explain. Although the question of whether teachers make a difference may seem trivial or obvious, it has been the source of considerable debate, both in everyday discourse and in the professional literature. On the one hand, anecdotal reports suggest that teachers can make a big difference, either positive or negative, in the lives of students. With awe in their voices, students tell of teachers who caused them to love mathematics or hate mathematics, to select one career over another, or to adopt a whole new philosophy of life! Despite these inspiring testimonials, there are educational writers who contend seriously that teachers make little or no difference in amount learned by students. Coleman et al (1966), for example, concluded that 95 percent of between-school variance in student achievement in elementary and secondary schools is attributable to student ability and family background, whereas less than 5 percent is due to differences in teacher quality. Sanders (1986) argues that since teaching is a commonplace, easily acquired activity akin to cooking or talking, there is no reason to expect significant variations in teaching effectiveness among normal adults.

Perhaps the most useful context in which to resolve the issue of whether teachers make a difference is a course in which students are assigned at random to multiple class sections (to ensure section equivalence in student aptitude), and in which all sections write a common, objectively scored final examination. Under these conditions the mean examination score of students taught by a given teacher can be taken as an index of teacher impact on student learning, and the extent to which mean scores vary across class sections is an index of differential teacher effectiveness. Investigators using this research paradigm have reported estimates of the differential impact of teachers ranging in magnitude from modest to very large. Murray (1983b) reported that the range from lowest to highest section mean score on a common final exam in an introductory psychology course, although statistically significant, was typically no larger than 7 or 8 percentage points in a given year. Frey (1973), on the other hand, found section mean scores varying from 70.5 percent to 89.2 percent, a range of nearly 19 percentage points, in a freshman calculus course at Northwestern University.

Although data are limited, it would appear that teachers do make a difference in the amount learned by students, and in some cases this difference is quite large. When affective or attitudinal outcome measures are used, teacher effects tend to be larger and more reliable than those reported for final exam scores. Murray (1983b) found that teachers accounted for more variance in non-cognitive measures such as course and instructor ratings and subsequent course enrollment than in final examination performance. It may be, then, that teachers not only influence student learning, but more importantly, influence student motivation for further learning.

Research Methods

Research on classroom teaching behaviors can be divided into two general categories according to methodological approach. In studies using an *observational* approach, teaching behaviors are observed and recorded in their natural setting, with the investigator making no attempt to manipulate or control variables. Correlations are then drawn between teaching behaviors and outcome measures such as achievement test scores, attitudes toward learning, or instructional ratings. An advantage of this approach is that research findings are obtained with real teachers in real classrooms, and thus are generalizable or applicable to everyday problems of teaching. A disadvantage of the observational approach is that, because variables are allowed to vary freely and naturally, correlations found between teaching behaviors and student outcomes are difficult to interpret in cause–effect terms. For example, if we find a positive correlation between teacher enthusiasm and student learning, we can conclude that students of enthusiastic teachers learn more than students of non-enthusiastic teachers, but we cannot conclude unequivocally that teacher enthusiasm is the cause of improved student learning. It is possible that high levels of student learning cause teachers to become more enthusiastic, or alternatively, that a third variable (e.g., interesting subject matter) causes concurrent increases in both teacher enthusiasm and student learning (Woolfolk, 1987). Because of interpretive ambiguities such as these, many investigators have opted for a second approach to research on teaching, the *experimental* approach. This approach is characterized by deliberate manipulation and control of variables, rather than observation and measurement alone. In a "true experiment" on classroom teaching, the investigator systematically manipulates one or more teaching behaviors while holding all other factors constant. Since teaching behaviors are the only factor that varies across experimental conditions, any differences between conditions in student outcome measures are assumed to be caused by teaching behaviors. In some studies, teaching behavior is manipulated by training some teachers, but not others, to exhibit certain behaviors in their classrooms. In other studies, teaching behaviors are manipulated by creating videotaped instructional segments that either incorporate or do not incorporate a particular pattern of behavior. The chief advantage of the experimental approach is that relations among variables are more readily interpretable in cause–effect terms. A disadvantage of this approach is that research findings are obtained under somewhat "contrived" or "artificial" conditions, and thus may not generalize to real teachers in real classrooms. The latter problem is less pronounced in "field" experiments than in "lab" experiments.

Observational and experimental studies of classroom teaching are treated separately in the review that follows. Despite this dichotomy, an ideal research strategy would be to investigate teaching behaviors concurrently in observational and experimental designs. Teaching behaviors could be screened in preliminary observational/correlational studies, and then analyzed in more depth and checked for causal status in experimental studies. In terms of practical application, there are reasons for having more confidence in teaching behaviors identified as significant in both observational and experimental studies.

OBSERVATIONAL STUDIES

The first large-scale observational study of low-inference teaching behaviors in the college classroom appears to have been that of Solomon, Rosenberg, and Bezdek (1964). Classroom teaching behaviors were investigated in relation to student learning and student evaluation of teaching in a sample of 24 political science instructors. Class enrollment ranged from 11 to 38. Although not stated by the investigators, the method of instruction was presumably a combination of lecture and discussion. Classroom teaching behaviors were observed by the following techniques: audiotape recording, teacher self-report questionnaire, descriptive rating form completed by students, and reports of two observers who visited each teacher's class on separate occasions. A total of 169 variables were derived from these four data sources. Many of the derived variables referred to non-classroom characteristics (e.g., teacher goals), or to global, high-inference dimensions of classroom performance (e.g., "clarity," "informality," "flexibility"). However, approximately one third of the classroom variables were low-inference in nature (e.g., "expresses approval of student work," and "asks questions about subject matter"). A principal-components factor analysis of the 169 teaching variables (see Solomon, Bezdek, and Rosenberg, 1964) yielded the following 8 factors or underlying dimensions: (1) control vs. permissiveness, (2) lethargy vs. energy, (3) protectiveness vs. aggressiveness, (4) vagueness vs. clarity, (5) encouragement of student cognitive growth, (6) dryness vs. flamboyance, (7) encouragement of student expressive participation, and (8) coldness vs. warmth. Table 1 shows examples of low-inference teaching behaviors loading on each of these factors. Student learning was measured by pretest-to-posttest gain scores on two separate achievement tests: a 35-item multiple-choice test of factual knowledge of American Government, and a 10-item test of reading comprehension in the same field. Student evaluation of teaching was measured by a 7-item rating form assessing various aspects of the course and instructor. The 24 teachers were assigned factor scores on each of the 8 teaching behavior factors defined above, and these scores studied in relation to mean student rating scores and mean gain scores on the two achievement tests.

The major findings are summarized in Table 1. Factor 4 (vagueness vs. clarity) correlated significantly with mean student gain in factual knowledge and with mean student rating of instructor overall effectiveness. Factor 2 (lethargy vs. energy) and Factor 6 (dryness vs. flamboyance) showed significant linear correlations with mean gain score on the comprehension test, whereas Factor 1 (control vs. permissiveness) showed a curvilinear relationship with comprehension gain (not shown in Table 1), such that maximum gain was associated with an intermediate level of permissiveness. The only other significant correlation was between Factor 8 (coldness vs. warmth) and mean student rating of instructor effectiveness.

Another finding of interest was that mean student rating of instructor effectiveness correlated significantly ($r = .46$) with mean gain in factual knowledge. This result is consistent with Cohen's (1981) conclusion that student ratings are moderately valid as predictors of student knowledge gains. Unfortunately, student ratings did not correlate with comprehension gain scores in the Solomon et al study, nor did comprehension gains correlate with factual knowledge gains.

The results of the Solomon, Rosenberg, and Bezdek study suggest that what the teacher does in the classroom is indeed related to student cognitive and affective development. The strong points of this study include the use of pre- and posttests to obtain more precise estimates of student achievement, and the use of multiple data sources in the observation of classroom teaching. An important drawback is that most of the teaching variables were global or high-inference in nature, thus making it difficult to interpret the results in specific, behavioral terms.

A follow-up to the Solomon, Rosenberg, and Bezdek study was reported by Solomon (1966). Since student ratings correlated significantly with student learning gains in the previous study, only the former measure of teaching effectiveness was used here. Classroom teaching behaviors were measured by a 69-item descriptive questionnaire administered to students at the end of the academic term. The sample of teachers included 229 instructors of small-enrollment evening courses in a variety of academic disciplines at 5 different universities. A factor analysis of instructor mean scores on the 69 teaching behavior items yielded the following 10 factors: (1) lecturing vs. encouragement of student participation, (2) energy, clarity vs. lethargy, vagueness, (3) criticism vs. tolerance, (4) control vs. permissiveness, (5) warmth vs. coldness, (6) obscurity vs. clarity, (7) dryness vs. flamboyance, (8) organization vs.

informality, (9) nervousness vs. relaxation, and (10) impersonality vs. personal expression. In general, these factors are similar to those identified in the Solomon, Rosenberg, and Bezdek study. Teachers were assigned factor scores on the 10 teaching behavior factors, and these scores correlated with mean student ratings of overall instructor effectiveness. Only 2 of the 10 factors correlated significantly with student ratings, namely Factor 1 (lecturing vs. encouragement of student participation) and Factor 2 (energy, clarity vs. lethargy, vagueness). Specific teaching behaviors loading on Factor 1 included solicitation of student opinion, approval of student comments, and asking questions of class. Teaching behaviors loading on Factor 2 included vocal expressiveness, clarity of speech, and showing interest in topic..

TABLE 1. Correlations Between Teaching Behaviors and Outcome Measures in the Solomon, Rosenberg, and Bezdek (1964) Study

Teaching behavior factors and sample behaviors	Correlations with outcome measures		
	Instructor rating	Knowledge gain	Comprehension gain
Control vs. Permissiveness (Factor 1) encourages argument shifts between lecture and discussion frequency of student-student	.13	.19	.32
Lethargy vs. Energy (Factor 2) rapidity of speech movement uses overstatement and exaggeration	.16	.23	.44*
Protectiveness vs. Aggressiveness (Factor 3) ridicules students asks questions about subject matter flippant toward students	−.03	−.13	.15
Vagueness vs. Clarity (Factor 4) understands student statements speaks clearly and understandably well-organized	.75*	.58*	.04
Emphasis on Student Growth (Factor 5) uses student work as basis for discussion uses discussion-lecture sequence encourages student contributions	.08	.12	−.13
Dryness vs. Flamboyance (Factor 6) expresses opinions about material uses humor as stimulus for learning refers to self	.07	−.08	−.42*
Emphasis on Participation (Factor 7) encourages free expression questions students regarding experiences tries to get all students to participate	−.04	−.06	.20
Coldness vs. Warmth (Factor 8) demonstrates methods of analysis expresses approval of student work uses humor as distraction	.49*	−.04	.17

*Statistically significant at .05 level.

In summary, the Solomon study provided further evidence that perceived teaching effectiveness is predictable from specific classroom behaviors of the instructor. Teaching behaviors relating to clarity, enthusiasm, and encouragement of student participation were critical in determining perceived effectiveness. A significant methodological weakness of the Solomon study is that the same individuals (namely students) served both as observers of classroom behavior and as raters of overall teaching effectiveness. Under these conditions, it is possible that process-product correlations are due in part to rater biases such as "halo effect." Halo effect is the tendency of a rater to form an overall positive impression of the person being rated, and on this basis assign indiscriminantly high ratings to all dimensions of performance, including those that, in reality, are statistically independent. Inflation of process-product correlations due to halo effect is presumably more likely under conditions where the same rater judges both specific teacher characteristics and overall teaching effectiveness. A second limitation of the Solomon study, shared with all other observational studies, is that the results are purely correlational in nature, and thus do not necessarily imply a cause–effect relationship between classroom teaching behaviors and student outcomes.

Tom and Cushman (1975) studied classroom teaching behaviors in relation to student self-ratings of amount learned in university agriculture courses. Students estimated their instructor's frequency of use of 45 different low-inference classroom behaviors, and rated their own progress in achieving course goals in 7 different areas, including factual knowledge, logical thinking, and development of favorable attitude toward subject. Both behavior ratings and outcome ratings were made on 5-point scales. Data were obtained from 12,792 students in 402 class sections at 10 different universities (mean class size = 31.8). The split-half reliability of student ratings of low-inference teaching behaviors ranged from .44 to .96 and averaged .84, indicating high interrater reliability for most behaviors. Mean student ratings of 28 of 45 teaching behaviors correlated significantly across class sections with self-rated achievement of one or more educational goals. As a general rule, teaching behaviors showed stronger and more consistent correlations with affective student outcomes (e.g., developing favorable attitudes) than with cognitive outcomes (e.g., gaining factual knowledge). Another finding of interest was that teaching behaviors tended to be differentially suited to different course objectives, rather than being uniformly effective or ineffective for all objectives. For example, "promoted teacher-student discussion" correlated significantly with self-rated progress in creative thinking and communication skill, but did not correlate with perceived gains in factual or conceptual knowledge. On the other hand, "presented well-organized lectures" was a significant predictor of factual and conceptual knowledge gains, but was unrelated to development of problem solving, creative thinking, or communication skills.

Contrary to the results of most other research, teaching behaviors reflecting instructor enthusiasm or expressiveness (e.g., movement and gesture, vocal variation) did not correlate strongly or consistently with student outcome measures in the Tom and Cushman study. Only one such behavior, "spoke with expressiveness and variety in tone of voice," was a significant predictor of self-rated learning, and it correlated with only 1 of 7 outcome measures. Significant correlations with self-rated progress in three or more areas were found for the following low-inference behaviors reflecting teacher clarity and task orientation: "pointed out what was important to learn in each class session," "gave step-by-step instructions when needed by students," and "gave students practice in recalling principles and concepts."

In summary, the Tom and Cushman study used a novel method of assessing student learning—namely, self-ratings of progress toward educational goals, but nonetheless confirmed previous evidence that student learning is significantly related to specific classroom behaviors of the instructor. A methodological weakness of this study is that teaching behaviors and student outcomes were concurrently assessed by the same group of raters (i.e., students), thus leaving open the possibility of inflated correlations due to rater beliefs or biases.

Further evidence that perceived teaching effectiveness is related to specific classroom behaviors of the instructor was provided by Mintzes (1979). Students in introductory psychology tutorials taught by teaching assistants rated 12 global dimensions of instructional quality (e.g., clarity of presentation, fairness of grading), and estimated the frequency with which their instructors exhibited 20 low-inference teaching behaviors. Multiple regression analysis showed that approximately 32 percent of the variance in student ratings of instructor effectiveness was attributable to the 20 low-inference classroom behaviors $R = .57$). The teaching behavior correlating highest with instructor clarity was "uses concrete examples," whereas the best predictor of instructor rapport was "addresses individual students by name," and the behavior correlating highest with ability to maintain student attention was "speaks expressively or dramatically." Methodological problems in this study include lack of procedural independence in the assessment of "process" and "product" measures, and use of individual student ratings rather than teacher (or class) mean ratings as the unit of statistical analysis. Use of the individual student as the unit of analysis fails to isolate the teacher as the source of variance (and covariance) in independent and dependent variables. Variations in student learning among members of the same class are obviously not attributable to between-teacher differences in classroom teaching behavior.

Cranton and Hillgartner (1981) used videotaping to record the classroom teaching behaviors of 28 faculty members at McGill University. Observations were made at 5-second intervals to obtain frequency counts for 15 categories of teaching behavior. Class size ranged from 20 to 100, and instructors came from a variety of academic disciplines. Quality of teaching was measured by mean student ratings on the 38-item Teaching Analysis by Students (TABS) questionnaire. Several significant correlations were found between categories of teaching behavior and student ratings of specific TABS items. For example, teachers who showed a high frequency of "structuring" and "management" behaviors tended to receive high ratings for clarity of objectives. Similarly, instructors who asked questions, elaborated on student answers, and praised students for good ideas tended to be highly rated as discussion leaders. Overall, a multiple correlation of .81 was found between the 15 categories of teaching behavior and student self-ratings of amount learned from the instructor. These results provide further confirmation that low-inference teaching behaviors account for a large proportion of variance in perceived quality of teaching. As in the Tom and Cushman study, there is evidence here that different teaching behaviors are important for different educational goals or activities (e.g., stating objectives vs. facilitating discussion). A strong point of the Cranton and Hillgartner study is that teaching behaviors and overall teaching effectiveness were assessed separately and independently (one by videotaping, the other by student ratings). A possible weakness is that teaching behaviors recorded by videotaping may not be entirely representative of those that occur under normal day-to-day classroom conditions.

Beginning in the early 1980s, the present writer (Murray, 1983a, 1983b, 1985; Erdle and Murray, 1986) undertook a series of studies designed to extend the scope and improve the methodology of prior research on low-inference teaching behaviors. As noted above, a methodological weakness of most studies in this area is that the same individuals (namely, students) have served both as observers of classroom teaching and as raters of instructional outcomes. This procedure leaves open the possibility that obtained behavior-outcome correlations reflect rater beliefs or biases rather than actual covariation of teaching behaviors with student outcomes. For example, a student rater who (1) believes that effective teachers exhibit behavior X, and (2) has just rated teacher A as "highly effective," may tend to rate teacher A high on behavior X regardless of whether this rating is justified by direct observational evidence. Some investigators (e.g., Cranton and Hillgartner, 1981) have tried to circumvent this problem through videotape recording of classroom teaching. However, videotaping itself can be highly "obtrusive" or "reactive," and results obtained with videotaping may or may not be representative of what occurs in normal classrooms. To rectify these methodological limitations, Murray (1983a) measured global teaching effectiveness in terms of archival student ratings and recorded low-inference teaching behaviors by way of trained observers who unobtrusively visited regular classes taught by participating instructors. It was assumed that this procedure would permit unobtrusive classroom observation while at the same time avoiding contamination of results due to use of the same individuals as judges of both "process" and "outcome" variables.

The sample of teachers in the Murray (1983a) study consisted of 54 professors in the Faculty of Social Sciences, University of Western Ontario. Each participating instructor had consistently received either low, medium, or high student ratings in previous courses, and each was scheduled to teach a lecture or lecture/discussion course with an enrollment of at least 30 students during the period of investigation. Each of the 54 teachers was observed in 3 separate one-hour class periods by each of 6 to 8 trained classroom observers. The observers were students in an undergraduate psychology course who, prior to visiting classes, received 4 hours of group training in recording low-inference teaching behaviors from videotape samples. Observers were instructed to focus solely on what the instructor actually *did* in the classroom, and to be as unobtrusive as possible during classroom visits. Following their 3 hours of observation of a given instructor, observers completed a standardized assessment form, the Teacher Behaviors Inventory (TBI), which required ratings of 60 low-inference teaching behaviors on a 5-point frequency-of-occurrence scale (1 = almost never, 5 = almost always). Ratings were averaged across observers to obtain mean frequency estimates of 60 teaching behaviors for each of 54 instructors.

Preliminary interrater reliability analysis indicated that classroom observers showed substantial agreement in their frequency estimates of low-inference teaching behaviors. The reliability of item mean ratings ranged from .24 to .97 for different TBI items, with a median value of .76. Three TBI items with reliability coefficients below .50 were deleted from further analysis, leaving a total of 57.

Follow-up analyses of variance showed that 26 of the 57 reliably judged teaching behaviors differed significantly in frequency of occurrence across groups of teachers receiving low, medium, and high student ratings in previous courses. Multiple regression analyses revealed that 36 to 59 percent of the variance in student ratings was predictable from frequency estimates of 10 teaching behaviors. Although significant group differences were found for teaching behaviors loading on 8 of the 9 factors identified in a principal-axis factor analysis of TBI items, group differences were largest and most frequent for behaviors loading on the Enthusiasm, Clarity, and Interaction factors. Significant behaviors loading on the Enthusiasm factor included: "moves about while lecturing," "speaks expressively," "uses humor," and "shows facial expressions." Significant behaviors associated with the Clarity factor included: "stresses important points," "gives multiple examples," and "suggests practical applications." Representative behaviors for the Interaction factor were: "encourages questions and comments," "addresses students by name," and "asks questions of individual students."

It is possible to account for the impact of enthusiasm, clarity, and interaction behaviors in terms of information-processing concepts from modern cognitive psychology (e.g., Mayer, 1987). Behaviors loading on the Enthusiasm factor share elements of spontaneity and stimulus variation, and thus are perhaps best interpreted as serving to elicit and maintain student attention to material presented in class. Research in cognitive psychology indicates that attention plays a pivotal role in virtually all forms of information processing, including that which occurs in the classroom. If the learner fails to pay attention, information is irretrievably lost in the early stages of processing, and is therefore not available for subsequent storage and retrieval. Apparently students are more likely to pay attention to teachers who exhibit expressive behaviors such as vocal variation, humor, and movement and gesture, and thus are more likely to respond positively to instruction and to learn the material that is presented.

Mayer (1987) argues that information is easier to encode in meaningful terms for storage in long-term memory if it is (1) internally coherent, and (2) related to prior knowledge already stored in memory. It is reasonable to assume that teaching behaviors loading on the Clarity factor have their impact on the encoding and storage stages of information processing. Behaviors such as "puts outline of lecture on blackboard" serve to structure the subject matter or provide internal connections, whereas behaviors such as "uses concrete examples" or "suggests practical applications" assist the learner in finding links (external connections) between new concepts and prior knowledge. A physics professor who explains principles of acoustics with reference to rock music is assisting in the integration of new knowledge with old knowledge, as is a psychology professor who explains learning and memory concepts in terms of student study habits.

TABLE 2. Results of Murray (1985) study

Teacher behavior factors and highest loading behaviors	Interrater reliability	Factor loading	Correlation with teacher rating
Enthusiasm (Factor 1)			
speaks expressively or emphatically	.78	.76	.63*
moves about while lecturing	.83	.67	.40*
gestures with hands and arms	.69	.65	.34*
shows facial expressions	.66	.65	.47*
uses humor	.84	.61	.49*
reads lecture verbatim from notes	.75	−.60	−.33*
Clarity (Factor 2)			
uses concrete examples of concepts	.66	.84	.17
gives multiple examples	.65	.79	.30*
points out practical applications	.67	.76	.26
stresses important points	.66	.75	.47*
repeats difficult ideas	.56	.68	.21
Interaction (Factor 3)			
addresses students by name	.92	.83	.32*
encourages questions and comments	.74	.77	.42*
talks with students after class	.69	.70	.13
praises students for good ideas	.76	.69	.37*
asks questions of class	.86	.64	.37*
Task orientation (Factor 4)			
advises students regarding exams	.67	.80	.04
provides sample exam questions	.85	.77	.15
proceeds at rapid pace	.73	.72	.22
digresses from theme of lecture	.64	−.69	−.13
states course objectives	.67	.63	−.07
Rapport (Factor 5)			
friendly, easy to talk to	.71	.74	.35*
shows concern for student progress	.69	.71	.45*
offers to help students with problems	.83	.66	.22
tolerant of other viewpoints	.72	.61	.11
Organization (Factor 6)			
puts outline of lecture on board	.81	.79	−.08
uses headings and subheadings	.79	.79	.01
gives preliminary overview of lecture	.72	.68	.24
signals transition to new topic	.66	.66	.31*
explains how each topic fits in	.65	.66	−.01

Teaching behaviors loading on the Interaction factor could be hypothesized to influence instructional outcomes by encouraging and rewarding active participation by students in the classroom. Research in cognitive psychology confirms that learning is more effective when the learner participates actively in all stages of information processing, including retrieval of information from long-term memory (Mayer, 1987). Teaching behaviors such as "addresses students by name" and "praises students for good ideas" would appear to be effective in encouraging participation by students in class, whereas behaviors such as "asks questions of individual students" provide specific practice in retrieval of knowledge from memory.

Although all of the above three categories of teaching behavior correlated significantly with student instructional ratings in the Murray (1983a) study, it was hypothesized that the impact of Clarity and Interaction behaviors was secondary to, or conditional upon, the impact of Enthusiasm behaviors. The rationale of this hypothesis is that teaching behaviors aimed at clarifying concepts or fostering student participation are not likely to be effective unless student attention has already been engaged by teacher enthusiasm or expressiveness. Consistent with such an interpretation, differences among low-, medium-, and high-rated teachers were larger for Enthusiasm behaviors than for any other category of teaching behavior. Furthermore, correlations between the Enthusiasm factor and student ratings were undiminished when the other two factors were statistically controlled through semi-partial correlation, whereas correlations of Clarity and Participation factors with student ratings were reduced to near-zero when Enthusiasm was statistically controlled.

In summary, Murray (1983a) found significant correlations between teaching behaviors and instructional outcomes in a research design that minimized rater biases operating in most previous studies. Consistent with prior research, teaching behaviors accounted for a sizable proportion of variance in student instructional ratings, and the behaviors discriminating most clearly between effective and ineffective teachers were those that reflected teacher enthusiasm, clarity of explanation, and encouragement of student participation. A strong point of the Murray (1983a) study is that an attempt was made to explain the impact of teaching behaviors in theoretical terms. A weak point is that teaching effectiveness was measured solely by student ratings, with no direct measure of amount learned or cognitive gain.

A follow-up study by Murray (1985) was similar in design to that described above, except that a 100-item (rather than 60-item) version of the Teacher Behaviors Inventory was used, and student ratings of overall teaching effectiveness were obtained from the same course in which classroom observations were made, rather than from previous courses. A factor analysis of instructor mean ratings of the 93 reliably judged TBI items yielded 6 major factors interpreted as Enthusiasm, Clarity, Interaction, Task Orientation, Rapport, and Organization. Table 2 lists the low-inference teaching behaviors loading highest on each of these factors. The multiple correlation between instructor scores on these 6 factors and mean end-of-term student ratings was .74, indicating that approximately 55 percent of between-teacher variance in student instructional ratings was attributable to classroom teaching behaviors. As may be noted in Table 2, significant correlations with student ratings were found for individual behaviors loading on 5 of the 6 major factors (all except Task Orientation), but, as in the Murray (1983a) study, correlations were largest and most frequent for behaviors loading on the Enthusiasm, Clarity, and Interaction factors. The following three behaviors loading on the Enthusiasm factor showed particularly high correlations with student global effectiveness ratings: "speaks expressively or emphatically," "uses humor," and "shows facial expressions." As noted above, these behaviors appear to serve an attention-getting role in classroom teaching. If a stimulus is unchanging and predictable, we tend to stop paying attention to it. An instructor who exhibits enthusiasm and expressiveness in the classroom is likely to be perceived as dynamic and spontaneous rather than as unchanging and predictable, and thus is unlikely to be "tuned out" by students.

Most research on low-inference college teaching behaviors, including that done by the present writer (Murray, 1983a, 1985), has relied solely on student instructional ratings as a measure of teaching effectiveness. It remains to be seen whether teaching behaviors that correlate with student ratings are similarly related to other, more ultimate criteria of effective teaching, such as gains in student knowledge and motivation. To address this issue, Murray (1983b) investigated low-inference teaching behaviors in relation to a full range of instructional outcome measures, including student learning and student motivation for further study. The research was conducted over a 5-year period in a multiple-section introductory psychology course (mean section size = 182). Students in this course were randomly assigned to class sections taught by different instructors, and all sections wrote a common, objectively scored final examination and completed standardized course evaluation forms. Under these conditions, it is reasonable to assume that class sections were initially equivalent in student aptitude and that any between-section differences in outcome measures were attributable to differences in teaching. Classroom teaching behaviors of the 36 participating instructors were recorded by trained observers who unobtrusively visited regular classes and completed the 100-item version of the Teacher Behaviors Inventory. A factor analysis of TBI items yielded a total of 12 factors, as listed in Table 3. Instructors were assigned factor scores on each of these 12 dimensions, and the latter were analyzed in relation to class mean scores on 6 different instructional outcome variables. The outcome variables included two measures of student satisfaction (course rating, instructor rating), two measures of student motivation (hours of studying per week, frequency of enrollment in senior psychology courses) and two measures of student learning (performance on common final examination, self-rating of amount learned).

The major findings of the Murray (1983b) study are summarized in Table 3. First, there was a significant overall relationship between teaching behaviors and instructional outcomes. Twenty-six of 72 individual correlations between teaching behavior factors and instructional outcome measures were statistically significant, and multiple regression analyses showed that the 12 factors taken collectively accounted for 38 to 85 percent of between-section variance in the various outcome measures. Second, teaching behavior factors tended to correlate higher with student ratings of the course and instructor (mean $r = .37$) than with measures of student learning (mean $r = .26$) or student motivation (mean $r = .20$). Third, teaching behavior dimensions tended to correlate differently (i.e., inconsistently) with different outcome measures. For example, both Rapport/Interaction and Conceptual Clarity correlated highly with student instructional ratings, but neither of these factors was significantly related to student studying, examination performance, or amount learned rating. Conversely, the factors that best predicted student achievement, namely Task Orientation and Use of Class Time, showed generally weak and non-significant correlations with student ratings of instructor and course. None of the 12 teaching behavior factors correlated significantly with all 6 instructional outcome measures, although Task Orientation correlated with 5 of 6 measures, and Enthusiasm/Expressiveness correlated with 4 of 6 outcomes, including final examination performance.

Table 3. Correlations between teacher behavior factors and criterion measures in Murray (1983b) study

	Criterion measures					
	Teacher rating	Course rating	Amount of studying	Senior course registration	Final exam performance	Amount learned rating
Rapport	.62[*]	.43[*]	.14	.34*	.27	.17
Conceptual clarity	.78*	.55*	.20	.36*	.16	.29
Enthusiasm	.72*	.57*	.25	.45*	.36*	.28
Task orientation	.27	.41*	.39*	.33*	.38*	.39*
Organization	.34*	.38*	.14	.14	.25	.17
Speech clarity	.64*	.36*	.05	.02	.29	.31
Use of class time	.22	.30	.12	.00	.41*	.25
Informality	.43*	.42*	.31	.35*	.08	.29
Nervousness	−.14	−.06	.13	.01	.24	.35*
Rate of speaking	.17	.20	.33*	.28	.31	.27
Use of media	.08	.17	.11	.20	−.23	.01
Criticism	−.34*	−.19	.01	−.21	−.25	−.20
Multiple R^2	.85*	.76*	.38*	.48*	.59*	.53*

*Statistically significant at .05 level.

Analysis of intercorrelations among the 6 different instructional outcome variables indicated a correlation of .30 between mean student rating of instructor quality and mean student performance on the common final examination, and a correlation of .55 between instructor rating and frequency of student enrollment in further courses. The first correlation, although statistically significant, is lower than the average correlation of .43 reported in Cohen's (1981) meta-analysis of studies using final examination performance as a validation criterion for student ratings. The second correlation coincides well with previous evidence that student ratings are valid predictors of continuing motivation to learn on the part of students (Bolton, Bonge, and Marr, 1979; Marsh and Overall, 1980).

The results of the Murray (1983b) study suggest that low-inference teaching behaviors are related to a wide range of cognitive and affective outcome measures. In other words, the extent to which a student enjoys the course, studies a lot or a little, does well on the final examination, and enrolls in further courses in the same subject area appears to be determined, at least in part, by specific classroom behaviors of the instructor. Although instructor behaviors are related to outcome measures, this relationship is by no means simple and straightforward. Teaching behaviors that correlate with one outcome measure may not correlate in similar ways with other outcome measures. The only teaching behavior factors to correlate consistently with a wide range of outcome measures in the Murray (1983b) study were Enthusiasm/Expressiveness (e.g., "speaks expressively," "moves about while lecturing") and Task Orientation (e.g., "states teaching objectives," "provides sample exam questions"). Perhaps teachers who exhibit these behaviors motivate their students both to participate actively in class and to work hard out of class, thus leading to high scores on a number of different outcome measures. It is surprising, both on intuitive grounds and in light of previous findings, that neither the Conceptual Clarity nor the Organization factor correlated with cognitive or motivation outcomes. Significant correlations between teacher clarity and study learning were reported in previous studies by Solomon, Rosenberg, and Bezdek (1964) and Tom and Cushman (1975), and in Feldman's (1989) recent review of student rating dimensions in relation to student achievement.

Yet another observational study of classroom teaching was conducted by Erdle and Murray (1986). The goal of this study was to determine whether there are differences among academic disciplines in (1) the frequency of occurrence of various classroom teaching behaviors, and (2) the correlation of these behaviors with perceived teaching effectiveness. The sample of teachers consisted of 124 faculty members at the University of Western Ontario holding positions in Arts and Humanities, Social Sciences, or Natural Sciences. Classroom behavior observations and end-of-term student ratings of instructor effectiveness were obtained as in Murray (1983a, 1983b, 1985). A principal-components factor analysis of teacher mean TBI data yielded a total of 14 factors, some of which (e.g., Pacing, Interest, Mannerisms) had not been found in previous studies. Analysis of variance indicated that 7 of 14 teaching behavior factors differed significantly in estimated frequency of occurrence across academic disciplines. For example, behaviors loading on the Rapport and Interaction factors occurred more frequently in Arts and Humanities than in Natural Sciences teachers, whereas behaviors reflecting use of graphs and rapid pacing in lecturing were more frequent in Science than in Arts teachers. Despite these differences in frequency of occurrence, correlations between teaching behaviors and student instructional ratings were surprisingly similar across academic disciplines. Only 2 of 14 teaching behavior factors showed significant differences among disciplines in magnitude of correlation with student ratings. Factor 2 (Interest) correlated higher with student ratings in the Social Sciences than in the Natural Sciences ($r = .71$ and $.37$ respectively), whereas Factor 3 (Disclosure) contributed more strongly to perceived effectiveness in Natural Science teachers than in Arts or Social Science teachers ($r = .65$, $.30$, and $.25$ respectively). In sum, the Erdle and Murray study provided no support for the theory, popular in faculty coffee lounges, that the constituents of effective teaching vary markedly for different academic disciplines.

The majority of studies reviewed to this point were carried out in the context of either a lecture or lecture-discussion method of teaching. Thus the question arises as to whether teaching behaviors identified as effective in these studies can be shown to be similarly effective with other methods of teaching, such as small-group discussion and one-to-one tutoring.

Smith (1977) and Andrews (1980) studied the impact of specific teaching behaviors in small-group discussion classes. Smith used a modified version of Flanders' (1970) Interaction Analysis to code student and teacher behaviors from audiotapes of classes taught by 12 liberal arts instructors. Teaching effectiveness was measured by student pretest-to-posttest gain scores on the Watson-Glaser Critical Thinking Appraisal, a paper-and-pencil test assessing 5 aspects of critical thinking ability. Although the mean gain in critical thinking for all classes combined was not statistically significant, significant correlations were reported across class sections between instructor behaviors and student gain in critical thinking. In particular, instructors whose students showed above-average gain scores were more likely to ask questions and encourage student-teacher and student-student interaction.

Andrews (1980) analyzed videotapes of discussion sections in first-year humanities courses at the University of California, San Diego. It was found that quality of class discussion, as measured by objective indices such as number of students participating and frequency of student-to-student interaction, was related to the types of questions asked by instructors. For example, "divergent" or open-ended questions led to higher quality discussion than "convergent" questions (i.e., questions for which there is a single correct answer), and focused questions produced better discussion than unfocused questions.

The teaching behaviors identified as effective in the Smith (1977) and Andrews (1980) studies overlap to some extent with behaviors loading on Interaction and Rapport factors in previous studies of lecture-style teaching. Other factors reported as significant in lecture-based research, such as Clarity and Enthusiasm, were not included in the Smith and Andrews studies.

Roberts and Becker (1976) investigated the teaching behaviors of 123 instructors engaged in one-on-one vocational and technical teaching in high schools, technical schools, and community colleges. Teaching behaviors were measured by classroom (shop) observations, rating scales, and narrative summaries. Two classroom observers were trained to the point where they showed adequate interrater reliability ($r = .75$), then each observer was assigned to observe the teaching of half of the sample of teachers. Overall teaching effectiveness was measured by end-of-term ratings from students and supervisors. It was found that teachers receiving high ratings from supervisors and/or students were more likely to: spend time in direct face-to-face contact with students; exhibit various expressive behaviors such as body movement, eye contact, and vocal variation; address students by name; and use praise rather than criticism in interactions with students. Despite some notable differences (e.g., face-to-face contact with students), there are obvious parallels between these behaviors and the Enthusiasm and Rapport factors identified in previous lecture-based studies.

In summary, very little research has been done on low-inference teaching behaviors in contexts other than lecturing, and the few studies reported have typically failed to include a full range of teaching behaviors comparable to those investigated in lecture-based research. These problems notwithstanding, available evidence indicates at least some degree of overlap between teaching behaviors important in lecturing and teaching behaviors important in small-group discussion and one-to-one tutoring.

Conclusions

The observational studies reviewed above support the following general conclusions concerning low-inference teaching behaviors in the college classroom:

1. Assessment of low-inference classroom behaviors, either by direct observation or by coding from videotape, has been found to show high levels of interrater reliability, indicating that low-inference behavioral data are objective and accurate.
2. Classroom teaching behaviors have been shown in a variety of research designs to make a significant difference in student attitudes, learning of course content, and motivation for further learning. In some cases, classroom behaviors have accounted for as much as 70 to 80 percent of between-class variance in non-cognitive outcome measures.
3. Three dimensions of teaching behavior have consistently emerged as strong predictors of instructional outcomes, namely Enthusiasm/Expressiveness, Clarity of Explanation and Rapport/Interaction. Across all studies reviewed above, the mean correlation between teacher enthusiasm (or facsimile) and various outcome measures was .37. Comparable figures for teacher clarity and teacher interaction were .35 and .28 respectively.
4. The impact of classroom teaching behaviors on student development can be interpreted in terms of cognitive theories of information-processing and learning. Murray (1983a) proposed that teacher enthusiasm plays an attention-getting role in information-processing, whereas teacher clarity facilitates the encoding of information in long-term memory, and teacher interaction encourages active responding and memory retrieval.
5. Teaching behaviors have typically shown an uneven profile of correlations with different instructional outcomes. For example, behaviors that correlate with affective outcome measures often fail to correlate similarly with cognitive outcomes, while behaviors that predict cognitive gain may fail to predict affective development.
6. It remains to be seen whether classroom behaviors found to be effective in the lecture method of teaching are similarly effective in non-lecture contexts. It is possible that some categories of teaching behavior (e.g., enthusiasm) are effective in all or nearly all teaching methods, while other categories (e.g., questioning) are specific to one or two methods only.

7. Within the traditional lecture method, available evidence suggests that specific teaching behaviors contribute similarly to overall teaching effectiveness in different academic disciplines.

EXPERIMENTAL STUDIES

Experimental studies of low-inference teaching behaviors in higher education can be traced back to Jones' (1923) pioneering research on college teaching. Rather than attempting an exhaustive review of research to date, this paper will focus on experimental studies that supplement or complement previously reported observational research. Since either teacher enthusiasm or teacher clarity has been the topic of nearly all experimental research, the present review is organized in terms of these two categories.

One way that experimental studies of teaching can supplement observational studies is by clarifying cause–effect relationships. Although the observational research reviewed above shows that teaching behaviors are correlated with instructional outcomes, it provides no basis for concluding that teaching behaviors are causes of instructional outcomes. As noted previously, a significant correlation between teaching behavior X and instructional outcome Y might be interpreted to mean that X causes Y, but could just as easily reflect reverse causation (Y causes X) or third-variable causation (Z causes concurrent variation of both X and Y). Ambiguities of this sort have serious consequences, both theoretically and practically. They are important theoretically because they prevent us from gaining a clear understanding of what causes what in classroom teaching. They are important practically because they make it difficult to provide teachers with reliable advice on how to teach effectively. A teacher who is advised on the basis of correlational evidence to increase his or her frequency of teaching behavior X, and who then discovers that this innovation makes no difference in instructional outcome Y, is likely to be reluctant to accept further research-based advice on teaching. The best way to confirm or disconfirm the causal status of a classroom teaching behavior is by way of a "true experiment" in which the behavior in question is systematically manipulated while all other conditions are held constant. All of the studies reviewed in this section involve such manipulation and control.

A second way in which experimental studies of classroom teaching can supplement prior observational research is by providing needed data on cognitive outcome measures. Only three of the observational studies reviewed above used objective measures of student learning. Thus it is difficult, on the basis of these studies alone, to make firm conclusions about the cognitive impact of classroom teaching behaviors. Fortunately, all of the experimental studies reviewed in this section included measures of amount learned by students.

Teacher enthusiasm

Several investigators, dating back to Coats and Smidchens (1966), have conducted laboratory or field experiments testing the effects of teacher enthusiasm on student learning of academic material. The subjects in the Coats and Smidchens experiment were 184 students enrolled in 8 introductory speech classes at the University of Michigan. Two instructors, graduate students in education, gave 10-minute guest lectures in 4 classes each. Lecture content was identical for all classes taught by a given instructor, but the lecture was presented in a "dynamic" fashion in two (randomly selected) classes, and in a "static" fashion in the two remaining classes. The dynamic condition included the usual behavioral ingredients of teacher enthusiasm: movement, gesturing, eye contact with students, vocal inflection, and minimal reliance on lecture notes. The static lecture was presented with good diction and volume, but was read verbatim from a manuscript, and included a minimum of eye contact, vocal inflection, and animation. Immediately following the lecture, students in all classes completed a 10-item multiple-choice recall test based on lecture material. Half of the students taught by each instructor (one class per treatment condition) were forewarned of the recall test, and half were not warned. It was found that, regardless of forewarning, students in the dynamic condition performed better on the recall test than students in the static condition. Mean recall was approximately 20 percent higher for dynamic lectures than for static lectures, and teacher enthusiasm accounted for 36 percent of the total variance in student recall scores.

In addition to confirming prior observational evidence that teacher enthusiasm is related to objective measures of student learning (e.g., Solomon, Rosenberg, and Bezdek, 1964), the Coats and Smidchens experiment suggests that enthusiastic teaching is a cause (rather than merely a correlate) of amount learned by students. The fact that this experiment was conducted under field conditions increases our faith that the results are applicable to real-world classrooms.

Further evidence of the importance of teacher enthusiasm in the college classroom was provided by the famous "Dr. Fox" experiments. In one of the early experiments in this series, Ware and Williams (1975) presented six versions of the same videotaped lecture, varying both in information coverage and lecturer enthusiasm, to six matched groups of students in a general studies course. The lecture was 20 minutes long and covered the topic of biochemistry of memory. All six versions of the lecture were produced by the same individual, a professional actor referred to as "Dr. Fox." The lectures were either low, medium, or high in information coverage (either 4, 14, or 26 substantive points presented in 20 minutes), and were presented at either a low or a high level of "seductiveness" (3 x 2 factorial design). The high seductiveness condition was defined by expressive teaching behaviors such as humor, movement and gesture, and charisma. The low seductiveness condition was characterized by a more businesslike, take-it-or-leave-it attitude. Following the lecture, all students rated the effectiveness of the instructor on an 18-item questionnaire, and completed a 26-item multiple-choice test based on lecture content. It was found that both student instructional ratings and student performance on the multiple-choice recall test were higher for enthusiastically presented lectures than for nonenthusiastic lectures, and higher for high-information than for medium- or low-information lectures. Thus, the Ware and Williams study provides further confirmation that expressive or enthusiastic teaching behaviors are causal antecedents of both student instructional ratings and student learning of academic content.

Further analysis of student rating data in the Ware and Williams experiment revealed that ratings differed significantly as a function of information coverage under the low seductiveness condition but not under the high seductiveness condition. The authors argued that the lack of relationship between ratings and information coverage under the high seductiveness condition (the "Dr. Fox effect") demonstrates that students can be "seduced" into giving high ratings to teachers who say next to nothing but do so in a very enthusiastic way. On this basis, Ware and Williams not only questioned the validity of student ratings, but also placed a negative connotation on teacher enthusiasm or expressiveness as a characteristic of classroom teaching. An alternative interpretation of the Ware and Williams data is that since teacher expressiveness contributed to high levels of both student ratings and student learning, (who could ask for anything more?), it must be viewed as an important classroom variable that should be taken seriously by any instructor seeking to enhance his or her teaching performance.

Follow-up experiments in the Dr. Fox series sometimes did (e.g., Williams and Ware, 1977) and sometimes did not (e.g., Perry, Abrami, and Leventhal, 1979) yield the same results as the original Ware and Williams (1975) experiment. A meta-analysis of research in this area by Abrami, Leventhal and Perry (1982) indicated that, across all experiments, instructor enthusiasm had a substantial impact on student instructional ratings (estimated mean variance accounted for = 28.5%), but a much smaller impact on student retention of lecture content (mean variance accounted for = 4.3%). Information coverage, on the other hand, had a large impact on student achievement (mean variance accounted for = 15.8%), but a much smaller impact on student instructional ratings (mean variance accounted for = 4.6%). This pattern of results is consistent with Murray's (1983b) finding that teacher enthusiasm correlated more highly with student ratings than with student final examination performance, whereas teacher task orientation (which might be viewed as analogous to content coverage) correlated more highly with exam performance than with student ratings. The effect of teacher enthusiasm on student recall scores was significant in only 5 of 10 experiments reviewed by Abrami, Leventhal and Perry, and the largest estimate of variance due to teacher enthusiasm in any one experiment was 10.5 percent. This result reminds us that, despite its widespread significance as a factor in teaching effectiveness, teacher enthusiasm sometimes fails to influence instructional outcomes. On the other hand, it should be noted that "effect size" estimates for teacher enthusiasm tend to be larger in observational studies (e.g., Solomon, Rosenberg, and Bezdek, 1964) and in experimental studies done under field conditions (e.g., Coats and Smidchens, 1966) than in the laboratory experiments conducted on the Dr. Fox effect. One possible reason for this difference is that a wider range of variations in teacher enthusiasm are present in real classrooms than in laboratory simulations. Another possibility is that field studies have typically used teacher or class mean scores in calculating outcome variances, whereas laboratory studies have used individual student data, which of course contain more "noise" or "error" variation.

Other experiments on teacher enthusiasm, using procedures similar to those described above but conducted outside the Dr. Fox tradition, have yielded generally positive results. Andersen and Withrow (1981) presented videotaped lectures incorporating low, medium, and high levels of lecturer nonverbal expressiveness to randomly assigned groups of students in a speech communication course. The lecture was 10 minutes in length and covered the topic of organizational theory. The high-expressiveness version of the lecture included vocal variation, gestures, facial animation, eye contact, minimal use of notes, and movement away from the lectern. The low-expressiveness lecture featured a monotone voice, little facial expression, and eyes fixed on lecture notes. All other factors, including lecture content, room conditions, and lecturer appearance, were held constant across treatment conditions. Data analysis revealed that lecturer expressiveness had a significant positive impact on perceived teaching effectiveness, accounting for 22 percent of the variance in student ratings of the lecture and lecturer. However, groups receiving low, medium, and high expressiveness lectures did not differ significantly on either an immediate or a delayed multiple-choice test based on lecture content.

Whereas Andersen and Withrow found that teacher enthusiasm influenced student ratings but not student achievement, Slater (1981) reported large effects of teacher enthusiasm on both ratings and achievement measures, and on student motivation for further learning as well. Four versions of a 12-minute videotaped lecture on the teacher expectation effect, varying in both vocal and nonvocal expressiveness (2 x 2 factorial design), were presented to randomly assigned groups of university students under simulated classroom conditions. Following the lecture, students completed an instructional rating form, wrote essay and multiple-choice tests keyed to lecture content, and were asked to sign their name and provide a mailing address plus money for postage (which was subsequently refunded) if they wished to receive further reading material on the topic of the lecture. The latter was viewed as a strict behavioral test of student motivation for further learning! Analyses of variance showed that high levels of teacher expressiveness resulted in more positive student ratings, higher scores on both multiple-choice and essay achievement tests, and larger numbers of students requesting (and paying for) further reading on the lecture topic. The frequency of students requesting further reading ranged from 28 percent in the High Vocal/High Nonvocal Expressiveness group to 5 percent in the Low Vocal/Low Nonvocal group. Although there were exceptions, nonvocal expressive behaviors (e.g., body movement) tended to have a bigger impact on outcome measures than vocal expressive behaviors (e.g., pitch variation).

Recent research by Perry and his associates (e.g., Perry, 1985; Perry and Magnusson, 1987) on "perceived control" in the college classroom has provided additional evidence of the diverse effects of teacher enthusiasm. Using experimental procedures similar to those described above, Perry has shown that expressive teaching behaviors not only lead to higher levels of student achievement, but also, at least under certain conditions, cause students to develop a stronger sense of personal control over classroom events. In other words, students taught by an expressive instructor believe they can predict and influence what happens in the classroom, whereas students taught by a non-expressive instructor are less likely to develop positive self-attributions. Moreover, a recent experiment by Perry and Penner (1990) showed that teacher expressiveness led to higher student achievement on a homework assignment done outside of class as a follow-up to a videotaped lecture presentation.

In summary, experimental studies confirm that expressive, enthusiastic teaching behaviors are causally related to a variety of instructional outcome measures, including student ratings and student learning. Recent evidence suggests that the impact of teacher enthusiasm extends to outcomes such as student attributions, motivation for further learning, and individual study outside the classroom. It is not clear that these wide-ranging effects of teacher enthusiasm can be explained solely in terms of maintenance of student attention in the classroom. Perhaps students tend to model or imitate the energy and commitment of an enthusiastic instructor, thereby increasing their own motivation for study outside the classroom.

Teacher Clarity

As was the case with teacher enthusiasm, low-inference classroom behaviors contributing to teacher clarity have been investigated in several experimental studies, and have been found to have robust effects on both student ratings and student learning. Land (1985) reviewed 10 experiments reporting significant effects of teacher clarity, 3 of which are discussed here. Land (1979) evaluated the combined impact of 6 low-inference teacher clarity variables, including vagueness terms (i.e., inexact statements), transition signals (i.e., cues that mark the end of one topic and the beginning of another), and verbal mazes (i.e., false starts or halts in speech). Two versions of the same videotaped lesson, varying only in the presence or absence of the 6 clarity behaviors, were presented to students in an introductory education course. Students were told to take notes during the lesson, but were not allowed to use their notes during subsequent testing. The achievement test, consisting of 30 multiple-choice items written at the comprehension level of Bloom's taxonomy, was completed either immediately following the lesson or after a delay of one week. Statistical analysis showed that, for both immediate and delayed testing, comprehension scores were higher for the high-clarity lesson than for the low-clarity lesson. The author hypothesized that the use of explicit transition signals in classroom teaching assists students in organizing the subject matter, whereas the use of vagueness terms causes students to lose confidence in the instructor and thus in themselves.

Land and Combs (1981) constructed 10 videotaped lectures varying in the frequency of occurrence of the following teacher vagueness behaviors: false starts or halts in speech, redundantly spoken words, and tangles of words. An attempt was made to approximate the range of teacher clarity levels found under real-world conditions. Separate randomly assigned groups of students viewed each of the videotaped lectures, then all students rated quality of teaching on a 10-item evaluation form and completed a multiple-choice examination keyed to lecture content. Teacher clarity was found to have a significant impact on both student instructional ratings and student examination performance, accounting for 35 percent of variance in the first measure and 5 percent of variance in the latter. Thus, as in the Dr. Fox experiments reviewed by Abrami, Leventhal, and Perry (1982) and in Murray's (1983b) classroom observation study, teaching behaviors correlated more highly with student ratings of teaching than with objective indicators of student learning. Further analyses showed that student exam performance correlated more highly with student perceptions of teacher clarity than with actual (planned) variation of clarity behaviors. This result suggests that the relationship between teacher clarity and student achievement is mediated by student perceptions of teacher clarity behaviors.

Hines, Cruickshank, and Kennedy (1985) investigated teacher clarity in a research design best described as a quasi-experiment rather than a true experiment. Although factors such as the context and content of instruction were carefully controlled, teaching behaviors were allowed to vary naturally rather than being experimentally manipulated. The sample of instructors consisted of 32 education students enrolled in an experimental peer teaching program. Each instructor was provided with a standard set of objectives and materials on the topic of matrix multiplication, and was allowed 2 days in which to prepare a 25-minute lesson to be presented to a group of 4 to 6 fellow students. Two observers viewed videotapes of the 32 mini-lessons and either counted or rated the frequency of occurrence of 29 low-inference teacher clarity behaviors. Additional data on teaching behaviors were obtained from student ratings and instructor self-ratings. Following instruction, students in each peer group rated their degree of satisfaction with the lesson and wrote a completion-type achievement test on matrix multiplication. Canonical correlation analysis revealed that teacher clarity behaviors as a set were significantly related to outcome measures as a set. Follow-up multiple regression analyses showed that observer estimates of low-inference clarity behaviors accounted for 36 percent of the variance in student instructional ratings and 52 percent of the variance in student achievement. This result runs counter to the general rule (see above) that teaching behaviors correlate higher with student ratings than with student learning. The teacher clarity behaviors showing the strongest relationships to student ratings and student achievement included the following: "uses relevant examples," "asks questions of students," "reviews material," "repeats points when students do not understand," "teaches in a step-by-step manner," and "provides frequent examples." These behaviors are similar to items loading on Clarity of Explanation factors identified in observational studies reviewed above (e.g., Murray, 1983b, 1985). As previously noted, such behaviors might be hypothesized to influence student learning by facilitating the encoding of information in long-term memory.

Conclusions

The experimental studies reviewed above support the following general conclusions regarding low-inference classroom teaching behaviors:

1. Classroom teaching behaviors, at least in the enthusiasm and clarity domains, appear to be causal antecedents (rather than mere correlates) of various instructional outcome measures.
2. Low-inference teaching behaviors have been shown to influence not only student instructional ratings, but objective measures of student learning as well.

3. As in observational studies, teaching behaviors accounted for a sizable proportion of outcome measure variance in most experiments. As a general rule, teaching behaviors accounted for more variance in student instructional ratings than in objective measures of student learning.

4. The specific teaching behaviors used to define teacher enthusiasm and teacher clarity manipulations in experimental studies were similar to behaviors loading on corresponding Enthusiasm and Clarity factors in observational studies.

5. Recent evidence suggests that enthusiastic or expressive classroom teaching behaviors may affect student motivational and attributional processes that extend far beyond the classroom.

IMPLICATIONS AND APPLICATIONS

The research reviewed above indicates that there are specific, concrete teaching behaviors that make a difference in the college classroom. They make a difference in the sense that they are causally related to student satisfaction, student learning of course content, and student motivation for further learning. To date, low-inference classroom behaviors have been studied mainly in the context of lecture and lecture-discussion styles of teaching. However, within this context, research findings have been remarkably consistent across different methods of study, academic disciplines, geographical areas, and types of students. Also, it seems likely that at least some of the teaching behaviors identified as effective in lecturing will turn out to be equally effective in non-lecture methods of teaching.

The teaching behaviors showing the strongest and most consistent relationships with instructional outcome measures have been those associated with the dimensions of teacher enthusiasm, teacher clarity, and teacher-student interaction. Low-inference behaviors, associated with the teacher enthusiasm dimension include vocal variation, movement and gesture, facial expression, and use of humor. Behaviors contributing to teacher clarity include use of concrete examples, providing an outline, repeating difficult points, and signaling the transition from one topic to the next. Behaviors that foster teacher-student interaction include asking questions, addressing students by name, soliciting questions and comments, and praising students for good ideas.

Given that the teaching behaviors found to be effective in prior research are specific, concrete, denotable, and presumably acquirable, the most obvious implication of this research is that college and university instructors can improve their classroom performance simply by exhibiting these behaviors with greater frequency. Although there are no "money-back guarantees," research evidence provides teachers with a strong basis for expecting significant improvement in student satisfaction, motivation, and learning if appropriate teaching behaviors are acquired and implemented. There are, however, some important cautions and caveats associated with this "behavioral" prescription for teaching improvement. The first caveat is that some low-inference teaching behaviors are easy to acquire, while others are extremely difficult to acquire. It is fairly easy to adopt the behavior of putting an outline on the blackboard, but not at all easy to develop effective speech behaviors such as pitch variation and vocal expressiveness. The second caveat is that teachers should be selective and judicious in adopting low-inference teaching behaviors. Rather than trying to mechanically emulate a wide array of teaching behaviors, instructors would be better advised to focus on a small subset of behaviors that are compatible with the instructor's basic traits, abilities, and educational values, and are relevant to areas of needed improvement. The third caveat is that there is more to effective college teaching than effective classroom behaviors. An instructor who teaches clearly and enthusiastically, but is seriously lacking in knowledge of subject, academic standards, or curriculum coverage, is not an effective instructor. This fact, parenthetically, supports the argument that student instructional ratings, when used for summative purposes, should always be supplemented by colleague assessment of "content" or "substance" aspects of instruction. The fourth and final caveat is that there is resistance in the minds of many faculty members to the idea of implementing certain teaching behaviors, particularly expressive or enthusiastic behaviors, in the college classroom. Faculty members are disturbed that they are being asked to "put on a show" for students, or turn their lectures into "Hollywood productions." The traditional faculty view is that it is the responsibility of the student, not the instructor, to maintain a high level of student attention and motivation in the classroom. Although the present writer has some sympathy for this viewpoint (especially on Monday mornings), there are at least two counterarguments that can be offered on behalf of expressive teaching behaviors. First, there are reasons for proposing that responsibility for student attentiveness should be shared, at least in part, by the instructor. Expressive teaching behaviors have been shown to play more than a mere cosmetic role in the classroom, in that they influence student learning as well as teacher "popularity." If it is the teacher's responsibility to create conditions that facilitate student learning, then conveying enthusiasm in the classroom could be viewed as a major component of teacher responsibility. Secondly, there is no reason to believe that expressive teaching behaviors are in any way incompatible with more traditional criteria of effective teaching, such as content coverage and high academic standards. In fact, it can be argued that the best teachers of all are those who excel in both "content" and "delivery" aspects of instruction.

The above caveats notwithstanding, there is evidence that research on low-inference teaching behaviors can be successfully applied to the improvement of college and university teaching. The remainder of this chapter reviews recent attempts, involving either feedback or training, to improve teaching effectiveness through modification of instructors' specific classroom behaviors.

Behavioral Feedback

One way in which research on low-inference behaviors can be applied to improvement of teaching is through the development of better procedures for providing diagnostic feedback to instructors. This type of application can be achieved by two separate routes. On the one hand, knowledge of specific teaching behaviors contributing to student instructional ratings can provide a basis for more meaningful interpretation of the typical "high-inference" student rating forms in current use. In the absence of this knowledge, an instructor who receives poor ratings on global dimensions such as "clarity" and "rapport" is unlikely to be aware of the specific teaching behaviors that led to these ratings, or the specific changes that need to be made to bring about improvement. A second, and perhaps more fruitful, approach to improvement of diagnostic feedback is to construct student rating forms that focus directly on low-inference classroom behaviors, and thus provide clearer prescriptions for remedial action. Low ratings on items such as "maintains eye contact with students" or "signals the transition from one topic to the next" provide the instructor with clear signals as to what is wrong and what remedial action is needed.

Although behavioral feedback forms similar to those described above are probably too long, detailed, and idiosyncratic for use in administrative personnel decisions, they would appear to be both appropriate and effective for formative, self-improvement purposes. Contrary to this hypothesis, early attempts to demonstrate beneficial effects of behavioral feedback met with limited success. Froman and Owen (1980) compared randomly assigned groups of teachers who, at mid-semester, received either no student feedback, feedback on 10 general characteristics such as "stimulates interest," feedback on 68 specific instructional behaviors such as "presents material at too fast a pace," or feedback on both general characteristics and specific behaviors. No significant differences were found among these groups in end-of-term student ratings of overall instructor effectiveness. One possible reason for the nonsignificant results of the Froman and Owen study is that classroom teaching behaviors that are acquired gradually over a period of many years are unlikely to change significantly within a post-feedback interval of only 6 to 8 weeks. Second, the feedback provided on specific instructional behaviors was very limited in terms of implications for improvement. Only those classroom behaviors checked by at least 25 percent of students as "particularly notable" were reported to the instructor as feedback. For example, an instructor might be informed that 32 percent of students viewed "stresses important points" as a notable characteristic of his or her classroom teaching. This type of feedback is of limited value for formative purposes, as it fails to specify whether the behavior in question is in need of improvement, and if so, whether the behavior needs to be increased in frequency or decreased in frequency. Also, no information was provided on teaching behaviors checked by less than 25 percent of students.

In a second study of the impact of midterm behavioral feedback, McLean (1979) obtained weekly student ratings of overall teaching effectiveness for volunteer experimental and control teachers during 6-week periods preceding and following the receipt of behavioral feedback by experimental teachers. Feedback consisted of mean frequency-of-occurrence estimates of 100 specific classroom behaviors. Frequency estimates were accompanied by: (1) percentile norms which allowed instructors to compare themselves to others teaching similar courses, and (2) information on the magnitude and direction of correlations between teaching behaviors and overall effectiveness ratings in previous research. Although experimental teachers expressed generally favorable attitudes toward behavioral feedback and believed that their teaching had improved as a result of feedback, there was no significant difference between experimental and control teachers in pretest-to-posttest gains in rated teaching effectiveness. However, follow-up analysis showed that experimental teachers whose prefeedback ratings ranked in the bottom third of the sample showed significant improvement following feedback, whereas middle- and high-rated teachers showed no significant improvement. McLean suggested that poorer teachers tend to be unaware of their own classroom behaviors and thus are more in need of specific behavioral feedback than their higher-rated colleagues. Statistical regression was not seen as a viable interpretation of the improved performance of low-rated teachers, because performance gains were restricted to observation periods following the introduction of feedback, and were not apparent in repeated prefeedback observations.

In summary, the McLean study yielded slightly more positive results than the Froman and Owen study, but the case for behavioral feedback was still rather weak. Moreover, the same methodological limitations cited above in relation to the Froman and Owen study seem to apply with equal force to the McLean study. First, McLean used a postfeedback period of only 6 weeks, which is probably too short for detecting changes in well-established teaching behaviors. Second, although behavioral feedback was thorough and well-structured in the McLean study, it is possible that the quantitative information provided, which included elaborate statistical norms, was too complex and difficult to interpret to be useful for improvement of teaching.

More recently, Murray and Smith (1989) reported more clearcut effects of behavioral feedback in a study using a diagnostic behavioral rating form (the Teacher Behaviors Inventory: Diagnostic Version) that incorporated several design improvements suggested by previous negative findings. The diagnostic version of the TBI consists of 50 items, each referring to a specific classroom teaching behavior that had been found in previous research to show adequate interrater reliability and to correlate significantly with student evaluation of overall teaching effectiveness. Students rate each of the 50 classroom teaching behaviors on a 5-point scale to indicate whether, for purposes of instructional improvement, the behavior in question needs to be increased in frequency of occurrence (rating of +1 or +2), decreased in frequency (rating of |m-1 or |m-2), or unchanged in frequency (zero rating). The diagnostic TBI is intended to provide behavioral feedback that is simple, direct, easy to interpret, and obvious in its implications for improvement. With ratings averaged across students, the instructor can obtain feedback on which behaviors to change, and in what direction, simply by identifying TBI items whose mean ratings deviate noticeably from zero.

The sample of instructors in the Murray and Smith (1989) experiment consisted of 60 teaching assistants in geography, psychology, and English at the University of Western Ontario. Half of the instructors in each discipline were randomly assigned to receive midterm behavioral feedback, whereas the other half received no feedback. Behavioral feedback consisted of the mean and standard deviation of student ratings for each item of the diagnostic TBI, plus brief instructions for interpreting the data provided. The experiment was conducted over an 8-month (September to April) academic term, with behavioral feedback provided at the approximate midpoint (late December). Thus the post-feedback interval was at least 4 months, or 2 to 3 times longer than that used by Froman and Owen (1980) and McLean (1979). The impact of feedback was measured by mean midterm to end-of-term gains in student ratings of overall teaching effectiveness, and by mean end-of-term student ratings of amount of teaching improvement. Scores on both measures were significantly higher for experimental than for control instructors, indicating that midterm behavioral feedback led to significant improvement in classroom teaching performance. Furthermore, the estimated effect size for behavioral feedback was .73 standard deviation units, which is considerably higher than the average effect size of .20 reported by Cohen (1980) for student feedback of a more global nature.

Thus, despite the pessimistic outcomes of earlier research, the Murray and Smith study suggests that, under the right conditions, behavioral feedback can contribute significantly to improvement of classroom teaching. More research is needed to confirm or disconfirm the effectiveness of behavioral feedback, both in comparison to absence of feedback and in comparison to obvious alternatives, such as global feedback.

Behavioral Training

A second way in which research on low-inference teaching behaviors can be applied to improvement of instruction is through intensive training of faculty on a limited subset of classroom behaviors known to contribute significantly to instructional outcome measures. As one example of a program of this sort, Murray and Lawrence (1980) assessed the impact of speech and drama training for lecturers as an aid in classroom communication. The rationale of this program was that the same expressive behaviors used by actors to convey meaning on the stage—for example, vocal variation, movement and gesture, facial expression, and spontaneity—can be used by lecturers to communicate more effectively in the classroom. Given that expressive teaching behaviors have been found to correlate highly with student instructional ratings, it was expected that training of these behaviors would produce significant improvement in rated teaching effectiveness. This hypothesis was tested by a nonequivalent control group, pretest–posttest design. The participating instructors were 24 full-time faculty members in the Departments of Psychology, Sociology, and Physics at the University of Western Ontario. Experimental teachers ($n = 12$) participated in a series of 20 two-hour training sessions taught by a professional speech and drama instructor. Specific activities in weekly sessions included breathing and voice exercises, reading of monologues, acting out of short scenes from plays, and delivery of videotaped mini-lectures with corrective feedback from the instructor during playback. In all of these activities, participants were encouraged to make full use of expressive communication behaviors. Experimental teachers volunteered for the acting lessons program and paid a fee to defray expenses. Control teachers $n = 12$) were matched with experimentals in terms of academic discipline and years of teaching, but received no behavioral training. Student ratings of classroom teaching were obtained just prior to and immediately following the 20-week training program for both experimental and control teachers. Experimental teachers showed significant gains in student ratings from pretest to posttest, whereas control teachers showed no measurable change. Although this result suggests that behavioral training did in fact produce significant improvement in classroom teaching effectiveness, it could be argued that experimental teachers, who volunteered for the speech and drama program, were more motivated to improve than controls, and thus would have shown significant pretest-to-posttest gains even in the absence of training. This interpretation was ruled out on the grounds that experimental teachers had shown no significant improvement in student ratings across successive courses taught prior to the onset of behavioral training. Yet another alternative hypothesis is that the superiority of the experimental group reflected a generalized "placebo" effect, resulting perhaps from group interaction or novelty, rather than a specific effect of training. This hypothesis was discounted on the grounds that pretest-to-posttest gains occurred only for target (trained) teaching behaviors, and not for nontarget (control) behaviors.

Given that training of expressive teaching behaviors appears to have produced improved teaching performance, further questions arise concerning the cost effectiveness and long-term persistence of training. On the issue of cost effectiveness, it must first be acknowledged that the gains in student ratings observed in the Murray and Lawrence study were not large in absolute terms, averaging approximately .20 points on a 5-point rating scale. On the other hand, considering that the standard deviation of mean teacher ratings among members of a given department may be as small as .30, a gain of .20 points is actually quite large in relative terms and could be of critical importance in a tenure or promotion decision. Viewed from this perspective, or from that of an administrator seeking institution- or department-wide improvement in teaching, the training program would appear to be well worth the time, effort, and money (approximately $600.00) expended. Whether or not the improved performance of experimental teachers persisted beyond the time frame of the training program has not been determined. However, one reason for being optimistic on this point is that teachers who show increased enthusiasm and expressiveness in the classroom are likely to be positively reinforced for their efforts, thus initiating a self-perpetuating reinforcement cycle.

A second example of a training program focusing on low-inference teaching behaviors is Brown's (1982) two-day workshop on clarity of explanation in lecturing. Working in small groups, faculty participants prepare, analyze, and present a series of mini-lectures on topics from their own areas of expertise. Mini-lectures are videotaped and followed by videotape analysis and feedback from fellow participants. Emphasis is placed on the following low-inference teaching behaviors assumed to contribute to clarity of explanation: (1) *signposts*, or preliminary statements of the overall structure of a presentation; (2) *frames*, which are similar to "signaling the transition from one topic to the next" in previous research on classroom behaviors; (3) *foci*, which correspond to "stresses important points" in previous research; and (4) *links*, defined as words such as "because," "therefore," and "however" that clarify connections or relations among ideas within a topic. Limited evidence is available on the impact of the clarity workshop on classroom teaching effectiveness. One study showed that workshop participants rated the program favorably and reported that they had become more critically aware of the factors involved in giving clear explanations. A second study compared the rated clarity of participants' first and second mini-lectures within the workshop setting. Ratings were provided by trained observers who viewed videotapes of the two presentations in random order. Results indicated a significant gain in clarity of explanation from pretest to posttest.

In summary, there is limited evidence that in-service training programs that focus on low-inference teaching behaviors can contribute significantly to perceived teaching effectiveness. It goes without saying that more research is needed on the impact and generality of behavioral training for teachers.

FUTURE PROSPECTS

The research reviewed in this chapter indicates that college teaching effectiveness is predictable from specific, low-inference classroom behaviors of the instructor, and is improvable, at least to an extent, by feedback and training procedures designed to modify these low-inference behaviors. As noted at the outset, the rationale for studying low-inference teaching behaviors is that classroom teaching is both easier to understand and easier to improve if we focus on specific observable actions rather than intractable generalities. In support of this rationale, research on low-inference teaching in relation to instructional outcome measures has yielded surprisingly consistent results, and this research has been applied with some success to improvement of instruction. Despite these successes, there are some serious weaknesses and limitations in research on low-inference teaching that will require the attention of future researchers. The remainder of this section outlines the problems most in need of resolution in future research on classroom teaching.

1. Most of the research on low-inference teaching behaviors has been carried out in an entirely atheoretical way, with no attempt made to test hypotheses about underlying mechanisms or cognitive processes. We need to know more about the "how" and "why" of process-product relationships, and, in particular, the ways in which teaching behaviors affect student information-processing. It seems obvious, for example, that the impact of teaching behaviors must depend at least in part on how those behaviors are perceived or interpreted by students, and furthermore, on how they affect the encoding and storage of information in memory. Perry's (1991) research in the present volume represents an important first step toward a theoretical understanding of student cognitive and affective reactions to classroom teaching.

2. Research on classroom teaching behaviors has ignored not only students' thought processes, but teachers' thought processes as well. In other words, there has been little or no emphasis on teacher goals, planning, and decision making as background factors related to classroom teaching. What the teacher does in the classroom is obviously important, but a complete understanding of teaching requires that we also know why and how the teacher selected certain classroom behaviors and ignored others.

3. As noted previously, nearly all research to date on specific teaching behaviors has been done in relation to the lecture method of teaching. Data are needed on the impact of low-inference behaviors in small-group discussion, laboratory instruction, one-to-one tutoring, and other nontraditional contexts.

4. Probably for reasons of expedience and practicality, both observational and experimental studies of low-inference teaching have relied almost exclusively on final exams and recall as cognitive outcome measures. Only two of the studies reviewed in this chapter (Tom and Cushman, 1975; Smith, 1977) examined teaching behaviors in relation to gains in student thinking or problem solving skills. While recall of facts and comprehension of concepts are important educational outcomes, it could be argued that the most important goal of higher education is to teach students to think for themselves. It would be interesting to know the extent to which progress toward this goal is influenced by specific behaviors of the instructor.

5. More research is needed on the impact of teaching improvement programs that provide feedback or training on low-inference teaching behaviors. Most observers would agree that the ultimate test of any theory, model, or approach to teaching is the extent to which it can be successfully applied to improvement of teaching. Although results to date are very promising, the ultimate case for the low-inference behavioral approach is yet to be fully made.

References

Abrami, P. C., Leventhal, L., and Perry, R. P. (1982). Educational seduction. *Review of Educational Research* 52: 446–464.

Andersen, J. F., and Withrow, J. G. (1981). The impact of lecturer nonverbal expressiveness on improving mediated instruction. *Communication Education* 30: 342–353.

Andrews, J. D. W. (1980). The verbal structure of teacher questions: Its impact on class discussion. *Professional and Organizational Development Quarterly* 2: 129–163.

Bolton, B., Bonge, D., and Marr, J. (1979). Ratings of instruction, examination performance, and subsequent enrollment in psychology courses. *Teaching of Psychology* 6: 82–85.

Brophy, J., and Good, T. L. (1986). Teacher behavior and student achievement. In M. C. Wittrock (ed.), *Handbook of Research on Teaching*, Third Edition. New York: Macmillan.

Brown, G. A. (1982). Two days on explaining and lecturing. *Studies in Higher Education* 7: 93–103.

Coats, W. D. and Smidchens, U. (1966). Audience recall as a function of speaker dynamism. *Journal of Educational Psychology* 57: 189–191.

Cohen, P. A. (1980). Effectiveness of student rating feedback for improving college instruction: A meta-analysis of findings. *Research in Higher Education* 13: 321–341.

Cohen, P. A. (1981). Student ratings of instruction and student achievement: A meta-analysis of multisection validity studies. *Review of Educational Research* 51: 281–309.

Coleman, J. S., Campbell, J., Wood, A. M., Weinfeld, F. D., and York, R. L. (1966). *Equality of Educational Opportunity*. Washington: United States Department of Health, Education and Welfare.

Cranton, P. A., and Hillgartner, W. (1981). The relationship between student ratings and instructor behavior: Implications for improving teaching. *Canadian Journal of Higher Education* 11: 73–81.

Dunkin, M. J., and Biddle, B. J. (1974). *The Study of Teaching*. New York: Holt, Rinehart and Winston.

Erdle, S., and Murray, H. G. (1986). Interfaculty differences in classroom teaching behaviors and their relationship to student instructional ratings. *Research in Higher Education* 24: 115–127.

Feldman, K. A. (1989). The association between student ratings of specific instructional dimensions and student achievement: Refining and extending the synthesis of data from multisection validity studies. *Research in Higher Education* 30: 583–645.

Flanders, N. A. (1970). *Analyzing Teacher Behavior.* Reading, MA: Addison-Welsey.

Frey, P. W. (1973). Student ratings of teaching: Validity of several rating factors. *Science* 182: 83–85.

Froman, R. D., and Owen, S. V. (1980). Influence of different types of student ratings feedback upon later instructional behavior. Paper presented at annual meeting of American Educational Research Association, Boston.

Hines, C. V., Cruickshank, D. R., and Kennedy, J. J. (1985). Teacher clarity and its relationship to student achievement and satisfaction. *American Educational Research Journal* 22: 87–99.

Jones, H. E. (1923). Experimental studies of college teaching. *Archives of Psychology* 68.

Kulik, J. A., and Kulik, C. C. (1979). College teaching. In P.L. Peterson and H.J. Walberg (eds.), *Research on Teaching.* Berkeley, California: McCutchan.

Land, M. L. (1979). Low-inference variables of teacher clarity: Effects on student concept learning. *Journal of Educational* Psychology, 71: 795–799.

Land, M. L. (1985). Vagueness and clarity in the classroom. In T. Husen and T. N. Postlethwaite (eds.), *International Encyclopedia of Education: Research and Studies.* Oxford: Pergamon Press.

Land, M. L., and Combs, A. (1981). Teacher clarity, student instructional ratings, and student performance. Paper presented at annual meeting of American Educational Research Association, Los Angeles.

Marsh, H. W. (1984). Students' evaluation of university teaching: Dimensionality, reliability, validity, potential biases, and utility *Journal of Educational Psychology* 76: 707–754.

Marsh, H. W. and Overall, J. U. (1980). Validity of students' evaluation of teaching effectiveness: Cognitive and affective criteria. *Journal of Educational Psychology* 72: 468–475.

Mayer, R. E. (1987). *Educational Psychology: A Cognitive Approach.* Boston: Little, Brown.

McKeachie, W. J. (1979). Student ratings of faculty: A reprise. *Academe* 62: 384–397.

McLean, D. F. (1979). The effect of mid-semester feedback upon weekly evaluations of university instructors. Unpublished master's thesis, University of Western Ontario, London, Canada.

Mintzes, J. J. (1979). Overt teaching behaviors and student ratings of instructors. *Journal of Experimental Education* 48: 145–153.

Murray, H. G. (1983a). Low-inference classroom teaching behaviors and student ratings of college teaching effectiveness. *Journal of Educational Psychology* 75, 138–149.

Murray, H. G. (1983b). Low-inference classroom teaching behaviors in relation to six measures of college teaching effectiveness. In J. G. Donald (ed.), *Proceedings of the Conference on the Evaluation and Improvement of University Teaching: The Canadian Experience* Montreal: Centre for Teaching and Learning Services, McGill University.

Murray, H. G. (1985). Classroom teaching behaviors related to college teaching effectiveness. In J. G. Donald and A. M. Sullivan (eds.), *Using Research to Improve Teaching.* San Francisco: Jossey-Bass.

Murray, H. G. (1987). Acquiring student feedback that improves instruction. In M. G. Weimer (ed.), *Teaching Large Classes Well.* San Francisco: Jossey-Bass.

Murray, H. G. and Lawrence, C. (1980). Speech and drama training for lecturers as a means of improving university teaching. *Research in Higher Education* 13: 73–90.

Murray, H. G. and Smith, T. A. (1989). Effects of midterm behavioral feedback on end-of-term ratings of instructor effectiveness. Paper presented at annual meeting of American Education Research Association, San Francisco.

Perry, R. P. (1985). Instructor expressiveness: Implications for improving teaching. In J. G. Donald and A. M. Sullivan (eds.), *Using Research to Improve Teaching.* San Francisco: Jossey-Bass.

Perry, R. P. (1991). Perceived control in college students: Implications for instruction in higher education. In J. Smart (ed.), *Higher Education: Handbook of Theory and Research,* Vol. 7. New York: Agathon Press. (*Reprinted in this volume.*)

Perry, R. P., Abrami, P. C., and Leventhal, L. (1979). Educational seduction: The effect of instructor expressiveness and lecture content on student ratings and achievement. *Journal of Educational Psychology* 71: 107–116.

Perry, R. P., and Magnusson, J.-L. (1987). Effective instruction and students' perceptions of control in the college classroom: Multiple-lectures effects. *Journal of Educational Psychology* 79: 453–460.

Perry, R. P., and Penner, K. (1990). Enhancing academic achievement in college students through attributional retraining and instruction. *Journal of Educational Psychology* 82: 262–271.

Roberts, C. L., and Becker, S. L. (1976). Communication and teaching effectiveness. *American Educational Research Journal* 13: 181–197.

Rosenshine, B., and Furst, N. F. (1971). Research on teacher performance criteria. In B. O. Smith (ed.), *Research in Teacher Education: A Symposium.* Englewood Cliffs, New Jersey: Prentice Hall.

Sanders, J. T. (1986). Why teaching cannot (and need not) be improved. *McGill Journal of Education* 21: 5–13.

Slater, L. (1981). Lecturer enthusiasm: A study of the effects of vocal and nonvocal enthusiasm on student ratings and achievement. Unpublished honors thesis, University of Western Ontario, London, Canada.

Smith, D. G. (1977). College classroom interactions and critical thinking. *Journal of Educational Psychology* 69: 180–190.

Solomon, D. (1966). Teacher behavior dimensions, course characteristics, and student evaluations of teachers. *American Educational Research Journal* 3: 35–47.

Solomon, D., Bezdek, W. E., and Rosenberg, L. (1964). Dimensions of teacher behavior. *Journal of Experimental Education* 33: 23–401.

Solomon, D., Rosenberg, L., and Bezdek, W. E. (1964). Teacher behavior and student learning. *Journal of Educational Psychology* 55: 23–30.

Tom, F. K. T., and Cushman, H. R. (1975). The Cornell Diagnostic Observation and Reporting System for Student Description of College Teaching. *Search* 5 (8): 1–27.

Ware, J. E., Jr., and Williams, R. G. (1975). The Dr. Fox effect: A study of lecturer effectiveness and ratings of instruction. *Journal of Medical Education* 50: 149–156.

Williams, R. G., and Ware, J. E., Jr. (1977). An extended visit with Dr. Fox: Validity of student ratings of instruction after repeated exposures to a lecturer. *American Educational Research Journal* 14:449–457.

Woolfolk, A. E. (1987). *Educational Psychology,* Third Edition. Englewood Cliffs, New Jersey: Prentice-Hall.

Instructional Interventions:
A Review of the Literature on Efforts
to Improve Instruction

Maryellen Weimer and Lisa Firing Lenze

INTRODUCTION

Efforts to improve college teaching continue. In some instances these are efforts of individual faculty members occurring independent of institutional involvement or support. In other instances institutions are engaged in activities designed to support and encourage faculty efforts in the classroom. Continuing concern about quality undergraduate education signals that interest in these efforts, particularly those at the institutional level, will remain high. Institutions need to know which resources and activities most positively affect instructional quality. Therefore, it is appropriate that the literature on efforts to improve instruction be reviewed frequently and regularly.

The bulk of these efforts at the institutional level occur via various "interventions," organized, systematic activities designed to impact, in a positive way, the instruction of an individual faculty member. A workshop on participation strategies or consultation with a faculty member over student evaluation data illustrate what is meant by intervention. It is important to note that the interventions, in and of themselves, do not improve instruction. They are the methods used to motivate and inform instructional change, but the faculty member alone implements the alterations. For example, the workshop on participation strategies may propose and describe a variety of techniques which effectively increase student involvement, but the faculty member is in charge of deciding whether or not to use any of the techniques in class tomorrow. Moreover, there is no guarantee that all change affects teaching performance positively. A consultant may offer bad advice, a faculty member may implement change at the wrong time, or it may be poorly suited for the student group to which it is directed.

This leads to the question: how then are the effects of the instructional interventions to be assessed? In the first review of this literature, Levinson-Rose and Menges (1981) used five categories which will be used in this review as well: 1) teacher attitude from self-report (participants offer opinions as to the effectiveness of the intervention); 2) teacher knowledge from tests or observer (pre- and post-tests or observations document any changes in teacher knowledge); 3) teacher skill from observer (instructional observation reports on changes in skill levels); 4) student attitude from self-report (student evaluation evidences change in teacher performance); and 5) student learning from tests or observer reports (tests or observation attest to changes in student learning). As Levinson-Rose and Menges (1981) note, "the strongest evidence for most interventions is impact on students (the last two categories), and the weakest is self-reported opinion of participants (the first category)" (p. 403).

Continuing interest in instructional improvement mandates an update of the 1981 review focusing on literature published during the intervening years. Moreover, while many of the instructional interventions originally considered are still widely used, various emphases have changed necessitating a different categorization than that used by Levinson-Rose and Menges (1981). Five interventions will be considered in this review; workshops, consultation, instructional grants, distribution of resource material, and efforts of colleagues on behalf of each other's instruction. Each of these interventions will be introduced briefly at this point and their inclusion justified as a means of illustrating how efforts to improve instruction have changed during the '80s.

As was the case in 1981, workshops, seminars, and programs continue to be the most widely used of all instructional interventions. They range from hour-long sessions, to week-long retreats, to year-long programs. They offer advice and information on virtually every aspect of instruction. They employ a wide range of instructional methods including lecture, discussion, and collaborative learning. More so during this decade than previous ones, workshop programs are complex. They use a variety of interventions in the context of a single program; like a three-day orientation activity for new faculty with lectures on instructional techniques, individual consultation, and the possibility of a microteaching experience.

During the decade, the use of consultation has grown. Here an instructional expert, most often a faculty or instructional developer, offers individual advice and information to faculty members, usually in the context of a face-to-face interview. It typically occurs in three arenas: over student ratings, over a videotaped teaching sample or microteaching experience, or over a more general instructional issue or concern. The Levinson-Rose and Menges (1981) review does not consider consultation as an independent intervention. However, research on consultation over student ratings is considered as part of a larger intervention labeled "feedback from ratings by students." Analysis and critique of microteaching experiences is considered separately. The consideration of consultation as an independent intervention reflects a change in practice that has occurred during the decade.

As was true in 1981, instructional grants continue to be used as a faculty development intervention. Most often now the grants are of small amounts and are awarded competitively to individual faculty members. Monies are targeted to some instructional, often course-related project. New materials may be designed, a new set of assignments conceived, course content significantly revised, or a computer component developed for the course.

It is difficult to document the extent to which resource materials aimed at improving instruction were being distributed to faculty prior to 1981. However, their widespread use today justifies their consideration as an improvement intervention. To illustrate, many instructional and faculty development centers publish newsletters; others distribute published articles to faculty; several new interdisciplinary and disciplinary pedagogical journals are being published; and marketed resource manuals, workbooks, and sourcebooks offer advice on everything from test construction to discussion techniques.

Although not reviewed previously, the effect of resource materials like these on instructional quality merits review.

Finally, although not used as widely as the previous interventions and not considered in the Levinson-Rose and Menges (1981) review, increasingly colleagues are being used to intervene in the instruction of each other. Their use in part reflects the chronic lack of staff in many instructional and faculty development units. Faculty volunteers were commandeered to help, but what was quickly discovered was their effectiveness as instructional improvers. Most often they are being used to observe other faculty teach, not as evaluators, but as colleagues interested in exploring the impact of a set of instructional policies and practices on student learning.

To summarize, this review considers two interventions considered by Levinson-Rose and Menges (1981), it recategorizes activities associated with the consultation intervention, and it adds two new interventions. It does not consider feedback from ratings independent of consultation since it has been shown that summative rating feedback alone has much less impact on instructional improvement (Murray, 1984), and it does not consider concept-based training since data do not document the prevalent use of this intervention.

One other change in efforts to improve instruction has occurred since 1981. Current efforts are being targeted at particular faculty groups more than they were previously. Specifically, if instructional and faculty development units exist at institutions where teaching assistants are employed, chances are those units sponsor, coordinate, or work closely with other academic departments in activities designed to prepare teaching assistants for instructional responsibilities. TA training existed before 1981. The difference here is one of degree. Instructional interventions with TAs are far more widespread than they used to be.

The interest in the instructional preparation of TAs has spawned efforts directed at a target group not previously focused on by those interested in instructional improvement—new faculty. Many of the programs and activities first offered teaching assistants are now being extended to new faculty.

Why are TAs and new faculty being targeted for instructional interventions more than other faculty groups? Is their instruction less effective? Certainly they are less experienced, and experience is seen as one of the conditions contributing to the development of pedagogical prowess. They are also the faculty groups an institution has most control over and are therefore the easiest to "require" to participate in efforts to improve instruction. Does that have an impact on the effectiveness of these interventions?

The attention focused on TAs and new faculty may also stem from larger issues confronting higher education. Many are concerned with the impending change in faculty populations. Most institutions anticipate significant percentages of retirements in the decade. This is seen not so much as a problem as an opportunity—the chance to intervene in instruction of faculty and potential faculty at the beginning of their careers. Germane to this review is the implicit assumption that somehow it is easier and more effective to "intervene" at this point in a teaching career. Does research evidence substantiate that assumption?

As the activities, programs, and resources offered TAs and new faculty are reviewed, it is readily apparent that the interventions most often used are those being considered in this review. In other words, no special, unique, or different interventions are being used despite the distinctions between TAs and new faculty, and other faculty groups. Are these interventions the most effective ones for TAs and new faculty?

Questions like these make it clear why efforts to target interventions at specific subgroups within the larger faculty population merit review and assessment. Research and other relevant literature on the effects of these interventions with new faculty will be considered in this review. A recent review of research on training TAs has been published, so literature in that area will be summarized and relevant references included.

This review is modeled on the original work of Levinson-Rose and Menges (1981), but with several important distinctions. It is a more comprehensive look at the literature. Levinson-Rose and Menges (1981) elected not to include description or discussion of studies where evaluation occurred only at the level of teacher attitude from self-report and teacher knowledge. A number of these are considered in this review and for several reasons. First, the extent of evaluation at this level warrants documentation. Second and considerably more important, efforts to improve instruction are occurring within the realm of practice. That is, practice is preceding research. Unlike the arena of student evaluation, where sizable research effort occurred first and stimulated to a large degree the adoption and adaptation of the evaluative practices, instructional interventions are being used prior to rigorous empirical exploration. Of concern is the considerable delay between implementation and exploration. It is hoped that by including some of what qualifies more as a literature of practice than a literature of research, the much needed research effort will be stimulated. These are cases and ongoing operations that could be studied. It is further hoped that by recognizing what is occurring in the arenas of both practice and research, those interested in one will see the merit of the other and be encouraged to collaborate.

A second distinction between this review and the Levinson-Rose and Menges (1981) effort is the more detailed description of inquiries that aim to assess the impact of the interventions at the more significant levels of observable change in classroom behaviors and student outcomes. First, the limited number of studies at this level permits it, and it is hoped the more detailed descriptions will serve as models, again to stimulate more rigorous investigation.

Finally, the conclusions as to the effectiveness of any single intervention are more qualitative than quantitative. No statistical methods of comparison were employed, primarily because the number of available studies precludes them. Rather the intent is to offer more general conclusions with specific and elaborate calls for more research.

The individual interventions are considered separately. For each a brief history is included. Current data documenting the prevalence of the practice precede a general but detailed description of the intervention, including specific, published examples of programs. An assessment of studies and results follows. Consideration of the intervention concludes with a discussion section. New faculty and TAs are considered following review of all the interventions. The review concludes with a recommendation and discussion section.

WORKSHOPS, SEMINARS, AND PROGRAMS

History

In early efforts to improve college teaching, the workshop was the main staple in the instructional improver's cupboard. Centra's (1978) first survey of those responsible for improvement efforts yielded 45 different instructional development practices. Oblique (promax) rotation of the data suggested four major categories of practices, and one of those, labeled "high faculty involvement," included a variety of workshop, seminar, and program activities.

Levinson-Rose and Menges (1981) assert, "workshops and seminars are probably the most frequent but least evaluated instructional improvement activities" (p. 406). Their review assessed research done primarily with graduate teaching assistants. The impact of workshops and seminars on teaching was assessed in three different areas: student ratings, observer ratings, and student learning. As to the overall effectiveness of this intervention they conclude: "Workshops and seminars are useful to motivate and to raise consciousness under certain conditions. But most workshops and seminars, even those with specific training goals, are unlikely to produce lasting changes in teacher behavior or lasting impact on students unless participants continue skill practice and receive critical feedback on their efforts" (p. 419).

Prevalence

Early reliance on workshops, seminars, and programs has continued in the years since the Levinson-Rose and Menges (1981) review. Konrad's (1983) replication of the Centra survey in 25 Canadian universities documented "fairly common" (p. 24) use of workshops with programs exploring "various methods or techniques of instruction, ...testing and evaluating student performance,...[and] new or different approaches to develop curricula" (p. 18). Of the 687 community colleges responding to Smith's (1981) survey of 1,315 of these institutions, 236 report using workshops to promote effective instruction. Of the 36 Illinois community colleges responding to Hansen's (1983) survey, 89 percent reported doing single session workshops, making them the most common faculty development activity listed. Seventy-five percent reported doing multisession workshops/seminars. Richardson and Moore (1987) surveyed 62 community colleges in Texas; of the 52 which responded, 69 percent reported using single-session workshops and 62 percent used all-day programs for full-time faculty, making this intervention the most common after orientation activities (many of which also used the workshop programming). Erickson (1986) reports that of the 630 four-year institutions responding to his survey, 63 percent offered workshops on various methods of instruction, 55 percent gave sessions on academic advising and counseling, and 36 percent sponsored programs on understanding college students and how they learn.

Most recently Bland and Schmitz (1988) reviewed literature which offered "either strategies or recommendations for developing full-time faculty members, departments or institutions" (p. 191). In their collection of 288 references they identified 49 different strategies and found that workshops were the most frequent strategy, mentioned in 73 sources.

Description

As might be expected with continued use of an intervention across better than 20 years now, a considerable amount of diversification has occurred. Workshop programs now vary across several important dimensions. First, they vary as to the topics presented. Sessions share information on subjects as diverse as cooperative learning, time management, learning disabilities, and cultural diversity. Recent literature does not document which of these and many other topics are used most commonly.

Second, these programs vary as to the instructional methods used to deliver the content. The large orientation sessions for TAs rely on traditional lecture methods, sessions for seasoned faculty tend more toward interactive modes, and some workshop sponsors try the collaborative/cooperative techniques they recommend to faculty. In recent years more elaborate programs that combine a variety of methods, content, and even interventions themselves have been used. Herr (1988) describes a semester-long workshop used at Colorado State University. Seventeen faculty enrolled in the program that focused on weekly observation in the courses of award-winning faculty. Participants observed in pairs and met privately to discuss the observation. During meetings (held every other week) the group explored the characteristics of the effective teaching they were observing. They also discussed, received information about, and participated in activities related to a number of other instructional issues such as mid-term evaluation and teaching assumptions.

Third, in recent years workshops have been directed to target populations within the larger faculty group. Since 1981, as already mentioned, both the number and scope of programs for TAs, many relying heavily on the workshop intervention (Weimer, Svinicki, and Bauer, 1990), have increased dramatically, witnessed by two national conferences on the training and employment of TAs, both with published proceedings (Chism, 1987, and Nyquist, Abbott, Wulff and Sprague, in press). In addition to workshops, seminars, and minicourses designed for TAs, in recent years programs for new faculty have also proliferated. Again, most commonly these are orientation workshops and seminars, although increasingly these are evolving into the more involved programs mentioned earlier. A number of specific examples appear in the section on new faculty as a target group. Reliance on part-time, adjunct, and fixed-term faculty has also grown during the past decade, necessitating workshop programs for this faculty population. Less common but not unusual are workshops designed for faculty populations who share instructional settings; for example, those who teach large courses, those who teach required introductory courses to nonmajors, and those who teach lab courses.

Finally, workshop programs vary in length—all the way from two-hour, one-shot sessions to semester-, and in a few cases, year-long programs. Between are half-day, full-day, two-day, week-long, biweekly, monthly, and weekly meetings of faculty groups which explore single or multiple instructional issues.

Assessment

Given the diversity of current workshop programming, assessment is difficult in any sort of general way. What is the impact of workshops on instructional effectiveness? The question is too broad. Programs for new faculty may work, but sessions less than four hours may not have measurable effects across the life of a course, for example. In other words, the research on workshops needs to be analyzed across different dimensions. This review begins that more detailed assessment by looking at workshops (in this section) of varying length and (in a subsequent section) targeted to different faculty populations. Unfortunately, the actual research on workshop effectiveness is so meager that it makes assessment across any dimension a moot point. However, the diversity of the phenomenon in question demands this more detailed analysis. Perhaps the categorization will stimulate subsequent investigation.

Short-term Programs: those less than four hours in length. Despite the prevalence of these programs, no published research assesses the effectiveness of these programs in any of the categories being used: 1) teacher attitude from self-report, 2) teacher knowledge from tests or observer, 3) teacher skill from observer, 4) student attitude from self-report (evaluations), and 5) student learning from tests or observer reports.

Long Programs: those between four hours and six days in duration. Brown and Daines (1983) report on a the effectiveness of a two-day program on lecturing and explaining which incorporated microteaching experiences. Sixty-six videotapes of new lecturers' explanations given during the workshop were rated by two trained independent observers. "The results indicate that, for this group of lecturers, the course yielded perceptible and significant improvements in the opening moves of an explanation, its structure and interest, and in the use of audiovisual aids" (p. 67). In addition, Brown and Daines studied transcripts of 65 explanations, also recorded during the program. Analysis of six variables via regression techniques documented "significant changes in structuring tactics such as the use of explaining links, signposts, and frames but not in the use of foci. The frequency of hesitations, stumbles, and incomplete sentences were reduced but not significantly" (p. 68).

Long, Sadker, and Sadker (1986) report on the effectiveness of a two-and-a-half-day training session that focused on the elimination of sex-biased teacher-student interactions in the classroom and the distribution, precision, and quality of teacher responses to students' verbal behavior. The 46 faculty participants were divided into experimental and control groups. Training included review of videotapes demonstrating both the desired and undesirable behaviors and a microteaching experience. Participants were observed teaching three times by five trained observers. The researchers summarized the results. "Training increased interaction by 38 percent, reduced the percentage of salient students who monopolize interaction, and also reduced the percentage of silent or non-participating students" (p. 3). As for gender issues, "this study revealed significant bias in favor of male students in the control group while the experimental group approached equity" (p. 3).

Mini Courses: longer than six days and incorporating more than one instructional intervention. Friedman and Stomper (1983) studied the effectiveness of a semester-long training program for selected mathematics faculty aimed at improving student achievement in a basic mathematics course. Five faculty members were selected for the training sessions; eight others constituted a control group. The training program encouraged the use of several instructional strategies, advocated responding to designated student needs, and provided feedback on videotaped teaching samples. Investigators controlled for the entry status of students in the classes used. In the experimental group, 59.1 percent of the students passed compared with 49.4 percent in the control group. The group average for test score means was 59.4 for the experimental group and 51.5 for the control group. These differences were corroborated by two additional videotaped recordings made at the beginning and end of the course for those in the experimental group. Analysis documented behavior changes in the direction of the strategies proposed. Investigators conclude that this program resulted in "large differences in student achievement in favor of the experimental group" (p. 60).

Menges and others (1988) report on a program of interdisciplinary faculty renewal workshops. Faculty from different institutions took part in two-week summer sessions conducted by Stanford faculty on a common humanistic and interdisciplinary theme. Participants were invited to return for a weekend "reunion" one or two years (or both) after the original session. Surveys were sent to all 189 participants with 123 returning them. Generally high levels of satisfaction appear in the responses. Most highly impacted were "knowledge of my discipline," "knowledge of related disciplines," and "scholarly enthusiasm" (p. 295), although when assessing results of participation, 57 percent indicated their teaching had been impacted.

As already described, Herr (1988) reports on a workshop-observation program used with 15 faculty at Colorado State University to identify the characteristics of effective teaching. Eleven of those participants returned evaluations. Of those, 91 percent indicated the workshop had met their expectation and 100 percent recommended it be repeated.

Gibbs, Browne, and Keeley (1989) report on a program designed to teach faculty critical thinking skills. Program participants (who received $200 for their involvement) had to: 1) attend six four-hour programs, 2) create a three- to four-page plan for integrating critical thinking into a course to be taught during the semester immediately following the program, 3) share plans with other participants, and 4) cooperate in evaluating the program. Seventy-two participants were randomly assigned to either an experimental and control group. In addition to qualitative data, investigators collected quantitative data via The Watson-Glaser Critical Thinking Appraisal Test administered to faculty prior to participation to determine whether the two groups differed on initial critical thinking ability. They did not. Following the fifth session, faculty completed the Ennis-Weir Critical Thinking Test as a post-test. Those in the control group had statistically significant higher post-test scores than those in the experimental group. During the term in which the plan for teaching critical thinking was being integrated into the course, a randomly selected student sample completed the Watson-Glaser Test and the Class Activities Questionnaire. Students selected from the classes of the experimental group did not differ significantly from those in the control group on either measure. The investigators maintain the findings have limited implications for a number of reasons, among them their sense that even a workshop of this length was too short to significantly change critical thinking abilities for faculty, and that the intervention period may have been too brief for changes in student outcomes to manifest themselves.

Some of those surveying institutions about faculty and instructional development activities have collected general assessments of the effectiveness of the intervention. In Hansen's (1983) survey of 36 Illinois community colleges a rating of good or excellent was given by 75 percent of those holding one-day workshops, by 78 percent conducting day-long programs and by 80 percent of those offering multisession workshops. In Richardson and Moore's survey of 56 Texas community colleges, a rating of good or excellent was given by 76 percent of those holding one day workshops, by 100 percent of those conducting day-long programs, and by 93 percent of those offering multisession workshops. Moses (1985) surveyed 17 directors of academic development units in Australia asking, "What three approaches to improvement of teaching have worked best in your institution?" (p. 77) Workshops and seminars were mentioned by 15, making them, in the judgment of these unit heads, the best way to improve instruction.

Discussion

In addition to the assessment of specific programs and general conclusions, other relevant information about the the evaluation of workshops exists. Hansen (1983) summarizes evaluation methods used to assess the effectiveness of workshop programs: "There was heavy dependence on verbal feedback and questionnaire evaluative techniques. Only three respondents indicated the use of classroom observation to see if improved instruction was occurring as a result of faculty development activities. Testing of students as a measure of improvement of instruction was never used as an evaluative device" (p. 223). Richardson and Moore (1987) asked the Texas Community College respondents to their survey how many of them were evaluating programs and what assessment methods they were employing. For workshop activities of varying sorts, 62 to 71 percent reported they were using evaluation. As for specifics, 57 to 71 percent reported using verbal feedback, 29 to 50 percent said they had participants respond to questionnaires, 4 to 6 percent used pre- and post-tests, 4 percent tested student outcomes, and zero percent reported using classroom observation.

Returning to the five levels of intervention assessment proposed by Levinson-Rose and Menges (1981), as was the case at the time of that review, the bulk of program assessment, if it occurs at all, occurs at the level of faculty attitude as reported by them. That's the bad news. As Levinson-Rose and Menges (1981), Richardson and Moore (1987), and others have consistently pointed out, this is the least significant way to measure the effectiveness of these programs. These data mean that in the opinion of the faculty participants the programs were useful, relevant, or informative. It does not prove that the programs caused them to change any of their instructional behaviors, nor does it establish any relationship between program participation and significantly improved learning outcomes.

There is some good news. At least faculty surveyed in these studies do respond favorably to workshop programming. They see the programs as contributing to their instructional effectiveness. And although the accuracy of that perception remains unproven, faculty attitudes toward teaching do affect their instructional policies and practices. What remains unclear is how long or to what degree new or recharged attitudes influence what happens in the classroom.

And added to the small number of studies in the Levinson-Rose and Menges (1981) that assess impact across the other four levels are a few additional studies completed during this decade. Brown and Daines (1983) and Gibbs, Browne, and Keeley (1989) did test participant knowledge. Brown and Daines (1983), Friedman and Stomper (1983), and Long, Sadker, and Sadker (1986) assessed changes in skill levels through independent observation. And Friedman and Stomper (1983) and Gibbs, Browne, and Keeley (1989) did test student achievement affected by program participation. Although the data pool is too small to warrant any conclusions, all studies except Gibbs, Browne, and Keeley (1989) report positive results, meaning the workshop, seminar, or program effectively improved instruction.

These studies have been categorized by the length of the program even though the amount of research makes it impossible to tell whether that dimension has an effect on the intervention. It is interesting to note that the programs reviewed here with positive effects, excepting Gibbs, Browne, and Keeley (1989), do tend to be longer and to involve more than one intervention. This provides further corroboration of the earlier Levinson-Rose and Menges (1981) conclusion that programs with more lasting impacts are those in which participants continue to practice and receive feedback on their efforts. However, short programs remain unstudied, so this trend in the research may be noted but its significance remains to be determined.

Despite this modest "good news," discussion of this intervention cannot be concluded without considerable concern again expressed about the extensive use of a method to improve instruction with so little corroboration of its effectiveness. Those who have reviewed these interventions previously, among them Richardson and Moore (1983), have warned that in times of tight budgets instructional and faculty development efforts will have to justify the methods used. Perhaps budgets are not tight enough yet, but to date that call for solid proof has not come from those who supply the funds. It seems the interest in documenting the effectiveness of an intervention ought to be more intrinsic. Why are those using the intervention not more interested in finding out whether or not what they are doing impacts instruction? Most of them do work hard at designing and presenting these programs. Assessing their effectiveness seems the next logical step. However, it is not just those who rely on the intervention who are ignoring its study. The same could be said of those who study teaching, learning, and its improvement in post-secondary education. If ever there was a case in point illustrating the need for greater collaboration between those who research and those who practice, the study and use of workshops to improve instruction demonstrates it.

CONSULTATION

History

Like workshops and seminars, consulting has been a common faculty development intervention. Centra (1978) found instructional consultation among the practices under a factor labeled, "high faculty involvement." He concluded that consultations "involve a high proportion of the faculty at the colleges that use them" (p. 154).

Much of what is known about consulting has been learned via experience and not research. Several different authors articulate the theoretical foundations and models that underlie current practice. Boud and McDonald (1981) describe consultants' original purpose as providing "solutions to educational problems," "carrying out a survey or a study for an individual or for a whole institution," or, simply, functioning as "experts" (p. 2). They outline three traditional models consultants initially adopted: the Professional Service Model, in which the consultant brings "organizational or technical expertise" (p. 3) to the consultation; the Counseling Model, in which the consultant aims to help the teacher-client realize his or her teaching problems and devise a plan to deal with the problem; and the Collegial Model, in which two peers serve as consultants for one another, "each taking equal responsibility and each having the same stake in the outcomes" (p. 5). However, Boud and McDonald (1981) point out that faculty often see consultants who ascribe to these models as "technicians," "shrinks," or "blind leading the blind." Consequently, they propose an Eclectic Model, which is to say that "the educational consultant needs to draw from each of these [previous] models...to work flexibly and eclectically in order to respond to the unique demands of *each situation*" (p. 5).

Lewis (1988) suggests that consultants must wear the "many hats" (p. 76) of data collector, data manager, facilitator, support system, counselor, and information source in order to meet the particular needs of each teacher-client. In a slightly more prescriptive sense, Nyquist and Wulff (1988) also depart from the traditional models of consultancy, proposing that the consulting process be viewed through a research perspective. Like Boud and McDonald's Eclectic Model, Nyquist and Wulff's (1988) Research Perspective draws on many of the *skills* used in preceding models (e.g., collecting and interpreting data, working collaboratively, etc.), but then recommends four specific steps (paralleling the steps in the research process) which will focus attention on the individual teacher-client and her or his unique teaching style and situation.

Taylor-Way (1988) also acknowledges the importance of "analyzing, reflecting on, and evaluating" specific teaching "events" (p. 161) when consulting with faculty. Murray (1985) provides empirical support for addressing individual teaching behaviors when consulting with faculty for the purpose of improving teaching. Thus, the current focus for instructional consultation has evolved out of practice. It involves looking at, interpreting, and analyzing the individual teacher-client's unique teaching behaviors in a collaborative, investigative fashion.

Prevalence

Widespread use of consultation continues, documented by all the survey data collected in the 1980s except Konrad (1983) whose survey of 25 Canadian universities showed that only eight percent of the institutions surveyed indicated use, by over 20 percent of their faculty, of consultations "by faculty with expertise." Contrastingly, in Hansen's (1983) survey of 36 Illinois community colleges, 64 percent offered "individual informal consultations." In Richardson and Moore's (1987) survey of 56 Texas community colleges, 44 percent offered "individual teaching consultations." Interestingly, in his survey of 630 four-year United States institutions, Erickson (1986) notes, separately, the percentage that use consultations over student evaluations, the percentage that use consultations over observations, and the percentage of institutions that use consultations over teaching issues, in general. Erikson found that only 38 percent of the 95 percent who used student evaluations offered consultations in conjunction with the evaluation data. More encouragingly, 51.5 percent of the respondents in his survey reported using consultations with videotaping of classroom instruction; and 49.5 percent reported using consultations for discussing teaching issues, in general.

Description

Although the discussion of faculty consultation has focused only on instructional improvement, a subset of a larger consulting arena, even this single area of instructional consulting (henceforth to be referred to simply as "consultation") must be subdivided. Face-to-face interactions between teacher-clients and consultants occur over three main issues: student evaluation data, a videotaped teaching sample or microteaching experience, and instructional concerns in general.

Other models of instructional consultation occur: when the consultant visits an actual classroom and offers feedback (more often colleagues fulfill this role and that contributions is described in a subsequent section), when students are trained to observe and offer feedback (Helling and Kuhlmann, 1988), when the consultation is part of a larger inquiry into the classroom teaching (Provlacs, 1988), and when small student groups offer input (Tiberius, 1988). Although these models propose innovative ways of using instructional consultation, they are not the norm and are therefore not considered in this review.

Although Erikson's (1986) survey indicates that receiving student evaluation feedback in conjunction with consultation is not as *prevalent* as receiving student evaluation feedback alone, consultation over student evaluations has been shown to be significantly more *effective* in improving teaching than receiving student evaluation feedback without consultation. Levinson-Rose and Menges (1981) report five of seven studies reviewed, with regard to "ratings with consultation," support the conclusion that consultation over student evaluation data improves teaching. The case is further supported by more recent research reviewed by Murray (1984).

But what does consultation over student evaluation entail? It may involve either a visit to the consultant's office or to the teacher-client's office to discuss the results of a mid-semester or end-of-semester student evaluation. The most productive discussions often focus on the instructor's behaviors; for when talking about specific, individual, observable behaviors, instructors acquire concrete suggestions to put into action when trying to implement change (Murray, 1984; Wilson, 1986). The consultant may request that the teacher-client bring with him or her past student evaluations, so as to compare performance across semesters. In all cases where improvement of teaching is the goal, the object of the consultation should be to work collaboratively to translate student data into teacher practices, or principles (Taylor-Way, 1988), that the client can use to maintain, modify, or eliminate certain elements of his or her teaching style.

Probably the most inhibiting of the three types of consultation involves recording a sample of teaching on videotape which the teacher-client and consultant then critique, or teaching a mini-lesson before a small audience of peers and/or consultants who then critique the instruction. This second method is usually called microteaching. Much more has been written about consultation over a videotaped teaching sample than microteaching experiences. Most often microteaching experiences are embedded in a longer seminar or program.

Consultation over videotape requires instructors to confront themselves as others actually see them (rather than as they think others see them). Taylor-Way (1988) suggests that videotaping allows the teacher-client to focus on the actual classroom behaviors observed (which allows the client to "own" the experience), rather than only on the particular behaviors noted in the observer-consultant's or colleague's notes (as is most often the case with personal observations). However, as he notes, instructors wishing to improve their teaching should not be forced into being videotaped; thus, in class observation (although not as descriptive as videotaping) is sometimes used to provide an unbiased account of the instructor's teaching behaviors. Often this feedback takes the form of a checklist with the observer-consultant's or colleague's notes attached.

The last, and the least well described, form of consultation is consultation over instructional issues in general. This type of consultation usually takes place in the consultant's office, and the teacher-client determines the content of the conversation. Issues raised may range from eliciting student participation, to dealing with classroom management issues, to improving presentational skills. This type of consultation also varies in the amount of time the instructor and consultant spend working together. The time period may consist of one meeting or may extend across the course of a semester.

Assessment

As was the case with workshops and seminars, much of the assessment as to whether consultations improve teacher effectiveness is at the attitudinal level. With regard to consultations generally, Centra (1978) found that 56 percent of college coordinators surveyed perceived "classroom visitations by an instructional resource person, simulation procedures to help faculty practice new skills, and the use of in-class videotapes" as effective. Centra also noted that in terms of perceived effectiveness, consultations and the other intervention strategies within the category "instructional assistance practices" ranked second out of six total categories of interventions (second only to the category "grants and travel funds").

Also regarding consultations in general, Moses (1985) surveyed 17 directors of academic development units in Australia and asked them what three approaches to improving teaching worked best in their institution. "Individual consultation" ranked third (behind workshops and student evaluations). Moses explained that "individual consultations were judged to be effective because they are based on the needs of individual teachers, they are initiated by them, and follow-up is feasible and usually occurs....Thus, it is often possible to observe a change in teaching or in student reaction to teaching" (p. 79). Similarly, in Konrad's (1983) survey of Canadian universities, he found that, although not the most widely utilized, "assessment practices followed by some types of consultation appeared to be among the most effective for development purposes."

These attitudinal studies all focused on consultation in general. There are, however, a few studies that report on the individual types of consultation and their ability to increase instructional effectiveness.

Consultation Over Student Evaluation Data
Since the Levinson-Rose and Menges (1981) review, research on the impact of consultation over ratings has continued to be explored. In Murray's (1984) review of the impact of student evaluation on improvement, he states that although "the weight of evidence suggests that feedback from student ratings produces a small but significant improvement in teaching effectiveness...student feedback supplemented by expert consultation produces a much larger improvement in teaching" (p. 124). Two more recent studies add still more support.

Wilson (1986) studied the effects of a consultation process that focused on teaching behaviors. Before consulting with client-teachers about their student evaluations, he asked award-winning teachers to identify their teaching behaviors. From the interviews, Wilson compiled a list of behaviors that conveyed certain characteristics of effective teaching. Wilson next conducted student evaluations with a group of teacher-clients. He then consulted with each client about his or her teaching behaviors, careful to incorporate suggestions (from the list of behaviors generated by the master teachers) of other possible behaviors to try. After an intervening semester a second evaluation was administered. He found no difference in evaluation ratings for a comparison group who administered two evaluations but received no consultation. However, the teacher-client consultations were "associated with statistically important change in overall teaching effectiveness ratings for 52 percent of the faculty clients" (p. 209). In addition, the data showed that the "items on which the greatest number of faculty showed statistically important change were those for which the suggestions were most concrete, specific and behavioral" (p. 209).

In another study, Stevens and Aleamoni (1985) conducted a retrospective analysis to assess the effectiveness of consultations promoting instructional improvement over a 14-year intervening period. The original study (Aleamoni, 1978) compared the instructional improvement of teachers who received student evaluation feedback with consultation and teachers who received student evaluation feedback without consultation. The second study looked at the student evaluation ratings of 17 of the original study's participants at two time intervals; seven years after the initial study, and 14 years after the initial study. The results showed that "provision of consultation in addition to student ratings feedback resulted in an increase in student ratings that was maintained over time" (p. 303). On the other hand, the evaluations of instructors who had not originally received consultation with their student evaluation data did not result in consistent increases.

Stevens and Aleamoni (1985) call for further longitudinal research in the area of consultations over student evaluation data to further substantiate these findings and suggest that student evaluation feedback "must be integrated with a system of instructor training and available instructional support services" (p. 303).

Consultation Over Videotaping and Microteaching

There is little direct evidence establishing the effectiveness of consultation over a videotaped teaching sample or microteaching experience. However, the support Levinson-Rose and Menges (1981) summoned for microteaching and the indirect evidence of the intervening decade establish a strong potential for this improvement intervention.

Perlberg (1983) draws on research and theory related to effective use of video feedback and consultation in other contexts to propose potential uses in higher education as an improvement strategy. Perlberg concludes: "To exploit the full potential of video as an adjunct to a consultant's interventions, and in some cases as the focus of training and consultation, we need more research on its effectiveness and optimal uses" (p. 659).

The most significant evidence of the impact of video as an intervention has been collected in efforts to train teaching assistants. Sharp (1981) showed that TAs who viewed a tape modeling effective lecturing techniques did teach differently than those who did not see the tape. The differences were documented by trained observers who reviewed a videotape of a microteaching experience scheduled after the tape had been viewed. The Long, Sadker, and Sadker (1986) study described in the workshop section also supports Sharp's findings. Dalgaard (1982) videotaped 22 inexperienced TAs prior to a training program that included feedback over the initial tape and workshop presentations designed to help TAs plan and organize course content and involve students. TAs were taped again after the training, and teaching experts who rated the tapes documented significantly higher ratings for those who participated in the training as compared with a control group who did not.

Personal testimony to the Taylor-Way Videotape Recall method (1988) suggests that consultation over videotaping is very effective. Taylor-Way (1988) reports that "in most cases I can see specific improvement even from the first to the second videotaping and this perception is equally shared by the teacher involved" (p. 187). He elaborates, "The primary sources of data I have to support this statement are the completed recall forms of my clients (cognitive and affective indices) and their teaching behaviors comparing first and second videotapes (behavioral indiced)" (p. 187).

Finally, as general evidence of the effectiveness of this intervention in Konrad's (1983) small sample of universities, he found that 33 percent of the institutions that used analysis of in-class video tapes rated the practice effective.

Consultation Over Teaching Issues, in General
Studies assessing consultation over teaching issues, in general, are by far the scarcest. Again, in Konrad's (1983) survey of 25 Canadian universities, he noted that of institutions which do practice consultation over general teaching issues, 31 percent rated this practice effective. Hansen's (1983) survey of 36 Illinois community colleges provides more support for the perceived usefulness of general consultations. In Hansen's study, 73 percent of the 64 percent that use individual informal consultations rated this practice as good or excellent in terms of its usefulness. In Richardson and Moore's (1987) survey of 56 Texas community colleges, 86 percent of the 44 percent that use individual teaching consultations rated them as good or excellent in terms of usefulness. Once again empirical research is needed to verify the perceptions of those who use this intervention.

Discussion
Evidence continues to support the effectiveness of consultation over ratings in positively affecting subsequent evaluations. Certainly enough evidence exists to strongly commend the practice to those who use student evaluation and are interested in increasing its impact on instruction. Despite the solid evidence supporting the effectiveness of this intervention some important questions remain unanswered. What exactly is it about the addition of a consultation session to student evaluation feedback that makes instructors improve? Murray (1985), Wilson (1986), and others who suggest translating evaluation data into behaviors, seem to suggest that talking about behaviors is the key. In addition Wilson (1986) states, "it may be…that interpersonal expectations established in the consultation sessions create for some faculty a desire to fulfill an implied contract with their consultant" (p. 211). Gil (1987) suggests that it is simply "the human element" (p. 59)—the fact that someone takes an interest—that provides the impetus for change. Obviously, further research is needed to clarify which of these elements, or combination of elements, it may be that helps faculty use student evaluation data to make instructional changes.

In addition, research to date has not yet addressed how long consultative sessions ought to be, how soon after the evaluative event they should be scheduled, if continuing consultation across several semesters adds to the impact, or if consultation works more effectively with certain groups of faculty, i.e. those with low or high ratings, those with limited or extensive teaching experience, and so on. The Stevens and Aleamoni (1985) call for further research as to effects of rating consultation over time needs response as well. At this point, consultation over ratings has been shown to make a difference; the scope, nature, and variables contributing to that impact remain to be discovered.

Evidence documenting the effectiveness of videotaping and microteaching as instructional improvement interventions continues to offer tantalizing possibilities. Unfortunately, most of the evidence is peripheral to the larger and more direct question: Does a videotape or microteaching experience with consultation improve instruction? The peripheral evidence provided by research done in this decade coupled with research on microteaching reported earlier seems to indicate a positive impact, but once again the extent of that impact, its continued effect over time, what the consultative component adds to the intervention, all remain unclear. As with consultation over student evaluation results, the effects of videotaping and microteaching on learning outcomes remains untested. Research in both these areas does tend to go beyond the level of faculty attitudes and knowledge, but to date it does not show that these interventions cause students to learn more.

In terms of consultations over general teaching issues, much remains unknown. For example, to name a few unresolved questions: What are the most common issues brought to the consultant? What are the implications in terms of effects of the models proposed in the historical section? Does experience and/or training of the consultant make a difference? Are the effects of consultation sustainable across time?

The use of instructional consultation as it occurs over ratings, over videotaped teaching samples and microteaching experiences, and over general instructional issues has grown during the '80s. In terms of the criteria being used to assess research on the interventions, more of the research in this area has occurred at the level of observable behavior changes and changes in student evaluation. Unfortunately, the body of research remains small, in some cases only peripherally related to the intervention and to date not at all assessing the effects of consultation on student learning outcomes. Much needed work in this area remains to be done.

GRANTS FOR INSTRUCTIONAL IMPROVEMENT PROJECTS

History

Generally small grants, in most cases available from the institution, have been used as an instructional intervention from the beginning of the instructional and faculty development efforts that started in the '60s. In the first survey of instructional improvement activities, Centra (1978) reports that of the 756 two- and four-year institutions responding to his survey, 58 percent indicated they had a grants program. Levinson-Rose and Menges (1981) reviewed instructional grants programs in terms of interinstitutional projects, campus-wide programs and individual faculty projects at the national (some offered by the professional associations of particular disciplines) and state level, as well as those offered by local institutions. They reference some survey studies completed in the '70s where those associated with grant programs were queried as to methods of evaluation. Only a small percentage went beyond soliciting faculty reactions. Centra's

(1978) data indicate that fewer than one-fifth of those with grants programs had attempted evaluation and most of those used unsophisticated designs. Levinson-Rose and Menges summarize the status of research on the grant intervention in 1981. "Few generalizations about effective granting programs can be made on the basis of this research. Such programs possess face validity, since persons completing a grant-supported project are likely to have gained new knowledge and skills. Nevertheless, impact on students remains to be studied in relation to specific features of particular programs" (p. 406).

Prevalence

Throughout the '80s, institutions continued to use small grants programs to intervene in the quality of instruction at the institution. Smith (1981), using a survey design modeled on Centra's (1978), asked 1,315 community colleges about staff development goals and activities. Of the 413 institutions having organized staff development programs, 324 used grants to faculty "for developing new or different approaches to courses or teaching" (p. 214). Hansen (1983) reports that 50 percent of the community colleges in Illinois who responded to a survey of faculty development activities and their impact used "institutional grants for instructional projects" (p. 218). Richardson and Moore (1987) found similarly in their survey of Texas community colleges. Forty-nine percent of the 56 institutions reported making grants available to support instructional programs. Of the 25 Canadian institutions responding to Konrad's (1983) survey, 40 percent indicated that "summer grants for projects to improve instruction or courses" existed. In Erickson's (1986) survey of four-year institutions, including responses from 630 colleges and universities, 60 percent had "summer grants for projects to improve instruction or courses" and 64.5 percent had "grants for faculty members developing new or different approaches to courses or teaching" (p. 188). The sum of this evidence warrants this conclusion: the use of grants as an intervention to improve instruction continues in all types of post-secondary institutions.

Description

Although no data were located which document the extent to which these programs share design details, there is a general sense among faculty and instructional developers that during this decade there are fewer interinstitutional projects, fewer campus-wide programs, and more institutional grants to individual faculty. In general, these grants tend to be small, ranging between $500 and $5,000. They are awarded competitively, with faculty writing grant proposals and faculty-administrative committees awarding the funds. Funds are used to purchase instructional materials, pay personnel, support travel, provide access to consultants, or buy release time.

Jacobsen's (1989) study of the impact of faculty incentive grants on teaching effectiveness at a college in Pennsylvania was the only published study of a particular grant program located during this review of up to $5,000 each annually to four instructors. Faculty members must submit "student evaluations of teaching performance during the preceding calendar year,...evidence of effective advising,...a course evaluation that has been completed by a fellow faculty member,...a letter from the department chair indicating quality performance in both teaching and advising,...and a proposal for how the award money will be used" (p. 4). Summarized in the assessment section are Jacobsen's findings with regard to the effect of this program on faculty members' student evaluations.

Assessment

Most of the assessment of the effectiveness of grants as an instructional intervention is general data collected in the survey's mentioned throughout this review. In other words, those who oversee or have knowledge of an institution's instructional grants program (not faculty who received the grants) offer opinions as to their effectiveness. Of Smith's (1981) community college respondents, 70 percent saw the use of grants by faculty as effective or very effective. Of Hansen's (1983) Illinois community college respondents, 89 percent gave grants excellent or good ratings, making them the highest evaluated improvement activity. Furthermore, 84 percent gave release time to develop instructional projects excellent or good ratings, making them the second most highly evaluated activity. Of Richardson and Moore's (1987) Texas community college respondents, 88 percent gave institutional grants for instructional projects excellent or good ratings; 90 percent gave the same ratings to release time to develop instructional projects. In Konrad's (1983) survey of Canadian institutions, 50 percent felt summer grants programs were effective. Erickson (1986) did not ask the faculty and instructional developers he surveyed to assess the effectiveness of the interventions they reported using.

Only two other assessments of grants as instructional intervention were located. The first appears in a book by Eble and McKeachie (1985) which describes and evaluates the Bush Foundation Faculty Development Project in Minnesota and the Dakotas. The foundation aimed to improve undergraduate education by supporting a variety of different programs (24 for the first three years) at a variety of different institutions in the region. Using interview and survey techniques, Eble and McKeachie (1985) compare and contrast individual programs and the interventions they employed. They write: "Projects involving *course development* and *curricular change* were also rated as highly productive by our faculty respondents" (p.198). Later they qualify: "Grant programs are unlikely to affect norms unless a purposeful effort is made to use the grants as catalysts for institutional change through faculty forums, newsletters, and follow-up activities drawing upon the experience of the grantees and relating their learning to the interests and needs of other faculty members....Our impression is that the degree to which faculty grants eventually affected teaching and learning was related to the degree to which a faculty development committee or officer consulted with grantees about teaching and the relevance of the grant to teaching" (p. 199).

The second assessment of grants as an instructional intervention appeared in the already mentioned Jacobsen (1989) study. Jacobsen defines the "Excellence in Teaching" grant as a reward (rather than incentive) grant since faculty members applying for the grant must supply proof of effective teaching and advising, in addition to a grant proposal. Jacobsen compared, over two time periods (pre-grant program and post-grant program), student evaluations for those instructors who received grants, those who applied for but did not receive grants, and those who did not apply for grants. She found that, overall, pre- and post-grant program evaluations for the whole college remained constant; instructors who were awarded grants were better teachers than their colleagues; instructors with grants did not see improved evaluations as a result of the grant received; and those who did see improved evaluations were the instructors who applied for a grant and did not receive one.

Additionally, she interviewed ten faculty members (some who received grants, some who applied but did not receive grants, and some who did not apply) and asked them, among other questions, "What effect has the Excellence in Teaching Award program had on teaching effectiveness at this college?" (p. 16). She found that no one indicated a positive effect, six reported no effect, and four indicated a negative effect.

Discussion

The evidence found to support the effectiveness of grants as an instructional improvement intervention justifies no conclusion. Most of it fails to meet even the first category of assessment proposed by Levinson-Rose and Menges (1981). Here even faculty participants have only rarely been asked to offer self-reports of instructional experiences related to receipt of a grant. More often those who administer the grant, perhaps have even had a hand in designing the program, have been asked for general opinions as to the effectiveness of the intervention. The only study that did assess faculty improvement (Jacobsen, 1989) reported that grants did not increase recipients' student evaluations. For this review no evidence was discovered which substantiates that grants change faculty instructional knowledge, in-class instructional behaviors, that they change student evaluations of instruction, or that they in any way change learning outcomes. It seems almost unbelievable that an intervention so widely used and that involves measurable amounts of money (to say nothing of time and effort) remains so unstudied. The decade has produced gains in experience, although even those have not been shared in a published form, but it has produced no gains in research-based knowledge. Whether or not grants have any measurable effects on instructional quality is still not known.

RESOURCE MATERIALS

History

Neither Centra (1978) nor Levinson-Rose and Menges (1981) considered those efforts to intervene in instructional quality by distributing to faculty various materials about teaching and learning. Therefore, no evidence as to the prevalence or effectiveness of this intervention has been reviewed previously. However, materials on teaching have been available and circulated to faculty prior to this decade. A number of discipline-specific pedagogical journals, *The Journal of Chemical Education* and *Teaching Psychology*, to name just two of many, have been published for decades. The interdisciplinary journal *College Teaching* began publication in the '50s. Early instructional and faculty development units did prepare and circulate local newsletters and other resources on teaching and learning.

Prevalence

Some of the survey data collected during the '80s does document the extent to which this intervention is used. In Konrad's (1983) survey of Canadian universities, 80 percent of those responding indicated that newsletters and articles pertinent to teaching were circulated. Of the 630 four-year institutions responding to Erickson's (1986) survey, 48 percent indicated they did circulate newsletters and articles on instructional issues.

Description

Materials on teaching and learning circulated to faculty take a variety of different forms. Newsletters are probably the most frequently discussed in faculty and instructional development circles. In a newsletter on writing newsletters Border and Fisch (1988) propose that these publications can achieve a number of important goals: present information about effective teaching, stimulate discussion and promote the sharing of good ideas, provide instructional support, and showcase examples of instructional excellence, among others. Besides infusing the instruction of faculty with new and pertinent information, newsletters also call attention to those units offering instructional resources and services.

Some instructional and faculty development units circulate articles to faculty or make them available upon faculty request. These articles may address teaching effectiveness generally or may relate to a specific instructional issue like constructing multiple-choice exams, or getting students participating in discussion, or using clear examples.

Some programs develop their own materials, perhaps a resource book for new faculty, or a monograph on test construction, or a bibliography of sources on how students learn. These may be distributed to faculty at large, to those who request them, or they may be part of a larger collection of instructional resources generally housed in the instructional or faculty development unit.

Assessment

This review uncovered no inquiry into the effectiveness of instructional materials distributed to faculty. Of those who use them in Canadian universities, according to Konrad (1983), only 30 percent list them as effective.

Weimer (1988), in an article written for faculty, offers a number of reasons why reading ought to improve instruction, among them that it infuses teaching with a stream of concrete, practical, new ideas; that it forces faculty to become aware of how they teach and how they might teach differently; and that it can help to alleviate some of the psychological burnout associated with teaching by providing motivational descriptions of teaching and learning. She does point out, however, that none of these claims have been subjected to empirical inquiry.

Discussion

No conclusions can be drawn as to the effectiveness of resource materials on instructional quality. In the case of this intervention as with others in this review, a fairly extensive use of an intervention can be documented, and yet for all intents and purposes absolutely no evidence exists supporting its effectiveness in the improvement of instruction. Perhaps a larger body of research can be summoned to make the case. Students of all sorts can and do learn by reading materials. There is nothing to indicate that faculty reading materials on teaching and learning are different than any other students who learn by reading, but that qualifies as general support, not the specific evidence needed to establish the efficacy of the case in point.

COLLEAGUES HELPING COLLEAGUES

History

Neither the Centra (1978) or Levinson-Rose and Menges (1981) review considered the effects of colleague interventions on teaching quality. The practice was not widespread in early instructional and faculty development efforts. The use of colleague intervention increased when understaffed and underfunded instructional and faculty development units began using faculty volunteers and discovered the benefits of their involvement, and when reviews of literature like Cohen and McKeachie's (1980) concluded that colleagues would do best by intervening formatively in the instructional efforts of one another.

Prevalence

The prevalence of this activity is currently difficult to document. Those collecting data on instructional and faculty development practices do not always clearly differentiate between the presence of colleagues in each other's classrooms for the purposes of preparing an evaluation to be used in a promotion and tenure decision, and the presence of colleagues in each other's classrooms for the purpose of instructional improvement. This may account for the low effectiveness rating given by community college personnel responding to Smith's (1981) survey. Only 38 percent of the 255 of them who reported using "formal assessments by colleagues for teaching or course improvement" (p. 216) labeled it an effective practice. In Erickson's (1986) survey, 64.5 percent of the four-year institutions who responded reported using classroom observation by peers as an instructional improvement intervention.

Description

Instructional and faculty developers are using colleagues to intervene with each other in a variety of ways. Most often they observe each other teach; sometimes one (possibly trained and experienced) observes the other, and sometimes the visitation is reciprocal. After the visitation there is a discussion of what was observed with suggestions offered for improvement. Faculty are sometimes used to offer input on course materials, or to respond to an instructional concern they have faced (for example, teaching a large, lower division, required course), or a practice they use (for example, student managed tutoring groups).

Millis (1989) describes a program typical in many respects of the kind of activities being used in this instructional intervention. At the University of Maryland a group of peer visitors are selected from a group of faculty who have distinguished themselves in the classroom as indicated by student evaluations and administrative recommendations. They are trained both in the observation of instruction and the communication of feedback. These peer visitors attend one class session of several target faculty groups: those new to the university, those nominated for teaching awards, randomly selected experienced faculty, and faculty perceived as needing assistance. Although some resistance occurs from faculty in the last two categories, most respond favorably to the opportunity.

Probably the most elaborate colleague instructional intervention is one described by Katz and Henry (1988). Their model was developed in two separate projects: one funded by FIPSE and the other by the Ford Foundation. It involves colleagues in an elaborate and comprehensive inquiry into the learning experiences of students in their courses. Colleagues attend class and then individually interview selected students from the class as to how they are attempting to learn course content. Those learning experiences are then related to the professor teaching the class and the two colleagues explore what instructional policies and practices might more effectively impact student learning experiences. Versions of this program have been used at a variety of different institutions throughout the country, most recently in the institutions in New Jersey's Department of Higher Education. Participants are asked to prepare a paper describing what knowledge they have gained through their interviews, observations, and discussions. A published assessment of those outcomes was not located for this review.

Assessment

Evaluation of the effects of colleagues interventions is spotty. Annis (1989) reports on a project at Ball State University where nine colleague pairs observed and interacted with each other for two quarters. Students completed a Teaching Analysis By Students (TABS) evaluation instrument prior to the program's start and once again at its conclusion. Comparisons between average student responses on the pre- and post-evaluations revealed improvement on six of seven primary teaching components. In a case study, two English professors (Rorschach and Whitney, 1986) describe the positive effects of a course-long observation experience in each other's composition courses.

Discussion

Despite the growing number of colleague interventions, the effectiveness of this means to improve instruction remains for all intents and purposes unstudied. Theoretical grounding for the intervention exists, as does experience in a number of different programs and activities. What remains unproven is the effect of colleague interventions on the instructional practices of each other, on student evaluations, and on learning outcomes.

TARGET GROUP: NEW FACULTY

Background and Current Status

A focus on the instructional efforts of new faculty stems from two assumptions. First, since the graduate school experiences continues to ignore instructional preparation (except perhaps for those with teaching assistantships), new faculty come to college teaching with little or no prior experience or training, and it is assumed that instructional quality suffers as a consequence. That assumption rests on some evidence, described subsequently, but mostly on the prior experience of faculty who teach in college today. Few wish to repeat (or even recall) their early teaching experiences. Second, since new faculty generally do not come to an institution with tenure, it is assumed the institution is in a better position to "encourage" these faculty to do "something" about teaching effectiveness during these years.

Neither of these two assumptions, however, can explain the current surge of interest in new faculty. It may be an extension of the concern about teaching assistants. *All* new college teachers face many of the same challenges: preparing course materials, constructing a syllabus, establishing credibility and control, devising equitable grading systems, to name a few. Instructional and faculty developers, and their institutions have discovered what concerns TAs is equally needed and of interest to new faculty. Or, current interest may be in anticipation of the large numbers of new faculty who will join colleges and universities in the '90s to replace retirees. Institutions have an opportunity to intervene with faculty over instruction to to an extent unknown in recent decades. Whatever the reason, interest in instructional interventions with new faculty is on the rise, as witnessed by several studies focusing on the instructional experiences of new faculty, published pieces describing and assessing the use of various interventions with them, and new materials being developed for them.

To date, the prevalence of activities targeted for new faculty has been partially documented. Hansen (1983) surveyed chief academic officers of Illinois community colleges and found that of the 36 institutions responding, 94 percent conducted orientation activities (mostly workshops) for new faculty. Richardson and Moore (1987) found that in the 56 Texas community colleges responding to their survey 89 percent reported having orientation activities (most often workshops) for full-time, new faculty. In Konrad's (1983) survey of 25 Canadian universities, 20 percent of the institutions indicated they gave new faculty lighter than normal teaching loads for the first year. Only 40 percent assessed it an "effective" practice. Likewise in the Smith (1981) survey of 413 community colleges nationwide, this technique fell in the "least favorable" category with only 32 percent listing it as "effective."

However, recent research on new faculty reflects current interest in this target group. Fink (1984) studied nearly 100 beginning college teachers in geography collecting information on their "origin, distribution, preparation, situation and performance...from the new teachers themselves, their colleagues, from students, and from site visits by the research director" (p. 95). Interestingly, in light of previous assessments of lighter loads for new faculty, Fink found that student evaluations revealed that "an increase in the number of separate preparations during a single term had a strong, straight-line negative effect on teaching performance" (p. 99). Participants were also asked to indicate whether they had found "intellectual companionship" (p. 100) with colleagues. One third said yes, one half said only to a limited degree, and one sixth said no. "The less companionship they found, the lower was their average teaching evaluation score" (p. 100). Also of interest to the topic of instructional improvement were Fink's attempts to assess the instructional performance of these first-year faculty. He summarizes, "The student ratings and the self-rating both indicated that one sixth of the new teachers performed well above average compared with other, experienced teachers. One half did about average, and one third had problems. In other words, there was a range in their performance, but the distribution was overrepresented in the lower half of the scale" (p. 102).

Sorcinelli (1988) interviewed 54 new tenure-track appointments at a large midwestern university. About half her sample reported stresses in teaching. "The major culprit was the time it took to develop courses (several designed four new courses their first year), teach, evaluate, and advise students" (p. 126). New faculty in this survey also reported a "lack of collegial relations as the most surprising and disappointing aspect of their first year" (p. 126).

Turner and Boice (1989) report on a large interview/observation project undertaken across the first four semesters 100 new faculty were at a large regional university. "The study's goals included collection of information about how new faculty reacted to recruiting and orienting practices, how they coped with pressures to master teaching while initiating research and scholarly writing, how they were socialized to departmental and campus mores, how they perceived the stresses and satisfactions of new faculty status, and their perceptions of senior faculty as sources of collegiality and intellectual stimulation" (p. 52).

Specifically, in regard to teaching most new professors in this survey reported spending from 16 to 20 hours a week preparing their lectures and other course materials. The majority received "good" or excellent" student evaluations. Those not teaching well seemed to share a common pattern. "They reported feeling highly motivated but notably insecure in their own knowledge and skills. They reported spending 35 hours a week preparing lectures. And, they came across as stiff, formal, and generally uncomfortable in the classroom" (p. 54) With regard to colleagues, "nearly 50% of all new tenure track faculty rated the overall quality of collegial relations in their department as only 'fair' or 'poor'" (p. 55).

Interventions

Three of the instructional interventions under consideration in this review are being used in efforts designed for new faculty: workshop programming, consultation (almost exclusively via some form of mentoring model), and resource materials. Each of these interventions will be considered separately in terms of the prevalence of its use (provided an indication of this exists), a general description and specific illustrations of the intervention, and the assessment measures being used to determine its effectiveness.

Workshop, Seminars, and Programs

Many of these occur under the rubric of orientation activities, and the prevalence of those has been mentioned previously. Additionally, Eison (1989) reports data from a survey of faculty developers at 70 different institutions where 85 percent of the respondents report providing a special workshop or program for new faculty. Approximately one third of those programs are less than a day in length, one third last one full day, and the final third are longer than one day.

Typically orientation activities for new faculty occur just prior to or shortly after the first teaching experience at the institution. The shorter orientations include introductions to various aspects of the institution and a review of relevant policies and practices, with some instructional "survival skills" thrown in for good measure. The longer programs tend to include more information on teaching and rely on a greater variety of instructional methods and interventions.

A particularly complete description of the development, implementation, and evolution of a week-long, mandatory workshop for new faculty is provided by Bonwell and Eison (1987) and Eison (1989). This workshop seeks to accomplish four goals: 1) to convey the university's view that teaching excellence should be the number one goal of the faculty, 2) to create a positive first impression of the university, faculty, staff, and community, 3) to provide new faculty with an opportunity to develop the attitudes, knowledge base, and pedagogical skills associated with instructional excellence, and 4) to provide new faculty with an opportunity to meet and work with each other, and with faculty members recognized as excellent teachers. Based on their discovery that not all new hired faculty are new to teaching, that mandatory attendance sometimes engenders defensiveness, and that participants wanted information about all sorts of issues in addition to instructional ones, program organizers have continued to revise what they offer new faculty and how they offer it. Participants each year in the program evaluate it via open and closed-ended instruments. Those assessments reported in 1989 are favorable.

Foster and Moore (1987) describe an orientation workshop for new faculty first offered at their institution in the 1960s. Forty percent of the content of the current workshop focuses on teaching methods. Participants also prepare and are videotaped delivering a 10- to 15-minute lesson. The group evaluates each presentation. Assessments of the activity delivered in group discussion sessions and in written comments indicate the "large majority of participants are enthusiastic about the workshop" (p. 749).

Certainly one of the most comprehensive and oldest programmatic interventions with new faculty is a fellowship program supported by the Lilly Endowment. Begun in 1974, the Teaching Fellows Programs offer research institutions a way to assist junior, untenured faculty members to learn about, reflect on, and develop teaching expertise, while they simultaneously pursue research activities at their institution of appointment. Yearly grants are awarded to institutions with the possibility of renewal for three years. Although the programs at the individual institutions vary, typically they involve regular group meetings to discuss teaching-related topics, individual projects focused on teaching, some release time from usual course responsibilities, and, often, senior faculty mentors. At least five Fellows must be appointed annually. A recent evaluation of the program completed by Austin (1990) assessed the impact of the program on individual Fellows, on their institutions, and on higher education policy issues. The 568 former Fellows were surveyed, all with a written instrument, some with phone interviews. All program directors were surveyed and interviewed as well as archival material studied. As for impact on the individual participants, Austin concludes: "In sum, evidence from the Fellows, the Program Directors, Deans, and Department Chairs leads to the unmistakable conclusion that, with only a few exceptions, the Teaching Fellows Program typically affects faculty participants in important, positive, identifiable ways" (p. 3). At the 30 universities where programs have been located, nine have continued the program with internal funding. Eighteen (some included in the nine) have established other faculty development programs that are the result, partially or fully, of the Lilly program.

Some general assessment of the effectiveness of the workshop activity with new faculty has occurred. Hansen (1983) asked those surveyed in Illinois community colleges if they considered orientation activities for new faculty to be useful for the improvement of instruction. Seventy-eight percent considered them to be an excellent or good way to improve instruction. Richardson and Moore (1987) report that 63 percent of the community colleges in Texas report they do evaluate their orientation activities for new faculty. Seventy-two percent evaluate via verbal feedback from participants; 57 percent use written feedback. Virtually no other form of assessment is reported by those surveyed.

Consultation via Mentoring Models

This review located very little material documenting the prevalence of this intervention with new faculty. Konrad's (1983) survey of Canadian institutions reported that 44 percent of those interviewed did not use this intervention, but of those who did (percentage not reported), 43 percent considered it an effective practice.

The interest in mentoring models for new faculty probably stems from a variety of different sources. Mentoring activities for newcomers in an organization are popular in various contexts right now. It appeals particularly to faculty who harbor traditions of collegiality and rely on experience for much of what they have learned about effective instruction. Perhaps those who propose it are attempting to respond to the earlier evidence documenting dissatisfaction on the part of new faculty with collegial experiences. Whatever its cause, a variety different programs and approaches are being taken which share two common objectives: help new faculty better understand an institution's goals and objectives, and get them started on activities designed to meet those goals.

Several published descriptions of programs exist. Boice and Turner (1989) report on an elaborate FIPSE supported mentoring project undertaken with faculty at California State University, Long Beach. Fourteen new faculty were given faculty mentors, picked "on the basis of our observations of their prowess and balance as teachers, researchers, and colleagues" (p. 119). New faculty were selected for the project based on "our judgments about their need for mentoring and their willingness, eventually, to become mentors themselves" (p. 119). During this year-long program mentors and mentees agreed to: 1) meet in mentor-mentee meetings at least weekly for an academic year, 2) attend monthly meetings of all project pairs, 3) keep regular records of their pair meetings, and 4) submit to weekly or biweekly observations and surveys conducted by project directors. Mentoring pairs reported they discussed research/scholarship/publication most often during the year, and teaching second most often. They reported the following as most helpful aspects of the experience (in rank order): help with academic policies, emotional support, help with faculty, help with scholarship, and time management/goal setting.

Freudenthal and DiGiorgio (1989) report on a new faculty program at Trenton State College where the institution assumes the mentor role. An advisory committee of selected faculty, department chairs, deans, and an administrative representative designed a formal mentoring program aimed at impacting the teaching, research, and service activities of new faculty members, including both those new to college teaching and new to the institution, and supporting faculty efforts throughout their entire first year. The program has five components: mentoring meetings (biweekly), departmental mentoring, development of a scholarly plan, "paper" mentoring that includes providing in an organized and coherent collection all published information about the college, and a one course reduction in teaching load. Participants have responded favorably to surveys asking for their feedback about the program.

Holmes (1988) reports on a mentoring component of a larger new faculty orientation program at the University of Wisconsin, Stevens Point. Here new faculty are assigned mentors from within their departments. In her survey of 44 mentors, Holmes found that most mentors reported spending six to fifteen hours with the mentee during the first semester and zero to five the second semester. The most frequently discussed topics by the pairs included talking about teaching, about the department, about testing and grading, about the administration, about the local community, and about research and scholarly activity. Surprisingly, since mentoring programs are generally constructed to benefit the mentee, Holmes' mentors reported several significant benefits had occurred to them as well. Thirty-eight percent reported and increased enthusiasm for teaching. Twenty-three percent indicated that they had in fact modified their own teaching style as a result of the program.

Resource Materials

No evidence was located that establishes the prevalence or use of materials written especially for new faculty. However, materials do exist, not the least of which is a text, *Tips for Teachers: A Guidebook for Beginning College Teachers* by Wilbert McKeachie (1986). This particular book, currently available in its eighth edition, holds the distinction of being the only book on college teaching. More recently an anthology of readings for new faculty has been published, *Teaching College: Collected Readings for the New Instructor*, edited by Weimer and Neff (1990). Two recent articles have also appeared, "Confidence in the Classroom: Ten Maxims for New Teachers" by Eison (1990) and "Achieving Excellence: Advice to New Teachers" by Browne and Keeley (1985). This review of instructional interventions uncovered no study of the effectiveness of these published materials on the improvement of the instruction of new faculty.

Discussion

In assessing the effectiveness of these three interventions with new faculty against the five levels proposed by Levinson-Rose and Menges (1981), it becomes clear quickly that no general statement as to the effectiveness of any or all the new faculty interventions can be offered. Empirical evidence establishing the effect of these interventions on faculty classroom behaviors and learning outcomes simply does not exist. In this case, the only evidence exists at the level of faculty attitude as reported by them. For orientation workshop programming there is some evidence that faculty "like" these programs and see them as useful and relevant to their initial experiences at the institution. In the case of consultation via mentoring, there is some of the same evidence as reported by both mentors and mentees depending on the published report.

As the summary of the literature described in this section shows, this is not the literature of research, but the literature of practice. To date no one has attempted to design and test a new faculty intervention using experimental controls, nor has anyone tried to assess an existing intervention in terms of its effects at these more objective, measurable levels. This, despite the fact that research cited in this section documents the need for such interventions, and the survey results reported document a widespread use of activities designed to improve the instruction of new faculty.

TARGET GROUP: TEACHING ASSISTANTS

Two reviews of research describe the status of current research on efforts to prepare teaching assistants for their instructional responsibilities. Carroll (1980) reviewed the research in terms of the effects of training on TA and student variables. For TA variables, he reports on eight studies which assessed TA feedback about the program (the Levinson-Rose and Menges category of attitude by self-report). Programs were evaluated favorably. Inconclusive evidence existed to determine whether or not training programs effectively changed TA knowledge, or TA attitudes toward specific methods and techniques. More evidence documented the success of TA training programs at changing observed teaching behavior. With student variables, Carroll concludes: "Quasi-experimental research has indicated that training programs covering a wide range of teaching skills generally improved student attitudes, achievement, and ratings of instruction. However, studies with true experimental designs have tended to isolate a narrow set of teaching skills, and the results have been inconsistent" (p. 177).

Recently, Abbott, Wulff, and Szego (1989) attempted to update the Carroll (1980) review. They focused on training programs studied via a research design that manipulated variables with training and no training groups, or employed pre- and post-testing. They found studies which met this criteria in the area of student ratings with consultation or interpretation, and conclude that the evidence there suggests that "consultation based on student rating can be useful in helping TAs improve their teaching" (p. 113). With general training combined with videotaping, the evidence reviewed also suggests that these interventions can be effective in producing change in TAs. Two studies were assessed which attempted training in specific disciplines. Both were successful. Two additional studies focused on training TAs in specific instructional approaches and both were successful.

Authors of this recent review summarize the current status of research on TA training efforts:

> *Empirical research on TA training is still lacking.* Carroll (1980) suggested that there was a paucity of research that dealt specifically with training TAs. That deficiency still exists. We originally planned to report the results of our review in a meta-analysis and to make recommendations based on effect sizes, but we identified too few relevant studies to undertake such a procedure. Our review also discovered few case studies that employed modern qualitative approaches to examine TA training, and little research examining the generalizability of results across disciplines. (p. 120)

Nonetheless, by comparison more research has studied the effects of TA training on instructional improvement than has studied efforts with new faculty. To date, though, none of the assumptions underlying efforts to reach particular parts of the larger faculty population are being tested. Is the beginning of the teaching career the best time to intervene? Are the interventions considered in this review the best means to intervene? Until those questions are addressed efforts directed at these target teacher groups remain on questionable ground.

DISCUSSION AND RECOMMENDATIONS

Based on this description and assessment of the literature in the 1980s on the effectiveness of five interventions to improve instruction (workshops, consultation, grants, resource materials, and colleagues helping colleagues), and the effectiveness of efforts to use these interventions with two target groups (new faculty and teaching assistants), concluding remarks and recommendations for future research can be offered.

First and most fundamentally, *more research must be undertaken.* That is probably the most obvious, but nonetheless most important conclusion of this review. In colleges and universities across this country and others, instructional interventions are being used with virtually no empirical justification as to their effectiveness. They have become the "traditional" and "customary" means of intervening to improve instruction. This is not to denigrate unnecessarily the wisdom of practice and the voice of experience present in the literature. Instructional and faculty developers are trained and experienced professionals. Their assessment of the effectiveness of these interventions should not be discounted, nor should the opinions of faculty participants be ignored. The problem is simply that they are not enough. The involvement and vested interest of these professionals in the success of the interventions place them in a biased position. The same may be said of faculty participants themselves who attend a workshop or experience visitation from a colleague. There is an inherent bias in favor of those experiences. All who support efforts to improve instruction will benefit from further evidence documenting how, why, and the extent to which these interventions succeed or fail.

Why has so little research on instructional interventions been conducted during this decade and the years preceding it? Those who use the interventions should not be excused from their lack of research, but to some degree it can be explained. Faculty and instructional developers for the most part are practitioners, not researchers. Many are faculty from other academic disciplines, assuming positions as heads and directors of faculty and instructional development units out of deep love for and concern about teaching. They are not familiar with educational research, either in terms of what is known about teaching or learning or in terms of methodology. Most also run offices chronically underfunded and understaffed. There is simply no time to do research beyond the most pragmatic levels—Did faculty like the program? Will they come if we sponsor one like it next year?

Despite these realities, during this decade the calls for more research and more comprehensive program evaluations are being made in the professional associations of these groups. Published materials are appearing which point out the need and value and then propose models and methods. Menges and Svinicki (1989) illustrate.

As much as more research is needed, *greater sophistication in empirical design is needed* even more. Granted, on some of the interventions reviewed (distribution of resource material, for example) any evidence would be an improvement, but for most of the interventions, evidence which does more than collect and summarize self-reported attitudes is essential. Favorable attitudes do not guarantee what is in fact needed if instruction is to be improved. Faculty must change what they do in class. Those changes must be obvious to independent observers, students, and must result in measurable differences in student learning. In other words, the effects of instructional interventions in these substantive realms must be established before any definitive claim can be made about current efforts to improve instruction.

Design sophistication also relates to the complexity that has come to characterize the use of a number of these interventions. Workshops and consultation provide the most compelling examples. Each of these interventions needs to be studied across different dimensions. Does the length of a workshop program correlate with its ability to change faculty behaviors? Do certain topics accomplish better results than other topics? What about consultation? Is it more effective over student evaluation results or a videotaped teaching sample? Individual interventions need to be studied across the different dimensions that have come to characterize their use.

In addition to deeper study of the interventions themselves, their relative strengths and weaknesses in the improvement process need to be assessed. It remains unclear, for example, whether participation in workshop programs more efficiently and permanently changes teaching behaviors than, say, consultation over a videotaped teaching sample. To date the association of more than one intervention in a packaged program—a week-long orientation to college teaching that combines, e. g., seminars, a microteaching experience, and consultation—remains unstudied. Does their power as impetuses to improve instruction grow or diminish by virtue of their association with each other? More sophisticated designs are needed if important questions like these are to be explored.

Finally, the targeting of instructional interventions to certain faculty groups needs study. Are efforts to intervene in the instruction of TAs and new faculty only occurring because those are the most "captive" of faculty groups? Stronger justification would include evidence that interventions like the ones reviewed in this study are effective in changing the behaviors, student assessments, and learning outcomes in the classes of faculty in these groups. More specific evidence would identify which of the interventions are most successful for each target group.

The call of this review for more rigorous empirical inquiry is not new. It has been made previously. Why are these interventions not being studied? First, as previously noted, those who use them are not qualified to complete the needed research agenda. Those with the qualifications may be avoiding the research because these are not easy phenomena to study. Researchers seldom have access to faculty subjects and even those who do quickly learn how difficult it is to "require" faculty to do anything. Moreover, the interventions themselves are difficult to study. Many intervening and confounding variables cloud results. It is easy to understand, by comparison, why the plethora of research on student evaluation continues. There vast quantities of data can be collected in much more tightly controlled environments. The study of instructional interventions requires field research with all its confounding logistical liabilities.

Do these realities preclude all possibilities of completing this research agenda? No. A closer collaboration between those who use the interventions and those interested in studying them could help to overcome a number of obstacles. Those associated with faculty and instructional development programs do have access to faculty subjects. Most would be amenable to using interventions in the more structured and systematic way research treatments require. Most also are part of a network of fellow professionals who might add to the potential number of subjects and the data pool. This interinstitutional collaboration would help to alleviate still another weakness of this research, identified by Levinson-Rose and Menges (1981). "Cross-campus collaboration is absent. Most studies are isolated efforts of investigators on individual campuses. Intercampus research networks are potentially powerful tools for dealing with several of these problems, particularly random assignment and small numbers" (p.419).

For years calls have been made for greater cooperation between those who research and those who practice. Here is yet another illustration of how that association could profitably benefit both groups. But will it occur? It will if those who research and those who practice, who do in fact share common goals and objectives, determine to make it so.

In addition to the need for more research and more rigorous empirical design of the research, there is also *a need for different kinds of inquiry.* Quantitative inquiries are not enough. They are by their nature ill-suited to answer all that needs to be known. Here little can be done but to re-echo the call made in the previous review. Levinson-Rose and Menges (1981) observe that quantitative methods "tend to distance researcher from participants in the name of objectivity and to oversimplify teaching and learning in the name of control.... To advance the field we need careful classroom ethnographies, disciplined case studies, and sensitive clinical interview as well as rigorous experimentation" (p. 419).

Finally, *the study of instructional interventions needs to derive from theoretical or conceptual bases.* In the research to date the underlying assumptions and grounding principles are rarely made explicit. Virtually no attempt is made to connect these interventions to related fields of knowledge. Several examples will illustrate. Faculty learning to teach more effectively are adult learners confronted with a new learning task. Much is known about how adults learn, what instructional strategies work best with them, and what learning activities they respond to favorably, but seldom is that knowledge applied to the use of instructional interventions with faculty. After an initial exploration of the applicability of adult learning theory to faculty development efforts, Geis and Smith (1989) conclude: "...we come away from this exploration of Adult Education and its application to the concerns and problems of faculty development with optimism and vitality. We suggest that much can be learned from the Adult Education literature, especially that part produced by those involved with continuing education in the professions"(p. 162).

Even closer to the sphere in which instructional interventions function is the work applying diffusion of innovation theories to faculty who adopt instructional innovations. Kozma's pioneering efforts (1978 and 1985) of faculty who adopted instructional technology innovations has large implications for the design and use of instructional interventions. Building on his work, Stevens' (1989) small but significant interview project with faculty innovators proposes a theoretical framework ripe for testing with more structured inquiries involving the interventions reviewed here.

Finally, work on motivation, specifically as it applies to the motivation faculty, do or do not have for teaching has large implications for the improvement of instruction. Bess' (1977) initial work in this area remains unapplied to improvement efforts, although the issues he identified have been repeated and reinforced by other literature; Berman and Skeff (1988), for example.

Interest in instructional improvement has continued unabated during the '80s. That interest shows no signs of impending decline. As more time, effort, and money are devoted to better college teaching, the contribution of various instructional interventions remains an issue. Do these efforts to stimulate faculty attention to teaching make a difference in the realms, like student learning, that matter most? Research reviewed here offers some support for them, but it is feeble, inconclusive support at best. Regrettably, this is the conclusion arrived at by virtually everyone who has assessed the literature. Hopefully those who review the literature at the end of this decade will tell a different story.

References

Abbott, R. D., Wulff, D. A. and Szego, C. K. (1989). Review of research on TA training. In J. D. Nyquist, R. D. Abbott and D. H. Wulff (eds.), *New Directions for Teaching and Learning: Teaching Assistant Training in the 1990s*. San Francisco: Jossey-Bass.

Aleamoni, L. M. (1978). The usefulness of student evaluations in improving college teaching. *Instructional Science* 7: 95–105.

Annis, L. F. (1989). Partners in teaching improvement. *Journal of Staff, Program, and Organizational Development* 7(1): 7–12.

Austin, A. E. (1990). To leave an indelible mark: encouraging good teaching in universities through faculty development. A report for the Lilly Foundation presented at the Annual Meeting of the American Association of Higher Education, San Francisco, March.

Berman, J., and Skeff, K. M. (1988). Developing the motivation for improving university teaching. *Innovative Higher Education* 12: 114–125.

Bess, J. L. (1977). The motivation to teach. *Journal of Higher Education* 48(3): 243–258.

Bland, C., and Schmitz, C. C. (1988). Faculty vitality on review: retrospect and prospect. *Journal of Higher Education* 59(2): 190–224.

Boice, R., and Turner, J. L. (1989). The FIPSE-CSULB mentoring project for new faculty. *To Improve the Academy* 8: 117–139.

Bonwell, C., and Eison, J. (1987). Mandatory teaching effectiveness workshops for new faculty: lessons learned the hard way. *The Journal of Staff, Program, and Organizational Development* 5(3): 114–118.

Border, L., and Fisch, L. (1988). A newsletter on newsletters. In E. Wadsworth (ed.), *A Handbook for New Practitioners.* Stillwater, OK: New Forums Press.

Boud, D., and McDonald, R. (1981). *Educational Development Through Consultancy.* Surrey, England: Society for Research into Higher Education.

Brown, G., and Daines, J. (1983). Creating a course on lecturing and explaining. *Programmed Learning and Educational Technology* 20: 64–69.

Browne, M. N., and Keeley, S. M. (1985). Achieving excellence: advice to new teachers. *College Teaching* 33(2): 78–83.

Carroll, J. G. (1980). Effects of training programs for university teaching assistants. *Journal of Higher Education* 51(2): 167–183.

Centra, J. A. (1978). Types of faculty development programs. *Journal of Higher Education* 49: 151–162.

Chism, N. (ed.) (1987) *Employment and Education of Teaching Assistants: Readings from a National Conference.* Columbus, Ohio: The Ohio State University.

Cohen, P. A., and McKeachie, W. (1980). The role of colleagues in the evaluation of college teaching. *Improving College and University Teaching* 28(4): 147–154.

Dalgaard, K. A. (1982). Some effects of training on teaching effectiveness of untrained university teaching assistants. *Research in Higher Education* 17(1): 39–50.

Eble, K., and McKeachie, W. (1985). *Improving Undergraduate Education Through Faculty Development.* San Francisco: Jossey-Bass.

Eison, J. A. (1990). Confidence in the classroom: ten maxims for new teachers. *College Teaching* 38(1): 21–25.

Eison, J. A. (1989). Mandatory teaching effectiveness workshops for new faculty: what a difference three years make. *The Journal of Staff, Program, and Organizational Development* 7(2): 59–66.

Erickson, G. (1986). A survey of faculty development practices. *To Improve the Academy* 5: 182–194.

Fink, L. D. (1984). *New Directions for Teaching and Learning: The First Year of College Teaching.* San Francisco: Jossey-Bass.

Foster, J. M., and Moore, R. M. (1987). A workshop for new faculty. *Engineering Education* 77(7/8): 748–749.

Freudenthal, N. R., and DiGiorgio, A. J. (1989). New faculty mentoring: the institution as mentor. *The Journal of Staff, Program, and Organizational Development* 7(2): 67–72.

Friedman, M., and Stomper, C. (1983). The effectiveness of a faculty development program: a process-product experimental study. *The Review of Higher Education* 7(1): 49–65.

Geis, G. L., and Smith, R. A. (1989). If professors are adults. *The Journal of Staff, Program, and Organizational Development* 7(4): 155–163.

Gibbs, L. E., Browne, M. N., and Keeley, S. M. (1989). Critical thinking: a study\'s outcome. *The Journal of Professional Studies* 13(1): 44–59.

Gil, D. H. (1987). Instructional evaluation as a feedback process. In L. M. Aleamoni (ed.), *New Directions for Teaching and Learning: Techniques for Evaluating and Improving Instruction.* San Francisco: Jossey-Bass.

Hansen, D. W. (1983). Faculty development activities in the Illinois Community College System. *Community/Junior College Quarterly* 7: 207–230.

Helling, B., and Kuhlmann, D. (1988). The faculty visitor program: helping teachers see themselves. In K. G. Lewis (ed.), *Face to Face.* Stillwater, OK: New Forums Press.

Herr, K. U. (1988). Exploring excellence in teaching: it can be done! *The Journal of Staff, Program, and Organization Development* 6(1): 11–16.

Holmes, S. K. (1988). New faculty mentoring: benefits to the mentor. *The Journal of Staff, Program, and*

Organization Development 6(1): 17–20.

Jacobsen, R. H. (1989). The impact of faculty incentive grants on teaching. A paper given at the Annual Meeting of the American Educational Research Association, San Francisco, March.

Katz, J., and Henry, M. (1988). *Turning Professors into Teachers.* New York: Macmillan.

Konrad, A. C. (1983). Faculty development practices in Canadian Universities. *The Canadian Journal of Higher Education* 13(2): 13–25.

Kozma, R. B. (1985). A grounded theory of instructional innovation in higher education. *Journal of Higher Education* 56(3): 300–319.

Kozma, R. B. (1978). Faculty development and the adoption and diffusion of classroom innovations. *Journal of Higher Education* 49(5): 438–449.

Levinson-Rose, J., and Menges, R. F. (1981). Improving college teaching: a critical review of research. *Review of Educational Research* 51(3): 403–434.

Lewis, K. G. (1988). Individual consultation: its importance to faculty development programs. In E. Wadsworth (ed.), *A Handbook for New Practitioners.* Stillwater, Oklahoma: New Forums Press.

Long, J. E., Sadker, D., and Sadker, M. (1986). The effects of teacher sex equity and effectiveness training on classroom interaction at the university level. Paper given at the Annual Meeting of the American Educational Research Association, San Francisco, April.

McKeachie, W. J. (1986). *Tips for Teachers: A Guidebook for Beginning College Teachers.* Lexington, Mass.: Heath.

Menges, R. J., and Svinicki, M. (1989). Designing program evaluations: a circular model. *To Improve The Academy* 8: 81–97.

Menges, R. J., and others. (1988). Strengthening professional development. *Journal of Higher Education* 59(3): 291–304.

Millis, B. J. (1989). Colleagues helping colleagues: a peer observation program model. *The Journal of Staff, Program, and Organizational Development* 7(1): 15–21.

Moses, I. (1985). Academic development units and the improvement of teaching. *Higher Education* 14: 75–100.

Murray, H. G. (1985). Classroom behaviors related to college teaching effectiveness. In J. G. Donald and A. M. Sullivan (eds.), *New Directions for Teaching and Learning: Using Research to Improve Teaching.* San Francisco: Jossey-Bass.

Murray, H. G. (1984). The impact of formative and summative evaluation of teaching in North American universities. *Assessment and Evaluation in Higher Education* 9(2): 117–132.

Nyquist, J., Abbott, B., Wulff, D., and Sprague, J. (in press). *Preparing the Professoriate of Tomorrow to Teach: Selected Readings on TA Training.* Dubuque, Iowa: Kendall Hunt.

Nyquist, J. D., and Wulff, D. H. (1988). Consultation using a research perspective. In K.G. Lewis (ed.), *Face to Face.* Stillwater, Oklahoma: New Forum Press.

Perlberg, A. (1983). When professors confront themselves: towards a theoretical conceptualization of video self-confrontation in higher education. *Higher Education* 12: 633–63.

Provlacs, J. (1988). The teaching analysis program and the role of the consultant. In K. G. Lewis (ed.), *Face to Face.* Stillwater, Oklahoma: New Forums Press.

Richardson, R., and Moore, W. (1987). Faculty development and evaluation in Texas Community Colleges. *Community/Junior College Quarterly of Research and Practice* 11(1): 19–32.

Rorschach, E., and Whitney, R. (1986). Relearning to teach: peer observation as a means of professional development. *English Education* 18: 159–172.

Sharp, G. (1981). Acquisition of lecturing skills by university teaching assistants: some effects of interest, topic relevance, and viewing a model videotape. *American Educational Research Journal* 18(4): 491–502.

Sorcinelli, M. D. (1988). Satisfactions and concerns of new university teachers. *To Improve the Academy* 7: 121–133.

Smith, A. (1981). Staff development goals and practices in U.S. community colleges. *Community/Junior College Research Quarterly* 2: 209–225.

Stevens, E. (1989). Explorations in faculty innovation. *The Journal of Staff, Program, and Organization Development* 7(4): 191–200.

Stevens, J. J., and Aleamoni, L. M. (1985). The use of evaluative feedback for instructional improvement: a longitudinal perspective. *Instructional Science* 13: 285–304.

Taylor-Way, D. (1988). Consultation with video: memory management through stimulated recall. In K.G. Lewis (ed.), *Face to Face*. Stillwater: New Forums Press. (159–191). (ed.) *Face to Face*. Stillwater, Oklahoma: New Forums Press.

Tiberius, R. (1988). The use of the discussion group for the fine-tuning of teaching. In K. G. Lewis (ed.) *Face to Face*. Stillwater, OK: New Forums Press.

Turner, J. L., and Boice, R. (1989). Experiences of new faculty. *The Journal of Staff, Program, and Organizational Development* 7(2): 51–57.

Weimer, M. (1988). Reading your way to better teaching. *College Teaching* 36(2): 48–51.

Weimer, M., and Neff, R. A. (1990). *Teaching College: Collected Readings for the New Instructor.* Madison: Magna Publications.

Weimer, M., Svinicki, M., and Bauer, G. (1990). Designing programs to prepare TAs to teach. In J.D. Nyquist, R. D. Abbott, and D. H. Wulff (eds.), *New Directions for Teaching and Learning: Teaching Assistant Training in the 1990s.* San Francisco: Jossey-Bass.

Wilson, R. (1986). Improving faculty teaching: effective use of student evaluations and consultants. *Journal of Higher Education* 57: 196–211.

Students' Evaluations of University Teaching: A Multidimensional Perspective[*]

Herbert W. Marsh and Michael J. Dunkin

INTRODUCTION

The Purposes of Students' Evaluations of Teaching Effectiveness

The most widely noted purposes for collecting students' evaluations of teaching effectiveness (SETs) are variously to provide: (1) diagnostic feedback to faculty about the effectiveness of their teaching that will be useful for the improvement of teaching; (2) a measure of teaching effectiveness to be used in administrative decision making; (3) information for students to use in the selection of courses and instructors; and (4) an outcome or a process description for research on teaching. The first purpose is nearly universal, but the next three are not. At many universities systematic student input is required before faculty are even considered for promotion, while at others the inclusion of SETs is optional or not encouraged at all. Similarly, in some universities the results of SETs are sold to students in university bookstores as an aid to the selection of courses or instructors, whereas the results are considered to be strictly confidential at other universities.

The fourth purpose of SETs, their use in research on teaching, has not been systematically examined, and this is unfortunate. Research on teaching involves at least three major questions (Gage, 1963; Dunkin, 1986; also see Braskamp, Brandenburg and Ory, 1985; Doyle, 1975, 1983): How do teachers behave? Why do they behave as they do? and What are the effects of their behavior? Dunkin goes on to conceptualize this research in terms of: a) process variables (global teaching methods and specific teaching behaviors); b) presage variables (characteristics of teachers and students); c) context variables (substantive, physical and institutional environments); and d) product variables (student academic/professional achievement, attitudes, and evaluations). McKeachie, Pintrich,

---

[*]The authors would like to acknowledge the helpful comments from Philip Abrami, Kenneth Feldman, Dennis Hocevar, and Wilbert McKeachie on earlier versions of this chapter.

Lin, Smith, and Sharma (1990) have blended this approach with a cognitive approach that includes student motivation, student cognition, and student involvement in self-regulated learning as well as student learning as important educational outcomes. SETs are important both as a process-description measure and as a product measure. This dual role played by SETs, as a process description and as a product of the process, is also inherent in their use as diagnostic feedback, as input for tenure promotion decisions, and as information for students to use in course selection. However, Dunkin's presage and context variables also have a substantial impact on both the process and the product, and herein lies a dilemma. SETs, as either a process or a product measure, should reflect the valid effects of presage and context measures. Nevertheless, since many presage and context variables may be beyond the control of the instructor, such influences may represent a source of unfairness in the evaluation of teaching effectiveness—particularly when SETs are used for personnel decisions (see subsequent discussion).

SETs are sometimes used to infer course quality. It is argued here, however, that responses to instruments such as SEEQ are probably not very useful for this purpose. Research indicates that the ratings are primarily a function of the instructor who teaches the course rather than the course that is being taught (see later discussion), and thus provide little information that is specific to the course. This conclusion should not be interpreted to mean that student input is not valuable for such purposes, but only that the student responses to instruments such as SEEQ are not appropriate as a source of student input into questions of course, as opposed to teacher, evaluations.

A Construct Validation Approach to the Study of Students' Evaluations

Particularly in the last 20 years, the study of SETs has been one of the most frequently emphasized areas in American educational research. Literally thousands of papers have been written and a comprehensive review is beyond the scope of this chapter. The reader is referred to reviews by Aleamoni (1981), Braskamp, Brandenburg, and Ory (1985), Cashin (1988) Centra (1979, 1989), Cohen (1980, 1981), Costin, Greenough and Menges (1971), de Wolf (1974), Doyle (1975, 1983), Feldman (1976a, 1976b, 1977, 1978, 1979, 1983, 1984, 1986, 1987, 1988, 1989a, 1989b), Kulik and McKeachie (1975), Marsh (1982b, 1984b, 1985, 1987), McKeachie (1963, 1973, 1979), Murray (1980), Overall and Marsh (1982), and Remmers (1958, 1963).

In the early 1970s there was a huge increase in the collection of SETs at North American universities that led to a concomitant increase in research. The ERIC system contains over 1,300 entries under the heading "student evaluation of teacher performance" and Feldman (1990b) noted that his collection of books and articles contained about 2,000 items. In the 1970s, however, there were few well-established research paradigms and methodological guidelines to guide this early research, and insufficient attention was given to those that were available. Many studies conducted during this period were methodologically unsound, but their conclusions were nevertheless used as the basis of policy and subsequent research. Richard Schutz, editor of the *American Educational Research Journal* during the late 1970s, commented that the major educational research journals may have erred in accepting for publication so many SET studies of questionable quality during this period (personal communication, 1979). In the 1980s there were fewer articles published in major research journals than in the late 1970s, but they were typically of a better quality. Based on ERIC citations, however, the number of SET studies from all sources declined only moderately during this period, methodologically flawed studies continue to be reported, and the quality of papers presented at conferences and published in less prestigious journals is still quite varied. During the late 1970s, and particularly the 1980s, research paradigms and methodological standards evolved, but they are presented in a piecemeal fashion in journal articles. Hence, an important aim of this chapter is to present the research paradigms and methodological standards that have evolved in SET research.

Validating interpretations of SETs involves an ongoing interplay between construct interpretations, instrument development, data collection, and logic. Each interpretation must be considered a tentative hypothesis to be challenged in different contexts and with different approaches. This process corresponds to defining a nomological network (Cronbach, 1971) in which differentiable components of SETs are related to each other and to other constructs. Within-network studies attempt to ascertain whether SETs consist of distinct components and, if so, what these components are. This involves logical approaches such as content analysis and empirical approaches such as factor analysis and multitrait-multimethod (MTMM) analysis. Some clarification of within-network issues must logically precede between-network studies where SETs are related to external variables. Several perspectives about SET underlie this construct validity approach (see Marsh, 1987, for more detail): effective teaching and SETs designed to reflect teaching effectiveness are multidimensional; no single criterion of effective teaching is sufficient; and tentative interpretations of relations with validity criteria and with potential biases should be evaluated critically in different contexts and in relation to multiple criteria of effective teaching.

DIMENSIONALITY OF STUDENTS' EVALUATIONS

In this section we examine the multidimensionality of SETs and appropriate dimensions to be included, emphasizing in particular the SEEQ instrument. Three overlapping approaches to this problem are considered: (1) an empirical approach emphasizing statistical techniques such as factor analysis and MTMM analysis; (2) a logical analysis of the content of effective teaching and the purposes the ratings are intended to serve, supplemented by reviews of previous research and feedback from students and instructors; and (3) a theory of teaching and learning. In practice, most instruments are based on the first two approaches—particularly the second—and the third approach seems not to have been used in the SET literature. Here, we offer support for the content of the SEEQ scales using all three approaches.

The Need for a Multidimensional Approach

Effective teaching is a multidimensional construct (e.g., a teacher may be organized but lack enthusiasm). Thus, it is not surprising that a considerable body of research has also shown that SETs are multidimensional (see Marsh, 1987). Information from SETs depends upon the content of the items. Poorly worded or inappropriate items will not provide useful information. If a survey instrument contains an ill-defined hodgepodge of different items and SETs are summarized by an average of these items, then there is no basis for knowing what is being measured. Particularly when the purpose of the ratings is formative, it is important that careful attention be given to the components of teaching effectiveness that are to be measured. Surveys should contain separate groups of related items that are derived from a logical analysis of the content of effective teaching and the purposes that the ratings are to serve, and that are supported on the basis of theory and previous research and by empirical procedures such as factor analysis and MTMM analysis.

Support for the claim that SETs are most appropriately considered a multidimensional construct must be evaluated—at least in part—in relation to the purposes that the ratings are to serve. As noted above, SETs are broadly recommended for four purposes. For personnel decisions, there is considerable controversy as to whether a multidimensional profile of scores or a single summary score is more useful (Abrami, 1989a, 1989b; Abrami and d'Apollonia, 1991; Marsh, 1987, 1991a). For feedback to teachers, for use in student course selection, and for use in research on teaching, however, there appears to be general agreement that a profile of distinct components of SET based on an appropriately constructed multidimensional instrument is more useful than a single summary score.

The Content of Factor Analytically Based SET Instruments

The SET literature contains examples of instruments that have a well defined factor structure and that provide measures of distinct components of teaching effectiveness. In addition to SEEQ, some of these instruments (the actual instruments are presented by Marsh, 1987) include: Frey's Endeavor instrument (Frey, Leonard and Beatty, 1975; also see Marsh, 1981a, 1987); The Student Description of Teaching questionnaire developed by Hildebrand, Wilson and Dienst (1971); and the Michigan State SIRS instrument (Warrington, 1973). Factor analyses of responses to each of these instruments identified the factors that each was intended to measure, demonstrating that SETs do measure distinct components of teaching effectiveness. The systematic approach used in the development of these instruments, and the similarity of the factors that they measure, support their construct validity. The strongest support for the multidimensionality of SETs apparently comes from research using SEEQ.

The SEEQ Instrument

In the development of SEEQ: 1) a large item pool was obtained from a literature review, forms in current usage, and interviews with faculty and students about what they saw as effective teaching; 2) students and faculty were asked to rate the importance of items; 3) faculty were asked to judge the potential usefulness of the items as a basis for feedback; and 4) open-ended student comments were examined to determine if important aspects had been excluded. These criteria, along with psychometric properties, were used to select items and revise subsequent versions, thus supporting the content validity of SEEQ responses (the SEEQ scales and the items in each scale are presented in Table 1).

TABLE 1. Factor analyses of students' evaluations of teaching effectiveness (S) and the corresponding faculty self-evaluations of their own teaching (F) in 329 courses. (*Reprinted from Marsh [1984b] by permission of the American Psychological Association.*)

Evaluation items (paraphrased)	Factor pattern loadings																	
	1		**2**		**3**		**4**		**5**		**6**		**7**		**8**		**9**	
	S	F	S	F	S	F	S	F	S	F	S	F	S	F	S	F	S	F
1. Learning/Value																		
Course challenging/stimulating	42	40	23	25	09	-10	04	04	00	-03	15	27	09	05	16	23	29	20
Learned something valuable	53	77	15	02	10	-02	09	04	01	01	10	08	10	04	17	09	16	06
Increased subject interest	57	70	12	05	08	07	08	07	02	03	18	-01	03	-04	19	05	14	-02
Learned/understood subject matter	55	52	12	12	13	12	05	03	03	11	02	08	19	07	14	-04	-23	-11
Overall course rating	36	33	25	29	16	09	12	08	09	02	12	16	13	-08	14	27	08	16
2. Enthusiasm																		
Enthusiastic about teaching	15	29	55	42	16	00	07	02	21	15	10	00	05	16	01	09	05	06
Dynamic & energetic	08	03	60	70	15	01	11	06	08	05	06	05	07	16	01	-08	06	03
Enhanced presentations with humor	10	04	66	58	-04	06	05	01	13	02	12	02	14	07	02	-18	-07	-10
Teaching style held your interest	09	12	59	64	23	20	16	04	06	00	03	14	10	05	06	03	-02	-03
Overall instructor rating	12	27	40	54	23	09	14	08	23	02	11	16	10	-08	05	27	05	16
3. Organization																		
Instructor explanations clear	12	00	07	24	55	42	20	09	05	04	10	06	13	01	06	23	-08	-03
Course materials prepared & clear	06	06	03	-02	73	69	09	01	10	-02	09	04	12	03	10	03	01	12
Objectives stated & pursued	19	12	-05	-08	49	41	03	05	08	05	14	08	25	27	06	05	06	06
Lectures facilitated note taking	-03	02	20	09	58	53	-17	07	-02	05	14	04	15	06	08	01	-04	-05
4. Group Interaction																		
Encouraged class discussions	04	06	10	02	01	03	84	86	03	00	00	00	06	00	06	-05	00	-03
Students shared ideas/knowledge	02	08	06	-07	-04	-01	85	88	05	13	05	01	07	-02	08	-10	-02	01
Encouraged questions & answers	03	-04	06	09	14	06	62	69	16	-02	15	03	07	11	08	21	00	01
Encouraged expression of ideas	07	01	02	06	01	-11	73	75	20	09	05	07	09	12	05	09	00	-02
5. Individual Rapport																		
Friendly towards students	-04	10	17	06	00	-06	13	12	68	78	-01	-05	13	02	10	-05	-07	01
Welcomed seeking help/advice	04	-10	05	02	02	07	06	00	85	75	-04	04	12	06	05	20	03	-04
Interested in individual students	04	10	11	09	00	01	14	07	69	77	-01	-09	14	03	08	09	04	09
Accessible to individual students	02	-13	-11	-11	16	09	09	-02	62	43	20	25	08	13	00	14	04	07
6. Breadth of Coverage																		
Contrasted implications	-05	02	12	01	05	03	08	01	-03	01	72	84	08	-03	14	02	08	-06
Gave background of ideas/concepts	08	03	08	10	16	07	-03	-02	02	-02	71	78	01	08	11	-01	03	03
Gave different points of view	04	-06	04	09	11	11	08	16	06	01	72	55	07	17	01	-06	04	08
Discussed current developments	23	29	08	-04	-04	-04	05	12	00	00	50	48	06	05	16	10	-01	-02
7. Examinations/Grading																		
Examination feedback valuable	-03	01	08	09	06	-11	09	05	08	12	-04	03	72	62	05	-03	09	03
Eval. methods fair/appropriate	06	02	00	-03	03	14	07	06	14	00	10	17	69	64	11	11	-08	04
Tested emphasized course content	08	00	-01	04	11	21	01	01	06	00	11	-04	70	58	07	10	-02	-03
8. Assignments																		
Reading/texts valuable	-06	09	06	-01	03	07	-01	-06	03	01	07	-07	01	11	91	70	02	04
Added to course understanding	12	01	-09	-01	01	04	09	21	01	17	-02	08	07	05	81	56	06	10
9. Workload/Difficulty																		
Course difficulty (Easy-Hard)	-06	00	06	-01	04	-05	02	02	-01	00	08	00	-04	08	10	04	85	74
Course workload (Light-Heavy)	14	-04	12	00	03	02	07	05	00	04	06	01	00	01	08	-04	88	86
Course pace (Too Slow-Too Fast)	-20	07	07	00	04	18	-12	-09	06	02	-03	-07	03	-08	05	-04	62	32
Hours/week outside of class	14	00	07	00	-11	00	07	02	00	02	-04	03	03	-08	05	21	73	46

Note. Factor loadings in boxes are the loadings for items designed to measure each factor. All loadings are presented without decimal points. Factor analyses of student ratings and instructor self-ratings consisted of a principal-components analysis, Kaiser normalization, and rotation to a direct oblimin criterion. The analyses were performed with the commercially available Statistical Package for the Social Sciences (SPSS) routine (see Nie, Hull, Jenkins, Steinbrenner, & Bent, 1975).

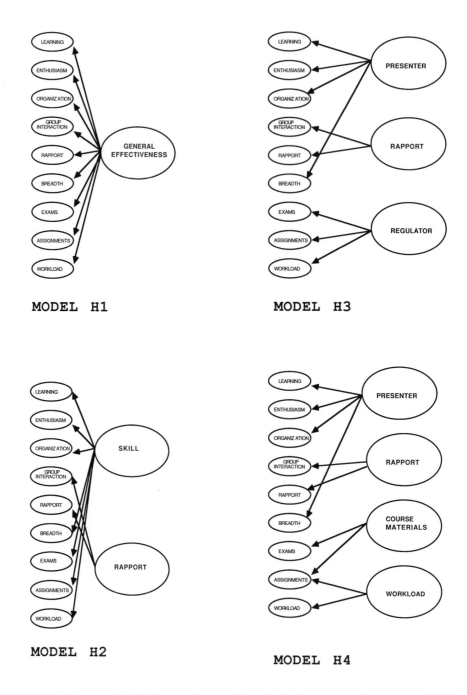

FIGURE 1. Four a priori higher-order models of relations among first-order SEEQ factors. Each first-order factor is inferred from multiple indications (i.e., items). In order to avoid clutter, the multiple indicators of the first-order factors and correlations among the higher-order factors are not presented. (*Reprinted from Marsh (1991a) by permission of American Psychological Association.*)

Factor Analysis of SEEQ Responses

Factor analytic support for the SEEQ scales is particularly strong. To date, more than 30 published factor analyses of SEEQ responses have identified the factors that SEEQ is designed to measure (e.g., Marsh, 1982b, 1983, 1984b, 1987, 1991b; Marsh and Hocevar, 1984, 1991a). Marsh and Hocevar (1991a) described the archive of SEEQ responses that contains ratings of 50,000 classes (representing responses to nearly 1 million SEEQ surveys). From this archive, 24,158 courses were selected and classified into one of 21 different subgroups varying in terms of teacher rank (teaching assistant or regular staff), level of instruction (undergraduate or graduate), and academic discipline. Twenty-two separate factor analyses of the total sample and each of the subsamples all identified the nine factors that SEEQ is designed to measure. For each of the 24,158 sets of ratings, two sets of factor scores were computed: one based on the factor analysis of responses to the particular subgroup to which the set belonged and one based on the factor analysis across the total group (across the 21 subgroups). Within all 21 subgroups correlations among the two sets of factor scores were very high and the median correlation was greater than $r=.99$. Because of large number and diversity of classes in this study, the results provided very strong support for the generality of the factor structure underlying SETs. When instructors evaluated their own teaching effectiveness on the same SEEQ form as completed by their students, factor analyses of SETs and instructor self-evaluations each identified the same SEEQ factors (Marsh, 1982c; Marsh and Hocevar, 1983; Marsh, Overall and Kesler, 1979b). The results from the largest of these studies, based on evaluations of instructors in 329 courses, are presented in Table 1. These studies demonstrate that the SEEQ factors identified in factor analyses of SETs also generalize to instructor self-evaluations.

Higher-Order SEEQ Factors

Factor analytic studies demonstrate that SEEQ measures distinct dimensions of teaching effectiveness, but some researchers argue that SETs should be considered as a relatively unidimensional construct for some purposes. Abrami (1985; also see Abrami and d'Apollonia, 1991; Marsh, 1991a) proposed a compromise analogous to the intelligence hierarchy in which there are distinct first-order factors, but a single higher-order factor. Marsh (1987) suggested that Abrami's proposal could be tested using recent advances in the application of confirmatory factor analysis (CFA) and hierarchical CFA (HCFA) that are summarized below. Whereas no previous research had formally tested the higher-order structure of SETs, Marsh (1991b) reviewed studies by Abrami (1985, 1989a, 1989b), Frey (1978), Feldman (1976b), and others to derive higher-order models positing 1, 2, 3, and 4 higher-order factors that are summarized in Table 2 and Figure 1.

The model with one higher-order factor tests Abrami's suggestion that there is only one higher-order factor. The two higher-order factor model is based on Frey's (1978) claim that specific dimensions of his Endeavor instrument can be explained in terms of two global dimensions called Skill and Empathy (see Table 2). The three higher-order factor model follows from Feldman's (1976b) suggestion that his specific categories of effective teaching could be classified into three global categories (see Table 2) related to the instructor's role as a presenter (actor or communicator), facilitator (interactor or reciprocator), and manager (director or regulator). Comparison of the content of these global components (Table 2) suggests that Frey's Rapport and Feldman's facilitator represent similar constructs. The four higher-order factor model is based on the observation that Workload/Difficulty is relatively uncorrelated with any of the other SEEQ factors except, perhaps, Assignments.

TABLE 2. Categories of effective teaching adapted from Feldman (1976b, 1983, 1984) and the students' evaluations of educational quality (SEEQ) and endeavor factors most closely related to each category (*adapted from Marsh [1991a], by permission of the American Psychological Association*).

Feldman's Categories[a]	SEEQ Factors	Endeavor Factors
1)Stimulation of interest (I)	Instructor Enthusiasm	None
2) Enthusiasm (I)	Instructor Enthusiasm	None
3) Subject knowledge (I)	Breadth of Coverage[b]	None
4) Intellectual expansiveness (I)	Breadth of Coverage	None
5) Preparation and organization (I)	Organization/Clarity	Organization/Planning (I)
6) Clarity and understandableness (I)	Organization/Clarity	Presentation Clarity (I/II)
7) Elocutionary skills (I)	None	None
8) Sensitivity to class progress (I/II) None	None	None
9) Clarity of objectives (III)	Organization/Clarity	Organization/Planning (I)
10) Value of course materials (III)	Assignments/Readings	None
11) Supplementary materials (III)	Assignments/Readings	None
12) Perceived outcome/impact	Learning/Value	Student Accomplishments (I/II)
13) Fairness, impartiality (III)	Examinations/Grading	Grading/Exams (II/I)
14) Classroom management (III)	None	None[b]
15) Feedback to students (III)	Examinations/Grading	Grading/Exams (II/I)[b]
16) Class discussion (II)	Group Interaction	Class Discussion (II)
17) Intellectual challenge (II)	Learning/Value	Student Accomplishments (I/II)
18) Respect for students (II)	Individual Rapport	Personal Attention (II/I)
19) Availability/helpfulness (II)	Individual Rapport	Personal Attention (II/I)
20) Difficulty/workload (III)	Workload/Difficulty	Workload (I)

[a]The actual categories used by Feldman in different studies (e.g., Feldman, 1976, 1983, 1984) varied somewhat. Categories 14 and 20 were included by Feldman (1976) but not in subsequent studies. Feldman (1976b) also proposed three higher-order clusters of categories that are identified by I (presentation), II (facilitation), and III (regulation) in parentheses following each category. Frey (1978) proposed two higher-order clusters of categories for factors from his Endeavor instrument that are identified by I (skill) and II (rapport) in parentheses following each Endeavor factor. When one of Feldman's categories or one of Frey's factors is associated with more than one higher-order cluster, the one that it is most strongly associated is presented first.

[b]Whereas these factors most closely match the corresponding categories, the match is apparently not particularly close.

It is important to emphasize that each of the higher-order models is predicated on the assumption that there is a well-defined set of first-order factors. Hence, Marsh (1991b) initially used CFA to test the first-order structure of SEEQ responses. Consistent with previous exploratory factor analyses, these results provided support for the 9 first-order factors that SEEQ is designed to measure. First-order models positing 1, 2, 3, or 4 first-order similar to the second-order factors were not able to fit the data.

The purpose of HCFA is to determine whether a smaller number of second-order factors can be used to explain relations among first-order factors (for further discussion of HCFA see Marsh, 1991b; Marsh and Hocevar, 1985). Conceptually, it is like doing a second factor analysis based on correlations among the first-order factors. Comparing the ability of the four HCFA models to fit the data, the four higher-order factor model was found to be the best. For even this model with four higher-order factors, however, much of the true score variance in first-order factors was not explained by the higher-order factors. The results demonstrate that the SEEQ responses cannot be adequately explained by one or even a few summary scores. Furthermore, the results of the higher-order factor models need to be evaluated carefully. If the purpose of the HCFA is to examine relations among the first-order factors, then the results of this study are useful. If, however, the purpose of the HCFA is to justify the use of a smaller number of second-order factors to summarize SEEQ responses instead of the nine first-order factors, then the results are not particularly useful.

The Applicability Paradigm

SETs are commonly collected and frequently studied at North American universities, but not in most other parts of the world. Because of the extensive exposure of North American research, there is a danger that North American instruments will be used in new settings without first studying their applicability. In order to address this issue, Marsh (1981a) described a new paradigm for studying the applicability of two North American instruments (SEEQ and Endeavor; see Table 2) that was used with Australian students at the University of Sydney. This applicability paradigm was subsequently used in five other studies: Hayton (1983) with Australian students in Technical and Further Education schools; Marsh, Touron and Wheeler (1985) with students from the Universidad de Navarra in Spain; Clarkson (1984) with students from the Papua New Guinea University of Technology; Watkins, Marsh, and Young (1985) with students from the University of Canterbury in New Zealand, and Marsh and Roche (1991) with Australian students in the newly established University of Western Sydney.

In these studies students from a cross-section of disciplines selected "one of the best" and "one of the worst" lecturers they had experienced (or a "good," an "average,"and a "poor" teacher in later studies), and rated each with the SEEQ and Endeavor items. As part of the study, students were asked to indicate "inappropriate" items, and to select up to five items that they "felt were most important in describing either positive or negative aspects of the overall learning experience in this instructional sequence" for each instructor they evaluated. Analyses included: a) a discrimination analysis of the ability of items and factors to differentiate between "best" and "worst" instructors; b) a summary of "not appropriate" responses; c) a summary of "most important item" responses; d) factor analyses of the SEEQ and Endeavor items; and e) a MTMM analysis of agreement between SEEQ and Endeavor scales that are posited to be matching (see Table 2). A detailed evaluation of this set of studies is beyond the scope of this chapter and the reader is referred to Marsh (1986, 1987). The results of these six studies—particularly the factor analyses and MTMM analyses—suggest that students from some different countries do differentiate among different components of teaching effectiveness, that the specific components do generalize across different nationalities, and that students differentiate among dimensions of effective teaching in a similar manner when responding to SEEQ and Endeavor. Across the studies the findings support the applicability and construct validity of the SEEQ and Endeavor when administered to university students in very different settings.

Feldman's Categories of Effective Teaching

Feldman (1976b; also see Feldman, 1983, 1984) derived the different components of effective teaching by categorizing the characteristics of the superior university teacher from the student's point of view. He reviewed research that either asked students to specify these characteristics or inferred them on the basis of correlations with global SETs. His list of categories (Table 2) provides the most extensive set of characteristics that are likely to underlie SETs. Nevertheless, Feldman used primarily a logical analysis based on his examination of the student evaluations literature, and his results do not imply that students can differentiate these categories. His categories, however, provide a useful basis for evaluating the comprehensiveness of SET factors on a given instrument.

Feldman (1976b) noted that factors identified by factor analysis typically corresponded to more than one of his categories. In Table 2 we have attempted to match Feldman's categories with the empirical factors identified in responses to the SEEQ and Endeavor instruments that are used in the present investigation. There is substantial overlap in the empirical factors from the two instruments (also see Marsh, 1986). Most of Feldman's categories are associated with empirical factors from the two instruments, although SEEQ factors represent Feldman's categories more comprehensively than do Endeavor factors. All of the factors in SEEQ and Endeavor represent at least one of Feldman's categories and most reflect two or more categories. In contrast, none of Feldman's categories reflects more than one of the empirical factors. This logical content analysis demonstrates that there is substantial overlap between Feldman's categories and the empirical factors but that Feldman's categories reflect more narrowly defined constructs than do the empirical factors.

Teaching-Learning Theories as a Basis of SEEQ Scales

SET instruments are typically not based on theories of teaching and learning. Furthermore, there is a surprising absence of evaluation of the content of SET scales in relation such theories. The instructional elements represented in the rating instruments should, however, be consistent with principles of effective teaching and learning established on the basis of accepted theory and research. It is important, therefore, that the factors underlying instruments such as SEEQ be inspected to see if they conform to principles of teaching and learning emerging from attempts to synthesize knowledge of teaching effectiveness.

For this analysis it is appropriate to focus upon theory and research in adult education, since SETs are most commonly obtained in post-secondary school situations. While Dubin and Okun (1973) were unable to find a single theory of learning that provided adequate guidance for teachers of adults, Mackie (1981) was satisfied that from the writings of behaviorists, cognitivists and personality theorists, 10 principles could be derived: (a) The learner must be motivated to learn; (b) The learning situation should take account of individual differences in learning capacities and learning style; (c) New learning should take into account the learner's present knowledge and attitudes; (d) What is to be learned should be reinforced; (e) The learning situation should give opportunities for practice; (f) The learner should be an active participant trying out new responses rather than just listening; (g) The material to be learned should be divided into learnable units and given in appropriately paced sequence; (h) Coaching or guidance should be given in the development of new responses; (i) What is learned should be capable of being successfully generalized from the learning situation; and (j) The material to be learned should be presented in a way that will emphasize the characteristics to be learned and do so in a way which is as meaningful as possible to the learner.

These principles were subsequently endorsed by Stephens (1985) and Brookfield (1989). Fincher (1985) engaged in a similar process of extracting "well-intended generalizations or working hypotheses" from the literature. He went on to trace the skepticism that developed regarding attempts to formulate such general principles but concluded that "most general principles of learning would not seem disconfirmed as much as they appear forgotten" and to express the belief "that efforts on the part of college instructors to adapt and to apply general principles of learning would be in the best interests of learners" (p. 92). Fincher's list was very similar to Mackie's, but included specific mention of the importance of the learner's experiences of success and failure. On the bases of the above, it seems appropriate to compare the content of the SEEQ factors with the general principles of teaching and learning put forward by Mackie and Fincher.

1. Learning/Value. In essence this factor denotes subjective feelings of success obtained through participation in a course and/or at the hands of a particular teacher. Students who are challenged and stimulated, who consider their learning through the course to have been worthwhile, whose interest in the subject was increased, who are conscious of having understood the subject-matter, and who generally rate the course highly are clearly expressing feelings of accomplishment on challenging learning tasks.

2. Instructor Enthusiasm. A minimal condition for learning is that attention be aroused. Stimulus salience, that is, the extent to which a stimulus stands out against a background, is known to be crucial in evoking interest and attention. It is to be expected, therefore, that teachers who impress students with their enthusiasm, dynamism, and energy and who make judicious use of humor will have students who are interested and attentive. Moreover, teacher enthusiasm can vicariously induce enthusiasm for the subject in students. Students who rate their teacher highly are more likely to model their behavior toward a subject based upon that teacher. Thus, the latter's enthusiasm can be acquired by students. Students whose interest in and enthusiasm for a subject are aroused are likely to have enhanced achievement in learning the subject. This factor is especially relevant to the principle that learners must be motivated to learn.

3. Organization/Clarity. The essential ingredients of this factor are structure and clarity. By cuing learners about the organization of subject matter, by providing advance organizers, by scheduling student exercises, and assignments appropriately and by inducing appropriate cognitive schemata, teachers assist students' memory retrieval and formation of linkages between new material and material previously learned. These principles of teaching and learning are time-honored and widely accepted elements of information processing theories of learning. While clarity is clearly an expected outcome of careful preparation and good organization, it can be important as a correlate of teacher knowledge of the subject, with teacher uncertainty producing vagueness which inhibits student understanding. Students who perceive instruction to be well organized and clear are, thus, likely to enjoy enhanced knowledge and understanding of course material. The Organization factor is pertinent to several accepted principles of teaching and learning.

4. Group Interaction. Learning in institutionalized educational contexts is a social phenomenon. That is, except in rare cases of individual tuition, instruction is given to groups of students ranging from small to very large in size. This factor refers to verbal interaction in classrooms in the form of questions and answers facilitating the expression and sharing of ideas and knowledge. Higher ratings on items comprising this factor suggest that the motivational potential of social interaction with others in learning contexts is being capitalized upon and also that the classroom context is being exploited as a venue for activity in practicing and testing ideas and obtaining feedback. As such the Group Interaction factor has a strong basis in principles of teaching and learning.

5. Individual Rapport. Opportunities to provide for individual differences in capacity and to take account of learners' present knowledge and attitudes in higher education depend heavily upon individual contacts with instructors. Furthermore, individual tuition and guidance are available to the extent that instructors are interested in and accessible to individual students. Students who feel welcome also have greater access to motivationally significant opportunities such as face-to-face reinforcement and encouragement. The Individual Rapport factor is consistent with several of Mackie's (1981) principles.

6. Breadth of Coverage. This factor reflects students' responses to items concerning the contrasting of implications of various theories, the provision of the backgrounds of ideas and concepts, the presentation of different points of view, and the discussion of current developments. These all have to do with substantive qualities of instruction. Each would seem to have the potential to increase student knowledge and understanding through facilitating generalization beyond the confines of the specific situation, to clarify the material to be learned and its meaningfulness to the learner. This factor relates closely to principles (i) and (j) above.

7. Examinations/Grading. The instructional value of examinations and grading lies in the quality of the feedback and in the stimulus to study they provide. The items comprising this factor apply specifically to feedback and less specifically to motivational issues. Students' perceptions of fairness and relevance of assessment procedures are probably associated with their motivation to learn. However, this factor's main basis in principles of learning is reinforcement in the form of knowledge of results and affective consequences of that knowledge.

8. *Assignments/Readings.* Student work in higher education especially is largely oriented to the completion of assignments, including required readings. Thus, positive SETs of the texts and supplementary readings and of other assignments probably indicate that activity in learning was found to be valuable and that the learning experiences involved were meaningful. Assignments provide students with opportunities to practice new knowledge and skills. Furthermore, learning tasks that constitute assignments are often presented in learnable units even if they are not always completed in an appropriately paced sequence. The Assignments factor, too, seems consistent with sound principles of learning.

9. *Workload/Difficulty.* Work that is seen by students to be too much or too difficult is almost by definition given without consideration of learners' capacities and prior learnings. Moreover, such work can not be appropriately paced or presented in desirably learnable units. Overloaded students find it difficult to experience subjective feelings of success and receive little or no reinforcement. They are likely to be forced into adopting learning strategies that minimize their ability to understand and generalize from the specific learning situation. On the other hand, students for whom success is too easily won lose motivation to succeed and are unlikely to value such learning highly. It would seem that student would value more highly achievement that involved them in overcoming substantial obstacles and that have necessitated relatively enduring commitments. This suggests the possibility of nonlinear relations between Workload/Difficulty and other indicators of teaching effectiveness such as student learning. There can be little or no doubt that the Workload factor is consistent with accepted principles of teaching and learning.

Summary of the Dimensionality of Students' Evaluations

In summary, many SET instruments are not developed using a theory of teaching and learning, a systematic logical approach that ensures content validity, or empirical techniques such as factor analysis. The evaluation instruments discussed above and particularly research based on SEEQ provide clear support for the multidimensionality of the SET construct. The debate about which specific components of teaching effectiveness can and should be measured has not been resolved, although there seems to be consistency in those that are identified in responses to the most carefully designed instruments such as SEEQ and Endeavor. Furthermore, the SEEQ factors are apparently applicable to a wide diversity of educational settings. SETs cannot be adequately understood if this multidimensionality is ignored. Many orderly, logical relationships are misinterpreted or cannot be consistently replicated because of this failure, and the substantiation of this claim will constitute a major focus of the remainder of this Chapter. SET instruments, particularly those used for research purposes, should be designed to measure separate components of teaching effectiveness, and support for both the content and the construct validity of the multiple dimensions should be evaluated.

RELIABILITY, STABILITY AND GENERALIZABILITY

Traditionally, reliability and validity are seen as opposite ends of a continuum of generalizability. Reliability refers to the generalizability of scores representing the same construct collected under maximally similar situations (e.g., internal consistency, alternative form correlations, and test-retest correlations), whereas validity refers to the generalizability of scores representing different constructs that are hypothesized to be related (e.g., SETs and student learning). As is obvious in this review, however, the separation is not so easy. The agreement between responses to matching SEEQ and Endeavor scales, for example, could be argued to reflect either reliability or validity. Short-term stability is typically interpreted to be an indication of reliability, but long-term stability could be argued to reflect either reliability or validity. Because of the limitations in the reliability/validity distinction, the broader term generalizability is useful. For present purposes we review studies of relations between two or more sets of SETs in this section on reliability and generalizability, and review relations between SETs and other constructs in the next section on validity.

Reliability

The reliability of SETs is commonly determined from the results of item analyses (i.e., correlations among responses to different items designed to measure the same component of effective teaching) and from studies of interrater agreement (i.e., agreement among ratings by different students in the same class). The internal consistency among responses to items designed to measure the same component of effective teaching is consistently high. However, such internal consistency estimates provide an inflated estimate of reliability since they ignore the substantial portion of error due to the lack of agreement among different students within the same course, and so they generally should not be used to measure the reliability of SETs (see Gilmore, Kane, and Naccarato, 1978, for further discussion).

The correlation between responses by any two students in the same class (i.e., the single rater reliability) is typically in the .20's but the reliability of the class-average response depends upon the number of students rating the class, as originally described by Remmers (1931; also see Feldman, 1977, for a review of methodological issues and empirical findings). For example, the estimated reliability for SEEQ factors is about .95 for the average response from 50 students, .90 from 25 students, .74 from 10 students, .60 from five students, and only .23 for one student. Given a sufficient number of students, the reliability of class-average SETs compares favorably with that of the best objective tests. In most applications, this reliability of the class-average response, based on agreement among all the different students within each class, is the appropriate method for assessing reliability. Recent applications of generalizability theory demonstrate how error due to differences between items and error due to differences between ratings of different students can both be incorporated into the same analysis, but the error due to differences between items appears to be quite small (Gilmore, Kane, and Naccarato, 1978).

Generalizability: The Perspective of Former Students

Some critics suggest that students cannot recognize effective teaching until after being called upon to apply their mastery in further coursework or after graduation. According to this argument, SETs completed by former students who evaluate courses with this added perspective will differ systematically from those by students who have just completed a course. Drucker and Remmers (1950) originally countered this contention with a cross-sectional study showing that responses by ten-year alumni agreed with those of current students. More recent cross-sectional studies (Centra, 1979; Howard, Conway and Maxwell, 1985; Marsh, 1977) have also shown good correlational agreement between the retrospective ratings of former students and those of currently enrolled students.

In a true longitudinal study (Marsh and Overall, 1979a; Overall and Marsh, 1980) the same students evaluated classes at the end of a course and again several years later, at least one year after graduation. End-of-class ratings in 100 courses correlated .83 with the retrospective ratings (a correlation approaching the reliability of the ratings), and the median rating at each time was nearly the same. Firth (1979) asked students to evaluate classes at the time of graduation from their university (rather than at the end of each class) and one year after graduation, and he also found good agreement between the two sets of ratings by the same students. These studies demonstrate that SETs are quite stable over time, and argue that added perspective does not alter the ratings given at the end of a course. Hence, these findings not only provide support for the long-term stability of SETs, but they also provide support for their construct validity.

In the same longitudinal study, Marsh and Overall (1979a) demonstrated that, consistent with previous research, the single-rater reliabilities were generally in the .20's for both end-of-course and retrospective ratings. (Interestingly, the single-rater reliabilities were somewhat higher for the retrospective ratings.) However, the median correlation between end-of-class and retrospective ratings, when based on responses by individual students instead of class-average responses, was .59. The explanation for this apparent paradox is the manner in which systematic unique variance, as opposed to random error variance, is handled in determining the single rater reliability estimate and the stability coefficient. Variance that is systematic, but unique to the responses of a particular student, is taken to be error variance in the computation of the single-rater reliability. However, if this systematic variance was stable over the several year period between the end-of-course and retrospective ratings for an individual student, a demanding criterion, then it is taken to be systematic variance rather than error variance in the computation of the stability coefficient. Hence, there is an enduring source of systematic variation in individual student SETs that is not captured by internal consistency measures. This also argues that while the process of averaging across the ratings produces a more reliable measure, it also masks much of the systematic variance in individual SETs, and that there may be systematic differences in ratings linked to specific subgroups of students within a class (also see Feldman, 1977; Centra, 1989). Various subgroups of students within the same class may view teaching effectiveness differently, and may be differentially affected by the instruction which they receive, but there has been surprisingly little systematic research to examine this possibility.

Generalizability—Teacher and Course Effects

Researchers have also asked how highly correlated SETs are in two different courses taught by the same instructor or in the same course taught by different teachers on two different occasions. This research examines the generality of SETs, and the relative importance of the effects of the instructor who teaches a class and the particular class being taught.

Marsh (1981b) arranged ratings of 1,364 courses into 341 sets such that each set contained ratings of: the same instructor teaching the same course on two occasions, the same instructor teaching two different courses, the same course taught by two different instructors, and two different courses taught by different instructors (Table 3). For the overall instructor rating, the correlation between ratings of different instructors teaching the same course (i.e., a course effect) was –.05, while correlations for the same instructor in different courses (.61) and in two different offerings of the same course (.72) were much larger (Table 3). While this pattern was observed in each of the SEEQ factors, the correlation between ratings of different instructors in the same course was slightly higher for some evaluation factors (e.g., Workload/Difficulty, Assignments, and Group Interaction) but had a mean of only .14 across all the factors. In marked contrast, correlations between background variables in different sets of courses (e.g., prior subject interest, class size, reason for taking the course) were higher for the same course taught by two different instructors than for two different courses taught by the same instructor (Table 3). Based on a path analysis of these results, Marsh argued that the effect of the teacher on SETs is much larger than is the effect of the course being taught, and that there is a small portion of reliable variance that is unique to a particular instructor in a particular course that generalizes across different offerings of the same course taught by the same instructor. SETs primarily reflect the effectiveness of the instructor rather than the influence of the course, and some teachers may be uniquely suited to teaching some specific courses. A systematic examination of the suggestion that some teachers are better suited for some specific courses, and that this can be identified from the results from a longitudinal archive of SETs, is an important area for further research.

These results provide support for the generality of SETs across different courses taught by the same instructor, but provide no support for the use of SETs to evaluate the course. Even SETs of the overall course were primarily a function of the instructor who taught the course, and not the particular course that was being evaluated. In fact, the predominance of the instructor effect over the course effect was virtually the same for both the overall instructor rating and the overall course rating. This finding probably reflects the autonomy that university instructors typically have in conducting the courses that they teach, and may not generalize to a setting in which instructors have little autonomy. Nevertheless, the findings provide no support for the validity of SETs based on instruments like SEEQ as a measure of the course that is independent of the instructor who teaches the course.

TABLE 3. Teacher and course effects: Correlations among different sets of classes for student ratings and background characteristics. (Reprinted from Marsh [1984b] by permission of the American Psychological Association.)

Measure	Same teacher, same course	Same teacher, different course	Different teacher, same course	Different teacher, different course
Student rating				
Learning/Value	.696	.563	.232	.069
Enthusiasm	.734	.613	.011	.028
Organization/Clarity	.676	.540	−.023	−.063
Group interaction	.699	.540	.291	.224
Individual rapport	.726	.542	.180	.146
Breadth of coverage	.727	.481	.117	.067
Examinations/Grading	.633	.512	.066	−.004
Assignments	.681	.428	.332	.112
Workload/Difficulty	.733	.400	.392	.215
Overall course	.712	.591	−.011	−.065
Overall instructor	.719	.607	−.051	−.059
Mean coefficient	.707	.523	.140	.061
Background characteristic				
Prior subject interest	.635	.312	.563	.209
Reason for taking course (percent indicating general interest	.770	.448	.671	.383
Class average expected grade	.709	.405	.483	.356
Workload/Difficulty	.773	.400	.392	.215
Course enrollment	.846	.312	.593	.058
Percent attendance on day evaluations administered	.406	.164	.214	.045
Mean coefficient	.690	.340	.491	.211

Marsh and Overall (1981) examined the effect of course and instructor in a setting where all students were required to take all the same courses, thus eliminating many of the problems of self-selection that plague most studies. The same students evaluated instructors at the end of each course and again one year after graduation from the program. For both end-of-course and follow-up ratings, the particular instructor teaching the course accounted for 5 to 10 times as much variance as the course. These findings again demonstrated that the instructor is the primary determinant of SETs rather than the course he or she teaches.

Murray, Rushton, and Paunonen (1990) used archive data to examine overall instructor ratings of 46 psychology instructors in as many as 6 different course types including 5 categories of undergraduate courses and a single category for graduate level courses. Because the graduate and undergraduate courses were evaluated on 7- and 5-point response scales respectively, ratings within each of the six course types were standardized separately. Included in the analysis were ratings of instructors teaching at least two courses within the same category. The number of teachers included in each category varied from 29 to 40. Correlations among mean ratings of the same teacher within the same course type over different years (mean r = .86) was very high. The consistency in ratings of the same instructor across the five undergraduate course types (rs of .78 to .52, mean = .66) was also very high, but the consistency between the five undergraduate course types and graduate level courses was much lower (rs of .06 to .33, mean = 1.15). Because scores within each course type were standardized separately, mean differences in ratings of different course types could not be considered. These values—except for consistency across graduate and undergraduate courses—are higher than reported elsewhere (e.g., Marsh, 1981b) due in part to the fact that scores were aggregated across several courses within the same course type and because variance due to different course types was removed through standardization within course types. Except for the ratings of graduate level courses, these results are generally consistent with Marsh's (1981b) findings. The suggestion that SETs of the same instructor in undergraduate and graduate level courses are only modestly correlated is not consistent with SEEQ research, and may be idiosyncratic to Murray's study of teachers within a single psychology department and the different instruments used to assess undergraduate and graduate level classes.

Gilmore, Kane, and Naccarato (1978), applying generalizability theory to SETs, also found that the influence of the instructor who teaches the course is much larger than that of the course that is being taught. They suggested that ratings for a given instructor should be averaged across different courses to enhance generalizability. If it is likely that an instructor will teach many different classes during his or her subsequent career, then tenure decisions should be based upon as many different courses as possible—Gilmore, Kane, and Naccarato, suggest at least five. However, if it is likely that an instructor will continue to teach the same courses in which he or she has already been evaluated, then results from at least two different offerings of each of these courses was recommended. These recommendations require that a longitudinal archive of SETs be maintained for personnel decisions. These data would provide for more generalizable summaries, the assessment of changes over time, and the determination of which particular courses are best taught by a specific instructor. It is indeed unfortunate that some universities systematically collect SETs, but fail to keep a longitudinal archive of the results. Such an archive would help overcome some of the objections to SETs (e.g., idiosyncratic occurrences in one particular set of ratings), would enhance their usefulness, and would provide an important data base for further research.

Generalizability of Ratings Over Time

The two most common approaches to the study of stability and change refer to the stability of means over time (mean stability) and to the stability of individual differences over time (covariance stability). Research in the last section considered the generalizability of individual differences across different courses; the results indicated that teachers rated highly in one course tend to be rated highly in all the courses that they teach. Research described here focuses on the mean stability over time.

Most studies of the mean stability of teaching effectiveness are based on cross-sectional studies at the primary and secondary school level and have not used SETs as an indicator of teaching effectiveness. In an early review of this research, Ryans (1960) reported an overall negative relation between teaching experience and teaching effectiveness. He suggested, however, that there was an initial increase in effectiveness during the first few years, a leveling out period, and then a period of gradual decline. In her review of research since the early 1960s, Barnes (1985) reached a similar conclusion. She further reported that teaching experience beyond the first few years was associated with a tendency for teachers to reject innovations and changes in educational policy.

At the university level, Feldman (1983) reviewed studies relating overall and content-specific dimensions of SETs to teacher age, teaching experience, and academic rank. He reported that SETs were only weakly related to these three measures of seniority, but that distinct patterns were evident. Overall evaluations tended to be negatively correlated with age and—to a lesser extent—years of teaching experience, but tended to be positively correlated with academic rank. Thus, younger teachers, teachers with less teaching experience, and teachers with higher academic ranks tended to receive somewhat higher evaluations. Age and teaching experience showed reasonably similar patterns of correlations with overall and content-specific dimensions. Academic rank, however, had a more varied pattern of relations with the content-specific dimensions. Academic rank tended to be positively correlated with some characteristics such as subject knowledge, intellectual expansiveness, and value of course materials, but negatively correlated with other characteristics such as class discussion, respect for students, helpfulness and availability to students. Consistent with the reviews by Ryans (1960) and Barnes (1985), Feldman noted that in the few studies that specifically examined nonlinear relations, there was some suggestion of an inverted U-shaped relation in which ratings improved initially, peaked at some early point, and then declined slowly thereafter.

Most SET research has considered ratings collected in one specific course on a single occasion and there is surprisingly little research on the stability of mean ratings received by the same instructor over an extended period of time. Cross-sectional studies like those reviewed by Feldman (1983) provide a poor basis for inferring what ratings younger, less-experienced teachers will receive later in their careers or what ratings older, more-experienced teachers would have received if evaluated earlier in their careers. Clearly, there are important limitations in the use of cross-sectional data for evaluating how ratings of the same instructor varies over time. For this reason, Marsh and Hocevar (1991b) examined changes in ratings of a large number of teachers who had been evaluated continuously over a 13-year period with SEEQ.

Using the SEEQ archive consisting of evaluations of 50,000 courses collected over a 13-year period, Marsh and Hocevar (1991b) selected all teachers who were evaluated at least once during each of 10 different years between 1976 and 1988. This process identified 195 different teachers who had been evaluated in a total of 6,024 different courses (an average of 30.9 classes per teacher) from a total of 31 different academic departments. All SETs for the same instructor at the same level (graduate or undergraduate) offered in the same year were then averaged, resulting in 3,135 unique combinations of instructor, year, and course level. In order to evaluate the influence of the instructor the mean rating of each instructor over all undergraduate classes and over all graduate classes was computed. In the main regression models considered (Table 4), these instructor mean ratings were included along with the linear and nonlinear components of the year (1976–1988), the course level (2=graduate, 1=undergraduate), and their interactions. Hence, the effects of the individual instructor were controlled in evaluating the effects of the other variables. As has been found previously, the individual instructor accounted for most of the variance in each of the different SEEQ scores. There were almost no systematic changes in ratings over time. Year accounted for no more than 1/4 of 1 percent in any of the evaluation scores, and—despite the large N and powerful design—only reached statistical significance for 2 of 11 scores (see Table 4).

TABLE 4. Changes in Multiple Dimensions of Students Evaluations Over Time for Ratings of the Same instructor: The Effects of Instructor, Year (1976-1988), Level (undergraduate and graduate), and their Interaction (N=3135). (*Reprinted from Marsh and Hocevar [1991] by permission of Pergamon Press*).

Dimension	r for Instr	Standardized Beta Weights For:						
		Instr	Year	Year2	Level	YrxLev	YrxLev	Mult R
Factor Scores								
Learning/Value	.701[**]	.703[**]	.001	−.045[**]	−.023	.018	.025	.703[**]
Enthusiasm	.822[**]	.822[**]	−.016	−.019	−.003	.010	.006	.822[**]
Organization	.770[**]	.770[**]	−.048[**]	−.025	.000	.017	−.004	.772[**]
Group Interact	.814[**]	.815[**]	−.012	−.020	−.009	−.013	.010	.815[**]
Indiv Rapport	.747[**]	.746[**]	−.026	.016	.006	.006	−.009	.748[**]
Breadth	.735[**]	.735[**]	.005	−.011	.000	.009	−.007	.736[**]
Exams	.678[**]	.678[**]	−.028	−.017	.006	−.008	−.014	.678[**]
Assignments	.704[**]	.704[**]	−.004	−.024	−.008	.012	.006	.704[**]
Workload	.797[**]	.797[**]	−.020	−.009	.010	−.009	.007	.797[**]
Overall Ratings								
Course	.725[**]	.725[**]	−.031	−.028	−.013	−.031	.019	.726[**]
Instructor	.756[**]	.755[**]	−.048[**]	−.020	−.010	.009	.015	.758[**]

* p < .05; ** p < .01.

Note. The Instructor (instr) component was obtained by taking the mean of the instructor ratings for undergraduate classes and for graduate classes, and then including these means in the prediction of ratings. Because these means were computed separately for graduate and undergraduate level courses, it has the effect of eliminating variance due to course level.

The Marsh and Hocevar (1991b) study showed that the mean stability of SETs of the same teachers over a 13-year period of time was remarkably strong. The mean ratings for their cohort of 195 teachers showed almost no systematic changes over this period. Supplemental analyses suggested that the standards that students used apparently did not change over this period. The nonlinear effects suggested from cross-sectional studies were not observed for either the total sample, or subsamples of teachers with little, intermediate, or substantial amounts of teaching experience at the start of the 13-year longitudinal study. These results are important because this was apparently the only study to examine the mean stability of faculty ratings using a longitudinal design with a large and diverse group of teachers over such a long period of time.

Generalizability: Profile Analysis

Thus far, we have considered only the generalizability of individual SEEQ scales. Marsh (1987), however, noted the need to examine profiles of SEEQ scores as well as the individual scales that make up the profile. More specifically he suggested that each instructor has a distinguishable profile of SEEQ scales (e.g., high on organization and low on enthusiasm) that generalizes over different course offerings and is distinct from the profiles of other instructors. Marsh and Bailey (in press), because no other research known to them had evaluated SET profiles in this manner, conducted a profile analysis of ratings selected from the large SEEQ archive. They considered 3,079 sets of class-average responses for 123 instructors—an average of 25 classes per instructor—who had been evaluated regularly over a 13-year period. Because there were so many sets of ratings for each instructor, it was possible to determine a characteristic profile of SEEQ scores for each instructor by averaging across all his or her ratings. In profile analyses, it is important to distinguish between the level of scores (whether an instructor receives high or low ratings) and the shape of the profile (e.g., relatively higher on organization and relatively lower on enthusiasm). Although both are important considerations, the focus of the Marsh and Bailey study was on profile shape.

The profile of 9 SEEQ scales (e.g., Enthusiasm, Organization, Group Interaction) for each instructor was shown to be distinct from the profiles of other instructors, generalized across course offerings over the 13-year period, and generalized across undergraduate and graduate level courses. This support for the existence of a distinguishable profile that is specific to each instructor has important implications for the use of SETs as feedback and for the relation of SETs to other criteria such as student learning. Thus, for example, it may be that being organized and enthusiastic is very conducive to student learning, whereas being organized (but not enthusiastic) or enthusiastic (but not organized) has little effect on student learning. Although such possibilities were not specifically considered in the Marsh and Bailey (in press) study, this is an important direction for further research. The results also provide further support for the multidimensionality of SETs.

Student Written Comments—Generality Across Different Response Form
Braskamp and his colleagues (Braskamp, Brandenburg, and Ory, 1985; Braskamp, Ory, and Pieper, 1981; Ory, Braskamp, and Pieper, 1980) have examined the usefulness of students' written comments and their relation to responses to rating items. Student comments were scored for overall favorability with reasonable reliability and these overall scores correlated with responses to the overall rating item (r=.93) close to the limits of the reliability of the two indicators (Ory, Braskamp, and Pieper, 1980). Braskamp, Ory, and Pieper (1981) sorted student comments into one of 22 content categories and evalu-

ated comments in terms of favorability. The comment favorability was again highly correlated with the overall instructor rating (0.75). In a related study, Ory and Braskamp (1981) simulated results about a hypothetical instructor consisting of written comments in their original unedited form and rating items—both global and specific. The rating items were judged as easier to interpret and more comprehensive for both personnel decisions and self-improvement, but other aspects of the written comments were judged to be more useful for purposes of self-improvement. Speculating on these results, the authors suggested that "the nonstandardized, unique, personal written comments by students are perceived as too subjective for important personnel decisions. However, this highly idiosyncratic information about a particular course is viewed as useful diagnostic information for making course changes" (pp. 280–281). Murray (1987), however, reported on a survey at the University of Western Ontario in which faculty were asked to evaluate the usefulness of SETs as feedback; 54 percent, 65 percent, and 78 percent endorsed the usefulness of global SETs, student comments, and ratings of specific teaching behaviors respectively.

Lin, McKeachie and Tucker (1984) compared statistical summaries of SETs and written comments in promotion and salary decisions. Previous research had shown that teaching ability in general, and statistical summaries of SETs in particular, had little effect on promotion decisions compared to research productivity. Based on theories of influence developed in social psychology, they reasoned that more vivid and concrete presentations of SETs might increase their importance in promotion decisions. In their experimental design, simulated promotion dossiers were prepared in which evidence for teaching ability was presented as statistical summaries alone or as statistical summaries supplemented by direct quotations of student comments that were consistent with the statistical information. Staff in the dossiers were depicted to be of high or medium teaching ability. Their results showed that for the most able teachers, the effects of statistical summaries and comments were more positive than statistical summaries alone. For the less able teachers, the effects of statistical summaries and comments were more negative than statistical summaries alone. Thus, the student comments seemed to increase the credibility and enhance the impact—for good or for bad—of the statistical summaries. Because the researchers did not consider comments alone or comments that were inconsistent with the statistical summaries, there was no basis for comparing the relative impact of the two sources of information.

The research by Braskamp and his colleagues demonstrates that student comments, at least on a global basis, can be reliably scored and that these scores agree substantially with students' responses to overall rating items. This supports the generality of the ratings. Their findings supported the usefulness of student comments (in addition to rating items) for purposes of diagnostic feedback, but did not indicate the relative usefulness of the unedited, original comments as opposed to the results of detailed content analyses. Both the Murray survey results and the Lin, McKeachie and Tucker experimental study suggest that student comments may be more useful than global ratings, but Murray's study suggests that ratings on specific components may be even more useful. Perhaps, as may be implied by Ory and Braskamp (1981), the useful information from comments that cannot be obtained from rating items is idiosyncratic information that cannot easily be classified into generalizable categories, that is so specific that its value would be lost if it was sorted into broader categories, or that cannot be easily interpreted without knowledge of the particular context. From this perspective, the attempt to systematically analyze student comments may be counterproductive. If such analyses are to be pursued, then further research is needed to demonstrate that this lengthy and time consuming exercise will provide useful and reliable information that is not obtainable from the more cost effective rating items.

VALIDITY

The Construct Validation Approach to Validity

Abrami, d'Apollonia, and Cohen (1990) note that there are two disparate views on how to validate SETs. In one, students are seen as the consumers of teaching and SETs provide a measure of consumer satisfaction. From this perspective the ratings are valid so long as they accurately reflect student feelings. In the other view, SETs are valid if they accurately reflect teaching effectiveness. This second perspective is more controversial, is the focus of most validity research, and is the emphasis here.

SETs, as one measure of teaching effectiveness, are difficult to validate since no single criterion of effective teaching is sufficient. Historically, researchers have emphasized a narrow, criterion-related approach to validity in which student learning is viewed as the only criterion of effective teaching. Such a restrictive framework, however, inhibits a better understanding of what is being measured by SETs, of what can be inferred from SETs, and how findings from diverse studies can be understood within a common framework. Instead, Marsh (1984b, 1987) advocated a construct validation approach, in which SETs are posited be positively related to a wide variety of other indicators of effective teaching and specific rating factors are required to be most highly correlated with variables to which they are most logically and theoretically related. Within this framework, evidence for the long-term stability of SETs, the generalizability of ratings of the same instructor in different courses, the agreement of SETs and student written comments, and the agreement in matching scales from two different SET instruments can be interpreted as support for the validity of SETs. The most widely accepted criterion of effective teaching is student learning, but other criteria include changes in student behaviors, instructor self-evaluations, the evaluations of peers and/or administrators who actually attend class sessions, the frequency of occurrence of specific behaviors observed by trained observers, and the effects of experimental manipulations. A construct validity approach to the study of SETs now appears to be widely accepted (e.g., Cashin, 1988; Howard, Conway, and Maxwell, 1985).

In this section we examine empirical relations between SETs and other potential indicators of effective teaching. The intent is not specifically to evaluate the construct validity of these other criteria as indicators of effective teaching, but to some extent this is inevitable. One of the most difficult problems in validating interpretations of a measure is to obtain suitable criterion measures. To the extent that criterion measures are not reliably measured, or do not validly reflect effective teaching, then they will not be useful for testing the construct validity of SETs. More generally, criterion measures that lack reliability or validity should not be used as indicators of effective teaching for research, policy formation, feedback to faculty, or administrative decision making.

Student Learning—The Multisection Validity Study

Student learning, particularly if inferred from an objective, reliable, and valid test, is probably the most widely accepted criterion of effective teaching. Learning, however, is not generally appropriate as an indicator of effective teaching in universities. Examination scores cannot be compared across departments, across different courses within the same departments, or—except in special circumstances—even across offerings of the same course taught by different teachers. It may be reasonable to compare pretest and post-test scores as an indicator of learning, but it is not valid to compare the pretest-post-test changes in different courses. It may be useful to determine the percentage of students who successfully master behavioral objectives, but it is not valid to compare percentages obtained from different courses. In a very specialized, highly controlled setting it may be valid to compare teachers in terms of operationally defined learning, and this is the intent of multisection validity studies. Most university teaching, however, does not take place in such a setting. SETs are related to learning in such a limited setting on the assumption that such results will generalize to settings where learning is not an adequate basis for assessing effective teaching, and not to demonstrate the appropriateness of learning as a criterion of effective teaching in those other settings.

The Multisection Validity Paradigm

In the ideal multisection validity study: a) there are many sections of a large multisection course; b) students are randomly assigned to sections, or at least enroll without any knowledge about the sections or who will teach them, so as to minimize initial differences between sections; c) there are pretest measures that correlate substantially with final course performance for individual students that are used as covariates; d) each section is taught completely by a separate instructor; e) each section has the same course outline, textbooks, course objectives, and final examination; f) the final examination is constructed to reflect the common objectives by some person who does not actually teach any of the sections, and, if there is a subjective component, it is graded by an external person; g) students in each section evaluate teaching effectiveness on a standardized evaluation instrument, preferably before they know their final course grade and without knowing how performances in their section compares with that of students in other sections; and h) section-average SETs are related to section-average examination performance, (see Yunker, 1983, for discussion on the unit-of-analysis issue) after controlling for pretest measures (for general discussion see Abrami, d'Apollonia, and Cohen, 1990; Benton, 1979; Cohen, 1981, 1987; Marsh, 1984b, 1987; Marsh and Overall, 1980; Yunker, 1983). Support for the validity of the SETs is demonstrated when the sections that evaluate the teaching as most effective near the end of the course are also the sections that perform best on standardized final examinations, and when plausible counter explanations are not viable.

Methodological Problems

Rodin and Rodin (1972) reported a negative correlation between section-average grade and section-average evaluations of graduate students teaching different quiz sections. Ironically, this highly publicized study did not constitute a multisection validity study as described above, and contained serious methodological problems (e.g., Cohen, 1987; Doyle, 1975; Frey, 1978; Marsh, 1987): the ratings were not of the instructor in charge of the course but of teaching assistants who played an ancillary role; a negative correlation might be expected since it would be the less able students who would have the most need for the supplemental services provided by the teaching assistants; the study was conducted during the third term of a year-long course and students were free to change teaching assistants between terms and were not even required always to attend sections led by the same teaching assistant during the third term; there was no adequate measure of end-of-course achievement in that performance was evaluated with problems given at the end of each segment of the course, and students could repeat each exam as many as six times without penalty; and these negative findings are generally inconsistent with the findings of subsequent research. In reviewing this study, Doyle (1975) stated that "to put the matter bluntly, the attention received by the Rodin and Rodin study seems disproportionate to its rigor, and their data provide little if any guidance in the validation of student ratings." (p.59). In retrospect, the most interesting aspect of this study was that such a methodologically flawed study received so much attention.

Even when the design of multisection validity studies is more adequate, numerous methodological problems may still exist. First, the sample size in any given study is usually small—about 15 sections—and produces extremely large sampling errors. As noted by Abrami, d'Apollonia, and Cohen (1990), however, this problem can be overcome in part by meta-analyses of all such studies. Second, most variance in achievement scores at all levels of education is attributable to student presage variables and researchers are generally unable to find appreciable effects due to differences in teacher, school practice, or teaching method (Cooley and Lohnes, 1976; McKeachie, 1963). Thus it may be that instructors have only a limited effect on what students learn. In multisection validity studies, however, so many characteristics of the setting are held constant, that differences in student learning due to differences in teaching effectiveness are even further attenuated in relation to likely effects in more representative settings. Hence, although the design is defensible, it is also quite weak for obtaining instructor produced achievement differences that are used to validate SETs. Third, the comparison of findings across different multisection validity studies is problematic, given the lack of consistency in measures of course achievement and student rating instruments. Although it may be possible to code study-level differences so as to evaluate their impact, comprehensive schemes (Abrami, d'Apollonia, and Cohen, 1990) are so complicated that this problem may not be resolvable. Fourth, performance on objectively scored examinations that have been the focus of multisection validity studies may be an unduly limited criterion of effective teaching

(Dowell and Neal, 1982; Marsh and Overall, 1980). Other criteria of teaching effectiveness besides student learning—defined largely by multiple choice tests that measure lower-level objectives such as memory of facts and definition—should be considered. For example, Marsh and Overall (1980) found that sections who rated their teacher most highly were more likely to pursue further coursework in the area and to join the local computer club (the course was an introduction to computer programming), and that these criteria of effective teaching were not significantly correlated with student learning. Fifth, presage variables such as initial student motivation and particularly ability level must be equated across sections for comparisons to be valid. Even random assignment becomes ineffective at accomplishing this when the number of sections is large and the number of students within each section is small, because chance alone will create differences among the sections. This paradigm does not constitute an experimental design in which students are randomly assigned to treatment groups that are varied systematically in terms of experimentally manipulated variables, and so the advantages of random assignment are not so clear as in a standard experimental design.[*] Furthermore, the assumption of truly random assignment of students to classes in large scale field studies is almost always compromised by time-scheduling problems, students dropping out of a course after the initial assignment, missing data, etc. For multisection validity studies the lack of initial equivalence is particularly critical, since initial presage variables are likely to be a primary determinant of end-of-course achievement. For this reason it is important to have effective pretest measures even when there is random assignment. In summary, the multisection validity design is inherently weak and there are many methodological complications in its actual application.

Meta-analyses

Cohen (1981) conducted what appears to have been the most influential meta-analysis of multisection validity studies. In his review he included all known studies, regardless of methodological problems such as found in the Rodin and Rodin study. Across 68 multisection courses, student achievement was consistently correlated with SETs of Skill (.50), Overall Course (.47), Structure (.47), Student Progress (.47), and Overall Instructor (.43). Only ratings of Workload/Difficulty were unrelated to achievement. (The relation between Difficulty and achievement may be nonlinear but this possibility was apparently not considered.) The correlations were higher when ratings were of full-

---

[*]The value of random assignment is frequently misunderstood in student evaluation research, and particularly in the multisection validity study. Random assignment is not an end, but merely a means to control for initial differences in treatment groups that would otherwise complicate the interpretation of treatment effects. The effectiveness of random assignment is positively related to the number of cases in each treatment group, but negatively related to the number of different treatment groups. In the multisection validity study the instruction provided by each teacher is a separate treatment, his or her students are the treatment group, and there is usually no a priori basis for establishing which of the many treatments is more or less effective. Hence, even with random assignment it is likely that some sections will have students who are systematically more able (prepared, motivated, etc.) than others, and this is likely to bias the results (also see Yunker, 1983).

time teachers, when students knew their final grade before rating instructors, and when achievement tests were evaluated by an external evaluator. Other study characteristics (e.g., random assignment, course content, availability of pretest data) were not significantly related to the results. Many of the criticisms of the multisection validity study are at least partially answered by this meta-analysis, particularly problems due to small sample sizes and, perhaps, the issue of the multiplicity of achievement measures and student rating instruments. These results provide strong support for the validity of SETs.

Cohen updated this meta-analysis in 1986 and provided a critical analysis and reanalysis in 1987 (see Cohen, 1987). In his 1987 reanalysis, Cohen placed more emphasis on the multidimensional nature of the SETs. For example, he distinguished between summary ratings that were aggregates across specific components and global ratings, he more critically evaluated the classification of specific dimensions, and he distinguished between specific dimensions inferred from single items and from multi-item scales. The reanalysis suggested that achievement/SET correlations were higher for global rating items than aggregated summary scores and for multi-item scales representing specific dimensions than single-item ratings of specific dimensions (presumably because multi-item scales are more reliable; see Rushton, Brainerd, and Pressley, 1983). Cohen (1987) also presented results for a subset of 41 "well-designed" studies; correlations between achievement and different SET components were Structure (.55), Interaction (.52), Skill (.50), Overall Course (.49), Overall Instructor (.45), Learning (.39), Rapport (.32), Evaluation (.30), Feedback (.28), Interest/Motivation (.15), and Difficulty (-.04), in which all but the last two were statistically significant. For an even more restrictive set of 25 "high quality" studies, the validity coefficients were somewhat lower, but the small N (less than 10 for all but the overall instructor rating) made comparisons dubious. On the basis of his meta-analyses, Cohen (1987, p.12) concluded that "I am confident that global ratings of the instructor and course, and certain rating dimensions such as skill, rapport, structure, interaction, evaluation, and student's self-rating of their learning can be used effectively as an integral component of a teaching evaluation system."

Feldman (1989a), based in part on earlier work by d'Apollonia and Abrami (1987) and Abrami, Cohen, and d'Apollonia (1988; see Feldman, 1990a), extended Cohen's (1981, 1987) meta-analysis by increasing the number of specific dimensions from 9 to 28. Cohen's 9 dimensions were represented by 16 dimensions in Feldman's analysis. For example, Cohen's conglomerate "skill" category—which correlated .51 with achievement—was represented by 3 dimensions in Feldman's analysis that correlated with achievement .34 (instructor's knowledge of the subject), .56 (clarity and understandableness), and .30 (teacher sensitivity to class level and progress). Hence, the strong correlation between skill and achievement in Cohen's study was primarily due to instructor clarity and understandableness. Similarly, the high correlation between structure and achievement in Cohen's study (r=.55) is more a function of teacher preparation and organization of the course (r=.57) than clarity of course objectives (r=.35) in Feldman's (1989a) reanalysis. Feldman also considered specific dimensions that he indicated were not represented in any of Cohen's dimensions, and some of these were significantly correlated with achievement: pursued and met objectives (.38), elocutionary skills (.38), enthusiasm (.29), personality characteristics(.25),intellectual challenge (.25), classroom management (.24), pleasantness of classroom atmosphere (.24), and nature, quality and frequency of feedback (.23). Both Feldman's and Cohen's reviews were based on a mix of studies using single-item and multi-item scales, and in this sense they are comparable. It should be noted, however, that single-item scales are less reliable than multi-item scales and thus likely to be less correlated with achievement (as noted by Cohen, 1987). Hence, the results of both reviews probably underestimate relations that would be obtained with a carefully constructed set of multi-item scales. Curiously, Feldman (1989a) chose not to interpret his results as an attempt to validate the specific dimensions. He noted, for example, that the specific dimensions are not alternative indicators of student learning. Whereas this is an appropriate rationale if validity is narrowly defined to be criterion-related validity, it is not appropriate within the broader perspective of construct validation that is emphasized here.

Particularly the Cohen (1987) and Feldman (1989a) meta-analyses indicate that some specific dimensions of the ratings are more highly correlated with achievement than are overall instructor ratings, further supporting the contention that SETs cannot be adequately understood if their multidimensionality is ignored. It also follows, as a statistical necessity, that an optimally weighted combination of specific components and the global ratings would be even more highly correlated with achievement. An important limitation in these meta-analyses, however, was their inability to determine the size of this optimal correlation based on multiple scores or the optimal weights for each dimension and the global ratings. Because of the lack of a uniform set of evaluation components in SET research, this problem is unlikely to be resolved in further meta-analytic research.

Counter Explanations.
The grading satisfaction hypothesis. Marsh (1984b, 1987; Marsh, Fleiner and Thomas, 1975; Marsh and Overall, 1980; also see Palmer, Carliner, and Romer, 1978) identified an alternative explanation for positive results in multisection validity studies that he called the grading satisfaction hypothesis (or a grading leniency effect). When course grades (known or expected) and performance on the final exam are significantly correlated, then higher evaluations may be due to: a) more effective teaching that produces greater learning and higher evaluations by students; b) increased student satisfaction with higher grades which causes them to "reward" the instructor with higher ratings independent of more effective teaching or greater learning; or c) initial differences in student characteristics (e.g., prior subject interest, motivation, and ability) that affect both teaching effectiveness and performance. The first hypothesis argues for the validity of SETs as a measure of teaching effectiveness, the second represents an undesirable bias in the ratings, and the third is the effect of presage variables that may be accurately reflected by the SETs.

Even when there are no initial differences between sections (and there are always at least random differences), either of the first two explanations is viable. Cohen (1987), for example, found that validity correlations were substantially higher when students already knew their final course grade, and noted that "a potential source of bias—are good teachers receiving high ratings or are students rewarding teachers who give high grades?—was empirically demonstrated to affect the correlational effect size." Palmer, Carliner, and Romer (1978) made similar distinctions but their research has typically been discussed in relation to the potential biasing effect of expected grades (also see Howard and Maxwell, 1980, 1982) rather than multisection validity studies. Dowell and Neal (1982) also suggest such distinctions, but then apparently confound the effects of grading leniency and initial differences in section-average ability in their review of multisection validity studies.

Abrami, d'Apollonia, and Cohen (1990) specifically cite Marsh's (1987) discussion of the grading satisfaction hypothesis, but then dismiss it so long as "section differences in students and instructor grading practices, including timing, are uniform across classes" (p.221). Whereas these are desirable characteristics and prerequisites of a good multisection validity study, they do not rule out the grading satisfaction hypothesis. Typically, there is no way of unconfounding the teaching effectiveness that supposedly led to the (good or poor) grades and (high or low) satisfaction with the grades if the grades and satisfaction are correlated. Abrami, Cohen, and d'Apollonia argue that "the alleged effect of grading satisfaction will operate consistently, if at all, in each section of a multisection course unless instructors first produce differences in student learning. Under these conditions, grading satisfaction cannot explain mean section differences in either student ratings or student achievement" (p.221). There are, however, several problems in this reasoning. First, there is an implicit assumption that all section differences in criterion test performance—systematic and random—are instructor-produced effects. This assumption is completely unrealistic and cannot even be tested without assessing teaching effectiveness independent of student learning and SETs. If there are section-average differences in test performance that are not due to the instructor—even random effects—and the resulting higher or lower course grades affect satisfaction, then the grading satisfaction hypothesis is likely to inflate the validity coefficients. Second, even if all section differences in criterion test performance did reflect instructor effects, there still is no way to unconfound the influences of grades and satisfaction with grades. This may be a moot issue if teaching effectiveness and satisfaction with grades are perfectly correlated—another dubious assumption in the Abrami Cohen, and d'Apollonia argument—but this is unlikely even in a tightly controlled multisection validity study. So long as there are section-average differences in satisfaction with grades that are independent of teaching effectiveness, the grading satisfaction hypothesis is viable. Third, as noted by Abrami, d'Apollonia, and Cohen (1990), "the problem is especially pronounced when one is studying multiple classes outside the multisection paradigm where there is more variability in grading practices" (p.221). Thus, if the results from the multisection paradigm are to generalize, it is important to know how much of the grade/SET correlation is due to teaching effectiveness and to satisfaction with grades. This can only be examined in a setting in which the effects of effective teaching and satisfaction with grades are established separately.

In the two SEEQ studies (Marsh, Fleiner and Thomas, 1975; Marsh and Overall, 1980), the grading satisfaction hypothesis was not a viable alternative to the validity hypothesis. The researchers reasoned that in order for satisfaction with higher grades to affect SETs at the section-average level, section-average expected grades must differ at the time the student evaluations are completed. In both these studies SETs were collected before the final examination, and student performance measures administered prior to the final examination were not standardized across sections. Hence, while each student knew approximately how his or her performance compared to other students within the same section, there was no basis for knowing how the section-average performance of any one section compared with that of other sections, and thus there was no basis for differences between the sections in their satisfaction with expected grades. Consistent with this suggestion, section-average expected grades indicated by students at the time the ratings were collected did not differ significantly from one section to the next, and were not significantly correlated with section-average performance on the final examination (even though individual expected grades within each section were substantially correlated with examination performance). Since section-average expected grades at the time the ratings were collected did not vary, they could not be the direct cause of higher SETs that were positively correlated with student performance, or the indirect cause of the higher ratings as a consequence of increased student satisfaction with higher grades. Marsh (1987) further noted that since the grading satisfaction hypothesis can only be explained in terms of expected grades the use of actual grades may be dubious unless students already know their final grades when the SETs are collected. In studies where section-average expected grades and section-average exam performance are positively correlated, the grading satisfaction hypothesis cannot be so easily countered.

Reliability of section-average achievement differences. Surprisingly, the reliability of section-average differences in achievement is a critical problem that is largely ignored in multisection validity studies. For example, in their critique of multisection validity studies, Abrami, d'Apollonia, and Cohen (1990) noted that only about one third of the studies reported the reliability of individual achievement test scores, but they apparently failed to recognize that the more critical concern is the reliability of section-average achievement scores. Even if individual achievement scores are perfectly reliable, the reliability of section-average achievement scores will be zero if the average achievement score is similar in each section.[*] Because much of the variance in individ-

---

[*]The intra-class correlation can be used to assess the reliability of section-average achievement in the same way that it is used to assess the reliability of section-average student ratings (see earlier discussion; also see Feldman, 1977). This can be accomplished with a one-way ANOVA that divides variability in individual student scores into within-section and between-section components. If section-average differences are no larger than expected by chance, then the reliability of section-average scores is—by definition—zero. Estimates of reliability for section-average scores are higher when there are larger differences between sections, smaller differences within sections, and larger numbers of students within each section. Whereas these reliability estimates are not typically reported, the reliability should be higher when the average number of students in each section is larger (all other factors being equal—always a worrisome assumption) and this relation could be tested in meta-analyses.

ual achievement is due to individual student characteristics, most of the variance is probably attributable to within-section differences. Hence, section-average achievement scores are likely to be much less reliable than section-average SETs.

If section-average differences in achievement are small or unreliable, then a modest SET/achievement correlation is the best that can be expected. It is only when there are large and reliable section-average differences in achievement that a small achievement/SET correlation reflects negatively on the validity of the SETs. Thus, the size and reliability of section-average differences in learning place an upper limit on the size of SET/achievement correlations. A more realistic estimate of the true SET/achievement relation would be a correlation that is corrected for unreliability in the section-average achievement and, perhaps, the section-average SETs. Because this issue is largely unexplored in individual studies and meta-analyses, there is no way determine how much higher the true validity coefficients—appropriately corrected for unreliability—would be than those that have been reported. We suspect, however, that the differences are substantial in some studies and large enough to be substantively important in most studies. It is clear that existing research has underestimated—seriously we suspect—the true correlation between section-average SETs and section-average achievement.

Student Study Strategies and Learning Outcomes

Prosser and Trigwell (1990, 1991) discussed the multisection validity paradigm and proposed that SETs should be evaluated in relation to student study strategies (e.g., deep vs. surface) and the quality of learning outcomes (varying from simple and concrete understanding to complex and abstract understanding). In a study of 11 classes from different disciplines, Prosser and Trigwell (1990) reported significant and positive correlations between global SETs and students adopting deeper study strategies. In the second study (Prosser and Trigwell, 1991), students from 11 sections of a Communications course completed SETs, a common final examination, and standardized instruments assessing study strategies and learning outcomes. Global ratings were negatively related (nonsignificantly) to final exam performance but were significantly and positively related to study strategies and to the learning outcome measure. Characterizing the learning outcome measure as the quality of learning and the exam score as the quantity of learning, the authors noted that the two components of learning were almost unrelated. The authors, noting limitations in these studies, indicate that the results should be interpreted cautiously. Nevertheless, the research is heuristic and demonstrates one direction for expanding the nature of outcome variables in multisection validity studies.

Implications for Further Research

Multisection validity studies should be designed according to the criteria discussed earlier. The interpretation of multisection validity studies may be substantially affected by section-average differences in pretest scores, the type of achievement tests used to infer student learning, the quality of SETs used to infer instructional effectiveness, the expected grades at the time students evaluate teaching effectiveness, and the reliability of section-average differences in student achievement. Hence it is important to test for the statistical significance of such differences and to provide some indication of effect size or variance explained. Pretest measures should be substantially related to final examination performance of individual students, and multiple regressions relating pretest scores to examination scores should be summarized. Nevertheless, if initial section-average differences are large, then the statistical correction for such initial differences may be problematic. Furthermore, if section-average expected grades are significantly correlated with section-average examination performance, and if the size of the validity coefficient is substantially reduced when the effects of expected grades are controlled, then grading satisfaction may be a viable alternative explanation of the results. Further research is needed to evaluate the potential confounding between teaching effectiveness, student learning, satisfaction with grades, and SETs. Finally, there is need to expand the range of outcome measures to include other criteria such as student learning at different levels in the Bloom taxonomy, quality of learning and study strategies, and affective outcomes.

The reliability of section-average achievement scores is a critical concern that has been largely ignored in multisection validity studies. This problem reflects a negative bias—one that makes SETs appear to be less valid—in all existing research and meta-analyses. Because these reliability estimates are not reported, the size of this negative bias cannot be accurately estimated and cannot be corrected in meta-analyses. Nevertheless, we suspect that the negative bias is substantial. This is an important concern that must be considered in future research or reanalyses of existing research.

Abrami, d'Apollonia, and Cohen (1990) summarized problems with the implementation of meta-analyses of multi-section validity studies and provided a set of 75 study features that may influence the results. Existing research, however, is not adequate to establish the effects of these features leading the authors to conclude that many more studies are needed that are more fully documented in relation to their coding scheme. Whereas we fully endorse this recommendation, it is relevant to point out that few multisection validity studies have been conducted in the last decade. Hence, whereas problems identified by Abrami, Cohen, and d'Apollonia may not be inherent weaknesses in the multisection validity design, it may be a very long time before there is a sufficient body of research to resolve the problems. From a practical perspective, the size of the task of evaluating these study effects may be consistent with our conclusion that the paradigm is inherently weak.

The methodologically flawed study by Rodin and Rodin aroused considerable interest in multisection validity studies, and focused attention on the methodological weaknesses of the design. Perhaps more than any other type of study, the credibility of SETs has rested on this paradigm. Researchers' preoccupation with the multisection validity study has had both positive and negative aspects. The notoriety of the Rodin and Rodin study required that further research be conducted. Despite methodological problems and difficulties in the interpretation of results, meta-analyses demonstrate that sections for which instructors are evaluated more highly by students tend to do better on standardized examinations; a finding which has been taken as strong support for the use of the ratings. Furthermore, because the lack of reliability of section-average achievement scores have not been taken into account, SET/achievement correlations in existing research are likely to underestimate—substantially we believe—true SET/achievement correlations. Nevertheless, the limited generality of the setting, the inherent weakness of the design, and the possibility of alternative explanations all dictate that it is important to consider other criterion measures and other paradigms in student-evaluation research.

Evaluations of Teaching Effectiveness by Different Evaluators

Most researchers emphasize that teaching effectiveness should be measured from multiple perspectives and with multiple criteria. Braskamp, Brandenburg, and Ory (1985) identify four sources of information for evaluating teaching effectiveness: students, colleagues, alumni, and instructor self-ratings. Ratings by students and alumni are substantially correlated, and ratings by each of these sources appear to be moderately correlated with self-evaluations. However, ratings by colleagues based on classroom observations do not seem to be systematically related to ratings by the other three sources. Braskamp, Brandenburg, and Ory recommend that colleagues should be used to review classroom materials such as course syllabi, assignments, tests, texts, and Scriven (1981) suggests that such evaluations should be done by staff from the same academic discipline from another institution in a trading of services arrangement that eliminates costs. While this use of colleagues is potentially valuable, we know of no systematic research that demonstrates the reliability or validity of such ratings.

Instructor Self-Evaluations

Validity paradigms in student evaluation research are often limited to a specialized setting (e.g., large multisection courses) or use criteria such as the retrospective ratings of former students that are unlikely to convince skeptics. Hence, the validity of SETs will continue to be questioned until criteria are utilized that are both applicable across a wide range of courses and widely accepted as a indicator of teaching effectiveness (see Braskamp, Brandenburg, and Ory, 1985 for further discussion). Instructors' self-evaluations of their own teaching effectiveness is a criterion which satisfies both of these requirements. Furthermore, instructors can be asked to evaluate themselves with the same instrument used by their students, thereby testing the convergent and divergent validity of the different rating factors. Also, there is evidence to suggest that providing instructors with the discrepancies between their own self-evaluations and SETs by their students provides more incentive to improve teaching effectiveness than the SETs alone (see Marsh, 1987).

Despite the apparent appeal of instructor self-evaluations as a criterion of effective teaching, it has had limited application and many studies are not readily available in published form. In his meta-analysis based on 19 studies, Feldman (1989a) reported a mean r of .29 for overall ratings and mean rs of .15 to .42 in specific components of teaching effectiveness. Marsh (1982c; Marsh, Overall and Kesler, 1979b) apparently conducted the only studies where faculty in a large number of courses (81 and 329) were asked to evaluate their own teaching on the same multifaceted evaluation instrument that was completed by students. In both studies: a) separate factor analyses of teacher and student responses identified the same evaluation factors (see Table 1, p. 245); b) student-teacher agreement on every dimension was significant (median rs of .49 and .45; Table 5) and typically larger than agreement on overall teaching effectiveness (rs of .32 in both studies); 3) mean differences between student and faculty responses were small and not statistically significant for most items, and were unsystematic when differences were significant (i.e., SETs were higher than faculty self-evaluations for some items but lower for others).

In MTMM studies, multiple traits (the student rating factors) are assessed by multiple methods (SETs and instructor self-evaluations). Consistent with the construct validation approach discussed earlier, correlations (see Table 5 for MTMM matrix from Marsh's 1982c study) between SETs and instructor self-evaluations on the same dimension (i.e., convergent validities—median rs of .49 and .45) were higher than correlations between ratings on nonmatching dimensions (median rs of −.04 and .02), and this is taken as support for the divergent validity of the ratings. In the second study, separate analyses were also performed for courses taught by teaching assistants, undergraduate level courses taught by faculty, and graduate level courses. Support for both the convergent and divergent validity of the ratings was found in each set of courses (also see Howard, Conway, and Maxwell, 1985).

Feldman (1988) reviewed studies that evaluated a different aspect of agreement between student and faculty perspectives. He examined 31 studies in which both students and instructors indicated the specific components of teaching effectiveness that are most important to effective instruction. The average correlation of .71 between the patterns of importance ratings indicated substantial agreement between the two groups. There were, however, some systematic differences: students placed somewhat more importance on teachers stimulating interest, having good elocutionary skills, and being available and helpful, whereas faculty placed somewhat more emphasis on challenging students, motivating students, encouraging self-initiated learning, and setting high standards. These findings are important in countering the frequently voiced concern that students and instructors differ substantially on what constitutes effective teaching. Because students and faculty do agree on the relative importance of different components of effective teaching, this research offers additional support for the construct validity of SETs and for the importance of considering their multidimensionality. It is also interesting to note that the pattern of correlations between specific dimensions and achievement in multisection validity studies (Feldman, 1989a) is not very highly correlated with the pattern of importance ratings by either students (.42) or faculty (.31).

This research on instructors' self-evaluations has important implications. First, the fact that SETs show significant agreement with instructor self-evaluations provides clear evidence for their validity, and this agreement can be examined in nearly all instructional settings. Second, there is good evidence for the validity of SETs for both undergraduate and graduate level courses (Marsh, 1982c). Third, support for the divergent validity demonstrates the validity of each specific rating factor as well as of the ratings in general, and argues for the importance of using systematically developed, multifactor evaluation instruments.

TABLE 5. Multitrait-multimethod Matrix: Correlations Between Student Ratings and Faculty Self-evaluations in 329 Courses.
(Reprinted from Marsh [1984b] by permission of the American Psychological Association.)

Factor	Instructor self-evaluation factor									Student evaluation factor								
	1	2	3	4	5	6	7	8	9	10	11	12	13	14	15	16	17	18
Instructor self-evaluations																		
1. Learning/Value	(83)																	
2. Enthusiasm	29	(82)																
3. Organization	12	01	(74)															
4. Group Interaction	01	03	-15	(90)														
5. Individual Rapport	-07	-01	07	02	(82)													
6. Breadth	13	12	14	11	-01	(84)												
7. Examinations	-01	08	26	09	15	20	(76)											
8. Assignments	24	-01	17	05	22	09	22	(70)										
9. Workload/Difficulty	03	-01	12	-09	06	-04	09	21	(70)									
Student Evaluations																		
10. Learning/Value	**46**	10	-01	08	-12	09	-04	08	02	(94)								
11. Enthusiasm	21	**54**	-04	-01	-02	-01	-03	-09	-09	45	(96)							
12. Organization	17	13	**30**	-03	04	07	09	00	-05	52	49	(93)						
13. Group Interaction	19	05	-20	**52**	00	-02	-14	-04	-08	37	30	21	(98)					
14. Individual Rapport	03	03	-05	13	**28**	-19	-03	-02	00	22	35	33	42	(96)				
15. Breadth	26	15	09	00	-14	**42**	00	09	02	49	34	56	17	15	(94)			
16. Examinations	18	09	01	-01	06	-09	**17**	-02	-06	48	42	57	34	50	33	(93)		
17. Assignments	20	03	02	09	-01	04	-01	**45**	12	52	21	34	30	29	40	42	(92)	
18. Workload/Difficulty	-06	-03	04	00	03	-03	12	22	**69**	06	02	-05	-05	08	18	-02	20	(87)

Note: Values in parentheses in the diagonals of the upper left and lower right matrices, are reliability (coefficient alpha) coefficients (see Hull & Nie, 1981). The underlined values in the diagonal of the lower left matrix, the square matrix, are convergent validity coefficients that have been corrected for unreliability according to the Spearman Brown equation. The nine uncorrected validity coefficients, starting with Learning, would be .41, .48, .25, .46, .25, .37, .13, .36, & .54. All correlation coefficients are presented without decimal points. Correlations greater than .10 are statistically significant.

In discussing instructor self-evaluations, Centra speculated that prior experience with SETs may influence self-evaluations (Centra, 1975, 1979, 1989). In particular, he suggested that instructors may initially overestimate their teaching effectiveness and that they may lower their self-evaluations as a consequence of having been previously evaluated by students so that their ratings would be expected to be more consistent with SETs (Centra, 1979). If instructors were asked to predict how students would evaluate them, then Centra's suggestion might constitute an important methodological problem for self-evaluation studies. However, both SEEQ studies specifically instructed the faculty to rate their own teaching effectiveness as they perceived it even it they felt that their students would disagree, and not to report how their students would rate them. Hence, the fact that most of the instructors in these studies had been previously evaluated does not seem to be a source of invalidity in the interpretation of the results (also see Doyle, 1983). Furthermore, given that the average of SETs is a little over 4 on a 5-point response scale, if instructor self-evaluations are substantially higher than SETs before they receive any feedback from SETs as suggested by Centra, then faculty on average may have unrealistically high self-perceptions of their own teaching effectiveness. A critical issue is whether exposure to prior SETs enhances or diminishes the validity of instructor self-evaluations. A systematic examination of how instructor self-perceptions change, or do not change, as a consequence of student feedback is a fruitful area for further research.

Ratings by Peers

Peer ratings, based on actual classroom visitation, are often proposed as indicators of effective teaching (Braskamp, Brandenburg, and Ory, 1985; Centra, 1979; Cohen and McKeachie, 1980; French-Lazovich, 1981; also see Aleamoni, 1985), and hence a criterion for validating SETs. In studies where peer ratings are *not* based upon classroom visitation (e.g., Blackburn and Clark, 1975; Guthrie, 1954; Maslow and Zimmerman, 1956), SETs and peer ratings are substantially correlated, but it is likely that peer ratings are based on information from students. Centra (1975) compared peer ratings based on classroom visitation and SETs at a newly established university, thus reducing the probable confounding of the two sources of information. Three different peers evaluated each teacher on two occasions, but there was a relative lack of agreement among peers (mean r = .26) which calls into question their value as a criterion of effective teaching and precluded any good correspondence with SETs (r = .20).

Morsh, Burgess, and Smith (1956)[*] correlated SETs, student achievement, peer ratings, and supervisor ratings in a large multisection course. SETs correlated with achievement, supporting their validity. Peer and supervisor ratings, though significantly correlated with each other, were not related to either SETs or to achievement, suggesting that peer ratings may not have value as an indicator of effective teaching. Webb and Nolan (1955)[*] reported good correspondence between SETs and instructor self-evaluations, but neither of these indicators was positively correlated with supervisor ratings

---

[*]These two studies were conducted in a military settings which may limit their generality. Feldman (1989b), for example, specifically excluded them in his review of research within a university setting.

(which the authors indicated to be like peer ratings). Howard, Conway, and Maxwell (1985) found moderate correlations between SETs and instructor self-evaluations, but ratings by colleagues were not significantly correlated with SETs, self-evaluations, or the ratings of trained observers.

Other reviews of the peer evaluation process in higher education settings (e.g., Centra, 1979; Cohen and McKeachie, 1980; Braskamp, Brandenburg, and Ory, 1985; French-Lazovich, 1981) have also failed to cite studies that provide empirical support for the validity of peer ratings based on classroom visitation as an indicator of effective college teaching or as a criterion for SETs. Cohen and McKeachie (1980) and Braskamp, Brandenburg, and Ory (1985) suggested that peer ratings may be suitable for formative evaluation, but suggested that they may not be sufficiently reliable and valid to serve as a summative measure. Murray (1980), in comparing SETs and peer ratings, found peer ratings to be "(1) less sensitive, reliable, and valid; (2) more threatening and disruptive of faculty morale: and (3) more affected by non-instructional factors such as research productivity" (p.45) than SETs. Ward, Clark and Harrison (1981; also see Braskamp, Brandenburg, and Ory, 1985) suggested a methodological problem with the collection of peer ratings in that the presence of a colleague in the classroom apparently affects the classroom performance of the instructor and provides a threat to the external validity of the procedure. In summary, peer ratings based on classroom visitation do not appear to be very reliable or to correlate substantially with SETs or with any other indicator of effective teaching. While these findings neither support nor refute the validity of SETs, they clearly indicate that the use of peer evaluations of university teaching for personnel decisions is unwarranted (see Scriven, 1981 for further discussion).

Behavioral Observations By External Observers
At the precollege level, observational records compiled by specially trained observers are frequently found to be positively correlated with both SETs of teaching effectiveness and student achievement (see Rosenshine, 1971; Rosenshine and Furst, 1973 for reviews), and similar studies at the tertiary level are also encouraging (see Dunkin, 1986; Murray, 1980). Murray (1976) found high positive correlations between observers' frequency-of-occurrence estimates of specific teaching behaviors and an overall student rating. Cranton and Hillgarten (1981) examined relationships between SETs and specific teaching behaviors observed on videotaped lectures in a naturalistic setting; SETs of effectiveness of discussion were higher "when professors praised student behavior, asked questions and clarified or elaborated student responses" (p.73); SETs of organization were higher "when instructors spent time structuring classes and explaining relationships"(p.73). Murray (1980) concluded that SETs "can be accurately predicted from outside observer reports of specific classroom teaching behaviors" (p.31).

In one of the most ambitious observation studies, Murray (1983) trained observers to estimate the frequency of occurrence of specific teaching behaviors of 54 university instructors who had previously obtained high, medium or low SETs in other classes. A total of 18-to-24 sets of observer reports were collected for each instructor. The median of single-rater reliabilities (i.e., the correlation between two sets of observational reports) was .32, but the median reliability for the average response across the 18-24 reports for each instructor was .77. Factor analysis of the observations revealed nine factors, and their content resembled factors in SETs described earlier (e.g., Clarity, Enthusiasm, Interaction, Rapport, Organization). The observations significantly differentiated among the three criterion groups of instructors, but were also modestly correlated with a set of background variables (e.g., sex, age, rank, class size). Unfortunately, Murray only considered SETs on an overall instructor rating item, and these were based upon ratings from a previous course rather than the one that was observed. Hence, MTMM-type analyses could not be used to determine if specific observational factors were most highly correlated with matching student rating factors. The findings do show, however, that instructors who are rated differently by students do exhibit systematically different observable teaching behaviors.

Systematic observations by trained observers are positively correlated with both SETs and student achievement, even though peer ratings apparently are not systematically correlated with either SETs or student achievement. A plausible reason for this difference lies in the reliability of the different indicators. Class-average SETs are quite reliable, but the average agreement between ratings by any two students (i.e., the single rater reliability) is generally in the .20s. Hence, it is not surprising that agreement between two peer visitors who attend only a single lecture and respond to very general items is low. When observers are systematically trained and asked to rate the frequency of very specific behaviors, and there is a sufficient number of ratings of each teacher by different observers, then it is reasonable that their observations will be more reliable than peer ratings and more substantially correlated with SETs. However, further research is needed to clarify this suggestion. For example, Howard, Conway, and Maxwell (1985) examined both external observer ratings by trained graduate students and colleague ratings by untrained peers, but found that neither was significantly correlated with the other, with instructor self-evaluations, or with SETs. While peer ratings and behavioral observations have been considered as separate in the present article, the distinction may not be so clear in actual practice; peers can be trained to estimate the frequency of specific behaviors and some behavior observation schedules look like rating instruments.

The agreement between multifaceted observation schedules and multiple dimensions of SETs appears to be an important area for future research. However, a word of caution must be noted. The finding that specific teaching behaviors can be reliably observed and do vary from teacher to teacher, does not mean that they are important. Here, as with SETs, specific behaviors and observational factors must also be related to external indicators of effective teaching. In this respect the simultaneous collection of several indicators of effective teaching is important.

The Comparison of Ratings by Different Groups

Feldman (1989b) conducted an important review and meta-analysis of studies correlating overall evaluations of teaching effectiveness by current students, former students, colleagues, administrators, external observers, and instructor self-evaluations. Inspection of Table 6 (below the main diagonal) indicates that there are many combinations in which there are very few or no relevant studies. Of greater relevance to this chapter, the results are consistent with some conclusions offered here but appear to conflict with others. Consistent with research summarized here, the 3 highest correlations involve SETs by current students (the highest being the correlation between current and former students) whereas those involving self-evaluations are more modest. In contradiction to conclusions offered here, however, SETs were more highly correlated with ratings by colleagues, external observers, and administrators than with self-evaluations.

TABLE 6. Correlations between overall evaluations of teaching effectiveness by different groups based on Feldman's (1989a) review (below main diagonal) and on the Howard, Conway, and Maxwell (1985) study.

		1	2	3	4	5	6
1 Current Students	Mean r	1	.74**	.19	.24	—	.34*
	No.						
2 Former Students	Mean r	.69**	1	.33*	.08	—	.31*
	No.	6					
3 Colleagues	Mean r	.55**	.33[a]	1	−.12	—	-.13
	No.	14					
4 External Observers	Mean r	.50**	.08[b]	−.12[b]	1	—	.18
	No.	5	1	1			
5 Administrators	Mean r	.39**	c	.48**	c	1	—
	No.	11	c	5	c		
6 Self-Evaluations	Mean r	.29**	.31[a]	.15*	.22[b]	.08	1
	No.	19	1	6	2	5	

[a] There were insufficient studies to compute significance across studies, but the correlation within each study was statistically significant.

[b] There were insufficient studies to compute significance the correlation within each study was not statistically significant.

[c] There were no studies of this relation.

Note. Coefficients below the main diagonal are a summary of information Feldman's (1989a, Table 1 and Figure 1) review and readers should refer to that study for further information. Feldman reported relations as rs based on overall ratings or an average r for specific components. A single r from each study is used in the averages and for computing statistical significance (two-tailed p-levels) across the studies. Coefficients from the Howard, Conway, Maxwell study are based on evaluations of the same set of 43 instructors by different raters (administrator ratings were not included in this study).

Important limitations noted by Feldman (1989b) in interpreting his results in terms of validity issues need to be considered. The most appropriate tests of validity are based on studies in which ratings by different groups are independent of knowledge of ratings by other groups. This is clearly not the case in most studies of colleague and administrator ratings. Feldman noted that SET/colleague and SET/administrator relations in his review were infrequently based on actual classroom observation, and the relations were probably inflated by colleagues and administrators basing their ratings in part on information from students (e.g., prior SETs, discussion with students, or discussions with the instructor about prior SETs). Feldman did not specifically take this issue into account in his review (i.e., did not relate results to a between-study variable reflecting this issue) in part because of the paucity of relevant studies, whereas conclusions in this chapter focus more specifically on studies actually based on classroom observation. In this sense, the two sets of conclusions are not comparable. Also, in some self-evaluation studies considered by Feldman, instructors made ratings of their teaching effectiveness in general rather than ratings in relation to the specific class that was evaluated by students (e.g., Blackburn and Clark, 1975) whereas the focus in this chapter has been on SETs and self-evaluations of the same course at the end of the term (also see earlier discussion).

The Howard, Conway, and Maxwell (1985) study is particularly relevant to understanding the apparent discrepancies between conclusions offered here and by Feldman because it simultaneously considered 5 of 6 sources included in Feldman's review (all but administrator ratings). Howard, Conway, and Maxwell contrasted SEEQ construct validity research like that summarized in this chapter that usually considers only two or three indicators of teaching effectiveness for large samples with their study that examined five different indicators in a single study for a small sample. Forty-three instructors from a variety of disciplines were each evaluated in one course by: current students in the course (mean N=34 per class); former students who had previously taken the same course or one selected by the instructor as being similar (minimum N=5); one colleague who was knowledgeable of the course content and who attended two class sessions; and 8 advanced graduate students specifically trained in judging teaching effectiveness who attended two class sessions. Howard, Conway, and Maxwell concluded (see Table 6, above the main diagonal) that "former-students and student ratings evidence substantially greater validity coefficients of teaching effectiveness than do self-report, colleague and trained observer ratings" (p.195). Whereas self-evaluations were modestly correlated with current SETs (.34) and former SETs (.31), colleague and observer ratings were not significantly correlated with each other, current SETs, or self-evaluations (colleague ratings were significantly correlated with ratings by former students but not current students). Howard, Conway, and Maxwell's conclusions are generally consistent with the present conclusions but less consistent with those based on the Feldman (1989b) review. The critical difference, apparently, is that the present conclusions and those by Howard, Conway and Maxwell are based on evaluations of teaching effectiveness in a particular classroom whereas those by Feldman—at least for ratings by nonstudents—are infrequently based on actual classroom observation. The apparent inconsistencies in methodology, results, and interpretations require more empirical studies like that of Howard, Conway, and Maxwell and more detailed meta-analyses that take into account between-study differences.

Experimental Manipulations

Researchers have considered the effects of experimentally manipulated components of teaching effectiveness on SETs and other indicators of effective teaching. Whereas some of this research has focused on the effects of potential biases to SETs (see subsequent discussion), studies of teacher clarity (Land, 1985; Land and Combs, 1981; Marsh, 1987) and teacher expressiveness (Abrami, Leventhal, and Perry, 1982; Marsh and Ware, 1982; Marsh, 1987) demonstrate the important potential of this approach. Both these teaching behaviors are amenable to experimental and correlational designs, can be reliably judged by students and by external observers, are judged to be important components of teaching effectiveness by students and by teachers, and are related to student achievement in naturalistic and experimental studies. In experimental settings, scripted lessons which differ in these teaching behaviors are videotaped, and randomly assigned groups of subjects view different lectures, evaluate teaching effectiveness, and complete achievement tests. In studies of teacher clarity and teacher expressiveness, the manipulated teaching behaviors have been found to be systematically related to SETs and student achievement. Dunkin (1986), and Rosenshine and Furst (1973) were particularly impressed with the robustness of teacher clarity effects and their generality across different instruments, different raters, and different levels of education. The effects of teacher expressiveness are positively related to student achievement in both multisection validity studies already considered and the Dr. Fox studies considered below. Furthermore, when multiple dimensions of teaching effectiveness are evaluated, manipulations of these specific behaviors are substantially more strongly related to matching SET dimensions than to nonmatching SET dimensions. These patterns of findings support the inclusion of clarity and expressiveness on SET instruments, demonstrates that SETs are sensitive to natural and experimentally manipulated differences in these teaching behaviors, and support the construct validity of the SETs with respect to these teaching behaviors.

Research Productivity

Teaching and research are typically seen as the most important products of university faculty. Research helps instructors to keep abreast of new developments in their field and to stimulate their thinking, and this in turn provides one basis for predicting a positive correlation between research activity and SETs of teaching effectiveness. However, Blackburn (1974) caricatured two diametrically opposed opinions about the direction of the teaching/research relationship: (a) a professor cannot be a first rate teacher if he/she is not actively engaged in scholarship; and (b) unsatisfactory classroom performance results from the professor neglecting teaching responsibilities for the sake of publications. Marsh (1979, 1987; also see Centra, 1983; Feldman, 1987), in a review of studies that mostly used SETs as an indicator of teaching effectiveness, reported that there was virtually no evidence for a negative relationship between effectiveness in teaching and research; most studies found no significant relationship, and a few studies reported weak positive correlations. Marsh (1987; also see Frey, 1978) reported that the specific SET components most logically related to research were more highly correlated to research, but even these correlations were not substantial.

In trying to explain this lack of relation between teaching and research, Marsh (1987) argued that ability, effort, and reward structure were all critical variables. In a theoretical model of these relations, Marsh (1979, 1987) proposed that: a) the ability to be effective at teaching and research are *positively* correlated (a view consistent with the first opinion presented by Blackburn); b) time spent on research and teaching are *negatively correlated* (a view consistent with the second opinion presented by Blackburn) and may be influenced by a reward structure which systematically favors one over the other; c) effectiveness, in both teaching and research, is a function of both ability and time allocation; d) the positive relationship between abilities in the two areas and the negative correlation in time spent in the two areas will result in little or no correlation in measures of effectiveness in the two areas. Marsh reported some support for hypotheses (b), (c), and (d). In his review, Feldman (1987) found some indication that research productivity was positively correlated with time or effort devoted to research and, perhaps, negatively correlated with time or effort devoted to teaching. However, he found almost no support for the contention teaching effectiveness was related to time or effort devoted to either research or teaching. Thus, whereas there is some support for Marsh's model, important linkages were not supported and require further research.

In summary there appears to be a zero to low-positive correlation between measures of research productivity and SETs or other indicators of effective teaching, although correlations may be somewhat higher for student rating dimensions which are most logically related to research effectiveness. While these findings seem neither to support nor refute the validity of SETs, they do demonstrate that measures of research productivity cannot be used to infer teaching effectiveness or vice versa.

Summary and Implications of Validity Research

Effective teaching is a hypothetical construct for which there is no adequate single indicator. Hence, the validity of SETs or of any other indicator of effective teaching must be demonstrated through a construct validation approach. SETs are significantly and consistently related to a number of varied criteria including the ratings of former students, student achievement in multisection validity studies, faculty self-evaluations of their own teaching effectiveness, and, perhaps, the observations of trained observers on specific processes such as teacher clarity. This provides support for the construct validity of the ratings. Colleague and administrator ratings not based on classroom observation show substantial agreement with SETs, but these results must be interpreted cautiously. In contrast, colleague and administrator ratings that were based on classroom visitation, and research productivity, were shown to have little correlation with SETs, and since they are also relatively uncorrelated with other indicators of effective teaching, their validity as measures of effective teaching is problematic.

Nearly all researchers argue strongly that it is absolutely necessary to have multiple indicators of effective teaching whenever the evaluation of teaching effectiveness is to be used for personnel/tenure decisions. This emphasis on multiple indicators is clearly reflected in research described in this chapter. However, it is critical that the validity of all indicators of teaching effectiveness, not just SETs, be systematically examined before they are actually used. It seems ironic that researchers who argue that the validity of SETs has not been sufficiently demonstrated, despite the preponderance of research supporting their validity, are so willing to accept other indicators which have not been tested or have been shown to have little validity.

Researchers seem less concerned about the validity of information that is given to instructors for formative purposes such as feedback for the improvement of teaching effectiveness. This perspective may be justified, pending the outcome of further research, since there are fewer immediate consequences and legal implications. Nevertheless, even for formative purposes, the continued use of any sort of information about teaching effectiveness is not justified unless there is systematic research that supports its validity and aids in its interpretation. The implicit assumption that instructors will be able to separate valid and useful information from that which is not when evaluating formative feedback, while administrators will be unable to make this distinction when evaluating summative material, seems dubious.

Marsh and Overall (1980) distinguished between cognitive and affective criteria of effective teaching, arguing for the importance of affective outcomes as well as cognitive outcomes. Those findings indicate that cognitive and affective criteria need not be substantially correlated, and appear to be differentially related to different SET components. Cognitive criteria have typically been limited to student learning as measured in the multisection validity paradigm, and there are problems with such a narrow definition. In contrast, affective criteria have been defined as anything that seems to be noncognitive, and there are even more problems with such an open-ended definition. Further research is needed to define more systematically what is meant by affective criteria, perhaps in terms of the affective domains described elsewhere (e.g., Krathwohl, Bloom, and Masia, 1964), to operationally define indicators of these criteria, and to relate these to multiple student rating dimensions (Abrami, 1985). The affective side of effective teaching has not been given sufficient attention in SET research or, perhaps, in the study of teaching in general.

The disproportionate amount of attention given to the narrow definition of teaching effectiveness as student learning has apparently stifled research on a wide variety of criteria that are acceptable in the construct validation approach. While this broader approach to validation will undoubtedly provide an umbrella for dubious research as suggested by Doyle (1983), it also promises to bring new vigor and better understanding to SET research. In particular, there is a need for studies that consider many different indicators of teaching effectiveness in a single study. In his recent review of teaching and learning in the college classroom, McKeachie et al. (1990) emphasized the need to expand traditional models to include recent emphases on student cognition and other educational outcomes such as motivation, self-concept, and self-regulated learning. Elaborating on this point, McKeachie (personal communication, 19 March, 1991) noted that "as I see it one of our major problems is that we've typically used final examinations constructed by instructors as the measure of learning or educational achievement." He indicated that there was insufficient research considering relations between a diverse array of educational outcomes (e.g., taking advanced coursework, independent reading, problem solving skills, attitude changes) and specific SET components. In future research, it is imperative that SET researchers substantially expand the range of validity criteria that are related to SETs.

POTENTIAL BIASES IN STUDENTS' EVALUATIONS

The study of potential biases to SETs is voluminous, typically atheoretical, frequently methodologically flawed, and often not based on an articulated definition of what constitutes a bias. This is, however, an important area of SET research. To the extent that

SETs are biased it is important to understand the nature of the biases and how they can be controlled. Even though research suggests that SETs are not substantially biased, there is a belief among faculty that they are. For example, Marsh and Overall (1979b), consistent with other surveys of faculty (e.g., Jacobs, 1987), reported that faculty wanted teaching to be evaluated, but believed that SETs—as well as other indicators of effective teaching—were biased. Hence, it is important to counter such misconceptions. A comprehensive review of this research is beyond the scope of this chapter and interested readers are directed to the excellent series of articles by Feldman (1976a, 1976b, 1977, 1978, 1979, 1983, 1984, 1987, 1989a, 1989b), other review papers by Aubrect (1981), Cashin (1988), Marsh (1983, 1984b, 1985, 1987), and McKeachie (1973, 1979), monographs by Braskamp, Brandenburg, and Ory (1985), Centra (1979, 1989; Centra and Creech, 1976) and Murray (1980), and a chapter by Aleamoni (1981). Older reviews by Costin, Greenough and Menges (1971), Kulik and McKeachie (1975), and the annotated bibliography by de Wolf (1974) are also valuable.

Large-scale Empirical Studies

Marsh (1987) reviewed several large studies that have looked at the multivariate relationship between a comprehensive set of background characteristics and SETs. Between 5 percent and 25 percent of the variance in SETs could be explained, depending upon the nature of the SET items, the background characteristics, perhaps the academic discipline, and perhaps the institution(s) where the study was conducted. In comprehensive multivariate studies, Marsh (1980, 1983) found that a set of 16 background characteristics explained about 13 percent of the variance in the set of SEEQ dimensions. However, the amount of variance explained varied from more than 20 percent in the Overall Course rating and the Learning/Value dimension, to about 2 percent of the Organization and Individual Rapport dimensions. Four background variables were most important and could account for most of the explained variance; more favorable ratings were correlated with higher prior subject interest, higher expected grades, higher levels of Workload/Difficulty, and a higher percentage of students taking the course for General Interest Only. A path analysis demonstrated that prior subject interest had the strongest impact on SETs, and that this variable also accounted for about one-third of the relationship between expected grades and SETs. Marsh (1983) demonstrated a similar pattern of results in five different sets of courses (one of which was the set of courses used in the 1980 study) representing diverse academic disciplines at the graduate and undergraduate level, although the importance of a particular characteristic varied somewhat with the academic setting.

A Construct Approach to the Study of Bias

The finding that a background characteristic is correlated with SETs does not mean that the ratings are biased. Support for a bias hypothesis, as with the study of validity, must be based on a construct approach. This approach requires that the background characteristics that are hypothesized to bias SETs are examined in studies which are relatively free from methodological flaws using different approaches, and interpreted in relation to a specific definition of bias. Important and common methodological problems in the search for potential biases to SETs include the following:

6. Using correlation to argue for causation—the implication that some variable biases SETs argues that causation has been demonstrated, whereas correlation only implies that a concomitant relation exists.

7. Neglect of the distinction between practical and statistical significance—all conclusions should be based upon some index of effect size as well as on tests of statistical significance.

8. Failure to consider the multivariate nature of both SETs and a set of potential biases.

9. Selection of an inappropriate unit of analysis. Since nearly all applications of SETs are based upon class-average responses, this is nearly always the appropriate unit of analysis. The size and even the direction of correlations based on class-average responses may be different from correlations obtained when the analysis is performed on responses by individual students. Hence, effects based on individual students as the unit of analysis must also be demonstrated to operate at the class-average level.

10. Failure to examine the replicability of findings in a similar setting and their generalizability to different settings—particularly in studies based on small sample sizes or a single academic department at a single institution.

11. The lack of an explicit definition of bias against which to evaluate effects—if a variable actually affects teaching effectiveness and this effect is accurately reflected in SETs, then the influence is not a bias.

12. Questions of the appropriateness of experimental manipulations—studies that attempt to simulate hypothesized biases with operationally defined experimental manipulations must demonstrate that the size and nature of the manipulation and the observed effects are representative of those that occur in natural settings (i.e., they must examine threats to the external validity of the findings).

Theoretical Definitions of Bias

Inadequate definition of what constitutes a bias has hindered research. Demonstrating a relation—even a causal relation—is insufficient. For example, research reviewed earlier suggests that teacher clarity is causally related to SETs (as well as student achievement), but it makes no sense to argue that teacher clarity biases SETs. Support for a bias hypothesis must be based on a theoretically defensible definition of what constitutes a bias. Marsh (1987) reviewed alternative definitions of bias and their weaknesses. One common definition, for example, suggests that SETs are biased to the extent that they are affected by variables not under the control of the teacher. According to this definition, however, grading leniency (students giving better-than-deserved ratings to instructors as a consequence of instructors giving better-than-deserved grades to students) is not a bias, since grading leniency is clearly under the control of the instructor. This definition also confuses bias with what Marsh referred to as "fairness." If a variable X legitimately influences the effectiveness of instruction and this influence is validly represented in SETs, then the influence of X should not be interpreted as a bias. For example, prior subject interest apparently affects teaching effectiveness in a way that is accurately reflected by SETs (see discussion below). In this respect, prior subject interest is not a bias to SETs. It may not, however, be "fair" to compare ratings in courses that differ substantially in prior subject interest for personnel decisions unless the influence is removed using statistical control or appropriately constructed norm groups. While there is need for further clarification of the issues of bias and fairness, it is also important to distinguish between these two concepts so that they are not confused. The "fairness" of SETs needs to be examined separately from, or in addition to, their validity and susceptibility to bias. Some researchers (e.g., Hoyt, Owens, and Grouling, 1973; Brandenburg, Slindle, and Batista, 1977; also see Howard and Bray, 1979) seem to circumvent the problem of defining bias by statistically controlling for potential biases with multiple regression techniques or by forming normative (cohort) groups that are homogeneous with respect to potential biases (e.g., class size). Whereas this procedure may be appropriate in some instances, its use requires that a causal relation has been demonstrated and must still be defended in relation to a theoretically defensible definition of bias or fairness. Consistent with this approach, for purposes of feedback from SEEQ, separate normative comparisons are made within each academic unit for teaching assistants, for undergraduate courses, and for graduate level courses so long as each resulting norm group has a sufficient number of classes.

Approaches to Exploring for Potential Biases

McKeachie (1973) argued that SETs could be better understood if researchers did not concentrate exclusively on trying to interpret background relations as biases, but instead examined the meaning of specific relations. Following this orientation, several approaches to the study of background influences have been utilized. The most frequently employed approach is simply to correlate class-average SETs with a class-average measure of a background variable hypothesized to bias SETs. Such an approach can be heuristic, but in isolation it can never be used to demonstrate a bias. Instead, hypotheses generated from these correlational studies should be explored in further research that more fully tests the construct validity of bias interpretations.

One approach is to isolate a specific variable, simulate the variable with an experimental manipulation, and examine its effect in experimental studies where students are randomly assigned to treatment conditions. The internal validity (see Campbell and Stanley, 1973, for a discussion of internal and external threats to validity) of interpretations is greatly enhanced since many counter explanations that typically exist in correlational studies can be eliminated. However, this can only be accomplished at the expense of many threats to the external validity of interpretations: the experimental setting or the manipulation may be so contrived that the finding has little generalizability to the actual application of SETs; the size of the experimental manipulation may be unrealistic; the nature of the variable in question may be seriously distorted in its "operationalization"; and effects shown to exist when the individual student is the unit-of-analysis may not generalize when the class-average is used as the unit-of-analysis. Consequently, while the results of such studies can be very valuable, it is still incumbent upon the researcher to explore the external validity of the interpretations and to demonstrate that similar effects exist in real settings where SETs are actually employed. The most fully documented use of this technique is the series of "Dr. Fox" studies that are discussed below.

An alternative approach—a construct approach—recommended by Marsh (1987) has been the basis of much SEEQ research. Two aspects of this approach were emphasized. First, consistent with the multidimensionality of the SETs, specific variables should be differentially related to SEEQ factors. For example, class size is most logically related (inversely) to the Group Interaction and Individual Rapport factors, and this logical relation is empirically testable. Support for the predicted pattern of findings argues for the construct validity of the ratings. The second aspect is based upon the assumption that a "bias" that is specific to SETs should have little impact on other indicators of effective teaching. If a variable is related both to SETs and to other indicators of effective teaching, then the validity of the ratings is supported. Employing this approach, Marsh asked instructors in a large number of classes to evaluate their own teaching effectiveness with the same SEEQ form used by their students, and the SEEQ factors derived from both groups were correlated with background characteristics. Support for the interpretation of a bias in this situation requires that some variable be substantially correlated with SETs, but not with instructor self-evaluations of their own teaching (also see Feldman, 1984). Of course, even when a variable is substantially correlated with both student and instructor self-evaluations, it is still possible that the variable biases both SETs and instructor self-evaluations (Abrami, d'Apollonia, and Cohen, 1990), but such an interpretation requires that the variable is not substantially correlated with yet other valid indicators of effective teaching. Also, when the pattern of correlations between a specific variable and the SEEQ factors for students response is similar to the pattern based on faculty self-evaluations using SEEQ, there is further support for the validity of the SETs.

Effects of Specific Background Characteristics Emphasized in SEEQ Research

Results summarized below emphasize the description and explanation of the multivariate relations that exist between specific background characteristics and multiple dimensions of SETs. This is a summary of findings based upon some of the most frequently studied and/or the most important background characteristics, and of different approaches to understanding the relationships. In this section the effects of the five background characteristics that have been most extensively examined and shown to be related to some SET components in SEEQ research are examined: class size; workload/difficulty; prior subject interest; expected grades; reason for taking a course.

Class Size
Class size is moderately correlated with Group Interaction and Individual Rapport (negatively, rs as large as –.30), but not with other SEEQ dimensions or with the overall rat-

ings of course or instructor (Centra and Creech, 1976; Feldman, 1978, 1984; Marsh, Overall, and Kesler, 1979a; Marsh, 1980, 1983). There is also a significant nonlinear component to this relation in which small and very large classes were evaluated more favorably. However, since the majority of class sizes occur in the range where the relation is negative, the overall correlation is negative. A similar pattern of results was found between class size and instructor self-evaluations of their own teaching (Marsh, Overall, and Kesler, 1979a; also see Table 7). The specificity of the class size effect to dimensions most logically related to this variable, and the similarity of findings based on SETs and faculty self-evaluations argue that this effect is not a "bias" to SETs; rather, class size does have moderate effects on the aspects of effective teaching (primarily Group Interaction and Individual Rapport) to which it is most logically related and these effects are accurately reflected in the SETs. This discussion of the class size effect clearly illustrates why SETs cannot be adequately understood if their multidimensionality is ignored (also see Feldman, 1984; Frey, 1978) and why it is important to evaluate potential biases within a construct approach.

Prior Subject Interest

Marsh (1987; Marsh and Cooper, 1981; also see Feldman, 1977; Howard and Maxwell, 1980; Howard and Schmeck, 1979) reviewed previous studies of the relation of prior subject interest to SETs and faculty self-evaluations. The effect of prior subject interest on SEEQ scores was greater than that of any of the 15 other background variables considered by Marsh (1980, 1983). In different studies prior subject interest was consistently more highly correlated with Learning/Value (rs about .4) than with any other SEEQ dimensions (rs between .3 and −.12). Instructor self-evaluations of their own teaching were also positively correlated with both their own and their students' perceptions of students' prior subject interest (see Table 7). The self-evaluation dimensions that were most highly correlated with prior subject interest, particularly Learning/Value, were the same as with SETs. The specificity of the prior subject interest effect to dimensions most logically related to this variable, and the similarity of findings based on SETs and faculty self-evaluations argue that this effect is not a "bias" to SETs. Rather, prior subject interest is a variable that influences some aspects of effective teaching, particularly Learning/Value, and these effects are accurately reflected in both the SETs and instructor self-evaluations. Higher student interest in the subject apparently creates a more favorable learning environment and facilitates effective teaching, and this effect is validly reflected in SETs as well as faculty self-evaluations.

Prior subject interest apparently influences teaching effectiveness in a way that is validly reflected in SETs, and so the influence should not be interpreted as a bias to SETs. However, to the extent that the influence is inherent in a particular course content, it may represent a source of "unfairness" when ratings are used for personnel decisions. If further research confirms these interpretations, then it may be appropriate to use normative comparisons or cohort groups to correct for this influence.

TABLE 7. Background characteristics: Correlations with student ratings (S) and faculty self-evaluations (F) of their own teaching effectiveness (n = 183 undergraduate courses). (*Reprinted from Marsh [1984b by permission of the American Psychological Association.*)

Background Characteristics	Learn	Enthus	Organ	Group	Individ	Brdth	Exams	Assign	Wrkld	Over Crse	Over Instr
Faculty Rating "Scholarly production in their discipline" (1 = *well below average to 5 = well above average*)											
S	17	07	18	04	06	21	04	17	11	14	16
F	28	20	40	09	11	26	25	25	10	40	41
Students Rating Course Workload/Difficulty (1 = *low to 5 = high*)											
S	20	08	01	04	06	18	04	23	53	26	16
F	-03	-04	03	03	00	00	21	15	—	17	09
Faculty Rating Course Workload/Difficulty (1 = *low to 5 = high*)											
S	08	02	01	-03	04	02	05	12	—	15	08
F	07	03	15	-09	10	-06	21	21	53	29	16
Students Rating expected course grade (1 = *F to 5 = A*)											
S	28	20	05	38	16	01	28	24	-25	26	27
F	11	-03	-07	17	-10	-11	-11	02	-19	-01	00
Faculty Rating of "Grading Leniency" (1 = *easy/lenient to 5 = hard/strict*)											
S	-04	-16	-06	06	-08	-05	-05	-02	26	-06	-10
F	00	04	06	16	14	08	32	19	28	14	03
Class size/enrollment (actual number of students enrolled)											
S	-24	-04	-13	-36	-21	-09	-22	-09	-07	-18	-20
F	-02	03	10	-43	-17	-03	-03	-11	-04	-04	-09
Faculty rating "Enjoy teaching relative to other duties" (1 = *extremely unenjoyable to 5 = extremely enjoyable*)											
S	25	34	18	22	33	00	20	09	03	29	32
F	24	39	01	10	12	-21	-20	03	-03	15	22
Faculty Rating "Ease of teaching particular course" (1 = *very easy to 5 = very difficult*)											
S	07	-01	10	11	06	09	09	01	05	03	08
F	-12	-16	-07	17	12	06	05	04	17	-14	-10

SEEQ factor*

Note. SEEQ = Students' Evaluations of Educational Quality. Correlations are presented without decimal points; all those greater than .15 are statistically significant. For more detail, see Marsh and Overall (1979b).

*See Table 1 for full factor names.

Workload/Difficulty

Workload/Difficulty is frequently cited by faculty as a potential bias to SETs in the belief that offering less demanding courses will lead to better SETs. For this reason, Workload/Difficulty has been considered as a potential bias in SEEQ studies even though it is also one of the SEEQ factors. Whereas the Workload/Difficulty effect was one of the largest in SEEQ research, the direction of the effect was opposite to that expected if this variable was a bias; Workload/Difficulty was positively correlated with SETS. Other research reviewed by Marsh (1987) was generally consistent with SEEQ results. Marsh and Overall (1979b) also reported that instructor self-evaluations of their own teaching effectiveness tended to be positively related to Workload/Difficulty (see Table 7). Results based on the large, multi-institution data base for the IDEA instrument suggest that SETs are even more positively related to Workload/Difficulty than are SEEQ results (see Cashin, 1988). Since the direction of the Workload/Difficulty effect is opposite to that predicted as a potential bias, and since this finding is consistent for both SETs and instructor self-evaluations, Workload/Difficulty does not appear to constitute a bias to SETs.

Expected Grades

SEEQ research and literature reviews (e.g., Centra, 1979; Feldman, 1976a; Marsh, Overall, and Thomas, 1976) have typically found class-average expected grades to be positively correlated with SETs. The critical issue is how this relation should be interpreted, and there are three quite different explanations for this finding. (1) The grading leniency hypothesis proposes that instructors who give higher-than-deserved grades will be rewarded with higher-than-deserved SETs, and this constitutes a serious bias to SETs. (2) The validity hypothesis proposes that better expected grades reflect better student learning, and that a positive correlation between student learning and SETs supports the validity of SETs. In multisection validity studies, for example, relations between grades and SETs were interpreted as support for the validity of SETs although the grading leniency hypothesis may be a viable counter-explanation. (3) The student characteristics hypothesis proposes that preexisting student presage variables such as prior subject interest may affect student learning, student grades, and teaching effectiveness, so that the expected grade effect is spurious. While these explanations of the expected grade effect have quite different implications, it should be noted that grades, actual or expected, must surely reflect some combination of student learning, the grading standards employed by an instructor, and preexisting presage *Path analyses.* Marsh (1980, 1983) examined the relations among expected grades, prior subject interest, and SETs in a path analysis (also see Aubrect, 1981; Feldman, 1976a). Across all rating dimensions, nearly one-third of the expected grade effect could be explained in terms of prior subject interest. Since prior subject interest precedes expected grades, a large part of the expected grade effect is apparently spurious, and this finding supports the student characteristic hypothesis. Marsh, however, interpreted the results as support for the validity hypothesis in that prior subject interest is likely to impact student performance in a class, but is unlikely to affect grading leniency. Hence, support for the student characteristics hypothesis may also constitute support for the validity hypothesis; prior subject interest produces more effective teaching which leads to better student learning, better grades, and higher evaluations. This interpretation, however, depends on a definition of bias in which SETs are not "biased" to the extent that they reflect variables which actually influence effectiveness of teaching.

In a similar analysis, Howard and Maxwell (1980; also see Howard and Maxwell, 1982), found that most of the covariation between expected grades and class-average overall ratings was eliminated by controlling for prior student motivation and student progress ratings. In their path analysis, prior student motivation had a causal impact on expected grades that was nearly the same as reported in SEEQ research and a causal effect on overall ratings which was even larger, while the causal effect of expected grades on SETs was smaller than that found in SEEQ research. They concluded that "the influence of student motivation upon student performance, grades, and satisfaction appears to be a more potent contributor to the covariation between grades and satisfaction than does the direct contaminating effect of grades upon student satisfaction" (p. 818).

Faculty self-evaluations. Marsh and Overall (1979b) examined correlations among SETs and instructor self-evaluations of teaching effectiveness, SETs of expected grades, and teacher self-evaluations of their own "grading leniency" (see Table 7). Correlations between expected grades and SETs were positive and modest (rs between .01 and .28) for all SEEQ factors except Group Interaction (r=.38) and Workload/Difficulty (r=−25). Correlations between expected grades and faculty self-evaluations were close to zero (rs between −.11 and .11) except for Group Interaction (r=.17) and Workload/Difficulty (r=−.19). Correlations between faculty self-perceptions of their own "grading leniency" (on an "easy/lenient grader" to "hard/strict grader" scale) with both student and teacher evaluations of effective teaching were small (rs between −.16 and .19) except for ratings of Workload/Difficulty (rs of .26 and .28) and faculty self-evaluations of Examinations/Grading (r=.32). In a separate study Marsh (1976) also reported small, generally nonsignificant correlations between faculty self-evaluations of their grading leniency and SETs, but found that "easy" graders received somewhat (significantly) lower overall course and Learning/value ratings. The correlations between grading leniency and SETs, and the similarity in the pattern of correlations between expected grades and ratings by students and by faculty, seem to argue against the interpretation of the expected grade effect as a bias. Nevertheless, the fact that expected grades were more positively correlated with SETs than with faculty self-evaluations may provide some support for a grading leniency bias.

Experimental manipulation of expected grades. Some researchers have argued that the expected grade effect can be better examined by randomly assigning students to different groups which are given systematically different grade expectations. Marsh (1987; also see Abrami, Dickens, Perry, and Leventhal, 1980) reviewed studies of this sort in which grades were experimentally manipulated by assigning grades that were different from the ones that students had earned or expected, or using different grading standards in different sections of the same course. Particularly when students received grades that were different from what they had earned, the nature of the experimental manipulations did not seem to match naturally occurring differences in grading standards. Even when grading standards were manipulated for different sections of the same course, it is likely that students from different sections realized they were being graded according to different standards.

Abrami et al. (1980) conducted what appears to be the most methodologically sound study of the effects of experimentally manipulated grading standards on SETs. After reviewing previous research they described two "Dr. Fox" type experiments in which grading standards were experimentally manipulated. Groups of students viewed a videotaped lecture, rated teacher effectiveness, and completed an objective exam. Students returned two weeks later when they were given their examination results and a grade based on their actual performance but scaled according to different grading standards (i.e., an "average" grade earning a B, C+, or C). The subjects then viewed a similar videotaped lecture by the same instructor, again evaluated teacher effectiveness, and took a test on the content of the second lecture. The manipulation of grading standards had no effect on performance on the second achievement test and weak inconsistent effects on SETs. There were also other manipulations (e.g., instructor expressiveness, content, and incentive), but the effect of grading standards accounted for no more than 2 percent of the variance in SETs for any of the conditions, and failed to reach statistical significance in some. Not even the direction of the effect was consistent across conditions, and stricter grading standards occasionally resulted in higher ratings. These findings fail to support the contention that grading leniency produces an effect that is of practical significance, although the external validity of this interpretation may also be *Other approaches*. Marsh (1982a) compared differences in expected grades with differences in SETs for pairs of offerings of the same course taught by the same instructor on two different occasions. He reasoned that differences in expected grades in this situation probably represent differences in student performance, since grading standards are likely to remain constant, and differences in prior subject interest were small and relatively uncorrelated with differences in SETs. He found even in this context that students in the more favorably evaluated course tended to have higher expected grades, which argued against the grading leniency hypothesis. It should be noted, however, that while this study is in a setting where differences due to grading leniency are minimized, there is no basis for contending that the grading leniency effect does not operate in other situations. Also, the interpretation is based on the untested assumption that differences in expected grades reflected primarily differences in student performance rather than differences in the grading standards by the instructor.

Peterson and Cooper (1980) compared SETs of the same instructors by students who received grades and those who did not. The study was conducted at two colleges where students were free to cross-enroll, but where students from one college were assigned grades but those from the other were not. Class-average ratings were determined separately for students in each class who received grades and those who did not, and there was substantial agreement with evaluations by the two groups of students. Hence, even though class-average grades of those students who received grades were correlated with their class-average evaluations and showed the expected grade effect, their class-average evaluations were in substantial agreement with those of students who did not receive grades. This suggests that the expected grade effect was not due to grading leniency, since grading leniency was unlikely to affect ratings by students who did not receive grades.

Gigliotti and Buchtel (1990) tested SETs for a self-serving bias, an attributional effect in which individuals take credit for their successes (good grades) but attribute their failures (poor grades) to external causes. Thus, for example, students who do poorly or more poorly than they expect, may rate instructors more poorly than they deserve. Interestingly, this approach does not predict a grading-leniency bias in that students who do well or better than expected will take credit for their successes and not attribute them to the instructor. However, analyses based on the course grade and on differences between expected and actual course grades provided little consistent evidence for a self-serving bias. Expected grades, actual grades, and grade violations were all unrelated to class-average ratings of instructor skills, instructor support, fairness of the course, and overall instructor ratings. Class-average grades were, however, related to ratings of "personal fit" (e.g., usefulness of course) and impact on self-feelings (e.g., how course affected feelings of self), but not in a way that was predicted by a self-serving bias. The authors interpreted their results as supporting Marsh's (1984) conclusion about the relative lack of bias in SETs due to actual or expected grades.

Summary. Evidence from a variety of different types of research clearly supports the validity hypothesis and the student characteristics hypothesis, but does not rule out the possibility that a grading leniency effect operates simultaneously. Support for the grading leniency effect was found with some experimental studies, but these effects were typically weak and inconsistent, may not generalize to nonexperimental settings where SETs are actually used, and in some instances may be due to the violation of grade expectations that students had falsely been led to expect or that were applied to other students in the same course. Consequently, while it is possible that a grading leniency effect may produce some bias in SETs, support for this suggestion is weak and the size of such an effect is likely to be insubstantial in the actual use of SETs.

Reason for Taking a Course

Courses are often classified as being elective or required courses, but preliminary SEEQ research indicated that this dichotomy may be too simplistic. On SEEQ students indicate one of the following as the reason why they took the course: a) major requirement; b) major elective; c) general interest; d) general education requirement; e) minor/related field; or f) other. All SEEQ factors tended to be positively correlated with the percentage of students taking a course for general interest and as a major elective, but tended to be negatively correlated with the percentage of students taking a course as a major requirement or as a general education requirement. After controlling for the effects of the set of 16 background characteristics, however, general interest was the only reason to have a substantial effect on ratings and it accounted for most of the variance that could be explained by the subset of five reasons. The percentage of students taking a course for general interest was also one of the four background variables selected from the set of 16 as having the largest impact on SETs and included in Marsh's (1980, 1983) path analyses. Marsh (1980, 1983) consistently found the percentage taking a course for general interest to be positively correlated with each of the SEEQ factors in different academic disciplines. However, the sizes of the correlations were modest, usually less than .20, and the effect of this variable was smaller than that of the other three variables (prior subject interest, expected grades, and workload/difficulty) considered in his path analyses. The correlations were somewhat larger for Learning/value, Breadth of Coverage, Assignments, Organization and overall course ratings than for the other SEEQ dimensions, but only the correlations with Breadth of Coverage were as large as or larger than those of the other variables considered in the path analysis.

Other researchers have typically compared elective courses with required courses, or have related the percentage of students taking a course as an elective (or a requirement) to SETs, but these approaches may not be directly comparable to SEEQ research. Large empirical studies have typically found that a course's electivity is positively correlated to student rating (e.g., Brandenburg, Slindle, and Batista, 1977; Pohlman, 1975; but also see Centra and Creech, 1976). These findings are also consistent with Feldman's 1978 review. Thus, these generalizations appear to be consistent with the SEEQ research.

Effects of Specific Background Characteristics Not Emphasized in SEEQ Research

Marsh (1980, 1983) examined the relations between a wide variety of background characteristics, but concluded that most of the variance in SETs that could be accounted for by the entire set could be explained by those characteristics discussed above. The effects of other characteristics, though much smaller, are considered briefly below. A few additional characteristics were examined in particular SEEQ studies (e.g., the faculty self-evaluation studies) that were not available for the large scale studies, and these are also discussed below. Finally, the results are compared with the findings of other investigators, particularly those summarized in Feldman's set of review articles.

Instructor Rank and Years Teaching Experience

SEEQ research has found that teaching assistants receive lower ratings than regular faculty for most rating dimensions and overall rating items, but that they may receive slightly higher ratings for Individual Rapport and perhaps Group Interaction (e.g., Marsh, 1976, 1980; Marsh and Overall, 1979b). Marsh and Overall (1979b) found this same pattern in a comparison of self-evaluations by teaching assistants and self-evaluations by regular faculty. Large empirical studies by Centra and Creech (1976) and by Brandenburg, Slindle, and Batista (1977) and Feldman's 1983 review also indicate that teaching assistants tend to receive lower evaluations than do other faculty (although Feldman also reported some exceptions).

Once teaching assistants are excluded from the analysis, relations between rank and SETs are much smaller in SEEQ research. There is almost no relation between rank and global ratings, while faculty rank is somewhat positively correlated with Breadth of Coverage and somewhat negatively correlated with Group Interaction. These results for the global ratings are consistent with large empirical studies (e.g., Aleamoni and Yimer, 1973; Brandenburg, Slindle, and Batista, 1977; Centra and Creech, 1976). Feldman (1983) reported that a majority of the studies in his review found no significant effect of instructor rank on global ratings, but that the significant relations that were found were generally positive. Feldman also reported that rank was not significantly related to more specific rating dimensions in a majority of studies, but that positive relations tended to be more likely for dimensions related to instructor knowledge and intellectual expansiveness whereas negative relations were more likely for ratings of encouragement of discussion, openness, and concern for students. Marsh and Hocevar (1991b; see earlier discussion) found that the ratings received by the same cohort of teachers who were evaluated continuously over a 13-year period showed little or no changes over this period.

Course Level

In SEEQ research, higher level courses—particularly graduate level courses—tend to receive slightly higher ratings (e.g., Marsh, 1976, 1980, 1983; Marsh and Overall, 1979b). Marsh and Overall (1979b) found that both SETs and faculty self-evaluations tended to be higher in graduate level courses than undergraduate courses. Marsh and Hocevar (1991b) also found this relation even when comparing SETs of the same teachers in graduate and undergraduate classes. In his review of this relation, Feldman (1978) also found that SETs tended to be positively related to course level. The effect of course level is typically diminished and may even disappear when other background variables are controlled (see Braskamp, Brandenburg, and Ory, 1985; Feldman, 1978; Marsh, 1980) but this finding is difficult to interpret without a specific model of the causal ordering of such variables.

Sex of Students and/or Instructor

Empirical studies (e.g., Centra and Creech, 1976; Pohlman, 1975) and Feldman's 1977 review indicate that student sex has little effect on SETs, although Feldman notes that when significant effects are reported women may give slightly higher ratings than men. Similarly, large empirical studies (e.g., Brandenburg, Slindle, and Batista, 1977; Brown, 1976) and McKeachie's 1979 review suggest that the sex of the instructor has little relation to SETs, although Dukes and Victoria (1989) and Feldman suggest a weak tendency for women teachers to receive higher ratings.

Feldman (1977) also considered student-gender by teacher-gender interactions, but few of the studies in his review provided relevant information. Since his review, however, additional research has examined this interaction. Because it is difficult to disentangle true sex differences from sex biases in correlational studies, it is particularly interesting to consider experimental studies. In three studies (Basow, 1987; Basow and Distenfeld, 1985; Winocur, Schoen, and Sirowatka, 1989), Dr. Fox type designs were employed (see later discussion of Dr. Fox studies) in which male and female actors were videotaped presenting experimentally manipulated lessons and students were randomly assigned to different conditions. The design variables were student gender, teacher gender, and instructional style. Higher instructor ratings were associated with higher levels of instructor expressiveness in the two Basow studies and an affiliative (as opposed to an instrumental) presentation style in the Winocur study. The effects of teacher gender, student gender, and their interaction, however, were either nonsignificant or very small in all three studies. Dukes and Victoria (1989) presented written scenarios depicting a teacher who was either male or female. In different conditions, teachers were described as high or low in different components of teaching effectiveness (knowledge, enthusiasm, rapport, and organization) and differed in status (department chairperson or not). In none of the conditions were the effects of teacher gender, student gender or their interaction statistically significant. Dukes and Victoria concluded that ratings in their study were primarily a function of the components of teaching effectiveness rather than gender or status. These experimental studies are apparently consistent with survey studies in showing that student gender and teacher gender have little effect on SETs.

Administration and Stated Purpose of the Ratings
Feldman's 1979 review suggests that some aspects of the manner in which SETs are administered may influence the ratings. Feldman (also see Braskamp, Brandenburg, and Ory, 1985) reported that anonymous ratings tended to be somewhat lower than non-anonymous ratings, and this effect may be stronger when teachers are given the ratings before assigning grades, when students feel they may be called upon to justify or elaborate their responses, or, perhaps, when students view the instructor as vindictive. Feldman (1979) reported that ratings tend to be higher when they are to be used for administrative purposes than when used for feedback to faculty or for research purposes, but that the size of this effect may be very small (also see Centra, 1979; Frankhouser, 1984). Feldman (1979) reported that ratings tended to be similar whether collected in the middle of the term, near the end of the term, during the final exam or even after completion of the course. Marsh and Overall (1980), however, suggested that end-of-term ratings may be less valid than mid-term ratings. Whereas these influences may not be large, all aspects of the administration process should be standardized.

Academic Discipline
Feldman (1978) reviewed studies that compared ratings across disciplines and found that ratings are: somewhat higher than average in English, humanities, arts, languages, and, perhaps, education; somewhat lower than average in social sciences, physical sciences, mathematics and engineering, and business administration; and about average in biological sciences. The Centra and Creech 1976 study and the Cashin and Clegg (1987) studies are particularly important because they were based on a very large number of courses from many different institutions. Centra and Creech classified courses as natural sciences, social sciences and humanities and found that ratings were highest in humanities and lowest in natural sciences. However, even though these results were highly significant, the differences accounted for less than 1 percent of the variance in the SETs.

For global items, Cashin and Clegg (1987) reported a similar pattern of discipline differences to those reported by Feldman (1978): the highest ratings were for humanities and arts courses, followed by social science courses, with the lowest ratings for mathematics, science, and economics courses. Whereas discipline differences were not large for global summary items, there were large differences for SETs of their progress on particular objectives. For example, ratings of "developing skill in expressing myself orally and in writing" were substantially higher in English, Language, and Letters than other disciplines, ratings of "discovering the implications of the course materials for understanding myself" were higher in Arts, Letters, Psychology, and Sociology, whereas ratings of "gaining factual knowledge (terminology, classifications, methods, trends)" were higher in mathematics and Biology. Particularly for these progress items, there appears to be a logical correspondence between the item content and the observed differences. It should also be noted, however, that these items are not like those that typically appear on SET instruments.

Neumann and Neumann (1983), based on Biglan's 1973 theory, classified academic areas according to whether they had: a) a well-defined paradigm structure (hard/soft); b) an orientation towards application (applied/pure); and c) an orientation to living organisms (life/nonlife). Consistent with a priori predictions based on the nature of instruction in different combinations, the authors found that SETs were higher in soft, in pure, and in nonlife disciplines. While the effects of all three facets on SETs were significant, the effect of the hard/soft facet was largest. The authors indicated that teachers in paradigmatic areas where research procedures are not well-developed play a more major role than in paradigmatic areas where the content and method of research is well-developed. On the basis of this research, the authors argued that SETs should only be compared within similar disciplines and that campus-wide comparisons may be unwarranted since the role of teaching varies in different academic areas. The generality of these findings may be limited since the results were based on a single institution. Further tests of the generality of these findings are important. The findings also suggest that discipline differences observed in SETs may reflect the different roles of teaching in these disciplines that are accurately reflected in the SETs.

There may be consistent differences in SETs due to academic discipline, but the relations are generally small for typical SET items. Also, it is possible that such differences are inherent in the discipline rather than a function of differences in teaching effectiveness. Nevertheless, since there are few large, multi-institutional studies of this relation, conclusions must be tentative. The implications of such a relation, if it exists, depend on the use of the SETs. At institutions where SEEQ has been used, administrative use of the SETs is at the school or division level, and SETs are not compared across diverse academic disciplines. In such a situation, the relation between ratings and discipline may be less critical than in a setting where ratings are compared across all disciplines.

Personality of the Instructor
The relation between the personality of an instructor and SETs is important for at least two different reasons. First, there is sometimes the suspicion that the relation is substantial and that instructor personality has nothing to do with being an effective teacher, so that the relation should be interpreted as a bias to SETs. Second, if the relation is signif-

icant, then the results may have practical and theoretical importance for distinguishing between effective and ineffective teachers, and for a better understanding of teaching effectiveness and personality.

Feldman's review (1986), because of the limited number of studies, emphasized relations between overall SETs (rather than separate instructional dimensions) and 14 categories of personality as inferred from self-reports by the instructor or as inferred from ratings by others (students or colleagues). For studies of personality based on self-report measures, the only practically significant correlations were for "positive self-regard, self-esteem" (mean r=.30) and "energy and enthusiasm" (mean r=.27); the mean correlation was .15 or less between SETs of teaching effectiveness and each of the other 12 areas of personality. In contrast, when personality was inferred from ratings by students or colleagues, the correlations were much higher; the average correlations between SETs and most of the 14 categories of personality were between .3 and .6.

Murray, Rushton, and Paunonen (1990) conducted an important study of relations between teacher personality and SETs. Using archive data, overall ratings of 46 instructors in up to 6 different types of courses ranging from freshman lecture courses to graduate seminars were considered. For each instructor between 9 and 15 sets of colleague ratings were obtained on a set of 29 personality traits. Patterns of zero-order correlations varied substantially depending on course type; in a few instances the same personality trait (e.g., seeks help and advice) correlated significantly and in the opposite direction with teaching effectiveness for different course types. Stepwise multiple regressions conducted separately within each course type indicated that substantial proportions of the variance in overall ratings could be explained by the first five personality traits to enter the equation. Because the number of instructors representing each course type was small (ns of 29 to 40) relative to the number of personality traits, there is likely to be substantial capitalization on chance that was only partly controlled.[*] Factor analyses of the 29 personality traits identified five well-defined factors. Profiles of the instructors most effective in the various categories indicated substantial differences in the different course types—particularly undergraduate and graduate level courses. Instructors most effective in all undergraduate courses, for example, were high in Extroversion whereas instructors most effective in graduate level courses were only average in Extroversion.

Feldman's review and the Murray, Rushton, and Paunonen (1990) study suggest that there is a relation between SETs and at least some aspects of the instructor's personality,

---

[*]Using stepwise multiple regression, Murray, Rushton, and Paunonen (1990) used the best five of 29 personality traits to predict overall ratings of between 29 and 40 instructors for each course type. Recognizing the potential for capitalizing on chance, they presented adjusted R^2 values based on 5 predictor variables. In fact, however, there were 29 possible predictor variables—not 5—and so their correction substantially underestimated the likely capitalization on chance. Correcting for 29 predictor variables would result in trivial R^2, but this approach probably overcorrects for capitalization on chance. One better compromise would be to use the five personality factor scores (derived from the 29 traits) to predict overall ratings, but these results were not presented. Based on the information presented it is difficult to determine the strength of relations between personality ratings and SETs.

but does not indicate whether this is a valid source of influence or a source of bias. As noted with other sources of influence, if teacher personality characteristics influence other indicators of teaching effectiveness in a manner similar to their influence on SETs, then the relation should be viewed as supporting the validity of SETs. Murray, Rushton, and Paunonen interpreted their findings to mean that an instructor's personality is translated into specific teaching behaviors that are accurately reflected in SETs. In support of this claim, earlier research by Erdle, Murray and Rushton (1985) found that more than 50 percent of the relation between personality and SETs was mediated by specific classroom behaviors. Using a perspective similar to that used here, they argued that such relations support the validity of SETs and should not be viewed as a source of invalidity. Neither Feldman's review nor the Murray, Rushton, and Paunonen study examined the pattern of relations between specific components of personality and specific student evaluation factors, and this is unfortunate. Logically, some specific aspects of an instructor's personality should be systematically related to some specific student evaluation factors. For example, enthusiasm is frequently measured by personality inventories and SET instruments and so the two measures of enthusiasm should be substantially correlated. Feldman's review indicated that personality inferred by others—like those in the Murray, Rushton, and Paunonen study—is substantially more correlated with SETs than personality inferred from self-responses. This distinction would seem to be important in establishing the practical significance of these findings for SET research and the theoretical implications for personality research.

The Dr. Fox Paradigm

The Dr. Fox effect is defined as the overriding influence of instructor expressiveness on SETs. The results of Dr. Fox studies have been interpreted to mean that an enthusiastic lecturer can entice or seduce favorable evaluations, even though the lecture may be devoid of meaningful content. In the original Dr. Fox study by Naftulin, , J. E., and Donnelly (1973), a professional actor called "Dr. Fox" lectured to educators and graduate students in an enthusiastic and expressive manner, and teaching effectiveness was evaluated. Despite the fact that the lecture content was specifically designed to have little educational value, the ratings were favorable. The authors and critics agree that the study was fraught with methodological weaknesses, including the lack of any control group, a poor rating instrument, the brevity of the lecture compared to an actual course, the unfamiliar topic coupled with the lack of a textbook with which to compare the lecture, and so on (see Abrami, Leventhal, and Perry, 1982; Frey, 1979; Marsh, 1987; Marsh and Ware, 1982; Ware and Williams, 1975). Frey (1979) notes that "this study represents the kind of research that teachers make fun of during the first week of an introductory course in behavioral research methods. Almost every feature of the study is problematic" (p.1). Nevertheless, reminiscent of the Rodin and Rodin (1972) study described earlier, the results of this study were seized upon by critics as support for the invalidity of SETs.

To overcome some of the problems, Ware and Williams (Ware and Williams, 1975, 1977; Williams and Ware, 1976, 1977) developed the standard Dr. Fox paradigm where a series of six lectures, all presented by the same professional actor was videotaped. Each lecture represented one of three levels of course content (the number of substantive teaching points covered) and one of two levels of lecture expressiveness (the expressiveness with which the actor delivered the lecture). Students viewed one of the six lectures, evaluated teaching effectiveness on a typical multi-item rating form, and completed an achievement test based upon all the teaching points in the high content lecture. Ware and Williams (1979, 1980) reviewed their studies, and similar studies by other researchers, and concluded that differences in expressiveness consistently explained much more variance in SETs than did differences in content.

Reanalyses and Meta-analyses

A reanalysis. Marsh and Ware (1982) reanalyzed data from the Ware and Williams studies. A factor analysis of the rating instrument identified five evaluation factors which varied in the way they were affected by the experimental manipulations. In the condition most like the university classroom, where students were told before viewing the lecture that they would be tested on the materials and that they would be rewarded in accordance with the number of exam questions which they answered correctly (incentive before lecture), the Dr. Fox effect was *not* supported. The instructor expressiveness manipulation only affected ratings of Instructor Enthusiasm, the factor most logically related to that manipulation, and content coverage significantly affected ratings of Instructor Knowledge and Organization/Clarity, the factors most logically related to that manipulation. Research by Perry (see Perry, 1991; Perry and Magnusson, 1987; Perry and Penner, 1990) provides empirical support for the broader implications of this variable for student motivation and performance. When students were given no incentives to perform well, instructor expressiveness had more impact on all five student rating factors than when external incentives were present, though the effect on Instructor Enthusiasm was still largest. However, without external incentives, expressiveness also had a larger impact on student achievement scores than did the content manipulation (i.e., presentation style had more to do with how well students performed on the examination than did the number of questions that had been covered in the lecture). This finding demonstrated that, particularly when external incentives are weak, expressiveness can have an important impact on both SETs and achievement scores. In further analyses of the achievement scores Marsh (1984a, p.212) concluded that the study was one of the few to "show that more expressively presented lectures *cause* better examination performance in a study where there was random assignment to treatment conditions and lecturer expressiveness was experimentally manipulated." Across all the conditions, the effect of instructor expressiveness on ratings of Instructor Enthusiasm was larger than its effect on other student rating factors. Hence, as observed in the examination of potential biases to SETs, this reanalysis indicates the importance of considering the multidimensionality of SETs. An effect which has been interpreted as a "bias" to SETs seems more appropriately interpreted as support for their validity with respect to one component of effective teaching. Consistent with this interpretation, Feldman's (1988) review indicated that "teacher enthusiasm" was judged to be an important characteristic by both students (rated 5th of 18 components) and faculty (2nd) although it was only 11th highest in its relation with student achievement.

A meta-analysis. Abrami, Leventhal, and Perry (1982) conducted a review and a meta-analysis of all known Dr. Fox studies. On the basis of their meta-analysis, they concluded that expressiveness manipulations had a substantial impact on overall SETs and a small effect on achievement, while content manipulations had a substantial effect on achievement and a small effect on ratings. Consistent with the Marsh and Ware reanalysis, they also found that in the few studies that analyzed separate rating factors, the rating factors that were most logically related to the expressiveness manipulation were most affected by it. Finally, they concluded that while the expressiveness manipulation did interact with the content manipulation and a host of other variables examined in the Dr. Fox studies, none of these interactions accounted for more than 5 percent of the variance in SETs.

Extensions. The Dr. Fox paradigm is an apparently valuable procedure for studying a wide variety of teaching variables within the context of a controlled experimental design as demonstrated by the research program on college students perceptions of control conducted by Perry and his associates (see Perry, 1991, for an overview). The focus of this research was not the Dr. Fox effect nor even SETS, but how instructor expressiveness interacted with perceived control to influence achievement test scores. Within an educational context, perceived control is a student's perceived capacity to influence and predict events, particularly those contributing to academic achievement. An internal locus in which students take more responsibility for their outcomes is associated with more favorable academic behaviors and outcomes. Whereas perceived control is often conceptualized as a relatively stable individual difference variable, Perry (1991) demonstrated that perceived control is significantly lowered by giving students negative, noncontingent feedback on responses to multiple choice test items.

In Perry's (1991) basic paradigm, students completed individual difference instruments, were administered feedback manipulations designed to alter perceptions of control, were presented with Dr. Fox-type videotapes that varied in terms of instructor expressiveness, and then completed post-test materials consisting of a multiple choice achievement test and an attribution questionnaire. The results of different studies have consistently shown a aptitude-treatment interaction in which instructor expressiveness has no effect on achievement test scores for students who are low in perceived control whereas instructor expressiveness increases achievement test scores for other students.

Other research suggested that low perceived control that occurred naturally (i.e., an individual difference variable instead of the result of an experimental manipulation) produced a similar pattern of results. Interestingly, low perceived control that occurred naturally could be offset to some extent by the feedback manipulation and also by an attributional retraining program described by Perry and Penner (1990). Perry and Dickens (1984) also studied how this effect varied with the incentive level of students. In the no-incentive conditions, instructor expressiveness facilitated achievement for contingent-feedback (high perceived control) students but not for noncontingent-feedback (low perceived control) students. In the high incentive condition performance was consistently higher, but instructor expressiveness did not effect achievement performance for either contingent or noncontingent feedback conditions. Perry (1991), like Marsh and Ware (1982), concluded that under conditions of high external incentive, instructor expressiveness has little effect on achievement performance. Research by Perry and his associates is important in demonstrating that the effectiveness of the instructor expressiveness can vary systematically depending on individual differences of students within a class or environmental factors. More generally, the research demonstrates the broad applicability of the Dr. Fox paradigm to the study of teaching effectiveness.

Interpretations, Implications and Problems
How should the results of the Dr. Fox type studies be evaluated? Consistent with the present emphasis on the construct validity of multifaceted SETs, a particularly powerful test of the validity of SETs would be to show that each rating factor is strongly influenced by manipulations most logically associated with it and less influenced by other manipulations. This is the approach used in the Marsh and Ware reanalysis of the Dr. Fox data described above, and it offers strong support for the validity of ratings with respect to expressiveness and, perhaps, limited support for their validity with respect to content.

Multiple ratings factors have typically not been considered in Dr. Fox studies even though researchers typically collect ratings that do represent multiple rating dimensions (i.e., the same form as was shown to have five factors in the Marsh and Ware reanalysis, and/or items from the 1971 Hildebrand, Wilson and Dienst study). However, this makes no sense when researchers also emphasize the differential effects of the experimental manipulations on the total rating score and the achievement outcome. According to this approach, SETs may be invalid because they are "oversensitive" to expressiveness and "undersensitive" to content when compared with achievement scores (but see Abrami, Leventhal, and Perry, 1982).

It is hardly surprising that the number of examination questions answered in a lecture (only 4 of 26 exam questions are covered in the low content lecture, while all 26 are covered in the high content lecture) has a substantial impact on examination performance immediately after the lecture, and less impact on SETs; more relevant is the finding that content also impacts SETs. Nor is it surprising that manipulations of instructor expressiveness have a large impact on the total rating score when some of the items specifically ask students to judge the characteristic that is being manipulated; more relevant is the finding that some rating factors are relatively unaffected by expressiveness and that achievement scores are affected by expressiveness. SETs are multifaceted, the different rating factors do vary in the way they are affected by different manipulations, and any specific criterion can be more accurately predicted by differentially weighting the student rating dimensions. Since most of the Dr. Fox studies are based upon total scores instead of separate components, reanalyses of these studies, as was done in the Marsh and Ware study, should prove valuable.

Summary of the Search for Potential Biases
The search for potential biases to SETs is plagued by methodological problems and the lack of definition of what constitutes a bias. For most of the relations, the effects tend to

be small, the directions of the effects are sometimes inconsistent, and the attribution of a bias is typically unwarranted. There is clearly a need for meta-analyses, and systematic reviews such as those by Feldman, to provide more accurate estimates of the size of effects which have been reported, and the conditions under which they were found. Perhaps the best summary of this area is McKeachie's (1979) conclusion that a wide variety of variables that could potentially influence SETs apparently have little effect. Similar conclusions have been drawn by Centra (1979, 1989), Cashin (1988), Menges (1973), Marsh (1980, 1983, 1987), Murray (1980), Aleamoni (1981), and others.

There are, of course, nearly an infinite number of variables that could be related to SETs and could be posited as potential biases. However, any such claim must be seriously scrutinized in a series of studies that are relatively free from the common methodological shortcomings, are based upon an explicit and defensible definition of bias, and employ the type of logic used to examine the variables described here. Single studies of the predictive validity of psychological measures have largely been replaced by a series of construct validity studies, and a similar approach should also be taken in the study of potential biases. Simplistic arguments that a significant correlation between SETs and some variable "X" demonstrates a bias can no longer be tolerated, and are an injustice to the field. It is unfortunate that the cautious attitude to interpreting correlations between SETs and potential indicators of effective teaching as evidence of validity has not been adopted in the interpretation of correlations between SETs and potential biases as a source of invalidity.

UTILITY OF STUDENT RATINGS

Braskamp, Brandenburg, and Ory (1985) argued that it is important for universities and individual instructors to take evaluations seriously. They support this contention with a broad rationale based on organizational research. Key points are that institutional goals/values are reinforced through an evaluation process and that successful organizations are data-based and assessment-driven. In summarizing this perspective Braskamp et al. (p.14) stated that: "the clarity and pursuit of purpose is best done if the achievements are known. A course is charted and corrections are inevitable. Evaluation plays a role in the clarity of purpose and determining if the pursuit is on course." In a related perspective, Marsh (1984b, 1987) argued that the introduction of a broad institution-based, carefully planned program of SETs is likely to lead to the improvement of teaching. Faculty will give serious consideration to their own teaching in order to evaluate the merits of the program. Clear support of a program by the central administration will serve notice that teaching effectiveness is being taken seriously. The results of SETs, as one indicator of effective teaching, will provide a basis for informed administrative decisions and thereby increase the likelihood that quality teaching will be recognized and rewarded, and that good teachers will be given tenure. The social reinforcement of getting favorable ratings will provide added incentive for the improvement of teaching, even at the tenured faculty level. Finally, faculty report that the feedback from student evaluations is useful to their own efforts for the improvement of their teaching.

Murray (1987) presented a similar logic in making the case for why SETs improve teaching effectiveness, offering four reasons: (a) SETs provide useful feedback for diagnosing strengths and weaknesses, (b) feedback can provide the impetus for professional development aimed at improving teaching, (c) the use of SETs in personnel decisions provides a tangible incentive to improve teaching, and (d) the use of SETs in tenure decisions means that good teachers are more likely to be retained. In support of his argument, Murray (1987) summarized results of published surveys from seven universities that asked faculty whether SETs are useful for improving teaching and whether SETs have led to improved teaching. Across the seven studies, about 2/3 of the faculty said that SETs were useful and about 80 percent indicated that SETs led to improved teaching.

Dunkin (1990) looked at relations among sex, academic qualifications, teaching experience, the use of SETs, and self-perceived teaching effectiveness for newly appointed staff at an Australian University where the use of SETs was not required. Males, lecturers with doctorates, and lecturers with more teaching experience rated themselves as more competent teachers. Self-perceived teaching effectiveness, however, was negatively related to the use of SETs. This suggests that lecturers who perceived themselves to be poorer teachers chose to use SETs in the belief that they would provide a basis for improved teaching.

None of these observations, however, provides an empirical demonstration of improvement of teaching effectiveness resulting from SETs.

Changes in Teaching Effectiveness Due to Feedback from Student Ratings

In most studies of the effects of feedback from SETs, teachers are randomly assigned to experimental (feedback) and one or more control groups; SETs are collected during the term; ratings of the feedback teachers are returned to instructors as quickly as possible; and the various groups are compared at the end of the term on a second administration on SETs and sometimes on other variables as well. (There is considerable research on a wide variety of other techniques designed to improve teaching effectiveness which use SETs as an outcome measure; see Levinson-Rose and Menges, 1981).

SEEQ has been employed in two such feedback studies using multiple sections of the same course. In the first study results from an abbreviated form of the survey were simply returned to faculty, and the impact of the feedback was positive, but very modest (Marsh, Fleiner, and Thomas, 1975). In the second study (Overall and Marsh, 1979) researchers actually met with instructors in the feedback group to discuss the evaluations and possible strategies for improvement. In this study students in the feedback group subsequently performed better on a standardized final examination, rated teaching effectiveness more favorably at the end of the course, and experienced more favorable affective outcomes (i.e., feelings of course mastery, and plans to pursue and apply the subject). These two studies suggest that feedback, coupled with a candid discussion with an external consultant, can be an effective intervention for the improvement of teaching effectiveness. These SEEQ studies are atypical of most feedback research in which different courses from a variety of disciplines are considered so that student achievement normally cannot be considered as an outcome variable.

In his classic meta-analysis, Cohen (1980) found that instructors who received midterm feedback were subsequently rated about one-third of a standard deviation higher than controls on the Total Rating (an overall rating item or the average of multiple items), and even larger differences were observed for ratings of Instructor Skill, Attitude Toward Subject, and Feedback to Students. Studies that augmented feedback with consultation produced substantially larger differences, but other methodological variations had little effect. The results of this meta-analysis support the SEEQ findings described above and demonstrate that SET feedback, particularly when augmented by consultation, can lead to improvement in teaching effectiveness.

L'Hommediu, Menges, and Brinko (1990; also see L'Hommedieu, Menges, and Brinko, 1988) noted Dunkin's (1986) call for more research on the effects of SETs on changes in teacher processes and for meta-analyses of the influence of design and contextual effects. In response to Dunkin, the authors updated Cohen's (1980) meta-analysis and critically evaluated the methodology used in the 28 studies. They concluded that the overall effect size (.342) attributable to feedback was probably attenuated by threats to validity in existing research and developed methodological recommendations for future research. Among their many recommendations, they emphasized the need to: use a larger number of instructors, more critically evaluate findings within a construct validity framework as emphasized by Marsh (1987), more critically evaluate the assumed generalizability of midterm feedback to end-of-term feedback, and to base results on well-standardized instruments such as SEEQ. They also noted that teachers in many studies had previously received SET feedback so that feedback/no-feedback comparisons actually tested the additive effects of the additional feedback from that study. In this respect, the results are likely to underestimate the gain due to feedback compared to a control group that had never received SET feedback. This serious threat to the internal validity of results was not systematically evaluated in any of the studies, but the authors noted the need to consider previous experience with SETs in future research.

In their meta-analysis, L'Hommediu, Menges, and Brinko (1988) considered three forms of feedback that differed systematically in their effect sizes: written feedback consisting of printed summaries of SETs (Mean effect=.18, SD=.24, N=16); personal feedback consisting of summary material delivered in person, sometimes accompanied by interpretations, discussion, and advice (mean effect=.25, SD=.21, N=6); and consultative feedback that combines SET feedback and professional development (mean effect = .86, SD=.554, N=6). Consistent with Cohen (1980) they concluded that "the literature reveals a persistently positive, albeit small, effect from written feedback alone and a considerably increased effect when written feedback is augmented with personal consultation" (1990, p. 240), but that improved research that incorporated their suggestions would probably lead to larger, more robust effects.

Wilson (1986, 1987) described an alternative paradigm that appears to have considerable potential. A key element in his research was a set of 24 teaching packets that were keyed to the 24 items on the SET instrument used in his research. Each packet contained suggestions from teachers who had received Distinguished Teaching Awards or received multiple nominations as the "best teacher" by graduating seniors. Participants in the study were volunteers who had been evaluated previously in the same course they would again be teaching. Based on SETs and self-evaluations of their own teaching, participants nominated specific evaluation items on which they would like assistance at a preliminary consultation session. The main consultation was held shortly before the second time the instructors were to teach the same course. The consultant began the session by noting items on which the instructor received the highest ratings. The consultant then considered 3 to 5 items which the instructor had selected or had received the lowest ratings. For each item the three to six strategies from the corresponding teaching packet were described and the instructor was given copies of the two or three that were of most interest to the instructor. During the next week the consultant summarized the main consultation and strategies to be pursued in a letter that was sent to the instructor and subsequently telephoned the instructor during the term to ask how things were going. The results indicated that ratings were systematically better at time 2 for the targeted items—particularly those items that referred to concrete behaviors (e.g., states objectives for each class session)—and an overall rating item. Recognizing the need for a nonintervention comparison group, Wilson evaluated SETs for 101 courses that were taught by the same instructors (who had not volunteered to be in the study) on two occasions during the same period. For this large comparison group, there were no systematic changes in either specific or global SETs. Results for the comparison group supported Wilson's contention that SETS without a consultation intervention are not likely to lead to improved teaching. Wilson suggested that the key elements in the consultation intervention were providing instructors with information on how to improve teaching in areas in which they are weak and the interpersonal expectations that created for some instructors a desire to fulfill an implied contract with their consultant. Whereas there may be counter-interpretations[*] of the findings in this quasi-experimental study, the results suggest that this consultation intervention may be an effective method for improving teaching effectiveness.

The most robust finding from the feedback research reviewed here is that consultation augments the effects of written summaries of SETs. Other sources also support this conclusion. For example, in the Jacobs (1987) survey of Indiana University faculty, 70 percent of the respondents indicated that SETs had helped them improve their teaching but 63 percent indicated that even when teachers can interpret their ratings, they often do not know what to do in order to improve their teaching. Also, Franklin and Theall (1989), based on an 153 multiple-choice test of knowledge about SETs that was validated by experts in the field, concluded that many users lacked the knowledge to adequately use the SETs for summative or formative purposes. Nevertheless, insufficient attention in SET research has been given to nature of consultative feedback that is most effective (e.g., Wilson, 1986, 1987). This important deficit in existing research has tre-

---

[*]Wilson (1986, 1987) evaluated changes for only the specific rating items that had been targeted for change. Because these items were typically the ones on which instructors had the lowest ratings at time 1, regression effects alone would predict that changes in these items would more likely be positive than negative. This problem, however, apparently does not affect results for the overall rating items.

mendous practical implications and should prove a fruitful area for further research.

Several issues still remain unresolved in SET feedback research. First, whereas the combination of feedback and consultation is more effective than feedback alone, no studies have provided an adequate control for the effect of consultation without SETs (i.e., a placebo effect due to consultation, or a real effect due to consultation that does not depend upon feedback from SETs).[*] Second, the criterion of effective teaching in feedback studies is limited primarily to subsequent SETs; only the Overall and Marsh (1979) study demonstrated a significant effect of feedback on achievement (but also see McKeachie, et al., 1980). Most other studies were not based upon multiple sections of the same course, and so it was not possible to test the effect of feedback on achievement scores. Third, nearly all of the studies were based on midterm feedback from midterm ratings. This limitation probably weakens effects in that many instructional characteristics cannot be easily altered within the same semester. Furthermore, Marsh and Overall (1980) demonstrated in their multisection validity study midterm ratings were less valid than end-of-term ratings. Fourth, most of the research is based upon instructors who volunteer to participate; this further limits the generality of the effect, since volunteers are likely to be more motivated to use the feedback. In addition, reward structure is an important variable which has not been examined. Even if faculty are intrinsically motivated to improve their teaching effectiveness, potentially valuable feedback will be much less useful if there is no extrinsic motivation for faculty to improve. To the extent that salary, promotion, and prestige are based primarily on research productivity, the usefulness of SETs as feedback for the improvement of teaching may be limited. Hildebrand (1972, p.53) noted that: "The more I study teaching, however, the more convinced I become that the most important requirement for improvement is incorporation of effective evaluation of teaching into advancement procedures." Realistically, particularly for faculty trying to get tenure in research-oriented universities, it may be counterproductive to place too much emphasis on improving teaching if this is accomplished by a diminished publication record. Finally, future research needs to evaluate the validity threats outlined by L'Hommedieu, Menges, and Brinko (1990) and to incorporate their suggestions about how to counter these problems.

Nearly all feedback studies have considered the effects of feedback from SETs within a single term, and this is unfortunate. SETs are typically collected near the end of the term so that the more relevant question is the impact of end-of-term ratings. A few studies have considered long-term follow-ups of short-term interventions, but these were apparently not designed for this purpose and were sufficiently flawed that no generalizations are warranted (see Marsh, 1987). No research has examined the effects of continued SET feedback over a long period of time with a true experimental design, and such research may be ethically dubious and very difficult to conduct. The long-term effects of SET feedback may be amenable to quasi-experimental designs (e.g., Voght

---

[*] McKeachie (personal communication, 9 April, 1991) noted that he had conducted a follow-up study that used consultation alone and that consultation without student ratings was nearly as effective as consultation with student ratings.

and Lasher, 1973), but the difficulties inherent in the interpretation of such studies may preclude any firm generalizations. For short periods, however, it may be justifiable to withhold the SETs from randomly selected instructors or to require that some instructors not collect SETs at all. In particular, it is reasonable to evaluate the effects of feedback from end-of-term ratings—augmented, perhaps, with consultation—on SETs collected the next semester in relation to SETs for no-feedback controls. Particularly for ongoing programs that regularly collect SETs at the end of each semester, this type of study should be easier to conduct than the traditional midterm studies, and so it is surprising that this research design has not been implemented.

Usefulness in Tenure/Promotion Decisions

Since 1929, and particularly during the last 25 years a variety of surveys have been conducted to determine the importance of SETs and other indicators of teaching effectiveness in evaluating total faculty performance in North American universities. Reviews (Centra, 1979; Marsh, 1987; Leventhal, Perry, Abrami, Turcotte, and Kane, 1981; Seldin, 1975) suggest that the importance and usefulness of SETs as a measure of teaching effectiveness have increased dramatically during the last 60 years and particularly in the last two decades. Despite the strong reservations by some, faculty are apparently in favor of the use of SETs in personnel decisions—at least in comparison with other indicators of teaching effectiveness. For example, in a broad cross-section of colleges and universities, Rich (1976) reported that 75 percent of the respondents believed that SETs should be used in tenure decisions. Rich also noted that faculty at major research-oriented universities favored the use of SETs more strongly than faculty from small colleges, suggesting that SETs were more threatening at small colleges because teaching effectiveness is a more important determinant of personnel decisions. However, Braskamp, Brandenburg, and Ory (1985) noted that university faculty place more emphasis on striving for excellence and are more competitive than faculty at small colleges, and these differences might explain their stronger acceptance of SETs.

In order to experimentally evaluate the importance of teaching effectiveness in personnel decisions, Leventhal et al. (1981), and Salthouse, McKeachie, and Lin (1978) composed fictitious summaries of faculty performance that systematically varied reports of teaching and research effectiveness, and also varied the type of information given about teaching (chairperson's report or chairperson's report supplemented by summaries of SETs). Both studies found reports of research effectiveness to be more important in evaluating total faculty performance at research universities, although Leventhal, et al. found teaching and research to be of similar importance across a broader range of institutions. While teaching effectiveness as assessed by the chairperson's reports did make a significant difference in ratings of overall faculty performance, neither study found that supplementing the chairperson's report with SETs made any significant difference. However, neither study considered SETs alone or even suggested that the two sources of evidence about teaching effectiveness were independent. Information from the ratings and chairperson's report were always consistent so that one was redundant, and it would be reasonable for subjects in these studies to assume that the chairperson's report was at least partially based upon SETs. These studies demonstrate the importance of reports of teaching effectiveness, but apparently do not test the impact of SETs. As noted earlier, Lin, McKeachie, and Tucker (1984) used a similar design to compare the effects of statistical summaries of SETs and written comments. Those results suggested that written comments augmented the impact of statistical summaries—favorably for highly rated teachers and negatively for less highly rated teachers. Again, however, the researchers did not consider comments alone or comments that were inconsistent with the statistical summaries, so there was no basis for comparing the relative impact of the two sources of information. This paradigm, however, could be used to determine the most effective way to present information from SETs. These studies, for example, imply that augmenting the feedback provided by summaries of global SETs may increase their impact. An important, unresolved question that appears well suited to this paradigm is the comparison of global SET summaries recommended for personnel decisions by Abrami (1989a, 1989b, 1991; also see Marsh, 1991a) and profiles of SET scores like those resulting from SEEQ responses that are emphasized here.

Usefulness in Student Course Selection

Little empirical research has been conducted on the use of ratings by prospective students in the selection of courses. UCLA students reported that the Professor/Course Evaluation Survey was the second most frequently read of the many student publications, following the daily, campus newspaper (Marsh, 1987). Similarly, about half the Indiana University students in Jacobs' (1987) study generally consulted published ratings prior to taking a course. Leventhal, Abrami, Perry, and Breen (1975) found that students say that information about teaching effectiveness influences their course selection. Students who select a class on the basis of information about teaching effectiveness are more satisfied with the quality of teaching than are students who indicate other reasons (Centra and Creech, 1976; Leventhal, Abrami, and Perry, 1976). In an experimental field study, Coleman and McKeachie (1981) presented summaries of ratings of four comparable political science courses to randomly selected groups of students during preregistration meetings. One of the courses had received substantially higher ratings, and it was chosen more frequently by students in the experimental group than by those in the control group. Apparently, SETs are useful for students in the selection of instructors and courses.

Summary of Studies of the Utility of Student Ratings

With the possible exception of short-term studies of the effects of midterm ratings, studies of the usefulness of SETs are infrequent and often anecdotal. This is unfortunate, because this is an area of research that can have an important and constructive impact on policy and practice. Important, unresolved issues were identified that are in need of further research. For example, for administrative decisions SETs can be summarized by responses to a single global rating item, by a single score representing an optimally-weighted average of specific components, or a profile of multiple components, but there is no research to indicate which is most effective. If different components of SETs are to be combined to form a total score, how should the different components be weighted? Again there is no systematic research to inform policy makers. Debates about whether SETs have too much or too little impact on administrative decisions are seldom based upon any systematic evidence about the amount of impact they actually do have. Researchers often indicate that SETs are used as one basis for personnel decisions, but there is a dearth of research on the policy practices that are actually employed in the use of SETs. A plethora of policy questions exist (e.g., how to select courses to be evaluated, the manner in which rating instruments are administered, who is to be given access to the results, how ratings from different courses are considered, whether special circumstances exist where ratings for a particular course can be excluded either a priori or post-hoc, whether faculty have the right to offer their own interpretation of ratings, etc.) which are largely unexplored despite the apparently wide use of SETs.

Anecdotal reports often suggest that faculty find SETs useful, but there has been little systematic attempt to determine what form of feedback to faculty is most useful (although feedback studies do support the use of services by an external consultant) and how faculty actually use the results which they do receive. Some researchers have cited anecdotal evidence for negative effects of SETs (e.g., lowering grading standards or making courses easier) but these are also rarely documented with systematic research. Critics suggest that SETs lead to more conservative teaching styles, but Murray (1987) countered that highly rated teachers often use nontraditional approaches and that teaching is less traditional today than it was before SETs were used widely. McKeachie (personal communication, 19 March, 1991) noted that SETs are typically used constructively, encouraging instructors to think of alternative approaches and to try them out. He also suggested, however, that if SETs are used destructively so that teachers feel that they are in competition with each other—"that they must always be wary of the sword of student ratings hanging over their head"—poor ratings may increase anxiety and negative feelings about students so that teaching and learning may suffer. Again, research is needed to examine whether teachers react constructively or destructively to SETs and whether there are individual differences that influence these reactions. While SETs are sometimes used by students in their selection of courses, there is little guidance about the type of information which students want and whether this is the same as is needed for other uses of SETs. These, and a wide range of related questions about how SETs are actually used and how their usefulness can be enhanced, provide a rich field for further research.

OVERVIEW, SUMMARY, AND IMPLICATIONS

Research described in this chapter demonstrates that SETs are clearly multidimensional, quite reliable, reasonably valid, relatively unbiased, and seen to be useful by students, faculty, and administrators. The same findings also demonstrate, however, that SETs may have some halo effect, have at least some unreliability, have only modest agreement with some criteria of effective teaching, are probably affected by some potential sources of bias, and are viewed with some skepticism by faculty as a basis for personnel decisions. It should be noted that this level of uncertainty probably also exists in every area of applied psychology and for all personnel evaluation systems. Nevertheless, the reported results clearly demonstrate that a considerable amount of useful information can be obtained from SETs; useful for feedback to faculty, useful for personnel decisions, useful to students in the selection of courses, and useful for the study of teaching. As noted by Cashin (1988), "in general, student ratings tend to be statistically reliable, valid, and relatively free from bias, probably more so than any other data used for faculty evaluation" (p.5).

Despite the generally supportive research findings, SETs should be used cautiously, and there should be other forms of systematic input about teaching effectiveness, particularly when they are used for tenure/promotion decisions. Whereas there is good evidence to support the use of SETs as one indicator of effective teaching, there are few other indicators of teaching effectiveness whose use is systematically supported by research findings. Based upon the research reviewed here, other alternatives which may be valid include the ratings of previous students, instructor self-evaluations, and colleague ratings that are *not* based on actual classroom observation, but each of these has problems of its own. Alumni surveys typically have very low response rates and are still basically SETs. Faculty self-evaluations may be valid for some purposes, but probably not for personnel decisions. (Faculty should, however, be encouraged to have a systematic voice in the interpretation of their SETs.) Colleague ratings that are not based on classroom observation apparently reflect second-hand student perceptions or, in some cases, impressions based on summaries of SETs. Consequently, while extensive lists of alternative indicators of effective teaching are proposed (e.g., Centra, 1979), few are supported by systematic research, and none is as clearly supported as SETs.

Why then, if SETs are reasonably well supported by research findings, are they so controversial and so widely criticized? Several suggestions are obvious. University faculty have little or no formal training in teaching, yet find themselves in a position where their salary or even their job may depend upon their classroom teaching skills. Any procedure used to evaluate teaching effectiveness would prove to be threatening and therefore criticized. The threat is exacerbated by the realization that there are no clearly defined criteria of effective teaching, particularly when there continues to be considerable debate about the validity of SETs. Interestingly, measures of research productivity, the other major determinant of instructor effectiveness, are not nearly so highly criticized, despite the fact that the actual information used to represent them in tenure decisions is often quite subjective and there are serious problems with the interpretation of the objective measures of research productivity that are used. As demonstrated in this overview, much of the debate is based upon ill-founded fears about SETs, but the fears still persist. Indeed, the popularity of two of the more widely employed paradigms in student evaluation research, the multisection validity study and the Dr. Fox study, apparently stems from an initial notoriety produced by claims to have demonstrated that SETs are invalid. This occurred even though the two original studies (Rodin and Rodin, 1972 and Naftulin, Ware and Donnelly, 1973) were so fraught with methodological weaknesses as to be uninterpretable. Perhaps this should not be so surprising in the academic profession where faculty are better trained to find counter explanations for a wide variety of phenomena than to teach. Indeed, the state of affairs has resulted in a worthwhile and healthy scrutiny of SETs and was heuristic in generating important research. The bulk of research, however, has supported their continued use as well as advocating further scrutiny.

References

Abrami, P. C. (1985). Dimensions of effective college instruction. *Review of Higher Education* 8: 211–228.

Abrami, P. C. (1988). SEEQ and ye shall find: A review of Marsh's "Students' evaluations of university teaching." *Instructional Evaluation* 9(2): 19–27.

Abrami, P. C. (1989a). How should we use student ratings to evaluate teaching. *Research in Higher Education* 30: 221–227.

Abrami, P. C. (1989b). SEEQing the truth about student ratings of instruction. *Educational Researcher* 43: 43–45.

Abrami, P. C., Cohen, P. A., d'Apollonia, S. (1988). Implementation problems in meta-analysis. *Review of Educational Research* 58: 151–179.

Abrami, P. C., and d'Apollonia, S. (1991). Multidimensional students' evaluations of teaching effectiveness: Generalizability of N = 1 research: Comment on Marsh (1991). *Journal of Educational Psychology.*

Abrami, P. C., d'Apollonia, S., and Cohen, P. A., (1990). Validity of student ratings of instruction: What we know and what we do not. *Journal of Educational Psychology* 82: 219–231.

Abrami, P. C., Dickens, W. J., Perry, R. P., and Leventhal, L. (1980). Do teacher standards for assigning grades affect student evaluations of instruction? *Journal of Educational Psychology* 72: 107–118.

Abrami, P. C., Leventhal, L., and Perry, R. P. (1982). Educational seduction. *Review of Educational Research* 52: 446–464.

Aleamoni, L. M. (1981). Student ratings of instruction. In J. Millman (ed.), *Handbook of Teacher Evaluation.* Beverly Hills, CA: Sage. Aleamoni, L. M. (1985). Peer evaluation of instructors and instruction. *Instructional Evaluation* 8 (entire issue).

Aleamoni, L. M., and Yimer, M. (1973). An investigation of the relationship between colleague rating, student rating, research productivity, and academic rank in rating instructional effectiveness. *Journal of Educational Psychology* 64: 274–277.

Aubrect, J. D. (1981). Reliability, validity and generalizability of student ratings of instruction (IDEA Paper No.6). Kansas State University: Center for Faculty Evaluations and Development. (ERIC Document Reproduction Service No. ED 213 296).

Barnes, J. (1985). Experience and student achievement/teacher effectiveness. In T. Husen and T. N. Postlethwaite (eds.), *International Encyclopedia of Education: Research and Studies.* Oxford: Pergamon Press.

Basow, S. A. (August, 1987). Teacher expressiveness: Effects of teacher sex and student sex. Paper presented at the 1987 Annual Meeting of the American Psychological Association, New York, NY (ERIC Document No. ED 290 067).

Basow, S. A., and Distenfeld, M. S. (1985). Teacher expressiveness: More important for male teachers than female teachers? *Journal of Educational Psychology* 77: 45–52.

Benton, S. E. (1982). Rating college teaching: Criterion validity studies of student evaluation of instruction instruments. (ERIC ED 221 147)

Biglan, A. (1973). The characteristics of subject matter in different academic areas. *Journal of Applied Psychology* 57: 195–203.

Blackburn, R. T. (1974). The meaning of work in academia. In J. I. Doi (ed.), *Assessing Faculty Effort* (a special issue of New Directions for Institutional Research.) San Francisco: Jossey-Bass.

Blackburn, R. T., and Clark, M. J. (1975). An assessment of faculty performance: Some correlations between administrators, colleagues, student, and self–ratings. *Sociology of Education* 48: 242–256.

Brandenburg, D. C., Slindle, J. A., and Batista, E. E. (1977). Student ratings of instruction: Validity and normative interpretations. *Research in Higher Education* 7: 67–78.

Braskamp, L. A., Brandenburg, D. C. and Ory, J. C. (1985). *Evaluating teaching effectiveness: A practical guide*. Beverly Hills, CA: Sage.

Braskamp, L. A., Ory, J. C. and Pieper, D. M. (1981). Student written comments: Dimensions of instructional quality. *Journal of Educational Psychology* 73: 65–70.

Brookfield, S. (1989). Teacher Roles and Teaching Styles: Adult Education. In Husen, T. and Postlethwaite, T. N. (eds.) *The International Encyclopedia of Education*, Supplementary Volume 1. Oxford: Pergamon Press.

Brown, D. L. (1976). Faculty ratings and student grades: A university-wide multiple regression analysis. *Journal of Educational Psychology* 68: 573–578.

Campbell, D. T., and Stanley, J. C. (1963). Experimental and quasi-experimental designs for research on teaching. In N. L. Gage (ed.), *Handbook of Research on Teaching*. Chicago: Rand McNally.

Cashin, W. E. (1988). Student ratings of teaching. A summary of research. (IDEA paper No.20). Kansas State University, Division of Continuing Education. (ERIC Document Reproduction Service No. ED 302 567).

Cashin, W. E., and Clegg, V. L. (April, 1987). Are student ratings of different academic disciplines different? Paper presented at the 1987 Annual Meeting of the American Educational Research Association, Washington, DC. (ERIC Document Reproduction Service No. ED 289 935).

Centra, J. A. (1975). Colleagues as raters of classroom instruction. *Journal of Higher Education* 46: 327–337.

Centra, J. A. (1979). *Determining Faculty Effectiveness*. San Francisco: Jossey-Bass.

Centra, J. A. (1983). Research productivity and teaching effectiveness. *Research in Higher Education* 18: 379–389.

Centra, J. A. (1989) Faculty evaluation and faculty development in higher education. In J. C. Smart (ed.), *Higher Education: Handbook of Theory and Research*, Vol. V. New York: Agathon Press.

Centra, J. A., and Creech, F. R. (1976). The relationship between student, teacher, and course characteristics and student ratings of teacher effectiveness (Project Report 76–1). Princeton, NJ: Educational Testing Service.

Clarkson, P. C. (1984). Papua, New Guinea students' perceptions of mathematics lecturers. *Journal of Educational Psychology* 76: 1386–1395.

Cohen, P. A. (1980). Effectiveness of student–rating feedback for improving college instruction: a meta-analysis. *Research in Higher Education* 13: 321–341.

Cohen, P. A. (1981). Student ratings of instruction and student achievement: A meta-analysis of multisection validity studies. *Review of Educational Research* 51: 281–309.

Cohen, P. A. (April, 1987). A critical analysis and reanalysis of the multisection validity meta-analysis. Paper presented at the 1987 Annual Meeting of the American Educational Research Association, Washington, D. C. (ERIC Document Reproduction Service No. ED 283 876).

Cohen, P. A., and McKeachie, W. J. (1980). The role of colleagues in the evaluation of college teaching. *Improving College and University Teaching* 28: 147–154.

Coleman, J., and McKeachie, W. J. (1981). Effects of instructor/course evaluations on student course selection. *Journal of Educational Psychology* 73: 224–226.

Cooley, W. W., and Lohnes, P. R. (1976). *Evaluation Research in Education*. New York: Irvington.

Costin, F., Greenough, W. T., and Menges, R. J. (1971). Student ratings of college teaching: Reliability, validity and usefulness. *Review of Educational Research* 41: 511–536.

Cranton, P. A., and Hillgarten, W. (1981). The relationships between student ratings and instructor behavior: Implications for improving teaching. *Canadian Journal of Higher Education* 11: 73–81.

Cronbach, L. J. (1971). Test validation. In R. L. Thorndike (ed.), *Educational Measurement*. Washington, D. C.: American Council of Education.

d'Apollonia, S., and Abrami, P. C. (1987). An empirical critique of meta-analysis: The literature on sutdent ratings of instruction. Paper presented at the annual meeting of the American Educational Research Association.

de Wolf, W. A. (1974). Student ratings of instruction in post secondary institutions: A comprehensive annotated bibliography of research reported since 1968 (Vol.1). University of Washington Educational

Assessment Center.

Dowell, D. A., and Neal, J. A. (1982). A selective view of the validity of student ratings of teaching. *Journal of Higher Education* 53: 51–62.

Doyle, K. O. (1975). *Student Evaluation of Instruction*. Lexington, MA: D. C. Heath.

Doyle, K. O. (1983). *Evaluating Teaching*. Lexington, MA: Lexington Books.

Drucker, A. J., and Remmers, H. H. (1950). Do alumni and students differ in their attitudes toward instructors? *Purdue University Studies in Higher Education* 70: 62–74.

Dubin, S. S., and Okun, M. (1973). Implications of learning theories for adult instruction. *Adult Education* 21(1): 3–19.

Dukes, R. L., and Victoria, G. (1989). The effects of gender, status, and effective teaching on the evaluations of college instruction. *Teaching Sociology* 17: 447–457.

Dunkin, M. J. (1986). Research on teaching in higher education. In M. C. Wittrock (ed.), *Handbook of Research on Teaching* (3rd Edition). New York: Macmillan.

Dunkin, M. J. (1990). Willingness to obtain student evaluations as a criterion of academic staff performance. *Higher Education Research and Development* 9: 51–60.

Erdle, S., Murray, H. G., and Rushton, J. P. (1985). Personality, classroom behavior, and college teaching effectiveness: A path analysis. *Journal of Educational Psychology* 77: 394–407.

Feldman, K. A. (1976a). Grades and college students' evaluations of their courses and teachers. *Research in Higher Education* 4: 69–111.

Feldman, K. A. (1976b). The superior college teacher from the student's view. *Research in Higher Education* 5: 243–288.

Feldman, K. A. (1977). Consistency and variability among college students in rating their teachers and courses. *Research in Higher Education* 6: 223–274.

Feldman, K. A. (1978). Course characteristics and college students' ratings of their teachers and courses: What we know and what we don't. *Research in Higher Education* 9: 199–242.

Feldman, K. A. (1979). The significance of circumstances for college students' ratings of their teachers and courses. *Research in Higher Education* 10: 149–172.

Feldman, K. A. (1983). The seniority and instructional experience of college teachers as related to the evaluations they receive from their students. *Research in Higher Education* 18: 3–124.

Feldman, K. A. (1984). Class size and students' evaluations of college teacher and courses: A closer look. *Research in Higher Education* 21: 45–116.

Feldman, K. A. (1986). The perceived instructional effectiveness of college teachers as related to their personality and attitudinal characteristics: A review and synthesis. *Research in Higher Education* 24: 139–213.

Feldman, K. A. (1987). Research productivity and scholarly accomplishment: A review and exploration. *Research in Higher Education* 26: 227–298.

Feldman, K. A. (1988). Effective college teaching from the students' and faculty's view: Matched or mismatched priorities. *Research in Higher Education* 28: 291–344.

Feldman, K. A. (1989a). Instructional effectiveness of college teachers as judged by teachers themselves, current and former students, colleagues, administrators, and external (neutral) observers. *Research in Higher Education* 30: 137–194.

Feldman, K. A. (1989b). Association between student ratings of specific instructional dimensions and student achievement: Refining and extending the synthesis of data from multisection validity studies. *Research in Higher Education* 30: 583–645.

Feldman, K. A. (1990a). An afterword for \'\'the association between student ratings of specific instructional dimensions and student achievement: Refining and extending the synthesis of data from multisection validity studies". *Research in Higher Education* 31: 315–318.

Feldman, K. A. (1990b). Instructional evaluation. *The Teaching Professor*. (December): 5–7.

Fincher, C. (1985) Learning theory and research. In J. C. Smart (ed.), *Higher Education: Handbook of Theory and Research*, Vol. New York: Agathon Press.

Firth, M. (1979). Impact of work experience on the validity of student evaluations of teaching effectiveness. *Journal of Educational Psychology* 71: 726–730.

Franklin, J., and Theall, M. (March, 1989). Who reads ratings: Knowledge, attitude and practice of users of student ratings of instruction. Paper presented at the 1988 Annual Meeting of the American Educational Research Association, San Francisco, CA. (ERIC Document Reproduction Service No. ED 306 241).

Frankhouser, W. M. (1984). The effects of different oral directions as to disposition of results on student ratings of college instruction. *Research in Higher Education* 20: 367–374.

French–Lazovich, G. (1981). Peer review: Documentary evidence in the evaluation of teaching. In J. Millman (ed.), *Handbook of Teacher Evaluation*. Beverly Hills, CA: Sage.

Frey, P. W. (1978). A two dimensional analysis of student ratings of instruction. *Research in Higher Education* 9: 69–91.

Frey, P. W. (1979). The Dr. Fox effect and its implications. *Instructional Evaluation* 3: 1–5.

Frey, P. W., Leonard, D. W., and Beatty, W. W. (1975). Student ratings of instruction: Validation research. *American Educational Research Journal* 12: 327–336.

Gage, N. L. (1963). *Handbook on Research on Teaching*. Chicago: Rand McNally.

Gigliotti, R. J., and Buchtel, F. S. (1990). Attributional bias and course evaluations. *Journal of Educational Psychology* 82: 341–351.

Gilmore, G. M., Kane, M. T., and Naccarato, R. W. (1978). The generalizability of student ratings of instruction: Estimates of teacher and course components. *Journal of Educational Measurement* 15: 1–13.

Guthrie, E. R. (1954). *The Evaluation of Teaching: A Progress Report*. Seattle: University of Washington Press.

Hayton, G. E. (1983). An investigation of the applicability in technical and further education of a student evaluation of teaching instrument. An unpublished thesis. Department of Education, University of Sydney.

Hildebrand, M. (1972). How to recommend promotion of a mediocre teacher without actually lying. *Journal of Higher Education* 43: 44–62.

Hildebrand, M., Wilson, R. C., and Dienst, E. R. (1971). *Evaluating University Teaching*. Berkeley: Center for Research and Development in Higher Education, University of California, Berkeley.

Howard, G. S., and Bray, J. H. (1979). Use of norm groups to adjust student ratings of instruction: A warning. *Journal of Educational Psychology* 71: 58–63.

Howard, G. S., Conway, C. G.,and Maxwell, S. E. (1985). Construct validity of measures of college teaching effectiveness. *Journal of Educational Psychology* 77: 187–196.

Howard, G. S., and Maxwell, S. E. (1980). The correlation between student satisfaction and grades: A case of mistaken causation? *Journal of Educational Psychology* 72: 810–820.

Howard, G. S., and Maxwell, S. E. (1982). Do grades contaminate student evaluations of instruction. *Research in Higher Education* 16: 175–188.

Howard, G. S., and Schmeck, R. R. (1979). Relationship of changes in student motivation to student evaluations of instruction. *Research in Higher Education* 10: 305–315.

Hoyt, D. P., Owens, R. E., and Grouling, T. (1973). *Interpreting Student Feedback on Instruction and Courses*. Manhattan, KN: Kansas State University.

Jacobs, L. C. (1987). University faculty and students' opinions of student ratings. Bloomington IN: Bureau of Evaluative Studies and Testing. (ERIC Document Reproduction Service No. ED 291 291).

Krathwohl, D. R., Bloom, B. S., and Masia, B. B. (1964). *Taxonomy of Educational Objectives: The Classification of Educational Goals. Handbook 2. Affective Domain*. New York, McKay, 1964.

Kulik, J. A., and McKeachie, W. J. (1975). The evaluation of teachers in higher education. In Kerlinger (ed.), *Review of Research in Education*, (Vol.3). Itasca, IL: Peacock.

L'Hommedieu, R., Menges, R. J., and Brinko, K. T. (1988). The effects of student ratings feedback to college teachers: A meta-analysis and review of research. Unpublished manuscript, Northwestern University, Center for the Teaching Professions, Evanston, IL.

L'Hommedieu, R., Menges, R. J., and Brinko, K. T. (1990). Methodological explanations for the modest effects of feedback. *Journal of Educational Psychology* 82: 232–241.

Land, M. L. (1985). Vagueness and clarity in the classroom. In T. Husen and T. N. Postlethwaite (eds.), *International Encyclopedia of Education: Research and Studies*. Oxford: Pergamon Press.

Land, M. L., and Combs, A. (1981). Teacher clarity, student instructional ratings, and student performance.

Paper presented at the annual meeting of the American Educational Research Association, Los Angeles.

Leventhal, L., Abrami, P. C., Perry, R. P., and Breen L. J. (1975). Section selection in multi-section courses: Implications for the validation and use of student rating forms. *Educational and Psychological Measurement* 35: 885–895.

Leventhal, L., Abrami, P. C., and Perry, R. P. (1976). Teacher rating forms: Do students interested in quality instruction rate teachers differently. *Journal of Educational Psychology* 68: 441–445.

Leventhal, L., Perry, R. P., Abrami, P. C., Turcotte, S. J. C., and Kane, B. (1981, April). Experimental investigation of tenure/promotion in American and Canadian universities. Paper presented at the Annual Meeting of the American Educational Research Association, Los Angeles.

Levinson–Rose, J., and Menges, R. J. (1981). Improving college teaching: A critical review of research. *Review of Educational Research* 51: 403–434.

Lin, Y–G., McKeachie, W. J., and Tucker, D. G. (1984). The use of student ratings in promotion decisions. *Journal of Higher Education* 55: 583–589.

Mackie, K. (1981). The application of learning theory to adult teaching. *Adults: Psychological and Educational Perspectives Series*. Monograph No.2. University of Nottingham, Nottingham.

Marsh, H. W. (1976). The relationship between background variables and students' evaluations of instructional quality. OIS 76–9. Los Angeles, CA: Office of Institutional Studies, University of Southern California.

Marsh, H. W. (1977). The validity of students' evaluations: classroom evaluations of instructors independently nominated as best and worst teachers by graduating seniors. *American Educational Research Journal* 14: 441–447.

Marsh, H. W. (1979). Annotated bibliography of research on the relationship between quality of teaching and quality of research in higher education. Los Angeles: Office of Institutional Studies, University of Southern California.

Marsh, H. W. (1980) The influence of student, course and instructor characteristics on evaluations of university teaching. *American Educational Research Journal* 17: 219–237.

Marsh, H. W. (1981a). Students' evaluations of tertiary instruction: Testing the applicability of American surveys in an Australian setting. *Australian Journal of Education* 25: 177–192.

Marsh, H. W. (1981b). The use of path analysis to estimate teacher and course effects in student ratings of instructional effectiveness. *Applied Psychological Measurement* 6: 47–60.

Marsh, H. W. (1982a). Factors affecting students' evaluations of the same course taught by the same instructor on different occasions. *American Educational Research Journal* 19: 485–497.

Marsh, H. W. (1982b). SEEQ: A reliable, valid, and useful instrument for collecting students' evaluations of university teaching. *British Journal of Educational Psychology* 52: 77–95.

Marsh, H. W. (1982c). Validity of students' evaluations of college teaching: A multitrait-multimethod analysis. *Journal of Educational Psychology* 74: 264–279.

Marsh, H. W. (1983). Multidimensional ratings of teaching effectiveness by students from different academic settings and their relation to student/course/instructor characteristics. *Journal of Educational Psychology* 75: 150–166.

Marsh, H. W. (1984a). Experimental manipulations of university motivation and their effect on examination performance. *British Journal of Educational Psychology* 54: 206–213.

Marsh, H. W. (1984b). Students' evaluations of university teaching: dimensionality, reliability, validity, potential biases, and utility. *Journal of Educational Psychology* 76: 707–754.

Marsh, H. W. (1985). Students as evaluators of teaching. In T. Husen and T. N. Postlethwaite (eds.), *International Encyclopedia of Education: Research and Studies*. Oxford: Pergamon Press.

Marsh, H. W. (1986). Applicability paradigm: Students' evaluations of teaching effectiveness in different countries. *Journal of Educational Psychology* 78: 465–473.

Marsh, H. W. (1987). Students' evaluations of university teaching: Research findings, methodological issues, and directions for future research. *International Journal of Educational Research* 11: 253–388. (Whole Issue No.3)

Marsh, H. W. (1991a). Multidimensional students' evaluations of teaching effectiveness: A test of alternative higher-order structures. *Journal of Educational Psychology* 83: 285–296.

Marsh, H. W. (1991b). A multidimensional perspective on students' evaluations of teaching effectiveness: A reply to Abrami and d'Apollonia (1991). *Journal of Educational Psychology* 83: 416–421.

Marsh, H. W. and Bailey, M. (in press). Multidimensionality of students' evaluations of teaching effectiveness: A profile analysis. *Journal of Higher Education.*

Marsh, H. W., and Cooper, T. L. (1981). Prior subject interest, students' evaluations, and instructional effectiveness. *Multivariate Behavioral Research* 16: 82–104.

Marsh, H. W., Fleiner, H., and Thomas, C. S. Validity and usefulness of student evaluations of instructional quality. *Journal of Educational Psychology* 67: 833–839.

Marsh, H. W., and Hocevar, D. (1984). The factorial invariance of students' evaluations of college teaching. *American Educational Research Journal* 21: 341–366.

Marsh, H. W. and Hocevar, D. (1983). Confirmatory factor analysis of multitrait–multimethod matrices. *Journal of Educational Measurement* 20: 231–248.

Marsh, H. W. and Hocevar, D. (1985). The application of confirmatory factor analysis to the study of self–concept: First and higher order factor structures and their invariance across age groups. *Psychological Bulletin* 97: 562–582.

Marsh, H. W., and Hocevar, D. (1991a). The multidimensionality of students' evaluations of teaching effectiveness: The generality of factor structures across academic discipline, instructor level, and course level. *Teaching and Teacher Education* 7: 9–18.

Marsh, H. W., and Hocevar, D. (1991b). Students' evaluations of teaching effectiveness: The stability of mean ratings of the same teachers over a 13–year period. *Teaching and Teacher Education* 7: 303–314.

Marsh, H. W. and Overall, J. U. (1979a). Long–term stability of students' evaluations: A note on Feldman's "Consistency and variability among college students in rating their teachers and courses." *Research in Higher Education* 10: 139–147.

Marsh, H. W. and Overall, J. U. (1979b). Validity of students' evaluations of teaching: A comparison with instructor self evaluations by teaching assistants, undergraduate faculty, and graduate faculty. Paper presented at Annual Meeting of the American Educational Research Association, San Francisco (ERIC Document No. ED177 205).

Marsh, H. W. and Overall, J. U. (1980). Validity of students' evaluations of teaching effectiveness: Cognitive and affective criteria. *Journal of Educational Psychology* 72: 468–475.

Marsh, H. W. and Overall, J. U. (1981). The relative influence of course level, course type, and instructor on students' evaluations of college teaching. *American Educational Research Journal* 18: 103–112.

Marsh, H. W., Overall, J. U., and Kesler, S. P. (1979a). Class size, students' evaluations, instructional *American Educational Research Journal* 16: 57–60.

Marsh, H. W., Overall, J. U., and Kesler, S. P. (1979b). Validity of students' evaluations of instructional effectiveness: A comparison of faculty self–evaluations and evaluations by their students. *Journal of Educational Psychology* 71: 149–160.

Marsh, H. W., Overall, J. U., and Thomas, C. S. (1976). The relationship between students' evaluations of instruction and expected grades. Paper presented at the Annual Meeting of the American Educational Research Association, San Francisco. (ERIC Document No. ED 126 140).

Marsh, H. W. and Roche, L. (1991). The use of students' evaluations of university instructors in different settings: The applicability paradigm. (In review.)

Marsh, H. W., Touron, J., and Wheeler, B. (1985). Students' evaluations of university instructors: The applicability of American instruments in a Spanish setting. *Teaching and Teacher Education: An International Journal of Research and Studies* 1: 123–138.

Marsh, H. W., and Ware, J. E. (1982). Effects of expressiveness, content coverage, and incentive on multidimensional student rating scales: New interpretations of the Dr. Fox effect. *Journal of Educational Psychology* 74: 126–134.

Maslow, A. H., and Zimmerman, W. (1956). College teaching ability, scholarly activity, and personality. *Journal of Educational Psychology* 47: 185–189.

McKeachie, W. J. (1963). Research on teaching at the college and university level. In N. L. Gage (ed.), *Handbook of Research on Teaching.* Chicago: Rand McNally.

McKeachie, W. J. (1973). Correlates of student ratings. In A. L. Sockloff (ed.), *Proceedings: The First Invitational Conference on Faculty Effectiveness as Evaluated by Students.* Measurement and Research Center, Temple University.

McKeachie, W. J. (1979). Student ratings of faculty: A reprise. *Academe*: 384–397.

McKeachie, W. J., Lin, Y–G, Daugherty, M., Moffett, M. M., Neigler, C., Nork, J., Walz, M., and Baldwin, R. (1980). Using student ratings and consultation to improve instruction. *British Journal of Educational Psychology* 50: 168–174.

McKeachie, W. J., Pintrich, P. R., Lin, Y–G., Smith, D. A. F., and Sharma, R. (1990). *Teaching and Learning in the College Classroom: A Review of the Research Literature* (2nd ed.). School of Education, University of Michigan.

Menges, R. J. (1973). The new reporters: Students rate instruction. In C. R. Pace (ed.), *Evaluating Learning and Teaching*. San Francisco: Jossey-Bass.

Morsh, J. E., Burgess, G. G., and Smith, P. N. (1956). Student achievement as a measure of instructional effectiveness. *Journal of Educational Psychology* 47: 79–88.

Murray, H. G. (1976). How do good teachers teach? An observational study of the classroom teaching behaviors of Social Science professors receiving low, medium and high teacher ratings. Paper presented at the Canadian Psychological Association meeting.

Murray, H. G. (1980). *Evaluating University Teaching: A Review of Research*. Toronto, Canada: Ontario Confederation of University Faculty Associations.

Murray, H. G. (1983). Low inference classroom teaching behaviors and student ratings of college teaching effectiveness. *Journal of Educational Psychology* 71: 856–865.

Murray, H. G. (April, 1987). Impact of student instructions ratings on quality of teaching in higher education. Paper presented at the 1987 Annual Meeting of the American Educational Research Association, Washington, DC. (ERIC Document Reproduction Service No. ED 284 495).

Murray, H. G., Rushton, J. P., and Paunonen, S. V. (1990). Teacher personality traits and student instructional ratings in six types of university courses. *Journal of Educational Psychology* 82: 250–261.

Naftulin, D. H., Ware, J. E., and Donnelly, F. A. (1973). The Doctor Fox lecture: A paradigm of educational seduction. *Journal of Medical Education* 48: 630–635.

Neumann, L., and Neumann, Y. (1985). Determinants of students' instructional evaluation: A comparison of four levels of academic areas. *Journal of Educational Research* 78: 152–158.

Ory, J. C. and Braskamp, L. A. (1981). Faculty perceptions of the quality and usefulness of three types of evaluativeinformation. *Research in Higher Education* 15: 271–282.

Ory, J. C., Braskamp, L. A., and Pieper, D. M. (1980). Congruency of student evaluative information collected by three methods. *Journal of Educational Psychology* 72: 181–185.

Overall, J. U., and Marsh, H. W. (1979). Midterm feedback from students: Its relationship to instructional improvement and students' cognitive and affective outcomes. *Journal of Educational Psychology* 71: 856–865.

Overall, J. U., and Marsh, H. W. (1980). Students' evaluations of instruction: A longitudinal study of their stability. *Journal of Educational Psychology* 72: 321–325.

Overall, J. U., and Marsh, H. W. (1982). Students' evaluations of teaching: An update. *American Association for Higher Education Bulletin*: 35(4) 9–13.

Palmer, J., Carliner, G., and Romer, T. (1978). Learning, leniency, and evaluations. *Journal of Educational Psychology* 70: 855–863.

Perry, R. P. (1991). Perceived control in college students: implications for instruction in higher education. In J. C. Smart (ed.), *Higher Education: Handbook of Theory and Research*, Vol. 7. New York: Agathon Press. (*Reprinted in this volume.*)

Perry, R. P., and Dickens, W. J. (1984). Perceived control in the college classroom: Response–outcome contingency training and instructor expressiveness effects on student achievement and causal attributions. *Journal of Educational Psychology* 76: 966–981.

Perry, R. P., and Magnusson, J.-L. (1987). Effective instruction and students' perceptions of control in the college classroom: Multiple lecture effects. *Journal of Educational Psychology* 79: 453–460.

Perry, R. P., and Penner, K. S. (1990). Enhancing academic achievement in college students through attributional retraining and instruction. *Journal of Educational Psychology* 82: 262–271.

Peterson, C., and Cooper, S. (1980). Teacher evaluation by graded and ungraded students. *Journal of Educational Psychology* 72: 682–685.

Pohlman, J. T. (1975). A multivariate analysis of selected class characteristics and student ratings of instruction. *Multivariate Behavioral Research* 10: 81–91.

Prosser, M., and Trigwell, K. (1990). Student evaluations of teaching and courses: Student study strategies as a criterion of validity. *Higher Education* 20: 135–142.

Prosser, M., and Trigwell, K. (1991). Student evaluations of teaching and courses: Student learning approaches and outcomes as criteria of validity. Paper in review, University of Technology, Centre For Learning and Teaching, Sydney NSW Australia.

Remmers, H. H. (1931). The equivalence of judgments and test items in the sense of the Spearman–Brown formula. *Journal of Educational Psychology* 22: 66–71.

Remmers, H. H. (1958). On students' perceptions of teachers' effectiveness. In McKeachie (ed.), *The Appraisal of Teaching in Large Universities*. Ann Arbor: The University of Michigan.

Remmers, H. H. (1963). Teaching methods in research on teaching. In N. L. Gage (ed.), *Handbook on Teaching*. Chicago: Rand McNally. Rich, H. E. (1976). Attitudes of college and university faculty toward the use of student evaluation. *Educational Research Quarterly* 3: 17–28.

Rodin, M., and Rodin, B. (1972). Student evaluations of teachers. *Science* 177: 1164–1166.

Rosenshine, B. (1971). *Teaching Behaviors and Student Achievement*. London: National Foundation for Educational Research.

Rosenshine, B., and Furst, N. (1973). The use of direct observation to study teaching. In R. M. W. Travers (ed.), *Second Handbook of Research on Teaching*. Chicago: Rand McNally.

Rushton, J. P., Brainerd, C. J. and Pressley, M. (1983). Behavioral development and construct validity: The principle of aggregation. *Psychological Bulletin* 94: 18–38.

Ryans, D. G. (1960). Prediction of teacher effectiveness. In C. W. Harris (eds.), *Encyclopedia of Educational Research*. New York: Macmillan.

Salthouse, T. A., McKeachie, W. J., and Lin Y. G. (1978). An experimental investigation of factors affecting university promotion decisions. *Journal of Higher Education* 49: 177–183.

Scriven, M. (1981). Summative teacher evaluation. In J. Millman (ed.), *Handbook of Teacher Evaluation*. Beverly Hills, CA: Sage.

Seldin, P. (1975). *How Colleges Evaluate Professors: Current Policies and Practices in Evaluating Classroom Teaching Performance in Liberal Arts Colleges*. Croton–on–Hudson, New York: Blythe–Pennington, 1975.

Stephens, M. D. (1985). Teaching methods for adults. In T. Husen and T. N. Postlethwaite (eds.), *The International Encyclopedia of Education*, Vol 9. Oxford:Pergamon Press.

Voght, K. E. and Lasher, H. (1973). Does student evaluation stimulate improved teaching? Bowling Green, OH: Bowling Green University (ERIC ED 013 371)

Ward, M D., Clark, D. C., and Harrison, G. V. (1981, April). The observer effect in classroom visitation. Paper presented at the annual meeting of the American Educational Research Association, Los Angeles.

Ware, J. E., and Williams, R. G. (1975). The Dr. Fox effect: A study of lecturer expressiveness and ratings of instruction. *Journal of Medical Education* 5: 149–156.

Ware, J. E., and Williams, R. G. (1977). Discriminant analysis of student ratings as a means of identifying lecturers who differ in enthusiasm or information giving. *Educational and Psychological Measurement* 37: 627–639.

Ware, J. E., and Williams, R. G. (1979). Seeing through the Dr. Fox effect: A response to Frey. *Instructional Evaluation* 3: 6–10.

Ware, J. E., and Williams, R. G. (1980). A reanalysis of the Doctor Fox experiments. *Instructional Evaluation* 4: 15–18.

Warrington, W. G. (1973). Student evaluation of instruction at Michigan State University. In A. L. Sockloff (ed.), *Proceedings: The First Invitational Conference on Faculty Effectiveness as Evaluated by Students*. Philadelphia: Measurement and Research Center, Temple University.

Watkins, D., Marsh, H. W., and Young, D. (1987). Evaluating tertiary teaching: A New Zealand perspective. *Teaching and Teacher Education: An International Journal of Research and Studies* 3: 41–53.

Webb, W. B., and Nolan, C. Y. (1955). Student, supervisor, and self–ratings of instructional proficiency. *Journal of Educational Psychology* 46: 42–46.

Williams, R. G., and Ware, J. E. (1976). Validity of student ratings of instruction under different incentive conditions: A further study of the Dr. Fox effect. *Journal of Educational Psychology* 68: 48–56.

Williams, R. G., and Ware, J. E. (1977). An extended visit with Dr. Fox: Validity of student ratings of instruction after repeated exposures to a lecturer. *American Educational Research Journal* 14: 449–457.

Wilson, R. C. (1986). Improving faculty teaching: Effective use of student evaluations and consultants. *Journal of Higher Education* 57: 196–211.

Wilson, R. C. (1987). Toward excellence in teaching. In L. M. Aleamoni (ed.), *Technique for Evaluating and Improving Instruction*. New Direction for Teaching and Learning, no.31. San Francisco: Jossey-Bass.

Winocur, S., Schoen, L. G., and Sirowatka, A. H. (1989). Perceptions of male and female academics within a teaching context. *Research in Higher Education* 30: 317–329.

Yunker, J. A. (1983). Validity research on student evaluations of teaching effectiveness: Individual versus class mean observations. *Research in Higher Education* 19: 363–379.

The Dimensionality of Student Ratings of Instruction: What We Know and What We Do Not[1]

Philip C. Abrami, Sylvia d'Apollonia, and Steven Rosenfield

Sometime during the second half of almost all college and university courses offered in North America, a brief ritual occurs. Students take out their sharpened pencils (number two lead, if you please) and quickly answer a series of multiple choice questions covering a range of issues about the course and their instructor. Student rating forms often contain specific items, which are purported to reflect a number of distinct dimensions of instructional effectiveness, as well as a few global items, which reflect students' overall impressions of the instructor and the course. Examples of specific items include: "Does the instructor have a good command of the subject matter?" "Does the instructor use class time well?" "Is the instructor friendly?" "Does the instructor assign difficult reading?" "Does the instructor facilitate class discussion?" "Does the instructor keep students informed of their progress?" Examples of global items include: "How would you rate the instructor in overall ability?" "How would you rate the quality of this course?" "How much have you learned in this course compared to others?" Many student rating forms also provide students with the opportunity to provide narrative feedback about the course, the instructor, and their learning. While the rating ritual ends quickly, the implications of the results can be far reaching, for student ratings are used for a variety of important purposes.

In many circumstances ratings are the most influential or only source of information

[1]An earlier version of this paper was presented at the annual meeting of the American Educational Research Association, Atlanta, Georgia, April, 1993 as part of a symposium entitled: "Student ratings of instruction: Meta-analysis of their dimensionality."

This research was supported by grants from the Social Sciences and Humanities Research Council (Government of Canada) and Fonds pour la formation de chercheurs et l'aide a la recherche (Government of Quebec).

The authors gratefully acknowledge the constructive feedback received from Harris Cooper, Kenneth Feldman, Wilbert McKeachie, Herbert Marsh, Raymond Perry, and an anonymous reviewer who read earlier versions of this manuscript.

Address reprint requests to: Dr. Philip C. Abrami, Centre for the Study of Classroom Processes, Concordia University, 1455 DeMaisonneuve Blvd. W., Montreal, Quebec CANADA H3G 1M8.

on teaching available for decisions about promotion, tenure, or merit. Typically, personnel committees use ratings to judge teaching effectiveness by comparing individual faculty results with departmental norms. Ratings are also widely used for instructional improvement to provide feedback to instructors on the quality of their courses. Faculty use ratings feedback to identify both areas of strength that should be maintained and areas of weakness that require modification. Ratings are occasionally used by students as a guide to course selection. For example, some students may use ratings information to select the highest rated instructors, while others may use ratings information to select the easiest courses. Thus, student ratings serve widespread and important practical purposes.

Student ratings also serve important theoretical purposes by providing researchers with information on the teaching-learning process. For example, such information may be useful in assessing the effectiveness of innovative pedagogical techniques such as cooperative learning, in understanding the relationship between instructional preparation and delivery as they affect multiple outcomes of instruction, and in judging the impact of instructional strategies for different students, courses, and settings.

The practical and theoretical utility of student ratings depends on the extent to which ratings meet psychometric standards of excellence. Concerns about the reliability, validity, and generalizability of student ratings include: Are rating results consistent over time? Are students uniform in their assessments of instructors? Are ratings free from the influence of biasing characteristics? What is the dimensionality of student ratings? Are these dimensions consistent across students, courses, settings, and rating forms? Which dimensions reflect the impact of instruction on student learning and other outcomes?

This paper is concerned with the dimensionality of instruction as reflected in student ratings. Research on the dimensions of effective teaching is not new. There are numerous studies which have explored this issue and notable disagreements (e.g., Abrami and d'Apollonia, 1990; Marsh, 1987) regarding, in particular, whether and how data from multidimensional student rating forms should be used in summative decisions about teaching (e.g., promotion, merit, tenure, etc.). This paper critically examines many of these issues and reaches important conclusions about the dimensionality of teaching as reflected in student ratings, makes practical suggestions, as well as suggests directions for future research.

In the first section, three alternative definitions of effective teaching are presented and critically analyzed: the product definition, the process definition, and the process-product definition. We contend that the relationships between teaching processes and teaching products is of major interest to researchers and practitioners.

The second section provides a general discussion of methods for empirically determining effective teaching with special emphasis on the use of student ratings for each of the three definitions of effective teaching. We comment on the difficulties of directly assessing the products of instruction and suggest the use of a table of specifications as one way to develop a rating form to indirectly measure what and how students have learned. We suggest that students ratings as process measures must contain items which assess the relevant aspects of teaching accurately in each instructional context. We note that the dimensionality of student ratings varies with course characteristics and we suggest that some items which evaluate specific aspects of teaching vary in relevance across contexts. We show that multidimensional student rating forms do not contain items which evaluate the same, specific teaching qualities; the rating forms lack both comprehensiveness and uniformity. We conclude that since the qualities of teaching evaluated by different student rating forms appear to differ both in their nature and structure, it is of value to explore the forms further and determine if there are dimensions of teaching common to a collection of student rating forms.

The third section concentrates on the strengths and weaknesses of three validation designs—the laboratory design, the multisection validation design and the multitrait-multimethod design—for empirically determining the relationship between the processes and products of teaching. The laboratory design uses the experimental manipulation of instructional conditions to study the causal effects of instruction on students. It is often considered low in external validity. The multisection validation design uses multiple sections of the same course taught by different instructors employing common measures of student ratings and student learning. The correlations between course section means for student ratings and means for student achievement explore the relationship between instructional processes and an important instructional product. We consider the multisection design particularly strong because it reduces the probability of rival explanations to instructor impacts and is high in generalizability to classrooms. In the multitrait-multimethod design, student ratings and several criterion measures (e.g., instructor self-ratings) are collected across a wide range of courses, without controlling for biasing or extraneous influences. We consider this design weaker both in internal validity, since controls are lacking, and in external validity, since important product measures of instruction (e.g., student learning) are not included. We conclude that studies employing the multisection design are worthy of special attention.

The fourth section examines the quantitative reviews of the 43 multisection validity studies. We describe what we have learned from these studies and what remains to be learned of the relationship between what instructors do when they teach and how this affects student learning. We note that reviews to date suggest that the specific dimensions of teaching appear to differentially and, in some cases, poorly predict instructor impacts on learning compared to global ratings. We suggest that there are several limitations of prior reviews. First, the reviews include only a fraction of the findings from the original studies. Second, there is the lack of a comprehensive, empirically validated system for organizing the findings from different rating forms into a common framework. Third, study features which may explain the variability in study findings remain unexplored. Consequently, a more comprehensive research integration is called for using an empirically determined scheme for coding the findings from different rating forms

The fifth section summarizes our attempt to identify the common dimensions of effective teaching as reflected in student ratings. First, we summarize our re-analysis of Marsh in which we failed to find many specific teaching dimensions but found a general teaching factor instead. Since our ultimate goal is to explore the relationship between process and product, we concentrate on the rating forms used in the 43 multisection validity studies. We quantitatively integrate the results from 17 inter-item correlation matrices by: a) coding the items using a common scoring scheme, b) eliminating items which were heterogeneous within categories, and c) factor analyzing the aggregate correlation matrix.

Our factor analysis indicates that there is a common structure to instruction. Four factors emerged of which the largest ones were highly correlated. We conclude that existing analyses provide support for a large underlying general trait although it may not be the only trait. We also believe that effective teaching is multidimensional but that there are differences across rating forms concerning the specific dimensions which underlie effective instruction. These differences suggest that student ratings of specific teaching dimensions should not be used indiscriminately for summative decisions about teaching effectiveness. Now that we have identified the common structure of student ratings, the next phase of research will be to use the techniques of quantitative research integration to explore the relationship between this structure and teacher-produced student achievement as well as the substantive and methodological variables which explain inconsistencies in the relationships.

DEFINITIONS OF EFFECTIVE TEACHING

Effective teaching can be defined from several perspectives. In the first perspective, effective teaching is defined in terms of affecting student products. In the second perspective, effective teaching is defined in terms of the processes which instructors enact. These views are elaborated and contrasted below. The relationship between process and product views is also presented. The relationship between the process and product views of effective teaching seeks to find the links between what teachers do and whether and how students change as a result.

The Product Definition of Effective Teaching

Broadly speaking, effective teaching from the product view can be defined as the positive changes produced in students in relevant academic domains including the cognitive, affective, and occasionally the psychomotor ones (to use the general taxonomic classifications developed by Bloom et al., 1956). Included in the cognitive domain are both specific cognitive skills (e.g., subject matter expertise), general cognitive skills (e.g., analytical thinking), and meta-cognitive skills (e.g., error correction). Included in the affective domain are attitudes and interests toward the subject matter in particular and learning in general as well as interpersonal skills and abilities relevant to learning and working in a social context. Finally, included in the psychomotor domain are physical skills and abilities ranging from those acquired in a physical education to precise motor skills acquired in a fine arts education.

This definition concentrates on the products that effective teaching promotes in students. The definition has several corollaries. First, there is not a single product of effective teaching; there are many. Second, there is no *a priori* theoretical requirement that the products are interrelated either within or across domains. For example, it is not necessarily the case that increased student knowledge of basic facts will result in increased analytical and synthesis skills or vice versa. Third, the value attached to individual products is often situation-specific, requiring adjustments to meet the local needs described by students, departments, and colleges. Fourth, greater teaching effectiveness is not necessarily associated with the number of products affected. Fifth, the definition makes no prediction about the (casual) sequences or paths among products. For example, it does not explicate whether student casual beliefs about learning affect academic self-concept or vice versa.

The product definition of effective teaching recognizes that there is widespread disagreement in the academic community about both the objectives and goals of instruction and the ways to achieve them. For example in the social sciences, clinical practitioners may dispute experimental researchers about the importance of developing the affective skills of students. While almost all faculty will agree with the preeminence of developing the cognitive abilities of students, there is less general agreement over the form that development takes. For example, in the natural sciences physicists may dispute whether to teach about the many concepts of the discipline or how to teach students to discover a few fundamentals.

The Process Definition of Effective Teaching

The process definition of effective teaching emphasizes the acts of teaching rather than the consequences of those actions. The process definition is meant to include instructor activities which occur both before (preparatory) and during (delivery) teaching. Preparation may include such wide-ranging activities as: developing content expertise; preparing course outlines, activities, and objectives; selecting a teaching method; assigning course workload; and setting evaluation practices and procedures. The delivery procedures may include classroom activities and abilities such as organization, dynamism, enthusiasm, and rapport, and outside classroom activities such as availability to, and friendliness toward, students.

The process definition has several corollaries. First, there is not a single process of effective teaching; there are many. The definition recognizes that effective teaching is multidimensional consisting of numerous and apparently distinct acts. Second, the definition is tentative regarding the specific acts which constitute the process. One purpose of our research is to determine empirically whether there is uniformity and consistency to these acts. Third, it is also possible that these distinct acts represent different operationalizations of an underlying construct or constructs. For example, "instructor clarity" may consist of clarity of speech, audibility, pace, comprehensibility, etc. Furthermore, these constructs may be both additive and hierarchical. This is also an empirical question. Fifth, the term "effective teaching" means that there is an evaluative component to the process. This evaluative component regards both the instructor's choice of acts and the quality and quantity with which they are enacted. In other words, ineffective instructors may emphasize the wrong acts when they teach or enact them poorly.

It is also unclear whether generally static personal characteristics or traits (e.g., gender, race, age, personality, etc.) form part of the process definition. They are qualities which are beyond the control of the instructor but which may nevertheless indirectly influence both the acts of teaching and the products of teaching. These are sometimes referred to as biasing characteristics in recognition both of their potential for influence and the undesirability of that influence.

The Process-Product Definition of Effective Teaching

What activities differentiate good instructors from poor ones in promoting students' critical thinking, task engagement, and persistence? Is instructor enthusiasm an important teaching process because enthusiasm motivates students to learn? Important questions such as these speak to the inexorable link between teaching processes and products.

It is our contention that the relationships between teaching processes and teaching products is of major interest. The link between process and product raises new questions about the meaning of the term "effective teaching." Now, rather than effective teaching being defined only in terms of either process or product, we may combine the two. Doing so helps identify links between what teachers do and whether and how students change as a result.

Broadly speaking, effective teaching from the process-product view can be defined as the instructor activities which occur both before (preparatory) and during (delivery) teaching which produce positive changes in students in relevant academic domains including the cognitive, affective, and occasionally the psychomotor ones.

We hypothesize that the varied products of effective teaching are affected by different teaching processes. But we cannot describe with any great confidence the specific nature of these causal relationships.

We further hypothesize that the causal relationship between any one teaching process and any one teaching product will vary as a function of external influences including student, course, and setting influences. As stated previously, there appears to be important disagreements among faculty on what to teach and how to teach it.

To summarize, we have briefly explored three alternative definitions of effective teaching: the product definition, the process definition, and the process-product definition. We believe the relationship between teaching processes and teaching products is of major interest.

EMPIRICALLY DETERMINING EFFECTIVE TEACHING

In this section we consider ways to determine effective teaching empirically for the three definitions of teaching presented. We concentrate, in particular, on the use of student ratings for these purposes.

Empirically Determining the Products of Effective Teaching

According to the product definition, effective teaching produces changes in such student outcomes as content knowledge, analytic ability, academic self-concept, motivation to learn, aesthetic appreciation, and so on. Unfortunately, the authors are unaware of individual studies that attempt to systematically and inclusively describe college teaching from a product-based perspective. There are studies that explore outcomes singly, particularly those that examine the effects of teaching on (undifferentiated) student learning of course content. Therefore, it may be profitable to apply the techniques of quantitative research integration to the literature on instructional products to better and more completely understand the effects of teaching.

In recent years, Seldin (1991), Shore et al. (1986), and others have argued for the use of the teaching portfolio, a comprehensive collection of descriptive and evaluative information on individual faculty teaching, which might include a statement of teaching responsibilities, course syllabi, instructor self evaluations, a description of improvement efforts, peer assessments, participation in teaching conferences, videotapes of instruction, student exams and essays, alumni ratings, and so on. The portfolio is to be used both for teaching improvement purposes and for summative decisions.

Judging teaching effectiveness by examining the evidence of student accomplishments—tests, papers, and projects—generally requires that two criteria are met: a) the data presented are representative of the faculty member's effect on students and b) the results of faculty can be objectively compared. Meeting the first criterion requires examining the results either of all students or a random sample of students. Submitting the best student products as evidence of teaching effectiveness, a common practice, does little to allow accurate judgments of how well instructors promote student learning.

Meeting the second criterion requires measures of student productivity that can be compared across courses. Unfortunately, this has rarely been accomplished. For example, it is extremely difficult to compare the achievement of students enrolled in an introductory Physics course with the achievement of students enrolled in an advanced, upper-level Physics course in order to judge which instructor best promotes student learning. Are differences in achievement between the two courses due to the quality of the students enrolled? The difficulty of the tests used? The nature of the material learned? The quality of the instruction given? Similarly, it is tenuous to assume that changes from pretest examination scores at the beginning of term to posttest examination scores at the end reflect only the impacts of instruction. In contrast, it is less difficult to compare student achievement on a final, common examination when the students are enrolled in different sections of the same course, especially when it is reasonable to assume that students selected course sections more or less at random. Under circumstances resembling the latter, using product measures to compare and judge instruction seems quite defensible and its use should be more widespread. In general, however, product measures of effective teaching are seldom practical to use and rarely provide accurate data for judging quality teaching.

*Student ratings as **direct** product measures.* Student ratings measure directly one product of instruction; namely, student satisfaction with teaching. For many, measuring student satisfaction with teaching is a sufficient reason to use student ratings. Proponents of the use of ratings as satisfaction measures argue that if students are the consumers of the teaching process, then student satisfaction with teaching should be a component of instructional evaluation.

Otherwise, student ratings do not measure *directly* how much or how well a class of students has learned or any other aspect of achievement in the cognitive domain including how well the content is retained. Student ratings also do not often measure directly:

most affective products of instruction such as student expectations, beliefs, and concepts about themselves as learners; student attitudes, values, and interests toward the subject matter including enrolling in other courses in the area or adopting the area as a field of major study; student interpersonal and social skills generally and such skills within the context of executing a complex academic task; etc.

*Student ratings as **indirect** product measures.* Student ratings are often used as convenient alternative measures of most instructional products. Ratings are used to *infer* that highly rated instructors positively affect instructional products. Student ratings provide a basic yardstick for these judgments when product measures are unavailable, when the product measures are of questionable quality, or when conditions (such as differences in the level or type of course) do not allow for fair comparisons of products across instructors.

To what extent do student ratings reflect the impact of instructors on students learning of course content, their motivation to learn, development of interpersonal skills, and so on? There is a reasonable body of well-designed research, reviewed more extensively elsewhere in this paper, which suggests that, on average, there is a modest, positive relationship between global ratings of instruction and instructor-produced student learning of lower-level academic skills (e.g., knowledge of basic facts, simple comprehension, etc.). Much less is known about the validity of ratings as predictors of other outcomes of instruction.

*Improving student ratings as **indirect** product measures.* Consider the following item from a student rating form: "Rate the extent to which your instructor motivated you to learn." Does this item ask students to describe an instructional process or an instructional product? The item does not ask students to judge instructor preparation or delivery but the consequences of teaching. It is, therefore, not a measure of a teaching process. But is it is an accurate, *indirect* assessment of an instructional product? It is accurate only to the extent that student self-report of motivation reflects student persistence at learning, the intensity of student effort, student choice of tasks to learn, etc. Rating forms occasionally include items that ask students to assess the success of instructors at encouraging them to learn but seldom include items that assess the specific behaviors associated with that motivation.

Similarly, rating forms do not often contain items that ask students to assess an instructor's impact on specific cognitive and meta-cognitive achievements. Instead, rating forms more frequently ask students to rate: "How much have you learned in this course compared with others?" A questionnaire can be designed so that ratings items may be made more precise by asking students to judge how well they learned from the instructor in each content area of the course as well as the depth to which they learned. (See Table 1, p. 329.)

The table of specifications or teaching blueprint presented in Table 1 illustrates a student rating form for an undergraduate course in psychological statistics. The rows represent the content to be learned. The columns represent how the content is to be learned. The cells or boxes represent the combination of what is to be learned and how it is to be learned. Students may use this type of evaluation form to judge an instructor's effectiveness: overall in promoting student learning, in particular content areas of the course, and in promoting different types and levels of learning. The evaluation form also allows for very specific feedback on particular aspects of teaching. For example, was the instructor effective at promoting higher level skills in more complex areas of the course?

Not all the content areas of the course are equally important, nor is every type of learning of equal value and emphasis. For example, the instructor may need to spend considerable time on some topics (e.g., descriptive statistics) and not others (e.g., factorial ANOVA). Similarly, some topics may require substantial efforts devoted to basic knowledge and comprehension while other topics may require greater efforts devoted to analysis, synthesis, and evaluation.

TABLE 1. Table of Specifications for Student Ratings of Course Content in Psychological Statistics

Instructions: Please use this rating form to assess how well your instructor taught you the content of this course. Begin by assigning your instructor an overall rating for the amount you learned in the course. Use the box with the darkest shading for this purpose. The major content areas of the course are listed in the *rows* of the table. For each content area or row assign your instructor an *overall* rating using the scale shown below. For example, if your instructor taught you descriptive statistics extremely well assign an overall rating of 5 for descriptive statistics. The major cognitive objectives of the course are listed as *columns* in the table. For each cognitive objective or column assign your instructor an *overall* rating. For example, if your instructor taught you to apply the content extremely well assign an overall rating of 5 for application. Finally, use each box to give your instructor a rating for both what you learned and how you learned it. For example, assign your instructor a "4" if (s)he did a very good job teaching you to evaluate uses of the t-test.

Use the following rating scale in making your judgments:
1—Poor
2—Fair
3—Good
4—Very good
5—Excellent
NA—*Not applicable*

Course Content	How the Content Was Learned						OVERALL RATING
	Knowledge	Compre-hension	Applica-tion	Analysis	Synthesis	Evaluation	
Descrip-tive statis-tics							
The t-test							
Oneway Anova							
Factorial Anova							
Nonpara-metrics							
OVER-ALL RAT-ING							

Prior to the evaluation, the instructor and/or students may wish to estimate the amount of time devoted to each content area and type of learning. First, estimate the percent of course time devoted to each content area. The sum of the row percentages should be 100%. Next estimate the percent of course time devoted to each cognitive objective. The sum of the column percentages should be 100%. Next, fill in each cell or box percentage. Note that the precision of the table of specifications rating form in assessing student learning remains to be determined empirically.

Finally, not all rating items seem as logically defensible as indirect measures of instructional products as the self report items described above. For example, why should instructor friendliness and openness toward students necessarily reflect student understanding of thermodynamics? Indeed, we recall rather heated discussions by some faculty that they do not. Therefore, such items are better understood to reflect student ratings of the processes of effective teaching. An interest in whether such items and similar items can be used to assess instructor impacts on student learning and other outcomes is, consequently, an interest in the relationship between process and product.

Empirically Determining the Processes of Effective Teaching

Many studies have attempted to determine empirically the dimensions, clusters, factors or major characteristics that college instructors employ. Are these characteristics too many or too varied to describe succinctly? Do faculty and students agree on the characteristics they describe? Can these characteristics be grouped together?

A major portion of the research has relied on empirical methods for identifying teaching dimensions, chiefly through the use of factor analysis. Marsh (1987) summarized research on one instrument, Students' Evaluations of Educational Quality (SEEQ), which identified nine factors of instruction. Marsh (1987) argued for consideration of these nine factors when summative evaluations of teaching are made (e.g., for promotion and tenure decisions).

Feldman (1976) reviewed studies in which students were asked to describe the characteristics of best teachers, or of ideal teachers, or of good teaching. He identified 19 dimensions which he used to classify the descriptions. Later, Feldman (1988) reviewed studies comparing faculty and student specifications of the instructional characteristics they considered particularly important to good teaching and effective instruction. In the latter review, Feldman (1988) identified 22 instructional dimensions. The average correlation between students and faculty in their judgment of these components was +0.71. Feldman (1988) concluded that there was general agreement between faculty and students in their views of good teaching as reflected in the importance the two groups placed on the components of teaching.

Feldman (1976) and Kulik and McKeachie (1975) reviewed factor analytic research of student ratings of instruction. Feldman (1976) employed 19 categories to categorize the items from 60 studies. He then fit the dimensions into three major clusters. Kulik and McKeachie (1975) reviewed 11 studies and identified four commonly found factors.

In sum, there appeared to be encouraging evidence regarding the processes of effective teaching. Descriptions of teaching by students appeared to fit into a reasonably finite set of categories. Faculty and students showed reasonable agreement as to the characteristics they considered important. When students rated faculty on these characteristics, groups of items formed into factors that reviewers were able to organize further. In light of such findings, it seemed reasonable to ask students to rate faculty to measure teaching processes. After all, students had the greatest exposure to faculty teaching and should be in a good position to judge.

Such thinking, however, depended first on showing that students were accurate, consistent, and unbiased judges. Second, it depended on showing that the teaching qualities students were asked to judge were always relevant and appropriate and took into account innovative teaching methods[2]. It also depended on showing that different rating forms contained items which tapped the same teaching qualities. Finally, it depended on showing that the results of specific ratings could be effectively used.

The accuracy of student ratings. The validity of student ratings as process measures of effective teaching depends on showing that the ratings of students are accurate and reliable descriptions of preparation and delivery activities. The reliability of student ratings is not a contested issue: the stability of ratings over time and the consistency of ratings over students (especially in classes of ten or more) compares favorably with the best objective tests (Feldman, 1977; Marsh, 1987; Marsh and Dunkin, 1992).

The accuracy of student ratings of teaching process is a concern about criterion-related validity. Are students able to accurately judge whether (quantity) and how well (quality) instructors teach according to the dimensions specified on the rating form? In general, criterion-related validation studies require alternative measures of the teaching process in addition to student ratings. For example, to assess the criterion-related validity of ratings as process measures requires examining studies comparing faculty (peer) and chair ratings with student ratings, trained observers ratings with student ratings,

---

[2]Feldman (1976, 1988, 1989a, 1989b, 1990) among others has explored the relationship between global ratings of teaching effectiveness and dimensional ratings as a way of showing the validity of dimensional ratings as indices of teaching processes. The value of such an approach depends on making a case for the link between specific teaching processes and student perceptions of the general quality of teaching received. Feldman (1988) puts the case this way:

> If it is assumed that each student's overall evaluation of an instructor is an additive combination of the student's evaluation of specific aspects of the teacher and his or her instruction, weighted by the student's estimation of the relative importance of these aspects to good teaching, then it would be expected that students' overall assessment of instructors would be more highly associated with instructor characteristics that students generally consider to be important to good teaching than with those they consider to be less important (p. 314).

The assumption of a link between global ratings and specific ratings is, in our view, highly plausible but an assumption that can be challenged on both conceptual and empirical grounds. Is it not also plausible that students' impressions have either: a) a general component and specific components or b) only specific components? If either of these alternative views is plausible, it would be erroneous to invalidate ratings of teaching dimensions that do not correlate with global assessments. For example, the social psychology literature suggests several models of impression formation including the three dimensions of evaluative judgment (good-bad, weak-strong, and fast-slow) offered by Osgood, Suci, and Tannenbaum (1957) as well as the weighted averaging model of overall impressions (Anderson, 1968).

However, what is fundamentally important is not the structure of student impressions but the structure of what teachers actually do when they teach. Consequently, the plausibility of the assumption that students form general impressions may be reasonable for the *judgment* of teaching process that students utilize but the assumption becomes much less reasonable and much less plausible when one is utilizing student ratings to develop a theoretical *description* of the teaching process. Is teaching a series of discrete actions? Do these actions meld into a single collection of actions or several collections of actions? It remains uncertain which of these ways is best to describe teaching.

instructor self-ratings with student ratings, etc. The data suggest that students are reasonably accurate judges of most teaching processes (Marsh, 1987; Marsh and Dunkin, 1992).

The criterion validation of student ratings as measures of teaching processes is not to be confused with the validation of student ratings as measures of teaching products. As Doyle noted:

> In instructional evaluation validity studies, ratings of instructor characteristics are compared with student learning. But student learning is not an alternative measure of, say, an instructor's effectiveness in engaging student attention. Alternative measures of engaging student attention might include observer's counts of students dozing or staring out the window, or student reports of boredom, or even galvanic skin response (1981, p. 24).

The content validity of student ratings. The validity of student ratings as process measures of effective teaching also depends on showing that the items on the rating form have content validity and are a representative sample of items from the larger population of items. The requirement of content validity suggests that if a single form is used it is equally applicable in a variety of instructional contexts and not just the lecture format for which most rating forms were designed. These instructional contexts include different pedagogical methods (e.g., small and large class lecturing, tutoring and advising, studio classes, discussion and small group methods including cooperative learning, individualized and mastery learning, etc.), academic disciplines, student and setting characteristics, etc.

Abrami and d'Apollonia (1990) argued that a student rating form should contain items equally relevant to each of the instructional situations for which it was designed. Consequently, items such as "Students were encouraged to participate in class discussion" and "Instructor was friendly towards individual students" would not be equally relevant in small and large classes, regardless of whether those items retained the same interrelationship with other items across instructional contexts. For example, imagine several items (e.g., friendliness, openness, encouraging, and warmth) which assess instructor rapport. It is quite easy to see how scores on these items would be interrelated regardless of instructional context. If you are not very friendly, you are probably not seen as especially open, encouraging, or warm. This may explain why Marsh and Hocevar (1984, 1990) report some evidence of the factorial validity of the SEEQ.

But it is equally easy to envision how instructor rapport with students might be more critical in a small class than a large one. And it is also possible that because different teaching behaviors are important in different contexts, instructor mean ratings might vary across contexts. That is, instructors may concentrate on the qualities important in that context and receive higher ratings on context-relevant teaching skills. Fernald (1990) found that items on a multidimensional rating form varied greatly with regard to student perceptions of item relevance to the course. Furthermore, the degree of item relevance was correlated with student ratings of instruction: the higher the item relevance score, the higher the student rating score.

In our hypothetical example, rapport mean ratings would vary significantly in small classes versus large classes even though the underlying relationship among rapport items remained the same. Unfortunately, mean scores, not interitem correlations, are used by promotion committees to make summative decisions about effective teaching. In this case, irrelevant items bias the case against the instructor of large classes.

Comprehensiveness and uniformity of student rating forms. Another type of evidence concerning the validity of rating forms comes from comparisons of items on different rating forms. Abrami and d'Apollonia (1990) reasoned that if effective teaching was substantially invariant, then one would expect the same teaching qualities to emerge on each multidimensional rating form; there would not be substantial variability across forms in the factors of effective teaching which are assessed. Moreover, the relative type and proportion of items representing these factors would also not vary across forms.

To assess the comprehensiveness and uniformity of existing multidimensional rating forms, we used an early version of our coding scheme to sort the rating items found in 43 studies assessing the validity of student ratings to predict teacher-produced student learning. There were 154 study findings in the 43 studies (e.g., studies that report the findings for more than one course). There were 742 validity coefficients or correlations between scores on the rating forms and student learning. For example, a multidimensional rating form would yield several rating-achievement correlations. We first determined the number of times a category was found in the study findings. The comprehensiveness index represents the portion of times a teaching category is represented in the 154 findings. We then computed a uniformity index, which is a measure of the unidimensionality of reported validity coefficients across forms, for each instructional dimension. The uniformity index is the average proportion of items within a specific dimension, computed across 154 study findings. Thus, a high uniformity index indicates that the reported validity coefficients tend to represent a single dimension. The results of the uniformity and comprehensiveness analyses are presented in Table 2. The results suggest that both the items that appear on multidimensional student rating forms and the factors that these items represent vary across study findings. The uniformity indices for teaching dimensions were as low as 0.11 (instructor expansiveness ratings); these dimensional indices contrast with global indices that were 0.51 (overall course rating) and 0.61 (overall instructor rating). Especially at the level of asking specific questions about instruction (i.e., low-inference questions) multidimensional student rating forms are composed of a diverse collection of items. Furthermore, even as the items are organized into factors, a considerable lack of uniformity remains.

Student ratings and innovative teaching methods. As never before, college instructors are using innovative teaching methods in place of, or in addition to, the traditional lecture method. One method that shows special promise for enhancing student achievement as well as developing communication and interpersonal skills, is cooperative learning (Abrami et al., 1995; Cooper et al., 1990: Johnson, Johnson, and Smith, 1991). Cooperative learning relies on students learning actively and purposefully together in small groups. Two key elements of cooperative learning are positive interdependence and individual accountability. Positive interdependence exists when students perceive that their success at learning has a positive influence on their teammates' successes and vice versa. Individual accountability exists when students perceive that they are responsible for their own learning and for the learning of their teammates. The instructor's role in cooperative learning is different than in whole class instruction. Because students spend a considerable amount of time attending to their classmates, much less class time is devoted to lecturing. Instead, the instructor usually gives only a brief overview of important ideas and then allows student teams to explore these ideas further.

TABLE 2. Uniformity and Comprehensiveness Analysis of Student Rating Forms (N = 154 study findings)

Dimension	N	CI[1]	UI[2]
Stimulation of interest	88	0.57	0.25
Enthusiasm	30	0.19	0.23
Knowledge of the subject	43	0.28	0.36
Intellectual expansiveness	35	0.23	0.11
Preparation and organization	89	0.58	0.33
Clarity and understandableness	112	0.73	0.30
Elocutionary skills	54	0.35	0.13
Class level and progress	76	0.49	0.20
Clarity of course objectives	68	0.44	0.25
Relevance and value of materials	46	0.30	0.38
Supplementary materials	26	0.17	0.36
Workload	84	0.55	0.45
Perceived outcome	75	0.49	0.47
Fairness of evaluation	69	0.45	0.39
Classroom management	79	0.51	0.25
Personality characteristics	54	0.35	0.25
Feedback	66	0.43	0.24
Encouragement of discussion	90	0.58	0.35
Intellectual challenge	35	0.23	0.24
Concern and respect for students	75	0.49	0.22
Availability and helpfulness	68	0.44	0.29
Overall course	92	0.60	0.51
Overall instructor	109	0.71	0.61
Miscellaneous	47	0.31	0.23

[1]CI=Comprehensiveness Index [2]UI=Uniformity Index
Adapted from Abrami and d'Apollonia (1990).

The distinctiveness of cooperative learning compared with lecturing suggests that the specific instructional processes involved will be different. For example, in whole class instruction almost all of class time is devoted to the instructor talking and students listening. Clarity of explanation should be more important in classes designed for lecturing than in classes where the instructor presents for only a portion of the time.

In a cooperative classroom, the instructor's primary role is to insure that teams are viable and that teammates are effectively instructing one another. In particular, the instructor insures that group tasks are appropriate for learning and that students are operating together as a team with each member of the team holding a personal stake in the outcome. Furthermore, the instructor insures that each team has the necessary skills and abilities to learn. When necessary, the instructor may intervene to motivate students and to facilitate their learning. Thus, differences in instructional methods suggest that a student rating form consisting of one set of specific teaching dimensions will not have uniform content validity.

Factorial invariance? An underlying assumption of the multidimensional approach to the evaluation of instruction is that the characteristics of effective teaching are substantially invariant across situations (Marsh and Hocevar, 1984). In general, the qualities important to effective teaching are not expected to vary from course to course, from department to department, or from university to university. Marsh and Hocevar (1984, 1990) provide some evidence of the factorial invariance of one student rating form across different groups of students, academic disciplines, instructor levels, and course levels. That is, the factor structure of the rating form (i.e., the number and nature of the teaching dimensions found) and thus the relationships among perceived characteristics of teaching, was stable across contexts. However, differences in pedagogical methods were not explored for possible influences on factor structure.

A study by Smith and Cranton (1992) reached different conclusions about the influence of course characteristics. They found that student perceptions of the amount of improvement needed in the four dimensions of a student rating form differed significantly across levels of instruction and class size. They concluded that the relationships between course characteristics and student ratings are not general but specific to the instructional setting. They suggested several practical implications of their results. First, for instructional improvement, a faculty member should not assume that all items on a student rating form are of equal importance in planning changes. Second, faculty who want to determine criteria for the interpretation of their ratings by comparing themselves to others would likely be making a mistake. Third, personnel decisions using data from student ratings should not be based on a comparisons among faculty or across courses without considering the instructional setting.

Utility of student rating forms. Finally, one cannot expect untrained administrators or non-experts in evaluation to properly weigh the information provided by factor scores in arriving at a single decision about the quality of an instructor's teaching (Franklin and Theall, 1989). One cannot expect administrators to have the expertise of faculty developers, nor are there precise and defensible procedures for synthesizing the information from factor scores. Experience suggests that administrators weigh factor scores equally or look for particularly strong or weak areas of teaching. What if these low scores occurred because the dimensions were low in relevancy? Cashin and Downey (1992) studied the usefulness of global items in predicting weighted composite ratings with a sample of 17,183 classes from 105 institutions. Their results were that global items accounted for a substantial amount of the variance (more than 50%). They concluded: "The results of this study have supported that single, global items—as suggested by Abrami (1985)—can account for a great deal of the variance resulting from a weighted composite of many multidimensional student rating items"(Cashin and Downey, 1992, p. 569). They recommended that short student rating forms should be used for summative evaluations and longer forms should be reserved for teaching improvement.

Ratings and the processes of instruction: Where do we go from here? The interests of many researchers and practitioners alike appears to have focused on finding a rating form capable of identifying the major qualities or traits essential to the process of effective teaching. Analytical strategies such as factor analysis concentrate on identifying what is common to teaching and generally disregard what is unique.

The alternative view we argue for here suggests that the search for a collection of the invariant dimensions of effective instruction may underemphasize the importance of the local context. We are reminded, in particular, of the endless discussions among faculty over the merits of including particular items on student rating forms. Comments such as "What does _____ have to do with good teaching?" are reflections of the possible problems associated with employing a single definition of instruction when many are needed. Consequently, research and practice may need to be more sensitive to situational influences and make greater allowances for multiple approaches to the definition and evaluation of effectiveness.

Nevertheless, there are both theoretical and practical reasons to continue to examine, describe, and classify instructional processes. We decided, therefore, to explore further the research on the dimensionality of the processes of effective teaching by quantitatively integrating the results of many studies using a collection of different student rating forms. We believe that a systematic effort to integrate this corpus of research may better answer questions about teaching. Is there a core set of teaching qualities that emerge from every one of the studies? Do these qualities form into the same factors? How much does context matter? By integrating the existing research, we hoped to be better able to separate common dimensions of teaching from unique qualities that may only be appropriate for particular instructional context. We describe our findings in a later section. Before doing so, we consider research linking the processes and the products of effective teaching.

Empirically Determining the Links Between the Processes and Products of Effective Teaching

According to the process-product view of effective instruction, a valid student rating must assess accurately, if not directly, instructor impacts on both processes and products. That is, we wish to know not only the extent student ratings reflect what instructors do when they teach but also the extent to which students learn course content, are motivated, and develop critical skills as a result. Consequently, the principal consideration for a research design is that it allows one to assess the degree to which student ratings reflect what teachers do (process) and the impact teachers have on students (product). In particular, the design must control for plausible rival explanations to the causal effects of instructors.

Generally, these plausible rival explanations center around the effects of "biasing" characteristics, mainly student characteristics (e.g., ability), but also course and setting effects (e.g., size), and extraneous instructor characteristics (e.g., grading standards). Thus, our first consideration is that the design controls for plausible threats to internal validity (Campbell and Stanley, 1963).

Our second consideration is that the design allows us to generalize the results across students, instructors, courses and other setting characteristics, various rating instruments and importantly, different products of effective instruction. For example, we wish to conclude that ratings predict teacher impacts in a variety of courses and for a variety of instructor effectiveness measures. Thus, our second consideration is that the design controls for plausible threats to external validity (Campbell and Stanley, 1963). The strongest design will control for plausible threats to both internal and external validity.

In this section three research designs—the laboratory design, the multisection validation design and the multitrait-mutimethod design (MTMM)—are critically reviewed. In the typical laboratory design, students are randomly assigned to instructional treatment conditions that attempt to simulate certain classroom features. After a brief exposure to the treatment (often as short as 20 minutes), students are asked to complete ratings and other measures. In the multisection validation design, researchers correlate mean student ratings and mean student achievement on a common examination from multiple sections of a college course. A large positive correlation is taken as evidence of rating validity, establishing a link between what instructors do when they teach and their impact on students. In the MTMM design, student ratings factors and several criterion measures (e.g., instructor self-ratings) are collected across a wide range of courses, and the convergent and discriminant validity of ratings are assessed.

Laboratory Designs

To explore simply and conclusively the causal relationships between particular instructional processes and particular products requires experiments that manipulate what teachers do and that measure how students change as a result (see Murray, 1991, for a review). Laboratory designs are the strongest designs for controlling threats to internal validity because they manipulate instructional conditions and control for the effects of students through random assignment. However, they are the weakest designs for controlling for threats to external validity.

The laboratory studies on instructor expressiveness and lecture content (educational seduction or the Dr. Fox effect; Abrami, Leventhal, and Perry, 1982) examined the effects of two instructional delivery processes—expressiveness and content—on two instructional products—student satisfaction and low-level student learning. But Abrami et al. (1982) argued that these laboratory studies suffered shortcomings in both the comprehensiveness of the process variables studied and the representativeness of the values of the process variables manipulated. The laboratory studies lacked comprehensiveness because they failed to represent the many instructor characteristics that may affect ratings and learning. The laboratory manipulations of instructor characteristics lacked representativeness because they failed to represent actual differences among instructors in the field. The lack of both comprehensiveness and representativeness means that laboratory studies cannot be used to estimate the *extent* to which ratings predict student learning. For example, the laboratory findings that instructor expressiveness affects ratings substantially (r=.70) and achievement slightly (r=.12) suggests only that the correlation between ratings and achievement falls somewhere in the range of +.84 to -.56. Instead, laboratory studies are best used to explain *why* ratings and achievement are related by identifying the instructional processes which *causally* affect instructional products.

Multisection Validation Design

To date, more than 40 studies have appeared using the multisection validation design. The design has several features that make it high in internal validity. Using class section means rather than students (or students pooled across classes) as the units of analysis emphasizes instructor effects on ratings and achievement. Furthermore, in many of these studies, section differences in student characteristics were controlled experimentally, via random assignment, or statistically, using ability pretests. Similarly, section differences in setting effects were often minimized with the use of a common syllabus, common textbook, similar section sizes, and so on. Finally, the effect of instructor grading standards was reduced by the use of a common examination for all sections. Thus, the design minimizes the extent to which the correlation between student ratings and achievement can be explained by factors other than instructor influences. However, unlike laboratory studies, instructional variables are not manipulated but only measured by the student rating instrument.

One of the strongest features of the design is that the validity criterion, mean section examination performance, is relatively high in external validity. Examination scores are both a direct and important measure of one of the products of effective instruction, designed to assess what students have learned of the course material (and to assign grades). Consequently, we believe that multisection validation designs are especially useful in determining the extent to which ratings of particular instructional processes are valid indices of important instructional products, particularly student learning of course content.

Substantive criticisms of multisection validation designs. Feldman (1989a, 1990) expressed a different view of the value of multisection validity studies:

> Although the data for the present analysis comes from what are called "multisection validity studies," the analysis herein was not an attempt to validate specific ratings of instructors. While it makes sense to seek information about the validity of overall or global ratings of instructors by correlating these ratings with student achievement, it makes less sense to do so for specific ratings because student achievement is not necessarily a direct or meaningful validity criterion for each of the instructional dimensions...

> The present analysis accepted the specific rating items, scales, and factors of the studies under review as valid indicators of instructional characteristics. It sought to find out which of them are most highly associated with student achievement under the presumption that the higher the correlation the more facilitative is the instructional characteristic of student achievement (1989, pp. 624-625).

We do not share completely Feldman's interpretation of the value of multisection validity studies. We agree that understanding the relationship between global ratings and student achievement is extremely important and can be used in judging the validity of global ratings. However, we believe that understanding the relationship between specific ratings and student achievement is also important and can be used to judge the validity of specific ratings since it sheds light on the link between what instructors do when they teach and their impact on students. According to the process-product view, ratings dimensions *are* validated to the extent they reflect instructor-produced student learning.

Methodological criticisms of the multisection design. Abrami (Abrami, Cohen, and d'Apollonia, 1988; Abrami, d'Apollonia, and Cohen, 1990) and Marsh (1987; Marsh and Dunkin, 1992) disagree over the strengths of the multisection design. Marsh gives several reasons why the design of multisection validity studies is "inherently weak" and notes that "there are many methodological complications in its actual application" (1987, p. 289). First, the sample size of course sections in any study is almost always quite small, adversely affecting sampling error. Second, variance in achievement scores is mostly attributable to student variables (e.g., ability) and researchers are generally unable to find appreciable effects due to teachers, especially in multisection designs where many of the setting effects are held constant. In addition, the reliability of section average differences is unstudied but may be small and unreliable, attenuating the size of the ratings-achievement correlation. Third, the comparison of findings across different multisection validity studies is problematic since most use different operationalizations both of student ratings and achievement. Fourth, other criteria of teaching effectiveness besides objectively scored tests, and more generally student learning, need to be considered. Fifth, pretest scores on student ability should be used to statistically equate course sections even when students are randomly assigned to the sections, since randomization is not a guarantee of section equivalence. Furthermore, the multisection design does not constitute an experimental design in which students are randomly assigned to treatment groups that are varied systematically in terms of experimentally manipulated variables, and so the advantages of random assignment are not so clear. Finally, the grading satisfaction hypothesis may explain the ratings-achievement correlation. According to the grading satisfaction hypothesis students reward teachers who assign high grades by rating instructors highly regardless of how much students actually learned.

Response to criticisms of the multisection design. We agree with Marsh on several points. First, integrating the findings from the collection of multisection courses helps overcome sample size problems in analyzing single studies. The research we report here and elsewhere is an attempt at such integration. Second, the statistical control of student characteristics in combination with randomization can be superior to randomization alone. However, failing this and faced with a choice of design strategies, we prefer the use of experimental control of nuisance variables over statistical control for two reasons: a) the as-yet unstudied effect of poor randomization on the validity coefficient must certainly be less than when students self-select course sections; and b) statistical control requires that these nuisance variables are known and uncorrelated with instructor effects, while random assignment does not.

Third, we agree that the products of effective instruction are multidimensional. But a call for the inclusion of measures other than student learning is not, by itself, an identification of a methodological weakness in multisection designs. It does identify a limitation of existent studies and suggests a direction for future research. Furthermore, the learning measures studied in multisection investigations do represent multiple operationalizations of student learning since test item content varies from study-to-study. Finally, instructor self-ratings, colleague or peer ratings, and the ratings of trained observers could be incorporated into studies employing the multisection design.

We disagree with Marsh on several points. First, the restriction of range problem in the achievement criterion does not hold unless it can be shown that the sample of instructors studied is unrepresentative and the criterion measure lacks sensitivity to instructor effects. Otherwise the experimental control of extraneous influences which affect the criterion is desirable, not undesirable. In both laboratory and field investigations, Abrami (Abrami, Perry, and Leventhal, 1982; Abrami and Mizener, 1985) found that student ratings were more sensitive than student achievement to differences in instruction. Instructors may have genuinely small effects on what students learn. In addition, the use of locally developed or teacher-made tests in some of the validation studies is a double-edged sword. On the one hand, teacher-made tests are likely to be less psychometrically sound but, on the other hand, are often more sensitive to instructor effects than standardized tests.

Second, mono-operationalizations of measures (i.e., using the same instruments throughout) reduce, but do not eliminate, the interpretive problems involved in making inferences across multisection validity studies. Important uncontrolled differences in student, instructor, course, and setting characteristics may also be responsible for study-to-study differences therefore lowering the internal validity of cross-study comparisons. However, cross-study comparisons can be useful for judging the external validity of findings where it seems reasonable to explore whether different student ratings instruments are correlated with different student learning measures.

Third, the unsystematic nature of the treatment (i.e., differences in instruction) in multisection designs does not detract from the value of random assignment of students. Random assignment helps insure that the relationship between ratings and achievement was produced by differences in instruction rather than differences in students. This insurance of internal validity can be the starting point for further explorations of the treatment. For example, Sullivan and Skanes (1974) used the multisection design to explore the influence of instructor experience on the ratings-achievement relationship.

Finally, the grading satisfaction hypothesis may be one mechanism by which students rate faculty, but it is not an alternative explanation of the validity of ratings when section differences in students are controlled and instructor grading practices, including timing, are uniform across classes. The alleged effect of grading satisfaction will operate consistently, if at all, in each section of a multisection course unless instructors *first* produce differences in student learning. Under these conditions, grading satisfaction cannot explain mean section differences in either student ratings or student achievement. However, the problem is especially pronounced when one is studying multiple classes outside the multisection paradigm where there is more variability in instructor grading practices.[3]

Multitrait-Multimethod Designs

Marsh (1987) and others (Howard, Conway, and Maxwell; 1985) have argued in favor of a MTMM approach to the validation of ratings. To be superior to the multisection design, the MTMM design requires greater control of threats to internal validity, external validity, or both. Specifically, the design must reasonably show that threats to internal validity are controlled in order to attribute class mean differences in ratings and the criterion measures to instructors, and not to extraneous characteristics such as students, the course, and setting variables.

This can be partly achieved if the criterion measures of effective instruction—possibly instructor self-ratings, alumni or former student ratings, peer ratings, and ratings of trained observers—are less sensitive to extraneous influences than course examinations. If so, one may compute the validity correlation between student ratings and scores on the criterion measure(s) for a host of courses, not just multisection ones, and may thereby greatly enhance external validity. But without evidence to the contrary, designs which do not control statistically or experimentally for extraneous influences on the criterion do not represent good alternatives to the multisection validation design in concluding that differences in the criterion measure were caused by instructors. Furthermore, these designs do not

---

[3]Marsh and Dunkin (1992) suggest several fallacies with our reasoning: First, the implicit assumption that all section differences are instructor-produced is completely unrealistic. Even random differences in section mean examination performances will produce inflated validity coefficients due to grading satisfaction effects. Second, there is no way to unconfound the influence of grades and satisfaction with grades. Third, the problem *is* pronounced outside the multisection paradigm and, therefore, the paradigm is unrepresentative. Finally, the reliability of section-average differences in achievement is a critical problem when the section-average scores are similar to one another and within-section differences.

Our response follows: First, if there were unwanted systematic differences in section means they would be much smaller than validation designs without controls for student differences. (The point of our argument has always been that the multisection design is relatively one of the strongest designs, not that it is a perfect design.) It is also unclear what effect *random* differences in examination performance will have on the ratings-achievement relationship. In general, unsystematic differences tend to attenuate the size of a correlation, whereas Marsh and Dunkin (1992) claim the opposite will occur due to grading satisfaction. It is also the case that inferential statistics were conceived on the notion of random fluctuation both between and within groups. This random fluctuation or sampling error does not need to be zero for valid statistical tests to be performed, although reductions in error variability increase the power or sensitivity of the tests. Random or unsystematic fluctuation, a tolerable problem, is not to be confused with systematic bias or contaminants which are alternative explanations of teacher effects, a more serious problem.

Second, we agree that the grading satisfaction effect cannot be disentangled from the effect of grading per se in existing multisection studies although it could be incorporated into the design of future multisection studies. Our claim is that the temporal sequence of influence (i.e., instructor produced learning affects grades which affects satisfaction which may affect ratings) coupled with the use of uniform grading standards removes grading satisfaction as a source of bias. Marsh's claim is the influence of learning and grade satisfaction on ratings are dissimilar. For example, small differences in learning produce large differences in grading satisfaction which, in turn, have a meaningful impact on student ratings. Thus, if this were the case it would be seen in individual validation studies incorporating a grading standards variable or by comparing multisection validation studies where grading standards were not uniform with validation studies where grading standards were uniform.

Finally, we believe that Marsh's concern for the reliability of section mean differences in achievement should be extended both to all student ratings and criterion measures and to all designs, not only multisection validation designs, using the correct unit of analysis for exploring instructor influences which is the class mean or section average. For example, in 1990 we wrote: "if we adjusted a validity coefficient of .43 (which is the average value reported by P.A. Cohen, 1981, for overall instructor ratings) for the reliability of ratings (estimated to be .70), the corrected coefficient would be .51. If we then adjusted the validity coefficient further for an equal degree of error in the criterion measure, the corrected coefficient would be .61" (Abrami et al., 1990, p. 227).

control for extraneous influences on student ratings. Thus, even if it could be shown that the criterion was unaffected, the validity coefficient might be affected.

To show advantages in external validity, one must also show that the alternatives to student learning such as instructor self-ratings, former student ratings, and peer ratings represent adequate product measures of instruction. Yet whether these measures (and student ratings) represent adequate criteria of effective instruction has been seriously questioned (Gaski, 1987). Maxwell and Howard (1987) acknowledge these criticisms as well-taken (see also Feldman, 1989b). In our view, such measures help establish the validity of ratings as measures of teaching processes but not as measures of the products of instruction.

Thus, we conclude the MTMM validation designs provide weaker evidence for the validity of student ratings as measures of instructional effectiveness than multisection validation designs. The MTMM designs are generally weaker in internal validity and employ criterion measures which are either less defensible as or less important measures of good teaching than student learning.

The Choice of Designs

In choosing among research designs, one must consider whether threats to internal and external validity are addressed. The multisection validation design has advantages over MTMM designs in determining whether ratings reflect instructional processes and products. The multisection design is generally higher in internal validity and typically incorporates an important product measure of effective instruction, student learning, contributing to its external validity. The multisection design is also superior to laboratory studies when the validity question addresses the practical concern of the degree to which ratings predict teacher-produced outcomes in typical classroom settings. For these reasons, multisection validation studies are singularly important to concerns about validity and deserve special attention.

MULTISECTION VALIDITY STUDIES: WHAT HAVE THEY TOLD US SO FAR?

What can one conclude about the validity of ratings from multisection validation studies? Do global ratings predict student learning? Are there particular instructional processes, as reflected in student ratings, which are related to student learning or other outcomes? Are the findings from the collection of studies uniform? If not, are there substantive or methodological features that explain variability in study findings? Do reviewers agree on what the findings mean? Is there more to learn: Are there inadequacies in either the literature or reviews of the literature?

The Relationship Between Ratings and Student Learning

Abrami, Cohen, and d'Apollonia (1988) compared six published, quantitative reviews of the findings from multisection designs (Abrami, 1984; Cohen, 1981, 1982, 1983; Dowell and Neal, 1982; McCallum, 1984) to identify their agreements and disagreements. Unfortunately, the reviews differed in several important ways including: a) the specification of the criteria used to include studies; b) comprehensiveness or the extent to which each review included studies meeting inclusion criteria (where the proportion of studies included per review ranged from .13 to .88); c) the presence and completeness of study feature coding used to explain study-to-study variability; d) the extraction and calculation of individual study outcomes (where there was only 47% agreement among the reviews); and e) procedures for data analysis, especially variability in study outcomes. These difference help explain why the conclusions reached by the reviewers were markedly different:

> The present meta-analysis provides strong support for the validity of student ratings as measures of teaching effectiveness. Teachers whose students do well on achievement measures receive higher instructional ratings than teachers whose students do poorly. This study demonstrates that the relationship between ratings and achievement is slightly stronger and more consistent than was previously thought. (Cohen, 1981, pp.300-301).

> The literature can be seen as yielding unimpressive estimates of the validity of student ratings. The literature does not support claims that the validity of ratings is a consistent quantity across situations. Rather the evidence suggests that the validity of student ratings is modest at best and quite variable. (Dowell and Neal, 1982, p. 59).

There have been further attempts to summarize the findings from the multisection validity studies and analyze variability in study findings (Abrami and d'Apollonia, 1987, 1988; Abrami, d'Apollonia, and Cohen, 1990; Cohen, 1986, 1987; d'Apollonia and Abrami, 1987, 1988; Feldman, 1989a, 1990). The average validity coefficients found by the reviewers using two different coding schemes for categorizing the results from different rating forms are presented in Tables 3 and 4.

TABLE 3. Mean Validity Coefficients in the Multisection Validity Studies: Cohen Dimensions (Cohen, 1987)

Type	Dimension	N[1]	VC[2]	Mean	SE[3]	Range
Global	Overall Instructor Overall Course	59 21	0.44 0.48	0.45	0.012	[0.44, 0.48]
Specific	Skill	44	0.41			
	Rapport	35	0.30			
	Structure	29	0.55			
	Difficulty	25	0.00			
	Interaction	20	0.45	0.34	0.053	[0.00, 0.55]
	Feedback	7	0.29			
	Evaluation	25	0.23			
	Learning Progress	17	0.46			
	Interest/Motivation	12	0.26			

1. N=number of course findings. 2. VC=mean validity coefficients. 3. SE=standard error.

TABLE 4. Mean Validity Coefficients in the Multisection Validity Studies: Feldman Dimensions (d'Apollonia, and Abrami, 1988)

Type	Dimension	N[1]	VC[2]	Mean	SE[3]	Range
Global	Overall instructor Overall course	44 18	0.30 0.36	0.32	0.019	[0.30, 0.36]
Specific	Stimulates interest	34	0.37	0.20	0.015	[0.03, 0.45]
	Enthusiasm	11	0.25			
	Knowledge	12	0.21			
	Expansiveness	4	0.03			
	Preparation	33	0.43			
	Clarity/understandable	46	0.42			
	Elocutionary skills	8	0.26			
	Concern for progress	19	0.30			
	Clarity of objectives	25	0.33			
	Course materials	19	0.29			
	Supplemental materials	12	0.17			
	Perceived outcome	32	0.39			
	Instructor's fairness	29	0.31			
	Personality	4	0.45			
	Feedback	15	0.11			
	Openness	27	0.29			
	Intellectual challenge	11	0.34			
	Concern for students	26	0.24			
	Availability	22	0.30			
	Course difficulty/workload	29	0.03			
	Classroom management	13	0.13			
	General	16	0.31			

1. N= number of course findings.   2. VC=mean validity coefficients.   3. SE=standard error.

Collectively, the results of the reviews suggest that some specific rating dimensions, as well as student global ratings, are moderately correlated with student learning in multisection college courses. On average, there exists a reasonable, but far from perfect, relationship between some student ratings and learning. To a moderate extent, student ratings are able to identify those instructors whose students learn best. Furthermore, regardless of the coding scheme used, the average of global ratings of instructional effectiveness explains a greater percentage of variance in student learning than the average of specific ratings. It also appears that not all specific ratings are related to achievement; for example, ratings of course difficulty generally do not predict student achievement at all. Consequently, we recommend using the results of specific rating dimensions to judge which teachers best promote student learning with caution especially when making promotion and tenure decisions. The same caution is not necessary when using global ratings of instruction.

Finally, the nature and number of the specific rating dimensions used in the two schemes appears different. In the Cohen (1987) coding scheme, the findings are arranged according to two global dimensions and nine specific dimensions. This coding scheme is not without limitations. For example, it relies on the factor analytic findings from a single instrument (Isaacson et al., 1964) which may not allow the results from all instruments to be properly represented. This may have resulted in validity coefficients being either forced into categories, creating heterogeneous categories, or dropped from the meta-analysis.

d'Apollonia and Abrami (1988) used Feldman's scheme to report the average validity coefficients for 22 specific rating dimensions, more than twice the number reported by Cohen. This coding scheme has been used and refined repeatedly by Feldman (1976, 1983, 1984, 1989a) using a conceptual approach to comprehensively represent the items from many forms without preference toward any one instrument or its factor structure. Nevertheless, questions remain about which way to organize items and whether any coding scheme can be empirically validated.

d'Apollonia and Abrami (1988) and Abrami et al. (1990) also observed that the multisection studies contained a large number of validity coefficients that were not all represented when other reviewers reported mean coefficients. In 43 multisection validation studies we found a total of 742 ratings-achievement correlations reported. Yet only a small fraction of these correlations were included in other reviews.

Looking Further at the Multisection Validity Studies

Research integrations are seldom necessary when the findings in an area are uniform. Reviews become necessary especially when the results of research on a topic appear heterogeneous. The research findings from the multisection validity studies seem to vary widely. The range of reported validity coefficients is -0.75 to +0.92. There is one study finding of a strong negative relationship between ratings and achievement—the highest rated instructors had the lowest performing students. There is also one study finding showing the opposite, a near perfect positive relationship between ratings and achievement. In a quantitative review, the reviewer searches for ways to explain the variability in study findings. The range of findings in the multisection validity studies is a reason to explore the findings further to explain these inconsistencies.

Cohen (1981) was the first quantitative reviewer to attempt a systematic exploration of the variability in study findings. He explored the relationship between 20 study and methodological features of the primary research and the validity coefficients extracted from this research. Three of the features together accounted for approximately thirty percent of the variance in the validity coefficients for Overall Instructor ratings: control for bias in evaluating achievement (i.e., Was the test graded by the instructor?); time at which ratings were administered (i.e., Were the ratings collected before final grades?); and instructor experience (i.e., Were the instructors graduate students?).

Abrami et al. (1990) examined these findings further. First, they showed that individual study features did not explain a significant amount of variability in the validity coefficients because of low statistical power. The analyses often lacked the sensitivity necessary to identify characteristics that explain a medium size effect on the relationship between ratings and achievement. More of the study features might prove to be useful predictors in future if either additional primary studies are conducted or more powerful statistical procedures of research integration were employed. Until then, one can neither accept nor reject claims that these other explanatory factors are trivial.

Second, the 20 study features employed by Cohen (1981) to explain variability in validity outcomes did not generalize across global and specific aspects of teaching. Since rating factors are regarded by some as distinct and uncorrelated (e.g., Marsh, 1987) there is little reason to suspect that these factors will be uniformly affected by biasing characteristics. Characteristics that predicted the relationship between student perceptions of teaching and instructor impacts on learning varied with the aspect of teaching being investigated. Unfortunately, the precise nature of this pattern of effects could not be elaborated. (For one, the sample sizes were too small to confidently make fine distinctions.) However, the findings were sufficiently clear to urge users of multidimensional rating forms away from the common practice of universally controlling for "biasing" characteristics (e.g., course level) and further complicate the use of specific ratings in summative decisions about teaching.

Third, Abrami et al. (1990) employed nomological coding to identify the investigated, accounted for, and mentioned characteristics in the forty-three validity studies. They uncovered 75 study features that could be used to explain variability in the findings of the multisection validity studies. Since this was a substantial increase in the explanatory features used previously (almost four times the number of factors explored by Cohen, 1981), Abrami et al. (1990) concluded that prior reviews did not comprehensively identify potential predictive characteristics.

Where Do We Go From Here?

Reviews of the multisection validity studies on the relationship between ratings and achievement suggest there is much yet to be learned of the relationship between what instructors do when they teach and how this affects student learning and other products of instruction. Abrami et al. (1990) recommended that another quantitative review should be undertaken with alternative systems for coding the rating dimensions, the use of the 75 study features they identified, and more powerful analysis strategies (e.g., tests of homogeneity, Hedges and Olkin, 1985) using the 742 validity coefficients extracted from the literature. As a major step in this process, we first embarked on research to identify the common dimensions of teaching as represented in the rating forms used in the multisection validity studies. Before presenting the results of the integration of many forms, we discuss some of the complications with the factor analysis of a single form.

FACTOR ANALYSIS AND THE DIMENSIONS OF EFFECTIVE INSTRUCTION

Recent research by Marsh (1991) attempted to address questions about the dimensionality of student ratings through the application of confirmatory factor analysis (CFA). Using data from a single rating form—the SEEQ—Marsh (1991) evaluated four higher-order factor models. The results provided support for the nine first-order factors the SEEQ is designed to measure and, of the higher-order models, particularly for the four factor approach. Marsh concluded:

Considerable information is lost when the student ratings are summarized with a single score or even a small number of scores. The challenge for future research—particularly in terms of personnel decisions—is how to most appropriately use the information that is available in student ratings rather than throw it away. (Marsh, 1991, p.13).

The validity of this conclusion rests in large part on the adequacy of the SEEQ to represent the qualities of effective teaching. As is evident from Abrami and d'Apollonia (1990), different student rating forms assess different dimensions of effective instruction. This point is also demonstrated by Marsh (1991, see Table 1, p. 15) where the dimensional categories of the Endeavor rating form (Frey, 1978) were compared with the SEEQ and shown to be different. It is also not surprising that Marsh's (1991) confirmatory analyses generally conform to prior analyses with the same instrument—they amount to grand tests of instrument reliability. What is surprising is that the nine factor a priori model…"is not fully adequate" (Marsh, 1991, p.9).

In addition, note that Marsh (1991) was able to describe not one but four higher order models from prior research and reviews. But even these models do not adequately describe the diversity and complexity of findings regarding the dimensionality of instruction. In his reviews of student rating forms, Feldman (1976, 1988) noted that rating form items are often intercorrelated despite their apparent conceptual independence. For example, the instructor's stimulation of interest, clarity and comprehensibility, course preparation, and organization and enthusiasm are frequently highly correlated. Kulik and McKeachie's (1975) review of student ratings suggested a general Skill factor on which many items (including global items) load highly. Global items are included in the specific factors from the SEEQ: *Overall course rating* is included in the *Learning/ Value* factor and *Overall instructor rating* is included in the *Instructor Enthusiasm* factor. These interrelationships among items and between global items and specific factors create interpretive difficulties when one argues for the dimensionality of instruction. Should one interpret this covariance to mean that specific dimensional ratings predict global ratings or that students' responses to specific items are influenced by their overall assessments? Indeed, Feldman's reviews have often been predicated on the assumption that specific dimensional ratings should predict student global ratings.

Limitations of Factor Analysis

Implicit in Marsh's conclusion is that CFA can "disconfirm" the theory that a few general or global dimensions capture the structure of student ratings. An alternative conclusion is that it is not the theory which needs revision but the instruments and methods used in testing it.

The use of factor analysis alone to determine the structure of a phenomenon is inconclusive since different analysis methods are based on different assumptions. Each analysis is, therefore, designed to "discover" the structure favored by the assumptions. For example, principal components extraction, the most frequently used extraction method, was pioneered by Spearman to extract mutually independent components such that the first or principal component resolves the maximum amount of variance with subsequent factors explaining progressively less variance. Thus, factor analysis without rotation is designed to resolve one general or global component explaining most of the variance and a few less important, subsidiary components. Thurstone objected to this hierarchical interpretation of the components and developed rotation to redistribute the variance explained by the general factor over the subsidiary factors. This increased the variance the subsidiary factors explained.

The two solutions resolve exactly the same amount of total variance, therefore, which one "best" describes reality cannot be determined empirically. Moreover, both solutions are affected by the choice of items in the instrument(s) in question. The selection of unique items that are highly positively correlated favors a principal components solution while the selection of clusters of similar items favors a rotated solution elucidating a number of equally important factors. Clearly, the use of any one student rating form in a CFA is not an adequate test for the presence of a particular higher order factor structure. An adequate test requires the use of a diversity of student ratings.

Secondary Analyses of SEEQ Data

There are a number of decisions made during a factor analysis that affect the final results and their interpretation. Some of these are: a) the items included in the correlation matrix, b) the number of factors extracted, c) whether the axes are rotated, d) if rotated, whether rotated orthogonally or obliquely, and e) if oblique rotation is selected, the degree of obliqueness. In order to investigate the possibility that Marsh's conclusions reflected his methodological choices rather than the multidimensionality of instruction (as determined by the SEEQ), Abrami and d'Apollonia (1991) conducted a secondary analysis of the SEEQ data from Marsh and Hocevar (1984) and replicated in Marsh (1991). Marsh and Hocevar (1984) obtained a nine factor solution using oblique rotation with delta set at approximately -2.0.

Abrami and d'Apollonia (1991) reconstructed the reproduced correlation matrix by premultiplying the factor pattern correlation matrix by the oblique factor matrix and postmultiplying it by the transpose of the oblique factor pattern matrix (Tabachnick and Fidell, 1983). Abrami and d'Apollonia (1991) estimated the observed correlation matrix by replacing the diagonal elements of the reproduce correlation matrix with 1's. Since the communalities were very high, they were able to replicate the results within rounding error. They then factor analyzed the correlation matrix of the 35 items using SPSS (SPSS Inc., 1990).

The results of the Abrami and d'Apollonia re-analysis (see Table 5) were: a) Thirty-one of the items load highly on the principal component (> .63) with Overall Instructor and Overall Course being the most highly loading items (both .94), indicating that the first component was a general or global factor. This global factor explained almost 60% of the total variance in ratings. The four remaining items, concerning course difficulty and workload, loaded heavily on a second component which explained an additional 11% of the variance. Interestingly, Cohen (1981) found that course difficulty items were poor in construct validity, predicting student learning near zero. The remaining four components explained only 5%, 4%, 3%, and 2%, respectively, and did not contain any items that did not load heavily on one of the first two factors.

TABLE 5. Nonrotated Factor Pattern Matrix with Six Components Extracted via Principal Components Analysis[1]

SEEQ Item	Factor loadings on first six components					
	I	II	III	IV	V	VI
Course challenging	.893	.392	.017	−.109	.037	−.056
Learned something valuable	.873	.262	.021	−.148	.133	−.080
Increased subject interest	.868	.122	−.013	−.226	.153	−.031
Understood subject matter	.760	−.182	−.094	−.167	.201	−.142
Overall course rating	.940	.176	−.032	−.085	.017	−.120
Enthusiastic about teaching	.886	.017	.039	−.082	−.308	−.073
Dynamic and energetic	.875	.104	.045	−.133	−.324	−.156
Enhanced presentation with humor	.787	.009	.039	−.158	−.315	−.152
Teaching style held interest	.884	.075	.012	−.147	−.249	−.208
Overall instructor rating	.941	.058	−.037	−.024	−.181	−.105
Explanations clear	.868	−.057	−.180	−.076	−.072	−.121
Materials prepared and clear	.857	.065	−.300	.052	−.064	−.060
Objectives stated and pursued	.855	.130	−.255	.125	.056	−.094
Lectures facilitated note taking	.649	.153	−.485	.118	−.158	.043
Encouraged class discussions	.741	−.390	.389	−.233	.104	−.068
Students shared ideas/knowledge	.688	−.479	.394	−.226	.136	−.046
Encouraged questions and answers	.852	−.303	.237	−.108	.047	−.070
Encouraged expression of ideas	.780	−.414	.349	−.131	.084	−.016
Friendly towards students	.769	−.370	.256	.258	−.097	.117
Welcomed seeking help or advice	.756	−.310	.246	.393	−.122	.184
Interested in individual students	.817	−.277	.261	.303	−.089	.117
Accessible to individual students	.678	−.180	.138	.471	−.108	.298
Contrasted implications	.803	.010	−.205	−.156	−.016	.418
Gave background of ideas/concepts	.819	−.024	−.237	−.201	.033	.398
Gave different points of view	.818	−.107	−.207	−.158	.060	.375
Discussed current developments	.743	.035	−.142	−.270	.030	.340
Examination feedback valuable	.776	−.061	−.163	.336	.064	−.182
Examination methods fair	.808	−.149	−.163	.328	.069	−.146
Exams emphasized course content	.794	−.064	−.242	.289	.071	−.187
Readings/texts valuable	.639	.168	−.045	.131	.563	−.018
Added to course understanding	.754	.175	−.007	.122	.476	−.098
Course difficulty	.333	.840	.181	.075	−.068	.046
Course workload	.336	.793	.351	.037	.034	.065
Course pacing	.238	.794	.182	.092	−.100	.037
Hours/week outside class	.305	.726	.384	.068	.065	.115
Factor eigenvalues	20.67	3.95	1.75	1.42	1.18	1.05
% variance explained	59.1	11.3	5.0	4.0	3.4	1.9

Source: Abrami and d'Apollonia (1991), p. 414.

In response, Marsh (1991) claimed that the most serious problem with the critiques of Abrami and d'Apollonia (1991) and Abrami (1988, 1989a, 1989b) was the failure to operationalize criteria for unidimensionality or multidimensionality. Further, Marsh claimed that "…the most defensible approach to evaluating unidimensionality is to test the existence of one latent trait underlying the data" (Marsh, 1991, p. 417). Consequently, one purpose of our analysis of the collection of rating forms was to explore the underlying nature of student perceptions of instruction across many rating forms as the first step towards testing the existence of one global trait.

In the past, Abrami (1985, 1988, 1989a, 1989b) and Abrami and d'Apollonia (1990, 1991) have been critical of the methodological and substantive difficulties with factor-analytic research on student ratings. These problems have not led us to deny that teaching is multidimensional—it clearly is—but to suggest that research to date does not justify the use of factor scores from a single instrument in making summative decisions about teaching effectiveness. By determining whether there exists a "common" core among the collection of rating forms used in multisection validation studies we believe we will take a step toward overcoming some of the limitations described above.

THE DIMENSIONALITY OF INSTRUCTION: IS THERE A "COMMON" CORE?

In this section we explore the unidimensionality-multidimensionality issue further by applying the techniques of quantitative synthesis to a collection of student rating forms. In this way, we will be able to explore the dimensionality of ratings with a higher degree of generalizability than ever attempted before.

A problem that reviewers of the multisection validity literature face is that there appears no consensus, across student rating forms, of what constitutes the structure or dimensionality of instructional effectiveness as perceived by students. The effectiveness of postsecondary instruction is, like the elephant in *The Blind Men and the Elephant* (John Godfrey Saxe), a beast with many different characteristics. Each reviewer has attempted to examine this issue, and like the blind men of the poem, is convinced that he/she has discovered the true and accurate representation. What the following analysis attempts is to fit together the pieces to form a picture. But the analogy of the blind men and the elephant is not entirely correct. Each researcher does not hold only a unique piece of the puzzle but rather may hold some pieces in common with one or more other researchers, as well as some unique pieces.

The question of the dimensionality or structure of instructional effectiveness across student rating forms can be approached in two ways: conceptually or empirically. In a conceptual or logical approach, theoretical models are used to develop a hierarchical structure or taxonomy. Borich (1977) suggests three stages in the development of a valid system of evaluating teacher effectiveness. The first stage is to search the literature for significant relationships and rationally select promising behaviors and skills. The second stage is to build a nomological network indicating antecedent, intervening and terminal behaviors, to test the validity of the above relationships, and to sequentially order the behaviors and skills. The third stage is to construct a taxonomy or hierarchy of behaviors emphasizing the important distinctions and minimizing the superfluous ones. Thus, the three stages are: selecting variables on the basis of the literature, chunking variables on the basis of relationships, and proposing higher-order structures on the basis of theory. The proposed hierarchical relationships among variables can then be empirically tested on a second sample via confirmatory factor analysis (CFA) or linear structured relationships (LISREL) (Hill, 1984).

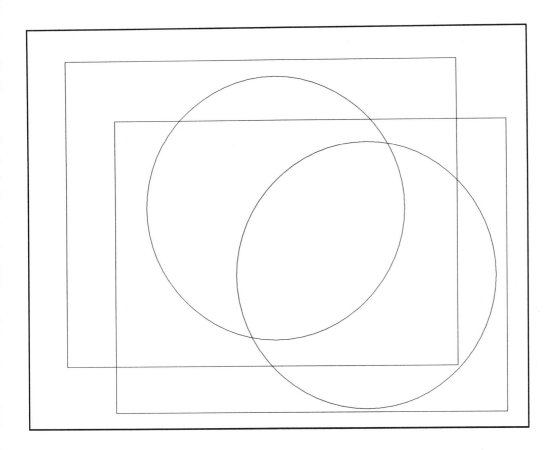

FIGURE 1. Hypothetical illustration of the underlying traits "common" to two rating forms.

There have been some studies attempting to elucidate empirically the structure of the student rating forms used in the multisection validity literature (Widlak, et al., 1973; Kulik and McKeachie, 1975; Marsh, 1987, 1991). However, in general, one student rating form is factor analyzed and no attempt is made to compare it's factor structure to those of other rating forms purporting to measure the same dimensions of effective instruction. One exception is Marsh (1987) who commented on the similarity of specific factors in a number of student rating forms. However, this was done on the basis of a logical analysis and not empirically. Marsh (1991) analyzed logically the correspondence among the SEEQ, the Endeavor and Feldman's categories. He concluded that: Feldman's categories were much more specific than factors from either the SEEQ or the Endeavor; the SEEQ represented more of Feldman's categories than the Endeavor represented; and many SEEQ factors contained more than one Feldman category.

In the last few years, we have been using multivariate approaches to meta-analysis to explore the "common" factor structure across multiple student rating forms (Rosenfield, d'Apollonia, and Abrami, 1993; d'Apollonia, Abrami, and Rosenfield, 1993). Thus, we have combined both conceptual and empirical approaches. Figure 1 illustrates our goals. Take the large rectangle that surrounds the illustration. This represents all the qualities of teaching that could be represented in student rating forms. Any one rating form is represented by a smaller rectangle. Hence, two rating forms are illustrated in the figure. Each rating form rectangle is a subset of the whole. Furthermore, the rating form rectangles do not perfectly overlap, suggesting they represent somewhat different aspects of instruction. The circle within each rating form rectangle represents the rating form variability explained by a particular factor analysis of student responses to the rating form. Finally, there is an area of overlap between the circles representing the two rating forms. This is what is common to the factor analyses of the two rating forms. The non-intersecting part of the two circles represents what is unique to each of the factor analyses.

Now, imagine a more complex figure with 17 rating form rectangles and their 17 circles within. Bits of intersecting circles represent what is common to two or more rating forms. But the union of all the circles represents the qualities of teaching represented by factors underlying all of the forms together.[4]

"Common" Dimensions of Teaching

We decided to employ the Feldman coding scheme to further explore the dimensionality of student ratings of instruction and the validity of those dimensions to predict the products of instruction, particularly, student achievement. We found several difficulties with the scheme: a) lack of operational definitions for the categories (use of exemplars only); b) high intercoder agreement by us (Cohen's kappa = .93) but lower agreement (.60) with items categorized by Feldman; and c) internal inconsistencies including ambiguity, multidimensionality, and overlap among the categories. Using Feldman's coding scheme as the basis of our work, we decided to revise the scheme using the following principles:

1. The coding scheme should not be ambiguous. The categories used to code items should be clear, comprehensive and succinct. The categories should be of more or less equal breadth.
2. The bipolar values of a category should be contained within it; for example, clear and unclear presentations, authoritarian and participatory class management, etc.
3. Both the product and the process orientations to a teaching behavior should be in the same category; for example, the instructor presenting the subject as interesting and the students being interested in the subject.
4. Since global evaluations (course instructor, perceived learning) are included, the remaining categories should only include specific statements.

We defined our coding scheme based upon the 1,184 items collected from the student rating forms used in the *multisection validity studies*. Two coders subsequently

---

[4]For methodological reasons associated with the aggregated correlation matrix, we were only able to examine that part of the union of the 17 circles that lay entirely encompassed within the largest circle.

coded the above items and obtained a 91.5% intercoder agreement. The items from the *factor analytic studies* are a subset of the above items. The definition of each category is presented in Appendix A, beginning on p. 358. The appendix also includes all items whose correlation were used to form the aggregate correlation matrix.

Collection of Factor Studies
We first collected studies that reported either complete factor matrices or correlation matrices for the student rating forms used in the multisection validity studies. We collected seventeen studies representing most of the rating forms in the validity set (excluding the in-house forms). One student rating form, the form used by Wherry (1951), supplied almost 50% of the items in the data set. It thus furnished a large portion of the interitem correlation coefficients. As expected, the global items are underrepresented in the factor set relative to the validity set.

Extraction and Coding of Outcomes
The outcome variables of interest for the integration of factor studies are the interitem correlation coefficients for each student rating form. These were estimated from the reproduced correlation matrices computed from the factor loading matrix of the items in the student rating forms (if rotated orthogonally), or from the pattern matrix and factor correlation matrix (if rotated obliquely). The 458 items from the factor studies were initially placed into 40 categories. These categories are listed and briefly defined in Appendix A .

Pruning and Synthesis of Aggregate Correlation Matrix
In order to aggregate the interitem correlation coefficients, one must first establish that the values being aggregated are homogeneous. If the set is not homogeneous, the (weighted) mean correlation does not properly represent the set of studies. There are a number of possible causes for heterogeneity: a) the items are ambiguous and/or multidimensional; b) the categories are ambiguous and/or multidimensional; and c) the relationship between items varies with setting, subject, etc.

The first two reasons speak to technical problems with the coding schema and certain student rating forms. Unfortunately, these problems confound questions concerning the dimensionality of effective instruction. Therefore, if one wishes to address the latter question, one must first reduce these technical problems. We therefore, eliminated (pruned) items and categories that were heterogeneous in the following manner.

We pruned items and categories from our data set in two stages. In the first stage we eliminated items that contributed to "poor" correlations between items belonging to the same category. We subdivided the complete set of interitem correlations (21,383 correlations) into 40 sets of interitem correlations between items belonging to the same category. We assumed that if the categories were unidimensional and generalizable, sets of interitem correlation coefficients should be uniform across student rating forms and the mean interitem correlation coefficient for the set should approach 1.0. In other words, the mean interitem correlation coefficient for the subset is analogous to a reliability coefficient. For each set, we identified items that contributed to correlations that were below 0.5, or that lowered the mean interitem correlation coefficient for a category consistently below .65. We scrutinized these items for ambiguous wording, reversed polarity, negative wording, compound statements, etc. We subsequently dropped these items. For each set, we continued pruning until the set was homogeneous (*i.e.* the coefficient of variability was .20 or less). We eliminated three categories, *appropriate use of materials*, *low-level cognitive outcomes*, and *overall learning* because of insufficient data.

In the second stage we eliminated items that contributed to heterogeneous correlations between items in different categories. This is a more difficult task in that since the correlations for items belonging to different categories are not known we can no longer assume that the correlations should approach 1. However, we can still expect that there should be a tight cluster of values about the weighted mean.

We subsequently subdivided the remaining 8,131 correlations into 666 sets representing the intercorrelations between items belonging to different categories. Taking one set at a time, we identified the items that contributed to correlations at the extremes of the distribution. We eliminated those items that consistently contributed to the heterogeneity of the set. Finally, after all pruning had been done, we reviewed all decisions to see if later decisions to drop items would allow us to reinsert some dropped items. Note that two items contributed to a correlation that was an "outlier." In some cases the "poor" item could be easily identified because of poor wording, double negatives, compound items, etc. However in other cases, the choice of item to be eliminated was somewhat arbitrary. That is, there is not one unique set of items which if eliminated produce homogeneous sets. Rather, there are a number of possible sets. Moreover, interitem correlations exist only between items in the same student rating form. Therefore the distribution of items per category/per rating form influences which items can be considered for elimination. That is, there have to be at least two items within a category from the same rating form for either item to be considered for pruning at the first stage. Therefore, some of the items that were retained at both pruning stages were retained not because they are "superior" items, but rather because they were never considered for elimination.

In addition, we eliminated two more categories, *time management* and *workload*, because we were not able to reduce the heterogeneity without deleting all the items in some sets. Less than 2% of the 595 sets that remained are heterogeneous. We decided not to drop any other categories or items since they did not consistently produce heterogeneity across all sets.

Thus, we constructed a 35 by 35 correlation matrix. This matrix represented the aggregation of 6,788 interitem correlations computed for 225 items from 17 rating forms. These items, sorted by category, are presented in Appendix A.

Of the 40 Feldman instructional categories, only five were missing from this correlation matrix because of either excessive heterogeneity or insufficient data. These five categories were: *appropriate use of methods/materials, low-level cognitive outcomes, overall learning, time management* and *workload*.

Factor Analysis

Factors were extracted from the aggregate correlation matrix produced above using SPSS (SPSS Inc., 1990). Factors with eigenvalues greater than 1.0 were extracted. The solution was then rotated obliquely using OBLIMIN with a delta of .2. Four factors were extracted via principal components extraction. The percent variance extracted by each factor, in decreasing magnitude, were 62.8%, 4.2%, 3.7, and 2.9%. Of the 35 categories, all except *course objectives, knowledge of domain,* and *supervision and disciplinary activities* had loadings of at least .62 on the first component. Thus there clearly is a large general factor which explains about 63% of the variance in student ratings.

In order to improve interpretability, the solution was rotated obliquely; thus, the variance was redistributed over the four factors. The four factors, in order of importance as judged by the sum of squared loadings, are described below.

Thirteen categories load on Factor 1 (loadings > .55): *choice of supplementary materials, relevance of instruction, overall course, monitoring learning, general knowledge and cultural attainment, research productivity and reputation, motivating students to greater effort, enthusiasm for teaching, high-level cognitive outcomes, clarity of instruction, stimulation of interest, preparation,* and *management style.* We note that most of these categories pertain to the instructor viewed in an instructional role. The sum of the squared loadings is 8.0 and, therefore, this factor appears to be the most important factor in instructional effectiveness.

Sixteen categories load on factor 2 (loadings > .38): *personal appearance, health, and attire, general attitudes, dramatic delivery, concern for students, vocal delivery, answering questions, knowledge of teaching, tolerance of diversity, availability, overall instructor, interaction and discussion, respect for others, enthusiasm for students, friendly classroom climate, enthusiasm for subject,* and *personality characteristics.* We note that most of these categories pertain to the instructor viewed as a person. The sum of the squared loadings is 5.6 and, therefore, the second factor is almost as important as the first factor.

Two categories load on Factor 3 (loadings > .75): *evaluation* and *feedback.* We note that these two categories pertain to the instructor viewed as a regulator. The sum of the squared loadings is 2.5 and, therefore, this factor is considerably less important than the previous two.

Four categories load on Factor 4. These are *supervision and disciplinary actions, knowledge of domain, choice of required materials,* and *objectives.* The sum of the squared loadings is 1.8 and, therefore, this factor is the least important factor. We note that it is difficult to interpret this factor, but it is considerably less important than the previous three and may not be stable. It is also the only factor that is not correlated with the other factors.

Since we aggregated items within categories and factor analyzed relatively homogeneous categories, one would expect to extract "higher-order" factors representing the "common" aspects of instruction across situations. We extracted 62.8% of the variance across the interitem correlations in the first principal component. All items load heavily on this component, suggesting it is an overall instructional skill factor. Such a general skill factor has been proposed by Kulik and McKeachie (1975). Rotation results in the redistribution of variance such that three correlated factors emerged, along with one subsidiary uncorrelated factor. These three correlated factors are similar to the three factors proposed by Widlak, McDaniel, and Feldhusen (1973) describing three roles: instructor, actor, and director. They subsequently factor analyzed responses to the 18 item Course-Instructor-Evaluation form from Purdue and obtained three highly correlated factors.

Feldman (1976) also investigated the pattern of relationships among factors from 60 factor studies. He reported that "despite the profusion of connections…, a fairly consistent and meaningful pattern does emerge: indeed, this pattern supports the view of Widlak et al. (1973) that instructors primarily enact three different roles." Feldman called these roles presentation, facilitation, and regulation.

To address concerns related to both the number of items pruned and the possibility of alternative pruned sets, we ran similar factor analyses of the complete data set, and alternative pruned sets. In all cases the same general factor emerged. Differences occurred primarily in those categories having moderate loadings (e.g., those mentioned above as loading on two factors).

Our factor analysis across the multiple rating forms indicates that there is a "common" structure to instructional effectiveness. Four factors were obtained, three of which were highly correlated. Global items were loaded highly on the first two factors.

The finding that the factors were correlated may obscure setting differences. For example, some students (e.g., engineering students in calculus classes) may respond favorably to the clarity of instruction and give especially high mean ratings for clarity, while other students (e.g., psychology students in clinical classes) may respond favorably to an interactive classroom climate and give especially high mean ratings for interaction and discussion. Despite situational differences in mean ratings, a "common" correlated factor structure would emerge.

Whatever the reason for the high correlations between the factors, the finding that there is such a large global component and that it is highly correlated with the other components argues against the utility of using specific factors or teaching categories to make summative assessments of instruction. We believe that the logical and empirical analyses already presented by us and others provide support for a large, underlying general trait "effective teaching" although it may not be the only trait. In addition, we believe that effective teaching is multidimensional but that there is inconsistency concerning the teaching dimensions, particularly across rating forms (i.e., operationalizations of different latent traits). This inconsistency suggests that any one of the existing multidimensional rating forms may not represent teaching for all instructors, courses, and settings. Therefore, we recommend that specific ratings should be used cautiously for summative decisions about teaching. If one uses an existing rating form, computing a composite score based on the categories and items that formed the general factor of our analysis would appear to be superior to using separate dimensional scores. If one prepares a customized form, only those items and categories that loaded highly on the first principal component of our analysis should be included and their scores averaged. Finally, it remains our opinion that the best alternative to averaging across specific items is to base summative decisions of teaching effectiveness on global ratings.

CONCLUSIONS

Numerous studies have explored the dimensions of effective college instruction. Yet there remain notable disagreements regarding whether and how data from multidimensional student rating forms should be used in summative decisions about teaching. This paper critically examined a host of issues associated with the dimensions of instructional effectiveness as reflected in student ratings of teaching. We discussed effective teaching from both product and process views. From the product view, effective teaching can be defined as the positive cognitive, affective, and/or psychomotor changes produced in students. From the process view, effective teaching can be defined as the teaching activities that occur both before (preparatory) and during (delivery) teaching. We subsequently discussed the need for research exploring the impact of process variables on product variables. The second section provided a general discussion of methods for empirically determining effective teaching. The third section concentrated on the strengths and weaknesses of three validation designs—the laboratory design, the multisection design and the multitrait-multimethod design. The fourth section summarized the quantitative literature reviews of the 43 multisection validity studies. Finally, the fifth section considered factor analysis and the dimensions of effective teaching. We summarized our attempts to quantitatively integrate the results from seventeen correlation matrices by coding the items using a common scoring scheme, eliminating items that were heterogeneous within categories, and factor analyzing the aggregated correlation matrix.

We conclude that existing analyses provide support for a large underlying general trait although it may not be the only trait. We also believe that effective teaching is multidimensional but that there are differences across rating forms concerning the specific dimensions that underlie effective instruction. These differences suggest that student ratings of specific teaching dimensions should not be used indiscriminately for summative decisions about teaching effectiveness.

In this paper we have presented many lines of evidence that suggest that although instructional effectiveness is multidimensional, global items should be used for the purposes of summative decisions. First, when examining many rating forms one is immediately struck by the fact that, despite their differences, what they share is a similar set of global items. Second, global items, more so than many specific instructional dimensions, have relatively high validity coefficients. Third, different instructional settings are likely to have larger effects on specific dimensions than on global items. Fourth, even in well designed multidimensional forms, such as the SEEQ, global items load most strongly on the first few factors. Finally, our factor analysis across seventeen rating forms confirms the four points listed above.

Appendix A: Student Rating Items and Their Categories

In the list below, categories are arranged alphabetically. The five categories not used in the final analysis are presented solely for completeness and are marked with an asterisk (*). These categories are listed with definitions while all other categories contain definitions as well as all items retained for final analysis. Note that items are presented as in original sources. If an item appeared in multiple sources it presented multiply. A quadruple of numbers appears immediately after the name of the category (used in the final analysis) to represent: a) the initial number of items code; b) the number of items retained through all stages; c) the number of items dropped at the stage when interitem correlations **within** each category were examined; and d) the number of items dropped at the stage when interitem correlations **between** categories were examined).

Answering Questions (9/6/2/1): The students are evaluating the extent to which the instructor encouraged students to ask questions and responded to students' questions appropriately.
Rate the instructor on the basis that he answers student's questions in a clear and concise manner.
Rate the extent to which the instructor responded effectively to student questions.
Encouraged questions and answers.
The instructor encouraged and readily responded to student questions.
Became angry when questions were asked.
No questions allowed between explanations.

*Appropriate Use of Methods/Materials (2/2/0/0): The students are evaluating the extent to which the instructor uses appropriate instructional methods and materials in class, including appropriate use of textbook and tests for learning.

Availability (7/4/0/3): The students are evaluating the extent to which the instructor was available outside of the classroom for assistance or extra-curricular activities.
Rate the instructor on the basis of the ease at which an office appointment can be made.
Welcomed seeking help and advice.
Accessible to individual students.
Welcomed conferences.

Choice of Required Materials (8/4/1/3): The students are evaluating the qualities of the required course materials including textbooks, assignments, etc.
The textbook was very good.
Readings and text valuable.
Assignments added to course understanding.
Did not go to trouble of making up assignments.

Choice of Supplementary Materials (4/2/0/2): The students are evaluating the qualities of the supplementary materials (e.g., film, audio-visuals, etc.). That is, they are evaluating whether they were interesting, valuable, or personally relevant. Unless explicitly labeled "supplementary" such materials are considered to be required.
The outside assignments for this course are just about the right length/somewhat too long/somewhat too short/much too long/much too short.
Had varied illustrations about topic covered.

Clarity of Instruction (25/15/3/7): The students are evaluating the extent to which the instructor delivers clear, concise, understandable and accurate instruction (e.g., lectures, laboratories, etc.).
Presentation of subject matter.
Rate the instructor on the basis of the organized class presentation.
Rate the instructor on the basis that she makes clear or simple the difficult ideas or concepts in this course.
The instructor did not synthesize ideas.
Rate the extent to which the instructor was successful in explaining the course material.
Presentations clarified material.
Presented clearly and summarized.
Instructor's explanations clear.

Presentation well prepared and integrated.
He explained clearly and his explanations were to the point.
Instructions not complete.
Covered subject well.
Made subject clear.
Presentations of materials especially good.
Students in constant state of uncertainty.

Concern for Students (8/6/0/2): The students are evaluating the extent to which the instructor was concerned and helpful about student difficulties
The instructor seemed genuinely concerned with student's progress and was actively helpful.
The instructor seemed to be concerned with whether the students learned the material.
Listened and willing to help.
Concerned about student difficulties.
The instructor maintained a generally helpful attitude toward students and their problems.
Too busy for talks with students.

Dramatic Delivery (5/3/2/0): The students are evaluating the extent to which the instructor delivered instruction in an expressive, dynamic, dramatic or exaggerated manner.
Dynamic and energetic.
Talked with back to class.
Hard to believe.

Enthusiasm for Students (11/9/2/0): The students are evaluating the extent to which the instructor communicates his/her enthusiasm, interest or liking for students as people.
Sympathetic attitude toward students.
Rate the instructor on the basis of the instructor's apparent interest in working with students.
The instructor seemed to be interested in students as persons.
Interested in individual students.
Was the instructor considerate of and interested in his students?
Always suspicious of students.
Afraid of students.
Lacked interest in students.
Kept up with student affairs.

Enthusiasm for Subject (3/3/0/0): The students are evaluating the extent to which the instructor communicates his/her enthusiasm, interest or liking for the subject.
Interest in subject.
The instructor was enthusiastic when presenting course material.
Interested in all aspects of subject.

Enthusiasm for Teaching (4/3/0/1): The students are evaluating the extent to which the instructor communicates his/her enthusiasm, interest or liking for teaching.
The instructor seemed to consider teaching as a chore or routine activity.
Enthusiastic about teaching.
Enjoyed teaching class.

Evaluation (27/8/11/8): The students are evaluating the extent to which the instructor's tests were appropriate in terms of content, frequency, time allocation, weight, difficulty, validity and learning opportunity. They are also evaluating the instructor's fairness and consistency in grading.
The types of test questions used were good.
Fair and impartial grading.
Grading reflected performance.
Grading indicated accomplishments.
Evaluation methods fair and appropriate.
Exams emphasized course content.
Tests indicated careful preparation.

Would not explain grading system.

Feedback (16/5/8/3): The students are evaluating the instructor's use of review and feedback (frequency, positive/negative) and its effect on students.

Instructor did not review promptly and in such a way that students could understand their weaknesses.

The instructor made helpful comments on papers or exams.

Rate the instructor on the basis of the information or feedback provided concerning the nature and quality of my work (considering all the factors involved in teaching this course).

Examination feedback valuable.

Reviewed test questions that majority of students missed.

Friendly Classroom Climate (8/6/2/0): The students are evaluating the extent to which the instructor modeled, encouraged and achieved a friendly and safe classroom.

He was friendly.

Friendly towards students.

Discouraged students

Made students feel very insecure.

Very much at ease with the class.

Students often returned to chat with teacher.

General Attitudes (4/3/1/0): The students are evaluating the instructor's general attitudes. (An attempt is first made to fit items into the other, more specific instructional dimensions. Only if they do not fit elsewhere are they classified here.)

Liberal and progressive attitude.

Had unethical attitudes.

Did not approve of extracurricular activities.

General Knowledge and Cultural Attainment (2/2/0/0): The students are evaluating the instructor's general knowledge and cultural attainment beyond the course.

Admired for great intelligence.

Large background of experience made subject more interesting.

High-level Cognitive Outcomes (32/11/21/0): The students are evaluating the extent to which the instructor is promoting high-level cognitive outcomes such as writing skills, reasoning, meta-cognition, problem solving, etc.

The instructor encouraged students to think for themselves.

The instructor encouraged the development of new viewpoints and appreciations.

Understand advanced material.

Ability to analyze issues.

I can think more coherently.

Developing a sense of personal responsibility (self-reliance, self-discipline).

Discovering the implications of the course material for understanding myself (interests, talents, values, etc.).

Developing specific skills, competencies and points of view that I can use later in life.

Intellectual curiosity in subject stimulated.

Gained general understanding of topic.

Encouraged students to think out answers.

Interaction and Discussion (15/6/1/8): The students are evaluating the extent to which the instructor modeled, encouraged and achieved interactive classes in which both students and instructor contributed to the class.

Encouraged class discussions.

Encouraged expression of ideas.

Students would not cooperate in class.

Group discussions encouraged.

Nothing accomplished in classroom discussions.

Very skillful in directing discussion.

Knowledge of Domain (4/1/2/1): The students are assessing the instructor's knowledge of the specific course subject matter and its applications.

Did not need notes.

Knowledge of Teaching and of Students (1/1/0/0): The students are evaluating the instructor's knowledge of pedagogy (e.g., knowledge of students, student learning, and/or of instructional methods).

No ability to handle students.

*Low-level Cognitive Outcomes: The students are evaluating the extent to which the instructor is promoting low-level cognitive outcomes (e.g., recall, recognition, knowledge, etc.).

Management Style (23/10/12/1): The students are evaluating the instructor's management style (e.g., authoritarian/participatory, formal/informal) and method of handling issues of classroom control (e.g., noise, order, seating, calling on students).

The demands of the students were not considered by the instructor.
He decided in detail what should be done and how it should be done.
He was permissive and flexible.
Knack in dealing with all types of problems.
Never deliberately forced own decisions on class.
Classes always orderly.
Conducted class smoothly.
Never considered what class wanted.
Maintained a well organized classroom.
Weak in leadership questions.

Monitoring Learning (7/5/1/1): The students are evaluating the extent to which the instructor monitored students' reactions and taught at the appropriate individual and class level .

The instructor was skilful in observing student reactions.
Skilled at bringing out special abilities of students.
Worked with students individually.
Aware of individual differences in pupils.
Sensed when students needed help.

Motivating Students to Greater Effort (18/9/3/6): The students are evaluating the extent to which the instructor motivated students to more effort, intellectual curiosity, love of learning, high academic aspirations, etc.

Stimulating intellectual curiosity.
Rate the instructor on the basis that the teaching methods inspire, stimulate or excite me intellectually.
Rate the instructor on the basis that she motivates me to think rather than just memorize material.
I developed motivation to do my best work.
Plan to take more courses.
Inspired many students to do better work.
Motivated students to work.
Instilled spirit of research.
Inspired class to learn.

Objectives (11/4/3/4): The students are evaluating the extent to which the instructor communicated performance criteria and deadlines for assignments and tests.

The direction of the course was adequately outlined.
Detailed course schedule.
The instructor was clear on what was expected regarding course requirements, assignments, exams, etc.
Students always knew what was coming up next day.

Overall Course (8/5/2/1): The students are evaluating the overall worth and quality of the course.

You generally enjoyed going to class.
Overall course rating.
How would you rate the overall value of this course?
Have you enjoyed taking this course?
Students discouraged with course.

Overall Instructor (13/12/1/0): The students are evaluating the overall effectiveness of the instructor.
Rate the overall teacher's effectiveness.
General teaching ability.
Attitudes about teaching.
Would you recommend this course from this instructor?
Overall instructor rating.
Would you recommend this course from this instructor?
How would you rate your instructor with respect to general (all-around) teaching ability?
Overall evaluation of instructor.
Would like instructor as personal friend.
Learned a lot from teacher.
Students avoided this teacher's class.
Not qualified as a teacher.

*Overall Learning: The students are evaluating the overall quality and relevance of the perceived learning that took place including the achievement of short and long term objectives.

Personal Appearance, Health, and Attire (11/5/6/0): The students are evaluating the instructor's personal appearance, health and attire.
Personal appearance.
Teacher very careless about dress.
Very pleasing appearance.
Wore wrinkled clothes.
Poor posture.

Personality Characteristics and Peculiarities (24/20/4/0): The students are evaluating the instructor's general personality characteristics and peculiarities not directly related to teaching (e.g., maturity, irritability, confidence, paranoia, cynicism, etc.).
Sense of proportion and humor.
Personal peculiarities.
Rate the instructor on the basis of poise and classroom mannerisms.
The instructor exhibited professional dignity and bearing in the classroom.
Enhanced presentations with humor.
Crabby.
Good natured.
Consistent.
A typical old maid (or bachelor) personality.
Immature emotionally.
Very prejudiced.
Considerate.
No sense of humor.
Tactless.
Wonderful sense of humor.
Cynical attitude repels students.
Did not inspire confidence.
Magnetic personality.
Tried to show off.
Well-rounded personality.

Preparation and Organization (13/8/2/3): The students are evaluating the extent to which the instructor prepared himself/herself for instruction. (This category only related to preparation, not presentation. Any items that are ambiguous in terms of whether they relate to preparation or presentation are classified as presentation are classified as presentation are classified as presentation since students judge on the basis of presentation.)

Course material was poorly organized.
Generally the course was well organized.
Rate the extent to which the instructor's lectures were well prepared.
The instructor was consistently prepared for class.
Rate the extent to which the instructor's lectures and other material were well prepared.
Absolutely no previous preparation for class.
Became confused in class.
Best organized of any class I have had.

Relevance of Instruction (11/7/3/1): The students are evaluating the extent to which the instructor emphasizes the relevance of the provided information, including recent research.

The instructor's use of examples or personal experiences helped to get points across in class.
Good use of examples.
Contrasted implications.
Gave background of ideas and concepts.
Gave different points of view.
Discussed current developments.
Related subject to everyday life.

Research Productivity and Reputation (3/2/1/0): The students are evaluating the instructor's research productivity and reputation.

Cooperative with other teachers.
Looked to for advice.

Respect for Others (28/15/13/0): The students are evaluating the extent to which the instructor modeled, encouraged and showed trust, respect, and consideration for others (e.g., listened without interruption, did not not belittle or criticize others' criticism, treated others as equals, was punctual, etc.).

The instructor's attendance and punctuality have been consistently good.
He listened attentively to what class members had to say.
Irritated easily.
Very impatient with less able students.
Carried friendliness outside of classroom.
Built up confidence in students.
Gained class confidence very quickly.
Made students feel at ease.
Sarcastic if disagreed with.
Students did things to make teacher mad.
Always very polite to students.
Humiliated students.
Publicly ridiculed some students.
Ridiculed students.
Very sincere when talking to students.

Stimulation of Interest in the Course (21/13/4/4): The students are evaluating the extent to which the instructor stimulated their interest in the course by using a variety of activities, manifested by the extent to which good attendance, increased interest, outside reading, and liking/enjoyment for the subject matter were exhibited.

Rate the instructor on the basis that she presents the material or content of this course in an interesting manner.
Rate the extent to which the instructor stimulated your interest in the course.
Increased subject interest.
Teaching style held your interest.
Rate the extent to which the instructor stimulated your interest in the course.
Do you now enjoy reading more than you used to?
Gained interest in American government.

Do more reading on topic.
Everyone attended regularly.
Knew how to hold attention in presenting materials.
Made lectures stimulating.
No attempt to make course interesting.
Students counted the minutes until class was dismissed.

Supervision and Disciplinary Actions (3/1/2/0): The students are evaluating the extent to which the instructor supervised tests and handled disciplinary actions when disruptions occurred.
Never had to discipline the students.

*Time Management: The students are evaluating the extent to which the instructor handled class time.

Tolerance of Diversity (12/6/3/3): The students are evaluating the extent to which the instructor modeled, encouraged and achieved tolerance for a diversity of opinions, ideas and viewpoints and an absence of prejudice in the classroom.
The instructor was open to other viewpoints.
Rate the instructor on the basis that he considers opposing viewpoints or ideas.
The instructor appeared receptive to new ideas and others' viewpoints.
Intolerant.
Presented both sides of every question.
Blinded to all viewpoints but own.

Vocal Delivery (7/5/2/0): The extent to which the instructor demonstrated skill in vocal delivery.
Rate the instructor on the basis that she speaks clearly and is easily heard.
The instructor is clear and audible.
Speech very fluent.
Lectured inaudibly.
Occasional bad grammar detracted from speech.

*Workload: The students are evaluating the performance standards and the workload (amount, difficulty) of the course and assignments.

References

Abrami, P.C. (1984, February). Using meta-analytic techniques to review the instructional evaluation literature. *Postsecondary Education Newsletter* 6: 8.

Abrami, P.C. (1985). Dimensions of effective college instruction. *Review of Higher Education* 8: 211-228.

Abrami, P.C. (1988). SEEQ and ye shall find: A review of Marsh's "Students' evaluation of university teaching." *Instructional Evaluation* 9(2): 19–27.

Abrami, P. C. (1989a). SEEQing the truth about student ratings of instruction. *Educational Researcher* 43(1): 43–45.

Abrami, P.C. (1989b). How should we use student ratings to evaluate teaching? *Research in Higher Education* 30: 221–227.

Abrami, P.C., Chambers, B., Poulsen, C., DeSimone, C., d'Apollonia, S., and Howden, J. (1995). *Classroom Connections: Understanding and Using Cooperative Learning.* Toronto, Ontario: Harcourt Brace.

Abrami, P.C., Cohen, P.A., and d'Apollonia, S. (1988). Implementation problems in meta-analysis. *Review of Educational Research* 58: 151–179.

Abrami, P.C., and d'Apollonia, S. (1987, April). A conceptual critique of meta-analysis: The literature on student ratings of instruction. Paper presented at the annual meeting of the American Educational Research Association, Washington, DC.

Abrami, P.C. and d'Apollonia, S. (1988, April). The literature on student ratings of instruction: A conceptual solution to some implementation problems of meta-analysis. Paper presented at the annual meeting of the American Educational Research Association, New Orleans, LA.

Abrami, P.C. and d'Apollonia, S. (1990). The dimensionality of ratings and their use in personnel decisions.

In M. Theall and J. Franklin (eds.) *Student Ratings of Instruction: Issues for Improving Practice. New Directions for Teaching and Learning.* Number 43, pp. 97–111. San Francisco: Jossey-Bass.

Abrami, P.C. and d'Apollonia, S. (1991). Multidimensional students' evaluations of teaching effectiveness–Generalizability of "N = 1" research: Comment on Marsh (1991). *Journal of Educational Psychology* 83: 411–415.

Abrami, P.C. d'Apollonia, S. and Cohen, P.A. (1990). The validity of student ratings of instruction: What we know and what we do not. *Journal of Educational Psychology* 82: 219–231.

Abrami, P.C., Leventhal, L., and Perry, R.P. (1982). Educational seduction. *Review of Educational Research* 52: 446–464.

Abrami, P.C., and Mizener, D.A. (1985). Student/instructor attitude similarity, student ratings, and course performance. *Journal of Educational Psychology* 77: 693–702.

Anderson, N.H. (1968). Likableness ratings of 555 personality-trait words. *Journal of Personality and Social Psychology* 9: 272–279.

Borich, G.D. (1977). *The Appraisal of Teaching: Concepts and Process.* Reading, MA.: Addison-Wesley

Bushman, B.J., Cooper, H.M., and Lemke, K.M. (1991). Meta-analysis of factor analyses: An illustration using the Buss-Durke Hostility Inventory. *Personality and Social Psychology Bulletin* 17: 344–349.

Bloom, B.S., Engelhart, M.D., Frost, E.J., Hill, W.H., and Krathwohl, D.R. (1956). *Taxonomy of Educational Objectives. Handbook I: Cognitive Domain.* New York: David McKay.

Campbell, D.T,. and Stanley, J.C. (1966). *Experimental and Quasi-experimental Designs for Research.* Boston: Houghton-Mifflin.

Cashin, W.E., and Downey, R.G. (1992). Using global student rating items for summative evaluations. *Journal of Educational Psychology* 84: 563–572.

Cohen, P.A. (1981). Student ratings of instruction and student achievement: A meta-analysis of multisection validity studies. *Review of Educational Research* 51: 281-309.

Cohen, P.A. (1982). Validity of student ratings in psychology courses: A meta-analysis of multisection validity studies. *Teaching of Psychology* 9: 78–82.

Cohen, P. A. (1983). Comment on a selective review of the validity of student ratings of teaching. *Journal of Higher Education* 54: 448–458.

Cohen, P.A. (1986, April). An updated and expanded meta-analysis of multisection student rating validity studies. Paper presented at the annual meeting of the American Educational Research Association, San Francisco. CA.

Cohen, P.A. (1987, April). A critical analysis and reanalysis of the multisection validity meta-analysis. Paper presented at the annual meeting of the American Educational Research Association, Washington, DC.

Cooper, J., Prescott, S., Cook, L., Smith, L., Mueck, R., and Cuseo, J. (1990). *Cooperative learning and College Instruction: Effective Use of Student Learning Teams.* Long Beach, CA: California State University Foundation on behalf of California State University Institute for Teaching and Learning, Office of the Chancellor.

d'Apollonia, S. and Abrami, P.C. (1987, April). An empirical critique of meta-analysis: The literature on student ratings of instruction. Paper presented at the annual meeting of the American Educational Research Association, Washington, DC.

d'Apollonia, S. and Abrami, P.C.(1988, April). The literature on student ratings of instruction: Yet another meta-analysis. Paper presented at the annual meeting of the American Educational Research Association, New Orleans, LA.

d'Apollonia, S., Abrami, P., and Rosenfield, S. (1993, April). The dimensionality of student ratings of instruction: a meta-analysis of the factor studies. Paper presented at the annual meeting of the American Educational Research Association, Atlanta, GA.

d'Apollonia, S., Abrami, P., and Rosenfield, S. (in preparation). A multivariate meta-analysis of the multisection validity studies.

Dowell, D.A., and Neal, J. A. (1982). A selective review of the validity of student ratings of teaching. *Journal of Higher Education* 53: 51–62.

Doyle, K.O., Jr. (1981). Validity and perplexity: An incomplete list of disturbing issues. *Instructional Evaluation, 6* (1): 23–25.

Doyle, K. O., and Crichton, L.I. (1978). Student, peer, and self-evaluations of college instructors. *Journal of*

Educational Psychology 5: 815–826.

Feldman, K.A. (1976). The superior college teacher from the student's view. *Research in Higher Education* 5: 243–288.

Feldman, K.A. (1977). Consistency and variability among college students in rating their teachers and courses: A review and analysis. *Research in Higher Education* 6: 223–274

Feldman, K.A. (1983). Seniority and experience of college teachers as related to evaluations they receive from students. *Research in Higher Education* 18: 3–214.

Feldman, K.A. (1984). Class size and college students' evaluations of teachers and courses: A closer look. *Research in Higher Education 21:* 45–116.

Feldman, K.A. (1988). Effective college teaching from the students' and faculty's view: Matched or mismatched priorities? *Research in Higher Education* 28: 291–344.

Feldman, K.A. (1989a). The association between student ratings of specific instructional dimensions and student achievement: Refining and extending the synthesis of data from multisection validity studies. *Research in Higher Education* 30: 583–645.

Feldman, K.A. (1989b). Instructional effectiveness of college teachers as judged by teachers themselves, current and former students, colleagues, administrators, and external (neutral) observers. *Research in Higher Education* 30: 137–194.

Feldman, K.A. (1990). An afterword for "The association between student ratings of specific instructional dimensions and student achievement: Refining and extending the synthesis of data from multisection validity studies." *Research in Higher Education* 31: 315–318.

Fernald, P.S. (1990). Students' ratings of instruction: Standardized and customized. *Teaching of Psychology* 17: 105–109.

Franklin, J,. and Theall, M. (1989, April). Rating the readers: Knowledge, attitude, and practice of users of student ratings of instruction. Paper presented at the Annual Meeting of the American Educational Research Association, San Francisco.

Frey, P.W. (1978). A two dimensional analysis of student ratings of instruction. *Research in Higher Education* 9: 69–91.

Gaski, J.F. (1987). On "Construct validity of measures of college teaching effectiveness." *Journal of Educational Psychology* 79: 326–330.

Gorsuch, R.I. (1983). *Factor Analysis.* Hillsdale, NJ: Lawrence Erlbaum.

Hedges, L.V., and Olkin, I. (1985). *Statistical Methods for Meta-analysis.* Orlando, FL: Academic Press.

Hill, P.W. (1984). Testing hierarchy in educational taxonomies: A theoretical and empirical investigation. *Evaluation Education* 8: 181–278.

Howard, G.S., Conway, C.G., and Maxwell, S.E. (1985). Construct validity of measures of college teaching effectiveness. *Journal of Educational Psychology* 77: 187–196.

Isaacson, R.L., McKeachie, W.J., Milholland, J.E., Lin, Y.G., Hofeller, M., Baerwaldt, J.W., and Zinn, K.L. (1964). Dimensions of student evaluations of teaching. *Journal of Educational Psychology* 55: 344–351.

Johnson, D. W., Johnson, R.T., and Smith, K.A. (1991). *Active Learning: Cooperation in the College Classroom* Edina, MN: Interaction Book Co.

Kaiser, H.F., Hunka, S., and Bianchini, J.C. (1969). *Relating factors between studies based upon different individuals.* In H.J. Eysenck (ed.), Personality Structure and Measurement. San Diego, CA: Knapp.

Kulik, J.A., and McKeachie, W.J. (1975). The evaluation of teachers in higher education. *Review of Research in Education* 3: 210–240.

Linn, R.L., Centra, J.A., and Tucker, L. (1975). Between, within, and total group factor analysis of student ratings of instruction. *Multivariate Behavioral Research* 10: 277–288.

Marsh, H.W. (1987). Students' evaluations of university teaching: Research findings, methodological issues, and directions for future research. *International Journal of Educational Research* 11:253–388.

Marsh, H. W. (1991). Multidimensional students' evaluations of teaching effectiveness: A test of alternative higher-order structures. *Journal of Educational Psychology* 83:285–296.

Marsh, H.W. (1991). A multidimensional perspective on students' evaluations of teaching effectiveness: Reply to Abrami and d'Apollonia (1991). *Journal of Educational Psychology* 83:416–421.

Marsh, H.W., and Dunkin, M.J. (1992). Students' evaluations of university teaching: A multidimensional perspective. In J. Smart (ed.), *Higher Education: Handbook of Theory and Research,* Vol. VIII. New

York: Agathon Press. (*Reprinted in this volume.*)

Marsh, H.W., and Hocevar, D. (1984). The factorial invariance of student evaluations of college teaching. *American Educational Research Journal* 21: 341–366.

Marsh, H.W., and Hocevar, D. (1991). The multidimensionality of students' evaluations of teaching effectiveness: The generality of factor structures across academic discipline, instructor level, and course level. *Teaching and Teacher Education* 7: 9–18.

Maxwell, S.E., and Howard, G. S. (1987). On the underdetermination of theory by evidence. *Journal of Educational Psychology* 79: 331–332.

McCallum, L.W. (1984). A meta-analysis of course evaluation data and its use in the tenure decision. *Research in Higher Education* 21:150–158.

Murray, H.G. (1991). Effective Teaching Behaviors in the College Classroom. In J. Smart (ed.), *Higher Education, Handbook of Theory and Research*, Vol. VII. New York: Agathon Press. (*Reprinted in this volume.*)

Murray, H.G., Rushton, J.P., Paunonen, S.V. (1990). Teacher personality traits and student instructional ratings in six types of university courses. *Journal of Educational Psychology* 82: 250–261.

Osgood, C.E., Suci, G.J., and Tannenbaum, P.H. (1957). *The Measurement of Meaning*. Urbana, IL: University of Illinois Press.

Rosenfield, S., d'Apollonia, S. and Abrami, P.C. (1993, April). The dimensionality of student ratings of instruction: Aggregating factor studies. Paper presented at the annual meeting of the American Educational Research Association, Atlanta, GA.

Seldin, P. (1991). *The Teaching Portfolio*. Bolton, MA: Anker Publishing Co.

Shore, B.M., Foster, S.F., Knapper, C.K., Nadeau, C.G., Neill, N., and Sim, V.W. (1986). *The Teaching Dossier: A Guide to Its Preparation and Use*. Ottawa: Canadian Association of University Teachers.

Smith, R.A., and Cranton, P.A. (1992). Students' perceptions of teaching skills and overall effectiveness across instructional settings. *Research in Higher Education* 33: 747.

Sullivan, A.M., and Skanes, G.R. (1974). Validity of student evaluations of teaching and the characteristics of successful instructors. *Journal of Educational Psychology* 66: 584–590.

Tabachnick, B.G., and Fidell, L.S. (1983). *Using Multivariate Statistics*. New York: Harper and Row.

Thomson, B. (1989). Meta-analysis of factor structure studies: A case study example with Bem's Androgyny measure. *Journal of Experimental Education* 57: 182:197.

Wherry, R.L. (1951). *The Control of Bias in Ratings: Factor Analysis of Rating Item Content*. Columbus: The Ohio State University Research Foundation, United States Army, AGO, Personnel Research Branch, PRB Report No. 919.

Widlak, F.W., McDaniel, E.D., and Feldhusen, J.F. (1973). Factor analyses of an instructor rating scale. Paper presented at the annual meeting of the American Educational Research Association, New Orleans. (ERIC Document Reproduction Service ED 079324).

Identifying Exemplary Teachers and Teaching: Evidence from Student Ratings[1]

Kenneth A. Feldman

Formal or systematic evaluation by college students of their teachers has long been used to help students in their selection of courses, to provide feedback to faculty about their teaching, and to supply information for administrators and personnel committees in their deliberations on the promotion and tenure of individual faculty members. Moreover, with the increasing emphasis that many colleges and universities are currently putting on good teaching and on designating, honoring, and rewarding good teachers, the use of student ratings is, if anything, likely to increase. Yet, for all their use, student ratings of instructors and instruction are hardly universally accepted. It is no secret, for example, that some college teachers have little regard for them. For these faculty, student evaluations of teachers (or courses)—whether sponsored by the university administration, faculty-development institutes, individual academic departments, or student-run organizations—are not reliable, valid, or useful, and may even be harmful. Others, of course, believe more or less the opposite; and still others fall somewhere in between these two poles of opinion.

If the credibility of teacher evaluations is to be based on more than mere opinion, one asks what the research on their use shows. This question turns out to be more difficult to answer than might be thought because, even apart from the substance of the pertinent research, the number of relevant studies is voluminous. A few years ago, in a letter to the editor in *The Chronicle of Higher Education* (Sept. 5, 1990), William

[1]This paper is based on an earlier one (Feldman, 1994) commissioned by the National Center on Postsecondary Teaching, Learning, and Assessment for presentation at the Second AAHE Conference on Faculty Roles & Rewards held in New Orleans (January 28-30, 1994). The earlier paper benefited by the thoughtful suggestions of Robert Menges and Maryellen Weimer. As for the present paper, I am grateful to Herbert Marsh, Harry Murray, and Raymond Perry for their helpful comments. A brief version of this paper is to appear in an issue of *New Directions for Teaching and Learning,* edited by Marill Svinicki and Robert Menges (Feldman, forthcoming).

Cashin pointed out that 1,300 citations could be found in the Educational Resources Information Center on "student evaluation of teacher performance" at the postsecondary level. This same year, my own collection of books and articles on instructional evaluation numbered about 2,000 items (Feldman, 1990b). This collection has grown still larger since then, of course. It is true that, at a guess, well over one-half of the items in this collection are opinion pieces (filled with insightful observations at best and uninformed polemics at worst). Even so, this still leaves a large number of research pieces.

Luckily, this research—either as a whole or subportions of it—has been reviewed relatively often (see, among others, Aubrect, 1981; Braskamp, Brandenburg and Ory, 1984; Braskamp and Ory, 1994; Centra, 1979, 1989, 1993; Costin, Greenough and Menges, 1971; Doyle, 1975, 1983; Kulik and McKeachie, 1975; Marsh, 1984, 1987; Marsh and Dunkin, 1992; McKeachie, 1979, Miller, 1972, 1974; and Murray, 1980). Cashin (1988, 1995) has even supplied particularly useful reviews of the major reviews. My own series of reviews started in the mid-1970s and has continued to the present. (See Feldman, 1976a, 1976b, 1977, 1978, 1979, 1983, 1984, 1986, 1987, 1989a, 1989b, 1990a, 1993; two other analyses—Feldman, 1988, 1992—are indirectly relevant.)

One of the best overviews in the area is that by Marsh (1987), which is an update and elaboration of an earlier review of his (Marsh, 1984). In this review, after 100 pages or so of careful, critical, and reflective analysis of the existing research and major reviews of student ratings of instruction, Marsh (1987) sums up his findings and observations, as follows:

> Research described in this article demonstrates that student ratings are clearly multidimensional, quite reliable, reasonably valid, relatively uncontaminated by many variables often seen as sources of potential bias, and are seen to be useful by students, faculty, and administrators. However, the same findings also demonstrate that student ratings may have some halo effect, have at least some unreliability, have only modest agreement with some criteria of effective teaching, are probably affected by some potential sources of bias and are viewed with some skepticism by faculty as a basis for personnel decisions. It should be noted that this level of uncertainty probably also exists in every area of applied psychology and for all personnel evaluation systems. Nevertheless, the reported results clearly demonstrate that a considerable amount of useful information can be obtained from student ratings; useful for feedback to faculty, useful for personnel decision, useful to students in the selection of courses, and useful for the study of teaching. Probably, students' evaluations of teaching effectiveness are the most thoroughly studied of all forms of personnel evaluation, and one of the best in terms of being supported by empirical research (p. 369).

Marsh's tempered conclusions set the stage for the present comments. This discussion first explores various interpretations that can be made of information gathered from students about their teachers (which includes a consideration of the possible half-truths and myths that continue to circulate about teacher and course evaluations). It then analyzes the differential importance of the individual items that constitute the rating forms used to evaluate teachers. The primary aim of this discussion is to see how student evaluations can be used to help identify exemplary teachers and instruction.

Truths, Half-truths, and Myths: Interpreting Student Ratings

The unease felt by some faculty, and perhaps by some administrators and students as well, in using teacher and course evaluations to help identify exemplary teachers and instruction may in part be due to the half-truths if not outright myths that have cropped up about these evaluations. Some of the myths can be laid to rest; and the half-truths can be more fully analyzed to separate the real from the imagined. To do so requires a consideration of certain factors or influences that have been said to "bias" ratings. At the moment there is no clear consensus on the definition of bias in the area of student ratings (see Marsh, 1984, 1987; and Marsh and Dunkin, 1992). I take bias to mean something other than (or more than) the fact that student ratings may be influenced by conditions not under the teacher's control or that conditions may somehow be "unfair" to the instructor (making it harder for him or her to teach well and thus to get high ratings compared to teachers in "easier" situations). Rather, bias here refers to one or more factors directly and somehow inappropriately influencing students' judgments about and evaluation of teachers or courses. In essence, the question is whether a condition or influence actually affects teachers and their instruction, which is then accurately reflected in students' evaluations (a case of *non*bias), or whether in some way this condition or influence only affects students' attitudes toward the course and students' perceptions of instructors (and their teaching) such that evaluations do not accurately reflect the instruction that students receive (a case of bias). (For a more extensive discussion of the meaning of bias as it pertains to student ratings, see Feldman, 1984, 1993; Marsh, 1987, and Marsh and Dunkin, 1992.) Implications and examples of this conceptualization of bias will be given as the discussion proceeds.

Myths

Aleamoni (1987) has listed a number of speculations, propositions, and generalizations about students' ratings of instructors and instruction that he declares "are (on the whole) myths." Although I would not go so far as to call each of the generalizations on his list a myth, some of them indeed are—at least as far as current research shows—as follows: students cannot make consistent judgments about the instructor and instruction because of their immaturity, lack of experience, and capriciousness (untrue); only colleagues with excellent publication records and expertise are qualified to teach and to evaluate their peers' instruction—good instruction and good research being so closely allied that it is unnecessary to evaluate them separately (untrue); most student rating schemes are nothing more than a popularity contest, with the warm, friendly, humorous instructor emerging as the winner every time (untrue); students are not able to make accurate judgments until they have been away from the course, and possibly away from the university for several years (untrue); student ratings are both unreliable and invalid (untrue); the time and day the course is offered affect student ratings (untrue); students cannot meaningfully be used to improve instruction (untrue). I call these statements untrue because supporting evidence was not found for them in one or another of the following research reviews: Abrami, Leventhal and Perry (1982); Cohen (1980b); Feldman (1977, 1978,

1987, 1989a, 1989b); Levinson-Rose and Menges (1981); L'Hommedieu, Menges and Brinko (1988, 1990); Marsh (1984, 1987); and Marsh and Dunkin (1992).

For the most part, Aleamoni (1987) also seems correct in calling the following statement a myth: "Gender of the student and the instructor affects student ratings." Consistent evidence cannot be found that either male or female college students routinely give higher ratings to teachers (Feldman, 1977). As for the gender of the teacher, a recent review (Feldman, 1993) of three dozen or so studies showed that a majority of these studies found male and female college teachers not to differ in the global ratings they receive from their students. In those studies in which statistically significant differences were found, more of them favored women than men. However, across all studies, the average association between gender and overall evaluation of the teacher, while favoring women, is so small (average $r = +.02$) as to be insignificant in practical terms. This would seem to show that the gender of the teacher does not bias students' ratings (unless, of course, it can be shown by *other* indicators of teachers' effectiveness that the ratings of one gender "should" be higher than the other to indicate the reality of this group's better teaching).

This said, it should also be noted that there is some indication of an interaction effect between the gender of the student and the gender of the teacher: across studies, there is some evidence to suggest that students may rate same-gendered teachers a little more highly they than do opposite-gendered teachers. What is unknown from the existing studies, however, is what part of this tendency is due to male and female students taking different classes (and thus having different teachers) and what part is due to differences in preferences of male and female students within classes (thus possibly indicating a bias in their ratings).

Half-truths and the Question of Bias in Ratings

Aleamoni (1987) also presents the following statements as candidates for the status of myth: the size of the class affects student ratings; the level of the course affects student ratings; the rank of the instructor affects student ratings; whether students take the course as a requirement or as an elective affects their ratings; whether students are majors or nonmajors affects their ratings. That these are myths is not clear-cut. Each of these course, instructor or student factors is, in fact, related to student evaluation. The real question is: "Why?"

Although the results of pertinent studies are somewhat mixed, some weak trends can be discerned: *slightly* higher ratings are given (a) to teachers of smaller rather than larger courses (Feldman, 1984; Marsh, 1987); (b) to teachers of upper-level rather than lower-level courses (Feldman, 1978); (c) to teachers of higher rather than lower academic ranks (Feldman, 1983; Marsh, 1987); (d) by students taking a course as an elective rather than as a requirement (Feldman, 1978; Marsh, 1987); and (e) by students taking a course that is in their major rather than one that is not (Feldman, 1978; Marsh, 1987). These associations do not prove causation, of course; each of these factors may not actually and directly "affect" ratings, but may simply be associated with the ratings due to their association with other factors affecting ratings.

Even if it can be shown that one or more of these factors actually and directly "affect" students' ratings, the ratings are not necessarily biased by these factors, as is often inferred when such associations are found (probably an important underlying worry of those prone to discount teacher or course evaluations). To give an example, at certain colleges and universities teachers of higher rank may in fact typically be somewhat better teachers, and thus "deserve" the slightly higher ratings they receive. To give another example, teachers in large classes may receive slightly lower ratings because they indeed are somewhat less effective in larger classes than they are in smaller classes, not because students take out their dislike of large classes by rating them a little lower than they otherwise would. So, while it may be somewhat "unfair" to compare teachers in classes of widely different sizes, the unfairness lies in the difference in teaching conditions, not in a rating bias as defined here.[2]

To put the matter in general terms, certain course characteristics and situational contexts—conditions that may not necessarily be under full control of the teachers—may indeed affect teaching effectiveness; and student ratings may then accurately reflect differences in teaching effectiveness. Although rating bias may not necessarily be involved, those interested in using teaching evaluations to help in decisions about promotions and teaching awards may well want to take into account the fact that it may be somewhat harder to be effective in some courses than in others. Along these lines, note that student ratings gathered from the Instructional Development and Effectiveness Assessment (IDEA) system are reported *separately* for four categories of class size—small (1-14 students), medium (15-34), large (35-99) and very large (100 or more)—as well as for five levels of student motivation for the class as a whole (determined by the average of the students' responses to the background question, "I have a strong desire to take this course"). The reason for this procedure is made clear to users of the evaluation instrument, as follows:

> In addition to using flexible criteria, the IDEA system also controls for *level of student motivation* of the students' desire to take the course . . . and the *size of the class*—two variables which the research has shown are correlated with student rating. . . . The IDEA system assumes that it is harder to teach large groups of students who do not want to take a course than it is to teach small groups of students who do want to take a course. IDEA controls for this by comparing an instructor's ratings, not all with "All" courses in the comparative data pool, but with "Similar" courses [same level of student motivation and same class size] as well (Cashin and Sixbury, 1993, pp. 1-2, emphasis in original).

Another candidate for the status of myth concerns students' grades. As Aleamoni (1987) words it, "the grades or marks students receive in the course are highly correlated with their ratings of the course and instructor." On the one hand, the word "highly" indeed makes the statement mythical; grades are not *highly* correlated with students' ratings. On the other hand, almost all of the available research does show a small or even modest positive association between grades and evaluation (usually a correlation somewhere between +.10 and +.30), whether the unit of analysis is the individual student or the class itself (see Feldman, 1976a, 1977; Stumpf and Freedman, 1979).

---

[2] Using a different definition of bias, Cashin (1988) would consider the size of class a source of bias if its correlation with student ratings of teachers were sufficiently large (but see Cashin, 1995).

Research has shown that some part of the positive correlation between students' grades (usually expected grades) and students' evaluation of teachers is due to "legitimate" reasons and therefore is unbiased: students who learn more earn higher grades and thus legitimately give higher evaluations. This has been called the "validity hypothesis" or "validity effect" (see Marsh, 1987, and Marsh and Dunkin, 1992). Moreover, some part of the association may be spurious, attributable to some third factor—for example, students' interest in the subject matter of the course—which has been referred to as the "student characteristics hypothesis" or "student characteristics effect" (see Marsh, 1989, and Marsh and Dunkin, 1992). Yet another part of the positive correlation may indeed be due to a rater bias in the ratings, although the bias might not be large. Researchers currently are trying to determine the degree to which an attributional bias (students' tendency to take credit for successes and avoid blame for failure) and a retributional bias (students "rewarding" teachers who give them higher grades by giving them higher evaluations, and "punishing" teachers who give them lower grades by giving them lower evaluations) are at work (see Gigliotti and Buchtel, 1990; Theall, Franklin, and Ludlow, 1990a, 1990b). The second of these two biases has been called a "grading leniency hypothesis" or "grading leniency effect" (Marsh, 1987; Marsh and Dunkin, 1992). In their review of research relating grades and teacher evaluations, Marsh and Dunkin (1992) conclude as follows:

> Evidence from a variety of different types of research clearly supports the validity hypothesis and the student characteristics hypothesis, but does not rule out the possibility that a grading leniency effect operates simultaneously. Support for the grading leniency effect was found with some experimental studies, but these effects were typically weak and inconsistent, may not generalize to nonexperimental settings where SETs [students' evaluations of teaching effectiveness] are actually used, and in some instances may be due to the violation of grade expectations that students had falsely been led to expect or that were applied to other students in the same course. Consequently, while it is possible that a grading leniency effect may produce some bias in SETs, support for this suggestion is weak and the size of such an effect is likely to be insubstantial in the actual use of SETs (p. 202).

Yet another correlate of—and, therefore, a possible influence on—teacher evaluations is not mentioned by Aleamoni (1987): academic discipline of the course. Reviewing eleven studies available at the time (Feldman, 1978), I found that teachers in different academic fields tend to be rated somewhat differently. Teachers in English, humanities, arts, and language courses tend to receive somewhat higher student ratings than those in social science courses (especially political sciences, sociology, psychology and economic courses); this latter group of teachers in turn receive somewhat higher ratings than teachers in the sciences (excepting certain subareas of biological sciences), mathematics and engineering courses. Recently, based on data from tens of thousands of classes either from the IDEA system only (Cashin and Clegg, 1987; Cashin and Sixbury, 1993) or from this system and the Student Instructional Report (SIR) of the Educational Testing Service combined (Cashin, 1990), differences among major fields similar to those in my review have been reported.

Cashin and his associates have suggested several possible causes that could be operating to produce these differences in ratings of teachers in different academic disciplines, including the following: some courses are harder to teach than others; some fields have better teachers than others; and students in different major fields rate differently because of possible differences in their attitudes, academic skills, goals, motivation, learning styles, and perceptions of the constituents of good teaching. The following practical advice given by Cashin and Sixbury (1993) is informative:

> There is increasing evidence that different academic fields are rated differently. What is not clear is why. Each institution should examine its own data to determine to what extent the differences found in the general research hold true at that particular institution. If an institution concludes that the differences found at that institution are *due to something other than the teaching effectiveness of the instructors*, e.g., because low rated courses are more difficult to teach, or reflect a stricter rating response set on the part of the students taking those courses, then some control for those differences should be instituted. Using the comparative data in this technical report is one possibility. If however, it is decided that the *differences in ratings primarily reflect differences in teaching effectiveness*, that is, that the low rated courses are so rated because they are *not* as well taught, then of course no adjustments should be made (pp. 2-3, emphases in original).

Identifying Instructional Dimensions Important to Effective Teaching

Thus far, I have explored how student ratings can be used to identify those persons who are seen by students as exemplary teachers (as well as those who are not), noting certain precautions in doing so. Now, I turn to the related topic of how exemplary teaching itself can be identified through the use of student ratings of specific pedagogical dispositions, behaviors and practices of teachers.[3] Teaching comprises many different elements—a multidimensionality that instruments of teacher evaluation usually attempt to capture. The construction of most of these instruments, as Marsh and Dunkin (1992) point out, is based on "a logical analysis of the content of effective teaching and the purposes the ratings are intended to serve, supplemented by reviews of previous research and feedback" (p. 146). Less often used is an empirical approach that emphasizes statistical techniques such as factor analysis or multitrait-multimethod analysis.

Marsh and Dunkin (1992) also note that "for feedback to teachers, for use in student course selection, and for use in research in teaching . . . there appears to be general agreement that a profile of distinct components of SETs [students' evaluations of teaching effectiveness] based on an appropriately constructed multidimensional instrument is more useful than a single summary score" (p. 146). However, whether a multidimensional profile score is more useful than a single summary score for personnel decisions has turned out to be more controversial (see Abrami, 1985, 1988, 1989a, 1989b; Abrami and d'Apollonia, 1991; Abrami, d'Apollonia and Rosenfield, 1993, 1996; Cashin and Downey, 1992; Cashin, Downey and Sixbury, 1994; Hativa and Raviv, 1993; and Marsh, 1987, 1991a, 1991b, 1994).

---

[3]As with overall evaluation of teachers, the characteristics of courses, of teachers themselves, and of situational contexts have all been found to correlate with specific evaluations. Those characteristics most frequently studied have been class size, teacher rank/experience and the gender of the teacher. Class size and the rank/experience of the teacher each correlate more highly with some specific evaluations than with others (for details, see Feldman, 1983, 1984). (The degree to which these factors actually affect teaching rather than "biasing" students in their ratings has yet to be determined.) With the possible exception of their sensitivity to and concern with class level and progress, male and female teachers do not consistently differ in the specific evaluations they receive across studies (Feldman, 1993).

In earlier reviews (Feldman, 1976b, 1983, 1984, 1987, 1989a), I used a set of roughly 20 instructional dimensions into which the teaching components of relevant studies could be categorized. In recent years, I extended this set in one way or another to include more dimensions (see Feldman, 1988, 1989b, 1993). The fullest set—28 dimensions—is given in the Appendix, along with specific examples of evaluation items that would be categorized in each dimension. Unlike studies using factor analyses or similar techniques to arrive at instructional dimensions, the categories are based on a logical analysis of the single items and multiple-item scales found in the research literature on students' views of effective teaching and on their evaluations of actual teachers. Over the years, I have found the system of categorization to be useful in classifying the characteristics of instruction analyzed in various empirical studies even though it may differ from the definitions and categories found in any one of these studies.[4]

Teaching That Is Associated with Student Learning

Although all 28 dimensions of instruction found in the Appendix would seem to be important to effective teaching, one would assume that some of them are more important than others. One way of establishing this differential importance is to see how various teaching dimensions relate to student learning, which Cohen (1980a, 1981, 1987) did in his well-known meta-analytic study of the relationships of student achievement with eight different instructional dimensions.[5] Based in large part on work by d'Apollonia and Abrami (1987, 1988) and Abrami, Cohen and d'Apollonia (1988), I extended Cohen's meta-analysis a few years ago by using less heterogeneous categories for coding the evaluation items and scales in the studies under review, widening the range of instructional dimensions under consideration, and preserving more of the information in the studies Cohen used in his meta-analysis (see Feldman, 1989b, l990a). To be included in Cohen's meta-analysis or my own, a study had to provide data from actual college classes rather than from experimental analogues of teaching. The unit of analysis in the study had to be the class or instructor and not the individual student. Its data had to be based on a multisection course with a common achievement measure used for all sections of the course (usually an end-of the course examination as it turned out). Finally, the study had to provide data from which a rating/achievement correlation could be calculated (if one was not given).

The correlations between specific evaluations and student achievement from the studies under review were distributed among 28 instructional dimensions (given in the present Appendix), with weighting procedures used to take into account evaluational items or scales that were coded in more than one dimension. Average correlations were calculated for each of the instructional dimensions having information from at least

---

[4] Abrami and d'Apollonia (1990) adapted these categories for use in their own work (also see d'Apollonia and Abrami, 1988). More recently, they have made more extensive refinements and modifications to the dimensions and concomitant coding scheme (Abrami, d'Apollonia and Rosenfield, 1993, 1996).

[5] These dimensions are labeled: Skill; Rapport; Structure; Difficulty; Interaction; Feedback; Evaluation; and Interest/Motivation.

three studies. These average correlations are given in Table 1, along with the percent of variance explained (r^2).[6]

TABLE 1. Average Correlations of Specific Evaluations of Teachers with Student Achievement

Percent Variance Explained		Instructional Dimension	Average r
30.0%-34.9%	No. 5	Teacher's Preparation; Organization of the Course	.57
	No. 6	Clarity and Understandableness	.56
25.0%-29.9%			
20.0%-24.9%	No. 28	Teacher Pursued and/or Met Course Objectives	.49
	No. 12	Perceived Outcome or Impact of Instruction	.46
15.0%-19.9%			
10.0%-14.9%	No. 1	Teacher's Stimulation of Interest in the Course and Its Subject Matter	.38
	No. 20	Teacher Motivates Students to Do Their Best; High Standard of Performance Required	.38
	No. 16	Teacher's Encouragement of Questions, and Openness to Opinions of Others	.36
	No. 19	Teacher's Availability and Helpfulness	.36
	No. 7	Teacher's Elocutionary Skills	.35
	No. 9	Clarity of Course Objectives and Requirements	.35
	No. 3	Teacher's Knowledge of the Subject	.34
5.0%-9.9%	No. 8	Teacher's Sensitivity to, and Concern with, Class Level and Progress	.30
	No. 2	Teacher's Enthusiasm (for Subject or for Teaching)	.27
	No. 13	Teacher's Fairness; Impartiality of Evaluation of Students; Quality of Examinations	.26
	No. 25	Classroom Management	.26
	No. 17	Intellectual Challenge and Encouragement of Independent Thought (by the Teacher and the Course)	.25
	No. 14	Personality Characteristics ("Personality") of the Teacher	.24
	No. 18	Teacher's Concern and Respect for Students; Friendliness of the Teacher	.23
	No. 15	Nature, Quality, and Frequency of Feedback from the Teacher to the Students	.23
	No. 26	Pleasantness of Classroom Atmosphere	.23
0.0%-4.9%	No. 10	Nature and Value of the Course (Including Its Usefulness and Relevance)	.17
	No. 23	Difficulty of the Course (and Workload)—Description	.09
	No. 24	Difficulty of the Course (and Workload)—Evaluation	.07
	No. 11	Nature and Usefulness of Supplementary Materials and Teaching Aids	-.11

Note: This table has been constructed from data given in Table 1 in Feldman (1989b), which itself was based on information in the following studies: Benton and Scott (1976); Bolton, Bonge and Marr (1979); Braskamp, Caulley and Costin (1979); Bryson (1974); Centra (1977); Chase and Keene (1979); Cohen and Berger (1970); Costin (1978); Doyle and Crichton (1978); Doyle and Whitely (1974); Elliott (1950); Ellis and Rickard (1977); Endo and Della-Piana (1976); Frey (1973); Frey (1976); Frey, Leonard and Beatty (1975); Greenwood, Hazelton, Smith, and Ware (1976); Grush and Costin (1975); Hoffman (L978); Marsh, Fleiner, and Thomas (1975); Marsh and Overall (1980); McKeachie, Lin, and Mann (1971); Mintzes (1976-77); Morgan and Vasché (1978); Morsh, Burgess, and Smith (1956); Murray (1983); Orpen

---

[6] The results given in Table 1 are similar to those shown in an analysis in d'Apollonia and Abrami (1988), although there are some differences (see Abrami, d'Apollonia and Rosenfield, 1996).

(1980); Rankin, Greenmun, and Tracy (1965); Remmers, Martin, and Elliott (1949); Rubinstein and Mitchell (1970); Solomon, Rosenberg, and Bezdek (1964); and Turner and Thompson (1974). Each r given in (or derived from information in individual studies was converted to a Fisher's Z transformation (z_r) and weighted by the inverse of the number of instructional dimensions in which it was coded. For each instructional dimension, the weighted z_r's were averaged and then backtransformed to produce the weighted average r's given in this table. These r's are shown only for those instructional dimensions having information from at least three studies; thus there are no entries for Dimensions 4, 21, 22 and 27. All correlations in this table are statistically significant except those for Dimensions 11, 23, and 24.

Note that average r's for the instructional dimensions range from +.57 to -.11. All but one (Dimension No. 11) are positive, and all but three (Dimensions No. 11, No. 23, No. 24) are statistically significant. The two highest correlations of .57 and .56—explained variance of over 30%—are for Dimensions No. 5 (teacher's preparation and course organization) and No. 6 (teacher's clarity and understandableness). The teacher's pursuit and/or meeting of course objectives and the student-perceived outcome or impact of the course (Dimensions No. 28 and No. 12) are the next most highly related dimensions with achievement (r = +.49 and +.46). Somewhat more moderately-sized correlations—indicating between roughly 10% and 15% of explained variance—were found for several instructional dimensions: teacher's stimulation of students' interest in the course and its subject (Instructional Dimension No. 1, average r = +.38); teacher's motivation of students to do their best (No. 20, +.38); teacher's encouragement of questions and discussion, and openness to the opinions of others (No. 16, +.36); teacher's availability and helpfulness (No. 19, +.36); teacher's elocutionary skills; teacher's knowledge of subject (No. 3, +.34) (No. 7, +.35); clarity of course objectives and requirements (No. 9, +.35); and teacher's knowledge of subject (No. 3, +.34).

Less strongly associated with student achievement are: the teacher's sensitivity to, and concern with, class level and progress (No. 8); teacher's enthusiasm (No. 2); teacher's fairness and impartiality of evaluation (No. 13); classroom management (No. 25); intellectual challenge and encouragement of students' independent thought (No. 17); teacher's "personality" (No. 14); teacher's friendliness and respect or concern for students (No. 18); the quality and frequency of teacher's feedback to students (No. 15); the pleasantness of the classroom atmosphere (No. 26); and the nature and value of the course material (No. 10). The nature and usefulness of supplementary materials and teaching aids as well as the difficulty and workload of the course (either as a description or as an evaluation by students) are not related to student achievement. Because of insufficient data in the set of studies under consideration, the relationship of the following dimensions to student achievement is not clear from these studies: No. 4 (teacher's intellectual expansiveness); No. 21 (teacher's encouragement of self-initiated learning); No. 22 (teacher's productivity in research); and No. 27 (individualization of teaching).

Do Certain Kinds of Teaching Actually Produce Student Achievement?

It is important to recognize that the associations between specific evaluations of teachers and student achievement by themselves do not establish the causal connections between the instructional characteristics under investigation and student achievement. For example, it is possible that the correlations that have been found in some proportion of the studies (whose results were used to create Table 1) do not necessarily indicate that the instructional characteristics were causal in producing the students' achievement. Rather, as Leventhal (1975) was one of the first to point out, some third variable such as student motivation, ability or aptitude of the class might independently affect both teacher performance and student learning, which would account for the correlations between instructional character- istics and student achievement even if there were no direct causal connection.

Leventhal (1975) has suggested that causality can be more clearly established in studies in which students are randomly assigned to sections of a multisection course rather than self-selected into them, for the "random assignment of students . . . pro- motes equivalence of the groups of students by disrupting the causal processes which ordinarily control student assignment" (p. 272). It is not always possible, however, to assign students randomly to class sections. In some of the studies reviewed by Cohen (and by Feldman, 1989b), students were randomly assigned to class sections, whereas in other studies they were not. Interestingly, in his meta-analysis, Cohen (1980a) found that, for each of the four instructional dimensions that he checked, studies in which students were randomly assigned to sections gave about the same results as did studies where students picked their own class sections. Cohen (1980a) also compared studies where the ability of students in class sections was statistically controlled with studies where it was not. Again, for each of the four instructional dimensions that he checked, the correlations for the two sets of studies did not differ. Results such as these increase the likelihood that the instructional characteristics and student achieve- ment are causally connected, although the possibility of spurious elements has not been altogether ruled out. Even with random assignment, the results of multisection validation studies may still permit certain elements of ambiguity in interpretation and generalization (Marsh, 1987; and Marsh and Dunkin, 1992; but see Abrami, d'Apollo- nia, and Rosenfield, 1993, 1996).

The results of experimental studies—whether field experiments or laboratory exper- iments—are obviously useful here, for they can help clarify cause-effect relationships in ways that the correlational studies just reviewed cannot. Relevant research has been reviewed (selectively) by Murray (1991), who notes in his analysis of pertinent studies that either teacher's enthusiasm/expressiveness or teacher clarity (or both) has been a concern in nearly all relevant experimental research, and that these studies usually include measures of amount learned by students. In his overview of this research, Mur- ray (1991) reports that "classroom teaching behaviors, at least in the enthusiasm and clarity domains, appear to be causal antecedents (rather than mere correlates) of various instructional outcome measures" (p. 161, emphasis added).

Although Murray's (1991) definitions of these domains are not completely identical with the definitions of pertinent dimensions of the present analysis, it is still of interest to compare his conclusions and the findings given here. Thus, in the present discussion, teacher clarity has also been shown to be of high importance to teaching, whether indi- cated by the correlation of teacher clarity with student achievement in the multisection correlational studies or, as will be seen in a later section of this paper, by the association of teacher clarity with the global evaluation of the teacher. As for the enthusiastic/ expressive attitudes and behaviors of teachers, highlighted in Murray's (1991) analysis, the instructional dimensions of "teachers enthusiasm (for subject or for teaching)" referred to in the present discussion is, in fact, associated with achievement in the multi-section correlational studies, but only moderately so compared to some of the other instructional dimensions. However, the instructional dimension of "teacher's elocution-ary skills," which assumedly is an aspect of enthusiasm/expressiveness is more strongly associated with achievement in the multisectional-correlational studies. Furthermore, note that Murray writes that "behaviors loading on the Enthusiasm [Expressive] factor share elements of spontaneity and stimulus variation, and thus are perhaps best inter-preted as serving to elicit and maintain student attention to material presented in class" (p. 146). Given this interpretation, it is of relevance that the instructional dimension of "teacher's stimulation of interest in the course and its subject matter" has been found to be rather highly correlated (albeit less so than the top four dimensions) with students' achievement in multisectional correlational studies; moreover, this particular dimension is highly associated, as well, with global evaluation of instruction relative to the other instructional dimensions (to be discussed in a later section of this paper).

Underlying Mechanisms and Other Considerations

Whether the associations between student learning and teacher's attitudes, behaviors, and practices are established by correlational studies or by experimental studies, the exact psychological and social psychological mechanisms by which these instructional characteristics influence student learning need to be more fully and systematically detailed than they have been. When a large association between an instructional charac-teristic and student achievement is found, the tendency is to see the finding as obvious—that is, as being a self-explanatory result. For example, given the size of the correlation involved, it would seem obvious that a teacher who is clear and understandable naturally facilitates students' achievement; little more needs to be said or explained, it might be thought. But, in a very real sense, the "obviousness" or "naturalness" of the connection appears only after the fact (of a substantial association). Were the correlation between dimension of "feedback" and student achievement a great deal larger than was found, then this instructional characteristic, too, would be seen by some as obviously facilita-tive of student achievement: naturally, teachers who give frequent and good feedback effect high cognitive achievement in their students. But, as previously noted, frequency and quality of feedback has not been found to correlate particularly highly with student achievement, and there is nothing natural or obvious about either a high or low associa-tion between feedback and students' achievement; and, in fact, to see either as natural or obvious ignores the specific psychological and social psychological mechanisms that may be involved in either a high or low correlation.

In short, although a case can be made that many of the different instructional charac-teristics could be expected to facilitate student learning (see, for example, Marsh and Dunkin, 1992, pp. 154-156 [pp. 251-253 herein]), what is needed are specific articula-tions about which particular dimensions of instruction theoretically and empirically are more likely and which less likely to produce achievement. A crucial aspect of this inter-est is specifying exactly how those dimensions that affect achievement do so—even when, at first glance, the mechanisms involved would seem to be obvious. Indeed, conceptually and empirically specifying such mechanisms in perhaps the most "obvious" connection of them all in this area—that between student achievement and the clarity and understandableness of instructors—has turned out to be particularly complex, not at all simple or obvious (see, for example, Land, 1979, 1981; Land and Combs, 1981, 1982, Land and Smith, 1979, 1981; and Smith and Land, 1980). Likewise, the mechanisms underlying the correlation between teacher's organization and student achievement have yet to be specifically and fully determined, although Perry (1991) has recently started the attempt by offering the following hypothetical linkages:

> Instructor organization…involves teaching activities intended to structure course material into units more readily accessible from students' long-term memory. An outline for the lecture provides encoding schemata and advanced organizers which enable students to incorporate new, incoming material into existing structures. Presenting linkages between content topics serves to increase the cognitive integration of the new material and to make it more meaningful, both of which should facilitate retrieval (p. 26).

One other consideration may be mentioned at this point. McKeachie (1987) has recently reminded educational researchers and practitioners that the achievement tests assessing student learning in the sorts of studies being considered here typically measure lower-level educational objectives such as memory of facts and definitions rather than the higher-level outcomes such as critical thinking and problem solving that are usually taken as important in higher education. He points out that "today cognitive and instructional psychologists are placing more and more emphasis upon the importance of the way in which knowledge is structured as well as upon skills and strategies for learning and problem solving" (p. 345). Moreover, although not a consideration of this paper, there are still other cognitive skills and intellectual dispositions as well as a variety of affective and behavioral outcomes of students that my be influenced in the college classroom (sees for example, discussions in Baxter Magolda, 1992; Bowen, 1977; Chickering and Reisser, 1993; Doyle, 1972; Ellner and Barnes, 1983; Feldman and Newcomb, 1969; Feldman and Paulsen, 1994; Hoyt, 1973; King and Kitchener, 1994; Marsh, 1987; Pascarella and Terenzini, 1991; Sanders and]Wiseman, 1990; Sockloff, 1973; and Turner, 1970).

Specific Aspects of Teaching as Related to Overall Evaluation of the Teacher

There is another way of determining the differential importance of various instructional dimensions, one that uses information internal to the evaluation form itself. If it is assumed that each student's overall evaluation of an instructor is an additive combination of the student's evaluation of specific aspects of the teacher and his or her instruction, weighted by the student's estimation of the relative importance of these aspects to good teaching, then it would be expected that students' overall assessment of teachers would be more highly associated with instructional characteristics that students generally consider to be more important to good teaching than with those they consider to be less important (cf. Crittenden and Norr, 1973). Thus, one way to establish the differential importance of various instructional characteristics is to compare the magnitudes of the correlations between the actual overall evaluations by students of their teachers and their ratings of each of the specific attitudinal and behavioral characteristics of these teachers. Otherwise put, the importance of an instructional dimension is indicated by its ability to discriminate among students' global assessment of teachers.[7]

In an analysis (Feldman, 1976b) done a while ago now, though one still of full relevance here, I located some 23 studies containing correlations (or comparable information showing the extent of the associations) between students' overall evaluations of their teachers and their ratings of specific attitudinal and behavioral characteristics of these teachers.

TABLE 2. Comparison of Instructional Dimensions on Two Different Indicators of Importance

Instructional Dimension	Importance Shown by Correlation with Student Achievement (1)	Importance Shown by Correlation with Overall Evaluations (2)
No. 5 — Teacher's Preparation; Organization of the Course	.57 (1)	.41 (6)
No. 6 — Clarity and Understandableness	.56 (2)	.25 (2)
No. 12 — Perceived Outcome or Impact of Instruction	.46 (3)	.28 (3)
No. 1 — Teacher's Stimulation of Interest in the Course and Its Subject Matter	.38 (4)	.20 (1)
No. 16 — Teacher's Encouragement of Questions and Discussion, and Openness to Opinions of Others	.36 (5.5)	.60 (11)
No. 19 — Teacher's Availability and Helpfulness	.3 6 (5.5)	.74 (16)
No. 7 — Teacher's Elocutionary Skills	.35 (7.5)	.49 (10)
No. 9 — Clarity of Course Objectives and Requirements	.35 (7.5)	.45 (7)
No. 3 — Teacher's Knowledge of the Subject	.34 (9)	.48 (9)
No. 8 — Teacher's Sensitivity to, and Concern with, Class Level and Progress	.30 (10)	.40 (5)
No. 2 — Teacher's Enthusiasm (for Subject or for Teaching)	.27 (11)	.46 (8)
No. 13 — Teacher's Fairness; Impartiality of Evaluation of Students; Quality of Examinations	.26 (12)	.72 (14.5)
No. 17 — Intellectual Challenge and Encouragement of Independent Thought (by the Teacher and the Course)	.25 (13)	.33 (4)
No. 18 — Teacher's Concern and Respect for Students; Friendliness of the Teacher	.23 (14.5)	.65 (12)
No. 15 — Nature, Quality, and Frequency of Feedback from the Teacher to Students	.23 (14.5)	.87 (17)
No. 10 — Nature and Value of the Course Material (Including Its Usefulness and Relevance)	.17 (16)	.70 (13)
No. 11 — Nature and Usefulness of Supplementary Materials and Teaching Aids	-.11 (17)	.72 (14.5)

Note: This table is adapted from Table 3 in Feldman (1989b). The correlations shown in Column 1 are the same as those in Table 1 of the present analysis. The higher the correlation, the more important the instructional dimension. The correlations have been ranked from 1 to 17 (with the ranks shown in parentheses). The average standardized ranks given in Column 2 originally were given in Feldman (1976b, see Table 2 and footnote 5), and are based on information in the following studies: Brooks, Tarver, Kelley, Liberty and Dickerson (1971); Centra (1975); Cobb (1956); French-Lazovik (1974, two studies); Garber (1964); Good (1971); Harry and Goldner (1972); Harvey and Barker (1970); Jioubu and Pollis (1974); Leftwich and Remmers (1962); Maas and Owen (1973); Owen (1967); Plant and Sawrey (1970); Remmers (1929); Remmers and Weisbrodt (1964); Rosenshine, Cohen and Furst (1973); Sagen (1974); Spencer (1967); Van Horn (1968); Walker (1968); Widlak, McDaniel and Feldhusen (1973); and Williams (1965). The lower the average standardized rank (that is, the smaller the fraction), the more important the dimension. The average standardized ranks in Column 2 have been ranked from 1 to 17 (with the ranks shown in parentheses). This table includes only those dimensions considered in both Feldman (1976b) and Feldman (1989b), and thus there are fewer dimensions in this table than there are in Table 1.

---

[7]Limitations of this approach to determining the importance of instructional dimensions are discussed in Feldman (1976b, 1988; also see Abrami, d'Apollonia and Rosenfield, 1993, 1996).

This information in each study was used to rank order the importance of these characteristics (in terms of size of its association with overall evaluation) and then to calculate for each study standardized ranks (rank of each item divided by the number of items ranked) for the specific evaluations in the study. Finally, for each of the instructional dimensions under consideration (see Feldman, 1976, Table 1 and note 5), standardized ranks were averaged across the pertinent studies.

These average standardized ranks are given in Column 2 of Table 2. Column 1 of this same table repeats those data previously given in Table 1 on the associations between instructional dimensions and student achievement for just those instructional dimensions considered in both analyses. The two analyses, each determining the importance of instructional dimensions in its own way, have eighteen instructional dimensions in common, although data for only seventeen of them are given in the table. Instructional Dimension No. 4 (teacher's intellectual expansiveness) has been left out, as it was in Table 1, because of insufficient data about the correlation between it and student achievement. Table 2 also shows (in parentheses) the rank in importance of each of the instructional dimensions that is produced by each of the two different methods of gauging importance of the dimensions.

There is no overlap in the studies on which the data in Columns 1 and 2 of Table 2 are based. Furthermore, because the studies considered in the student achievement analyses (Col. 1) are mostly of students in multisection courses of an introductory nature, these students and courses are less representative of college students and courses in general than are the students and courses in the second set of studies (Col. 2). Despite these circumstances, the rank-order correlation (rho) between the ranks shown in the two columns is +.61. Those specific instructional dimensions that are the most highly associated with student achievement tend to be the same ones that best discriminate among teachers with respect to the overall evaluation they receive from students. The correlation is not a perfect one, however. The largest discrepancies are for teacher's availability and helpfulness (relatively high importance in terms of its association with achievement and relatively low importance in terms of its association student's global evaluations) and for intellectual challenge and encouragement of students' independent thought (relatively low importance by the first indicator and relatively high importance by the second indicator). The other large "shifts" between the two indicators of importance are less dramatic: teacher's preparation and course organization (from Rank 1 to Rank 6, the latter still relatively high in importance), and teacher's encouragement of questions and openness to others' opinion (from rank 5.5 to rank 11).

If ranks 1 through 6 are thought of as indicating high importance (relative to the other dimensions), rank 7-12 as indicating moderate importance, and ranks 13-17 as indicating low importance (low, that is, relative to the other dimensions, not necessarily unimportant), then the two methods determining the importance of instructional dimensions show the following pattern. Both methods indicate that the teacher's preparation and course organization, the teacher's clarity and understandableness, the teacher's stimulation of students' interest and the students' perceived outcome or impact of the course are of high importance (relative to the other dimensions). Although the teacher's encouragement of questions and openness to others' opinion as well as his or her avail-ability and helpfulness are also of high importance in terms of the association of each with achievement, the first is only of moderate importance and the second of low impor-tance in terms of its association with global evaluation of teachers.

Both methods of determining the importance of the instructional dimensions show the following to be of moderate importance relative to other dimensions: teacher's elo-cutionary skill, clarity of course objective and requirements, teacher's knowledge of subject, and teacher's enthusiasm. The importance of the teacher's sensitivity to class level and progress is also moderate by the first indicator (association with student learn-ing) but high by the second (association with overall evaluation of the teacher), whereas the teacher's fairness and impartiality of evaluation is moderate by the first and low by the second. Each of the following five dimensions is of low relative importance in terms of its association with student achievement, although only the first three are also rela-tively low in importance in terms of their association with global evaluation: nature, quality and frequency of feedback to students; nature and value of course material; nature and usefulness of supplementary materials and teaching aids; intellectual chal-lenge and encouragement of independent thought (which is of relatively high impor-tance in the strength of its association with the global evaluation of teachers); and teacher's friendliness and concern/respect for student (of moderate importance in its association with global evaluation).

Table 3 offers a summary of the results of using the two different ways considered here of determining the importance of various instructional dimensions from student ratings of teachers. By averaging (when possible) the rank order of the dimensions produced by the two methods, information in Table 2 (and, in some cases, Table 1 as well) has been used to classify roughly the instructional dimensions into four catego-ries of importance: high importance; moderate importance; moderate-to-low impor-tance; and low (or no) importance. For most of the instructional dimensions, placement into the categories depended on information from both indicators of impor-tance (association with achievement and association with global rating); in the other cases, classification was based on information from only one indicator (association with achievement).

Although the present paper has concentrated on data derived from student ratings of actual teachers, I want to note briefly another way of determining the importance of various instructional dimensions using different information: Those most involved with teaching and learning can be asked directly about the importance of various components of instruction. In one analysis (Feldman, 1988), I collected thirty-one studies in which both students and faculty (separately) specified the instructional characteristics they considered particularly important to good teaching and effective instruction. Students and faculty were generally similar, though not identical, in their views, as indicated by an average correlation of +.71 between them in their valuation of various aspects of teaching. However, the ordering of the instructional dimensions by either of these groups shows differences (as well as some similarities) with that based on the two indicators of importance using student ratings of actual teachers.

TABLE 3. Summary of the Importance of Various Instructional Dimensions Based on Student Ratings

	High Importance	
(Two Sources)	No. 6	Clarity and Understandableness
(Two Sources)	No. 1	Teacher's Stimulation of Interest in the Course and Its Perceived Subject Matter
(Two Sources)	No. 12	Perceived Outcome of Impact of Instruction
(Two Sources)	No. 5	Teacher's Preparation; Organization of the Course
(One Source)	No. 28	Teacher Pursued and/or Met Course Objectives
(One Source)	No. 20	Teacher Motivates Students to Do Their Best; High Standard of Performance Required
	Moderate Importance	
(Two Sources)	No. 9	Clarity of Course Objectives and Requirements
(Two Sources)	No. 8	Teacher's Sensitivity to, and Concern with, Class Level and Progress
(Two Sources)	No. 16	Teacher's Encouragement of Questions and Discussion, and Openness to Opinions of Others
(Two Sources)	No. 17	Intellectual Challenge and Encouragement of Independent Thought
(Two Sources)	No. 7	Teacher's Elocutionary Skills
(Two Sources)	No. 3	Teacher's Knowledge of the Subject
(Two Sources)	No. 2	Teacher's Enthusiasm for the Subject
(Two Sources)	No. 19	Teacher's Availability and Helpfulness
	Moderate-to-Low Importance	
(Two Sources)	No. 13	Teacher's Fairness; Impartiality of Evaluation of Students; Quality of Examinations
(Two Sources)	No. 18	Teacher's Concern and Respect for Students; Friendliness of the Teacher
(One Source)	No. 25	Classroom Management
(One Source)	No. 14	Personality Characteristics ("Personality") of the Teacher
(One Source)	No. 26	Pleasantness of Classroom Atmosphere
	Low Importance or No Importance	
(Two Sources)	No. 10	Nature and Value of the Course (Including its Usefulness and Relevance)
(Two Sources)	No. 15	Nature, Quality, and Frequency of Feedback from the Teacher to the Student
(Two Sources)	No. 11	Nature and Usefulness of Supplementary Materials and Teaching Aids
(One Source)	No. 23	Difficulty of the Course (and Workload)—Description
(One Source)	No. 24	Difficulty of the Course (and Workload)—Evaluation

Note: By averaging (when possible) the rank ordering of dimensions produced by two different methods of determining importance of various instructional dimensions, information in Table 2 (and, in some cases, Table 1) has been used to classify instructional dimensions into one of the four categories shown in this table. As indicated in the table, for some instructional dimensions two sources of information were available (association of the instructional dimension with achievement and with global evaluations, as given in Table 2); for other instructional dimensions, only one source of information was available (association of the instructional dimension with achievement, as given in Table 1.)

A few examples may be given. Similar to the results shown in Table 3, Instructional Dimensions No. 5 (teacher's preparation and organization of the course) and No. 6 (clarity and understandableness) are of high importance to students and to faculty when these groups are asked directly about what is important to good teaching and effective instruction. Further, when asked directly, students again place high importance on Dimension No. 1 (teacher's stimulation of interest), but in this case faculty (when asked directly) see this aspect of teaching as less important than do the students (when asked directly) or by the two indicators of importance derived from student evaluations (summarized in Table 3). Moreover, compared to the importance determined by the analysis of data from student evaluations, students and faculty, when asked directly, place less importance on Instructional Dimension No. 12 (perceived outcome or impact of instruction) but more importance on Dimensions No. 8 (teacher's sensitivity to, and concern with, class level and progress), No. 3 (teacher's knowledge of subject matter), and No. 2 (teacher's enthusiasm).[8]

Concluding Comments

This paper was not intended as a comprehensive review of the research literature on evaluation of college students of their teachers or on the correlates of effective teaching in college. Indeed, several topics or areas usually explored in such reviews have not been considered in this paper. To take two instances, I have ignored an analysis of whether there is a connection between research productivity and teaching effectiveness as well as a discussion of the usefulness of student ratings as feedback to faculty to improve their teaching (other than to label as myths the statements that good instruction and good research are so closely allied as to make it unnecessary to evaluate them separately and that student ratings cannot meaningfully be used to improve teaching). Rather, I have somewhat single-mindedly focused on the use of student ratings to identify exemplary teachers and teaching. In doing so, I have drawn together relevant parts of my own work over the years in addition to incorporating findings and conclusions from selected others.

Nothing I have written in this paper is meant to imply that the use of teacher evaluations is the only means of identifying exemplary teachers and teaching at the college level. The recent discussion of the multitude of items that would be appropriate for "teaching portfolios" by itself suggests otherwise (see, among others, Centra, 1993, Edgerton, Hutchings and Quinlan, 1991, and Seldin, 1991). For instance, in a project sponsored by the Canadian Association of University Teachers to identify the kinds of information a faculty member might use as evidence of teaching effectiveness, some forty-nine specific items were suggested as possible items for inclusion in a dossier (Shore and associates, 1986); only one of these items referred to student ratings (listed as "student course and teaching evaluation data . . ."). Given the diverse ways noted in these dossiers of "capturing the scholarship of teaching," as Edgerton, Hutchings and Quinlan (1991) put it, gathering teacher evaluations may or may not be the one best way to identify excellence in teaching. But it is an important way; and current research evidence does show that when teacher evaluation forms are properly constructed and administered (Feldman, 1979), the global and specific ratings contained in them, as interpreted with appropriate caution, are undeniably helpful in identifying exemplary teachers and teaching.

---

[8]Other similarities and differences can be found in Feldman, 1989b (Table 3), where data for all four indicators of the importance of various instructional dimensions—association with achievement, association with global ratings, direct report of students, and direct report of faculty—are given.

References

Abrami, P. C. (1985). Dimensions of effective college instruction. *Review of Higher Education* 8: 211-228.

Abrami, P. C. (1988), SEEQ and ye shall find: A review of Marsh's "Students' evaluation of university teaching." *Instructional Evaluation* 9: 19-27.

Abrami, P. C. (1989a). How should we use student ratings to evaluate teaching? *Research in Higher Education* 30: 221-227.

Abrami, P. C. (1989b). SEEQing the truth about student ratings of instruction. *Educational Researcher* 43: 43-45.

Abrami, P. C., Cohen, P. A., and d'Apollonia, S. (1988). Implementation problems in meta-analysis. *Review of Educational Research* 58: 151-179.

Abrami, P. C., and d'Apollonia, S. (1990). The dimensionality of ratings and their use in personnel decisions. In M. Theall and J. Franklin (eds.), *Student Ratings of Instruction: Issues for Improving Practice* (New Directions for Teaching and Learning No. 43). San Francisco: Jossey-Bass.

Abrami, P. C., and d'Apollonia, S. (1991). Multidimensional students' evaluations of teaching effectiveness—generalizability of "N=1" research: Comments on Marsh (1991). *Journal of Educational Psychology* 83: 411-415.

Abrami, P. C., d'Apollonia, S., and Rosenfield, S. (1993). The dimensionality of student ratings of instruction: Introductory remarks. Paper presented at the annual meeting of the American Educational Research Association.

Abrami, P. C., d'Apollonia, S., and Rosenfield, S. (1996). The dimensionality of student ratings of instruction: What we know and what we do not. In J. C. Smart (ed.) *Higher Education: Handbook of Theory and Research* (Vol. 11). New York: Agathon Press. (*Reprinted in this volume.*)

Abrami, P. C., Leventhal, L., and Perry R. P. (1982). Educational seduction. *Review of Educational Research* 52: 446-464.

Aleamoni, L. (1987). Student rating myths versus research facts. *Journal of Personnel Evaluation in Education* 1: 111-119.

Aubrecht, J. D. (1981). Reliability, validity and generalizability of student ratings of instruction. (IDEA Paper No. 6). Manhattan, KS: Kansas State University, Center for Faculty Evaluation and Development. (ERIC Document Reproduction Service No. ED 213 296)

Baxter Magolda, M. B. (1992). *Knowing and Reasoning in College: Gender-Related Patterns in Students' Intellectual Development*. San Francisco: Jossey-Bass.

Benton, S. E., and Scott, O. (1976). A comparison of the criterion validity of two types of student response inventories for appraising instruction. Paper presented at the annual meeting of the National Council on Measurement in Education.

Bolton, B., Bonge, D., and Marr, J. (1979). Ratings of instruction, examination performance, and subsequent enrollment in psychology courses. *Teaching of Psychology* 6: 82-85.

Bowen, H. R. (1977). *Investment in Learning: The Individual and Social Value of American Higher Education*. San Francisco: Jossey-Bass.

Braskamp, L. A., Brandenburg, D. C., and Ory, J. C. (1984). *Evaluating Teaching Effectiveness: A Practical Guide*. Beverly Hills, Calif.: Sage.

Braskamp, L. A., Caulley, D., and Costin, F. (1979). Student ratings and instructor self-ratings and their relationship to student achievement. *American Educational Research Journal* 16: 295-306.

Braskamp, L. A., and Ory, J. C. (1994). *Assessing Faculty Work: Enhancing Individual and Institutional Performance*. San Francisco: Jossey-Bass.

Brooks, T. E., Tarver, D. A., Kelley, H. P., Liberty, P. G., Jr., and Dickerson, A. D. (1971). Dimensions underlying student ratings of courses and instructors at the University of Texas at Austin: Instructor Evaluation Form 2. (Research Bulletin RB-71-4). Austin, Texas: University of Texas at Austin, Measurement and Evaluation Center.

Bryson, R. (1974). Teacher evaluations and student learning: A reexamination. *Journal of Educational Research* 68: 11-14.

Cashin, W. E. (1988). Student ratings of teaching: A summary of the research. (IDEA Paper No. 20). Manhattan, KS: Kansas State University, Center for Faculty Evaluation and Development.

Cashin, W. E. (1990). Students do rate different academic fields differently. In M. Theall and J. Franklin (eds.), *Student Ratings of Instruction: Issues for Improving Practice* (New Directions for Teaching and Learning No. 43). San Francisco: Jossey-Bass.

Cashin, W. E. (1995). Student ratings of teaching: The research revisited. (IDEA Paper No. 32). Manhattan, KS: Kansas State University, Center for Faculty Evaluation and Development.

Cashin, W. E., and Clegg, V. L. (1987). Are student ratings of different academic fields different? Paper presented at the annual meeting of the American Educational Research Association. (ERIC Document Reproduction Service No. ED 286 935)

Cashin, W. E., and Downey, R. G. (1992). Using global student rating items for summative evaluation. *Journal of Educational Psychology* 84: 563-572.

Cashin, W. E., Downey, R. G., and Sixbury, G. R. (1994). Global and specific ratings of teaching effectiveness and their relation to course objectives: Reply to Marsh (1994). *Journal of Educational Psychology* 86: 649-657.

Cashin, W. E., and Sixbury, G. R. (1993). Comparative data by academic field. (IDEA Technical Report No. 8). Manhattan, KS: Kansas State University, Center for Faculty Evaluation and Development.

Centra, J. A. (1975). Colleagues as raters of classroom instruction. *Journal of Higher Education* 46: 327-337.

Centra, J. A. (1977). Student ratings of instruction and their relationship to student learning. *American Educational Research Journal* 14: 17-24.

Centra, J. A. (1979). *Determining Faculty Effectiveness: Assessing Teaching, Research, and Service for Personnel Decisions and Improvement.* San Francisco: Jossey-Bass.

Centra, J. A. (1989). Faculty evaluation and faculty development in higher education. In J. C. Smart (ed.), *Higher Education: Handbook of Theory and Research* (Vol. 5). New York: Agathon Press.

Centra, J. A. (1993). *Reflective Faculty Evaluation: Enhancing Teaching and Determining Faculty Effectiveness.* San Francisco: Jossey-Bass.

Chase, C. I., and Keene, J. M., Jr. (1979). Validity of student ratings of faculty. (Indiana Studies in Higher Education No. 40). Bloomington, Ind.: Indiana University, Bureau of Evaluation Studies and Testing, Division of Research and Development. (ERIC Document Reproduction Service No. ED 169 870).

Chickering, A. W., and Reisser, L. (1993). *Education and Identity* (2nd Ed.). San Francisco: Jossey-Bass.

Cobb, E. B. (1956). Construction of a forced-choice university instructor rating scale. Unpublished doctoral dissertation, University of Tennessee, Knoxville.

Cohen, P. A. (1980a). A meta-analysis of the relationship between student ratings of instruction and student achievement. Unpublished doctoral dissertation, University of Michigan, Ann Arbor.

Cohen, P. A. (1980b). Effectiveness of student-rating feedback for improving college instruction: A meta-analysis of findings. *Research in Higher Education* 13: 321-341.

Cohen, P. A. (1981). Student ratings of instruction and student achievement. *Review of Educational Research* 51: 281-309.

Cohen, P. A. (1987). A critical analysis and reanalysis of the multisection validity meta-analysis. Paper presented at the annual meeting of the American Educational Research Association. (ERIC Document Reproduction Service No. ED 283 876)

Cohen, S. H., and Berger, W. G. (1970). Dimensions of students' ratings of college instructors underlying subsequent achievement on course examinations. Proceedings of the 78th Annual Convention of the American Psychological Association 5: 605-606.

Costin, F. (1978). Do student ratings of college teachers predict student achievement? *Teaching of Psychology* 5: 86-88.

Costin, F., Greenough, W. T., and Menges, R. J. (1971). Student ratings of college teaching: Reliability, validity and usefulness. *Review of Educational Research* 41: 511-535.

Crittenden, K. S., and Norr, J. L. (1973). Student values and teacher evaluation: A problem in person perception. *Sociometry* 36: 143-151.

d'Apollonia, S., and Abrami, P. C. (1987). An empirical critique of metaanalysis: The literature on student ratings of instruction. Paper presented at the annual meeting of the American Educational Research Association.

d'Apollonia, S., and Abrami, P. C. (1988). The literature on student ratings of instruction: Yet another meta-analysis. Paper presented at the annual meeting of the American Educational Research Association.

d'Apollonia, S., Abrami, P. C., and Rosenfield, S. (1993). The dimensionality of student ratings of instruction: A meta-analysis of the factor studies. Paper presented at the annual meeting of the American Educational Research Association.

Doyle, K. O., Jr. (1972). Construction and evaluation of scale for rating college instructors. Unpublished doctoral dissertation, University of Minnesota, Minneapolis.

Doyle, K. O., Jr. (1975). *Student Evaluation of Instruction.* Lexington, Mass.: D. C. Heath.

Doyle, K. O., Jr. (1983). *Evaluating Teaching.* Lexington, Mass.: D. C. Heath.

Doyle, K. O., Jr., and Crichton, L. I. (1978). Student, peer, and self evaluation of college instruction. *Journal of Educational Psychology* 70: 815-826.

Doyle, K. O., Jr., and Whitely, S. E. (1974). Student ratings as criteria for effective teaching. *American Educational Research Journal* 11: 259-274.

Edgerton, R., Hutchings, P., and Quinlan, K. (1991). *The Teaching Portfolio: Capturing the Scholarship in Teaching.* Washington, D.C.: American Association for Higher Education.

Elliott, D. N. (1950). Characteristics and relationship of various criteria of college and university teaching. *Purdue University Studies in Higher Education* 70: 5-61.

Ellis, N. R., and Rickard, H. C. (1977). Evaluating the teaching of introductory psychology. *Teaching of Psychology* 4: 128-132.

Ellner, C. L., and Barnes, C. P. (1983). *Studies of College Teaching: Experimental Results, Theoretical Interpretations, and New Perspectives.* Lexington, Mass.: D. C. Heath.

Endo, G. T., and Della-Piana, G. (1976). A validation study of course evaluation ratings. *Improving College and University Teaching* 24: 84-86.

Feldman, K. A. (1976a). Grades and college students' evaluation of their courses and teachers. *Research in Higher Education* 4: 69-111.

Feldman, K. A. (1976b). The superior college teacher from the students' view. *Research in Higher Education* 5: 243-288.

Feldman, K. A. (1977). Consistency and variability among college students in rating their teachers and courses: A review and analysis. *Research in Higher Education* 6: 223-274.

Feldman, K. A. (1978). Course characteristics and college students' ratings of their teachers: What we know and what we don't. *Research in Higher Education* 9: 199-242.

Feldman, K. A. (1979). The significance of circumstances for college students' ratings of their teachers and courses. *Research in Higher Education* 10: 149-172.

Feldman, K. A. (1983). Seniority and experience of college teachers as related to evaluation they receive from students. *Research in Higher Education* 18: 3-124.

Feldman, K. A. (1984). Class size and college students' evaluations of teachers and courses: A closer look. *Research in Higher Education* 21: 45-116.

Feldman, K. A. (1986). The perceived instructional effectiveness of college teachers as related to their personality and attitudinal characteristics: A review and synthesis. *Research in Higher Education* 24: 139-213.

Feldman, K. A. (1987). Research productivity and scholarly accomplishment of college teachers as related to their instructional effectiveness: A review and exploration. *Research in Higher Education* 26: 227-298.

Feldman, K. A. (1988). Effective college teaching from the students' and faculty's view: Matched or mismatched priorities? *Research In Higher Education* 28: 291-344.

Feldman, K. A. (1989a). Instructional effectiveness of college teachers as judged by teachers themselves, current and former students, colleagues, administrators, and external (neutral) observers. *Research in Higher Education* 30: 137-194.

Feldman, K. A. (1989b). The association between student ratings of specific instructional dimensions and student achievement: Refining and extending the synthesis of data from multisection validity studies. *Research in Higher Education* 30: 583-645.

Feldman, K. A. (1990a). An afterword for "The association between student ratings of specific instructional dimensions and student achievement: Refining and extending the synthesis of data from multisection validity studies." *Research in Higher Education* 31: 315-318.

Feldman, K. A. (1990b). Instructional evaluation. *The Teaching Professor* 4: 5-7.

Feldman, K. A. (1992). College students' views of male and female college teachers: Part I—evidence from the social laboratory and experiments. *Research in Higher Education* 33: 317-375.

Feldman, K. A. (1993). College students' views of male and female college teachers: Part II—evidence from students' evaluations of their classroom teachers. *Research in Higher Education* 34: 151-211.

Feldman, K. A. (1994). Identifying exemplary teaching: Evidence from course and teacher evaluations. Paper commissioned by the National Center on Postsecondary Teaching, Learning, and Assessment for presentation at the Second AAHE Conference on Faculty Roles and Rewards.

Feldman, K. A. (forthcoming). Identifying exemplary teaching: Using data from course and teacher evaluations. In M. D. Svinicki and R. J. Menges (eds.), *Honoring Exemplary Teaching* (New Directions for Teaching and Learning). San Francisco: Jossey-Bass.

Feldman, K. A., and Newcomb, T. M. (1969). *The Impact of College on Students*. San Francisco: Jossey-Bass.

Feldman, K. A., and Paulsen, M. B. (eds.) (1994). *Teaching and Learning in the College Classroom*. Needham Heights, Mass.: Ginn Press.

French-Lazovik, G. (1974). Predictability of students' evaluation of college teachers from component ratings. *Journal of Educational Psychology* 66: 373-385.

Frey, P. W. (1973). Student ratings of teaching: Validity of several rating factors. *Science* 182: 83-85.

Frey, P. W. (1976). Validity of student instructional ratings as a function of their timing. *Journal of Higher Education* 47: 327-336.

Frey, P. W., Leonard, D. W., and Beatty, W. W. (1975). Student ratings of instruction: Validation research. *American Educational Research Journal* 12: 435-444.

Garber, H., 1964. Certain factors underlying the relationship between course grades and student judgments of college teachers. Unpublished doctoral dissertation, University of Connecticut, Storrs.

Gigliotti, R. J., and Buchtel, F. S. (1990). Attributional bias and course evaluation. *Journal of Educational Psychology* 82: 341-351.

Good, K. C. (1971). Similarity of student and instructor attitudes and student's attitudes toward instructors. Unpublished doctoral dissertation, Purdue University, West Lafayette.

Greenwood, G. E., Hazelton, A., Smith, A. B., and Ware, W. B. (1976). A study of the validity of four types of student ratings of college teaching assessed on a criterion of student achievement gains. *Research in Higher Education* 5: 171-178.

Grush, J. E., and Costin, F. (1975). The student as consumer of the teaching process. *American Educational Research Journal* 12: 55-66.

Harry, J., and Goldner, N. S. (1972). The null relationship between teaching and research. *Sociology of Education* 45: 47-60.

Harvey, J. N., and Barker, D. G. (1970). Student evaluation of teaching effectiveness. *Improving College and University Teaching* 18: 275-278.

Hativa, N., and Raviv, A. (1993). Using a single score for summative teacher evaluation by students. *Research in Higher Education* 34: 625-646.

Hoffman, R. G. (1978). Variables affecting university student ratings of instructor behavior. *American Educational Research Journal* 15: 287-299.

Hoyt, D. P. (1973). Measurement of instructional effectiveness. *Research in Higher Education* 1: 367-378.

Jiobu, R. M., and Pollis, C. A. (1971). Student evaluations of courses and instructors. *American Sociologist* 6: 317-321.

King, P. M., and Kitchener, K. S. (1994). *Developing Reflective Judgment: Understanding and Promoting Intellectual Growth and Critical Thinking in Adolescents and Adults*. San Francisco: Jossey-Bass

Kulik, M. A., and McKeachie, W. J. (1975). The evaluation of teachers in higher education. In F. N. Kerlinger (ed.), *Review of Research in Education* (Vol. 3). Itasca, Ill.: F. E. Peacock.

Land, M. L. (1979). Low-inference variables of teacher clarity: Effects on student concept learning. *Journal of Educational Psychology* 71: 795-799.

Land, M. L. (1981). Actual and perceived teacher clarity: Relations to student achievement in science. *Journal of Research in Science Teaching* 18: 139-143.

Land, M. L., and Combs, A. (1981). Teacher clarity, student instructional ratings, and student performance. Paper read at the annual meeting of the American Educational Research Association.

Land, M. L., and Combs, N. (1982). Teacher behavior and student ratings. *Educational and Psychological Research* 2: 63-68.

Land, M. L., and Smith, L. R. (1979). The effect of low inference teacher clarity inhibitors and student achievement. *Journal of Teacher Education* 30: 55-57.

Land, M. L., and Smith, L. R. (1981). College student ratings and teacher behavior: An Experimental Study. *Journal of Social Studies Research* 5: 19-22.

Leftwich, W. H., and Remmers, H. H. (1992). A comparison of graphic and forced-choice ratings of teaching performance at the college and university level. *Purdue Universities Studies in Higher Education* 92: 3-31.

Leventhal, L. (1975). Teacher rating forms: Critique and reformulation of previous validation designs. *Canadian Psychological Review* 16: 269-276.

Levinson-Rose, J., and Menges, R. L. (1981). Improving college teaching: A critical review of research. *Review of Educational Research* 51: 403-434.

L'Hommedieu, R., Menges, R. J., and Brinko, K. T. (1988). The effects of student ratings feedback to college teachers: A meta-analysis and review of research. Unpublished manuscript, Northwestern University, Center for the Teaching Professions, Evanston.

L'Hommedieu, R., Menges, R. J., and Brinko, K. T. (1990). Methodological explanations for the modest effects of feedback. *Journal of Educational Psychology* 82: 232-241.

Maas, J. B., and Owen, T. R. (1973). *Cornell Inventory for Student Appraisal of Teaching and Courses: Manual of Instructions*. Ithaca, NY: Cornell University, Center for Improvement of Undergraduate Education.

Marsh, H. W. (1984). Students' evaluations of university teaching: Dimensionality, reliability, validity, potential biases, and utility. *Journal of Educational Psychology* 76: 707-754.

Marsh, H. W. (1987). Students' evaluations of university teaching: Research findings, methodological issues, and directions for future research. *International Journal of Educational Research* 11: 253-388.

Marsh, H. W. (1991a). Multidimensional students' evaluation of teaching effectiveness: A test of alternative higher-order structures. *Journal of Educational Psychology* 83: 285-296.

Marsh, H. W. (1991b). A multidimensional perspective on students' evaluations of teaching effectiveness: A reply to Abrami and d'Apollonia (1991). *Journal of Educational Psychology* 83: 416-421.

Marsh, H. W. (in press). Weighting for the right criterion in the IDEA system: Global and specific ratings of teaching effectiveness and their relation to course objectives. *Journal of Educational Psychology*.

Marsh, H. W., and Dunkin, M. J. (1992). Students' evaluations of university teaching: A multidimensional approach. In J. C. Smart (ed.), *Higher Education: Handbook of Theory and Research* (Vol. 8). New York: Agathon Press. (*Reprinted in this volume.*)

Marsh, H. W., Fleiner, H., and Thomas, C. S. (1975). Validity and usefulness of student evaluations of instructional quality. *Journal of Educational Psychology* 67: 833-839.

Marsh, H. W., and Overall, J. U. (1980). Validity of students' evaluations of teaching effectiveness: Cognitive and affective criteria. *Journal of Educational Psychology* 72: 468-475.

McKeachie, W. J. (1979). Student ratings of faculty: A reprise. *Academe* 65: 384-397.

McKeachie, W. J. (1987). Instructional evaluation: Current issues and possible improvements. *Journal of Higher Education* 58: 344-350.

McKeachie, W. J., Lin, Y-G, and Mann, W. (1971). Student ratings of teacher effectiveness: Validity studies. *American Educational Research Association* 8: 435-445.

Miller, R. I. (1972). *Evaluating Faculty Performance*. San Francisco: Jossey-Bass.

Miller, R. I. (1974). *Developing Programs for Faculty Evaluation*. San Francisco: Jossey-Bass.

Mintzes, J. J., (1976-77). Field test and validation of a teaching evaluation instrument: The Student Opinion Survey of Teaching (A report submitted to the Senate Committee for Teaching and Learning, Faculty Senate, University of Windsor). Windsor, Ontario: University of Windsor.

Morgan, W. D., and Vasché, J. D. (1978). An Educational Production Function Approach to Teaching Effectiveness and Evaluation. *Journal of Economic Education* 9: 123-126.

Morsh, J. E., Burgess, G. G., and Smith, P. N. (1956). Student achievement as a measure of instructor effectiveness. *Journal of Educational Psychology* 47: 79-88.

Murray, H. G. (1980). *Evaluating University Teaching: A Review of Research*. Toronto: Ontario Confederation of University Faculty Associations.

Murray, H. G. (1983). Low-inference classroom teaching behaviors in relation to six measures of college teaching effectiveness. Proceedings of the Conference on the Evaluation and Improvement of University Teaching: The Canadian Experience (pp. 43-73). Montreal: McGill University, Centre for Teaching and Learning Service.

Murray, H. G. (1991). Effective teaching behaviors in the college classroom. In J. C. Smart (ed.), *Higher Education: Handbook of Theory and Research* (Vol. 7). New York: Agathon Press. (*Reprinted in this volume.*)

Orpen, C. (1980). Student evaluations of lecturers as an indicator of instructional quality: A validity study. *Journal of Educational Research* 74: 5-7.

Owen, P. H. (1967). Some dimensions of college teaching: An exploratory study using critical incidents and factor analyses of student ratings. Unpublished doctoral dissertation, University of Houston, Houston.

Pascarella, E. T., and Terenzini, P. T. (1991). *How College Affects Students: Findings and Insights from Twenty Years of Research.* San Francisco: Jossey-Bass.

Perry, R. P. (1991). Perceived control in college students: Implications for instruction in higher education. In J. C. Smart (ed.), *Higher Education: Handbook of Theory and Research* (Vol. 7). New York: Agathon Press. (*Reprinted in this volume.*)

Plant, W. T., and Sawrey, J. M. (1970). Student ratings of psychology professors as teachers and the research involvement of the professors rated. *The Clinical Psychologist* 23: 15-16, 19.

Rankin, E. F., Jr., Greenmun, R., and Tracy, R. J. (1965). Factors related to student evaluations of a college reading course. *Journal of Reading* 9: 10-15.

Remmers, H. H. (1929). The college professor as the student sees him. *Purdue University Studies in Higher Education* 11: 1-63.

Remmers, H. H., Martin, F. D., and Elliott, D. N. (1949). Are students' ratings of instructors related to their grades? *Purdue University Studies in Higher Education* 66: 17-26.

Remmers, H. H., and Weisbrodt, J. A. (1964). *Manual of Instructions for Purdue Rating Scale of Instruction.* West Lafayette, IN: Purdue Research Foundation.

Rosenshine, B., Cohen, A., and Furst, N. (1973). Correlates of student preference ratings. *Journal of College Student Personnel* 14: 269-272.

Rubinstein, J., and Mitchell, H. (1970). Feeling free, student involvement, and appreciation. *Proceedings of the 78th Annual Convention of the American Psychological Association* 5: 623-624.

Sagen, H. B. (1974). Student, faculty, and department chairmen ratings of instructors: Who agrees with whom? *Research in Higher Education* 2: 265272.

Sanders, J. A., and Wiseman, R. L. (1990). The effects of verbal and nonverbal teacher immediacy on perceived cognitive, affective, and behavioral learning in the multicultural classroom. *Communication Education* 39: 341-353.

Seldin, P. (1991). *The Teaching Portfolio.* Boston: Anker Publishing.

Shore, B. M., and associates (1986). The Teaching Dossier: A Guide to Its Preparation and Use (Rev. Ed.). Montreal: Canadian Association of University Teachers.

Smith, L. R., and Land, M. L. (1980). Student perception of teacher clarity in mathematics. *Journal for Research in Mathematics Education* 11: 137-146.

Sockloff, A. L. (1973). Instruments for student evaluation of faculty: Ideal and actual. In A. L. Sockloff (ed.), *Proceedings of the First Invitational Conference on Faculty Effectiveness as Evaluated by Students.* Philadelphia, PA.: Temple University, Measurement and Research Center.

Solomon, D., Rosenberg, L., and Bezdek, W. E. (1964). Teacher behavior and student learning. *Journal of Educational Psychology* 55: 23-30.

Spencer, R. E. (1967). Analysis of the Instructor Rating Form—General Engineering Department. (Research Report No. 253). Urbana, Ill.: University of Illinois, Measurement and Research Division, Office of Instructional Resources.

Stumpf, S. A., and Freedman, R. D. (1979). Expected grade covariation with student ratings of instruction: Individual versus class effects. *Journal of Educational Psychology* 71: 293-302.

Theall, M., Franklin, J., and Ludlow, L. (1990a). Attributions and retributions: Student ratings and the perceived causes of performance. *Instructional Evaluation* 11: 12-17.

Theall, M., Franklin, J., and Ludlow, L. (1990b). Attributions or retributions: Student ratings and the perceived causes of performance. Paper presented at the annual meeting of the American Educational Research Association.

Turner, R. L. (1970). Good teaching and its contexts. *Phi Delta Kappan* 52: 155-158.

Turner, R. L., and Thompson, R. P. (1974). Relationships between college student ratings of instructors and residual learning. Paper presented at the annual meeting of the American Educational Research Association.

Van Horn, C. *An Analysis of the 1968 Course and Instructor Evaluation Report.* (Institutional Research Bulletin No. 2-68). West Lafayette, Ind.: Purdue University, Measurement and Research Center.

Walker, B. D. (1968). An investigation of selected variables relative to the manner in which a population of junior college students evaluate their teachers. Unpublished doctoral dissertation, University of Houston,

Widlak, F. W., McDaniel, E. D., and Feldhusen, J. F. (1973). Factor analysis of an instructor rating scale. Paper presented at the annual meeting of the American Educational Research Association.

Williams, H. Y., Jr. (1965). College students' perceptions of the personal traits and instructional procedures of good and poor teachers. Unpublished doctoral dissertation, University of Minnesota, Minneapolis.

Appendix

This appendix, with its listing of 28 instructional dimensions, first appeared in Feldman (1989b) in a slightly different version. For each of the instructional dimensions, examples of evaluation items that would be classified into it are given. For refinements and modifications to this list of dimensions and attendant coding scheme, see d'Apollonia, Abrami and Rosenfield (1993) and Abrami, d'Apollonia and Rosenfield (1996).

No. 1 *Teacher's Stimulation of Interest in the Course and Its Subject Matter:* "the instructor puts material across in an interesting way"; "the instructor gets students interested in the subject"; "it was easy to remain attentive"; "the teacher stimulated intellectual curiosity"; etc.

No. 2 *Teacher's Enthusiasm (for Subject or for Teaching):* "the instructor shows interest and enthusiasm in the subject"; "the instructor seems to enjoy teaching"; "the teacher communicates a genuine desire to teach students"; "the instructor never showed boredom for teaching this class"; "the instructor shows energy and excitement"; etc.

No. 3 *Teacher's Knowledge of Subject Matter:* "the instructor has a good command of the subject material"; "the teacher has a thorough knowledge, basic and current, of the subject"; "the instructor has good knowledge about or beyond the textbook"; "the instructor knows the answers to questions students ask"; "the teacher keeps lecture material updated"; etc.

No. 4 *Teacher's Intellectual Expansiveness (and Intelligence):* "the teacher is well informed in all related fields"; "the teacher has respect for other subject areas and indicates their relationship to his or her own subject of presentation"; "the teacher exhibited a high degree of cultural attainment"; etc.

No. 5 *Teacher's Preparation; Organization of the Course:* "the teacher was well prepared for each day's lecture"; "the presentation of the material is well organized"; the overall development of the course had good continuity"; "the instructor planned the activities of each class period in detail"; etc.

No. 6 *Clarity and Understandableness:* "the instructor made clear explanations"; the instructor interprets abstract ideas and theories clearly"; "the instructor makes good use of examples and illustrations to get across difficult points"; "the teacher effectively synthesizes and summarizes the material"; "the teacher answers students' questions in a way that helps students to understand"; etc.

No. 7 *Teacher's Elocutionary Skills:* "the instructor has a good vocal delivery"; "the teacher speaks distinctly, fluently and without hesitation"; "the teacher varied the speech and tone of his or her voice"; "the teacher has the ability to speak distinctly and be clearly heard"; "the instructor changed pitch, volume, or quality of speech"; etc.

No. 8 *Teacher's Sensitivity to, and Concern with, Class Level and Progress:* "the teacher was skilled in observing student reactions"; "the teacher was aware when students failed to keep up in class"; "the instructor teaches near the class level"; "the teacher takes an active personal interest in the progress of the class and shows a desire for students to learn"; etc.

No. 9 *Clarity of Course Objectives and Rdequirements:* "the purposes and policies of the course were made clear to the student"; "the instructor gave a clear idea of the student requirements"; "the teacher clearly defined student responsibilities in the course"; "the teacher tells students which topics are most important and what they can expect on tests"; "the instructor gave clear assignments"; etc.

No. 10 *Nature and Value of the Course Material (Including Its Usefulness and Relevance):* "the teacher has the ability to apply material to real life"; "the instructor makes the course practical"; "there is worthwhile and informative material in lectures that doesn't duplicate the text"; "the course has excellent content"; "the class considers what we are learning worth learning"; etc.

No. 11 *Nature and Usefulness of Supplementary Materials and Teaching Aids:* "the homework assignments and supplementary readings were helpful in understanding the course"; "the teacher made good use of teaching aids such as films and other audio-visual materials"; "the instructor provided a variety of activities in class and used a variety of media (slides, films, projections, drawings) and outside resource persons"; etc.

No. 12 *Perceived Outcome or Impact of Instruction:* "gaining of new knowledge was facilitated by the instructor"; "I developed significant skills in the field"; "I developed increased sensitivity and evaluative judgment"; "the instructor has given me tools for attacking problems"; "the course has increased my general knowledge"; "apart from your personal feelings about the teacher, has he/she been instrumental in increasing knowledge of the course's subject matter"; etc.

No. 13 *Teacher's Fairness; Impartiality of Evaluation of Students; Quality of Examinations:* "grading in the course was fair"; "the instructor has definite standards and is impartial in grading"; "the exams reflect material emphasized in the course"; "test questions were clear"; "coverage of subject matter on exams was comprehensive"; etc.

No. 14 *Personality Characteristics ("Personality") of the Teacher:* "the teacher has a good sense of humor"; "the teacher was sincere and honest"; "the teacher is highly personable at all times in dress, voice, social grace, and manners"; "the instructor was free of personal peculiarities"; "the instructor is not autocratic and does not try to force us to accept his ideas and interpretations"; "the teacher exhibits a casual, informal attitude"; "the instructor laughed at his own mistakes"; etc.

No. 15 *Nature Quality, and Frequency of Feedback from the Teacher to Students:* "the teacher gave satisfactory feedback on graded material"; "criticism of papers was helpful to students"; "the teacher told students when they had done a good job"; "the teacher is prompt in returning tests and assignments"; etc.

No. 16 *Teacher's Encouragement of Questions and Discussion, and Openness to Opinions of*

Others: "students felt free to ask questions or express opinions"; the instructor stimulated class discussions"; "the teacher encouraged students to express differences of opinions and to evaluate each other's ideas"; "the instructor invited criticisms of his or her own ideas"; "the teacher appeared receptive to new ideas and the viewpoints of others"; etc.

No. 17 *Intellectual Challenge and Encouragement of Independent Thought (by the Teacher and the Course)*: "this course challenged students intellectually"; "the teacher encouraged students to think out answers and follow up ideas"; "the teacher attempts to stimulate creativity"; "the instructor raised challenging questions and problems"; etc.

No. 18 *Teacher's Concern and Respect for Students; Friendliness of the Teacher*: "the instructor seems to have a genuine interest in and concern for students"; "the teacher took students seriously"; "the instructor established good rapport with students"; "the teacher was friendly toward all students"; etc.

No. 19 *Teacher's Availability and Helpfulness*: "the instructor was willing to help students having difficulty"; "the instructor is willing to give individual attention"; "the teacher was available for consultation"; "the teacher was accessible to students outside of class"; etc.

No. 20 *Teacher Motivates Students to Do Their Best; High Standard of Performance Required:* "Instructor motivates students to do their best work"; "the instructor sets high standards of achievement for students"; "the teacher raises the aspirational level of students"; etc.

No. 21 *Teacher's Encouragement of Self-Initiated Learning:* "Students are encouraged to work independently"; "students assume much responsibility for their own learning"; "the general approach used in the course gives emphasis to learning on the students' own"; "the teacher does not suppress individual initiative"; etc.

No. 22 *Teacher's Productivity in Research Related Activities*: "The teacher talks about his own research"; "instructor displays high research accomplishments"; "the instructor publishes material related to his subject field"; etc.

No. 23 *Difficulty of the Course (and Workload)—Description:* "the workload and pace of the course was difficult"; "I spent a great many hours studying for this course"; "the amount of work required for this course was very heavy"; "this course required a lot of time"; "the instructor assigned very difficult reading"; etc.

No. 24 *Difficulty of the Course (and Workload)—Evaluation:* "the content of this course is too hard"; "the teacher's lectures and oral presentations are 'over my head' "; "the instructor often asked for more than students could get done"; "the instructor attempted to cover too much material and presented it too rapidly"; etc.

No. 25 *Classroom Management:* "the instructor controls class discussion to prevent rambling and confusion"; "the instructor maintained a classroom atmosphere conducive to learning"; "students are allowed to participate in deciding the course content"; "the teacher did not 'rule with an iron hand' "; etc.

No. 26 *Pleasantness of Classroom Atmosphere:* "the class does not make me nervous"; "I felt comfortable in this class"; "the instructor created an atmosphere in which students in the class seemed friendly"; "this was not one of those classes where students failed to laugh, joke, smile or show other signs of humor"; "the teacher is always criticizing and arguing with students"; etc.

No. 27 *Individualization of Teaching:* "instead of expecting every student to do the same thing, the instructor provides different activities for different students"; "my grade depends primarily upon my improvement over my past performance"; "in this class each student is accepted on his or her own merits"; "my grade is influenced by what is best for me as a person as well as by how much I have learned"; "the instructor evaluated each student as an individual"; etc.

No. 28 *Teacher Pursued and/or Met Course Objectives:* "the instructor accomplished what he or she set out to do"; "there was close agreement between the announced objectives of the course and what was actually taught"; "course objectives stated agreed with those actually pursued"; etc.

Good Teaching Makes a Difference —And We Know What It Is[1]

W. J. McKeachie

Harry Murray began his chapter with the question, "Do teachers differ significantly in their impact on student cognitive and affective development?" The preceding chapters clearly demonstrate that they do and that we can measure the differences and the impact that teaching makes.

The basic aim of this chapter is to review and highlight aspects of the previous chapters in ways that will be helpful to faculty developers or faculty members involved in programs for improving teaching and evaluation of teaching. However these chapters stimulated my thinking, as they no doubt have stimulated yours, and I include here some additional thoughts about the topics they covered. I should also state at the outset that what seemed a daunting task when I began reading these chapters in order to prepare my review turned out instead to be one of real delight. Each is excellent! My hope is that this chapter in no way diminishes the superb job they have done. I have organized the review around four questions:

1. Does teaching make a difference?
2. How do teachers differ from one another?
3. Can teachers learn how to be more effective?
4. Why do effective teaching methods result in better learning?

Does teaching make a difference?

One of the barriers to the improvement of teaching is the still not uncommon belief that all that is required for good college teaching is knowledge of the subject matter. This attitude was exemplified by one of the speakers at the 1993 Council meeting of the American Psychological Association. The Board of Educational Affairs had proposed that the Association's criteria for accreditation of doctoral programs should consider whether or not the program provided training for teaching. One Council member stated with great fervor, "Those who attempt to give training in methods of college and univer-

---

[1] I am grateful for the comments of Herb Marsh and Ray Perry on an earlier version of this chapter.

sity teaching are usually themselves poor teachers and certainly have nothing to offer to any professor who has a good command of the subject matter."

The average person would have no doubt that good teaching methods make a difference, but ever since the review by Dubin and Taveggia (1968) suggesting that most comparisons of teaching methods found no statistically significant differences, some academicians have argued that even though some teachers may make a difference for some students, on the average differences in teaching don't make much difference in student learning.

We thought we had pretty well silenced that argument by our review of the research literature (McKeachie and Birney, 1955) showing that even though many studies of teaching lacked sufficient statistical power to show differences at the 5% level of confidence, the direction of the results was quite consistent; e.g. classes taught by discussion were superior to lecture classes in 13 out of 14 comparisons that used measures of thinking, retention after the final examination, motivation, or attitude change. Similarly early studies of student ratings of teachers by Remmers and his students showed that teachers differ in effectiveness (Remmers, 1927, 1958). As we have also seen in the previous chapters, clearly teachers and teaching methods do make a difference!

Research on teaching flourished in the decades following World War II, but in the past couple of decades the focus of attention has shifted from teaching to the *learner*. While the earlier discounting of the importance of the teacher was largely a function of naïveté, current emphasis on the learner with less focus on teaching results from sophisticated research and theory. With the hegemony of cognitive psychology, we became more aware that learning was not simply a matter of stimulus-response-feedback, but rather that learners construct knowledge, actively seeking to understand—interpreting and encoding information in relation to their prior knowledge. Thus in any classroom, no two learners represent new knowledge in the same way. Some faculty members may take this to mean that the responsibility for learning is now solely that of students. Such an abdication of responsibility is, however, uncommon. Clearly teaching and learning are intimately intertwined (See Shuell, 1993). The great bulk of research on student studying, reading, writing, and experiencing has occurred in the last 20 years. This has given us much valuable knowledge about how students learn. Nonetheless, as Murray suggests, "what," "how," and "how much" a student studies is to some extent a function of the teaching. To the degree that teachers make challenging assignments, encourage competency, give thought-provoking tests, and use other means to promote active learning, students will make their learning meaningful so that it will stick with them for later use. If in recent years we have overemphasized learning at the expense of teaching, the chapters in this section help to restore the balance.

Each of the preceding chapters presents evidence that teaching makes a difference. Murray shows that low inference behaviors can reliably differentiate effective from less effective teachers; this is true both for cognitive and motivational outcomes. Feldman and Marsh and Dunkin give a wealth of evidence that effective teachers are different from less-effective teachers on dimensions that appear even in cross-cultural studies. This section of my chapter can be brief because the evidence in the previous chapters is compelling. Thus we can turn to the broader question of what makes the difference between effectiveness and ineffectiveness. To answer that question we need first to understand how teachers differ.

How do teachers differ from one another?

Marsh and Dunkin's analysis of primary and higher order factors found in student ratings to teaching clearly indicates the multi-dimensionality and complexity of teaching. Marsh's nine primary factors—Instructor enthusiasm, Breadth of coverage, Organization/clarity, Assignments/reading, Learning/value, Examinations/grading, Group interaction, Individual rapport, and Workload/difficulty—indicate that student ratings of teaching involve a mix of personality characteristics and characteristics related to the content and assessment of achievement, broadly paralleling the two factors—"Empathy" and "Professional Maturity"—found in the first factor analysis of student ratings (Smalzreid and Remmers, 1943). "Empathy" included "sympathetic attitude toward students" and "liberal and progressive attitude" while "Professional Maturity" included "presentation of subject-matter."

I like factor analysis, and I enjoyed thinking about the differences between Marsh's nine dimensions, Feldman's twenty-eight, and Abrami, d'Apollonia, and Rosenfeld's four. In many ways their disagreement parallels that between Spearman and Thurstone in the early factor analytic studies of intelligence. However, it seems to me that the key issue is how one wants to use these findings. For certain research and personnel purposes, only a general factor, such as Abrami, d'Apollonia and Rosenfield's general factor or Marsh's higher order factors may be sufficient; for analyzing a particular course, in helping a particular group of teachers to improve, or for research on the effect of interventions in teaching, a finer cut, such as Feldman's, may be more useful.

As Abrami, d'Apollonia and Rosenfield suggest, we need a theoretical description of the teaching process. Factor analysis is only one means to stimulate theoretical thinking; we need to approach theory not only through factor analysis but also from other approaches as well. Much of the work on student ratings deals not so much with process as with characteristics of teachers; we need also to think not only of teaching processes but also of cognitive processes of student learners. Following are examples of two approaches—one related to teacher characteristics; the other to cognitions of learners.

With respect to teacher characteristics one way of relating student rating dimensions to a larger body of research and theory would be to see how they fit with the "Big Five" dimensions of personality, (Norman, 1963; Tupes and Christal, 1961) which are now generally accepted as the basic taxonomic basis for research in personality structure.

While researchers differ somewhat in the names they attach to the Big Five, the following are reasonably acceptable labels:

    I. Extraversion-introversion
    II. Agreeableness
    III.Conscientiousness
    IV.Emotional stability-neuroticism
     V.Culture (Openness to experience).

Marsh's "Instructor enthusiasm" falls into Factor I—*extraversion.* "Organization" is found in Factor III—*conscientiousness,* and "Fairness in examinations and grading" also falls in Factor III. "Individual rapport" clearly belongs in *agreeableness.* "Breadth of coverage" might well fall in Factor V. Surprisingly *Emotional stability vs. neuroticism* doesn't appear in Marsh's list even though it seems likely that this dimension is also important in teaching effectiveness. Feldman's dimension 14, "Teacher personality," with items such as "good sense of humor," "sincere and honest," "highly personable," "casual, informal, attitude," and "free of personal peculiarities" seems to capture some of the emotional stability dimension.

Why should we care about relating our student ratings of teachers to the basic dimensions of personality? The practical implications are not immediately apparent. Yet, recognizing this relationship does help in giving us confidence that the dimensions found by Marsh and others are not arbitrary; they do make sense in terms of the basic theory of personality structure. While the Big 5 dimensions have been most often applied in personnel selection, personnel psychologists see them as also being valuable in performance appraisal and training (Barrick and Mount, 1991). Thus those who work in appraisal and training of college teachers may find useful relationships to the broader work in other areas. Equally important is that the Big 5 gives us access to the several thousand words describing the Big 5 personality characteristics, roles, and motives. This can give us a richer understanding of what is represented by the dimensions and how the items making up the dimensions of student rating scales are likely to be related to other human characteristics.

Another theoretical approach is to look at cognitive and instructional theory to see what tools they provide for thinking about the dimensions uncovered by factor analysis. For example, we might look at the dimensions revealed in Marsh's analysis to see how they relate to the major categories of theoretical variables that predict student learning—cognition and motivation. (Marsh and Dunkin's chapter relates their nine dimensions to principles of learning in adult education and have covered some of the points that I shall develop from a related but slightly different perspective.) While there are overlaps between motivational and cognitive aspects of the Marsh dimensions, most can be fairly easily classified as affecting either student motivation or cognition. I like the way Murray linked "enthusiasm" to attention, "clarity" to encoding and "interaction" to active learning. Moreover, I think we can go beyond this. Thus, "instructor enthusiasm" seems to me to affect student motivation as well as attention, while "organization/clarity" affects the meaningfulness and organization of student learning.

"Group interaction" has both motivational and cognitive effects. "Interaction" provides opportunities to reveal and clear up confusion, to practice problem solving, to permit elaboration or deep processing of the subject matter, and also to stimulate motivation by social facilitation and the opportunity to relate material to student interests. "Rapport" is also related to motivation for learning.

"Workload/difficulty" can pose cognitive problems, but also may be a factor either in stimulating curiosity and challenge or alternatively leading to discouragement and loss of motivation. Brady (1994) showed that in general students prefer professors who are demanding, a result reinforced by Feldman's finding that intellectual challenge is more positively related to mean student ratings of teaching effectiveness than to mean student achievement.

As an aside, I would note that Abrami, d'Apollonia, and Rosenfield's comment that "ratings of course difficulty do not predict student learning at all" is what one would expect on the basis of cognitive and motivational theory. The relationship between difficulty and learning should be curvilinear; i.e. the best learning should occur when a course is perceived as difficult enough to be achievable—challenging one to do well—but not when it is so easy that it is not challenging, or so difficult that mastery is hopeless. As a further aside, I would note that one of the difficulties with factor analysis, as well as with product-moment correlations, is that they assume linearity and are likely to miss curvilinear relationships.

In any case Marsh gives us a framework for looking at teacher differences. Both personality and cognitive theories as well as research evidence indicate that these dimensions are important in determining teacher effectiveness.

Can teachers learn how to be more effective?

Once again we can give a resoundingly positive answer. Each chapter presents encouraging evidence, ranging from the specific training of behavior by Murray through the feedback of student rating studies reviewed by Perry and Marsh to the more extensive programs of faculty development reviewed by Weimer and Lenze.

Although feedback of student ratings alone has positive but mixed effects, feedback with consultation or with written descriptions of strategies, such as the booklets developed by Wilson (1986) and Marsh and Roche (1993), enhances the likelihood of improvement.

The improvement in teaching demonstrated is encouraging, but I fully agree with Murray and Weimer and Lenze that we need more research on teacher thinking to get a better idea of how feedback and various forms of training are incorporated into planning and moment-to-moment decision making in the classroom. Is our training primarily effective through its effect upon teacher thinking? Upon development of skills? Or does it obtain its results through its effect on motivational variables such as goals and self-efficacy? Probably all occur, with different effects in different contexts.

In any case we have made significant gains since the early studies validating the importance of instructor enthusiasm and clarity. (Remmers, Martin, and Elliott, 1949; Morsh, Burgess, and Smith, 1956)

Murray shows the specific behaviors that mark the enthusiastic teacher—vocal variation, movement and gesture, facial expression, and humor. While I had always thought that changing a teacher's enthusiasm was well nigh impossible, I now believe that Murray has given us some handles that will help. Movement, gesture, and vocal variation are trainable characteristics. We are probably not going to transform a quiet, monotone into a manic who rushes up and down the aisles shouting, but we can move them toward the middle of the expressiveness scale and Murray's research demonstrates that such training produces significant changes in student ratings of effectiveness.

Teaching "clarity" is, I think, an easier task when we are given Murray's list of associated behaviors. Using concrete examples, providing an outline, signaling transitions—these are clearly teachable skills.

And I learned very early in training graduate teaching assistants that encouraging them to learn student names and to use the students' names when questioning or responding—such simple things made a significant difference in student-teacher "rapport."

Marsh and Dunkin's and Feldman's superb reviews of research on student ratings of teaching, together with Murray's research, should convince any rational person of the value of collecting student ratings, but college faculty members are not noted for their rationality in faculty debates about higher education policy. As one of my distinguished colleagues said when Herb Marsh mildly suggested that there was relevant research on the issue being discussed, "We don't care about the research findings. We have our own experience."

Such an attitude may help us understand why there is general acceptance of peer ratings of research as highly valid despite data indicating relatively low agreement among ratings of research articles while discounting the voluminous validity data presented by Marsh with respect to student ratings of teaching.

I suspect that the validity data for student ratings of instruction are about as extensive as for any psychological tests except intelligence tests. Nonetheless we still have points of vulnerability. Most validity studies relating mean student ratings to mean achievement of students are carried out in large multi-section courses at the introductory level. As Feldman notes, the typical criterion is a final examination consisting mostly of multiple-choice or true-false questions testing simple knowledge of isolated facts and involving little higher order thinking. This probably explains why Feldman found that ratings of "intellectual challenge" and "encouragement of students' independent thought" were highly correlated with students' overall evaluation of instruction but not highly correlated with mean student achievement. To me this indicates that students are more sophisticated in their view of the goals of education than we may have thought. They value an emphasis on thinking even if the criterion examinations on which they are graded do not require it.

Faculty resistance to student ratings: An aside. While the research on the impact of feedback from student ratings indicates that there is some improvement in teaching, the amount of improvement is small unless the feedback involves consultation. A major reason for this rather disappointing result is that many faculty members resist using them. Even though student ratings of teaching have been in widespread use at the University of Michigan for 45 years there is still much resistance and hostility toward their use. Yet our experience at the Center for Research on Learning and Teaching is that there is great faculty enthusiasm for *midterm* feedback from students. How can we account for this phenomenon?

Marsh and Dunkin analyze the problem of faculty resistance in some depth, and I shall simply endorse and elaborate on their discussion. As I see it, a major difference between end-of-term student ratings and collection of student reactions at mid-term is in the projected use of the student opinions. In the case of midterm feedback, the instructor has personal control of the use of the results. One can determine which aspects to attend to and which are less important. The use of the ratings is within the faculty member's own control—and autonomy is one of the motives that is particularly high for faculty members as compared with individuals in other occupations. Perry shows the importance of perceived personal control in student motivation, and faculty members are, if anything, even more motivated for personal control than the average person.

End-of-the-term ratings that may be used for determination of salary increases or promotion are quite another matter. Here the faculty member has no control over the interpretation or use of the ratings. As I wrote two decades ago, most humans do not enjoy being evaluated unless we are confident that the results will be highly positive (McKeachie, 1973). Ratings used for personnel decisions represent the power and control of the institution over the individual—a condition that is not conducive to positive feelings.

Why then do we accept peer evaluation of our research—a dimension of academic performance carrying even more weight in promotion decisions? The answer, I believe, is that these evaluations are almost always positive. As a department chair and member of our college executive committee, I have been involved in reviewing hundreds—probably well over a thousand—such letters. My experience (lacking knowledge of relevant research) is that negative letters are about as common as palm trees above the Arctic circle. It is true that one reads between the lines—even the absence of superlatives is sometimes taken to be negative—but I can never remember a letter stating bluntly that a candidate's research is poor.

Now as it happens, student ratings are also mostly positive. At the University of Michigan 90% of our faculty are rated as excellent by over half of their students. Why then are student ratings feared?

I believe that there are two reasons.

The first is that the ratings are on numerical scales that are normed. In the late 1940s, when the University of Michigan faculty first debated the used of student ratings, one faculty member argued that good teaching could not be measured. I argued that anything that existed, existed in a quantifiable fashion. Thus it was appropriate to use quantifiable ratings. I now feel that that was a mistake. Not that qualities of teaching are not quantifiable. Numbers are often useful. The fault is not in the numbers, but rather in their use. Once numbers are assigned, faculty promotion committees begin to make comparisons between teachers and assume that if one number is larger than another, there is a real difference between the teachers to whom the numbers have been assigned.

Moreover faculty members are supplied with norms indicating the average ratings on each item. Thus a faculty member whose students all "agree" that he or she is an excellent teacher will find that he or she is "below average" as a teacher because other faculty members have some students who "strongly agree" on that item. Finding that one is "below average" is unlikely to increase one's enthusiasm for teaching, and it certainly does not lead to greater enthusiasm for student ratings.

Nira Hativa, in a recent article in *Instructional Evaluation and Faculty Development* (Hativa, 1993), argues persuasively against comparative ratings. She suggests that we simply consider absolute levels of student satisfaction or, as I would prefer, judgments of learning. Abrami, d'Apollonia, and Rosenfield's chapter provides additional support for the notion that faculty members should not use student ratings to compare themselves with other teachers.

We do not assign numbers in our letters evaluating the research of a faculty member being considered for promotion to tenure. It is very unlikely that a solid, but not outstanding researcher, will be categorized as "below average." I believe that we should simply report the number of students at each point on the rating scale for each item rather than reporting means and norms. However using the distribution of student responses, or even mean ratings, to track one's improvement over time is a worthwhile use of numbers. Marsh and Bailey (1993) show how profile comparisons over time can be of value.

If one is concerned about using ratings to improve the quality of teaching, the finding that most faculty are rated positively should not be taken as a damning indictment of student ratings. Rather, even elementary motivation theory would say that this is exactly the sort of result that is likely to increase faculty member's motivation for teaching.

The second reason for the distrust of student ratings is that evaluation of teaching in many universities is seldom used as a positive factor in determining the promotion of faculty members. Rather, as Salthouse, Lin and I (1978) showed in our studies of the use of student ratings in promotion and salary decisions, poor ratings of teaching had a negative effect, but good ratings had little impact. Thus a teacher being evaluated runs the risk of negative results with little chance of positive rewards.

For decades those who study student ratings of faculty have suggested that we should make a cleaner separation between the formative and summative uses of student ratings of teaching. Rather than requiring that ratings be given routinely at the end of the semester, let us get feedback from students early in the term—perhaps at the end of the first month or at midterm. The feedback could well be on the sort of items studied by Murray or Marsh, could be on specific aspects of the course, or could be open-ended. For example, I sometimes ask my students or my teaching assistants' students two questions:

What have you liked about the course so far?
What suggestions do you have for improvement?

These questions are not likely to produce comments that will be devastating to the beginning teacher and usually provide useful ideas for improvement.

Similarly Bob Boice (1992) has developed a painless set of items for collecting student feedback. His "Informal Student Evaluation" form asks students to rate aspects of teaching that the instructor does well and the directions in which it might be changed (with no good or bad endpoints). Whatever the method of collecting feedback, improvement is more likely to occur if the feedback is discussed with a consultant.

End of the term student opinion need not be collected in every course to be valid data for personnel purposes. Faculty members should be asked to include data from several classes in their portfolio, but they should be free to opt out when they are trying new methods or developing a risky innovation, just as they are free to avoid publishing research that didn't pan out.

Helping faculty members and administrators become more sophisticated users of student ratings of teaching. Those of us involved in faculty development and evaluation of teaching have, I believe, done a creditable job in developing and validating forms for collecting student opinion. Students have generally done a fairly good job in filling out the forms. The problems encountered in evaluation of faculty seem to me to lie primarily on the doorsteps of faculty members, administrators, and faculty developers. As a faculty member, a sometime administrator and faculty developer, I admit culpability in all three roles.

The basic problem is that neither administrators, nor faculty members who serve on committees responsible for faculty evaluation, are well-trained for the task. Those of us responsible for evaluative decisions accept with little question letters about research that have limited reliability and unknown validity. In evaluating teaching we often fail to gather relevant data such as examinations, papers, reports, or other student products indicative of achievement, and only with the current popularity of the portfolio have many departments examined syllabi, reading lists, course requirements, and other evidence of course planning and content. We focus on classroom performance and neglect important out-of-class contributions to education. We look at mean ratings of teaching and because the results are reported statistically, the numbers are given magical significance. As Abrami, d'Apollonia and Rosenfield demonstrate, we include information from student rating items that are inappropriate for courses that do not fit the conventional classroom lecture format. We fail to take account of contextual variables.

Feldman's review of the myths and half-truths believed by many faculty members illustrates the seriousness of the problem of resistance by faculty members and misuse by faculty committees and administrators.

Nonetheless professionals in faculty development must share the blame. We have done all too little to supply information in ways that will reduce misuse; we have failed to provide training for personnel committees and administrators, not only in interpreting student ratings, but also in evaluating course materials and other kinds of evidence. We have not succeeded in helping faculty members understand the basic research and theories having to do with the goals of education and the nature of effective teaching and learning. We have done little to help students be better observers and judges of their own learning.

The ethics of evaluation of teaching. There is also an ethical problem in requiring student time for the collection of student opinions of teaching. I believe that if you are taking students' (or anyone's) time, you have an ethical obligation to insure that it is educational, interesting, fun, or in some way rewarding to them. For midterm evaluations, one can argue that the students will benefit from whatever improvements follow from their feedback. But I would argue that there is a more important value that we have failed to emphasize in our use of student ratings of teaching. This is the educational value to the student of filling out student rating forms.

Systems of student evaluation of teaching should encourage students to think about their own educational experiences—to develop clearer conceptions of the kinds of teaching and educational experiences that contribute most to their learning. The student opinion form could, and should, be educational in the highest sense—helping students gain a better understanding of the goals of education, stimulating them to think more metacognitively about their own learning, motivating them to continue learning, and encouraging them to accept responsibility for their learning.

I believe that we could do a much better job of introducing these educational objectives for filling out the rating forms. We can certainly create forms that encourage student metacognition. The form I developed and published in my book, *Teaching Tips*, (7th edition, 1978; 9th edition, 1994) asks students to think about the impact of the course upon their own gains on several dimensions of education. Items are also included dealing with the student's own responsibility for learning. I am pleased that Abrami, d'Apollonia and Rosenfeld also endorse this approach.

Discussion with students aimed at sensitizing them to evaluating their own learning and the conditions that contribute to learning is important in developing their ability to learn more effectively. Such a discussion before ratings are collected and discussion of the results after the ratings have been summarized should not only result in more useful feedback for teachers but also help students become better learners.

At this point we have linked dimensions of teaching and teaching behaviors to teaching effectiveness empirically, but we have only touched upon the theory underlying our conception of effective teaching. Let us now return to the theory of instruction.

Why do effective teaching methods result in better learning?

Even in the 1940's and 1950's we theorized about teaching effectiveness. In my doctoral dissertation (McKeachie, 1949) I talked about student "gut learning"—essentially the kind of learning that might now be labeled as "deep processing." We used terms like "groupiness" or "group cohesion" to describe the sense of trust, cooperation and motivation characterizing effective discussion groups. Today we emphasize the value of collaborative or cooperative learning, sometimes based upon cognitive theory of elaboration or levels of processing and upon motivation and social psychological theories of social facilitation, or sometimes simply on the practical argument that skills in cooperation are important in employment after college. Even though it might seem from comparing the research and theory of research in college teaching in the 1950's with that of the 1990's that the themes are much the same, there has been progress. As I see it, three areas of theoretical development have particular significance for our thinking about teaching.

One of these is the importance of ***context***. Feldman points out that many aspects of teaching that one would expect to be highly related to teaching effectiveness have rather modest correlations with outcomes. *Feedback*, for example, does not correlate particularly well with student achievement. But we now know that feedback can have unintended effects depending upon the context and the student's attributions. Criticism, for example, may be taken by a student as evidence that he or she lacks the ability to succeed, or it may be interpreted as evidence that the teacher thinks that one has the ability to improve. Thus the kind of feedback and the previous relationship between the teacher and the student may determine whether the feedback produces a reduction in motivation or increased motivation.

Similarly *organization* has a rather tricky relationship to student prior knowledge, the difficulty of the material, and the heterogeneity of the students in a class. Clearly students will remember better if they have some organized framework within which to encode facts and concepts. But they will remember the material best if they have developed the organization for themselves. Teachers with heterogeneous classes, therefore, are faced with the dilemma that if they provide a high level of organization, they diminish the learning of students with the ability to organize for themselves; if the teachers fail to provide an organization, students with less prior knowledge will be left in confusion. Hartley's comparisons of providing complete lecture notes, skeletal notes, or no notes suggest that skeletal notes are an effective compromise in the typical lecture class (Hartley and Davies, 1978), but clearly the value of organization is affected by the context.

A second area where we have made progress is in a much more detailed understanding of what is going on in the students' heads—the ***cognitive processes*** affected by teaching. As discussed earlier, teacher *enthusiasm* enhances student attention; teacher *clarity* aids encoding; *interaction* of students and teachers promotes the surfacing of misunderstanding, and permits clarification and elaboration.

Students create learning out of the interaction of what is already in their heads with the learning experiences we provide in and out of the classroom. Because only the students know what is in their minds, peer observations can never take the place of the students' own ratings of their educational experiences. This does not mean that student introspections are flawless, but they do provide information that is important for understanding teaching and learning.

Important as are the gains in our understanding of cognition, equally important progress has been made, as Perry suggests (Perry, 1991) in the area of ***motivation***. Both expectancy-value theory and attribution theory have given a better understanding of the way in which teaching affects motivation for learning.

Teacher *enthusiasm* has important motivational as well as cognitive effects. The teacher's enthusiasm about the interest and value of the subject acts as a model that influences the value students place upon learning the material; moreover, as Feldman notes, teacher enthusiasm includes spontaneity and variability, which not only affects attention but is also relevant to curiosity and interest.

Similarly *interaction* of students and teachers increases opportunity for students to feel a greater sense of personal control—an important motivational variable both in increasing the student's self-efficacy and expectancy of success and also in affecting attributions of success to one's own ability and effort rather than to external causes.

Motivation theory also helps us understand the problems of faculty motivation for teaching, such as the heavy extrinsic pressures exerted by evaluation for tenure, with a likely result of a loss of intrinsic satisfaction. (Deci, 1971)

Conclusion

So, we have seen that good teaching makes a difference. What can we do with the information?

There are a number of implications for teachers and academic administrators in the preceding chapters and I have mentioned several in this chapter. Like Mary Ellen Weimer I would call them tentative rather than hard and fast rules. Nonetheless I would take a somewhat more strongly positive stance than Weimer in encouraging teachers, administrators, and faculty developers to think about the implications suggested by the researchers and to try out their own versions, using the suggestions heuristically rather than as recipes for improvement. In any case here are some that are particularly worthy of the attention of administrators and faculty developers:

1. Workshops and other forms of training (as reviewed by Weimer and Lenze) can help faculty members communicate greater enthusiasm, teach them methods of establishing rapport, help develop greater skills in organization and clarity, assist in developing other skills, and enhance motivation.
2. Consultation (See Weimer and Lenze) can greatly improve the value of feedback from student ratings, videotapes, or other information gathering methods.
3. No one is too old to learn. With the end of mandatory retirement in the United States, it will become even more important that older faculty members maintain their vitality by developing new skills and understanding of teaching.
4. As Weimer and Lenze indicate, training in basic skills as well as continuing social support can increase the likelihood that the early teaching experiences of teaching assistants and new faculty members will be intrinsically satisfying. Just as intrinsic interest in learning and deeper processing of content reciprocally reinforce one another; so too intrinsic satisfactions in teaching and development as a teacher go hand in hand.
5. Weimer and Lenze, reviewing each of the categories of interventions designed to help teachers improve, repeatedly stress the necessity of better evaluative data particularly in actual teaching situations. I join in that plea. We can seldom do an ideal evaluation, but we should do much more than we have thus far in linking our efforts to changes in teacher motivation, thinking, and behavior that seem likely to result in better student learning. I would not ask that we always go to our ultimate criterion—student learning—because as I have pointed out elsewhere, (McKeachie, 1990) student learning is affected by so many variables that the effects of any one intervention are not likely to make a big difference, particularly in the relatively insensitive and marginally valid typical final examination.

Although there is still much to be done, we have come a long way since Remmers' 1927 monograph. I have no doubt that college and university teaching has improved and that we have gained enough knowledge to facilitate continued improvement.

References

Barrick, M. R., and Mount, M. K. (1991). The Big Five personality dimensions and job performance: A meta-analysis. *Personnel Psychology* 44: 1-26.

Boice, R. (1992) Countering common misbeliefs about student evaluations of teaching. *Chalkboard*. Fall 1992, University of Missouri-Columbia, Program for Excellence in Teaching.

Brady, P. J. (1994). How likeability and effectiveness ratings of college professors by their students are affected by course demands and professors' attitudes. *Psychological Reports* 74: 907-913.

Deci, E. L. (1971). *Intrinsic Motivation* New York: Plenum.

Dubin, R., and Taveggia, T. C. (1968). *The Teaching-Learning Paradox* Eugene, Oregon: University of Oregon.

Hartley, J. , and Davies, I. K. (1978). Note-taking: A critical review. *Programmed Learning and Educational Technology*. 15(3): 207-224.

Hativa, N. (1993) Student ratings: A non-comparative interpretation. *Instructional Evaluation and Faculty Development* 13(2), 1-4.

Marsh, H. W., and Bailey, M. (1993). Multidimensionality of students' evaluations of teaching effectiveness: A profile analysis. *Journal of Higher Education* 64: 1-18.

Marsh, H. W., and Roche, L. (1993). The use of students' evaluations and an individually structured intervention to enhance teaching effectiveness. *American Educational Research Journal* 30: 217-251.

McKeachie, W. J. (1949) Individual conformity to attitudes of classroom groups. Doctoral dissertation published in *Journal of Abnormal and Social Psychology*, 1954: 49, 282-289.

McKeachie, W. J. (1973). Resistances to evaluation of teaching. *Occasional Paper No. 2*. Evanston, IL: The Center for Teaching Professions, Northwestern University.

McKeachie, W. J. (1990). Learning, thinking, and Thorndike. *Educational Psychologist* 25(2): 127-141.

McKeachie, W. J. (1978, 1994) *Teaching Tips*. Lexington, MA: D.C.Heath.

McKeachie, W. J., and Birney, R. (1955). The teaching of psychology: A survey of research since 1942. *Psychological Bulletin* 51: 51-68.

Morsh, J. E., Burgess, G. G., and Smith, P. N. (1956). Student achievement as a measure of instructor effectiveness. *Journal of Educational Psychology* 47: 79-88.

Norman, W. T. (1963) Toward an adequate taxonomy of personality attributes: Replicated factor structure in peer nomination personality ratings. *Journal of Abnormal and Social Psychology* 66: 574-583.

Perry, R. P. (1991). Perceived control in college students: Implications for instruction in higher education. In Smart, J.C. (Ed.) *Higher Education: Handbook of Theory and Research*, Vol. VII. New York: Agathon Press *(included in this volume)*.

Remmers, H. H. (1927). The college professor as the student sees him. *Purdue University Studies in Higher Education* No.11.

Remmers, H. H. (1958) On students' perceptions of teacher effectiveness. In McKeachie, W.J. (Ed.) *The Appraisal of Teaching in Large Universities*. Ann Arbor: University of Michigan.

Remmers, H. H., Martin, F. D., and Elliott, D. N. (1949). Are students' ratings of instructors related to their grades? *Purdue Studies of Higher Education* 66:17-26.

Salthouse, T. A., McKeachie, W. J., and Lin, Y-G, (1978). An experimental investigation of factors affecting university promotion decisions: A brief report. *Journal of Higher Education* 49:177-183.

Shuell, T. J. (1993). Toward an integrated theory of teaching and learning. *Educational Psychologist* 28: (4), 291-311

Smalzreid, N. T. , and Remmers, H. H. (1943). A factor analysis of the Purdue rating scale for instructors. *Journal of Educational Psychology* 34: 363-367.

Tupes, E. C. , and Christal, R. E. (1961). Recurrent personality factors based on trait ratings. (USAF ASD Tech. Rep. No. 61-97). Lackland Air Force Base, TX: U.S. Air Force.

Wilson, R. C. (1986). Improving faculty teaching: Effective use of student evaluations and consultants. *Journal of Higher Education* 57:196-211.

CONCLUSION

Exploring the Implications: From Research to Practice[1]

Maryellen Weimer

INTRODUCTION

In something of a break with tradition, the editors of this volume, which focuses on research on teaching, commissioned a chapter that features no findings. The objective is a chapter that summarizes the research with an eye toward its implications. That does not mean watered down, diluted summaries of individual chapters, but distillations that accurately portray in accessible language the essence of the findings and implications.

The research reported here is replete with implications—some of which chapter authors clearly state, some of which they hint at, others which they do not articulate, and a few they propose with which this author disagrees. All of these implications are discussed in this chapter.

As with all social science findings, there are different degrees of "tentativeness" associated with these various areas of inquiry. Work on teaching, particularly in terms of student ratings, is well enough established to be more or less firm with regard to conclusions and what ought to be done in light of them. Less work has been done on college learners. It follows narrower lines and is not as well integrated across lines (in the way that Perry's work relates to Covington's and vice versa), which leads to more "tentativeness" when the implications are generalized to the diverse contexts of higher education.

And readers should bear this tentativeness in mind as they see how concrete policies and practices are extrapolated from work sometimes completed in constrained (as they need to be) research environments. What's proposed derives from a process of inference and sometimes intuition—what policies and/or practices the chapter authors and this author think might achieve the same result. Example: Perry's work shows that attributional retraining can change levels of perceived control, but can that effect be accomplished by what teachers say and do in a classroom full of students? If so, how?

---

[1]The author was a senior research associate in the Center for the Study of Higher Education at The Pennsylvania State University during the preparation of this chapter. She is currently a faculty member teaching communication courses at the Berks campus of Penn State.

Said differently, to know that a particular policy or practice has the same effect as that discovered vis-a-vis a research paradigm requires systematic empirical inquiry, and few in-the-field policies and practices have been so studied. Nonetheless, we still need to make policy and practice choices that are based on something other than what has always been done or what is the latest fad. This research offers that more solid foundation on which to build.

In addition to offering concrete policy and practice suggestions, this chapter organizes them in terms of groups for whom the research has implications. In these chapters, that is most often faculty, administrators, and students, although when there are implications for other groups, those are identified.

Finally, policies and practices, some of them common, that are at odds with the apparent implications of research reported here are identified and discussed in terms of their potential and in some cases realized negative consequences. It's never easy to be critical of policy and practice because most of it is well-intentioned; unfortunately too much of it is uninformed. We can and should do better. This chapter aims to show us how.

✳ ✳ ✳ ✳ ✳

Students' Evaluations of University Teaching:
A Multidimensional Perspective
by Herbert W. Marsh and Michael J. Dunkin

The Dimensionality of Student Ratings of Instruction:
What We Know and What We Do Not
by Philip C. Abrami, Sylvia d'Apollonia, and Steven Rosenfield

Identifying Exemplary Teaching:
Evidence from Student Ratings
by Kenneth A. Feldman

Summary

These three chapters address issues involving the assessment of instruction and teachers by student evaluations; two of them happen to be the longest chapters in the volume. And so it is important in this summary to begin by recognizing the enormousness of the task. Unlike other reviews in this volume where the domains of inquiry are more tightly bounded and in which much less work has actually been completed, in this area the sheer volume of studies result not in a painting to be viewed from across the room, but in a mural so wide that to stand on the other side is still to see only part of the panorama.

For specifics: Marsh and Dunkin report (page 242) (as does Cashin, 1988), that more than 1,300 studies are listed in the ERIC data base. Feldman (page 368) references an interview I conducted with him in 1990 in which he reports having 2,000 items in his collection of books, articles, monographs, and papers, and he notes that his collection has grown since. Is it not interesting that of all the areas of inquiry within higher education, this is the one that has been studied most?

These three reviews orient differently to the research area. The Marsh and Dunkin state-of-our-knowledge review is the most comprehensive of the three, noteworthy for its breadth and depth. It joins and builds on a notable number of other reviews (referenced by Marsh and Dunkin on page 247, and by Feldman on page 369), which makes this particular area of knowledge better summarized and organized than most.

Key to the Marsh and Dunkin summary is the fundamental premise that teaching is a multidimensional phenomenon. It has parts, distinct and separate dimensions, aspects and components, and these parts must be reflected on the instruments used to assess instructional effectiveness.

What are the factors? Marsh and Dunkin list nine (pages 251-253) that emerged when Marsh developed the Students' Evaluations of Educational Quality (SEEQ) instrument and have been confirmed in much subsequent research involving it. Feldman's work in this area (referenced in note 2 of his chapter) began with a summary of the dimensions as they appeared in studies where students were asked to identify the characteristics of best, ideal or good teachers. His original list of 20 dimensions has been extended (partly by the inclusion of studies reporting views other than students, like faculty colleagues and administrators) to the current 28 dimensions that appear in the appendix at the end of his chapter. In both of these reviews the dimensions of instruction "represent a common core" of items characteristic of all teachers, in all subjects, and at all kinds of institutions.

Feldman sorts and prioritizes the dimensions in two ways. First, he attempts to establish the relative importance of the dimensions by looking at them in terms of student achievement. He finds that all but three dimensions are positively correlated with achievement at statistically significant levels. Second, he looks at the relationship between specific items and global ratings in terms of correlations assuming that the "overall assessment of teachers would be more highly associated with instructional characteristics that students generally consider to be important to good teaching...." (page 380) Moreover, he finds high correlations between the most important dimensions as determined by the two separate methods.

In many respects a response to Marsh and Dunkin specifically and Feldman more generally, the Abrami, d'Apollonia, and Rosenfield review focuses on this dimensionality issue as well as several other contested areas. While Abrami, d'Apollonia, and Rosenfield agree that teaching is multidimensional, they do not accept the dimensions proposed in the other two chapters, particularly in terms of their universality. In their work they identified four factors, three of which are highly correlated, and all of which suggest a large global component that can alone be the basis for instructional judgment.

The Marsh and Dunkin review considers five other areas and issues addressed by the instructional evaluation research, one of which receives considerable coverage in all three reviews. First, Marsh and Dunkin establish that given attention to appropriate empirical considerations (like the number of students completing an evaluation, for example), evaluation instruments are reliable—meaning the instrument itself does not get in the way of what it intends to measure. Research confirms that reliable instruments are remarkably stable. They change little across time—demolishing the optimistic faculty assumption that if students object to a set of learning experiences, they will subsequently see and appreciate what the faculty member aimed to accomplish.

Second, research also confirms in a consistent and almost dramatic way the generalizability of the ratings—they are primarily a function of the *instructor* who teaches the course and not of the course that is taught.

Third, more complicated and contested are efforts to establish the validity of student ratings. What is being measured by the forms? Most fundamentally they measure student satisfaction with teaching. Important though that may be in these times of educational consumerism, is it enough? For some in higher education, yes; but most want to know more, e.g., if the instruction facilitates learning, and they want to differentiate between levels of instructional effectiveness—the level that leads to more learning contrasted with that with diminished impacts.

Establishing validity by means of this more meaningful criteria presents a number of challenges. First, the learning must be shown to be a consequence of the teaching. The teaching may be, for example, quite ineffective, but because the student is highly motivated and works hard, lots of learning may still result. Moreover, we in higher education don't agree on learning goals and objectives. So, it's not only that we have trouble defining effective instruction, we are equally at odds as to desired learning outcomes.

All three reviews devote considerable attention to a category of studies called multisection validity studies. Here multiple sections of the same course are evaluated by students and the class section averages correlated with class average scores on a standardized final exam. In general, strong positive correlations exist—meaning the courses with higher exam averages are taught by teachers with higher student rating scores. So, to sum the point, student evaluations of teaching are valid because more learning (as measured by exam scores) occurs when instructor evaluations are high.

Marsh and Dunkin are critical of this research paradigm for methodological reasons and because results rest on such narrow definitions of learning. Often end-of-course exams measure low level learning outcomes, like what and how much a student has memorized. Marsh and Dunkin look at larger conceptions of validity—like the relationships between self and peer ratings—and in most areas find other evidence of validity. That is, ratings are valid because faculty peer assessments as well as an instructor's own evaluations basically agree with the student assessments.

Abrami, d'Apollonia, and Rosenfield write in defense of the multisection validity work; countering methodological objections and pointing out the importance of process-product definitions of effective teaching. What the instructor does both before and during teaching should produce positive changes in students in relevant academic domains. This means a dimension of effective instruction such as enthusiasm is important not just for its own sake (a product orientation), but because it motivates students to learn (a process orientation). Looking at process-product definitions "helps identify links between what teachers do and whether and how students change as a result." (page 326)

Fourth, despite much evidence to the contrary, faculty continue to believe that student evaluations of teaching are likely to be biased, often by factors beyond their control, such as whether or not the course they teach is required. Marsh and Dunkin point out that voluminous research has been conducted and although some of it is atheoretical (meaning we don't have very good or clear definitions of bias) and methodologically flawed, little evidence of significant bias exists.

Feldman considers this issue, but in a broader context. Building on the work of Aleamoni (1987) who first proposed a list of myths, he confirms the existence of seven myths about instructional evaluation most of which go beyond the issue of bias. Feldman then considers five "half-truths," candidates for the status of myth, according to Aleamoni, most of which relate to issues of bias, such as the effect of class size, level of the course, rank of the instructor, for example. Here the evidence establishes that bias variables have small effects but the cases are still not closed.

Next on the bias topic, Feldman, as well as Marsh and Dunkin, spend time exploring the relationship between course grades and evaluations given instructors. They report the small but consistently positive correlations present in the research, but point out that some of the "bias" may be legitimate: students who learn more earn higher grades and thus legitimately give higher evaluations. Finally Feldman, points to evidence which documents that instructors in different academic fields tend to be rated somewhat differently.

Marsh and Dunkin conclude in the fifth area by exploring the usefulness of ratings in faculty efforts to improve, as part of the students' course selection process and in administrative personnel decision-making.

Implications

For faculty and administrators: Faculty and administrators continue to be largely ignorant of this research and that is difficult to excuse. That harsh accusation is justified in that ignorance in both camps is not benign. For faculty the myth and folklore they accept as fact about student evaluation excuses them from taking seriously important information about their teaching. The refusal to accept as legitimate, feedback from the persons who are the very objects of our teaching offers yet more implicit evidence of how faculty themselves devalue teaching.

As for administrators, it is most often at their initiative and under their leadership that an institution's policies and practices with respect to evaluation are formed and implemented. Taken together, I would venture a guess that the policies and practices used to assess instruction today are, conservatively, 20 years behind the research reported in this volume.

If faculty and administrators had only research reviews, summaries, and analyses like these from which to learn about instructional evaluation, perhaps they could be somewhat excused. These reviews are written to inform subsequent research. They are technical, complex, and with only occasional and generally oblique references to policy and practice implications. But keeping pace with the emerging research findings have been a family of books and articles *written for* faculty and administrators (Braskamp, Brandenburg, and Ory, 1985; Braskamp and Ory, 1994; Cashin, 1988; Centra, 1979 and 1993; McKeachie, 1979; Miller, 1975). Yes, it is true that faculty and administrators are busy with multiple demands on their time, but more troubling is the verdict they seem to have reached as evidenced by their neglect of these resources: *Teaching continues to be something we can afford to be uninformed about.* In darker moments one is tempted to propose radical solutions; like transforming the myth and half-truth list from the Feldman review into a quiz which every faculty member and administrator would be required to take and pass before using student evaluations.

One way to treat the area of implications is to identify policies and practices called for by research findings like these. That is the tack most often taken in the publications listed above. I have argued for some time now that since virtually all colleges and universities report the systematic use of student evaluation (Seldin, 1985), what we have to contend with is not a clean slate but an environment polluted with a hodgepodge of policies and practices most of which are born out of expediency and political necessity. They have not been without consequence and probably explain why the Marsh's (page 311) promise of instructional improvement and enhanced commitments to teaching resulting from student evaluation programs have yet to be realized at most institutions.

I propose to analyze current policy and practice in five areas; 1) instrument construction, 2) the amount and environment of evaluation, 3) the summative-formative relationship, 4) the comparability of ratings, and 5) the role of peers in the process. My goal is to assess commonplace procedures in light of the research reported here. I have framed each as a case, meaning the evidence and conclusions of the research argue against certain policies and practices.

The Case of the Camel Created by a Committee

The research spells out the importance of instrument design and development:

> Information from SETs (student evaluations of teaching) depends upon the content of the items. Poorly worded or inappropriate items will not provide useful information. If a survey instrument contains an ill-defined hodgepodge of different items and SETs are summarized by an average of these items, then there is no basis for knowing what is being measured. (Marsh and Dunkin, page 244)

I have a collection of approximately 75 instruments gathered nonscientifically in my travels to various colleges and universities and passed on by colleagues who know of my interest in this area. The collection has not been analyzed empirically, but even a casual observer would be impressed by the lack of convergence between what appears on these instruments and the research-identified dimensions in the Feldman categories or on the Marsh instrument. Some important dimensions aren't there; some unimportant ones are overrepresented; and some new dimensions appear to have been created. And those are just the problems with content validity. Inconsistently worded items, scales with anchors that don't apply to the items, and other such anomalies are common. All in all, it's not a very impressive collection.

The origins of these instruments to some extent account for their deficiencies. These are camels created by committees. Faculty tend to object strenuously to instruments developed externally. In the eight years I used Marsh's SEEQ instrument as part of a formative assessment activity at my own institution, the most common complaint was that it had been developed at UCLA and "you know, this place is not like UCLA."

The best way for an administrator to negotiate this minefield is to appoint a faculty committee and charge them with the task of creating an instrument. What results is an idiosyncratic measure that reflects the collected and negotiated priorities of the committee members involved. After considerable debate in the faculty senate, it passes, largely on the power of its home-grown quality.

The general quality of the instrumentation being used to assess instruction argues for the Abrami, d'Apollonia, and Rosenfield position in favor of a single overall rating. Unfortunately, faculty find it difficult to accept the notion that a "single number" can accurately reflect the complexity and variability of the teaching phenomenon. They also distrust the ability of administrators to use the numbers responsibly. Again, poor practices, such as ranking faculty according to overall scores and then targeting the bottom third for "development," contribute to faculty paranoia.

However, the bulk of instruments being used to evaluate instruction are multidimensional, generally with some overall comparative items. The problem is the dimensions that are and are not reflected and the lack of empirical rigor associated with the development process. Those interested in developing an instrument locally are well advised to note the multistep process used to develop Marsh's SEEQ instrument (Marsh and Dunkin, pages 244-249). Until instrumentation improves, the credibility of the rating feedback will continue to be compromised.

The Case Against Competition

Ours is a culture that thrives on competition and the need to outperform one another. Regrettably, the academy is like much of the rest of society. Here faculty compete for dwindling resources, are pressed by a business model where achievement is part of the drive toward quality and excellence, and are pushed toward accountability. Not all these forces are undesirable, but taken together they create a climate that is far more competitive than it is cooperative.

As evidence, most of our institutions have succumbed to a "more is better" mentality—more publications, more grants, more buildings, more visibility, and more instructional evaluation. How many times I've visited with administrators who tell me their institution values teaching, takes it seriously—and the evidence? "Why we evaluate every course every semester."

This practice stands in contradiction to clear research evidence that ratings are remarkably stable across time. Marsh and Dunkin describe a 13-year longitudinal study of individual faculty ratings in which "year accounted for no more than 1/4 of 1% in any of the evaluation scores." (page 260)

And the policy may have consequences. Is it possible for students to be asked to evaluate too often? Typically the evaluation occurs at the end of the course during the time when students are busiest and most stressed. Is the quality of the data compromised by the frequency with which it is solicited—especially if it is collected in an institutional environment where students do not see evidence that their evaluations are taken seriously (i.e., poor teachers teach on and some good ones are never promoted)? And how about faculty—do the results gain a certain commonplace status to the extent that the same instrument produces roughly the same results course after course?

The competitive environment at most institutions is reflected in the way student rating data are used. Frequently lists of overall scores are compiled and distributed. Generally faculty confidentiality is respected, but the impact of finding one's score at the top or bottom of the list is profound and personal. The practice does not foster collegiality and can be paralyzing for new faculty. The notion that a faculty member with a 5.13 overall score is decidedly better or instructionally different from a faculty member with a 5.07 overall score is not empirically defensible.

The Case of the Summative and Formative Confusion

In general, most institutions have in place a set of policies and practices that fail to differentiate between the summative and formative functions of evaluation. Clearly institutional interest (and one is tempted to add research interest) sides heavily on the summative—the use of student ratings in the personnel decision-making process.

There is a sad bit of irony here that should not be overlooked. Student rating information is widely collected, and almost universally included in promotion and tenure dossiers and in annual performance appraisals. And this research points out that, collected correctly, student rating data "tends to be statistically reliable, valid, and relatively free from bias, probably more so than any other data used for faculty evaluation." (Cashin in Marsh and Dunkin, page 311) In other words, most institutions have evidence they could use to justify tenuring, promoting, and rewarding good teachers, but very few in fact use it. Research and the data documenting scholarly productivity still count more than teaching excellence (Fairweather, 1993). Instructional evidence is generally ignored unless for some reason it is particularly notable.

The summative and formative confusion results from the widespread assumption that primarily end-of-course and generally global information can do double duty. It can inform the personnel decision-making process and give faculty the feedback they need to improve.

Unfortunately, what those of us who have worked with faculty on instructional improvement agendas have learned and what Murray's research (discussed subsequently) on low-inference behaviors documents, is that overall rating results may motivate improvement but they do not inform it. The reasons are mostly common sense. To know that compared with other instructors at your institution you are "below average," a 3 on a 1-to-7 negative to positive scale, is to know you should improve, but all this information tells you is to "do better" during the next course. If, on the other hand, if you receive a relatively low rating on an item such as "instructor's presentations facilitate notetaking," or "group work aids in understanding course content," at least you have a park in which to play ball. And so, when instructional change is the objective, multidimensional forms aid and direct the process.

The debate over global vs. multidimensional ratings can be resolved practically by using global ratings for summative purposes and multidimensional forms to accomplish formative ends. That argues for two separate sets of activities, which some of us believe could enhance the impact of both kinds of data on the improvement process (Weimer, 1990). This same conclusion is reached for different reasons in a subsequent discussion of Murray's work.

That the summative/formative confusion diminishes the impact of both kinds of feedback is also illustrated by a set of practices called for in the research but frequently missing from our policies. The opportunity to interact, to "consult" with someone about student rating results, enhances the impact of that feedback. Only rarely does such consultation occur, and when it does only rarely is the consultant a professional with training and experience relevant to delivering the feedback. More often the consultant is a department chair, functioning in a role that uncomfortably combines summative and formative activities. It is extremely difficult to sit in a position of judgment (pass out raises, for example) and at the same time offer the nurturing support often necessary to begin meaningful dialogue about teaching. Without the opportunity to interact, most faculty choose to muse privately over the frequently indecipherable computer printout which summarizes their most recent set of student ratings.

These problems in practice would be helped by greater consideration (by faculty, administrators, and researchers) of the role and usefulness of ratings in the improvement process. We are too preoccupied with the summative function—which until we redress the teaching-research reward imbalance renders even the best data ineffective.

The Case for the Comparable

Administrators are interested in comparisons of all sorts, including the comparison of teachers and teaching. For that reason, they do at times appear to be on a quest for the single best, bureaucratically efficient, machine-scorable, short form for their instructional evaluation program. Find it and it can be used to evaluate all faculty in all departments teaching all kinds of courses. I remember a number of years back being amazed to discover that my 15-week 400-level course was evaluated with the same form used to assess a 2-day, noncredit, continuing education workshop I taught for 15 human resources managers.

And so, in terms of policy, most institutions, if they do not have one already, aspire to a common form. As Abrami, d'Apollonia, and Rosenfield point out, "the search for a collection of the invariant dimensions of effective instruction may underemphasize the importance of local context." (page 326) Moreover, they too note (pages 333-334) that most forms are designed with the lecture method in mind and that some alternative instructional methods (like group work) are gaining in use across higher education.

The recommendation that institutions use multiple measures to assess teaching effectiveness is underscored by these reviews (Abrami, d'Apollonia, and Rosenfield, page 335 and Marsh and Dunkin, page 282) and that recommendation is generally heeded. That's the good news. The bad news involves the continuing untenable use of peers (to be discussed next) and the fact that, as Marsh and Dunkin note (page 277), little has been done to establish the validity of these alternative measures.

The Case Against Peers

The objection here is not to all forms of peer assessment, but rather specifically to the use of the commando-raid style instructional observations that are frequently a part of peer involvement in the promotion and tenure process. Although not the focus of any of these reviews, Marsh and Dunkin (pages 276-277) do reference relevant research as part of their validity discussion. This case is virtually a closed one. Peers who drop into the classroom of a colleague unannounced, observe with no criteria in mind, have little experience or training doing observations, and observe only once *do not* produce reliable assessments. In addition to providing assessments of questionable quality, using peers this way, and exclusively in summative contexts, hurts collegiality. It adds to the competitive environment, does not build trust, and reinforces our tendency to make teaching a private activity. And it results in a diminished role for colleagues in formative activities for which they are best qualified and most able to make constructive contributions.

These five areas are not unrelated. Poor practice in one compromises what occurs in the others, and puts the entire evaluation effort in a tenuous position, which is precisely where we are today. The systematic evaluation of instruction has been a part of the scene in higher education for more than 20 years now. Has teaching improved? Are we more effectively rewarding and recognizing instructional excellence? Are we using the data to mastermind the reform of higher education? Regrettably we must answer all three questions in the negative. How unfortunate and unnecessary. Policies and practices informed by research reported here could have a much more significant and substantive impact.

For students: This research gives students much more credit for making quality assessments of instruction than most faculty and administrators do. Objections are still regularly raised regarding student qualifications, and while students may not be in a good position to evaluate the best text for an introductory course, the research referenced here attests to their collective wisdom on instructional experiences. It verifies that in large measure, students take their evaluation responsibilities seriously and are able to sort through complicated issues like leniency and rigor. They may clap when an instructor cancels class but there is evidence in this research that the standards and rigor we seek to maintain are recognized and appreciated by our students. One would be hard pressed to read this data and conclude that Mickey Mouse courses and easy A's are the answer to high ratings. And so, to any institution still questioning the validity of instructional assessment reflected in collected student opinions, the evidence here comes down clearly and compellingly in favor of giving students a voice.

Marsh and Dunkin propose that rating information can be used by students as part of a course selection process. It is occasionally, but the practice is not widespread. In part this may be because students have difficulty disseminating the information, but one suspects it is more because students have difficulty accessing the information.

I will argue against this use of rating information on several grounds. First, presumably highly rated teachers "benefit" by having more students enrolled or wanting to enroll in their courses. More students inevitably means more work. Teachers rated poorly "benefit" by having few students in their classes. In these times of financial exigency, when smaller classes become less of a reality and more of a coveted prize, at an institution with the proposed policy in place, the "reward" conceivably goes to the poor teacher.

Second, many poor teachers have tenure. What is the impact of a policy like this one on their attitudes toward teaching and students? Conceivably the public shame of a poorly rated course will motivate improvement. However, given the continuing devaluing of teaching and the prevalence of poorly designed evaluation systems, equally conceivable (and regularly observable in my own work with faculty) is a defensive, hostile response to evaluation efforts and negative, counterproductive attitudes toward students. Faculty who respond in this way do not devote time to improving their courses but become dedicated defamers of student rating programs.

And, finally, what of a new teacher, probably not trained to teach and new to the institution, who may be teaching the course for the very first time and may not yet have the confidence and credibility necessary to teach well? Does publishing a set of inadequate ratings early in the career of such a teacher help to create the kind of constructive climate necessary for instructional growth and development?

Yes, students deserve quality course experiences. As consumers they have the right to a first-rate educational product. But the routine use of student ratings as a criterion in the course selection process is a cheap way to get it—a way that lets institutions ignore their responsibility to create conditions conducive to instructional health and well-being and to implement evaluation and reward systems that deal with both exemplary and inadequate instructional performance.

As Abrami, d'Apollonia, and Rosenfield note (page 330), most evaluation instruments do focus on the preparation and presentational activities of teaching. That puts the attention on the teaching, not on the learning, and students need to be directed more regularly to their learning experiences. Abrami, d'Apollonia, and Rosenfield sensibly suggest that we inquire about learning more often in terms of how it is affected by teaching, and the sample form and procedure they include are useful (page 328).

From the faculty perspective it is oftentimes less threatening and more motivational to put the focus on learning. The question is no longer, "Did students 'like' me and my course?" but rather "What is the impact of my instructional policies, practices and behaviors on student learning?" Researchers may continue to debate validity in terms of outcomes, but the interest in tying aspects of teaching such as enthusiasm to learning processes such as selective attention adds the credibility and significance faculty often find missing from evaluative endeavors. Items on the multidimensional forms are there for a reason.

Conclusion

Even this lengthy discussion of the student evaluation research has but scratched the surface of this domain of knowledge. One cannot read summaries like this, replete with multiple references, and not be impressed by the amount of empirical treatment of this area and the issues that surround it. It is also clear in even a casual review of the chapters in this volume that not all the issues have been resolved: significant areas of contested theory, methodology, and results remain. This should be viewed positively, a part of our growing understanding of a highly complex phenomenon. It should not be used as an excuse to defer development of research-based policies and practices. Yes, we do need clear research evidence on the global-multidimensional form debate, for example, but until it is forthcoming we can make informed choices in light of the potential ramifications these researchers have spelled out.

Moreover, as Marsh and Dunkin point out (page 311), not all studies have been of exemplary quality, but much of the work, like that which appears in this volume, is first rate. This is good science and those still contending that the artistic, ephemeral, and dynamic elements of teaching preclude its measurement are mistaken.

In fact, I will offer a radical conclusion. Done correctly, the evaluation of instruction is more sophisticated, objective, and accurate than our assessment of research productivity. There we measure by counting, always assuming that more is better, and we use as criteria of excellence the subjectively determined reputation of journal publications.

Regrettably, the policies and practices used to evaluate teaching do not regularly reflect what the research calls for and so too often contribute to the problem, when they could be part of an enhanced appreciation of and respect for effective teaching. Reviewing and revising our instructional evaluation policies and practices could contribute concretely to the current interest in undergraduate teaching. It would stand as substantive proof that teaching is important, and that we care enough to assess it with the best methods possible.

✳ ✳ ✳ ✳ ✳

"Effective Teaching Behaviors in the College Classroom"
by Harry G. Murray

Summary

Some simple yet profound assumptions ground Murray's orientation to effective teaching. He proposes that when the agenda is improvement we need to move away from highly inferential depictions of effectiveness to the concrete realities of behaviors. The latter—low-inference teaching behaviors—are concrete actions that observers can easily see and record.

In both observational and experimental studies, these behaviors have been shown to make a difference in student attitudes, in how well they learn course content, and in their motivation for subsequent learning. Behaviors in three areas—enthusiasm/expressiveness, clarity of explanation, and rapport/interaction—seem to be the most strongly related to changes in attitudes learning and motivation. Samples of low-inference behaviors in each of the categories include: "gestures with arms and hands," "signals the transition from one topic to the next," and "addresses individual students by name."

Implications

Murray addresses the issue of implications throughout his chapter. What follows here builds on and elaborates what he identifies as the pragmatic applications of this research.

For instructional improvement: As Murray notes (page 172 and page 195) the emphasis on behaviors has potent implications for instructional improvement whether those efforts are at the behest of the faculty member or under the direction of a faculty developer. The high inference descriptions of instructional effectiveness tend to focus on abstract characteristics often inextricably linked with what the teacher "is," e.g., enthusiastic, organized, and clear. In this case, the improvement message can be no more specific than "be enthusiastic, be organized, and be clear," which can sound like daunting tasks to teachers who does not perceive themselves as any of those things.

However, once the focus changes to behaviors, the advice gains power by virtue of being concrete (move around the room more, write out key points, use more examples) and of being "do-able." It doesn't take a Ph.D. to put a skeleton outline on the side of a board. Murray does point out (page 195) that not all behaviors are easily implementable and that effective instruction is indeed more than a set of concrete actions, but caveats accepted, the specifics of this research make the improvement agenda a much more manageable proposition.

For faculty: Research like this deals effectively with the all too common faculty (and sometimes administrative) assumption that teaching is a "gift", some sort of given "natural ability" that remains basically impervious to outside interventions. Often the thinking is bipolar; one is a "born" teacher or one is not, once again making the matter more or less beyond control. These mystical orientations to teaching are difficult to sustain in light of observable behaviors, any number of which are easily acquirable.

For administrators: Several important orientations to evaluation and improvement follow naturally from this work. First, efforts to improve need not necessarily rest on premises of remediation and deficiency. Murray's work ties these teaching behaviors to important learning outcomes involving content competence as well as positive motivational and attitudinal changes. Teachers then improve because of interest in and commitment to better learning. Their motivation becomes more intrinsic and less extrinsic.

Second, this work suggests something about the context in which efforts to improve may need to occur. To develop teaching skills vis-a-vis these behaviors requires practice, the opportunity to reflect, to solicit feedback, and to revise. At least initially, skills develop better in a formative, constructive environment.

Unfortunately, many current efforts to improve occur in the highly evaluative context already discussed. Faculty are prodded into improvement as a consequence of low student evaluations. They are motivated by little more than the need to get those ratings up. End-of-course summative assessments loom as an onerous conclusion to many courses, sometimes stifling innovation and change. Again, the argument for clearer differentiation between efforts to evaluate and efforts to improve needs to be made. Faculty ought to have the opportunity to try out low-inference behaviors. Some will work well, some will not, and others may need to be adapted. They all need to be tested in an environment that encourages faculty to experiment. The courage and sense of adventure experimentation requires is difficult to summon when one is fearful of evaluative outcomes.

✳ ✳ ✳ ✳ ✳

"Instructional Interventions: A Review of the Literature on Efforts to Improve Instruction"
by Maryellen Weimer and Lisa Firing Lenze

Summary

Five "instructional interventions" or methods commonly used in instructional improvement efforts are the focus of this review. Modeled after and built on a review of literature in this area completed ten years earlier (Levinson-Rose and Menges, 1981), this review considers five such interventions: 1) workshops, seminars, and programs, 2) consultation, 3) grants for instructional improvement projects, 4) resource material, and 5) colleagues helping colleagues.

Evidence cited in the review verifies the extent of use for all these interventions, with workshop programming and consultation the most commonly used according to the data. Workshops vary in the topics they cover, the instructional methods used to present the material and in duration. Consultation as reported in the research reviewed here generally occurs when an instructional development professional and the faculty member go over students' ratings, or discuss videotaped or actual instructional observation or some other general teaching issue. In addition, the review points to an instructional development practice that has gained acceptance during the past ten years—targeting certain faculty groups (like new faculty and TA's) for intervention.

Despite their widespread use, this review (like its predecessor) finds an alarming lack of evidence as to the impact and effectiveness of the interventions, particularly on students in terms of learning outcomes. Workshops, for example, have not been regularly or systematically linked to more or better learning by empirical measures, nor is there much empirical evidence that they change teaching behavior in any observable way. There is evidence that in the opinion of faculty participants they do have instructional impact, but the authors of this and the previous review worry that the most widely used intervention is the least evaluated.

The best empirical evidence for any intervention is that summoned on behalf of consultation over student ratings. The discussion of rating results by a consultant and faculty member has been shown to have a significant and positive impact on subsequent ratings that is sustained over time. This review and the Marsh and Dunkin review are duplicative in their coverage of this topic.

It is important to note that evidence does not disconfirm the effectiveness of the interventions. Studies do not prove that resource materials and/or instructional grants, for example, have *negative* effects. Rather, it is a case of no or little significant research being done on the ways we most frequently seek to improve instruction.

Implications

For researchers: Despite the focus of this chapter on the implications of research for practice, this review spells out the need for more research so convincingly that it cannot be ignored. The need is for more quantity, for research of more sophisticated design, for different kinds of inquiry, and for research grounded in conceptual frameworks and built on theoretical foundations.

This is not the first time the call has gone out. Will it be answered? Experience in the field makes it difficult not to be cynical. Those who do research are often just as uninformed and unresponsive to the needs of practitioners as practitioners are to relevant research findings. And even more discouraging than the lack of information is that, on both sides, ignorance is all too often accompanied by lack of respect.

As the authors note, our knowledge base in higher education (and elsewhere) continues to be hurt by the separation of research and practice. Trying to assign blame will not move us past the problem to solutions. The responsibility for establishing connections is a shared one. Researchers who wonder why their findings have so little impact on practice need to look at and be concerned with the relevance of research to those at the policy and implementation level. Those who make policy and implement programs should not tolerate uninformed and nonreflective practice.

For those who practice: There are important implications in this work for faculty developers. First, the choice of intervention ought to be informed, at least to some degree, by the research base on which it rests. The choice ought to rest much less on tradition and convention (what it is developers are expected to do), consequently decreasing the number of workshops offered and increasing the amount of consultation available.

Second, the continuing lack of research implies a responsibility on the part of developers to be more assessment-minded in their own work. Those who run faculty development centers, often on shoestring budgets and without enough staff, cannot be expected to conduct complex empirical inquires on the side, but they must use evaluative techniques that go beyond asking participants if they "liked" an intervention and "felt" it had impact. The lack of evidence linking intervention to change makes faculty development efforts vulnerable, especially in light of continuing rampant budget cutting and "restructuring." Both student instructional rating programs and faculty development centers need to better demonstrate how, why, and under what terms they make a difference.

✳ ✳ ✳ ✳ ✳

"A Motivational Analysis of Academic Life in College"
by Martin V. Covington

"Turning Work into Play: The Nature and Nurturing of Intrinsic Task Engagement"
by Martin V. Covington and Sonja Wiedenhaupt

Summary

Covington, with a number of different collaborators, has been studying student motivation since the mid 1970s. Out of this work comes a clearer understanding of what motivation is and how it affects college students. Covington shows how the traditional view of motives-as-drives sets up competitive climates where success and failure become inextricably linked to notions of ability. He proposes motives-as-goals as an alternative with "incentives that draw, not drive, individuals to action." (page 84)

Central to understanding the case against the traditional view is Covington's work that establishes "the importance of ability perceptions among college students as the most salient aspect of their academic self-definition." (page 69) In a 1984 study (completed with C. L. Omelich), students were asked to rate their ability to deal with the content in a course taken the previous semester, to estimate how hard they had worked, and to judge how much positive self-regard they enjoyed as a student. They reported their course grade as well. "By far the most important contributor to feelings of self-regard were self-estimates of ability, a factor which accounted for more than 50 percent of the variance." (page 69). Course grade and the amount of effort expended were a distant second and third.

With self-estimates of ability that important, it is easy to see why failure experiences have profound effects on students. To fail repeatedly is to confirm incompetence and the absence of ability. Consequently some students create elaborate contrivances to avoid that conclusion. They may procrastinate, writing an entire paper the night before it is due. A low grade results not because they lack the ability to write a term paper but because they didn't devote enough time to the assignment.

In his own work as well as in the work of others, Covington finds evidence of four groups of students who can be categorized by their response to failure. He labels them; failure-avoiding students, overstriving students, failure-accepting students, and success-oriented students.

Failure-avoiding students harbor serious doubts about their abilities and as a consequence work hard to avoid personal blame for failure. "I'd be doing better in this course if the teacher wasn't so bad." "I don't really care about these required classes. They aren't in my major." Covington reports that these students were often unprepared "even though on average they spent as much or more time studying (or at least going through the motions) as did success-oriented students." (page 78) The problem: they are burdened by pervasive feelings of self-doubt.

Overstriving students are intriguing. They do have good study skills and high ability, but are also plagued with relentless self-doubt. These students compensate by studying more. They dare not procrastinate. Tension mounts during exams, often causing these students to go blank, momentarily forgetting what they have painstakingly learned. They covet A's, unconsciously hoping that one more will settle the issue of ability.

Failure-accepting students have more or less given up. They are resigned to their fate. This pattern of behavior illustrates a psychological state known as "learned helplessness," which is characterized by a loss of hope and of the will to act. These students believe that no matter how hard they try, failure is the inevitable outcome.

Success-oriented students have confidence and good study skills and therefore experience comparatively little anxiety over their ability.

"The boundaries between groups are intended to be semipermeable, reflecting the fact that in real life students are often in flux and transition." (page 81) So long as their beliefs about their perceived incompetence have not crystallized students will continue to try.

It is easy to see how the highly competitive character of American higher education plays into this performance mode, where what motivates students is the drive to achieve for the sake of self-worth. Covington see that as problematic. "The real threat to learning occurs whenever the individual's sense of worth becomes tied to the ability to achieve competitively." He proposes an alternative basis for rewarding behavior, "one that shifts the payoff away from being competitive to becoming competent." (page 84) He describes (pages 85-86) how assignments, for example, might be designed so that they engage (motivate) students to reach for goals. The suggestions are concrete and highly contrastive to most of the work students are asked to complete.

Despite this proposal for a somewhat radical restructuring of the college classroom environment, Covington and Wiedenhaupt understand that "competitive grading is here to stay." (page 102) In their second chapter they focus on research that explores whether it is possible to involve student intrinsically in the highly extrinsic competitive reality of higher education. Based on results from several inquires, they find that "intrinsic motives, at least those associated with achieving a sense of mastery and the expression of personal interest, can emerge spontaneously and operate largely unfettered for most students in an achievement dominated by extrinsically driven rewards." (page 106)

They also explore the impact of novel tasks (like having students design a toy or game that will stimulate intellectual growth as defined by Piaget) and organizing learning around students' interests as ways of engaging intrinsic motivation. They found that both worked effectively, precipitating this more general conclusion that "students will gladly undertake academic work apart from any grade they might receive so long as it is seen as meaningful and valued." (page 112) Said even more succinctly, "grades need be only as important as instructors choose them to be." (page 112) "…performance meets or surpasses the prevailing (or absolute) standards of excellence." (page 86)

Implications

For students: Students would benefit enormously by knowing about this work. Much like faculty, students are often unaware of how they learn, what motivates them, and how that motivation may affect them. The behaviors Covington describes, such as procrastination, blaming others (like the teacher), or blaming things (like the test) for less than the desired performance are easily observed in virtually any student group. Equally observable is the palpable anxiety present in almost every class on exam day. Most students find the grade-getting game enormously stressful and ought to be taught that they may be playing a role in raising the stakes.

How will students find out about this work? They probably will not, unless faculty assume some responsibility for teaching students how they learn. Is that an implication of this research? Not directly, but for too long faculty have focused exclusively on transferring the content of a discipline, on the no longer valid assumption that college is the time for students to learn everything they need to know about a field. Knowledge is expanding too fast and technology has made information so accessible that instruction now ought to focus on helping students to develop sophisticated learning skills. This is not a call for content-free courses, but a plea for an orientation to teaching and learning that views the content as the means to teach skills, not an end in itself.

For faculty: This work has several important implications for faculty. The first is a clear-cut call to examine course-grading policies and practices in light of their impact on classroom environments and their effects on student motivation. Do students in a course regularly procrastinate? When they come to discuss a poor performance, do they blame external forces? Do they believe their efforts, or can faculty show that good study habits make a difference? Might some of Covington's findings explain the behaviors observed? Is the course- grading policy contributing to the problem?

Obviously the faculty response needs to be a measured one. Grades cannot be abandoned or otherwise discounted. They continue to provide or bar access to some of the most significant professional opportunities in our society—medical school, law school, graduate school, and various other advanced professional educational opportunities. They must remain meaningful measures of what a student knows and is able to do as a consequence of a given course.

Grades undoubtedly count for too much, but that is not the specific problem uncovered by this research. It is the competitive environment in which they are awarded. Students are pitted against, compared with, and measured by other students. Although a number of faculty have abandoned grading by a strict curve with its assumption of performance at all grade levels, many do still use a "modified curve" in which cutoff points are "adjusted" (maybe fewer F's than A's) in response to class performance and in which all the competitive consequences of concern to Covington still remain.

Our grading policies and practices signify an enormously complex array of interrelated factors. For example, despite the fact students are graded competitively, grade inflation exists. Course, class, and college GPAs have risen (as have high school grades) while at the same time SAT scores have declined. And while many college teachers may be giving higher grades, few admit to doing so. The public stance of faculty is strongly against inflated grades. To have a disproportionately high number of A's and B's in a course is *not* taken as a sign of successful teaching or much learning. Rather it is viewed with suspicion and the pretty strong hunch that this is a teacher who has abandoned standards and offers a course without rigor.

On the other hand, a proportionately balanced number of A's, B's, C's and so on may be taken as a sign of integrity and rigor. However, oftentimes perverse ways of thinking and acting are used to achieve the balance. Excessively difficult exams can and do squelch grade inflation. Low class averages (say 30 out of 100 points) may reflect standards but equally troubling is the fact that despite a good faith effort to teach, more than half the students have failed. It seems enormously myopic and elitist to see that only as an indication of weak students and not an indictment of instructional method.

To conclude, this work not only calls for a change in grading policies and practices, it requires a change in the way we think about grades—made all the more important in light of the kinds of students now entering our colleges and universities. Most of us who teach could easily verify a decline in the number of *success-oriented students* present in our classrooms and an increase in *failure-avoiding* and *failure-accepting students*. One might surmise that students in the last two categories are more likely to be our at-risk populations—first generation college students, those from underrepresented groups, those not well-prepared, those having to work to pay for college—those from segments of our society with absolutely the most to gain from attending college—those for whom a college education can literally mean a different quality of life. If our grading policies and practices systematically and differentially exclude these students from majors, programs, and degrees, that has ethical ramifications that should shake us to our very roots. The Covington research raises questions about who and how many students benefit from our competitive, ability-oriented assessments of performance. His practical suggestions on assignment design give us a concrete place to start anew. And his encouraging findings about intrinsic motivation give us reasons to try.

✳ ✳ ✳ ✳ ✳

"Perceived Control in College Students: Implications for Instruction in Higher Education"
by Raymond P. Perry

Summary

Perceived control refers to an "individual's perceived capacity to influence and to predict events in the environment." (page 12) It is *perceived* because, "some people believe they possess a greater capacity to influence and to predict events than they have in reality, while others believe they have less capacity than they actually have." (page 12**0**) Perry believes, and his work offers support, that perceived control plays "a pivotal role in students' educational attainment, possibly being as important as intelligence, social class, or discipline knowledge." (page 13)

In the academic context it works something like this: Students who believe that diligent study, focused attention, and personal application, among other things, improve their performance are at the "mastery" end of the perceived control continuum. At the "helplessness" end are students with low perceived control who believe that much of what happens to them is the result of luck or factors external to them over which they have no control (like how hard the teacher decides to make the test).

Perry began his work interested in the potential interaction between students' perceived control and instruction. "Does perceived control in college students influence performance differently depending on the quality of instruction they receive? What teaching methods are likely to increase students' mastery of course content given pre-existing levels of perceived control?" (page 14)

After reviewing the research on the dimensions of effective teaching, Perry chose to relate perceived control to instructor expressiveness, a dimension believed to "prime central information processing activities." (page 33) When teachers move about and vary their voice intonation, for example, they help students to selectively attend more effectively.

What he found is quite surprising: "Helpless students [those who experience a loss of control] performed no better with an expressive than with an unexpressive teacher." (page 33) In other words, this proven dimension of effective instruction had no impact on students who lacked a belief in their own ability to succeed.

Perry and various colleagues confirmed and manipulated feedback given to students with low and high levels of perceived control. They also aimed to discover ways the powerful influence of perceived control (particularly in helpless students) might be mitigated.

Among the most useful of the findings coming out of this work is the potential of attributional retraining to change students' levels of perceived control. This training involves a direct, personalized intervention that seeks to replace certain dysfunctional attributions, like a belief that test failures are caused by lack of ability rather than lack of effort. Students with low levels of perceived control who received the training did perform better on achievement tests than those who received no training.

The continuing research work also documented that when students' perception was that they had some control over test performances, effective teaching did enhance achievement. Additionally, Perry discovered the existence of a "buffer effect" involving certain cognitive schemata that appear to protect some students against the negative consequences of a loss of control. Students at the mastery ends of the perceived control continuum recovered quite quickly and efficiently even they were told that they had failed (regardless of how well they had in fact done).

Implications

For students: As with other research in this volume, students stand only to gain from knowledge of what Perry and his colleagues have discovered. Often students know that their behaviors are counterproductive. When asked in an office consultation what they think they might do to improve test performance, they speak against procrastination (for example) and indicate that they will try to study more regularly, not just prior to the exam. The proclivity to procrastinate could better be controlled by deeper understanding of some of the complicated motivations that may in fact be behind the behavior. Students as well as faculty need to learn about learning in terms of the various factors that influence academic achievement.

For faculty and administrators: These findings raise a number of questions about instructional practices related to our methods of evaluating students and delivering feedback on their performance. Students are moved to the helplessness end of the perceived control continuum by ambiguous assessment policies and practices. Anytime students do not clearly understand how their knowledge will be assessed, or take an exam with material they never expected to see, or receive an unexpected grade or one where no rationale is provided, their sense of perceived control is diminished. Here's a class where the time and effort put in just don't result in better grades—it's a matter of luck, having by accident decided to study the right things.

The implications involve practices like sharing sample exam questions with students before the exam, taking class time to equip students with the skills they need to differentiate levels of content and thereby make informed choices about what to study, making grading criteria for the course explicit, and engaging students in self-assessment activities that help them to more accurately predict their mastery of the material.

What of course worries faculty is the potential of practices like these to compromise academic standards. And it is true, one *can* handle assessment tasks so that all students do well. One *can* teach to the test, give grades that do not accurately differentiate levels of learning and never push students to excel. But this is one end of the continuum. Just as extreme and wrong are the practices at the other end that shroud grading criteria, testing methods, and content in mystery. Particularly worrisome are the assumptions of standards equated with this extreme position. Hard courses are good and in hard courses lots of students fail. That's desirable because a discipline must have its standards. The really bright students will figure out how to succeed, and those are the only ones we want in the discipline anyway.

What faculty must seek is a balance between these two positions. The position must recognize that exams and grades are measures of mastery, the means postsecondary educators use to certify levels of learning and knowledge. They must be meaningful to those who use them to determine entrance into graduate school, professional education and employment. But equally necessary is a position that recognizes that we also use exams and grades to *promote* learning, and this research helps us make better decisions as to the design and use of course assessment activities.

Less explicit in this work is a call for rethinking the faculty relationship with students. For a number of years those of us interested in instructional enhancement have been concerned with teaching: the aspects, components, dimensions of it and how those might be reflected in and measured by rating forms, how the dimensions relate to learning outcomes, and how teaching performance might be improved. By no means devaluing the relevance and importance of teaching concerns, this research establishes that for some students, the instructor's effectiveness has no impact; it does not overcome the power of their self-perceptions. What does make a difference is a direct intervention aimed at changing how and to what students attribute their success and failure.

We have known for some time now that the involvement of teachers with students is important, particularly at the beginning of a college experience. Perry's work underscores that importance and would justify faculty learning about their students, spending time talking with them, providing personal and constructive feedback, and moving students toward greater confidence in their own abilities as learners.

This leads quite naturally to the administrative and institutional implications of this work. Faculty cannot be expected to be involved with students when they are teaching large numbers of them. Realistically, however, the current budgetary facts of higher education make small, intimate classes an unaffordable luxury. Perhaps, then, it is smaller classes for some kinds of students (not just the beginning honors students who don't need them for reasons articulated by this research) or at least one small class for every beginning student. And along with the small class must go the incentives and rewards for faculty to get involved with students. Many prefer involvement with their content—it's a lot safer, quieter, and less emotionally demanding.

✳ ✳ ✳ ✳ ✳

"The Matrix Representation System: Orientation, Research, Theory and Application" by Kenneth A. Keiwra

Summary

This work focuses on "representing structural knowledge spatially so that the interrelationships among the ideas—the entire skeleton, the assembled puzzle—are apparent." (page 115) Keiwra objects to text and outline representations because they present information linearly, a single idea at a time, "like bones lined up across the floor. They often separate or conceal important relationships." (page 115)

Kiewra proposes and reports research testing the effectiveness of what he calls the matrix representation system, which displays information hierarchically, sequentially, and in matrix format. Among the advantages of configuring information in this manner are that it presents the information's overriding structure, and that within-topic relations are easily identifiable, as are across-topic relations and within-cell relations.

The matrix representation system facilitates learning because of how it relates to two sequential memory processes necessary for learning: attention and encoding. In terms of attention, the matrix facilitates pattern recognition because the structure of the knowledge is apparent at once. Also important during the attention step is selective attention during which attention is focused on a few ideas. A matrix, because it contains subsets, directs attention better than text material.

As for encoding, organization and integration are the key components. The purpose of a matrix is to organize information and help learners to connect ideas. The matrix supports integration in two ways: first, new information is assimilated more easily when an organized structure exists in the memory; and second, integration occurs when a completed matrix extends previously acquired knowledge and matrix representations can be easily modified.

In the review of research Kiewra summarizes work on matrices in terms of their effectiveness during the attention and encoding processes. As for attention, a variety of studies document that "spatial representations serve an attention focusing function relative to text or underlined text. They are, however, no more effective than outlines that select and display the same information. In terms of search time, however, a matrix representation is attended to more rapidly than an outline or text." (page 134)

The research on encoding, the process whereby new information is stored in memory, reviews how matrix representations affect memory for factual details, relational learning, written discourse, and problem solving. In all four cases, the research shows clear advantages to matrix representation based on a variety of outcomes and measures.

Implications

For students and faculty: Keiwra concludes the chapter with concrete advice on how to use matrix representations to help students acquire lecture and text information, and to aid in concept learning, problem solving and critical thinking, and writing. He also proposes how students can be taught to construct the matrix representations. In all categories the suggestions are detailed and specific. They are clearly written and do not need to be reformulated here.

The larger issue is one already visited in the context of implications of the work on students' perceived control and motivation. The work here makes clear there are preferred ways of learning—preferred because of their effects on memory and learning. It means we can teach students learning skills that will stand them in good stead after their college experience. The question is whether we will release our grip on course content enough to allow "coverage" of some of these process issues.

Kiewra proposes one solution: courses on study skills. But he notes they have one inherent flaw: they separate "the strategy from the content areas where it is applicable. The best place for study skills instruction is within the content areas." (page 150) He offers a metaphor that overcomes pitting course content against learning processes:

> The process of embedding strategy instruction into content instruction resembles that used by an experienced tradesperson who is training an apprentice. While the tradesperson works, he/she speaks aloud so that personal thoughts and actions become public and explicit for the watchful apprentice. (page 151)

The issues are probably more political than this. Coverage stands for rigor, standards, and reputation, but for the faculty member committed to doing what's possible to enhance student learning skills, the advice represents useful compromise.

Conclusion

After summarizing this research and thinking about it in terms of implications, are there any general conclusions, assessments, and observations that might be offered? I see three.

First, this research calls clearly for a greater emphasis on the *processes* inherently a part of both teaching and learning. In our practice to date we regularly view teaching concerns as secondary to content issues. It is always interesting to me when I ask faculty in workshops to identify the ingredients or dimensions of effective instruction, that the one almost always mentioned first is the content competence of the instructor. Our continuing lack of instructional training in graduate school experiences saturated in disciplinary content socializes us away from teaching concerns. Even the fact that we "train" teaching assistants how to teach, often in a brief orientation activity, further underscores the mistaken notion that teaching processes are irrelevant and unnecessary. The old adage may not be as publicly supported as it once was, but by our actions we continue to assume, "if you know it, you can teach it."

Equally absent in our instructional practice is an understanding of how students (particularly those in college today) learn. As this research so ably demonstrates, we have much to learn. And what this research teaches us first, is that we need to devote educational time to the development of learning skills. We can no longer assume that students learn to learn by osmosis, just by being in the presence of our content. Learning skills need to be taught explicitly, which brings us back to the content and our proclivity to cover it. The assumption of coverage must be challenged; more is not always better, there is too much any way and much of what there is will change during the lifetimes of our college students. The call is not for content-free courses, but courses that better balance content and process objectives.

A deeper and more complete understanding of how students learn, again as demonstrated by work in this volume, leads inevitably to a rethinking and revision of common instructional policies and practices; like assignment design, like exam objectives, and like grading standards and practices. The call here is not to abandon, but to revise and refocus what we do in light of the learning needs of our students.

The second observation has to do with the uneven distribution of research work across the areas of interest and issues of concern to those of us in the field. The clearest examples in this volume involve the work on summative student ratings and the research on instructional interventions. Although not all the research questions have been answered with regard to ratings, and some of the answers do not agree, one would be hard pressed to leave this work not knowing a lot about the design of quality rating assessment programs. Compare that with what can be concluded about interventions aimed at changing instructional quality. Could you leave work reported in this volume able to select, design and implement a set of instructional development activities with known impacts on teaching and learning?

The uneven distribution is at the same time a blessing and a curse. The blessing is the rigor, the complexity, and the detail. It is science to be proud of—science motivated to get to the bottom of an issue and understand it fully. The curse is the exclusion of other topics, the seeming inability of social science to decide when there's enough and move on. The uneven coverage relates to and is a function of the third conclusion.

Research does not inform practice, and those who practice do not inform research. The proverbial great gulf exists with pundits on either side pointing at each other. The vast majority of students, faculty, and administrators could not pass even an elementary quiz on the content of this volume, and I will venture, with less certainty since I am more on the practice side, that a vast majority of researchers could not list accurately the five most compelling questions of faculty who teach beginning students, of faculty about to be evaluated for the first time, or of administrators interested in creating climates for learning. And as noted, if it were just a question of ignorance, we might be able to overcome that, but often the ignorance is accompanied with a lack of respect. How sad, since both the work of research and practice bear consequences resulting from their suspicious separation.

Trying to assess who's to blame will not motivate either side to reach out. Let me offer two suggestions that might. First, both sides must realize that a role for translators exists. Researchers cannot be expected to speak or write the language of practice, but they must release their work to those who can and help them communicate the findings with integrity. Those who practice must be encouraged and helped to think about issues as research questions. I overhead a researcher leaving a town meeting discussion of assessment issues say to a colleague, "Well, the group generated 30 questions. I don't think more than two are researchable."

And those of us in the middle with a commitment to both camps must be recognized as doing legitimate work—scholarship, if you please. To do it well requires intellectual muscle, the opportunity to publish, and the chance for tenure and promotion.

Secondly, we reach out to one another when we realize that good work in both camps values teaching and learning. The issues of recognition and reward are real ones, but this valuing is a larger conception. It means those of us who study teaching and learning and those of us who do it see the intellectual intrigue as inherently a part of the phenomenon. Research like that reported on in this volume captures the complexity and stands in stark contrast to the tips, tricks, and techniques mentality that sees teaching and learning only in terms of the skills associated with their execution. Behind the nuts and bolts lies a vast domain of knowledge to be mapped by those who research and to be traveled by those who practice. Let us both recognize that we journey in the same land.

References

Aleamoni, L. (1987). Student rating myths versus research facts. *Journal of Personnel Evaluation in Education* 1: 111-119.

Braskamp, L. A., Brandenburg, D. C., and Ory, J. C. (1985). *Evaluating Teaching Effectiveness: A Practical Guide*. Beverly Hills, CA: Sage.

Braskamp, L. A., and Ory, J. C. (1994). *Assessing Faculty Work*. San Francisco: Jossey-Bass.

Cashin, W. E. (1988). *Student ratings of teaching: A summary of the research* (IDEA Paper No. 20). Manhattan, KS: Kansas State University, Center for Faculty Evaluation and Development.

Centra, J. A. (1979). *Determining Faculty Effectiveness*. San Francisco: Jossey-Bass.

Centra, J. A. (1993). *Reflective Faculty Evaluation*. San Francisco: Jossey-Bass.

Fairweather, J. S. (1993). *Teaching, Research and Faculty Rewards: A Summary of the Research Findings of the Faculty Profile Project*. The Pennsylvania State University: National Center on Postsecondary Teaching, Learning and Assessment.

Levinson-Rose, J., and Menges, R. F. (1981). Improving college teaching: A critical review of research. *Review of Educational Research* 51(3): 403-434.

McKeachie, W. J. (1979). Student ratings of faculty: A reprise. *Academe* 65: 384-97.

Miller, R. (1975). *Developing Programs for Faculty Evaluation*. San Francisco: Jossey-Bass.

Seldin, P. (1985). *Changing Practices in Faculty Evaluation*. San Francisco: Jossey-Bass.

Weimer, M. (1990). *Improving College Teaching*. San Francisco: Jossey-Bass.

Author Index

Abbott, B. 210
Abbott, R. D. 233
Abrahams, S. 80, 96
Abrami, P. C. 15, 25, 39, 50, 191, 193, 244,
    247, 263, 265, 267, 269, 270, 272, 280, 287,
    291, 292, 299, 302, 308, 309, 322, 332, 333,
    335, 337, 338, 340, 341, 342, 343, 345, 346,
    347, 348, 349, 350, 352, 370, 374, 375, 378,
    398
Abramson, L. Y. 79, 92
Abt, C. C. 86, 92
Aleamoni, L. M. 219, 220, 242, 276, 284, 303, 370,
    371, 372, 373, 415
Alexander, P. A. 112
Ames, C. 64, 86, 87, 90, 92
Ames, R. 64, 87, 92
Amiran, M. R. 138, 150
Andersen, J. F. 191, 192
Anderson, D. S. 55
Anderson, J. G. 77
Anderson, N. H. 331
Andrews, J. D. W. 187
Annis, L. F. 227
Archer, J. 90
Arkin, R. M. 66
Aronson, E. 56
Ashby, J. D. 73
Atkinson, J. W. 63, 64, 73
Aubrect, J. D. 284, 290
Austin, A. E. 230

Baerwaldt, J. W. 366
Bailey, M. 403
Bamberg, B. 140
Bandura A. 18, 19, 20, 159
Barker, D. G. 381
Barnard, J. W. 92
Barnes, C. P. 380
Barnes, J. 12, 57, 259
Barrick, M. R. 399
Basow, S. A. 295

Batista, E. E. 286, 294, 295
Battle, E. S. 66
Bauer, G. 210
Baxter Magolda, M. B. 380
Beatty, W. W. 244, 377
Becker, S. L. 187
Beery, R. G. 68, 70, 72, 102
Beissner, K. 115
Belz, D. 66
Benton 140, 150
Benton, S. E. 264, 377
Benton, S. L. 151
Berger, W. G. 377
Berglas, S. 70
Berman, J. 237
Bess, J. L. 237
Bezdek, W. E. 175, 186, 190, 191, 377
Biddle, B. J. 55, 171
Biglan, A. 297
Birney, R. C. 68, 72, 397
Blackburn, R. T. 276, 280, 281
Bland, C. 210
Block, J. H. 87
Bloom, B. S. 283, 324
Boggiano, A. K. 93
Boice, R. 4, 7, 229, 231, 403
Boli, J. 73
Bolles, R. C. 63, 84
Bolton, B. 185, 377
Bonge, D. 185, 377
Bonwell, C. 230
Border, L. 225
Borich, G. D. 350
Boud, D. 215
Bovenmeyer Lewis, A. 141
Bowen, H. R. 380
Bracht, G. H. 16
Brady, P. J. 399
Brainerd, C. J. 267
Brandenburg, D. C. 241, 242, 261, 273, 276, 277,
    284, 286, 294, 295, 296, 303, 308, 369, 415

Braskamp, L. A. 241, 242, 261, 262, 273, 276, 277, 284, 295, 296, 303, 308, 369, 377, 415
Bray, J. H. 286
Breen, L. J. 309
Brehm, J. W. 18, 19, 159
Brinko, K. T. 305, 307, 370
Brookfield, S. 251
Brooks, T. E. 381
Brophy, J. E. 21, 37, 171, 202
Brown, D. L. 295
Brown, G. A. 200, 211, 214
Brown, J. 67, 69
Browne, M. N. 212, 214, 232
Bryant, B. 87
Bryson, R. 377
Buchtel, F. S. 293, 373
Burdick, H. 68, 72
Burgess, G. G. 276, 377, 400
Burns, R. B. 87
Burton, D. 72
Butler, R. 88

Campbell, D. N. 89, 337
Campbell, D. T. 29, 286, 336
Campbell, J. 202
Carliner, G. 268, 269
Carlsmith, J. M. 56
Carnegie Foundation for the Advancement of Teaching 61, 93
Carroll, J. G. 233, 234
Carse, J. P. 93
Carver, C. S. 19, 78, 80, 159, 160
Cashin, W. E. 242, 263, 284, 290, 296, 303, 311, 335, 368, 369, 372, 373, 412, 415
Caulley, D. 377
Centra, J. A. 4, 25, 26, 209, 215, 218, 221, 224, 226, 242, 255, 276, 277, 281, 284, 288, 290, 294, 295, 296, 303, 308, 309, 311, 369, 377, 381, 385, 415
Chambers, B. 364
Chance, J. E. 20
Chase, C. I. 377
Check, J. 59
Chickering, A. W. 380
Christal, R. E. 398
Christian, D. 138, 139, 140
Clark, B. R. 72
Clark, D. C. 277
Clark, M. J. 276, 280
Clarkson, P. C. 249
Clegg, V. L. 296, 373

Coats, W. D. 189, 190
Cobb, E. B. 381
Cohen, A. 381
Cohen, J. 56, 152
Cohen, P. A. 26, 28, 39, 87, 122, 176, 185, 199, 226, 242, 263, 264, 265, 266, 267, 268, 269, 270, 272, 276, 277, 287, 305, 338, 341, 342, 343, 344, 345, 346, 348, 370, 375, 378
Cohen, S. H. 377
Coleman, J. S. 173, 309
Collins, J. R. 88
Combs, A. 64, 102, 193, 280
Combs, N. 379
Connell, J. P. 65
Conway, C. G. 255, 263, 274, 277, 278, 279, 280, 340
Cook, L. 365
Cook, R. 66
Cook, T. D. 29
Cooley, W. W. 265
Cooper, H. M. 65
Cooper, J. 333
Cooper, S. 292
Cooper, T. L. 288
Coopersmith, S. 82
Costin, F. 2, 242, 284, 369, 377
Covington, M. V. 20, 61, 64, 66, 67, 68, 69, 70, 71, 74, 76, 77, 79, 80, 82, 84, 87, 88, 102, 103, 104, 105, 107, 157
Cox, D. J. 22
Coyne, J. C. 79, 80
Crandall, V. C. 13, 22, 23
Crandall, V. J. 13, 22, 23
Cranton, P. A. 179, 180, 277, 335
Creech, F. R. 284, 288, 294, 295, 296, 309
Crichton, L. I. 377
Crittenden, K. S. 380
Crockenberg, S. 87
Cronbach, L. J. 16, 243
Cross, D. R. 126
Cruickshank, D. R. 194
Csikszentmihalyi, M. 94
Culler, R. E. 81
Cuseo, J. 365
Cushman, H. R. 178, 186, 202

Dahllof, U. 24, 37, 155
Daines, J. 211, 214
Dalgaard, K. A. 219
Dansereau, D. F. 126

d'Apollonia, S. 244, 247, 263, 265, 267, 269, 270, 272, 287, 322, 332, 333, 338, 342, 343, 345, 347, 348, 349, 350, 352, 374, 375, 378, 398
Davidson, W. 83
Davies, I. K. 406
Davis, K. E . 54
Day, R. S. 138, 146
De Charms, R. 18, 159
Deci, E. L. 88, 101
Deffenbacher, J. L. 81
De Groot, E. V. 65, 98
de Lange Jzn, J. 89
Della-Piana, G. 377
Dembo, M. H. 13, 64
Dembo, T. 97
Dennison, R. 140, 150
DeSimone, C. 364
Detchon, C. S. 66
Deutsch, M. 89, 102
De Volder, M. 65, 95
Dewey, J. 91
de Wolf, W. A. 242, 284
Dickens, W. J. 21, 22, 25, 38, 39, 42, 43, 51, 53, 55, 158, 291, 301
Dickerson, A. D. 381
Dienst, E. R. 244, 302
Diggory, J. C. 85
Distenfeld, M. S. 295
Domino, G. 17
Donnelly, F. A. 299, 311
Dowaliby, F. J. 17
Dowell, D. A. 266, 269, 342, 343
Downey, R. G. 335, 374
Doyle, K. O., Jr. 25, 37, 39, 241, 242, 265, 276, 283, 332, 369, 377, 380
Doyle, W. 56
Drucker, A. J. 255
Dubin, R. 397
Dubin, S. S. 251
Du Bois, N. F. 115, 122, 125, 130, 135, 138, 139, 140
Dukes, R. L. 295, 296
Dunkin, M. J. 12, 171, 241, 277, 281, 304, 305, 331, 332, 339, 341, 369, 370, 372, 373, 374, 378, 379, 397, 413
Dweck, C. S. 13, 18, 50, 51, 64, 83, 159

Eble, K. 223
Eccles, J. 65
Edgerton, R. 385

Eifferman, R. R. 95
Eison, J. A. 229, 230, 232
Elliott, D. N. 377, 400
Ellis, A. 71, 72
Ellis, N. R. 377
Ellner, C. L. 380
Elton, C. F. 73
Endo, G. T. 377
Enna, B. 83
Erdle, S. 26, 180, 186, 299
Erickson 216, 222, 223, 225
Erickson, G. 210, 216
Eswara, H. S. 68
Etheridge, B. 81
Evans, F. B. 77

Fairweather, J. S. 418
Fattaleh, D. L. 141
Feather, N. T. 73
Feldhusen, J. F. 356, 381
Feldman, K. A. 25, 26, 28, 163, 186, 242, 247, 248, 250, 254, 255, 259, 267, 268, 270, 273, 274, 276, 278, 279, 280, 281, 282, 284, 287, 288, 290, 294, 295, 296, 298, 299, 300, 330, 338, 342, 343, 345, 347, 352, 356, 368, 369, 370, 371, 372, 373, 374, 375, 377, 378, 380, 381, 384, 398, 412, 413
Felker, D. 87
Fernald, P. S. 332
Festinger, L. 64
Fincher, C. 251
Findley, M. J. 65
Fink, L. D. 228
Firth, M. 255
Fisch, L. 225
Flanders, N. A. 187
Fleiner, H. 270, 304, 268, 377
Fletcher, G. 54
Flower, L. S. 149
Folsom, C. H., Jr. 73
Fontaine, G. 67
Forsterling, F. 46
Foster, J. M. 230
Foster, S.F. 367
Frankhouser, W. M. 296
Franklin, J. 306, 335, 373
Frederiksen, N. 88
Freedman, R. D. 372
French-Lazovich, G. 276, 277, 381
Freudenthal, N. R. 231
Frey, P. W. 25, 174, 244, 247, 265, 281, 288, 347,

377
Friedman, M. 212, 214
Frieze, L. 99
Froman, R. D. 197, 199
Furst, N. F. 172, 277, 281, 381

Gage, N. L. 4, 29, 37, 241
Gagné, R. M. 144
Gallini, J. K. 125
Garber, H. 381
Garber, J., 13, 21
Garcia, T. 87
Gardner, J. W. 84
Gaski, J. F. 342
Geis, G. L. 237
Gibbs, L. E. 212, 214
Gibson, S. 13
Gigliotti, R. J. 293, 373
Gil, D. H. 220
Gilmore, G. M. 254, 255, 258
Glanzmann, P. 77
Glass, D. C. 18
Goldberg, L. R. 16, 88
Goldner, N. S. 381
Good, T. L. 29, 37, 171
Good, K. C. 381
Gowin, D. B. 126
Greenberg, P. J. 64
Greene, D. 111
Greenmun, R. 377
Greenough, W. T. 2, 7, 242, 284, 369
Greenwood, G. E. 377
Grouling, T. 286
Grush, J. E. 377
Guthrie, E. R. 57, 276

Hagtvet, K. A. 78
Halliday, M. A. K. 140
Handelsman, M. M. 71
Hansen, D. W. 209, 213, 216, 220, 222, 223, 228, 231
Harackiewicz, J. M. 96
Harari, O. 66
Harlow, J. F. 63
Harris, A. M. 86
Harrison, G. V. 277
Harry, J. 381
Hartley, J. 406
Harvey, J. N. 381
Hasan, R. 140

Hativa, N. 374, 403
Hayes, J. R. 149
Hayton, G. E. 249
Hazelton, A. 377
Hebb, D. O. 63
Heckhausen, H. 66, 68
Hedges, L. V. 346
Heider, F. 54, 82
Heist, P. A. 73
Helling, B. 216
Helmke, A. 53
Hembree, R. 81
Henry, M. 227
Herr, K. U. 210, 212
Hidi, S. 110
Hildebrand, M. 244, 302, 307
Hill, P. W. 350
Hillgarten, W. 179, 180, 277
Hines, C. V. 194
Hocevar, D. 247, 249, 259, 260, 295, 332, 335, 348
Hofeller, M. 366
Hoffman, M. L. 66
Hoffman, R. G. 377
Holahan, C. J. 94
Holland, J. L. 73
Hollandsworth, J. 81
Holley, C. D. 126
Holmes, S. K. 232
Howard, G. S. 255, 263, 269, 274, 277, 278, 279, 280, 286, 288, 291, 340, 342
Howden, J. 364
Hoyt, D. P. 286, 380
Hrabal, V. 66
Huesmann, L. R. 21
Hullfish, G. 91
Hutchings, P. 385
Hwang, Y. 136

Isaacson, R. L. 345

Jacobs, L. C. 306, 309
Jacobsen, R. H. 222, 223, 224
Jacoby, K. E. 87
Jansen, T. 99
Jerusalem, M. 66, 82
Jioubu, R. M. 381
Johnson, D. W. 333
Johnson, R. T. 333
Jonassen, D. H. 115, 116, 124, 125
Jones, B. F.54, 70, 82, 138, 150

Jones, E. E. 54, 70, 82
Jones, H. E. 189, 203

Kane, B. 308
Kane, M. T. 254, 255, 258
Kaplan, R. M. 89
Kassin, S. M. 111
Kasten, E. A. 16
Katchadourian, H. A. 73
Katims, M. 138, 150
Katkovsky, W. E. 13, 22
Katz, J. 227
Keeley, S. M. 212, 214, 232
Keene, J. M., Jr. 377
Kelley, H. H. 54
Kelley, H. P. 381
Kennedy, J. J. 194
Kesler, S. P. 247, 273, 288
Kiewra, K. A.115, 122, 125, 130, 134, 135, 139, 140, 150
Kim, S. 136
King, P. M. 380
Kirkland, K. 81
Kirst, M. 62
Kitchener, K. S. 380
Knapper, C. K. 367
Kobasa, S. C. 20
Kohn, A. 102, 103
Kolbasa, S. C. 19, 159
Konrad, A. C. 209, 216, 218, 220, 222, 225, 228, 231
Koran, M. L. 17
Korn, H. A. 73
Kozma, R. B. 237
Krapp, A. 110
Krathwohl, D. R. 283
Kraus, W. J. 71
Kuhl, J. 18, 22, 80, 159
Kuhlmann, D. 216
Kukla, A. 66, 67, 68
Kulik, C. C. 96, 172
Kulik, J. A. 26, 87, 172, 242, 330, 347, 351, 355
Kulikowich, J. M. 112

Lambiotte, J. G. 126
Land, M. L. 193, 280, 379
Langer, E. J. 18
Langer, J. A. 141
Larkin, J. H. 122, 135
Larson, J. R. 25
Laux, L. 77

Lave, J. 86
Lavelle, T. L. 80
Lawrence, C. 26, 173, 199
Lazarus, R. S. 79
Lefcourt, H. M. 21, 22, 23
Leftwich, W. H. 381
Lens, W. 65
Leonard, D. W. 244, 377
Lepper, M. R. 111
Leppin, A. 66
Leventhal, L. 15, 25, 39, 191, 193, 280, 291, 299, 301, 302, 308, 309, 337, 340, 370, 377
Levin, B. B. 89, 136
Levin, J. R. 136
Levinson-Rose, J. 205, 206, 207, 208, 209, 213, 214, 217, 218, 219, 221, 224, 226, 232, 233, 236, 304, 370, 424
Lewis, K. G. 64, 215
L'Hommedieu, R. 305, 307, 370
Liberty, P. G., Jr. 381
Liebert, R. M. 81
Lin, Y.-G. 241, 262, 308, 309, 366, 377, 403
Lipson, M. Y. 151
Litwin, G. H. 64, 92
Litwin, L. W. 73
Lohnes, P. R. 265
Long, J. E. 214, 219

Maas, J. B. 381
Mackie, K. 251, 252
Maehr, M. L. 101
Magnusson, J.-L. 14, 39, 42, 43, 44, 46, 47, 48, 51, 54, 55, 192, 300
Malone, T. W. 85
Man, F. 66
Manderlink, G. 96
Mandler, G. 81
Mandler, J. 115
Mann, W. 58, 377
Marr, J. 185, 377
Marsh, H. W. 15, 25, 26, 39, 172, 185, 242, 243, 244, 247, 249, 250, 255, 256, 257, 258, 260, 261, 263, 264, 265, 266, 269, 270, 273, 274, 280, 283, 284, 287, 288, 290, 291, 292, 293, 294, 295, 296, 300, 301, 302, 303, 304, 305, 307, 308, 309, 322, 330, 332, 335, 338, 340, 341, 346, 347, 348, 349, 351, 369, 370, 371, 372, 373, 374, 377, 378, 379, 380, 397, 400, 403, 413
Martens, R. 72
Martin, F. D. 377, 400

Maruyama, G. M. 66
Masia, B. B. 283
Maslow, A. H. 276
Matthews, K. A. 19, 45, 159, 160
Maxwell, S. E. 255, 263, 269, 274, 277, 278, 279, 280, 288, 291, 340, 342
Mayer, R. E. 125, 128, 135, 141, 143, 181, 183
McCallum, L. W. 342
McClelland, D. C. 63, 64
McDaniel 381
McDaniel, E. D. 356,
McDonald, F. 17
McDonald, R. 215
McGuinness, C. 142
McKeachie, W. J. 2, 8, 16, 17, 23, 26, 29, 55, 155, 172, 226, 232, 241, 242, 262, 265, 276, 277, 283, 284, 286, 295, 303, 307, 308, 309, 330, 347, 351, 355, 366, 369, 377, 380, 397, 402, 403, 405, 415
McLean, D. F. 197, 199
McLuhan, M. 1
McMahan, I. D. 67
McShane, A. 138, 139, 140
Medley 17
Medley, D. M. 58
Menec, V. H. 156
Menges, R. F. 205, 206, 207, 208, 209, 214, 217, 218, 219, 221, 222, 224, 226, 232, 233, 235, 236, 242, 284, 303, 304, 370, 424
Menges, R. J. 2, 4, 212, 235, 242, 284, 303, 305, 307, 369
Messick, S. 14
Metalsky, G. I. 80
Meyer, B. J. F. 66, 120
Meyer, W.-U. 66, 97
Meyerhoffer, M. 138, 139
Meyers, T. 136
Milholland, J.E. 366
Miller, I. W. 22, 38, 79
Miller, R. 415
Millis, B. J. 226
Mintzes, J. J. 179, 377
Mitchell, H. 377
Mizener, D. A. 340
Moore, R. M. 230
Moore, W. 209, 213, 214, 216, 220, 222, 223, 228, 231
Morgan, M. 111
Morgan, R. D. 66
Morgan, W. D. 377
Morris, L. W. 81

Morsh., J. E. 377, 400
Moses, I. 213, 218
Moulton, R. W. 64, 73
Mueck, R. 365
Murakami, J. 71
Murray, H. G. 24, 26, 37, 173, 180, 182, 183, 185, 186, 188, 191, 193, 194, 198, 199, 207, 216, 217, 218, 220, 242, 257, 262, 277, 284, 298, 299, 303, 304, 337, 369, 377, 378, 397
Musgrave, B. S. 122

Naccarato, R. W. 254, 255, 258
Nadeau, C.G. 367
Naftulin, D. H. 299, 311
Naveh-Benjamin, M. 81
Neal, J. A. 266, 269, 342, 343
Neff, R. A. 232
Neill, N. 367
Nelson, S. 83
Neumann, L. 297
Neumann, Y. 297
Newcomb, T. M. 380
Nicholls, J. G. 64, 83, 85
Nierenberg, R. 68
Nisan, M. 88
Nisbett, R. E. 82
Nolan, C. Y. 276
Norman, W. H. 22, 38, 79
Norman, W. T. 398
Norr, J. L. 380
Novak, J. D. 126
Novick, L. R. 143
Nowicki, S. 22
Nuttin, J. 65
Nyquist, J. D. 210, 215

Okun, M. 251
Olkin, I. 346
Olsen, C. 103
Olson, C. 81
Omelich, C. L. 64, 66, 68, 69, 70, 74, 76, 77, 79, 82, 87, 102, 104, 105, 107, 426
Orpen, C. 377
Ortony, A. 132
Ory, J. C. 241, 242, 261, 262, 273, 276, 277, 284, 295, 296, 303, 308, 369, 415
Osgood, C. E. 331
Osipow, S. H. 73
Overall, J. U. 185, 242, 247, 255, 257, 264, 266, 268, 270, 273, 283, 284, 288, 290, 291, 294, 295,

296, 304, 307, 377
Owen, S. V. 197, 199
Owen, P. H. 381
Owens, R. E. 286

Palmer, J. 268, 269
Parelius, A. P. 72, 95
Parelius, R. J. 72, 95
Paris, S. G. 151
Parsonson, K. 39, 43
Pascarella, E. 380
Paulsen, M. B. 380
Paunonen, S. V. 257, 298, 299
Payne, G. C. 66
Penner, K. S. 16, 45, 46, 52, 156, 192, 300, 301
Perkins, D. N. 150
Perlberg, A. 219
Perry, R. P. 14, 15, 21, 22, 23, 37, 39, 42, 43, 44, 46,
    47, 48, 51, 53, 54, 55, 156, 159, 191, 192, 280,
    291, 299, 300, 301, 302, 308, 309, 337, 340, 370,
    379, 406
Peterson, C. 19, 20, 21, 159, 292
Peterson, P. L. 17, 159
Peterson, R. E. 72
Phares, E. J. 20, 21
Pieper, D. M. 261
Pintrich, P. R. 65, 87, 241
Pittman, T. S. 93
Plant, W. T. 381
Pohlman, J. T. 25, 294, 295
Polich, J. M. 141
Pollis, C. A. 381
Poulsen, C. 364
Pratte, R. 91
Prescott, S. 365
Pressley, M. 267
Prosser, M. 271
Provlacs, J. 216

Quast, H.-H. 66
Quinlan, K. 385

Rankin, E. F., Jr. 377
Raviv, A. 374
Raynor, J. O. 65
Reagan, D. 78
Reed, L 99
Reisser, L. 380
Remmers, H. H. 3, 242, 255, 377, 381, 397, 400
Renandya, W. 136

Renninger, K. A. 110
Reppucci, N. D. 13
Rest, S. 68
Reynolds, S. B. 126
Richardson, R. 213, 214, 216, 220, 222, 223, 228,
    231
Rickard, H. C. 377
Roberts, B. 75, 80, 105
Roberts, C. L. 187
Robinson, D. H. 130, 133, 135, 141
Roche, L. 249, 400
Rodin, B. 265, 266, 299, 311
Rodin, M. 265, 266, 299, 311
Romer, T. 268, 269
Rorschach, E. 227
Rosenbaum, R. M. 67
Rosenberg, L. 175, 186, 190, 191, 377
Rosenfeld, C. 68, 83
Rosenfield, S. 352, 374, 375, 378, 398
Rosenshine, B. 172, 277, 281, 381
Roskelley, D. 138, 139
Ross, M. 54
Rothbaum, F. 18, 22, 38, 159
Rothblum, E. D. 71
Rotter, J. B. 18, 19, 20, 21, 22, 159, 160
Royce, J. D. 59
Rubinstein, J. 377
Rumelhart, D. E. 132
Rushton, J. P. 257, 267, 298, 299
Ryan, R. M. 88, 101
Ryans, D. G. 259

Sabini, J. 71
Sadker, D. 214, 219
Sadker, M. 211
Sagen, H. B. 381
Salamé, R. 77
Salomon, G. 16, 150
Salthouse, T. A. 308, 403
Sanders, J. A. 380
Sanders, J. T. 173, 204
Sansome, C. 112
Sarason, S. 81
Sawrey, J. M. 381
Schantz, S. 125
Scheier, M. F. 19, 78, 159, 160
Schmalt, H. D. 77
Schmeck, R. R. 288
Schmitz, C. C. 210
Schoen, L. G. 295

Schoenfeld, A. H. 98
Schulze, S. K. 112
Schuman, H. 81
Schumer, H. 17
Schunk, D. H. 13
Schürmann, M. 82
Schutz, R. 242
Schwartz, S. H. 141
Schwarzer, C. 80, 81, 82
Schwarzer, R. 66, 76, 80, 82
Scott, O. 377
Scriven, M. 277
Sears, P. 64
Seipp, B. 80
Seldin, P. 308, 327, 385, 416
Seligman, M. 13, 18, 19, 20, 21, 38, 79, 157, 159, 160
Shapiro, G. 86
Sharma, R. 242
Sharp, G. 219
Shearer, J. W. 60
Sherman, S. J. 83
Shore, B. M. 327, 385
Shuell, T. J. 397
Shulman, L. S. 37
Shwalb, B. J. 87
Silver, M. 99
Sim, V. W. 367
Simon, H. A. 122, 135
Sirowatka, A. H. 295
Sixbury, G. R. 372, 373
Skanes, G. R. 340
Skeff, K. M. 237
Skinner, E. A. 65
Slater, L. 192
Slavin, R. E. 86
Slindle, J. A. 286, 294, 295
Smalzreid, T. J. 398
Smidchens, U. 189, 190
Smith, A. B. 209, 222, 223, 228, 377
Smith, D. A. F. 242
Smith, D. G. 187, 202
Smith, L. R. 365, 379
Smith, P. N. 91, 276, 377, 400
Smith, R. A. 237, 333, 335
Smith, T. A. 26, 58, 198
Smith, T. W. 71, 99
Snow, R. E. 16, 17
Snyder, C. R. 71, 99
Snyder, M. L. 68, 83, 99

Snyder, S. S. 18, 159
Sobell, M. B. 70
Sockloff, A. L. 380
Solomon, D. 175, 186, 190, 191
Solomon, L. J. 71
Sorcinelli, M. D. 229
Spencer, R. E. 381
Sperling-Dennison, R. A. 130, 134, 138
Sprague, J. 210
Spratt, M. F. 70
Staley, R. K. 130, 135
Stallings, W. M. 101
Stanley, J. C. 286, 336, 337
Stephan, W. G. 68, 83
Stephens, M. D. 251
Stevens, E. 219, 237
Stevens, J. J. 220
Stiensmeier-Pelster, J. 82
Stiksrud, A. 82
Stipiek, D. J. 13, 65
Stomper, C. 212, 214
Streufert, S. 83
Strickland, B. R. 21, 22
Struthers, W. C. 156
Stumpf, S. A. 372
Suci, G. J. 331
Sullivan, A. M. 340
Svinicki, M. 210, 235
Swant, S. G. 89
Szego, C. K. 233

Tallmadge, G. 16
Tannenbaum, P. H. 331
Tarver, D. A. 381
Taveggia, T. C. 397
Taylor-Way, D. 215, 217, 219
Teasdale, J. D. 79
Teevan, R. C. 68, 72
Terenzini, P. T. 380
Theall, M. 306, 335, 373
Thomas, C. S. 268, 270, 290, 304, 377
Thompson, R. P. 377
Tiberius, R. 216
Till, A. 83
Tobias, S. 16, 76
Tom, F. K. T. 178, 186, 202
Topman, R. M. 99
Touron, J. 249
Tracy, R. J. 377
Travers, R. M. W. 17, 29

Trigwell, K. 271
Trow, M. 72
Tucker, D. G. 262, 309
Tucker, J. A. 70
Tukey, J. W. 130, 143
Tunna, K. 22, 45, 46
Tupes, E. C. 398
Turcotte, S. J. 308
Turner, J. L. 229, 231
Turner, R. L. 377, 380

Valle, V. A. 67
Van Horn, C. 381
Veroff, J. 64
Veroff, J. B. 99
Victoria, G. 295, 296
Von Baeyer, C. L. 22
Vuchinich, R. E. 70

Wageman, R. 80
Walker, B. D. 381
Wall, H. W. 73
Waller, R. 129
Walsh, E. 81
Ward, M. D. 277
Ware, J. E. 15, 190, 191, 280, 299, 300, 301, 302, 311
Ware, W. B. 377
Warren, J. R. 72
Warrington, W. G. 244
Watkins, D. 249
Webb, W. B. 276
Weidenhaupt, S. 167
Weimer, M. 167, 225, 232, 419
Weiner, B. 46, 47, 48, 54, 63, 65, 66, 67, 68, 69, 157
Weinert, F. E. 53
Weinfeld, F. D. 202
Weisbrodt, J. A. 381
Weiss, M. E. 125

Weisz, J. R. 13, 18, 65, 159
Wellborn, J. G. 65
Wheeler, B. 249
Wherry, R. L. 353
White, R. 18, 159
Whitely, S. E. 25, 39, 377
Whitener, E. M. 16
Whitfall, J. 140, 150
Whitney, R. 227
Wicker, F. W. 66
Widlak, E. W. 351, 356, 381
Wilce, L. 87
Williams, H. Y., Jr. 381
Williams, J. P. 87
Williams, R. G. 190, 191, 299
Wilson, R. 23, 217, 218, 220, 244, 302, 305, 306, 400
Winn, W. 123
Winocur, S. 295
Winter, D. G. 64
Wiseman, R. L. 380
Withrow, J. G. 191, 192
Wittrock, M. 17, 29
Wixon, K. K. 151
Wolosin, R. J. 83
Wood, A. M. 202
Woodworth, R. S. 63
Woolfolk, A. E. 174
Wortman, C. B. 18, 159
Wulff, D. A. 215, 233

Yacci, M. 115
Yonge, G. 73
York, R. L. 202
Yunker, J. A. 264, 266

Zimbardo, P. G. 92
Zimmerman, W. 276
Zinn, K. L. 366

Subject Index

A

Ability grouping 156
Ability perceptions 426
Achievement dynamics
  interactive model 77
Achievement measures 375
Achievement motivation, *see* Motivation
Administrators, and research on teaching 415
Affective domain 324
American Educational Research Association
    (AERA) 2
American Educational Research Journal 242
American Psychological Association 396
Applicability paradigm 249
Aptitude test performance 38
Aptitude-treatment interactions (ATIs) 16, 161
Assessment, success-oriented 88
Assignments, student evaluation of 253
Attribution theory 54, 65–68
  benefits 55
Attributional retraining 46, 53
Australian SET instruments 249
Authentic activities 86

B

Behavior, teacher, *see* Teacher behavior
Behavioral feedback 196
Behavioral training 199
Belief patterns 18
Berkeley Teaching/Learning Project 105
Bias in student ratings 372, 414
  theoretical definitions 285, 370
Bipolar model 103
Buffer effect 52
Bush Foundation Faculty Development Project 223

C

California State University 231
California, University of 1
California-San Diego, University of 187

Canada
  teacher training in 209, 231
  teaching improvement centers 1
Causation structure 121
Children's Locus of Control Scale 22
Clarity 193–194, 401
  student evaluation of 252
Class size 287, 431
  teacher-student rapport and 332
Classification of students 155
Cognition
  as learning predictor 399
Cognitive domain 324
Cognitive operations 34, 406
College Teaching 224
College teaching, literature on 2, 23
Collegial Model 215
Colorado State University 210, 212
Community colleges
  new faculty orientation 228
  teacher training in 209, 216, 222, 228, 231
Comparison structure 121
Comparisons, measurable 419
Competence motivation 18
Competition 13, 417, 427
Concept learning 145
Concept maps 126
Confirming interval 72
Consultation, in teacher training 215–221
Context 405
Cooperative learning 86
Cornell University 1
Correlation approach 26
  compared with descriptive approach 29
Counseling Model 215
Course difficulty 344, 348, 400
Course outline restructuring, effect of 165
Course selection
  and faculty ratings 309
  reasons 293
  student ratings and 322

Criterion-related validity 331
Critical thinking 213

D

Descriptive approach, compared with correlational
    approach 29
Diversity, challenge of 154
"Dr. Fox" effect 30, 190, 292
    paradigm 299–302
Dynamics of action model 64

E

Eclectic Model 215
Ecological validity 24
Educational Resources Information Center 369
Educational Seduction 50
    see also "Dr. Fox" effect
Effective teaching
    categories of 248, 250
    definitions 14, 324–326
    developing evaluation of 350–357
    dimensions of 23-32
    effect on students 173
    evaluation, *see* Feedback; SEEQ; SETs; Student
        ratings
    experience factor 259
    factor analysis 413
    factor ratings 355
    instructional dimensions 374
    invariance assumption 335
    methods 160–166
    multiple indicators 282, 419
    principles of success 251–253, 413
    process definition 325
    process-product links 336
    product definition 324
    research methods 173
    strategies for 155
    training for, *see* Teacher training
Ego-involvement 64
Encoding 134
Endeavor rating form 347, 352
Endeavor scales 254
Engaging tasks 85
Ennis-Weir Critical Thinking Test 213
Enthusiasm, teacher 25, 178, 189–193, 251, 359,
        379, 399, 406
    student evaluation of 251, 359
    training for 400
ERIC data base 242, 412

Evaluation, *see* Feedback; SEEQ; SETs; Student
        ratings
Examination scores, as achievement measure 327
Examinations, instructional value 252
Experience factor 259
    and instructor ranking 294
Experimental approach 29
Experimental research 174, 189
Expressiveness, teacher 14, 178
    and curriculum objectives 50
    definition 31
    effect on student performance 42, 44
    experimental analysis 34
External observers 277
Extrinsic motivation 103

F

Factor analyses of student ratings 27, 346
    utility 398
Faculty
    attitudes toward teaching research 415
    peer ratings 402
    promotion, effect of SETs 262
    ranking policies 417
    ratings of, *see* SETs; Student ratings
    self-evaluations 273, 291
    teaching portfolio 327
Faculty development 425
Faculty ratings, compared with student ratings 330
Failure acceptors 64, 74, 79, 106, 157, 426
Failure-avoiding strategies 70
Failure-avoiding students 77, 157, 426
Familiarity, as motivation 107
Feedback
    contingent 46
    correlations 405
    impact 419
    methods 403
    noncontingent 16, 21, 43, 44, 48
    norm-based 90
    variables 38
    see also SEEQ; SETs; Student ratings
Feldman coding scheme 352
Field studies 30
FIPSE 227
Foci 200
Follow Through 29
Ford Foundation 227
Frame-factors 24
Frames 200

Functional compensation 53

G
Gender issues
    in student ratings 295, 371
    in teacher training 212
Goal-setting 84
Grade focus 105
Grade-choice arrangement 87
Grades
    effect of 290, 341
    instructional value 252
    as motivation 88, 102 427
    and student ratings 372
Grading leniency hypothesis 373
Grading satisfaction hypothesis 268
Grading systems 87
Graduate students, teacher ratings by 265
Grants programs, in teacher training 221
Group Interaction factor 252, 287, 399
"Gut learning" 405

H
Head Start 29
Helpless-mastery continuum 159
Helplessness
    definition 32
    impact of 430
    learned 20, 36
    perceptions of 14
    theory 21
    types of 22
    uncontrollability and 43
Hierarchical representation 118

I
Individual Rapport factor 252, 287
Information structure 129, 130
Instruction methods 12, 23
    perceived control and 14
    teacher-centered 17
    see also Teacher behavior
Instructional Development and Effectiveness As-
        sessment (IDEA) system 372
Instructional dimensions 383, 392–395
Instructional Evaluation and Faculty Development
    403
Instructional improvement, *see* Teacher training
Instructor organization 34, 380, 406
    student evaluation 252

Instructor self-evaluations 273, 291
Integration of knowledge 132
Intellectual Achievement Responsibility Scale 13,
    22, 23
Interaction factor 182
Interest-centered learning 110
Interitem correlation coefficients 353
Internal-locus children, 13
Intrinsic engagement 105
Intrinsic motivation 103

J
Jenkins Activity Scale 23
Journal of Abnormal Psychology 21
Journal of Chemical Education, The 224
Journal of Educational Psychology 155

K
Knowledge
    integration 132
    structural 115

L
Laboratory analogs 30, 37
Laboratory design 337
Learned drives 63
Learned helplessness theory 157
Learning, student evaluation of 251
Learning processes 128
Lecturing, as teaching method 12, 24
Links 200
Low-inference teaching behavior 172

M
Mastery
    definition 32
    motive 106
    perceptions of 14
Mathematics teaching methods 86
Matrix
    definition 118
    forms 138
Matrix Representation System 115-151, 432–433
    advantages 116, 122
    analysis 162
    applications 143
    learning processes 128
    memory tests 135
    research on 133
McGill University 179

Mentoring, in teacher training 231
Miami-Dade community college system 1
Michigan State SIRS instrument 244
Michigan, University of 190, 402
Microteaching, vs. videotaping 219
Mnemonic pictures 136
Moon illusion 88
Motivation 406
    attribution model 67
    bipolar model 103
    as concept 61
    definitions 103
    as drives 62–83
    as goals 83–89
    grades and 291
    intrinsic vs. extrinsic 106
    as learning predictor 399
    levels 372
    quadripolar model 104
    and teaching behavior 422
    terminology 18
    traditional view 62, 426
Multidimensional-Multiattributional Causality
    Scale 22, 23
Multisection Validity Study 264, 338
Multitrait-multimethod (MTMM) analysis 274
    designs 340

N
Need achievement theory 63
    quadripolar model 157
Negative reinforcement 107
Note taking 134
    matrix system 139
Novelty, as motivation 107

O
Observational research 174, 175, 277
Oral communication 12
Organization, *see* Instructor organization
Outline representation 122
Overjustification effect 111
Overmotivation 84
Overstrivers 74, 79, 106, 157, 426

P
Pattern recognition 128, 129
Pedagogical methods 12
Pedagogy, *see* Instruction methods
Peer ratings 276, 402, 420

Perceived personal control 18–23, 429-431
    causal attributions 47
    cognitive origins 44
    definition 12
    enhancing 163
    environmental origins 39
    interaction analysis 32
    operational definition 51
    taxonomy for 19, 159
    typology 158
Performance mentality 64
Personal causation 18
Personality structure 398
Piagetian theory 105, 149
Placebo effect 200
Plasticity 52
Play, definition 101
Positive interdependence 333
Positive reinforcement 107, 119
Posttest examination scores 327
Praise, effect of 21
Pretest examination scores 327
Principal components extraction 347
Problem solving 146
Problem/solution structures 121
Procrastination 71
Professional and Organizational Development
    (POD) society 2
Professional Service Model 215
Promotion, student evaluation and 308
Psychomotor domain 324
Purdue University 3

Q
Quadripolar model 104

R
Random assignment 266
Rapport with students 34, 332
Readings, student evaluation of 253
Reflective inquiry 91
Relational learning 138
Research in Higher Education 155
Research on college teaching
    as basis for practice 155
    methodological problems 51
    methodologies 174
    need for 425
    teaching and 281
Review of Higher Education 155
Rules, learning 146

S

Section-average achievement scores 272
SEEQ (Students' Evaluations of Educational Quality) 330
  assessment of 347
  construct approach 287
  development of 244
  factor analysis table 25
  feedback studies 304
  first-order factors 246
  reliability 254
  scales 261
  secondary analysis of data 348
  teaching-learning theories and 250
  see also SETs; Student ratings
Selective attention 130
Self-efficacy 20
Self-mastery 85
Self-worth theory 68, 102, 156, 161, 426
  threats to learning 84
Semantic maps 125
Seminars, in teacher training 209
Sequential representation 118
SETs (Students' Evaluations of Teaching Effectiveness)
  achievement correlations 271
  dimensionality of 243
  effect on promotion 262
  experimental manipulations 280
  factor analysis 27, 245
  generalizability 255
  and learning outcomes 271
  potential biases 283
  purposes 241, 296
  reliability 254
  research activity and 281
  stability 258
  in tenure/promotion decisions 308
  utility 303–309
  validity 254, 263
  written 261
  see also SEEQ; Student ratings
Sex-biased teacher-student interactions 211
  see also Gender
Snap quiz, effect of 165
Spatial representation systems 124
Special Interest Group on Faculty Evaluation and Development (SIGFED) 3
Stanford University 212
Steering groups 155

Stimulus motives 63
Structural knowledge 115
  representation techniques 116
Structured formats 25
Student characteristics hypothesis 373
Student Description of Teaching questionnaire 244
Student Instructional Report (SIR) 373
Student learning
  as criterion of effective teaching 264
  measurement of 327
  and study skills 271
  teaching methods associated with 165, 375
  and teaching skills 397
Student rating forms, factor structure 352
Student ratings
  accuracy 331
  autonomy dimension 87
  consulation and 218
  compared with faculty ratings 330
  content validity 332
  as determinants of effective teaching 28, 326–342
  dimensionality 350, 398
  ethics of 404
  faculty attitudes 368
  faculty resistance 401
  feedback methods 403
  factor analysis of 346
  forms for 405
  global vs. specific 332
  institutional policy 416
  interpretation 370–374
  items and their categories 358–364
  learning and 342–345
  multidimensional forms 328–333
  myths about 370, 415
  as predictors 328, 346, 352
  purposes 321
  quantification 402
  rating bias 372
  student performance and 345
  teaching behaviors 28, 358-364
  utility of forms 335
  validity analysis 414, 420
  validity studies 401
Student typologies 72
Student-centered instruction 17
Students' Evaluations of Educational Quality, *see* SEEQ
Students' Evaluations of Teaching Effectiveness,

see SETs
Study skills 150
  and learning outcomes 271
Subject interest 288
Success-oriented students 80, 106, 157, 426
Supervisor ratings 276

T
Teacher and course effect 257
Teacher attributes, formats 25
Teacher behavior 172–202, 422–424
  consultation and 218
  correlation with student ratings 380–383
  effectiveness analysis 33
  high school 187
  information processing and 35
  instructional dimensions 392–395
  laboratory analog 37
  linkages 53
  observation studies 277
  student ratings of 28, 358-364
Teacher Behaviors Inventory (TBI) 26, 180, 184
Teacher personality 298, 398
Teacher training
  behavior adaptation 423
  colleague intervention 226
  effectiveness 400
  instructional consultation 215
  resistance to 396
  resource materials for 224
  seminars 209
  workshops 209, 424
Teaching effectiveness, *see* Effective teaching
Teaching Analysis by Students (TABS) question-
    naire 179
Teaching assistants
  graduate student ratings 265

ranking 294
training of 233
workshop training 210
*Teaching College: Collected Readings for the New
    Instructor* 232
Teaching methods, *see* Instruction methods
Teaching portfolio 327
Teaching Professor, The 3, 167
Teaching proficiency, lack of assistance for 2
Teaching Psychology 224
Teaching Tips 405
Teaching/learning principles 251–253, 413
  student ratings and 322
Tenure. and student ratings 308, 421
Test rescheduling, effect of 165
Test-taking anxiety 71, 105
Topic-repeatable category structure 122
Trenton State College 232
Type A/B behavior 18, 45, 160

V
Validity hypothesis 270
Verbal aptitude 88
Videotaped lectures 38, 179
  vs. microteaching 219
Visual argument 129

W
Watson-Glaser Critical Thinking Appraisal Test
    213
Western Ontario, University of 180, 262
Wisconsin-Stevens Point, University of 232
Work, definition 101
Workload/difficulty effect 253, 290, 399
Workshops, in teacher training 209–215, 424
Writing, matrix facilitation of 149